THE ROLE OF DOMESTIC COURTS IN TREATY ENFORCEMENT

A Comparative Study

This book examines the application of treaties by domestic courts in eleven countries. The central question is whether domestic courts actually provide remedies to private parties who are harmed by a violation of their treaty-based rights. The analysis shows that domestic courts in eight of the eleven countries – Australia, Canada, Germany, India, the Netherlands, Poland, South Africa, and the United Kingdom – generally do enforce treaty-based rights on behalf of private parties. On the other hand, the evidence is mixed for the other three countries: Israel, Russia, and the United States. In Israel and Russia, the trends are moving in the direction of greater judicial enforcement of treaties on behalf of private parties. The United States is the only country surveyed where the trend is moving in the opposite direction. U.S. courts' reluctance to enforce treaty-based rights undermines efforts to develop a more cooperative global order.

Professor David Sloss joined the faculty of Santa Clara University School of Law in 2008. He was a faculty member at Saint Louis University School of Law from 1999 to 2008. During his academic career, Professor Sloss has published approximately two dozen law review articles. Before embarking on an academic career, Professor Sloss spent nine years as a civil servant in the U.S. government. During that time, he participated in drafting and negotiating several important treaties and other international agreements. Professor Sloss earned his J.D. from Stanford Law School, his M.P.P. from Harvard University, and his B.A. from Hampshire College.

The Role of Domestic Courts in Treaty Enforcement

A COMPARATIVE STUDY

Edited by

DAVID SLOSS

Santa Clara University School of Law

CAMBRIDGE
UNIVERSITY PRESS

CAMBRIDGE UNIVERSITY PRESS
Cambridge, New York, Melbourne, Madrid, Cape Town, Singapore,
São Paulo, Delhi, Dubai, Tokyo

Cambridge University Press
32 Avenue of the Americas, New York, NY 10013-2473, USA

www.cambridge.org
Information on this title: www.cambridge.org/9780521877305

First published 2009

Printed in the United States of America

A catalog record for this publication is available from the British Library.

Library of Congress Cataloging in Publication data

The role of domestic courts in treaty enforcement : a comparative
study / edited by David Sloss.
p. cm.
Includes bibliographical references and index.
ISBN 978-0-521-87730-5 (hardback)
1. Treaties. 2. International and municipal law. 3. Jurisdiction.
4. Jurisdiction (International law) I. Sloss, David. II. Title.
KZ1303.R65 2009
341.3′7–dc22 2009010920

ISBN 978-0-521-87730-5 Hardback

Contents

Detailed Contents

Contributors

Anthony Aust studied law at the London School of Economics. For 35 years he was a full-time legal adviser with the Foreign and Commonwealth Office, retiring as Deputy Legal Adviser in 2002. From 1988 to 1991, he was the Legal Adviser of the U.K. Mission to the UN in New York. Later he advised the FCO's UN, Middle East, and Counter-Terrorism Departments, including working for ten years on the Lockerbie case before the ICJ. In 2007, Cambridge published the second edition of his *Modern Treaty Law and Practice*, and in 2005 his *Handbook of International Law* (he is now working on a second edition). He is a consultant with a U.K./U.S. law firm and privately; and he has taught international law at the London School of Economics and at other universities in London and abroad.

William E. Butler is the John Edward Fowler Distinguished Professor of Law, Dickinson School of Law at the Pennsylvania State University; Emeritus Professor of Comparative Law at the University of London; Foreign Member, National Academy of Sciences of Ukraine and the Russian Academy of Natural Sciences; Member, International Court of Commercial Arbitration (Moscow); and Associate, International Academy of Comparative Law. He has written and published extensively on Russian law and public and private international law.

John Dugard is Honorary Professor of Law at the Centre for Human Rights, University of Pretoria; Professor Emeritus at the University of Leiden; a member of the International Law Commission; a member of the Institute of International Law; and Judge ad hoc of the International Court of Justice. From 1968 to 1998 he was a Professor of Law at the University of the Witwatersrand. He is the author of *Human Rights and the South African Legal Order* (1978) and *International Law: A South African Perspective* (3d, ed. 2005).

Lech Garlicki is a Judge on the European Court of Human Rights, a position he has held since 2002. He previously served as a Judge of the Constitutional Court of Poland (1993–2001); the President of the Polish Association of Constitutional Law; a Professor of Law at the University of Warsaw; the Director of the American Studies Center at the University of Warsaw; a member of the Committee on Legal Sciences of the Polish Academy of Sciences; and a member of the Legislative Council in the Prime Minister's Office. Judge Garlicki is the author of numerous publications in the field of human rights. He has been a visiting professor at universities in Canada, France, Germany, and the United States.

Nihal Jayawickrama practiced law in Sri Lanka before serving as Attorney General, Secretary for Justice, and Vice Chairman of the Sri Lanka Delegation to the United Nations General Assembly. He was also a member of the Permanent Court of Arbitration at The Hague. After receiving his doctorate from the University of London in 1983, he taught constitutional and administrative law and the international law of human rights at the University of Hong Kong, and was Chairman of JUSTICE, the Hong Kong section of the International Commission of Jurists, until 1997. He was the Ariel F. Sallows Professor of Human Rights at the University of Saskatchewan from 1992 to 1993 and Executive Director of Transparency International in Berlin from 1997 to 2000. He is currently a consultant on governance and judicial reform, and coordinator of the Judicial Integrity Group of Chief Justices that drafted the Bangalore Principles of Judicial Conduct. He has published on a range of public law and human rights issues and is the author of *The Judicial Application of Human Rights Law* (Cambridge University Press, 2002).

David Kretzmer, LL.B, LL.M (Jerusalem), Dr. Jur. (York, Canada), Dr. Jur. h.c. (Potsdam), is Professor Emeritus of International Law at the Hebrew University of Jerusalem and Professor of Law at the Transitional Justice Institute, University of Ulster and the Academic Centre for Law and Business, Ramat Gan. He was a member of the UN Human Rights Committee from 1995 to 2002, serving as vice chairperson of the Committee in 2001 and 2002. Kretzmer's main fields of research are constitutional law, human rights, and international humanitarian law. His books include *The Occupation of Justice: The Supreme Court of Israel and the Occupied Territories* (SUNY Press, 2002); *The Concept of Human Dignity in Human Rights Discourse* (edited with E. Klein) (Kluwer International, 2002), and *The Legal Status of the Arabs in Israel* (2d ed., 2002).

Małgorzata Masternak-Kubiak is a Professor of Law in the Department of Constitutional Law at the University of Wrocław. She is also a Judge in the Regional Administrative Court; the Director of the Center of Postgraduate Studies of Legislation; the treasurer and a member of the Executive Board of the Polish Association of Constitutional Law; and a visiting scholar at the Institute of Comparative Law in Lausanne. Professor Masternak-Kubiak's scholarship focuses on the status of international law in the domestic legal order, judicial review, and systems of government.

Sean D. Murphy is the Patricia Roberts Harris Research Professor of Law at George Washington University Law School in Washington, DC, where he teaches international and foreign relations law. After receiving law degrees from Columbia and Cambridge, he served eleven years in the U.S. State Department Legal Adviser's Office, including as Legal Counselor of the U.S. Embassy in The Hague. He has published various articles in national and international law journals, receiving the *American Journal of International Law*'s (*AJIL*) 1994 Deák Prize for best scholarship by a younger author. Two of his books were awarded American Society of International Law certificates of merit. His most recent book is *Foreign Relations and National Security Law* (2008) (with Franck and Glennon). He is a member of the *AJIL* Board of Editors.

André Nollkaemper is Professor of Public International Law at the faculty of Law of the Universiteit van Amsterdam, the Netherlands. He is general editor of the *Netherlands Yearbook of International Law* and editor-in-chief of *International Law in Domestic Courts*. As counsel to the Amsterdam-based law firm Bohler Franken Koppen Wijngaarden, he has frequently been involved in litigation in international and Dutch courts. He has published widely on the application of international law in domestic courts, including "Internationally Wrongful Acts" in *Domestic Courts, American Journal of International Law* (2007); *New Perspectives on the Divide between International and National Law* (2007) (coeditor with Janne Nijman), and *Domestic Courts and the International Rule of Law* (forthcoming 2009).

Andreas L. Paulus is Professor of Public and International Law and director of the Institute of International and European Law at the Georg-August-University Göttingen, Germany. From 2000 to 2006, he was lecturer at the University of Munich and, in 2003–2004, Visiting Assistant Professor of Law at the University of Michigan Law School. Paulus holds a doctor's degree from the University of Munich. His publications deal with international legal theory, the law of the United Nations, international adjudication, and international criminal law. Paulus also served as counsel and advisor to Germany in cases before the International Court of Justice.

Donald R. Rothwell is Professor of International Law at the ANU College of Law, Australian National University, and was previously Challis Professor of International Law, University of Sydney. His major research interest is international law with a specific focus on law of the sea, law of the polar regions, dispute resolution, and international law in Australia and has published widely in those areas. He also actively contributes to media commentary on international law issues. Rothwell is the current coeditor of the *Australian Year Book of International Law*, and he chaired the Sydney (2006) and Canberra (2009) Panels reviewing the legality of Japan's Special Permit "Scientific" Whaling.

David Sloss is a Professor of Law and the Director of the Center for Global Law and Policy at Santa Clara University School of Law. He was a faculty member at Saint Louis University School of Law from 1999 to 2008. Professor Sloss has published numerous law review articles related to the domestic application of international law in U.S. courts. His articles have been published in leading journals, such as *Stanford Law Review, Cornell Law Review*, the *American Journal of International Law*, the *Yale Journal of International Law*, the *Virginia Journal of International Law*, and the *Columbia Journal of Transnational Law*. Before embarking on an academic career, Professor Sloss spent nine years as a civil servant in the U.S. government. During that time, he helped draft and negotiate several important treaties and other international agreements.

Michael P. Van Alstine is the Associate Dean for Faculty Development and a Professor of Law at the University of Maryland School of Law. His area of specialization is international and domestic private law. He has published widely in both English and German in the areas of contracts, commercial law, and international commercial transactions. His particular area of scholarly interest is the domestic law application of international law through the vehicle of treaties. Professor Van Alstine received Doctor of Laws and Masters of Comparative Law degrees summa cum laude from the University of Bonn, Germany, where his focus of study was comparative contract and commercial law, and a Juris Doctor degree from George Washington University.

Gib van Ert practices civil litigation and public law with Hunter Litigation Chambers, Vancouver. He holds law degrees from the Universities of Cambridge and Toronto. He is a former law clerk to Madam Justice Prowse of the Court of Appeal for British Columbia and to Justices Gonthier and Fish of the Supreme Court of Canada. His book, *Using International Law in Canadian Courts*, was published in 2002 and appeared in a second, revised edition in 2008. He has published numerous articles on the domestic reception of public international law in Canada and is the coauthor (with Mark Freeman) of the textbook *International Human Rights Law* (2004). Since 2004, he has prepared case notes on Canadian decisions in public international law for the *Canadian Yearbook of International Law.*

Krzysztof Wójtowicz has been a Professor of Law at the University of Wrocław, Poland, since 1997. He is the Head of the Department of International and European Law; the Director of the Center of Postgraduate Studies in Law and Economics of the European Union; and a former Vice Rector of the University of Wrocław for Research and Foreign Cooperation. His recent publications in English include "Constitution of Poland" in *Encyclopedia of World Constitutions* (2006) and "Proposed Changes in the Polish Constitution of 1997 Ahead of Poland's Accession to the European Union" in *Poland's Way to the European Union: Legal Aspects* (2002). He is an expert on European Union law and Polish constitutional law.

Preface

As I prepare to send this book to the printer, President Obama is evaluating potential nominees to fill Justice Souter's soon-to-be-vacant slot on the United States Supreme Court. The selection of the next Supreme Court Justice could have significant implications for the international legal system and for the United States' participation in that system.

The last two individuals appointed to the Supreme Court – Chief Justice Roberts and Justice Alito – view international law with a mixture of contempt and indifference, as evidenced by the Chief Justice's 2008 opinion in *Medellin v. Texas* (which Justice Alito joined). They apparently view their job, in part, as one of shielding the domestic legal system from the unwanted intrusion of international law. Their elevation to the nation's highest court exemplifies a broader trend in which the judicial branch in the United States has become a key obstacle to the nation's performance of its international treaty obligations.

This book demonstrates that U.S. judges are out-of-step with their counterparts in other modern democratic nations. In most of the nations surveyed in this volume, domestic courts play a constructive role in promoting compliance with national treaty obligations by providing remedies to private parties who are harmed by a violation of their treaty-based rights. For most of United States history, judges in this nation played a similar role: they routinely enforced treaties on behalf of private parties, as envisioned by the Constitution's founders. Unfortunately, over the past several decades, U.S. presidents have filled the courts with judges who have abandoned the judiciary's traditional mission of enforcing individual rights protected under international law.

President Obama has an historic opportunity to reverse this unfortunate trend by appointing judges who, like their counterparts in other free countries, will use their judicial power to promote compliance with international treaty obligations, rather than obstructing performance of those obligations. One Supreme Court Justice cannot transform the legal system overnight. But she can help nudge the courts toward an international-law-friendly perspective on the U.S. constitutional system. If this book makes a small contribution to that goal, the editor will be very gratified.

David Sloss
Santa Clara, California
May 2009

Acknowledgments

Numerous people deserve thanks and credit for the production of this book. I cannot possibly name all of them, but I want to take this opportunity to thank those who have made especially valuable contributions.

To begin, I want to thank the authors of the individual chapters in this book: Anthony Aust, William Butler, John Dugard, Lech Garlicki, Nihal Jayawickrama, David Kretzmer, Małgorzata Masternak-Kubiak, Sean Murphy, André Nollkaemper, Andreas Paulus, Donald Rothwell, Michael Van Alstine, Gib van Ert, and Krzysztof Wójtowicz. They all provided carefully researched, well-written, insightful chapters. They all demonstrated admirable patience during a lengthy and sometimes tedious editorial process. I learned a great deal from all their contributions.

The staff at Cambridge University Press and its affiliates have provided tremendous support and assistance throughout the entire project. I owe special thanks to John Berger at Cambridge, who has worked with me since the very inception of the project and has guided me through every step of the process. Thanks also to Brigitte Coulton at Aptara, who oversaw the final stages of the editorial process and helped transform a collection of separate chapters into a finished book.

As a professor, I am always thankful for the generosity of the Deans who support my scholarship. I began this project as a professor at Saint Louis University (SLU). I am grateful to Jeff Lewis, the Dean at SLU, for his consistent generosity in funding my research. I completed this project as a professor at Santa Clara University. Don Polden, the Dean at Santa Clara, has been equally generous in funding my work during the final stages of this project. I am very grateful for his support.

I have benefited greatly from the assistance provided by several excellent librarians and research assistants. In particular, I want to thank Lynn Hartke, a research librarian at Saint Louis University, and Mary Sexton, a research librarian at Santa Clara University. Special thanks also to Liz Culhane, who served as my research assistant during her third year of law school at Saint Louis University. Liz did a superb job creating a database of U.S. treaty cases that provided the basis for much of the analysis in the chapter on the United States.

I presented an early draft of the chapter on the United States in December 2007 at a meeting of the American Society of International Law interest group on international law in domestic courts. Several people at that meeting provided valuable feedback, including Curt Bradley, Jacob Cogan, Duncan Hollis, John McGinnis, Peggy McGuinness, Paul Stephan, David Stewart, Ed Swaine, Melissa Waters, Mark Weisburd, and Ingrid Wuerth. I made fairly drastic revisions in response to their insightful criticisms. I believe that the final chapter is much better, thanks to their comments. I also received valuable feedback on subsequent drafts of the chapter from Katherine Barnes, Robert Chesney, Marina Hsieh, Bradley Joondeph, and Chris Whytock. I thank all of them for their comments, suggestions, and insights. Of course, I alone am responsible for any deficiencies in the final chapter.

I presented a draft of Chapter 1 in December 2008 at a meeting of the Northern California International Law Scholars group. At that meeting, I received valuable comments from Diane Amann, John Barton, David Caron, Anupam Chander, Bill Dodge, Oona Hathaway, and Beth Van Schaack. Others who provided very helpful feedback on Chapter 1 include Anthony Aust, John Dugard, Duncan Hollis, Sean Murphy, John Parry, Andreas Paulus, and Gib van Ert. I am certain that the final product is much better as a result of their comments and suggestions. As above, I am solely responsible for any remaining errors, mistakes, or omissions.

Two people deserve special thanks here. I began this project as a joint venture with Derek Jinks. Derek was my coeditor during the early phases of the project. Although he withdrew midway through the project, I never would have begun the book without his participation. The entire book bears the stamp of his remarkable intellectual energy. Thank you, Derek – I could not have done this without you. Michael Van Alstine wrote the concluding chapter of this book (Chapter 14). Michael is the only person, other than myself, who read every chapter of this book more than once. Michael and I exchanged multiple drafts of Chapters 1 and 14 as we both read successive iterations of the other chapters. I learned a tremendous amount from this intellectual exchange; the final product is undoubtedly much improved as a result of this process.

Last, but certainly not least, I want to thank my wife, Heidi, and my two children, Dakin and Kamala. They have all supported me in countless ways throughout my entire academic career. Although I have devoted many evenings and weekends to my scholarly endeavors, they have rarely complained. Instead, they gently remind me that it is good for me to take a break from work to enjoy some quality time with my family. Heidi, Dakin, and Kamala – thank you for adding to the joy in my life.

1

Treaty Enforcement in Domestic Courts

A Comparative Analysis

David Sloss

Professor of Law and Director, Center for Global Law and Policy
Santa Clara University School of Law

International law today is not confined to regulating the relations between the states. Its scope continues to extend. Today matters of social concern, such as health, education, and economics apart from human rights fall within the ambit of international regulations. International law is more than ever aimed at individuals.[1]

This book presents a comparative analysis of the role of domestic courts in treaty application. In evaluating the role of domestic courts, it is helpful to distinguish among three types of treaty provisions. Horizontal treaty provisions regulate relations between states; vertical provisions regulate relations between states and private parties; and transnational provisions regulate relations among private parties that cut across national boundaries. Domestic courts are rarely invited to apply horizontal treaty provisions. However, private parties frequently seek access to domestic courts to vindicate rights that arise from vertical and/or transnational treaty provisions.

The use of treaties to regulate vertical and transnational relationships is not a new phenomenon. Two centuries ago, Chief Justice Marshall, writing for the U.S. Supreme Court, declared: "Each treaty stipulates something respecting the citizens of the two nations, and gives them rights. Whenever a right grows out of, or is protected by, a treaty, it is sanctioned against all the laws and judicial decisions of the states; and whoever may have this right, it is to be protected."[2] Although states have used treaties to regulate transnational and vertical relationships for centuries, there has been an exponential growth in treaty making in this area over the past few decades. The rapidly growing number of treaties that involve transnational and

[1] People's Union for Civil Liberties v. Union of India, 18 December 1996, [1999] 2 L.R.C. 1, at 12, per Kuldip Singh J.

[2] Owings v. Norwood's Lessee, 9 U.S. (5 Cranch) 344, 348 (1809).

vertical relationships is one reason it is important to understand the role of domestic courts in treaty enforcement.

Domestic adjudication is not the only mechanism for private parties to vindicate their treaty-based rights, but it is an important mechanism. On the international plane, there is frequently a gap between rights and remedies, because treaty provisions that are intended to protect the rights of private parties often do not grant the intended beneficiaries a right of access to international courts to adjudicate claims arising under those treaties. Insofar as treaties create private rights without granting private parties access to international tribunals, the effective enforcement of transnational and vertical treaty provisions may depend on the willingness of domestic courts to enforce treaty-based rights on behalf of private parties.

This book examines the application of treaties by domestic courts in eleven countries: Australia, Canada, Germany, India, Israel, the Netherlands, Poland, Russia, South Africa, the United Kingdom, and the United States. These eleven countries were not chosen at random: wealthy, democratic countries are overrepresented in the sample. It is difficult to draw reliable conclusions about more than 190 states in the world based on the eleven states analyzed in this volume. Even comparisons among the eleven countries are not wholly scientific. The book includes one chapter on each of the eleven countries; a different author has written each chapter. Comparisons across countries are invariably influenced, to some degree, by the individual authors' decisions about which points deserve emphasis. Despite these caveats, though, the analysis in the subsequent chapters does support several interesting conclusions.

The central question addressed in each of the eleven country chapters is this: do domestic courts provide remedies to private parties who are harmed by a violation of their treaty-based primary rights? I use the term *remedies* here, and throughout this introductory chapter, in a broad sense to include a judicial order designed to prevent an incipient treaty violation or to halt an ongoing violation, as well as orders designed to compensate victims for past harms. In brief, the most significant conclusions that emerge from this study are as follows:

- Domestic courts in eight of the eleven countries examined in this volume – Australia, Canada, Germany, India, the Netherlands, Poland, South Africa, and the United Kingdom – generally enforce treaty-based rights on behalf of private parties. However, the evidence is somewhat mixed for the other three countries: Israel, Russia, and the United States.

- In Israel and Russia, the trends are moving in the direction of greater judicial enforcement of treaties on behalf of private parties. The United States is the only country studied in this volume in which the trends are moving in the opposite direction.[3]
- The conventional wisdom is wrong, insofar as the conventional wisdom holds that direct judicial application of treaties is a more effective means of treaty enforcement than indirect application. In countries such as Canada and India, where domestic law precludes direct application of treaties, domestic courts play an active role in treaty enforcement by applying treaties indirectly. In contrast, in the United States, for example, although domestic courts have the authority to apply treaties directly in some cases, they rarely use their judicial power to remedy treaty violations committed by government actors.

Comparative analysis of the role of domestic courts in treaty enforcement is a topic that has received insufficient scholarly attention. Prior comparative studies of treaties within domestic legal systems have tended to focus primarily on the roles of the legislative and executive branches.[4] The most significant prior work that focused on the role of domestic courts is now more than twenty years old, and it dealt only with Western Europe and the United States.[5] In contrast, this book provides an updated analysis of the domestic judicial enforcement of treaties in countries from Africa, the Middle East, the Asia-Pacific region, Eastern and Western Europe, and North America.[6]

This book consists of fourteen chapters, including this introductory one. Chapters 3 through 13 provide detailed analyses of the judicial enforcement of treaties in the eleven countries identified previously. Chapter 2, written by Professor Sean Murphy, addresses the question whether international law obligates states to grant private parties access to national courts to vindicate

[3] Throughout the nineteenth century, U.S. courts routinely enforced treaties on behalf of private parties. *See* David Sloss, *When Do Treaties Create Individually Enforceable Rights?* 45 Colum. J. Trans'l L. 20 (2006). In recent years, though, U.S. courts have been far less hospitable to treaty claims. *See* chapter 13 in this volume.

[4] *See, e.g.*, National Treaty Law and Practice (Duncan B. Hollis, Merritt R. Blakeslee & L. Benjamin Ederington, eds.) (2005); Parliamentary Participation in the Making and Operation of Treaties: A Comparative Study (Stefan A. Riesenfeld & Frederick M. Abbott eds., 1994).

[5] The Effects of Treaties in Domestic Law (Francis G. Jacobs & Shelley Roberts eds., 1987).

[6] The project originally envisioned chapters on Argentina, Brazil, China, Mexico, Nigeria, and South Korea, in addition to the other countries noted herein. For various reasons, none of those chapters materialized.

treaty-based rights. Chapter 14, written by Professor Michael Van Alstine, provides an overall summary of the eleven country chapters.

In light of the contributions by Professors Murphy and Van Alstine, this introductory chapter is intended to accomplish three distinct tasks. Section I presents some general comments on the scope and relevance of the overall project. Section II provides a summary of the eleven country chapters, focusing on the question of whether domestic courts provide remedies to private parties harmed by a violation of their treaty-based rights. Section II differs from Professor Van Alstine's chapter in that he provides a broad-based overview of the materials presented in the eleven country chapters, whereas Section II draws selectively from the country chapters to provide a more narrowly focused analysis of a single question.

Section III presents an alternative perspective on some of the international law issues analyzed in Professor Murphy's chapter. In his contribution, Professor Murphy presents a very thorough and insightful analysis of the question of whether international law obligates "a state to open its courts for private persons to vindicate rights or benefits that a treaty accords to them."[7] He concludes that the answer is generally no, except insofar as a specific treaty creates an explicit or implicit obligation to do so. Section III frames the question in a slightly different way: it asks whether customary international law obligates states to provide remedies for private parties who are harmed by a violation of their treaty-based rights. By posing a different question, I reach a slightly different answer. Section III contends that international law sources provide some support for the proposition that customary international law obligates states to provide remedies for private parties who are harmed by a violation of their treaty-based rights. Ultimately, though, I agree with Professor Murphy that there is presently insufficient evidence of state practice or *opinio juris* to establish such a rule of customary international law. Professor Murphy contends, and I agree, that there may be an emerging rule of customary law along these lines.

I. PRELIMINARY ISSUES

The bulk of this introductory chapter is devoted to an analysis of judicial practice in the eleven states surveyed in this volume. Before turning to that subject, however, there are two points that merit brief preliminary comments.

[7] *See* Chapter 2, pg. 61.

A. *Domestic Courts as Transnational Actors*

There are at least three distinct reasons why it is important for domestic courts to provide remedies for individual victims of treaty violations. First, many modern treaties codify an agreed understanding about the content of universal moral norms. Human rights treaties and humanitarian law treaties, in particular, express the collective moral judgment of people from many different cultures about the standards of conduct that determine what are, and what are not, acceptable ways for governments to treat individual human beings. To the extent that domestic courts enforce the norms embodied in those treaties, governments are more likely to comply with those norms. Judicial enforcement by domestic courts is not the only factor that influences governmental compliance, but it is a significant factor. The better the record of governmental compliance, the closer we come to realizing in practice the humanitarian ideals that underlie contemporary human rights and humanitarian law.

Second, there are numerous treaties that do not reflect universal moral norms but that codify agreements designed to promote more efficient and effective transnational relations between and among private parties. For example, the New York Convention[8] facilitates arbitration of international business disputes by establishing rules that promote effective enforcement of arbitral awards in domestic courts. Similarly, the Warsaw Convention[9] facilitates international aviation by providing a set of agreed rules governing the liability of airlines for international transportation of cargo and passengers. The New York and Warsaw conventions are just two examples of broad-based, multilateral treaties that ultimately rely on domestic courts as a principal enforcement mechanism. These and other treaties help promote the growth of a global economy that provides economic benefits for billions of people. If domestic courts failed to enforce such treaties, the private actors whom the treaties are designed to benefit could be deprived of those benefits.

Third, as mentioned previously, the fact that many treaties create private rights without granting private parties access to international dispute resolution mechanisms creates a right-remedy gap on the international plane. Domestic courts are not the only actors capable of filling that gap, but they

[8] Convention on the Recognition and Enforcement of Foreign Arbitral Awards, June 10, 1958, 330 U.N.T.S. 38, U.N. Registration No. I-4739 [hereinafter, New York Convention].

[9] Convention for the Unification of Certain Rules Relating to International Carriage by Air, opened for signature Oct. 12, 1929, Registration No. LoN-3145 [hereinafter, Warsaw Convention].

states, private parties who are harmed by a violation of their treaty-based rights can generally obtain a domestic legal remedy.[19]

In the United States and Russia the evidence is somewhat mixed. To appreciate this point, it is helpful to distinguish between transnational cases, where private parties seek to enforce treaties against other private parties, and vertical cases, where private parties seek a remedy for an alleged treaty violation by a government actor. The country chapters show that domestic courts in the United States and Russia routinely apply treaties to help resolve transnational disputes between private actors.[20] However, domestic courts in Russia rarely grant judicial remedies to private parties who are the victims of treaty violations committed by the host government.[21] U.S. courts occasionally grant remedies to private actors in these types of cases, but U.S. courts frequently avoid holding government actors accountable for treaty violations by adopting an interpretive methodology that favors the government's interpretation of a treaty or by applying judicial avoidance doctrines to refrain from deciding the merits of a treaty-based claim.[22]

In sum, there does not appear to be any significant correlation between the monist-dualist dichotomy and the actual practice of domestic courts, except for the purely formal matter that courts in hybrid monist states sometimes apply treaties directly, whereas courts in dualist states apply treaties only indirectly. In terms of practical results, though, "[t]he attitude of courts themselves may be as important as the formal features of the constitutional system."[23]

II. AN ANALYSIS OF STATE PRACTICE

This section analyzes judicial practice in the eleven states surveyed in this volume, focusing on the question of whether domestic courts provide remedies to private parties who are harmed by a violation of their treaty-based primary rights. The first subsection analyzes state practice in three continental European states: Germany, Poland, and the Netherlands. The second subsection addresses three Commonwealth states: Australia, Canada, and the United Kingdom. The third subsection discusses judicial practice in two other Commonwealth states: India and South Africa. India and South Africa are unique because their highest courts have an established record of

[19] *See infra* Sections II.A and II.C.
[20] *See* Chapters 10 and 13 in this volume on Russia and the United States, respectively.
[21] *See infra* Section II.E.
[22] *See* Chapter 13.
[23] Chapter 8, pg. 369.

judicial activism. Domestic courts in these eight states generally do provide remedies for treaty violations.

The fourth subsection addresses Israel and the United States, countries with independent judiciaries that have been hesitant to play an active role in overseeing executive compliance with national treaty obligations. The final subsection analyzes judicial practice in Russia, a state that does not have a strong, independent judiciary. In Israel, the United States, and Russia, domestic courts generally do enforce transnational treaty obligations. However, with respect to vertical treaty obligations, domestic courts in Russia and the United States do not consistently provide remedies for private parties who are harmed by a violation of their treaty-based primary rights. In Israel, the problem of judicial underenforcement relates primarily to the Occupied Territories.

A. *Germany, Poland, and The Netherlands*

In Germany, Poland, and the Netherlands, domestic courts play an active role in promoting compliance with treaty obligations. Courts in those countries generally do provide remedies for individuals who are harmed by a violation of their treaty-based primary rights. There are four key features of these legal systems that help explain this judicial practice. First, in all three states, many treaties are a part of the domestic legal order. Second, the domestic courts in these states recognize that many treaties have direct effect and that individuals have standing to invoke treaties before domestic courts. Third, the courts in all three states often apply treaties indirectly to harmonize domestic law with the state's international obligations. Finally, all three states are members of the European Union. This subsection briefly analyzes the significance of each of these factors.

1. Treaties within the Domestic Legal Order. Under the constitutional systems of Germany, Poland, and the Netherlands, at least some treaties have the status of law within the domestic legal system. In the Netherlands, "[a]ll treaties that are binding on the Netherlands as a matter of international law are automatically incorporated and thus have the force of law in the domestic legal order."[24] In Germany, "[u]nder the prevailing interpretation of Article 59 of the Grundgesetz, duly ratified treaties are part of German law."[25] In Poland, "[a] ratified treaty becomes, by virtue of its ratification,

[24] *Id.*, pg. 331.
[25] Chapter 5, pg. 209.

a 'part of the domestic legal order.'"[26] However, "agreements of a purely administrative nature" that are binding on Poland as a matter of international law but enter into force without ratification are not part of the domestic legal order.[27]

Although many treaties are part of the domestic legal orders in Germany, Poland, and the Netherlands, the three states differ in terms of the status they accord to treaties. In the Netherlands, treaties have a higher rank than statutes: in the event of a conflict between a statute and a treaty, the treaty takes precedence, even with respect to a later-in-time statute.[28] Indeed, "the supremacy of treaties over domestic law applies even to the Constitution itself, at least in those cases where a treaty has been adopted pursuant to article 91(3) of the Constitution, which requires a two-thirds majority vote in both Chambers of Parliament."[29]

In Poland, the rank of a treaty within the domestic legal order depends on the process that precedes ratification. Certain important categories of treaties cannot be ratified without prior statutory authorization.[30] "Treaties ratified upon statutory authorization enjoy a suprastatutory rank.... This constitutional arrangement places the rank of treaties on a higher level than the rank of authorizing statutes."[31] In contrast, treaties ratified without statutory authorization do not take precedence over statutes. "[S]ome authors accept that such treaties have a rank equal to ordinary statutes; others assign them a sub-statutory position."[32]

In Germany, also, the rank of a treaty within the domestic legal system depends on the domestic process used to authorize ratification. Article 59 of the German Constitution authorizes the president to conclude treaties. However, "ratification requires the prior consent of the Parliament if the treaty deals with the 'political relations' of the Federation, or if it relates to matters that would require legislation when regulated domestically."[33] "The domestic rank of treaties concluded with legislative consent is equal to that of domestic legislation."[34] In contrast, treaties ratified without legislative consent have a lower rank.

[26] Chapter 9, pg. 378 (quoting art. 91, sec. 1 of the Constitution).
[27] *Id.*, pg. 376.
[28] *See* Chapter 8, pg. 334 (citing art. 94 of the Dutch Constitution).
[29] *Id.*
[30] *See* Chapter 9, pgs. 376–77.
[31] *Id.*, pg. 379.
[32] *Id.*, pg. 380.
[33] Chapter 5, pg. 214.
[34] *Id.*, pg. 217.

2. The Direct Effect of Treaties and the Rights of Private Parties. A treaty provision has *direct effect*, or is *directly applicable*, if domestic law authorizes a domestic court to apply that treaty provision as a rule of decision. A treaty provision is *invocable* by a private party if that person is empowered to invoke that provision before a domestic court.[35] Conceptually, invocability and direct effect are two distinct issues. However, the two issues are closely linked in the judicial practice of courts in Germany, Poland, and the Netherlands. In all three countries, treaty provisions that protect individual rights are generally considered directly applicable and invocable by private parties.

Article 93 of the Constitution of the Netherlands specifies that treaty provisions "that are binding on all persons by virtue of their contents shall become binding after they have been published."[36] This provision "has been interpreted in case law to mean that a treaty provision has to be sufficiently clear to function as 'objective law' in the domestic legal order."[37] Thus, treaty provisions have direct effect if they are "sufficiently clear, by virtue of their contents, that private parties can ascertain what conduct is permitted or prohibited."[38] By its terms, Article 93 specifies who is bound by a treaty provision; it does not specify who is entitled to invoke a treaty before a domestic court. "In practice, though, Article 93 is also interpreted and applied in such a way that individuals may invoke a" treaty only if it satisfies the requirements of Article 93.[39]

In the Netherlands, the question of whether a treaty provision protects individual rights is understood to be an issue of treaty interpretation. Dutch "courts ask whether the parties intended to grant rights to individuals. . . . If the intention of the parties is not clear from the treaty or its negotiating history, the court will analyze the nature and content of the treaty to ascertain whether its provisions are designed to protect the interests of individuals."[40] If a treaty is designed to protect the interests of private parties, the Dutch courts will say that it grants rights to private parties. Moreover, "[i]f a treaty does confer rights on private parties, then, as a matter of Dutch law and practice, those parties can invoke the treaty before a domestic court."[41] Thus, in the Netherlands, if a treaty grants rights to

[35] *See* Chapter 8, pgs. 345–48.
[36] Gw. art. 93 (quoted in Chapter 8, pg. 332).
[37] Chapter 8, pg. 333.
[38] *Id.*
[39] *See* Chapter 8, pgs. 345–48.
[40] *Id.*, pg. 347.
[41] *Id.*, pgs. 346–47.

private party P, P can invoke the treaty before a domestic court and the court will apply the treaty as a rule of decision in an appropriate case.

The situation in Poland is similar. The Polish Constitution specifies that a treaty provision is not directly applicable if it "depends on the enactment of a statute."[42] A treaty provision that depends on the enactment of a statute is *not self-executing*; other treaty provisions are *self-executing*. Polish case law establishes that a treaty provision is self-executing, and hence directly applicable, if it "has been drafted in a complete manner, (i.e., in a manner allowing its use as an exclusive legal basis for resolving an individual case or controversy)."[43] Moreover, if a treaty provision is self-executing, it is "regarded as conferring rights on individuals and, consequently, may (and should) be applied by the courts as an independent legal basis for judicial decisions."[44] Thus, in practice, Polish courts, as do Dutch courts, link the ideas of private rights, invocability, and direct effect. A treaty that confers rights on private parties is invocable by the right holder; it can also be applied directly by a court.

In Germany, as in Poland, courts distinguish between self-executing and non-self-executing treaties. A self-executing treaty is invocable by private parties and can be applied directly by the courts. In Germany, direct judicial application of treaties on behalf of private parties is "not considered controversial as long as [the treaty] create[s] rights and obligations in the relationship between the state and its citizens... when individual citizens claimed rights against the state on the basis of international law, it was quite natural that the state that had given its word to other states could be regarded also bound towards its own citizens."[45] In short, if a treaty grants rights to private parties and imposes corresponding duties on the state, the judiciary will enforce those rights on behalf of an aggrieved individual.

Courts in all three countries have stated (or assumed) that the European Convention on Human Rights (ECHR) is both directly applicable and invocable by individual litigants.[46] In addition, courts in the Netherlands "have identified a large number of international treaties and agreements

[42] Chapter 9, pg. 400.

[43] *Id.*

[44] *Id.*, pg. 379.

[45] Chapter 5, pg. 211.

[46] *See, e.g.*, Chapter 5, pg. 232 (quoting the Federal Constitutional Court for the proposition that the ECHR "must... be complied with by the judiciary"); Chapter 9, pg. 405 ("The direct applicability of the Convention seems so evident that the Supreme Court has simply assumed that the ECHR is directly applicable, without ever deciding that question explicitly"); Chapter 8, pg. 342 (Dutch courts have accepted that "all the substantive provisions of the ECHR and most of the substantive provisions of the International

that create individual rights that are invocable in domestic courts. These include all the conventions on human rights, the Convention relating to the Status of Refugees, various treaties covering social security and labor law, and numerous other agreements."[47] The Polish Supreme Court has held that Article 8 of the Paris Convention for the Protection of Industrial Property "is directly enforceable in the domestic legal system."[48] Similarly, Polish courts frequently apply the Hague Convention on the Civil Aspects of International Child Abduction as a self-executing treaty.[49]

In Germany, Poland, and the Netherlands, the fact that (some) treaties are part of the domestic legal order makes it possible for domestic courts to apply treaties directly. If a treaty provision is sufficiently clear, and if it is designed to benefit private parties, judicial practice establishes that the provision is invocable by private parties and directly applicable by the courts. This helps explain why judicial practice in these countries is generally consistent with the principle that private parties who are harmed by a violation of their treaty-based primary rights are ordinarily entitled to a judicial remedy for the harm they suffered.

3. **Friendly Interpretation and Indirect Application.** Although Germany, Poland, and the Netherlands all permit direct application of treaties by domestic courts, the courts in these countries also apply treaties indirectly to promote compliance with international obligations. Indirect application occurs when a court invokes a treaty as an aid to interpretation of a domestic constitutional or statutory provision.

Article 9 of the Polish Constitution specifies that "the Republic of Poland shall respect international law binding on it."[50] Accordingly, Polish courts accept that "domestic law (including the Constitution) should be interpreted in a manner 'friendly' towards obligations resulting from international and European law."[51] In Germany, the Constitution does not state explicitly that courts must respect international law. Nevertheless, the German Constitution is "famous for its 'friendliness' towards international legal relations."[52] Accordingly, the task of domestic courts "is to allow Germany to fulfill its international obligations by faithfully interpreting German law

Covenant on Civil and Political Rights (ICCPR)" should be given direct effect by Dutch courts).

[47] Chapter 8, pg. 347.

[48] Chapter 9, pg. 401 (quoting judgment of June 14, 1988).

[49] *Id.*, pgs. 406–07.

[50] Constitution of Poland, art. 9 (quoted in Chapter 9, at 375).

[51] Chapter 9, pg. 382.

[52] Chapter 5, pg. 209.

in accordance with Germany's international obligations, in particular treaty obligations."[53] Similarly, in the Netherlands, the Supreme Court has stated that "Dutch courts should, as far as is possible, interpret and apply Dutch law in such a way that the State meets its treaty obligations."[54]

In Germany, as noted previously, treaties and statutes have equal rank. Consequently, a later-in-time statute would theoretically take precedence over an earlier-in-time treaty under the *lex posterior* principle.[55] However, in cases where there is an apparent conflict between an earlier treaty and a later statute, German courts often apply the treaty as *lex specialis* to avoid a ruling that would place Germany in violation of its international obligations. "German courts assume that the legislature, had it anticipated a conflict between a treaty and a statute, would have provided a legislative exception to accommodate the treaty."[56] Thus, the German Constitutional Court has stated: "it cannot be assumed that the legislature, insofar as it has not clearly declared otherwise, wishes to deviate from the Federal Republic of Germany's international treaty commitments or to facilitate violation of such commitments."[57]

In Poland, it is more common for domestic courts to apply treaties indirectly than for courts to apply treaties directly.[58] As Professor Nollkaemper explains, courts may prefer indirect application, even in cases where they could apply a treaty directly, because direct application might produce a conflict with domestic law, and "courts usually prefer a conciliatory solution over the acknowledgment and resolution of a conflict of law."[59] By construing domestic law in a manner that is consistent with the state's treaty obligations, the courts in Germany, Poland, and the Netherlands promote national compliance with those obligations.

4. The Influence of European Law. European Union law exerts tremendous influence over the national legal systems of the twenty-seven countries that are members of the European Union. The most obvious reason for this influence is that "the case law of the European Court of Justice (ECJ) . . . establishes that European law requires the direct effect of

[53] *Id.*, pg. 210.
[54] Chapter 8, pgs. 348–49 (quoting Supreme Court judgment of November 16, 1990).
[55] *See* Chapter 5, pg. 228.
[56] *Id.*, pg. 229.
[57] *Id.* (quoting BVerfGE 74, 358 at 370).
[58] *See* Chapter 9, pg. 404 (noting that "coapplication of an international norm and a domestic norm" is "the most typical technique" of treaty application).
[59] Chapter 8, pg. 349.

community law in the domestic legal order."[60] Thus, the domestic courts in EU member states routinely give direct effect to European law – not only to primary law (which is codified in treaties and in laws enacted by the European Parliament) but also to the secondary law codified in regulations enacted by the European Commission.[61]

The ECJ not only demands the direct effect of EU law within national legal systems but also "demands supremacy of European law over domestic law."[62] Thus, domestic courts in EU member states routinely resolve conflicts between EU law and domestic statutes in favor of EU law.[63] In principle, domestic courts reserve the right to reject the ECJ's interpretation of a European law if it would "lead to results contradicting the explicit wording of constitutional norms or being irreconcilable with the minimum guarantee functions realised by the [national] Constitution."[64] The German Constitutional Court has maintained its prerogative "to overrule the ECJ... if human rights protection in the European Union breaks down... [and] in cases where European organs act beyond the scope of their legitimate authority."[65] However, the German Constitutional Court has never actually overruled an ECJ decision. Thus, in practice, Community law as interpreted by the ECJ "plays a paramount role in the" domestic legal systems of EU member states.[66]

Apart from the direct application of Community law, EU membership influences judicial application of international law by domestic courts in three other ways. First, as a practical matter, decisions of the European Court of Human Rights (ECtHR) have tremendous influence within domestic legal systems, even though, in contrast to ECJ decisions, ECtHR decisions do not have direct effect within national legal systems. For example, in the Netherlands, "[t]he practice of following interpretations of the ECtHR is such that, in practice, they have almost a dispositive effect."[67] Professor

[60] Chapter 5, pg. 210.
[61] *See* Chapter 9, pgs. 385–86; Chapter 5, pg. 225 (noting that individuals in Germany may raise a constitutional claim before the German Constitutional Court "against a lower court accused of disregarding its obligations under the" Treaty on the European Community).
[62] Chapter 5, pg. 210.
[63] *See* Chapter 5, pgs. 225–26; Chapter 9, pgs. 385–86 and 393–94; Chapter 8, pg. 365 (stating that "large sections of EC law have direct effect in the member states, taking precedence over contradictory rules in national law").
[64] Chapter 9, pg. 397 (quoting judgment of Constitutional Court of May 11, 2005).
[65] Chapter 5, pgs. 226–27.
[66] Chapter 9, pg. 385.
[67] Chapter 8, pg. 363. *See also* Chapter 5, pgs. 231–33; Chapter 9, pgs. 389–90 (stating that "the case law of the ECtHR is a binding part of the Convention").

Nollkaemper suggests that "the acceptance of the legal relevance of such interpretations has been enhanced by the fact that courts have become accustomed to" following decisions of the ECJ.[68]

Second, in at least some EU member states, domestic courts have become sufficiently accustomed to following ECJ decisions that their receptivity to decisions of international tribunals extends beyond European courts to other international courts. For example, "[i]n a 2006 chamber decision, the Federal Constitutional Court [in Germany] applied the reasoning of" a prior decision involving the ECHR "to the relationship between the International Court of Justice and the Federal Constitutional Court."[69] Under this approach, German courts do "not follow a path of complete subservience to international courts and tribunals," but "the principle of 'friendliness to international law' enshrined in the German constitution . . . require[s] domestic courts to 'take into account' decisions of the International Court of Justice that are binding on Germany."[70] Professor Paulus explains that "[t]he German Court's decision . . . emphasizes that international integration is also a constitutional value."[71]

Finally, it is important to bear in mind that the European Union itself is a member of the international community and subject to both customary and conventional international legal obligations. The ECJ "has ruled that international regulations in areas where the European Union exercises jurisdiction are automatically part of the EU legal order."[72]

> This situation has direct consequences for the national legal orders of the member states. It means that member states receive international law into their domestic legal systems not only directly (as independent members of the international community) but also indirectly, as members of the EU, because international obligations that form part of the European legal order are binding on member states as an element of core Community law.[73]

Consequently, "as member states transfer more and more powers to the European Union, they are increasingly incorporating international law into their own legal orders as a part of European law."[74]

[68] Chapter 8, pg. 363.
[69] Chapter 5, pg. 234.
[70] *Id.*, pgs. 234–35.
[71] *Id.*, pg. 235.
[72] Chapter 8, pg. 365.
[73] *Id.*, pg. 366.
[74] *Id.*, pg. 367. For further elaboration of this point, *see id.*, 365–68.

B. *Australia, Canada, and the United Kingdom*

Australia, Canada, and the United Kingdom are strict dualist states: a treaty has no legal force within their domestic legal systems unless the legislature has incorporated the treaty into domestic law. Consequently, domestic courts in these countries never apply treaties directly as law. Even so, courts routinely grant remedies to private parties who have been harmed by a violation of their treaty-based primary rights. Courts typically achieve this result by applying a statute that was enacted to implement a treaty or by interpreting a statute to conform to treaty obligations codified in an unincorporated treaty. This section analyzes the domestic application of treaties in Australia, Canada, and the United Kingdom. The first subsection addresses the legislature's role in incorporating treaties into domestic law. I then examine the judiciary's role in applying incorporated treaties, unincorporated treaties, and partially incorporated treaties. The final subsection addresses judicial application of treaties as an aid to constitutional interpretation.

1. Legislative Incorporation. The legal systems of Australia and Canada, like those of most other Commonwealth states, are based on the British model. Under this model, treaty making is understood to be an executive function; the executive does not need legislative approval to make a binding international treaty commitment on behalf of the nation. However, lawmaking is a legislative function. This is why treaties do not have the status of law in the domestic legal system, and why statutes that incorporate treaties into domestic law generally control the domestic effects of treaties.[75]

Not all treaties require legislative incorporation. "For those treaties that operate purely on the international plane, without requiring any domestic legal effect from the parties,"[76] legislative implementation is not necessary. Similarly, if a treaty obligates a state to protect certain private rights within its domestic legal system, but preexisting legislation already protects those rights to the full extent required by international law, additional legislation would be superfluous.[77] Thus, legislative action is needed only if a proposed treaty (1) does not operate purely on the international plane and (2) obligates the state to protect private rights that are not already protected by preexisting domestic law.

[75] *See* Chapter 12, pg. 477; Chapter 4, pgs. 167–68; Chapter 3, pg. 130 (quoting Minister of State for Immigration and Ethnic Affairs v. Teoh (1995) 128 ALR 353).

[76] Chapter 4, pg. 169.

[77] *Id.*, pg. 170 ("Another way of ensuring domestic conformity with treaty obligations, in many cases, is simply to retain laws that predate the treaty but that, as it happens, suffice to discharge the state's responsibilities under the supervening treaty.")

In all three states, the political branches try to ensure treaty compliance by enacting the legislation necessary to implement treaty obligations before the treaty enters into force on the international plane. For example, "the unwavering practice of the [British] Government is to" examine each treaty in detail "to see whether there will be any need for new legislation to enable a provision to be enforceable in domestic law. It is invariable British practice never to ratify a treaty until any such legislation has first been made."[78] Similarly, "[t]he usual Canadian practice is not to allow treaties requiring domestic implementation to enter into force for Canada until the federal government has ensured the treaty's implementation. The reason for this is simply that, where a treaty requires domestic legal action by states parties, failure to take that action may breach the treaty."[79]

Legislative incorporation can take many forms. The simplest case is when the legislature includes the text of a treaty as an attachment to a statute and declares that the attached treaty shall have the force of law in the domestic legal system.[80] In the alternative, the legislature might amend a preexisting statute "to bring it into conformity with the treaty's requirements"[81] or delegate authority to an executive official to adopt regulations to implement the treaty.[82] In Australia, if the legislature determines that the text of a treaty "is not suited to simple transportation into Australian law, . . . the Commonwealth and where necessary State legislation will seek to adapt the international instrument to Australian conditions."[83] This approach sometimes results in partial incorporation rather than total incorporation, a subject that is addressed below.

2. Full Incorporation of Treaties. If a treaty-based primary right has been fully incorporated into domestic law, domestic courts enforce that right in the same way that they enforce any other law. Thus, in Australia, "where municipal legislation imports international agreements, conventions and treaties, those international instruments will have operative effect."[84] Similarly, in Canada, "[w]here the treaty right upon which a claimant seeks to rely is implemented in Canadian law, there may be no need to refer to the international aspect of the right at all. The right has

[78] Chapter 12, pg. 486.
[79] Chapter 4, pg. 204.
[80] *See* Chapter 12, pg. 479; Chapter 4, pg. 169.
[81] Chapter 4, pgs. 169–70.
[82] *See* Chapter 12, pgs. 480–81.
[83] Chapter 3, pg. 159.
[84] *Id.*, at 158–59.

descended from the lofty heights of international law to the solid ground of domestic law and will be applied in the same way as any other domestic provision."[85]

If a treaty has been fully incorporated into domestic law, and a private claimant seeks a domestic judicial remedy for a treaty violation, the court will have to decide whether the implementing statute confers a primary right. If the claimant cannot show that the statute creates a primary right, he or she will not be entitled to a remedy.[86] Conversely, "if a court does find that the implementing legislation (not the treaty itself) does confer a private right, it would be rare indeed if it did not also find some sort of remedy."[87] As a formal matter, the court applies the statute, not the treaty. Even so, as a practical matter, if the treaty has been fully incorporated into domestic law, and if the treaty itself creates primary rights for private parties, the statute will also create primary rights for private parties and will generally be enforceable by the right holders.

When a treaty has been fully incorporated into domestic law, the courts are often called upon to interpret the treaty. The courts in Australia, Canada, and the United Kingdom interpret treaties in accordance with internationally agreed rules of treaty interpretation.[88] By looking primarily to international law rather than domestic law as a guide to treaty interpretation, the courts help promote compliance with the state's international obligations.

If the political branches had perfect foresight, and if treaty compliance was always the paramount objective, then every treaty requiring legislative implementation would be fully incorporated in a domestic statute, and such treaties would be privately enforceable in precisely the same way as other laws. However, foresight is not always perfect. Moreover, when enacting implementing legislation for treaties, legislatures sometimes try to balance the treaty goals with competing domestic objectives. As a result, some treaties that require domestic application remain unincorporated or partially incorporated. In recent years, courts in Australia, Canada, and the United Kingdom have begun to play a much more active role in enforcing these types of treaty provisions.

[85] Chapter 4, pg. 202.

[86] *See* Chapter 12, pg. 482.

[87] *Id.*, pg. 486.

[88] *See, e.g.*, Chapter 12, pg. 483 ("When a treaty has been incorporated by attaching all or part of it to legislation, since the treaty is a creation of international law the English courts will interpret it according to the rules of international law."). *See also* Chapter 3, pgs. 151–52; Chapter 4, pgs. 182–83 (suggesting that "international treaty interpretation rules supplant domestic interpretive rules where the two approaches differ").

3. Unincorporated Treaties. One of the features of a strict dualist system is that a conflict between a statute and an unincorporated treaty is invariably resolved in favor of the statute. "Nothing in the written constitution of Canada prevents Canadian legislatures from enacting laws contrary to the state's obligations under treaties."[89] The same is true for Australia's written constitution and the United Kingdom's (largely) unwritten constitution. Thus, if the legislature adopts a statute that conflicts with the state's treaty obligations, the state may well violate its treaty obligations, and individuals harmed by such a violation will have no remedy. However, courts in all three countries are hesitant to conclude that there is an irreconcilable conflict between a statute and a treaty, and they have developed a variety of mechanisms to apply even unincorporated treaties.

The most important mechanism for judicial application of unincorporated treaties is the presumption of conformity. "[W]hen construing domestic laws Canadian courts apply an interpretive presumption that those laws conform to the state's obligations under treaties and other sources of international law."[90] Similarly, "[u]nclear legislation will be interpreted in a way that is consistent with any applicable international obligations of the United Kingdom, including customary international law and unincorporated treaties."[91] And in Australia, "[i]n resolving ambiguity in a statute, courts favour a construction which accords with Australia's obligations under a treaty, on the basis that they presume that parliament intends to legislate in accordance with, rather than contrary to, its international obligations."[92]

All agree that the presumption of conformity applies when a statute is ambiguous. But how much ambiguity is needed to trigger application of the presumption? Before 1990, the prevailing view was "that courts could not invoke a treaty for interpretive purposes unless the statute under consideration was first determined to be ambiguous on its face."[93] However, the Supreme Court of Canada held in 1990 "that a court or tribunal may make reference to an international agreement at the very outset of the inquiry to determine whether there is any ambiguity, patent or latent, in the domestic legislation."[94] Since that time, Canadian courts "need not justify their resort to relevant treaties binding on the state by purporting to find some

[89] Chapter 4, pg. 190.
[90] *Id.*, pg. 188.
[91] Chapter 12, pg. 482.
[92] Chapter 3, pg. 153 (quoting Chief Justice Gleeson).
[93] Chapter 4, pg. 192.
[94] *Id.*

patent ambiguity on the face of the legislation."[95] Justice Kirby, a justice on the High Court of Australia, has forcefully advocated the adoption of a similar approach in Australia.[96] However, his view remains a minority view in Australia.[97] There is no indication that courts in the United Kingdom have deviated from the traditional view that there must be ambiguity on the face of the statute to justify reliance on an unincorporated treaty as an aid to statutory interpretation.

A separate question concerns the extent to which courts can or should apply unincorporated treaties in the context of judicial review of discretionary decisions by administrative agencies. The Australian High Court has endorsed the so-called legitimate expectations doctrine, first articulated in the famous *Teoh* case.[98] In that case, a Malaysian citizen facing deportation argued that immigration authorities should exercise their discretionary powers under federal statutes in accordance with Australia's obligations under the Convention on the Rights of the Child, an unincorporated treaty. The High Court stated: "[R]atification of a convention is a positive statement by the executive government . . . [that] its agencies will act in accordance with the Convention. The positive statement is an adequate foundation for a legitimate expectation, absent statutory or executive indications to the contrary, that administrative decision-makers will act in conformity with the Convention."[99] As applied by Australian courts, this doctrine does not compel an administrative decision maker to decide a case in a particular way, but it does require the decision maker to take account of unincorporated treaties in the process of making a decision.

British and Canadian courts have declined to follow the legitimate expectations doctrine.[100] In Canada, though, courts may have achieved essentially the same result by applying the presumption of conformity to review discretionary decisions by administrative decision makers. For example, *Baker v. Canada*,[101] like *Teoh*, was a case in which a foreign national facing deportation challenged an administrative decision on the grounds that immigration authorities "failed to give sufficient weight to . . . Canada's obligations under the 1989 Convention on the Rights of the Child."[102] The Supreme Court accepted that the convention had not been incorporated into Canadian law

[95] *Id.*, pg. 193.
[96] *See* Chapter 3, at 153–56.
[97] *See id.*, at 154–56.
[98] Teoh, 128 ALR 353.
[99] *Id.* (quoted in Chapter 3, pg. 148).
[100] *See* Chapter 12, note 37; Chapter 4, pg. 173.
[101] Baker v. Canada, [1999] 2 S.C.R. 817.
[102] Chapter 4, pgs. 194–95.

"but held nevertheless that the minister's decision was an unlawful exercise of discretion because . . . it unreasonably neglected . . . Canada's obligations under the Convention."[103] This approach has not gained wide traction in the United Kingdom, but in a 1997 decision, "one judge in the House of Lords was prepared to consider the legality of the exercise of a statutory power in the light of an unincorporated treaty, the Rights of the Child Convention."[104]

4. Partial Incorporation. The term *partial incorporation*, or *quasi-incorporation*, refers to two distinct types of domestic statutes. The first type includes "laws that are based . . . on international instruments and are clearly designed to give effect to international obligations"[105] but do not fully incorporate a treaty because the implementing statute adapts the treaty to domestic requirements. Judicial application of these types of statutes is similar to judicial application of fully incorporated treaties, insofar as the treaty is incorporated, and similar to judicial application of unincorporated treaties, insofar as the treaty is unincorporated.

A distinct variety of partial incorporation occurs when a statute requires an administrative decision maker to exercise his or her discretionary authority in conformity with treaty obligations. For example, in the *Project Blue Sky* case,[106] an Australian statute specifically directed the Australian Broadcasting Authority (ABA) "to perform its functions in a manner consistent with 'Australia's obligations under any convention to which Australia is a party or any agreement between Australia and a foreign country.'"[107] This situation differs from the legitimate expectations doctrine in *Teoh*, because in *Teoh* there was no statute that specifically instructed immigration authorities to exercise their discretion in conformity with the Convention on the Rights of the Child. The petitioners in *Project Blue Sky* argued that the ABA had violated the statute by enacting regulations that were inconsistent with a bilateral free-trade agreement between Australia and New Zealand.[108] The High Court held that the "ABA was precluded from making a standard inconsistent with the"[109] free-trade agreement, and that "the standard had been unlawfully made."[110] Consequently, even though the free-trade

[103] *Id.*, pg. 195.
[104] Chapter 12, pgs. 492–93.
[105] Chapter 3, pg. 159.
[106] Project Blue Sky Inc. v. Australian Broad. Auth. (1998) 153 ALR 490.
[107] Chapter 3, pg. 141 (quoting Broadcasting Services Act 1992).
[108] *See id.*, at 141–42.
[109] *Id.*, at 144.
[110] *Id.*, at 145.

agreement had not been incorporated into domestic law, the petitioners were able to obtain a remedy (i.e., a judicial order blocking enforcement of the regulation) by invoking a statute that referred indirectly to the treaty.

Project Blue Sky is not a unique case. "[T]here are other Commonwealth statutes which make reference to international instruments without directly incorporating those treaties into Australian law."[111] Similarly, the chapter on the United Kingdom discusses several cases where petitioners have obtained judicial remedies by invoking a statute that requires an administrative decision maker to exercise his or her authority in conformity with treaty obligations.[112] In some cases, the statute refers to one particular treaty or group of treaties.[113] In other cases, though, as in *Project Blue Sky*, the relevant statute imposes a more general requirement for the administrative decision maker to act in conformity with the state's treaty obligations. As the Australia chapter notes, "[r]equiring a statutory instrumentality to act in accordance with a state's international obligations without giving any precise direction as to which international obligations in particular may be relevant will potentially open the door for a vast array of international instruments to be considered" in actions for judicial review of administrative decisions.[114]

5. Treaties and Constitutional Interpretation. The preceding sections discussed the use of treaties as an aid to statutory interpretation. In Australia, Justice Kirby has advocated the use of treaties as an aid to constitutional interpretation to promote Australia's compliance with its treaty obligations.[115] However, the majority of justices on the High Court have firmly and consistently rejected the idea that unincorporated treaties provide a useful guide to issues of constitutional interpretation.

In contrast, the Supreme Court of Canada has apparently embraced the idea that the presumption of conformity applies not only to ordinary

[111] *Id.*, pg. 159 (citing examples).

[112] *See* Chapter 12, pgs. 490–91 (noting that "there have been numerous successful challenges by way of judicial review to [administrative] decisions on claims to refugee status"); *id.*, at 491–92 (discussing the *Quark* case); *id.*, at 492 (noting that "the Antarctic Act 1994... requires a permit from the Secretary of State to conduct various activities in Antarctica... [and] section 15 requires the Secretary of State to have regard to [a specific treaty] when considering a permit application").

[113] For analysis of a Canadian case that is similar, *see* Gib Van Ert, Using International Law in Canadian Courts 155–56 (2d ed. 2008) (discussing the Federal Court of Appeal decision in DeGuzman v. Canada (Minister of Citizenship and Immigration) [2005] 262 D.L.R. (4th) 13 (F.C.A.)).

[114] Chapter 3, pg. 161.

[115] *See id.*, at 156–58.

statutes but also to the Canadian Charter of Rights and Freedoms, a part of Canada's written constitution since 1982. Until recently, there was a lively debate within Canada about whether the presumption of conformity applied to the Charter.[116] However, "two recent decisions of the Supreme Court of Canada, released one day apart [in 2007], appear to establish the court's determination to subject the Charter to the same presumption of conformity that is applicable to the rest of Canadian law."[117]

There are two main reasons why this issue has not arisen in the United Kingdom. First, the British constitution is "mainly, but not entirely, unwritten."[118] Second, the 1998 Human Rights Act effectively incorporated the ECHR into British law. "The Act does not formally make the ECHR part of domestic law, but requires courts and public bodies to apply existing and future legislation 'so far as possible' in a way 'which is compatible with' rights under the ECHR."[119] The Human Rights Act has had far-reaching implications for the judicial protection of individual rights in the United Kingdom.[120] As a result of the Act, domestic courts routinely provide remedies for violations of internationally protected individual rights – rights that in many countries are protected by a written constitution – but they do so without reference to a written constitution.

*****

In sum, judicial practice in Australia, Canada, and the United Kingdom is generally consistent with the principle that states should provide remedies to private parties who are harmed by a violation of their treaty-based primary rights. Each state has reached this result in a slightly different manner. The United Kingdom relies heavily on legislative action to achieve total or partial incorporation of treaties; the 1998 Human Rights Act, in particular, has substantially expanded the judicial role in providing remedies for violations of internationally protected private rights. In Canada, the courts make fairly aggressive use of the presumption of conformity in both statutory and constitutional interpretation. In Australia, courts apply the legitimate expectations doctrine; they also play a fairly active role in supervising application of partially incorporated treaties. Even so, in all three states, dualist principles establish a clear limit to the judicial role in providing remedies: if the legislature enacts a statute that is clearly inconsistent with the state's treaty obligations, domestic courts will apply the statute.

116 *See* Chapter 4, pgs. 197–99.
117 *Id.*, at 199. *See also id.*, at 199–201.
118 Chapter 12, pg. 477.
119 *Id.*, at 487.
120 *See id.*, at 487–90.

C. *India and South Africa*

Like their counterparts in Australia, Canada, and the United Kingdom, domestic courts in India and South Africa apply treaties in cases where the legislature has incorporated a treaty into domestic law. They also apply unincorporated treaties in the context of statutory interpretation and judicial review of administrative action. However, India and South Africa differ from the states discussed previously because courts in India and South Africa make fairly aggressive use of international law as an aid to constitutional interpretation. By construing constitutional provisions to promote compliance with treaty obligations, they ultimately remedy treaty violations by enforcing the constitution.

This section summarizes judicial practice in India and South Africa. It begins with a brief review of the relevant constitutional background. It then discusses the use of international law generally, and treaties in particular, as an aid to constitutional interpretation. The next subsection explains how courts in India and South Africa have adapted traditional remedial and procedural mechanisms to promote aggressive enforcement of treaties. The final subsection touches briefly on judicial application of unincorporated treaties in the context of statutory interpretation and judicial review of administrative action.

1. **Constitutional Background.** At the end of the apartheid era, South Africa adopted an interim constitution in 1994, and it adopted its current constitution in 1996.[121] Section 231(4) of the 1996 Constitution states: "Any international agreement becomes law in the Republic when it is enacted into law by national legislation; but a self-executing provision of an agreement that has been approved by Parliament is law in the Republic unless it is inconsistent with the Constitution or an Act of Parliament."[122] The first clause makes clear that the South African system is largely dualist in that most treaties require legislative incorporation. The second clause provides that self-executing treaty provisions are automatically incorporated into domestic law without the need for legislative action, apart from legislative approval of the treaty itself, which is necessary for international entry into force.[123] To date, no South African court has actually held that a particular treaty provision is self-executing.[124] Thus, although the clause allowing for

[121] *See* Chapter 11, pg. 450.
[122] Sec. 231(4) of the 1996 Constitution (quoted in Chapter 11, pg. 452).
[123] *See* Chapter 11, pgs. 452–54.
[124] *See id.*, at 454.

self-executing treaties has generated substantial scholarly debate,[125] direct application of treaties by South African courts remains a theoretical option but not a practical reality.

Three other constitutional provisions exert a significant influence over the judicial application of treaties in South Africa. First, Section 233 stipulates: "When interpreting any legislation, every court must prefer any reasonable interpretation of the legislation that is consistent with international law over any alternative interpretation that is inconsistent with international law."[126] This provision effectively elevates the presumption of conformity to constitutional status. Next, Section 39(1) provides: "When interpreting the Bill of Rights, a court, tribunal or forum . . . must consider international law; and may consider foreign law."[127] This section requires courts to apply the presumption of conformity in the context of constitutional interpretation, at least when the Bill of Rights is at issue. Finally, Section 39(2) states: "When interpreting any legislation, and when developing the common law or customary law, every court, tribunal or forum must promote the spirit, purport and objects of the Bill of Rights."[128] The Constitutional Court has taken the view "that the spirit, purport and objects of the bill of rights . . . are inextricably linked to international law and the values and approaches of the international community."[129]

With respect to treaties, the Indian Constitution follows the British model. India is a traditional dualist state in which all treaties require legislative incorporation to give them the force of law within the domestic legal system.[130] Thus, in contrast to South Africa, direct application of treaties is not even a theoretical possibility in India because all treaties are non-self-executing.[131]

Part III of the Indian Constitution concerns fundamental rights. Part IV contains the "Directive Principles of State Policy." In contrast to the fundamental rights provisions, the directive principles are "not directly enforceable by any court."[132] Even so, the Supreme Court maintains that Parts III and IV "are supplementary and complementary to each other, and that the fundamental rights must be construed in light of the directive

[125] *See id.*, at 454–55.
[126] S. Afr. Const., sec. 233 (quoted in Chapter 11, pg. 457).
[127] *Id.*, at sec. 39(1) (quoted in Chapter 11, at 457–58).
[128] *Id.*, at sec. 39(2) (quoted in Chapter 11, at 458).
[129] Chapter 11, pg. 462 (quoting Neville Botha, *The Role of International Law in the Development of South African Common Law*, SAYIL 253, 259 (2001)).
[130] *See* Chapter 6, pg. 244.
[131] *See* Chapter 6, pgs. 244, 266.
[132] *Id.*, at 245.

principles."[133] For present purposes, the key directive principle is section 51(c), which provides: "The State shall endeavour to . . . foster respect for international law and treaty obligations in the dealings of organized peoples with one another."[134] In light of this directive principle, the Supreme Court's interpretive approach is "that any international convention not inconsistent with the fundamental rights provisions in the Constitution and in harmony with its spirit must be read into those provisions to enlarge the meaning and content thereof."[135] Thus, like Section 39 of the South African Constitution, Section 51(c) of the Indian Constitution, as interpreted by the Supreme Court, requires courts to construe individual rights provisions of the Constitution in accordance with international law.

2. International Law in Constitutional Interpretation. Both the Indian Supreme Court and the South African Constitutional Court make extensive use of international human rights law as a tool for interpreting individual rights provisions of their domestic constitutions. For example, the Indian Supreme Court has invoked the Convention on the Elimination of Discrimination Against Women (CEDAW) to support its interpretation of gender-equality provisions in the Indian Constitution.[136] Similarly, it has invoked Article 17 of the International Covenant on Civil and Political Rights (ICCPR) to support its holding that the constitutional guarantee of personal liberty includes a right to privacy,[137] and Article 9(5) of the ICCPR to support its holding that surviving family members of individuals killed in police custody have a constitutional right to monetary compensation.[138] Likewise, the South African Constitutional Court has relied heavily on international human rights norms to support holdings that the death penalty is unconstitutional, that corporal punishment is unconstitutional, that the state may not imprison a person for failure to pay a debt, that the constitution bars criminal punishment for sodomy, and that the state could not deport a person "to a country in which there was a real risk that he or she might be subjected to cruel, inhuman or degrading treatment."[139]

The South African Constitutional Court has stated explicitly that the constitutional requirement to consider international law "include[s] non-binding as well as binding law."[140] In accordance with this approach, the

[133] *Id.*, at 246.
[134] India Const., sec. 51 (quoted in Chapter 6, pg. 246).
[135] Chapter 6, pg. 246.
[136] *See* Chapter 6, pgs. 257–60.
[137] *See id.*, at 260–61.
[138] *See id.*, at 261–63.
[139] Chapter 11, pgs. 467–68 (citing cases).
[140] Chapter 11, pg. 458 (quoting S v. Makwanyane).

Constitutional Court and lower courts have routinely cited decisions of the UN Human Rights Committee, the European Court of Human Rights, and the European Commission of Human Rights as aids to constitutional interpretation, even though the decisions of those bodies have no binding force in South Africa.[141] The Indian Supreme Court also relies on both binding and nonbinding international norms. For example, in decisions construing constitutional provisions protecting gender equality, the Court has invoked the Beijing Principles (a nonbinding declaration) and the views of the CEDAW Committee (also nonbinding).[142] The Court relied on a nonbinding UN resolution, among other things, to support its conclusion that the right to life under Article 21 of the Constitution includes a right of access to clean drinking water.[143]

The courts' reliance on international law as a tool of constitutional interpretation is not limited to human rights law. For example, the South African "Constitutional Court considered the Convention Against Illicit Traffic in Narcotic Drugs and Psychotropic Substances of 1988, a treaty to which South Africa is a party, to help evaluate a claim that a Rastafarian was entitled to possess and use cannabis in the exercise of his freedom of religion."[144] The Indian Supreme Court referred to the same treaty in adjudicating a case in which the petitioner challenged the constitutional validity of a statute that precluded suspension or commutation of sentences for individuals convicted of drug offenses.[145]

Some scholars urge that international law is a primary tool of constitutional interpretation to be consulted in every case; others contend that courts should "consider only as an afterthought whether international law supports or is in conflict with" a particular interpretation.[146] Professor Dugard argues that the former view is correct "because there can be no 'proper' interpretation of the [South African] Constitution without a consideration of international law."[147] He cites the Constitutional Court's decision in *Azapo v. President of the Republic of South Africa*[148] in support of this viewpoint. It is unclear whether the Indian Supreme Court has directly addressed this question.

[141] *See* Chapter 11, pgs. 467–69 (citing numerous cases).
[142] *See* Chapter 6, pgs. 257–60.
[143] *See id.*, at 264.
[144] Chapter 11, pgs. 458–59.
[145] *See* Chapter 6, pgs. 264–65.
[146] Chapter 11, pg. 461.
[147] *Id.*, at 462.
[148] 1996 (4) SA 671 (CC).

3. Remedies and Procedure. Both the South African Constitutional Court and the Indian Supreme Court take a remarkably broad view of the judiciary's remedial powers. These courts use their power to fashion far-reaching remedial orders, primarily to remedy constitutional violations. However, since they routinely construe constitutional provisions to promote compliance with treaty obligations and other international norms, they ultimately provide remedies to victims of treaty violations by enforcing the constitution.

Courts in South Africa "are given wide powers to review administrative action and legislation."[149] In *Minister of Health v. Treatment Action Campaign*,[150] the Constitutional Court invoked the International Covenant on Economic, Social, and Cultural Rights (ICESCR) to support its holding that the government violated Sections 27(1) and 27(2) of the Constitution by failing "to devise and implement . . . a comprehensive and coordinated program to realize progressively the rights of pregnant women and their newborn children to have access to health services to combat mother-to-child transmission of HIV."[151] The Court announced a set of measures to combat mother-to-child transmission of HIV and ordered the government to implement those measures.[152] Similarly, in *Government of the RSA v. Grootboom*,[153] the Constitutional Court invoked the ICESCR in support of its holding that the government housing program "fell short of the obligations imposed upon the state by section 26(2) [of the Constitution] in that it failed to provide for any form of relief to those desperately in need of access to housing."[154] The Court issued a declaratory order requiring the government "to devise, fund, implement and supervise measures to provide relief to those in desperate need."[155]

The Indian Supreme Court has decided numerous cases in which it has invoked international law in support of a constitutional holding and then "legislated from the bench" to remedy the constitutional violation. For example, in *Basu v. State of West Bengal*,[156] a case involving deaths in police custody, the Court invoked the ICCPR in support of its constitutional holding.[157] It also issued a set of "eleven requirements to be followed

[149] Chapter 11, pg. 471.
[150] 2002 (5) SALR 721 (CC).
[151] *Id.*, para. 135(2).
[152] *Id.*, para. 135(3).
[153] 2001 (I) SALR 46 (CC).
[154] *Id.*, para. 95.
[155] *Id.*, para. 96.
[156] [1997] 2 LRC 1.
[157] *See* Chapter 6, pgs. 261–62.

in all cases of arrest or detention" and ordered those requirements to be disseminated to every police station throughout the country.[158] In *Visaka v. State of Rajasthan*,[159] the Court invoked CEDAW in support of its constitutional holding.[160] "The Court noted the absence of enacted law to provide for the effective enforcement of the basic human right of gender equality and guarantee against sexual harassment . . . at workplaces. Accordingly, the Court proceeded to lay down guidelines and norms for due observance at all workplaces and other institutions, until legislation is enacted for the purpose."[161]

The Indian Supreme Court has also adopted procedural innovations so that public interest litigation "now can be initiated not only by filing formal petitions in Court but also by writing letters and telegrams or when the Court takes notice of articles in newspapers."[162] The Court has "evolved the practice of appointing commissioners for the purpose of gathering facts and data in regard to a complaint of breach of a fundamental right made on behalf of the weaker sections of society."[163] The Court has explained its rationale as follows:

> [W]here a person or class of persons to whom legal injury is caused by reason of violation of a fundamental right is unable to approach the court for judicial redress on account of poverty or disability or socially or economically disadvantaged position, any member of the public acting *bona fide* can move the court for relief . . . so that the fundamental rights may become meaningful not only for the rich and well-to-do who have the means to approach the Court but also for large masses of people who are living a life of want and destitution and who are by reason of lack of awareness, assertiveness and resources unable to seek judicial redress.[164]

4. Statutory Interpretation and Other Matters. The aggressive use of international law in constitutional adjudication is perhaps the most unique feature of the Indian and South African systems. However, courts in those countries also utilize international law in statutory interpretation and common law adjudication to promote compliance with treaty-based norms and

[158] *See id.*, at 268–69.
[159] [1997] 3 LRC 361.
[160] *See* Chapter 6, pgs. 257–58.
[161] Chapter 6, pg. 270.
[162] *Id.*
[163] *Id.*, at 271 (quoting Bandhua Mukti Morcha v. Union of India, [1984] 2 SCR 67, at 111–12).
[164] *Id.* (quoting Bandhua Mukti Morcha, [1984] 2 SCR 67, at 105).

provide remedies to private parties who are harmed by a violation of their treaty-based primary rights.

As noted previously, Section 233 of the South African Constitution obligates courts, when interpreting legislation, to "prefer any reasonable interpretation of the legislation that is consistent with international law over any alternative interpretation that is inconsistent with international law."[165] Accordingly, South African courts apply a strong "presumption that the legislature, in enacting a law, did not intend to violate South Africa's international obligations."[166] Consistent with this principle, South Africa's legislature has enacted numerous statutes in which the law states explicitly that "the statute is to be interpreted to accord with international law."[167] This principle applies equally to incorporated and unincorporated treaties. Thus, South African courts refer to unincorporated treaties "in order to interpret an ambiguous statute" and in the context of adjudicating "a challenge to the validity of delegated legislation on the grounds of unreasonableness."[168]

The courts in India apply similar principles. "If two constructions of municipal law are possible, the court will lean in favour of adopting such construction as will bring the provisions of municipal law into harmony with international law or treaty obligations."[169] "This is because Parliament, prima facie, intends to give effect to India's obligations under international law."[170] The Indian Supreme Court applies these principles not only in cases involving statutory interpretation but also in the context of judicial review of discretionary decisions by state officers. For example, in a case where a public interest group challenged a governmental decision to permit a mining company to engage in mining activity in a national park, the Court cited the 1992 Convention on Biological Diversity, a treaty to which India is a party, and stated that it is "necessary for the Government to keep in view the international obligations while exercising discretionary powers under the Conservation Act unless there are compelling reasons to depart therefrom."[171] The Indian Supreme Court has also utilized its judicial power to create common law rules incorporating treaty norms codified in treaties that the Indian government has not ratified.[172]

[165] South African Const., sec. 233 (quoted in Chapter 11, pg. 457).
[166] Chapter 11, pg. 460.
[167] *Id.*, at 462. *See id.*, at 462–63 (citing examples).
[168] *Id.*, at 459.
[169] Chapter 6, pg. 247.
[170] *Id.*, at 250.
[171] Chinnappa v. Union of India, Judgment of Oct. 30, 2002 (quoted in Chapter 6, pgs. 252–53).
[172] *See* Chapter 6, pgs. 255–56.

D. *Israel and the United States*

As a formal matter, there are sharp differences between Israel and the United States with respect to the status of treaties in domestic law. Israel is a traditional dualist state; a treaty has no domestic legal force until the legislature enacts a statute to incorporate the treaty. The United States is a hybrid monist state; many treaties are automatically incorporated into the corpus of domestic law at the time of ratification. Despite these formal differences, there are striking similarities in judicial practice. In both states, the courts routinely apply doctrines that are designed to harmonize domestic law with the state's international treaty obligations. However, the courts also apply other doctrines that have the opposite effect: they shield government actors from judicial review of governmental compliance with treaty-based norms, thereby creating a free space in which executive officers can violate treaty obligations, if they so choose, without fear of judicial sanction.

The trends in Israel and the United States appear to be moving in different directions. Except for cases involving the Occupied Territories, Israeli courts are generally quite receptive to applying international law as a constraint on executive action. In contrast, U.S. courts have recently created new doctrines that effectively shield government actors from accountability for treaty violations. This section analyzes the application of treaties by domestic courts in Israel and the United States. The analysis is divided into three subsections. The first subsection discusses the formal status of treaties within the domestic legal systems of Israel and the United States. The next subsection analyzes the tools that courts employ to promote the domestic application of treaties. The final subsection examines the strategies that courts utilize to insulate government actors from judicial review of governmental compliance with treaty-based norms.

1. The Status of Treaties in Domestic Law. Israel does not have a single written constitution. The Israeli constitution consists of a set of Basic Laws enacted by the Knesset between 1958 and 1992, supplemented by judge-made common law. Initially, the Israeli Supreme Court held that most of the Basic Laws had the same status as ordinary legislation. However, after adoption of two Basic Laws in 1992, including one on "Human Dignity and Liberty," the Supreme Court reversed course and "held that all Basic Laws have constitutional status and may not be amended by ordinary legislation."[173]

The status of international law within the Israeli legal system is governed entirely by judge-made law because there are no statutes or Basic Laws

[173] Chapter 7, pg. 274.

that address the issue. The Israeli Supreme Court has endorsed three key principles, which are derived primarily from British law. First, legislation adopted by the Knesset takes precedence over international law; in the event of a conflict, the will of the legislature prevails.[174] Second, customary international law has the force of law within the domestic legal system, provided that it does not conflict with a valid statute.[175] Third, a treaty that is binding on Israel as a matter of international law lacks the force of law within the domestic legal system unless and until the Knesset enacts legislation to incorporate the treaty.[176] As in other traditional dualist states, the legislature employs a variety of techniques for incorporating treaties into domestic law.[177]

The U.S. Constitution states expressly that "all Treaties made, or which shall be made, under the Authority of the United States, shall be the supreme Law of the Land."[178] On its face, this language suggests that the United States is a purely monist system with respect to treaties; the text seems to say that all treaties have the force of law within the domestic legal system. However, judicial decisions distinguish between self-executing and non-self-executing treaties.[179] There is no generally agreed definition of these terms, but one version of the doctrine holds that non-self-executing treaties lack the force of law within the domestic legal system in the absence of implementing legislation.[180] The U.S. system is properly characterized as a hybrid monist system because some (but not all) treaties are automatically incorporated into domestic law at the time of ratification.

In the United States, a self-executing treaty has the same status as a federal statute. In the event of a conflict between a federal statute and a self-executing treaty, the last-in-time prevails.[181] Self-executing treaties take precedence over state laws because federal law generally trumps conflicting state law.[182] However, any conflict between a treaty and the

[174] *See id.*, pgs. 276–77.
[175] *See id.*, at 278. It is unclear whether customary international law takes precedence over delegated legislation promulgated by an administrative body. *See id.*, at 277.
[176] *See id.*, at 279–80.
[177] *See id.*, at 283–85 (identifying five different techniques for treaty incorporation). *Compare* Chapter 12, pgs. 479–81 (discussing various methods for incorporating a treaty into domestic law); Chapter 4, pgs. 169–70 (same).
[178] U.S. Const. art. VI, cl. 2.
[179] *See* Chapter 13, pgs. 509–14.
[180] *See id.*, at 510–11.
[181] *See id.*, at 509.
[182] *Id.*

Constitution will be resolved in favor of the Constitution, which is higher law.[183]

2. Harmonizing Domestic Law with Treaty Obligations. Courts and legislatures in Israel and the United States employ a variety of tools to harmonize domestic law with the state's international treaty obligations. These tools are similar to the techniques applied in the eight other countries discussed above. The primary tools are incorporation of a treaty into domestic law (either by preexisting legislation, by new legislation, or by self-execution); a judicially created presumption that domestic statutory and constitutional provisions should be interpreted in a manner that is consistent with the state's treaty obligations; and other interpretive strategies that promote harmony between the domestic and international interpretations of a particular treaty provision.

There are numerous treaties that have been incorporated into domestic law in both Israel and the United States. For example, Israel has enacted legislation[184] to incorporate the Warsaw Convention,[185] the CISG,[186] and the Hague Convention on Child Abduction.[187] The United States has also incorporated all three treaties into its domestic legal system. In the United States, the Warsaw Convention and the CISG are considered self-executing treaties.[188] Accordingly, they are incorporated into U.S. law by virtue of treaty ratification, without any separate legislative action. In contrast, Congress enacted a statute to regulate domestic implementation of the Hague Convention in the United States.[189]

Inasmuch as Israel is a traditional dualist state, legislative action is the sole means for domestic incorporation. Since the United States is a hybrid monist state, incorporation can be accomplished either by legislation or by self-execution. Regardless of whether a state incorporates a treaty by means of self-execution or by legislative action, the practical result is essentially the

[183] *Id.*, text at note 19.
[184] *See* Chapter 7, pgs. 283–85.
[185] Warsaw Convention, *supra* note 9.
[186] United Nations Convention on Contracts for the International Sale of Goods, 1489 U.N.T.S. 3, U.N. Registration No. I-25567.
[187] Hague Convention on the Civil Aspects of International Child Abduction, 1343 U.N.T.S. 49, U.N. Registration No. I-22514.
[188] *See, e.g.*, Trans World Airlines, Inc. v. Franklin Mint Corp., 466 U.S. 243, 252 (1984) (stating that the Warsaw Convention is self-executing); Chicago Prime Packers, Inc. v. Northam Food Trading Co., 408 F.3d 894, 897 (7th Cir. 2005) (stating that the CISG is a self-executing treaty).
[189] International Child Abduction Remedies Act, 42 U.S.C. § 11601 et seq. (first adopted in 1988).

same. In either case, courts apply the treaty in roughly same way that they apply domestic statutes.

Both U.S. and Israeli courts apply a presumption that domestic statutes should be construed in a manner that is compatible with the state's treaty obligations. In the United States, this principle is known as the *Charming Betsy* canon.[190] In Israel, courts refer to the "presumption of compatibility."[191] Although the label differs, the underlying concept is the same. If the text of a statute is open to two plausible interpretations, but one interpretation is inconsistent with the state's treaty obligations, courts prefer the interpretation that is consistent with the state's treaty obligations.

Israeli courts routinely apply the presumption of compatibility to harmonize domestic law with international obligations embodied in customary international law and unincorporated treaties. The presumption applies to judicial interpretation of "Basic Laws and ordinary legislation, as well as in discussing principles of Israel's common law."[192] Judicial application of the *Charming Betsy* canon in U.S. courts is generally similar, but there is one key difference. In the United States, the use of international law in constitutional interpretation is quite controversial: critics contend that it is illegitimate for courts to consult international and foreign law as an aid to constitutional interpretation.[193] In contrast, there appears to be a broad consensus in Israel that it is entirely legitimate for courts to consult international and foreign sources for guidance in interpreting Israel's "common law material constitution."[194]

In practice, judicial application of the *Charming Betsy* canon and the presumption of compatibility is uneven. In the United States, "there are numerous cases . . . where a court could have invoked the *Charming Betsy* canon but did not reference the canon explicitly."[195] In at least some of these cases, the courts reached results that appear to be inconsistent with the canon.[196] Similarly, Israeli courts periodically issue rulings that appear

[190] *See* Chapter 13, pgs. 526–27.
[191] *See* Chapter 7, pgs. 287–88.
[192] Chapter 7, pg. 298.
[193] *See, e.g.*, Roper v. Simmons, 543 U.S. 551, 575–78 (citing international and foreign law in support of the Court's holding that the Eighth Amendment prohibits capital punishment for individuals who were younger than eighteen years old when they committed their crimes); *id.* at 622–28 (Scalia, J., dissenting) (criticizing the Court's reliance on international and foreign law).
[194] *See* Chapter 7, pgs. 302–04.
[195] Chapter 13, pg. 527.
[196] *See id.*, note 91 (citing I.N.S. v. Aguirre-Aguirre, 526 U.S. 415 (1999); *In re* Automotive Refinishing Paint Antitrust Lit., 358 F.3d 288 (3d Cir. 2004)).

to deviate from the presumption of compatibility.[197] In sum, the evidence suggests that courts apply the presumption of compatibility (and the *Charming Betsy* canon) in many cases, but they conveniently ignore the presumption when they want to reach a result that is inconsistent with the presumption.

The same could be said with respect to the canon of good faith, which holds that courts should interpret treaties in accordance with the internationally agreed understanding of their terms.[198] The U.S. Supreme Court has repeatedly endorsed the principle that courts should construe treaties "in a manner consistent with the shared expectations of the contracting parties."[199] U.S. courts regularly consult international and foreign sources to help shed light on the shared understanding of the parties. Similarly, "[i]n interpreting a convention that has been incorporated into Israeli law, the courts refer extensively to decisions of courts in other jurisdictions relating to the convention."[200] The goal is "to achieve conformity with the interpretation adopted internationally."[201] While this principle is firmly established, courts in Israel and the United States disregard the canon of good faith when they want to adopt a treaty interpretation that deviates from the internationally agreed understanding.

The presumption of compatibility, the *Charming Betsy* canon, and the canon of good faith are "transnationalist" tools: they facilitate the domestic application of a treaty in accordance with the internationally agreed understanding of its terms. But domestic courts in Israel and the United States sometimes employ "nationalist" strategies that tend to inhibit the domestic application of treaties or to promote adoption of treaty interpretations that deviate from the international understanding. Moreover, the circumstances in which courts apply nationalist strategies are fairly predictable. The Supreme Court of Israel frequently applies nationalist strategies in cases involving the Occupied Territories (OT).[202] U.S. courts commonly apply transnationalist tools in treaty cases involving disputes between private parties; they are much more likely to apply nationalist strategies in treaty cases involving vertical relations between the government and private

[197] *See* Chapter 7, pgs. 288–90.
[198] *See* Chapter 13, pgs. 523–24.
[199] *Id.*, at 523.
[200] Chapter 7, pg. 291.
[201] *Id.*
[202] *See* Chapter 7, pg. 315 ("For a long time it seemed that the main function of the Court in petitions relating to the OT, including those in which issues of international law arose, had been to legitimize almost everything that the authorities wished to do.")

actors.[203] The following section examines the use of nationalist tools that tend to limit the domestic effects of treaties.

3. **Limiting the Domestic Effects of Treaties.** Domestic courts in Israel and the United States apply two different types of nationalist strategies to insulate government actors from judicial review of executive compliance with treaty-based norms. First, they sometimes adopt an interpretive approach that favors the government's preferred interpretation of a treaty. Second, they apply a variety of judicial avoidance strategies to avoid ruling on the merits of treaty-based claims.

In the United States, there is a well-established canon of deferencc to executive-branch treaty interpretations.[204] The canon states that "the meaning attributed to treaty provisions by the Government agencies charged with their negotiation and enforcement is entitled to great weight."[205] In theory, the canon applies in every case that presents a question of treaty interpretation. In practice, though, courts apply the canon primarily in cases where the U.S. government is a party or an amicus.[206] Whereas the canon of good faith encourages courts to adopt a treaty interpretation that is consistent with the internationally agreed meaning of the treaty, the canon of deference nudges courts in the direction of an interpretation that promotes unilateral U.S. policy interests.[207] When courts apply the canon of deference, the government almost always wins.[208]

The Israeli Supreme Court "has never officially subscribed to the view that it must accept the executive branch of government's interpretation of a treaty."[209] "Nevertheless, in cases relating to the [Occupied Territories], for a long time the Supreme Court in fact adopted the interpretation of [Geneva Convention IV] favored by the authorities, even when this meant changing the theory of interpretation from case to case."[210] At one point, the Court even suggested "that if there were two possible interpretations of a convention, the Court should adopt that interpretation which is least restrictive of state sovereignty."[211]

[203] *See* Chapter 13, Table 2, pg. 530.
[204] *See id.*, at 524.
[205] El Al Israel Airlines, Ltd. v. Tsui Yuan Tseng, 525 U.S. 155, 168 (1999) (quoting Sumitomo Shoji Am., Inc. v. Avagliano, 457 U.S. 176, 184–85 (1982)).
[206] *See* Chapter 13, Table 2A, pg. 533.
[207] *See* Chapter 13, pg. 524.
[208] *See* Chapter 13, Tables 4C and 4D, pgs. 545–46.
[209] Chapter 7, pg. 292.
[210] *Id.*
[211] *Id.*

The Israeli Supreme Court has also employed judicial avoidance strategies to avoid ruling on the merits of claims involving the Occupied Territories.

> [In cases] relating to the legality of Israeli settlements, the Court has leaned over backward to avoid having to rule on the issue. It has managed to do this by regarding the provision in Article 49, Paragraph 6, of GC IV, as an innovative provision that has not achieved the status of customary international law; by denying the standing of individual Palestinians to challenge the use of public land for settlements; by holding that a petition against the settlements submitted by an NGO was nonjusticiable; and by ruling that whether or not the settlements are lawful under international law is irrelevant in examining segments of the separation barrier whose object is to provide protection for settlers.[212]

Similarly, U.S. courts have developed two treaty-specific doctrines whose primary function is to "shield government actors from judicial review of government compliance with treaty-based norms."[213] First, U.S. courts sometimes apply a presumption that treaties do not create individually enforceable rights.[214] Second, U.S. courts sometimes hold that a treaty is not self-executing. Although the doctrine of non-self-execution has roots in the nineteenth century, the version of non-self-execution doctrine that emerged in the latter half of the twentieth century bears little resemblance to its nineteenth-century predecessor.[215] In practice, courts apply the doctrine of non-self-execution and the presumption against individually enforceable rights almost exclusively in circumstances where individuals seek to hold government actors accountable for treaty violations. By applying these doctrines, courts avoid ruling on the merits of treaty-based claims, thereby enabling government actors to escape accountability for treaty violations.[216]

Recent trends in judicial decision making in Israel and the United States appear to be moving in opposite directions: while U.S. courts are becoming increasingly nationalist, Israeli courts are becoming increasingly transnationalist. According to Professor Kretzmer: "In recent years . . . there has been a change in the [Israeli Supreme] Court's approach; it has made a sincere effort to interpret international law in a more credible fashion" in cases involving the Occupied Territories.[217] In contrast, the U.S. Supreme

[212] *Id.*, at 314.
[213] Chapter 13, pg. 539.
[214] *Id.*, at 526.
[215] *See* David Sloss, *Non-Self-Executing Treaties: Exposing a Constitutional Fallacy*, 36 U.C. Davis L. Rev. 1 (2002).
[216] *See* Chapter 13, pgs. 535–39.
[217] Chapter 7, pg. 315.

Court's recent decision in *Medellin v. Texas*[218] is indicative of a disturbing trend in which U.S. courts increasingly regard international treaties with barely disguised contempt.[219]

E. *Russia*

In the past two decades, Russia has taken significant steps to incorporate treaty norms into its domestic legal system. The 1993 Russian Constitution specifies that "international treaties of the Russian Federation shall be an integral part of its legal system."[220] Thus, on paper at least, Russian law gives substantial weight to treaties within the domestic legal system. However, the reality of law in action does not necessarily correspond to the law on paper. In Russia, private parties generally have access to the judicial system to enforce transnational treaty provisions in litigation against other private parties. However, there are significant constraints on the ability of individuals to utilize the judicial system to enforce vertical treaty provisions that regulate relationships between government actors and private parties.

The analysis in this section provides a brief snapshot of both the law on paper and the law in action. The first subsection summarizes the legal rules that govern the formal status of treaties in Russia's domestic legal system. The next subsection discusses the application of treaties by domestic courts to resolve disputes among private parties. The final subsection addresses constraints that limit judicial application of vertical treaty provisions in disputes involving government actors.

1. The Domestic Legal Status of Treaties. As noted previously, the 1993 Russian Constitution specifies that treaties are "an integral part" of the Russian legal system. The Constitution also states: "If other rules have been established by an international treaty of the Russian Federation than provided for by a law, the rules of the international treaty shall apply."[221] In other words, a conflict between a law and a treaty should be resolved in favor of the treaty. Russian law recognizes an important distinction among three types of treaties: interstate, intergovernmental, and interdepartmental.[222] Interstate treaties require legislative approval in the form of a federal law. In

[218] Medellin v. Texas, 128 S. Ct. 1346 (2008).
[219] *See* David Sloss, *Schizophrenic Treaty Law* 43 Tex. Int. L.J. 15 (2007) (providing a brief survey of the historical rise of nationalist doctrines and the concomitant decline of transnationalist doctrines).
[220] 1993 Russian Constitution, art. 15(4) (quoted in Chapter 10, pg. 410).
[221] 1993 Russian Constitution, art. 15(4) (quoted in Chapter 10, pgs. 410–11).
[222] *See* Chapter 10, pg. 416.

contrast, the government can make a legally binding international commitment in the form of an intergovernmental or interdepartmental treaty without obtaining prior legislative approval.[223]

The Russian Supreme Court has held that "not all treaties are of equal stature within the Russian legal system."[224] In particular, a treaty takes precedence over a law "only if consent to the treaty being binding upon Russia was given in the form of a federal law."[225] Thus, interstate treaties rank higher than federal laws, but intergovernmental and interdepartmental treaties rank lower than federal laws, because they are adopted without legislative approval. Certain commentators have criticized the Supreme Court's view that only interstate treaties outrank federal laws.[226] The Russian Constitutional Court has not ruled on this matter.

2. Judicial Application of Treaties. In Russia, judicial application of a treaty depends upon some prior action that accords domestic legal effect to the treaty. The prior action takes the form of a federal law approving ratification (for an interstate treaty), or a government decree confirming the treaty (for intergovernmental and interdepartmental treaties). "[T]here are thousands of laws of ratification or decrees of confirmation with respect to individual treaties."[227] These laws and decrees provide the foundation for judicial application of treaties.

In Russia, higher courts have issued judicial directives to guide the application of treaties by lower courts. For example, the plenum of the Supreme Court adopted Decree No. 5 to guide the application of treaties by courts of general jurisdiction.[228] Similarly, the plenum of the Supreme Arbitrazh Court issued Decree No. 8 to guide the application of treaties by Russian *arbitrazh* courts (which have jurisdiction over specific types of economic disputes).[229] These judicial directives are not intended to resolve a particular dispute between named parties. Rather, the directives, which are binding on the lower courts, provide general regulatory guidance for the application of treaties by lower courts.

Domestic courts in Russia apply treaties directly in appropriate cases to resolve legal disputes involving private parties.

[223] *See id.*, at 429.
[224] *Id.* at 421.
[225] *Id.*
[226] *See id.*, at 427–30.
[227] *Id.*, at 412.
[228] *See id.*, at 415–21.
[229] *See id.*, at 421–25.

> Few areas of law are untouched by treaties. Of those areas regulated by treaty, fewer still have not been affected by treaty enforcement in the Russian judicial and arbitral systems. . . . Individuals and juridical persons may invoke treaty rights directly in Russian courts pursuant to Article 15(4) of the Russian Constitution. . . . Published decisions of Russian courts include a significant number that cite treaties and other international acts. The Russian judicial system has become a central arena in which issues involving the application and enforcement of treaty rules are resolved.[230]

In Russia, private disputes that the parties have referred to arbitration frequently involve the domestic application of treaties. "There are hundreds of arbitration courts established in the Russian Federation."[231] The two most important are the International Court of Commercial Arbitration (MKAC) and the Maritime Arbitration Commission (MAK). The MKAC and MAK publish annual summaries of their decisions. Those summaries demonstrate that the MKAC and MAK routinely apply the UN Convention on Contracts for the International Sale of Goods, the New York Convention on the Recognition and Enforcement of Arbitration Awards, the European Convention on Foreign Trade Arbitration, and other relevant treaties.[232]

3. Treaty-Based Constraints on Government Action. The Russia chapter in this volume gives the reader the impression that domestic courts enforce treaties quite vigorously. Other sources, however, give rise to some doubts on this matter, especially insofar as private parties might seek to invoke treaties in litigation as a constraint on government action.

Russia is no longer an authoritarian state. But Russia is not fully democratic either. The Polity IV Project is a sophisticated scholarly endeavor that rates 162 countries on a scale from 10 (fully democratic) to –10 (wholly autocratic).[233] In the 2006 Polity IV ratings, Russia received a polity score of 7.[234] This places Russia in the midrange of the spectrum from democratic to autocratic, with sixty-nine states rated as more democratic and eighty-one states rated as more autocratic.[235] Professor Kahn notes that the new Russian Criminal Code "works a 180 degree turnaround from Soviet practice."[236] This is undoubtedly a positive development. However, he

[230] *Id.*, at 410–11.
[231] *Id.*, at 438.
[232] *See id.*, at 438–39.
[233] Polity IV Country Reports 2006, *available at* http://www.systemicpeace.org/polity/polity4.htm.
[234] *Id.*
[235] *See id.*
[236] Jeffrey Kahn, *Vladimir Putin and the Rule of Law in Russia*, 36 GA. J. INT'L & COMP. L. 511, 546 (2008).

cautions "that what is required by law does not always reflect what transpires on the ground."[237] He concludes that the state is willing "to ignore Code provisions in political cases.... Every time the system is abused in that way, the system corrodes and respect for the rule of law weakens."[238] Similarly, the U.S. State Department reports: "The law provides for an independent judiciary; however[,] the judicial branch did not consistently act as an effective counterweight to other branches of the government.... Judges allegedly remained subject to influence from the executive, military, and security forces, particularly in high profile or politically sensitive cases."[239]

The Russia chapter in this volume provides summaries of two cases where a Russian court ruled against the government on the basis of a treaty. In one case, the Supreme Arbitrazh Court ruled in favor of a "British juridical person [who] alleged that a tax had been levied in contravention of a bilateral tax treaty."[240] In another case, the Supreme Arbitrazh Court ruled against a customs collector who had imposed an import duty in violation of a free-trade agreement between Russia and Moldova.[241] These examples demonstrate that Russian courts do apply treaties as a constraint on government action in some cases.

However, the available evidence suggests that Russian courts do not regularly apply human rights or humanitarian treaties as a constraint on government action. The war in Chechnya created a "legal blackhole" in which Russian military officers have violated international humanitarian law with impunity, and the courts have done little or nothing to address this problem.[242] In the field of human rights, although there are forty-seven states subject to the jurisdiction of the European Court of Human Rights, cases from Russia account for roughly one-fourth of the Court's docket. In 2007, the Court received more than ten thousand cases from Russia.[243] When the Court decides cases from Russia, it almost always rules that Russia has violated its treaty obligations under the European Convention.[244] On the positive side, "Russia has paid every, single judgment assessed against it, without exception."[245] However, if domestic courts in Russia consistently

[237] *Id.*, at 547.
[238] *Id.*, at 548.
[239] Country Report on Human Rights Practices in Russia, 2007, *available at* http://www.state.gov/g/drl/rls/hrrpt/. in Russia, 2007.
[240] *See* Chapter 10, pg. 422.
[241] *See id.*, at 436–37.
[242] *See* Kahn, *supra* note 236, at 526–28.
[243] *Id.*, at 536.
[244] *See id.*, at 537.
[245] *Id.*, at 540.

enforced the Convention in cases where private parties alleged human rights violations by the government, there would not be so many cases against Russia in the European Court, and Russia would have a better win-loss record in those cases. Therefore, Russia's record before the European Court demonstrates that Russian courts have not been enforcing treaty-based human rights constraints on government actors.

III. THE CUSTOMARY INTERNATIONAL LAW OF REMEDIES

In Chapter 2 of this volume, Professor Murphy presents a detailed analysis of the question whether international law obligates "a state to open its courts for private persons to vindicate rights or benefits that a treaty accords to them."[246] He concludes that the answer is generally no, except insofar as a specific treaty creates an explicit or implicit obligation to do so. Professor Murphy's analysis is extremely thorough and very insightful. However, I submit, by framing the question in slightly different terms, it is possible to gain a somewhat different perspective on the issues presented.

Section III considers the question whether customary international law obligates states to provide remedies to private parties who are harmed by a violation of their treaty-based primary rights.[247] This question differs from the question posed by Professor Murphy in two significant respects. First, Professor Murphy highlights the distinction between obligations of result and obligations of conduct.[248] He correctly notes that customary international law generally creates obligations of result, not obligations of conduct. He conceives of the obligation to allow "individuals to invoke [a] treaty in the state's judicial system" as an obligation of conduct, not an obligation of result, and he argues that there is no such obligation of conduct under customary international law.[249] This argument is persuasive on its own terms, but it does not address the question whether states have an obligation of result to provide remedies for private parties who are harmed by a violation of their treaty-based rights.

Second, Professor Murphy argues that there is no general principle of law "that individuals are entitled to invoke treaties before national courts."[250] In

[246] *See* Chapter 2, pg. 61.

[247] As noted previously, I use the term *remedies* in a broad sense to include a judicial order designed to prevent an incipient treaty violation or to halt an ongoing violation, as well as orders designed to compensate victims for past harms.

[248] *See* Chapter 2, pgs. 74–79.

[249] *See id.*, at 78.

[250] *Id.*, at 79.

this portion of his argument, he relies heavily on the distinction between monism and dualism. He claims that "[t]he existence of a significant number of countries that generally fall into the 'dualist' camp makes it quite difficult to establish the existence of a general principle of international law that individuals may invoke treaty norms before national courts."[251] As Section II of this introductory chapter demonstrates, there are several dualist countries in which domestic courts consistently provide remedies to individuals who are harmed by a violation of their treaty-based rights. Individual victims do not care whether, as a formal matter, the court applies a statute rather than a treaty; they care whether they can obtain a remedy. Similarly, from the standpoint of international law, the critical question is whether the domestic court issues a ruling that promotes treaty compliance, not whether the court applies the treaty directly or indirectly. Hence, Section III focuses on the question whether states are obligated to provide remedies to private parties who are harmed by a violation of their treaty-based primary rights, rather than the (somewhat different) question whether states are obligated to permit private parties to invoke treaties before domestic courts.

Section III is divided into three parts. The first part contends that International Court of Justice decisions and International Law Commission documents provide substantial support for the proposition that customary international law obligates states to provide remedies for private parties who are harmed by a violation of their treaty-based primary rights. The second part shows that, at the present time, there is insufficient evidence of state practice or *opinio juris* to establish such a rule of customary international law. The final part endorses Professor Murphy's suggestion that there may be an emerging rule of customary law along these lines.[252] I contend that the emergence of such a rule is generally a positive development, but I recommend certain limitations on the emerging rule.

A. *Views of International Judges and Experts*

This subsection focuses on what Professor David Caron has called "trans-substantive rules": that is, "a set of rules present in [the law of] state responsibility independently of the particular substantive obligation in question."[253] The international legal system is decentralized; there are multiple institutions that issue pronouncements about the content of

[251] *Id.*, at 81.
[252] *See id.*, at 109–15.
[253] David D. Caron, *The ILC Articles on State Responsibility: The Paradoxical Relationship between Form and Authority*, 96 Am. J. Int'l L. 857, 871 (2002).

international law. However, there are very few international institutions that have articulated transsubstantive rules of state responsibility. The two most important such institutions are the International Court of Justice (ICJ) and the International Law Commission (ILC).[254] This section shows that ILC documents and ICJ decisions support the proposition that customary international law obligates states to provide remedies for private parties who are harmed by a violation of their treaty-based primary rights.

This subsection is divided into four further subsections. The first subsection explains the conceptual distinction between primary and secondary rules, a distinction that is "the central organizing idea"[255] of the ILC's Articles on State Responsibility.[256] Next, I provide a brief overview of articles 28–41 of the ILC Articles; these articles provide a concise summary of what I will call the *customary international law of remedies.* Then I show that the customary international law of remedies, as articulated by the ICJ and ILC, obligates state S to make reparation to private party P in any case where P has a primary right under a treaty, S violates that right, and P is injured as a result of that violation.[257] The final subsection shows that, under the ICJ decision in *Avena,*[258] there are some cases in which customary law also obligates state S to grant P access to a domestic court to assert his or her entitlement to a remedy. However, the ICJ decision in *Avena* leaves unanswered many questions about the scope of the customary legal rule requiring access to domestic courts.

1. Primary and Secondary Rules. Various scholars have offered different formulations for explaining the distinction between primary and

[254] The ICJ is "the principal judicial organ of the United Nations." U.N. Charter, art. 92. The ILC is a body of independent experts, initially created by the UN General Assembly in 1947, whose mandate is to promote "the progressive development of international law and its codification." Statute of the International Law Commission, art. 1, para. 1., *available at* http://untreaty.un.org/ilc/texts/instruments/english/statute/statute_e.pdf.

[255] James Crawford, The International Law Commission's Articles on State Responsibility: Introduction, Text and Commentaries 15 (2002).

[256] Draft Articles on Responsibility of States for Internationally Wrongful Acts (2001), *available at* http://www.un.org/law/ilc/index.htm [hereinafter ILC Articles].

[257] Although the final document produced by the ILC is labeled "Draft Articles," the ILC Articles effectively became final when the General Assembly adopted a resolution "taking note" of the ILC Articles. GA Res. 56/83 (Dec. 12, 2001). There continues to be substantial debate about whether the ILC Articles represent a genuine codification of customary international law. *See* Caron, *supra* note 253, at 861–68. Here, I do not express a view on that question, although my argument does suggest that certain portions of the ILC Articles lend support for a rule that is not firmly rooted in state practice or *opinio juris.*

[258] Avena and Other Mexican Nationals (Mex. v. U.S.), Judgment, I.C.J. Reports 2004.

secondary rules.[259] The distinction between primary and secondary rules that is reflected in the ILC Articles is largely the work of Roberto Ago, who served as the ILC Special Rapporteur for State Responsibility from 1963 to 1979. According to Ago, primary rules "place obligations on States, the violation of which may generate responsibility." In contrast, secondary rules, among other things, "determine whether that [primary] obligation has been violated and what should be the consequences of the violation."[260] The ILC Articles are concerned exclusively with secondary rules, not primary rules. Of particular importance for the present discussion, Part Two of the ILC Articles (Articles 28–41) addresses the legal consequences of an internationally wrongful act.[261] The secondary rules governing the legal consequences of an internationally wrongful act comprise the customary international law of remedies.

The question whether a private party has a primary right under a treaty is a question about primary rules, not secondary rules. In any particular case, the answer to this question is a matter of treaty interpretation. For example, in *LaGrand*,[262] the ICJ analyzed Article 36 of the Vienna Convention on Consular Relations and concluded, as a matter of treaty interpretation, "that Article 36, paragraph 1, creates individual rights."[263] Horizontal treaty provisions create obligations that a state party owes to another state or group of states; such treaty provisions do not create primary rights for private parties. However, vertical treaty provisions create obligations that a state party owes to private persons; such treaty provisions create primary rights for the class of persons to whom the obligation is owed.[264] Thus, to ascertain whether a particular treaty provision creates primary rights for private parties, a court or other tribunal must interpret the treaty provision to determine whether the primary obligation is owed to states, to private parties, or to both. A private party has a primary right under a treaty if the treaty imposes a duty on a state party to refrain from action that would burden that private party or to engage in affirmative action to benefit that

[259] *See, e.g.*, H.L.A. Hart, The Concept of Law (1961); Hans Kelsen, General Theory of Law and State (1945).

[260] Responsibility of States for Internationally Wrongful Acts, Official ILC Commentaries, para. 2 (*reproduced in* Crawford, *supra* note 255, at 74) (quoting Yearbook of the International Law Commission, 1970).

[261] *See* ILC Articles, art. 28 ("The international responsibility of a State which is entailed by an internationally wrongful act . . . involves legal consequences as set out in this Part.")

[262] LaGrand (Ger. v. U.S.), Judgment, I.C.J. Reports 2001, pg. 466.

[263] *Id.*, paras. 75–77.

[264] *See id.*, para. 77 ("The Court notes that Article 36, paragraph 1(b), spells out the obligations the receiving State has toward the detained person" and therefore creates individual rights for the detained person).

private party.[265] As used in this chapter, the statement that a treaty "protects private rights" means that a private party has a primary right under the treaty.

Assume that a tribunal concludes that a particular treaty provision creates primary rights for private party P, state S has violated those rights,[266] and P has been injured by that violation.[267] Is P entitled to a remedy for that violation? This is a question about secondary rules, not primary rules: it is a question about the legal consequences of a treaty violation. One could examine those legal consequences from the perspective of either domestic law or international law, because every domestic legal system, like the international legal system, has a set of secondary rules governing the availability of remedies. If P has brought his claim before a domestic court, the domestic court would presumably want to examine the relevant domestic secondary rules to determine whether P is entitled to a remedy as a matter of domestic law. If P is clearly entitled to a remedy as a matter of domestic law, the domestic court might not care whether international law obligates state S to provide a remedy for P. Similarly, if domestic law clearly prohibits the domestic court from granting a remedy to P, the domestic court would be unable to grant P a remedy, even if international law obligated S to provide a remedy.[268]

Suppose, though, that the relevant secondary rules of domestic law are open to different interpretations. In these circumstances, the domestic court might wish to know whether international law obligates state S to provide a remedy for P. The court could examine the treaty that S violated to determine whether that particular treaty obligates states to provide domestic legal remedies for private parties whose treaty-based primary rights are violated.

[265] One could also add a third category, if a treaty obligates a state to do something "if at all only in a prescribed way." *See* Sloss, *supra* note 3, at 29 (quoting Henry M. Hart Jr. & Albert M. Sacks, The Legal Process: Basic Problems in the Making and Application of Law 122 (1994)). *See also* Carlos Manuel Vazquez, *Treaty-Based Rights and Remedies of Individuals*, 92 Colum. L. Rev. 1082 (1992).

[266] To answer the question of whether state S violated P's rights, a tribunal would have to determine whether there was a violation, and if so, whether S was responsible for that violation. The question of whether S is responsible for a particular treaty violation implicates a different branch of the law of state responsibility, which is addressed in Part One of the ILC Articles.

[267] Whether P has been injured is essentially a factual question, but the question whether there is a sufficient causal link between the violation and the injury to say that the violation caused the injury is, at least partially, a question of law.

[268] Even in cases where a treaty expressly obligates a state party (as a matter of international law) to grant P a private right of action in its domestic courts, P will not actually have a private right of action (as a matter of domestic law) unless the state party has incorporated that treaty obligation into its domestic law.

Some treaties do contain secondary rules of this type.[269] However, most treaties that spell out primary rules governing the conduct of states say nothing about the secondary rules that determine the consequences that follow from a violation of those primary rules. If such a treaty becomes the subject of domestic litigation, and a domestic court wants to know whether international law obligates state S to provide a remedy for P, a knowledgeable court would look to the customary law of state responsibility for an answer.

In sum, it is important to bear in mind the conceptual distinction among three discrete issues: (1) whether P has a primary right under treaty T (a question about primary international rules whose answer depends on treaty interpretation), (2) whether P is entitled to enforce that primary right in a domestic court (a question about secondary domestic rules that is governed by domestic law), and (3) whether international law obligates state S to grant P a remedy when he or she is harmed by a violation of his or her treaty-based primary rights. The third issue involves a question about secondary international rules. Specific treaty provisions may answer this question in some cases. However, where a treaty is silent on this question (as is usually the case), the customary international law of remedies provides background rules that determine the remedial consequences of a treaty violation. The next section addresses the customary international law of remedies that applies between states. The following subsection addresses the application of those rules in cases where a state has allegedly violated the treaty-based primary rights of a private party.

2. The Customary International Law of Remedies. More than eighty years ago, in the *Chorzow Factory* case, the Permanent Court of International Justice (PCIJ) affirmed the principle that a breach of an international legal obligation gives rise to an additional "obligation to make reparation in an adequate form."[270] The Court added:

> The essential principle contained in the actual notion of an illegal act – a principle which seems to be established by international practice and in particular by the decisions of arbitral tribunals – is that reparation must, as far as possible, wipe out all the consequences of the illegal act and reestablish the situation which would, in all probability, have existed if that act had not been committed.[271]

[269] *See* Chapter 2, pgs. 88–95 (citing examples of treaties that require access to domestic courts). If a particular treaty explicitly addresses the domestic remedial consequences of a treaty violation, such *lex specialis* rules supplant the ILC Articles in cases arising under that treaty.

[270] Factory at Chorzow, Jurisdiction, 1927 P.C.I.J. (ser. A) No. 9, pg. 21.

[271] Factory at Chorzow, Merits, 1928 P.C.I.J. (ser. A) No. 17, pg. 47.

In short, when a state violates an international legal obligation – for example, by breaching a treaty – the state is obligated to "wipe out all the consequences of the illegal act," insofar as possible, and to restore the status quo ante.

The PCIJ decision in *Chorzow Factory* is the cornerstone of the customary international law of remedies. The ILC Articles build on that foundation (and on subsequent decisions) to provide a more systematic presentation of the customary international law of remedies. According to the ILC Articles, when a state breaches an international legal obligation, there are three key principles that come into play. First, the responsible state has a "continued duty ... to perform the obligation breached."[272] Second, if the violation is ongoing, the responsible state "is under an obligation to cease that act" and "to offer appropriate assurances and guarantees of non-repetition, if circumstances so require."[273] Third, "[t]he responsible State is under an obligation to make full reparation for the injury caused by the internationally wrongful act."[274]

Under the ILC Articles, there are three main forms of reparation: "restitution, compensation and satisfaction."[275] Restitution involves restoring the status quo ante.[276] Restitution is the preferred form of reparation: it is required in every case unless it is "materially impossible" or involves "a burden out of all proportion to the benefit."[277] In cases where restitution is impossible or would impose a disproportionate burden, the responsible state "is under an obligation to compensate for the damage caused" by the violation. "The compensation shall cover any financially assessable damage."[278] Satisfaction is the least favored form of reparation. The state responsible for a violation is obligated to provide satisfaction only if "the injury caused by that act ... cannot be made good by restitution or compensation."[279] "Satisfaction may consist in an acknowledgement of the breach, an expression of regret, a formal apology or another appropriate modality."[280]

[272] ILC Articles, *supra* note 256, art. 29.
[273] *Id.*, art. 30.
[274] *Id.*, art. 31.
[275] *Id.*, art. 34.
[276] *Id.*, art. 35 ("A State responsible for an internationally wrongful act is under an obligation to make restitution, that is, to re-establish the situation which existed before the wrongful act was committed.").
[277] *Id.*
[278] *Id.*, art. 36.
[279] *Id.*, art. 37, para. 1.
[280] *Id.*, art. 37, para. 2.

The secondary rules summarized above apply to all breaches of primary international obligations, regardless of whether those obligations are derived from a treaty or from customary international law. The ILC Articles are chiefly concerned with secondary rules that apply when a state breaches a horizontal legal obligation owed to another state or group of states. The principles summarized above are not controversial insofar as they apply to horizontal relations between states. However, there is disagreement about whether the same rules apply when a state breaches an international legal duty owed to a private party – that is, when a state violates a primary right of a private party that is protected by international law. The next section addresses that issue.

3. The Duty to Make Reparations to Private Parties. To begin this analysis, it is helpful to distinguish between two discrete issues. The first issue concerns the scope of a state's duty to make reparations for an injury to a private party caused by that state's violation of a primary international legal obligation. The second issue concerns the scope of a state's duty to grant private persons access to domestic tribunals to pursue a claim for reparations. This section addresses the first issue. The next subsection addresses the second issue.

As noted previously, the fundamental principle of the customary international law of remedies is the principle articulated by the PCIJ in the *Chorzow Factory* case: the responsible state has an obligation to "wipe out all the consequences of the illegal act and reestablish the situation which would, in all probability, have existed if that act had not been committed."[281] As a matter of simple logic, it is difficult to limit this principle exclusively to interstate injuries. If state S violates an international legal obligation, and private party P suffers an injury as a result of that violation, S's secondary obligation to wipe out the consequences of the violation would seemingly entail an obligation to remedy the harm caused to P. If state S does not remedy the harm caused to P, it has arguably failed to "wipe out all the consequences of the illegal act."[282]

In *Chorzow Factory*, Poland breached a treaty obligation by seizing property owned by two private companies; the private companies sustained monetary damage as a result of Poland's treaty violation. Consequently,

[281] Factory at Chorzow, Merits, 1928 P.C.I.J. (ser. A) No. 17, pg. 47.

[282] *Accord* André Nollkaemper, *Internationally Wrongful Acts in Domestic Courts*, 101 AJIL 760, 782 (2007) ("The general principle that the breach of a right entails the obligation to provide reparation is irrefutable and as such appears applicable to the legal relationship between states and individuals.").

the court held, the Polish government was "under an obligation to pay, as reparation . . . compensation corresponding to the damage sustained by the said Companies as a result of" the treaty violation.[283] As a formal matter, Poland owed compensation to the German government, not to the private companies directly. Nevertheless, the amount of compensation was measured by the harm sustained by the private companies and the goal of the court's remedial order was to compensate the private companies for the injury they suffered.

In subsequent decisions, the ICJ has tacitly assumed that the fundamental remedial principle articulated in *Chorzow Factory* also applies to cases where international law creates vertical obligations that a state or international organization owes to private parties. For example, in an advisory opinion concerning the rights of a disgruntled former employee who had lost his job with the United Nations, the ICJ quoted *Chorzow Factory* in support of the principle "that reparation must, as far as possible, wipe out all the consequences of the illegal act and re-establish the situation which would, in all probability, have existed if that act had not been committed."[284] In this advisory opinion, as Professor Shelton has noted, the ICJ thought it was axiomatic "that the basic principle of reparation articulated in the *Chorzow Factory* case applies to reparation for injury to individuals."[285]

Similarly, in the process of drafting the Articles on State Responsibility, the ILC assumed that the basic remedial principle articulated in *Chorzow Factory* also applies in cases where the right-holder is a private party, rather than a state. Hence, although the ILC Articles focus primarily on inter-state responsibility, Article 33(2) stipulates: "This part is without prejudice to any right, arising from the international responsibility of a State, which may accrue directly to any person or entity other than a State."[286] James Crawford, the Special Rapporteur on State Responsibility who supervised the final stages of drafting the ILC Articles, explains that this provision is "a saving clause" designed to avoid the implication "that all secondary obligations were owed to states or collectives of states."[287] Moreover, he adds, Article 33(2) "clearly envisages that some 'person or entity other than a State'

[283] Factory at Chorzow, Merits, pg. 63.
[284] Application for Review of Judgement No. 158 of the UN Administrative Tribunal, Advisory Opinion, 1973 ICJ Rep. 166, 197 (July 12).
[285] Dinah Shelton, *Righting Wrongs: Reparations in the Articles on State Responsibility*, 96 AJIL 833, 834 n.8 (2002).
[286] ILC Articles, *supra* note 256, art. 33, para. 2.
[287] James Crawford, *The ILC's Articles on Responsibility of States for Internationally Wrongful Acts: A Retrospect*, 96 AJIL 874, 887 (2002).

may be directly entitled to claim reparation arising from an internationally wrongful act of a state."[288]

The official ILC commentary explains that it is "a matter for the particular primary rule to determine whether and to what extent persons or entities other than States are entitled to invoke responsibility on their own account."[289] In other words, if a treaty creates a primary obligation that state S owes to private party P, and S violates that primary obligation, thereby violating P's primary right, the violation by S triggers a secondary obligation for S to make reparation to P for any material injury caused by the violation. This follows from the fact that the treaty creates a primary obligation that S owes to P. As noted previously, this conclusion is somewhat controversial. Regardless, the ILC Articles and *Chorzow Factory* do support such a secondary rule of international law. Moreover, as discussed below, the ICJ analysis in *Avena* assumes the validity of such a secondary rule.

4. The Duty to Grant Private Parties Access to Domestic Tribunals. The preceding section suggests that, in cases where private party P has a primary right under a treaty, and state S violates P's primary right, the customary international law of remedies may obligate state S to make reparations to P for any material injury caused by the violation. This conclusion raises a further question. Does the alleged obligation to make reparations entail a further obligation to provide a domestic legal mechanism to enable P to bring a claim before a domestic tribunal to assert his entitlement to reparations? I contend that the best explanation of the ICJ decision in *Avena* is that the Court thought there are some cases in which customary international law obligates state S to provide a domestic judicial forum to adjudicate P's claim for reparation.

In the *Avena* case,[290] the ICJ applied the customary international law of remedies to determine the nature and scope of the secondary obligations resulting from the United States' violation of Article 36 of the VCCR. The Court first held that the United States had violated the rights of fifty-one Mexican nationals, under Article 36(1)(b), to be informed about their right to obtain assistance from the Mexican consulate.[291] It then held "that the remedy to make good these violations should consist in an obligation on

288 *Id.*
289 Official Commentary to art. 33 (*reprinted in* Crawford, *supra* note 255, at 210).
290 Avena, *supra* note 258, pg. 12.
291 *Id.*, para. 106.

the United States to permit review and reconsideration of these nationals' cases by the United States courts."[292]

The ICJ had previously held in the *LaGrand* case that the United States was obligated to provide "review and reconsideration" for German nationals whose rights under Article 36(1) of the VCCR had been violated.[293] The ICJ decision in *LaGrand* could plausibly be interpreted to say that the obligation to provide "review and reconsideration" is itself rooted in Article 36(2) of the VCCR.[294] However, the logic and structure of the ICJ's decision in *Avena* makes clear that the U.S. obligation "to permit review and reconsideration" of the Mexican nationals' criminal convictions and sentences is not derived from Article 36(2). Rather, that obligation is derived from the customary international law of remedies.

In *Avena*, the ICJ divided its analysis of the merits into three main parts. First, the ICJ addressed allegations that the United States had violated Article 36, Paragraph 1; it concluded that the United States had violated this provision with respect to fifty-one Mexican nationals.[295] Second, the ICJ addressed allegations that the United States violated Article 36(2); it concluded that the United States breached this provision with respect to only three Mexican nationals.[296] In the final major section of its opinion, the ICJ concluded that the United States was obligated to provide "review and reconsideration" of the convictions and sentences of all fifty-one Mexican nationals whose rights under Article 36(1)(b) had been violated.[297]

It is obvious that the obligation to provide "review and reconsideration" for fifty-one Mexican nationals cannot be derived from Article 36(2), because the ICJ said that the United States breached Article 36(2) with respect to only three of those fifty-one individuals. The headings that the ICJ used to organize its analysis reinforce this point. The heading "Article 36, Paragraph 1" introduces the analysis in Paragraphs 49 to 106. The heading "Article 36, Paragraph 2" introduces the analysis in Paragraphs 107 to 114. The heading "Legal Consequences of the Breach" introduces the analysis in

[292] *Id.*, para. 121.

[293] *See LaGrand, supra* note 262.

[294] Some passages in the ICJ decisions in *LaGrand* and *Avena* suggest that, in certain circumstances, the obligation to provide review and reconsideration is linked to art. 36(2) of the VCCR. *See, e.g., LaGrand, supra* note 262, para. 128(4); *Avena, supra* note 258, para. 153(8). As explained below, though, this rationale does not apply to the forty-eight Mexican nationals in *Avena* whose rights under art. 36(1) were violated but whose rights under art. 36(2) were not violated.

[295] *Avena, supra* note 258, paras. 49–106.

[296] *Id.*, paras. 107–14.

[297] *Id.*, paras. 115–50.

Paragraphs 115 to 150. This heading, when compared to the other two headings, makes clear that the analysis in this section is not based on a specific treaty provision. Moreover, the phrase "legal consequences of the breach" is almost identical to the phrase used in Article 28 of the ILC Articles.[298] Article 28 is the first article in Part Two of the ILC Articles: it is the opening provision for that portion of the ILC Articles that addresses the customary international law of remedies. Thus, the ICJ's choice of terminology reinforces the point that the analysis in Paragraphs 115 to 150 of the *Avena* judgment is based on the customary international law of remedies, not on Article 36(2).

To clarify the underlying rationale in *Avena*, it is worth quoting one passage at length:

> [T]he Court's task is to determine what would be adequate reparation for the violations of Article 36. It should be clear from what has been observed above that the internationally wrongful acts committed by the United States were the failure of its competent authorities to inform the Mexican nationals concerned, to notify Mexican consular posts and to enable Mexico to provide consular assistance. It follows that the remedy to make good these violations should consist in an obligation on the United States to permit review and reconsideration of these nationals' cases by the United States courts... with a view to ascertaining whether in each case the violation of Article 36 committed by the competent authorities caused actual prejudice to the defendant in the process of administration of criminal justice.[299]

Several points merit comment here. First, the second sentence of the passage quoted above refers to three distinct U.S. violations: the failure to inform Mexican nationals, to notify Mexican consulates, and to enable Mexico to provide consular assistance. All three violations relate to Article 36(1), not Article 36(2).[300]

Second, the Court states explicitly that its "task is to determine what would be adequate reparation for" these violations. This statement follows shortly after a paragraph in which the ICJ quotes *Chorzow Factory* for the proposition "that reparation must, as far as possible, wipe out all the consequences of the illegal act."[301] Thus, it is clear that the ICJ's analysis of

[298] Art. 28 is entitled "Legal consequences of an internationally wrongful act." ILC Articles, *supra* note 256, art. 28.
[299] *Avena, supra* note 258, para. 121.
[300] *See id.*, para. 106.
[301] *Id.*, para. 119 (quoting *Chorzow Factory*).

reparation is guided by the principles articulated in *Chorzow Factory* (i.e., the customary international law of remedies).

Third, the passage quoted above makes clear that the purpose of "review and reconsideration" is to ascertain "whether in each case the violation of Article 36 . . . caused actual prejudice to the defendant." The underlying logic involves a straightforward application of *Chorzow Factory*. To identify the steps required to "wipe out all the consequences of the illegal act," it is first necessary to determine what those consequences were. Specifically, it is necessary to determine whether the illegal act "caused actual prejudice to the defendant."[302] If the violation of Article 36 did not cause any actual prejudice to defendant A, then no further action is necessary to wipe out the consequences of that violation. However, if the violation of Article 36 did cause actual prejudice to defendant B, the United States would be obligated to remedy that injury. In sum, the ICJ ordered the United States to provide "review and reconsideration" to determine the consequences of the Article 36 violations for each individual defendant. Only after determining those consequences could the United States take steps to wipe out those consequences, in accordance with its secondary obligations under the customary international law of remedies.

Finally, in the above-quoted passage, the ICJ stated explicitly that "United States courts" must provide review and reconsideration. In its submissions to the Court, Mexico argued explicitly that the obligation to provide review and reconsideration "cannot be satisfied by means of clemency proceedings."[303] The ICJ specifically rejected U.S. arguments to the contrary. It held that "the clemency process" is "not sufficient,"[304] and that "it is the judicial process that is suited to this task" of providing review and reconsideration.[305] This makes perfect sense, because the goal of review and reconsideration is to ascertain whether a particular defendant was prejudiced by the violation of his or her Article 36 rights, and the clemency process is not designed to accomplish this task. Thus, assuming that the ICJ was correct, *Avena* demonstrates that there are some cases in which customary international law obligates states to grant private parties access to domestic tribunals to seek reparations for treaty violations. Unfortunately,

[302] Subsequent portions of the opinion make clear that the Court is concerned with prejudice caused by the art. 36 violation, not with prejudice caused by anything else. *See id.*, paras. 131–34. This reinforces the point that the whole purpose is to "wipe out the consequences" of the violation, not to remedy some other harm.

[303] *Avena*, *supra* note 258, para. 135.

[304] *Id.*, para. 143.

[305] *Id.*, para. 140.

Avena tells us very little about how to distinguish between cases where states are obligated to grant access to domestic tribunals and cases where states are not so obligated.

In sum, *Avena* is a case in which individual Mexican nationals had primary rights under a treaty, the United States violated those rights, but the relevant treaty said nothing about the secondary obligations that arose as a consequence of the U.S. violations of its primary obligations. Accordingly, the ICJ applied the customary international law of remedies to determine the nature and scope of those secondary obligations. The Court decided that the United States had a duty under customary international law (1) to make reparations to individual Mexican nationals who were prejudiced by the treaty violations and (2) to grant individual Mexican nationals access to U.S. courts so that they would have an opportunity to demonstrate that they were prejudiced by the violation of their treaty-based primary rights.

B. *State Practice and* Opinio Juris

To prove the existence of a rule of customary international law, it is necessary to establish two points: (1) that state conduct generally conforms to the asserted rule and (2) that states follow the rule because they believe they are legally obligated to do so (*opinio juris*).[306] The preceding section showed that ILC documents and ICJ decisions support the claim that customary international law obligates state S to make reparations to private party P in cases where P has a primary right under a treaty, S violates P's primary right, and P suffers a material injury as a result of that violation. Section II showed that eight of the eleven states surveyed in this volume generally behave in accordance with this rule. Even so, at the present time, there is not sufficient evidence of state practice or *opinio juris* to prove the existence of the asserted rule.

First, consider *opinio juris*. The ILC Articles and the ICJ decisions summarized previously provide evidence that international judges and international law experts believe that states are obligated to conform their conduct to the asserted rule. The critical question, though, is whether states believe that they are bound by that obligation. Most states would probably acknowledge that they have a duty under international law to prevent incipient treaty violations and to halt ongoing violations. This much is implicit in the *pacta sunt servanda* principle.[307] However, international law does not obligate

[306] *See* Brownlie, *supra* note 13, at 7–10.

[307] *See* Vienna Convention on the Law of Treaties, art. 26 (obligating states to perform treaties in good faith).

states to organize their domestic legal systems in a manner that empowers domestic courts to prevent or halt treaty violations affecting private rights. Moreover, there is scant evidence that states construe the *pacta sunt servanda* principle to include a duty to compensate individual victims of treaty violations.

The country chapters in this volume – even the chapters on international-law-friendly states – do not maintain that domestic courts provide remedies to individual victims of treaty violations because international law obligates them to do so. It is possible that domestic courts provide remedies to private parties who have suffered legally cognizable harms because domestic law requires (or, perhaps, empowers) them to do so. Alternatively, domestic courts may provide remedies for treaty violations because they believe that it is in the national interest to comply with treaty obligations, or because they believe that the political branches value compliance with treaty obligations. To present a rigorous proof of *opinio juris*, one would have to exclude these alternative explanations of judicial behavior.

The UN Guidelines on the Right to a Remedy,[308] adopted by the UN General Assembly in 2005, provide some evidence of *opinio juris*. That document specifies that states are obligated to provide "equal and effective access to justice" and "effective remedies" for individuals who have suffered "substantial impairment of their fundamental rights, through acts or omissions that constitute gross violations of international human rights law, or serious violations of international humanitarian law."[309] However, there is an ongoing debate about how much weight to attribute to General Assembly resolutions in evaluating evidence of *opinio juris*. Moreover, the Guidelines on the Right to a Remedy is merely a single resolution. At best, it shows that states acknowledge a duty to provide remedies for a certain narrow class of treaty violations.

The evidence of state practice is equally thin. To evaluate state practice, it is helpful to draw upon the Polity IV Country Reports.[310] The Polity IV Project rates 162 countries on a scale from 10 (fully democratic) to –10 (a pure autocracy). To simplify the analysis, we can classify these 162 countries into three groups: democracies (with a polity score of 8, 9, or 10); autocracies (with a negative polity score) and mixed systems (with a score between 0

[308] Basic Principles and Guidelines on the Right to a Remedy and Reparation for Victims of Gross Violations of International Human Rights Law and Serious Violations of International Humanitarian Law, G.A. Res. 60/147, U.N. Doc. A/RES/60/147 (Dec. 2005).

[309] *See id.*, paras. 3(c), 3(d), and 8.

[310] Polity IV Country Reports 2006, *available at* http://www.systemicpeace.org/polity/polity4.htm.

and 7, inclusive). Using this rubric, the 162 states rated by the Polity IV Project include sixty-nine democracies, fifty-three autocracies, and forty mixed systems.

The fifty-three autocratic states generally do not have strong, independent judiciaries staffed by professional judges who believe that they have an institutional duty to protect the rights of private parties from government infringement. Thus, it is reasonable to assume that domestic courts in those fifty-three states play a fairly limited role in enforcing treaty-based constraints on government action. The fact that there are fifty-three autocratic states in the world whose behavior probably does not conform to the asserted rule arguably demonstrates that there is insufficient evidence of state practice to prove the asserted rule.

C. *Is There an Emerging Rule?*

In Chapter 2, Professor Murphy says that "[t]he arc of the development of international law may point in the direction of a more general obligation to allow invocation of treaty norms by individuals in national courts in situations where the treaty contains provisions that are protective of individuals."[311] He provides an excellent summary of the current trends that support this emerging rule.[312] There is no value in repeating his argument here, but it is worthwhile to add two points that reinforce his analysis.

First, the information in this volume demonstrates that there is a clear trend toward greater use of domestic courts to enforce treaty-based private rights. That trend is present in eight of the eleven states discussed in this volume: Australia, Canada, India, Israel, Poland, Russia, South Africa, and the United Kingdom. Germany and the Netherlands are excluded from this list because both countries have a long-standing tradition of openness to international law that, for many years, has facilitated domestic judicial enforcement of treaties. The United States is the only country featured in this volume where the trend is moving in the opposite direction. Thus, the country chapters in this volume support Professor Murphy's claim that there may be an emerging rule of customary international law along the lines suggested here.[313]

Second, in recent years, there has been a rapid growth in the number of states that have voluntarily subjected themselves to the jurisdiction of regional courts. At present, there are twenty-seven EU member states that

[311] Chapter 2, pg. 109.
[312] *Id.*, at 109–15.
[313] Professor Murphy makes a similar point. *See* Chapter 2, pgs. 110–15.

are subject to the jurisdiction of the European Court of Justice;[314] forty-seven Council of Europe member states that are subject to the jurisdiction of the European Court of Human Rights;[315] and twenty-two states subject to the jurisdiction of the Inter-American Court of Human Rights.[316] African states recently adopted a Protocol creating the African Court of Justice and Human Rights.[317] The chapters in this volume on Germany, Poland, and the Netherlands show that a state's membership in the European Union and the Council of Europe tends to induce domestic courts in that state to be more receptive to domestic adjudication of claims based on bilateral and global treaties.[318] If states subject to the jurisdiction of regional courts in Africa and the Americas follow a similar pattern of development, one can expect that domestic courts in those states will become increasingly receptive to domestic adjudication of treaty-based claims.

Professor Murphy expresses concern that that there may be some unwanted negative consequences if the aforementioned emerging rule crystallizes into an established rule of international law.[319] Those concerns are not unwarranted. Even so, for the reasons articulated in Section I.A of this chapter, I believe that the trend toward greater use of domestic courts to enforce treaty-based private rights is generally a positive development. In closing, though, it may be helpful to identify appropriate limits on the emerging rule. In my view, the emerging rule should be subject to five key limitations.[320] First, horizontal treaty provisions are excluded from the scope of the rule because they do not protect primary private rights. Second, a treaty provision must be "formulated in sufficiently specific terms [that] it can be invoked by private persons."[321] If "the treaty expresses a benefit or protection for individuals that is highly inchoate or aspirational in nature," judicial application may be inappropriate.[322] Third, the right to a private

[314] *See* http://europa.eu/abc/european_countries/index_en.htm.

[315] *See* http://www.coe.int/T/E/Com/About_Coe/Member_states/default.asp. (listing Member States of Council of Europe).

[316] *See* http://www.cidh.oas.org/Basicos/English/Basic4.Amer.Conv.Ratif.htm.

[317] *Available at* http://www.hurisa.org.za/Advocacy/AfricanCourt/Single_Legal_Instument.pdf.

[318] *See supra* notes 60–74 and accompanying text.

[319] *See* Chapter 2, pgs. 115–18.

[320] There is some overlap between my list of five limitations and Professor Murphy's discussion of situations where, in his view, it would be inappropriate for a domestic court to conclude that there is an implied right for individuals to invoke a treaty in national courts. *See id.*, at 105–09.

[321] Chapter 8, pg. 346.

[322] Chapter 2, pg. 105. *See also* Chapter 9, pg. 400 (stating that a treaty provision is not judicially enforceable unless it "has been drafted in a complete manner").

remedy does not necessarily imply a right of access to domestic courts; states could fulfill the purposes of the emerging rule by creating administrative tribunals that have the authority to adjudicate claims within the scope of the rule.

Fourth, domestic courts should not enforce a treaty that expressly precludes domestic judicial enforcement. Similarly, if a treaty creates an alternative mechanism for private parties to vindicate their treaty-based primary rights, a court might reasonably conclude that the treaty drafters implicitly precluded domestic judicial enforcement.[323] (However, courts should not infer an implied limitation on domestic judicial enforcement if the alternative mechanism is accessible only to states, not private parties.) Finally, the right to a remedy for treaty violations is subject to limitations in cases where the private party waits too long to seek a remedy,[324] fails to follow the prescribed procedure,[325] or is otherwise at fault for the failure to obtain a remedy that the legal system made available.

[323] *Accord* Chapter 2, pgs. 107–08.

[324] Virtually all domestic legal systems include statutes of limitations to address this type of problem. Similarly, the ILC Articles provide that a state loses its right to bring a claim if it "validly acquiesced in the lapse of the claim." ILC Articles, *supra* note 256, art. 45(b).

[325] *See* ILC Articles, *supra* note 256, art. 44.

2

Does International Law Obligate States to Open Their National Courts to Persons for the Invocation of Treaty Norms That Protect or Benefit Persons?

Sean D. Murphy

Patricia Roberts Harris Research Professor of Law
George Washington University Law School

I. INTRODUCTION

In its decisions in the *LaGrand*[1] and *Avena*[2] cases, the International Court of Justice (hereinafter, ICJ or the Court) determined that Article 36 of the Vienna Convention on Consular Relations (VCCR)[3] creates "individual rights" (as opposed to just rights of states) and that the United States has an obligation to provide an individual with meaningful access to U.S. courts to vindicate those rights. On the basis of those determinations, it might be thought that international law generally obligates a state to open its courts for private persons to vindicate rights or benefits that a treaty accords to them, whether or not the treaty expressly provides for such a remedy. Such a proposition, however, is overbroad and does not follow from a close reading of the ICJ's decisions or from a more general assessment of the international legal system. This chapter seeks to provide a more nuanced assessment of whether international law generally obligates states to open their national courts to persons in such situations.

Because of the equal sovereign status of states, it is generally accepted in international law that a state cannot and should not sue another state in national courts to vindicate a treaty right. Instead, states normally address the matter through resort to international negotiation or dispute settlement. By contrast, the invocation of treaties in national courts usually arises in

[1] LaGrand Case (Ger. v. U.S.), 2001 I.C.J. 466 (June 27), *reprinted in* 40 I.L.M. 1069 (2001); *see* William J. Aceves, Case Report, 96 AM. J. INT'L L. 210 (2002).

[2] Avena and Other Mexican Nationals (Mex. v. U.S.), 2004 I.C.J. 12 (Mar. 31), *reprinted in* 43 I.L.M. 581 (2004); *see* Dinah L. Shelton, Case Report, 98 AM. J. INT'L L. 559 (2004).

[3] Vienna Convention on Consular Relations, Apr. 24, 1963, 21 U.S.T. 77, 596 U.N.T.S. 261 [hereinafter VCCR].

the context of actions by or against nonstate actors or private parties (i.e., persons or companies). In considering such actions, it is useful to note that treaty provisions may seek to regulate three different types of relationships: interstate relationships (e.g., a treaty provision that commits the state parties to maintain a limit on nuclear weapons), relationships among private parties (e.g., a treaty provision setting rules on the sale of goods across borders), and the relationship between private parties and a state (e.g., treaty provisions protecting against expropriation or a denial of human rights).

With respect to the first type of provision, only on rare occasions will a nonstate entity bring suit in a national court in an effort to force a state to comply with a treaty provision that regulates an interstate relationship.[4] It is much more common for individuals to seek to invoke a treaty-based norm in national courts for the two other types of provisions, where the treaty seeks to regulate relationships between private parties or between a private party and a state. When this happens, it is not necessarily the case that the private party is directly invoking the treaty before the national court. The individual may be invoking a national constitution or statutory provision that serves to implement the treaty obligation. The individual may be using the treaty provision as a matter of national contract law, such as when a sales contract, a bill of lading, or an airline ticket makes express reference to the rules set forth in a treaty. In other instances, the individual may be using the treaty as a vehicle for dictating a particular choice of law, as might occur in matters relating to family law. For the purposes of this chapter, "invoking of the treaty" is meant to encompass the whole range of ways in which an individual may seek to secure the protection or benefit recognized in the treaty.

For cases in which the treaty is regulating relations between two private parties, invocation of the treaty in national courts is usually not controversial; it is generally accepted that such treaties are intended to serve as a basis for adjudication of disputes among private parties in national courts. More contentious is the situation involving a treaty provision that protects or provides benefits to individuals against governmental action. If those protections or benefits are denied, the person may wish to invoke the relevant treaty provision before a national court, especially a court of the recalcitrant state party, but the government may resist the litigation by denying that the treaty may be so invoked. The person may be invoking the treaty provision for various reasons: to support injunctive relief against ongoing or anticipated

[4] *See, e.g.*, Natural Resources Def. Council v. Envtl. Prot. Agency, 464 F.3d 1, 2–11 (D.C. Cir. 2006) (suit by environmental group to force U.S. government to comply with its obligations under the Montreal Protocol on Substances That Deplete the Ozone Layer, Sept. 16, 1987, 1522 U.N.T.S. 3, S. Treaty Doc. 100–10 (1987)).

state action; to support a civil action for harm incurred from violation of the treaty; as a defense to a criminal charge; as a basis for challenging a state's right to detain, deport, or extradite the person; or for some other reason.

Regardless of why the treaty norm is being invoked by an individual, the national court may be confronted with either allowing or precluding reliance on the treaty as a source of national law (if there is no national statute or other source of law applying the norm). In reaching that decision, the national court may consider it relevant whether international law obligates a state to open its national courts for invocation of the treaty by individuals. If international law carries great weight in the national legal system, trumping other forms of national law (perhaps even the national constitution), the national court will care deeply about what international law requires. Alternatively, international law may not carry great weight in the national legal system, in which case the court may look solely to its national rules, without concern for what international law has to say on the matter. Yet even then, international law remains of relevance for that state, as the state will be regarded by other states as having breached international law if it fails to uphold an obligation to allow invocation of the treaty in national courts.

Consequently, it is important to consider carefully whether international law obligates states to open their national courts to persons for the invocation of treaty provisions that are protective of or beneficial to individuals. Section II of this chapter begins by explaining why, at the broadest level, there is no general obligation under international law for states to open their courts to individuals for this purpose. There is no such obligation under the Vienna Convention on the Law of Treaties (VCLT),[5] whether as a component of *pacta sunt servanda* or any other general norm of treaty law. To the extent that the VCLT is regarded as largely codifying the core rules of customary international law on treaties, no such obligation exists as a matter of customary international law either. Rather, the standard view is that customary international law permits states to abide by their substantive treaty obligations through whatever procedural means they choose. So long as the state achieves the substantive objective set forth in the treaty, the mechanism by which that compliance occurs is left to the state. The state can

[5] Vienna Convention on the Law of Treaties, May 23, 1969, 1155 U.N.T.S. 331 [hereinafter VCLT]. For treaties involving an international organization as a party, see Vienna Convention on the Law of Treaties between States and International Organizations or between International Organizations, Mar. 21, 1986, 25 I.L.M. 543. This convention has not yet entered into force, but its provisions (which parallel those of the VCLT) are generally regarded as expressing customary international law.

choose to allow individuals to invoke a treaty in its courts, and doing so may assist the state in fulfilling its treaty obligation, but such access to national courts need not be provided as a matter of customary international law. If the state fails to achieve the substantive objective of the treaty, international law speaks to possible remedies available on the international plane, but generally leaves issues concerning national judicial remedies to principles of national remedial law. While the terms of any specific treaty may include an express or implied obligation relating to the ability to invoke treaty provisions in national courts, it is those particular treaty obligations that govern the issue, not general international law.

Similarly, there does not appear to be any basis for finding a general principle of international law that obligates states to open their courts for invocation of treaty norms by individuals. As is clear from many of the chapters in this volume, no such legal principle operates uniformly across the major legal systems of the world; indeed, many dualist states reject reliance on treaties as operating ex proprio vigore (by their own strength) in national law and instead insist on only national measures (e.g., a statute) as providing the basis for enforcement of the relevant treaty norm. The Roman law principle of *ubi jus, ibi remedium* (where there is a right, there is a remedy) may be regarded as a feature of international law, but not in the sense of establishing a right to compulsory dispute settlement at either the international or the national level, even in situations where the right holder is a nonstate actor. Indeed, in most situations, violations of international law, including violations of treaties, have not been addressed by compulsory recourse to judicial or arbitral fora.

The broad conclusions reached in Section II are not controversial, but they are important in establishing the general backdrop of the international legal system. The remainder of the chapter turns to more difficult questions that can arise in the context of particular treaty regimes, when states may assume an express or implied obligation to allow persons to invoke treaty norms in the state's national courts. First, as discussed in Section III, a treaty may expressly require that individuals be able to invoke a treaty norm before national courts. When this occurs, the state is obligated as a matter of international law to allow private parties to have such access in the national system.

Second, as discussed in Section IV, even if a treaty does not expressly oblige a state party to allow individuals to invoke a treaty norm in the state's national courts, such an obligation may be implicit in the treaty. Determining whether such an obligation is implicit in the treaty requires careful analysis of the language of the treaty, in the context and in light of the treaty's object and purpose as well as the practice of state parties subsequent to the treaty's entry into force, and possibly the treaty's negotiating history. The ICJ engaged in such an analysis and found an implied right to invoke a treaty in national courts, in the course of rendering its decisions in *LaGrand* and *Avena* with respect to VCCR Article 36.

Section V suggests that implying a right of access to national courts to vindicate a treaty norm should not occur in certain circumstances. Where the treaty expresses a benefit or protection for individuals that is highly inchoate or aspirational in nature, and thus implicitly anticipates some further action by states to clarify and implement the treaty provision, then it is improper to imply a right of access to national courts to vindicate the treaty provision. Further, if there are similar treaties between similar parties, some of which expressly provide for access to national courts and some of which do not, a right of access usually should not be implied in the latter. If a treaty provides a particular mechanism for individuals to vindicate their rights other than through national courts, then usually a right of access to national courts should not be implied. Finally, if when joining a treaty a state issues an uncontested understanding, or some other definitive statement, to the effect that no private right of action is created by virtue of the state's ratification of the treaty, then access to that state's national courts to vindicate a right under the treaty should not be implied.

Section VI concludes by speculating that, while the ICJ's decisions in *LaGrand* and *Avena* should not be read as evidence of a general rule of international law obliging states to allow individuals to invoke treaty norms in national courts, the Court's decisions may nevertheless represent an incremental step in the evolution of international law in that direction. As international law increasingly establishes rights protective of the individual, and increasingly develops avenues for individuals to enforce their rights (including before international tribunals), there may emerge a settled expectation that invocation of treaty norms by individuals in national courts is the logical consequence of embedding protections for individuals in treaty regimes, regardless of whether it is expressly or implicitly envisaged by the particular treaty. Such a development may not be optimal; although it may have a valid normative goal (promoting and protecting the rights of individuals), there would likely be confusion about the contours of the right of access to national courts, there might be adverse consequences for the creation and development of treaty regimes that are protective of individuals, it may result in excessive deference to unreliable national fora, and it may be out of step with other, more effective mechanisms for vindication of individual rights.

II. INVOCATION OF TREATY NORMS BY INDIVIDUALS IN NATIONAL COURTS UNDER GENERAL INTERNATIONAL LAW

In determining whether international law generally obligates a state to open its national courts for the invocation of treaty norms, a standard analysis should consider whether the obligation exists as a matter of general treaty law, customary international law, or general principles of law, as evidenced in part by judicial decisions and the writings of highly qualified publicists.[6] As the subsequent discussion indicates, none of those traditional sources of international law supports the proposition that such a general obligation exists.

A. *Vienna Convention on the Law of Treaties*

The background (or secondary) rules that govern the conclusion, operation, interpretation, and termination of treaties emerged over the centuries from the practice of states. The 1969 VCLT codified and, in some instances, developed these background rules in a single treaty, which is sometimes referred to as the "treaty on treaties." As of 2007, the VCLT directly binds, as a matter of treaty law, the 108 states that have adhered to it with respect to treaties among those states, so long as the relevant treaty was concluded after the date the VCLT entered into force for the parties to the treaty.[7] For treaties concluded prior to that date, and for treaties concluded by or with states that have not yet ratified the VCLT, the VCLT does not directly apply.

The VCLT addresses in some detail the manner in which a state may react to a breach of a treaty by another state, principally through termination or suspension of the treaty.[8] Further, disputes over such reactions are to be resolved through standard methods of international dispute settlement.[9] The VCLT, however, contains no provision requiring states to open their national courts for invocation of treaty norms, either by other states or by individuals.

Traditionally, states alone have been viewed as the subjects of international law and, as noted in the introduction to this chapter, many treaties concern matters that are solely interstate in nature. At the same time, individuals have been accorded benefits or protections under international law,

[6] *See* Statute of the International Court of Justice, June 26, 1945, art. 38(1), 59 Stat. 1055.
[7] VCLT, *supra* note 5, art. 4.
[8] *Id.*, arts. 60 & 65.
[9] *Id.*, art. 66(a). An annex to the VCLT outlines a process for conciliation through use of the UN secretary-general. *See id.*, art. 66(b) & Annex.

such that they have been described as "objects" of international law.[10] There are numerous treaties that accord such protections or benefits: protections for diplomats and consular officials; protections for aliens visiting or residing in a host state; protections for transnational commercial activities, such as foreign investments or franchises; and, of course, contemporary human rights treaties that restrain governments from infringing on basic civil, political, economic, social, and cultural rights of individuals. Even so, while treaties can be broadly grouped as those that involve states alone and those that involve individuals along with states, the VCLT draws no distinction among treaties on that basis, and hence suggests no differential treatment among them on the issue of access to national courts.

One might postulate that the fundamental obligation of a state to perform treaties in good faith (*pacta sunt servanda*)[11] means that all of the organs of a state – the executive, legislative, and judicial organs – that have the power to bring the state into compliance with the treaty must exercise that power to compel compliance.[12] As the ICJ has stated, *pacta sunt servanda* obliges states to apply a treaty "in a reasonable way and in such a manner that its purpose can be realized,"[13] and in some circumstances perhaps the only reasonable way to apply a treaty that protects or benefits individuals is for national courts to be available for individuals to litigate claims arising from the treaty. There is some intuitive appeal to such an argument, as the conduct of all organs of a state, whether by means of commission or omission of an action, is attributable to the state under the laws of state responsibility.[14]

[10] *See, e.g.*, George Manner, *The Object Theory of the Individual in International Law*, 46 AM. J. INT'L L. 428 (1952); CARL A. NØRGAARD, THE POSITION OF THE INDIVIDUAL IN INTERNATIONAL LAW (1962).

[11] VCLT, *supra* note 5, art. 26.

[12] *See* ARNOLD MCNAIR, THE LAW OF TREATIES 78 (2d ed. 1961) (finding that it "is the duty of a party to a treaty to see to it that its municipal law enables it to give effect to the treaty and that its organs – executive and judicial – are properly equipped with the powers required for that purpose."). At the same time, Lord McNair noted the "great differences between the legal systems and practices of different States" on this point, *see id.* at 79, and explained his native system as one that did not recognize any rights for individuals to invoke treaties in municipal courts. *See infra* note 54.

[13] Gabcikovo-Nagymaros Project (Hung.-Slovk.), 1997 I.C.J. 7, 79 (Judgment of Sept. 25).

[14] *See* Draft Articles on Responsibility of States for Internationally Wrongful Acts, *in* Report of the ILC on the Work of Its Fifty-third Session, U.N. GAOR, 56th Sess., Supp. No. 10, U.N. Doc. A/56/10, arts. 2 & 4 (2001) [hereinafter ILC Articles] ("There is an internationally wrongful act of a State when conduct consisting of an action or omission ... is attributable to the State under international law; and ... constitutes a breach of an international obligation of the State") ("The conduct of any State organ shall be considered an act of that State under international law, whether the organ exercises legislative, executive, judicial or

There are certain problems, however, with this line of argument. First, the VCLT itself contains no language expressly endorsing this approach; there is no reference in the VCLT to the means under internal law by which states are to fulfill treaty obligations. In Article 27, the VCLT addresses the issue of "internal law and observance of treaties," but provides only that a "party may not invoke the provisions of its internal law as justification for its failure to perform a treaty."[15] Thus, the VCLT precludes a party from asserting that its national courts are unwilling to uphold a treaty obligation as a means of escaping from that treaty obligation, but the VCLT does not compel the party to use national courts to secure adherence to a treaty obligation.

Second, nothing in the preparatory work of the International Law Commission or the negotiating record of the two sessions of the 1968–69 Vienna Conference,[16] in the associated commentaries on the VCLT,[17] or in the practice of states under the VCLT[18] support interpreting the general obligation of *pacta sunt servanda* as requiring the use of national courts to uphold treaty obligations, including those protective of individual rights. Shortly after adoption of the VCLT, D. P. O'Connell reiterated the conventional view that, notwithstanding the binding nature of a treaty,

> A treaty is a contract, not law. It lays down rules for the parties, and these should be promulgated to the individual before he should be bound by them. Hence, many countries have a rule that treaties must be legislated

any other functions"). The UN General Assembly has commended the ILC Articles to the attention of governments, but they have not been transformed into a treaty and are not themselves binding on states. *See* G.A. Res. 56/83, ¶ 3, U.N. Doc. A/RES/56/83 (Dec. 12, 2001); G.A. Res. 59/35, ¶ 1, U.N. Doc. A/RES/59/35 (Dec. 2, 2004).

[15] VCLT, *supra* note 5, art. 27. Art. 27 was not included in the ILC draft articles; rather, it was introduced at the first session of the diplomatic conference. Separately, art. 46 addresses provisions of internal law concerning competence to conclude treaties. *See id.*, art. 46.

[16] For citations to the relevant documents of both the ILC's preparatory work and the negotiating sessions of the diplomatic conference on what became art. 26, see SHABTAI ROSENNE, THE LAW OF TREATIES: A GUIDE TO THE LEGISLATIVE HISTORY OF THE VIENNA CONVENTION 196–99 (1970); THE VIENNA CONVENTION ON THE LAW OF TREATIES: TRAVAUX PRÉPARATOIRES 209–14 (Ralf Wetzel & Dietrich Rausching eds., 1978). In the two decades of the ILC's work, there were a series of reports by the ILC's esteemed rapporteurs: Brierly (1950–1952), Lauterpacht (1953–1954), Fitzmaurice (1956–1960), and Waldock (1962–1966).

[17] *See, e.g.*, Richard D. Kearney & Robert E. Dalton, *The Treaty on Treaties*, 64 AM. J. INT'L L. 495, 516–17 (1970); 1 D. P. O'CONNELL, INTERNATIONAL LAW 55–57, 265 (2d ed. 1970); IAN SINCLAIR, THE VIENNA CONVENTION ON THE LAW OF TREATIES 83–84 (2d ed. 1984).

[18] *See* Walter Kälin, *Implementing Treaties in Domestic Law: From "Pacta Sunt Servanda" to "Anything Goes"?* in MULTILATERAL TREATY-MAKING 111, 112–18 (Vera Gowlland-Debbas ed., 2000) (noting various techniques of states to soften the effects of ratifying a treaty, including "the exclusion of the self-executing character of the treaty without enacting implementing legislation to avoid the possibility that individuals will invoke it vis-à-vis authorities and courts in domestic procedures.").

> upon to be internally operative. Even when they have no such rules their courts can only apply the treaty as law when it was the intention of the signatories that it should be internally operative.[19]

Third, when an individual seeks to invoke a treaty norm, the individual does so as a third party, as persons are never parties to treaties. The general rule under the VCLT is that a treaty applies only as between the parties to it (*pacta tertiis nec nocent nec prosunt*);[20] exceptions to this rule were controversial in the VCLT negotiations. Nevertheless, the VCLT is cognizant of the possibility of third-party rights (and obligations), but it recognizes those rights only in the context of third-party states.[21] Under the VCLT, a third-party right can arise when there is an intent of the treaty parties to create such a right and the third party assents to the right, though assent generally may be presumed.[22] The third-party state may exercise the right only in conformity with the "conditions for its exercise provided for in the treaty or established in conformity with the treaty."[23] In short, recognition of third-party rights by the VCLT was contentious, was limited to states, and calls for close attention to the particular treaty in question when determining how it is that the third party may seek to exercise or vindicate the right. This approach would appear to disfavor a general rule, under the law of treaties, granting private parties the right to invoke a treaty, and at best it calls for careful scrutiny of the language and intent of the treaty being invoked by the individual rather than reference to a more general norm of treaty law.[24]

To gain traction, an argument in favor of a state's obligation to open its national courts for invocation of a treaty must shift to norms outside the realm of treaty law, such as those present in the law of state responsibility. Those norms are discussed in greater detail in the subsequent section, but for present purposes it must be noted that rules on attribution of conduct in state responsibility are not viewed as establishing whether there is a breach of an obligation under international law: the two concepts are distinct.[25] In other words, the fact that the organs of a state can include a wide array of

[19] O'Connell, *supra* note 17, at 54.
[20] VCLT, *supra* note 5, art. 34; *see* Christine Chinkin, Third Parties in International Law 25–88 (1993).
[21] *See* Anthony Aust, Modern Treaty Law and Practice 207–11 (2000).
[22] VCLT, *supra* note 5, art. 36(1).
[23] *Id.*, art. 36(2).
[24] As discussed in Section V, this treaty-specific approach was the one taken by both the parties and the ICJ in the *LaGrand* and *Avena* cases.
[25] ILC Articles, *supra* note 14, art. 2.

collective or individual entities, central or peripheral to the government, has not been viewed as transforming treaty-based obligations into obligations that are to be performed by all such state organs. A legislature may have the power under national law to enact a law that compels executive compliance with a treaty obligation, or courts may have the power to allow lawsuits by state or nonstate actors that compel compliance, but the fact that such organs have not acted in a given situation traditionally has not been viewed as constituting the violation of international law. Rather, in the absence of a specific treaty obligation that directs itself to national courts, international law concerns itself only with the broader failure of the state as a whole to bring itself into compliance with the treaty obligation. As Antonio Cassese has explained:

> When a State breaches an international obligation because the national legislation necessary for implementing the rule is lacking or inadequate, other States claim cessation of the wrongdoing or reparation only for that breach, without enquiring about the reasons for non-compliance or protesting at the lack or inadequacy of legislation. In other words, States are only interested in the final result: fulfilment or non-fulfilment of an obligation. They show no interest in the factors that brought about that result.... [T]his state of affairs reflects the individualistic structure of the international community and the paramount importance of respect for other States' internal affairs.[26]

Although Cassese acknowledges some exceptions, he concludes that international law generally "leaves each country *complete freedom* with regard to how it fulfils, nationally, its international obligations."[27]

This unwillingness to impose, under general international law, an obligation on any specific organ to enforce a treaty obligation is no doubt recognition that adoption of such a rule would potentially impose an obligation on courts to enforce the vast array of treaty obligations that are purely interstate by their nature. In other words, if the state is obligated to comply with the treaty obligation, and courts have the power to order executive authorities to do so, there would appear to be no reason, conceptually, to limit the courts' obligation to only those treaties protective of individuals. Further, the unwillingness to go in this direction is likely an acknowledgment that when relief is being sought in courts, it may well be for purposes of challenging a decision already taken by a different national organ (the

[26] Antonio Cassese, International Law 218 (2d ed. 2005).
[27] *Id.*, at 219 (emphasis in original).

executive or the legislature). How the state internally resolves that issue is not of concern to international law: what is of concern is determining the nature of the obligation in the context of a specific treaty and whether the state as a whole has violated that obligation. The following section further develops the interface of custom with treaty law on this point.

B. *Customary International Law*

Does customary international law obligate a state to open its national courts for the invocation of treaty norms by individuals? Many states and international tribunals regard the VCLT as largely reflecting the customary treaty practice of states, and thus they accept the VCLT as relevant when considering how states should behave in their treaty relations under customary international law. The lack of provisions in the VCLT requiring states to open their national courts for invocation of treaty norms by individuals demonstrates a lack of conviction at the time the VCLT was drafted that such a rule existed as a matter of customary international law.

Looking beyond the VCLT, there are two further concepts that have helped shape customary international law that also cast doubt on the proposition that customary international law generally requires states to allow persons to invoke treaties in national courts. The first is the principle (borne out by consistent state practice) that disputes between states, including those arising from treaties, should not be settled in the national courts of one of them. As discussed here, this principle may have somewhat less traction in the context of treaty provisions that regulate relations between private parties and a state or solely between private parties, but the sentiments that animate the principle are sometimes relevant for even those types of treaty provisions. In any event, the principle suggests that a general customary rule allowing invocation of treaties in national courts cannot be sustained; rather, one needs to focus on the specific treaty at issue.

The second relevant concept is the general understanding that treaty obligations may, by their nature, be of a kind that requires a state to achieve a particular result, without requiring that the state do so by any particular means. The distinction between obligations of result and obligations of conduct can be confusing and has led to disagreements among scholars as to the exact meaning of the terms, but there appears to be acceptance that there exists a category of international obligations, including within it treaty obligations, that cannot be said to require a state to achieve a particular objective through use of a particular means, such as by allowing access to national courts by individuals. To the extent that this is true, it reinforces the difficulty of maintaining that there is a general customary rule allowing invocation of treaties in national courts; again, one needs to focus on the specific treaty at issue instead.

1. ***Par in Parem Non Habet Jurisdictionem.*** The general practice of states has been that, when disputes arise among them (including treaty disputes), those disputes are resolved through recourse to negotiation or other forms of international dispute settlement, not through litigation in national courts. Indeed, the ancient feudal principle *par in parem non habet jurisdictionem* or *par in parem imperium non habet* is often invoked in support of the proposition that states – as sovereigns of equal standing – "cannot have their disputes settled in the national courts of one of them."[28]

The *par in parem non habet jurisdictionem* principle is relevant to the issue of invocation of treaty norms in national courts by an individual in situations where the individual is suing a foreign sovereign. The principle serves as the foundation for the doctrine of sovereign immunity, as well as the act-of-state doctrine,[29] which essentially exist to promote stable relations among states and nonintervention of states in the affairs of other states.[30] While the absolute theory of immunity of states has largely given way to a more restrictive theory of immunity (whereby foreign sovereigns are not immune from suit in national courts in certain circumstances, such as when they engage in commercial relations),[31] even under the latter theory states habitually refrain from suing other states in national courts. The restrictive theory of immunity does contemplate persons suing foreign sovereigns in national courts, but adoption of the restrictive theory is not compelled as a matter of international law; indeed, a few states (notably

[28] Ian Brownlie, Principles of Public International Law 321 (6th ed. 2003).

[29] Under the act-of-state doctrine, national courts decline to sit in judgment on the acts of a foreign government when those acts are taken within the foreign government's territory. The principal motivation for this self-restraint appears to be a desire that disputes involving the acts of foreign governments in their own territories be resolved through diplomatic means, not through litigation in national courts. *See generally* Oppenheim's International Law 365–71 (Robert Jennings & Arthur Watts eds., 9th ed., 1992).

[30] *See* Hazel Fox, *International Law and Restraints on the Exercise of Jurisdiction by National Courts of States*, in International Law 361, 361–65 (Malcolm Evans ed., 2d ed. 2006); *see generally* Hazel Fox, The Law of State Immunity (2002).

[31] *See* U.N. Convention on Jurisdictional Immunities of States and Their Property, G.A. Res. 59/38, Annex, U.N. Doc. A/RES/59/38 (Dec. 2, 2004); Andrew Dickinson et al., State Immunity: Selected Materials and Commentary (2004); Joseph W. Dellapenna, Suing Foreign Governments and Their Corporations (2d ed. 2003).

China) continue to follow the absolute theory of immunity, barring all suits against foreign sovereigns in their courts.[32]

When a foreign sovereign fails to accord the required protection or benefit to an individual, international law allows the state of that individual's nationality to react to the breach by exercising a right of diplomatic protection of the national. In such a circumstance, the state espouses the right of its national and pursues the matter through whatever means are available, whether international negotiation or otherwise. Espousal, however, is recognized as a discretionary power of the state; if a state chooses not to espouse the claim, international law accepts that the protection accorded to the national may remain unfulfilled.[33] The inability of the individual to pursue the claim does not deprive the individual of the underlying right; as D. P. O'Connell noted: "He may not be able to pursue his claims and take action to protect his property without the intervention of his own State, but it is still his claim and still his interest which the machinery of enforcement is designed to facilitate."[34]

The *par in parem non habet jurisdictionem* principle is not directly relevant to the issue of invocation of treaty norms in national courts by an individual for purposes of suing the local sovereign, for in that instance the sovereign is sitting in judgment on itself. In contrast, to the extent that the principle is designed in part to preclude states from interfering in the internal relations of another state (by not letting their national courts sit in judgment on a foreign sovereign's conduct undertaken in its own country), the same concern presumably arises if states are insisting that a foreign sovereign conduct its national legal system in a certain fashion. If so, the same sentiment that animates the *par in parem non habet jurisdictionem* principle would seem to disfavor a general obligation under customary international law that a state must allow itself to be exposed to treaty claims in its own courts.

The *par in parem non habet jurisdictionem* principle is also of less significance when an individual invokes treaty norms in national courts against another individual, as may occur in the context of treaties regulating private international law. The lack of direct state involvement in such cases likely explains why those cases tend not to evoke any controversy, even when the parties' positions are based directly on the treaty (as opposed to being based on an implementing statute or some other instrument). Yet even here, in

[32] *See, e.g.*, Huang Jin & Ma Jingsheng, *Immunities of States and Their Property: The Practice of the People's Republic of China*, 1 Hague Y.B. Int'l L. 163 (1988).

[33] *See* Cassese, *supra* note 26, at 232.

[34] 1 O'Connell, *supra* note 17, at 108.

some instances, the *par in parem non habet jurisdictionem* principle may have traction, such as when the individual is impugning the legality of the conduct of a foreign sovereign undertaken in its own territory. In that instance, a national court might apply the act-of-state doctrine, or some other avoidance doctrine, so as to dismiss the claim, even though it is arising as between private parties, because of a concern that the national court's decision might disrupt interstate relations.[35]

Although the application of the *par in parem non habet jurisdictionem* principle may have differing relevance depending on the type of treaty provision at issue, the existence of the principle for at least a broad range of treaties makes it difficult to sustain an argument that there is a general customary rule requiring states to allow invocation of treaties in their national courts. At best, presence of the principle suggests that the critical factor is not the existence of a general norm but a norm emanating from the specific treaty at issue before the court.

2. **Obligations of Result and Obligations of Conduct.** As may be surmised from some of the foregoing discussion, customary international law on treaties as it relates to invocation before national courts can also be viewed through a prism that differentiates the existence in treaties of obligations of result and obligations of conduct.[36] The result-conduct distinction in international law is one that can be confusing, both in its relationship to the result-conduct distinction as understood in civil law systems and in its application to treaty provisions that contain elements of both forms of obligations.[37] Nevertheless, the distinction is generally accepted as correctly

[35] For a discussion of such avoidance doctrines, *see* Eyal Benvenisti, *Judicial Misgivings Regarding the Application of International Law: An Analysis of Attitudes of National Courts*, 4 EUR. J. INT'L L. 159, 169–75 (1993).

[36] The distinction between obligations of result and obligations of conduct was made famous through the work of Roberto Ago as the special rapporteur for the work of the International Law Commission (ILC) on the rules of state responsibility. Ultimately, the articles on state responsibility adopted by the ILC refrained from relying on the distinction, not because the distinction was inherently invalid, but because it was not useful in addressing the consequences that flow from a breach of international law (the subject of the ILC's work). *See* JAMES CRAWFORD, THE INTERNATIONAL LAW COMMISSION'S ARTICLES ON STATE RESPONSIBILITY: INTRODUCTION, TEXT AND COMMENTARIES 21–22 (2002) (stating that the conduct-result distinction has "become an accepted part of the language of international law" but that no "substantive consequences" flowed from the distinction for the ILC Articles).

[37] *See, e.g.*, Pierre-Marie Dupuy, *Reviewing the Difficulties of Codification: On Ago's Classification of Obligations of Means and Obligations of Result in Relation to State Responsibility*, 10 EUR. J. INT'L L. 371, 374–78 (1999); IAN BROWNLIE, SYSTEM OF THE LAW OF NATIONS: STATE RESPONSIBILITY (PART ONE) 241 (1983).

distinguishing, at a general level, two different ways that states might be bound under international law.

On the one hand, treaty obligations often speak to a specific result that must be achieved by each treaty party rather than a particular course of conduct that the party must undertake. Thus, treaties such as the Montreal Protocol on Substances That Deplete the Ozone Layer (Montreal Protocol)[38] or the Kyoto Protocol on climate change[39] establish quotas on the emission of certain gases but leave it to states to determine how such limits should be reached. The obligation might be met by (1) adopting a national statute that prohibits emissions in excess of the threshold requirement, (2) regarding the treaty as itself creating a norm within the national legal system that binds governmental authorities to that end, (3) having the national government simply exercise its regulatory discretion so as to preclude the emissions, (4) creating private rights of action whereby persons may sue the government or other private parties in national courts to enforce compliance with the treaty,[40] or (5) some other means for promoting treaty compliance. Such a treaty obligation is often referred to as an obligation of result. How the state party reaches the result is not the focus of the treaty obligation; so long as the state party reaches the result by some means or conduct, the treaty obligation is satisfied.

On the other hand, it is possible for any given treaty to require that a state follow a certain course of conduct, which might include allowing access to its courts for individuals for the purpose of promoting the treaty's objective, in which case the state has undertaken an obligation of conduct. For example, under the Vienna Convention on Diplomatic Relations, the state parties are obligated to "take all appropriate steps to protect the premises of the mission

[38] Montreal Protocol on Substances That Deplete the Ozone Layer, Sept. 16, 1987, 1522 U.N.T.S. 3, S. Treaty Doc. No. 100–10 (1987). The Montreal Protocol provides for the progressive reduction by specified dates of the production and consumption of certain types of ozone-depleting chemicals – such as chlorofluorocarbons and halons – listed in annexes to the Protocol.

[39] *See* Kyoto Protocol to the U.N. Framework Convention on Climate Change, Dec. 10, 1997, U.N. Doc. FCCC/CP/197/L.7, *reprinted in* 37 I.L.M. 22 (1998). The Kyoto Protocol binds to specific targets and timetables for the reduction of greenhouse gases that are regarded as responsible for long-term global warming.

[40] To the extent that national courts are utilized, it should be noted that such courts are organs of the state, and hence are obligated to issue judgments that are consistent with the international obligation of the state. *See* Difference Relating to Immunity from Legal Process of a Special Rapporteur of the Commission of Human Rights, 1999 I.C.J. 62, 88 (Apr. 29) ("the conduct of an organ of a State – even an organ independent of the executive power – must be regarded as an act of that State").

against any intrusion or damage."[41] Such an obligation is in the nature of an obligation of conduct. The fact that damage occurs to the mission alone does not constitute a violation of the treaty provision; rather, it is the state's failure to undertake a particular course of conduct ("appropriate steps to protect the premises") so as to avoid such damage that leads to the violation. Some scholars have characterized obligations of conduct as referring only to obligations to pursue best efforts or due diligence in trying to achieve a particular outcome (such as the Vienna Convention example),[42] while others have included in this concept obligations that are fairly specific about the course of conduct expected, including steps that must be taken within the internal legal sphere of the state.[43] For example, the obligation in Article 2(c) of the Convention on the Elimination of All Forms of Discrimination against Women (CEDAW), which provides that states undertake to "ensure through competent national tribunals and other public institutions the effective protection of women against any act of discrimination," has been characterized as an obligation of conduct or means.[44] The purpose of this chapter is not to definitively resolve the proper scope of obligations of conduct but simply to underscore the different nature of treaty obligations that exist in the international sphere.[45]

The concepts of obligations of result and obligations of conduct are linked to the doctrine of margin of appreciation in international law. That doctrine – which has its origins in French and German law and is best known internationally for its application by the European Court of Human

[41] Vienna Convention on Diplomatic Relations, art. 22(2), Apr. 18, 1961, 500 U.N.T.S. 95, 23 U.S.T. 3227.

[42] *See, e.g.*, Dupuy, *supra* note 37, at 381–82.

[43] *See, e.g.*, 2 Y.B. I.L.C. at 31 (1977) (examples by Professor Ago).

[44] Convention on the Elimination of All Forms of Discrimination against Women, Dec. 18, 1979, 1249 U.N.T.S. 13 [hereinafter CEDAW]; *see* Rebecca J. Cook, *State Accountability under the Convention on the Elimination of All Forms of Discrimination against Women*, in HUMAN RIGHTS OF WOMEN: NATIONAL AND INTERNATIONAL PERSPECTIVES 228, 232 (Rebecca J. Cook ed., 1994).

[45] A well-known institutionalization of the distinction between obligations of result and obligations of conduct may be seen in the secondary legislation created by the institutions of the European Community. Consistent with the concept of obligations of result, EC directives bind EC member states to objectives that must be achieved within a certain time limit but leave to national authorities the means for achieving those objectives. Directives have to be implemented in national law but only in accordance with the procedures of individual member states. By contrast, and consistent with the concept of obligations of conduct, EC regulations are binding in their entirety and directly applicable to all EC member states; there is no room provided for EC states to apply the directive selectively or through alternative approaches; indeed, there is no need for any national implementing legislation to support an EC regulation. *See* P.S.R.F. MATHIJSEN, A GUIDE TO EUROPEAN UNION LAW 26–27 (8th ed. 2004).

Rights (ECtHR)[46] – generally may be viewed as comprising two elements: (1) an acceptance that certain international norms are open ended or unsettled (normative flexibility) and (2) a consequent willingness of international courts to exercise restraint when reviewing the decisions of national authorities that interpret such norms (judicial deference).[47] When an international norm calls for a particular result, the margin-of-appreciation doctrine is largely unnecessary; since the norm is not regulating the national means by which the end should be secured, there is no need to resort to the doctrine (deference to the means is already built into the norm). Nevertheless, the doctrine may be useful when determining whether an international norm is in fact an obligation of result, since the policy reasons supporting the doctrine are the same ones that would support viewing an ambiguous norm as an obligation of result.[48] Those policy reasons are a desire to promote pluralism and diversity in the application of law, within appropriate limits; a preference for empowering decision makers at the lowest possible level, as they are closest to and most accountable to the persons being governed (often referred to as the principle of subsidiarity); and a concern with the quality, ability, and cost of decision making at the international level.[49]

When an international norm calls for particular conduct, the margin-of-appreciation doctrine is squarely implicated, for the doctrine is concerned with the level of discretion to be afforded states when undertaking that conduct. Hence, if an international norm calls for particular state conduct but qualifies the obligation through use of terms such as *appropriate, reasonable, proportionate, necessary*, or *not arbitrary*, then – under the margin-of-appreciation doctrine – the norm may be viewed as preserving a zone of legality within which states bound to the norm may operate, thereby allowing multiple states to pursue somewhat different avenues of action, all

[46] *See* Yutaka Arai-Takahashi, The Margin of Appreciation Doctrine and the Principle of Proportionality in the Jurisprudence of the ECHR 2–5 (2002); Oren Gross & Fionnuala Ní Aoláin, *From Discretion to Scrutiny: Revisiting the Application of the Margin of Appreciation Doctrine in the Context of Article 15 of the European Convention on Human Rights*, 23 Hum. Rts. Q. 625 (2001).

[47] *See* Yuval Shany, *Toward a General Margin of Appreciation Doctrine in International Law?* 16 Eur. J. Int'l L. 907, 909–11 (2005); *see also* Eyal Benvenisti, *Margin of Appreciation, Consensus, and Universal Standards*, 31 N.Y.U. J. Int'l L. & Pol. 843 (1999).

[48] *See* Shany, *supra* note 47, at 917.

[49] *Id.*, at 918–22. For a discussion in the context of decision making within the European communities, see Leonard F.M. Besselink, *Entrapped by the Maximum Standard: On Fundamental Rights, Pluralism and Subsidiarity in the European Union*, 35 Common Mkt. L. Rev. 629 (1998).

of which are intended to satisfy the conduct required by the norm.[50] This preservation of state autonomy, to the extent possible under international law, is consistent with the background principle most famously articulated in the *Lotus* case:[51] states, as a general matter, should be able to engage in their preferred course of action unless international law prohibits them from doing so.[52]

Turning to the relevance of the results-conduct distinction for this chapter, when a state accepts in a treaty an obligation of result, international law generally does not require that the state fulfill that obligation by allowing individuals to invoke the treaty in the state's judicial system, even in a situation where the treaty provides a benefit to or protects the interests of individuals. If the primary treaty obligation is simply to benefit or protect the individual, then, so long as the state complies with that obligation, the mechanism by which that compliance occurs is left to the state. Of course, the state can choose as a matter of convenience to allow access to local courts for this purpose, and doing so may assist the state in fulfilling its treaty obligation,[53] but such access to courts or other measures under national law generally need not be provided as a matter of international law. It cannot be said that the treaty is violated simply because steps have not been taken to provide access for individuals to national courts for enforcement of the treaty protections. Indeed, as indicated by the previous quote of Antonio Cassese,[54] the failure to bring national law into conformance with international law alone is normally not a breach of international law (let alone the failure to provide access to national courts); a breach normally

[50] *See* Shany, *supra* note 47, at 910 (citing *Vo v. France*, Eur. Ct. H.R., Judgment, July 8, 2004, ¶ 82).

[51] Lotus Case (Fr. v. Turk.), 1927 P.C.I.J. (ser. A) No. 10, at 18–19.

[52] *See, e.g.*, S.D. Myers, Inc. v. Canada, NAFTA Ch. 11 Arb. Trib., ¶ 263 (Nov. 12, 2001), *reprinted in* NAFTA Arbitration Reports (2003) *and reprinted in* 40 I.L.M. 1408, 1438 (2001) ("a breach of Article 1105 occurs only when it is shown that an investor has been treated in such an unjust or arbitrary manner that the treatment rises to the level that is unacceptable from the international perspective. That determination must be made in the light of the high measure of deference that international law generally extends to the right of domestic authorities to regulate matters within their own borders.").

[53] *See* McNair, *supra* note 12, at 322:

> The British view appears to be . . . that a treaty creates obligations between the contracting parties solely . . . and not between one party and the nationals of another, or between the nationals of two or more parties; though, as we shall see, in practice it is often, and indeed usually, convenient to allow the assertion by or against individuals in municipal courts of right or liabilities which their State has obtained for them or imposed upon them by treaty.

[54] *See supra* note 26.

occurs only when the state fails to observe its treaty obligation on a specific occasion.[55]

If the state does breach the treaty obligation, then customary international law speaks to the remedies available on the international plane, largely through rules on pacific settlement of disputes, (including diplomatic protection of nationals), on treaty termination or suspension, or on nonforcible countermeasures. In cases where the affected persons are nationals of the transgressing state, the traditional remedies available under general international law become problematic, but international legal theory does recognize the concept of a limited number of *erga omnes* obligations (obligations owed to the international community as a whole), such as obligations not to engage in genocide, slavery, or racial discrimination.[56]

Of course, any given treaty may expressly or by implication oblige a state to achieve or aspire to a particular outcome through a particular means, such as by permitting individuals to invoke a treaty norm in national courts. That possibility is the subject of Sections III and IV herein.

C. *General Principles of International Law*

If it were possible to show relatively uniform adoption within national legal systems of a principle that individuals are entitled to invoke treaties before national courts, then it might be said that a general principle of international law exists to that effect as well. General principles of law are, of course, one of the classic sources of international law (after treaties and custom), and such principles can be established if they operate in the national laws of states worldwide.[57] Yet, as the ensuing chapters in this volume indicate, national legal systems worldwide are not sufficiently uniform on this point; many national legal systems do not operate on the basis of a legal principle whereby individuals can readily invoke treaties in national courts. The lack of uniformity among national legal systems worldwide on this issue is related to the structural relationship of international law to national law, which is typically discussed in the context of dualism and monism.

Some countries, such as the common law and Scandinavian countries, tend to view international law and national law as separate, distinguishable

[55] *See* Brownlie, *supra* note 28, at 35.

[56] *See* Barcelona Traction, Light & Power Co., Ltd. (Belg. v. Spain), Second Phase, 1970 I.C.J. 3, 32, ¶ 34 (Feb. 5); East Timor (Port. v. Austl.), 1995 I.C.J. 90, 102, ¶ 29 (June 30); Application of the Convention on the Prevention and Punishment of the Crime of Genocide, Judgment on Preliminary Objections to Jurisdiction, 1996 I.C.J. 595, 615–16, ¶ 31 (July 11).

[57] *See* Oscar Schachter, International Law in Theory and Practice 50–55 (1991).

bodies of law (the dualist approach). Thus, in countries such as Canada or the United Kingdom, no treaty has any direct effect on internal law; only with the passage of implementing legislation by the national legislative body does the internal law change.[58] Consequently, there is no legal principle recognized in such countries whereby individuals have a general right to invoke treaties before national courts. For example, in *UL Canada v. Quebec (Attorney General)*, the Court of Appeal for Quebec in 2003 rejected the argument that trade treaties to which Canada was a party could be used by a private litigant to strike down a Quebec food regulation. According to the court:

> An international treaty does not have force in internal law unless it is incorporated into internal law by the legislative body having jurisdiction under the Constitution. Quebec's [trade agreement] implementation Acts set out a statement of fact and enunciate a truism with respect to legislative competence. They do not express an intent to make the free trade agreements part of Quebec's domestic law, and such an intent could not be inferred from their text. These Acts state only approval for the free trade agreements, and that approval was not sufficient to support the conclusion that the National Assembly intended to incorporate the entire text of the free trade agreements into Quebec law. The trial judge correctly ruled that the international free trade agreements had not been incorporated into Quebec law and could not, therefore, be invoked to invalidate the section.[59]

[58] *See* AUST, *supra* note 21, at 150–56; Gaetano Arangio-Ruiz, *International and Interindividual Law*, in NEW PERSPECTIVES ON THE DIVIDE BETWEEN NATIONAL AND INTERNATIONAL LAW 15, 19 (Janne Nijman & André Nollkaemper eds., 2007) (noting that the dualist view "is that the *key* to the implementation of international law within the framework of national law is in the hands of national law itself, as impersonated by the constituent, the legislator, or the courts, in the exercise of powers they respectively derive from national law, and . . . just from that law."). For a discussion of early British cases on how treaties affecting private rights have no force of law before U.K. courts absent confirmation by parliamentary statute, *see* SAMUEL B. CRANDALL, TREATIES: THEIR MAKING AND ENFORCEMENT 289–92 (2d ed. 1916). For recent cases in U.K. courts involving violations of the European Convention on Human Rights and Fundamental Freedoms, where no remedy of compensation was found available under U.K. law, *see* Ian Leigh & Laurence Lustgarten, *Making Rights Real: The Courts, Remedies, and the Human Rights Act*, 58 CAMBRIDGE L.J. 509, 527–31 (1999).

[59] UL Canada, Inc. v. Quebec (Attorney General), 2003 R.J.Q. 2729, 2003 Carswell Que. Cases 2247 (Westlaw); *see* Council of Canadians v. Canada (Attorney General), No. 01-CV-208141, 2005 Carswell Ont. Cases 2973, paras. 41–43 (Ont. Sup. Ct. Justice, July 8, 2005) (finding that international wrongs are to be addressed in international courts); *see generally* THE GLOBALIZED RULE OF LAW: RELATIONSHIPS BETWEEN INTERNATIONAL AND DOMESTIC LAW (Oonagh E. Fitzgerald ed., 2006).

The existence of a significant number of countries that generally fall into the dualist camp makes it quite difficult to establish the existence of a general principle of international law that individuals may invoke treaty norms before national courts.

In contrast, some countries do view international law and national law as part of the same system of law (the monist approach), such that international law is automatically a part of the national legal system. Thus, in several civil law countries, treaties are regarded as part of the internal law as soon as they are ratified.[60] Indeed, in some countries, such as the Netherlands, treaties have the same rank as constitutional law, and thus are paramount even with respect to subsequent legislation.[61] Yet even in those countries, courts are sometimes reluctant to allow treaties to be invoked by private litigants in the absence of language within the treaty to that effect. An example of that reluctance is the 2001 case of *X. v. Japan* before the Tokyo High Court, where the plaintiffs sought compensation from the government of Japan for acts committed in Hong Kong during World War II that arguably violated provisions of the 1907 Hague Convention (and its annexed regulations). According to the Tokyo High Court, even though the Hague regulations contain many provisions that directly protect individuals' interests, nevertheless

> since international law by its nature regulates relations between States, legal subjectivity in principle is recognized for States, not for individuals. In order for individual rights to be recognized under international law, individuals need to be recognized as having the standing to exercise their rights as a party under a certain treaty, and moreover, procedures for realizing such rights need to be provided under international law. However, the Hague Convention has no such stipulations that recognize the ability of individuals to exercise their rights or that provide procedures for realizing such rights. Thus, the Hague Convention cannot be interpreted as a convention which sets individuals' private rights as interests seeking to be protected by the Convention and which aims to restrain acts that violate those private rights by putting upon a belligerent party [who is] in violation [of] the obligation for compensation.[62]

[60] For a brief survey of some monist systems, *see* AUST, *supra* note 21, at 146–50.

[61] *See* GRONDWET [CONSTITUTION OF THE KINGDOM OF THE NETHERLANDS], art. 94 ("Statutory regulations in force within the Kingdom shall not be applicable if such application is in conflict with provisions of treaties that are binding on all persons or of resolutions by international institutions.").

[62] X v. Japan, Tokyo High Court, Judgment, Feb. 8, 2001, *reprinted in* 2002 JAP. ANN. INT'L L. 142, 143–44; *see also* X v. State, Osaka High Court, Judgment, Oct. 15, 1999, *reprinted in* 2001 JAP. ANN. INT'L L. 171 (no ability to sue for violation of rights under the International

Further, even in monist countries, there may be significant obstacles to invocation of treaties before national courts because of the avoidance doctrines referred to previously, especially as against the government.[63]

Where a country has incorporated a treaty into its national law by statute, it is usually the statute (and background constitutional principles) that serve as the touchstone for the national court's decision making, not an implied right for individuals to invoke the treaty norm. For example, Professor Hofman describes the reasoning by the German Federal Constitutional Court (FCC) in the 2004 *Görgülu* case on the relationship of the European Convention on Human Rights (ECHR) to German law as follows:

> The Second Senate of the FCC sets out by stating that the ECHR and its protocols have been transformed, by pertinent Acts passed by the legislature . . . into German law and therefore have the rank of federal statute law. Therefore, German courts must observe and apply the ECHR within the limits of a methodologically justifiable interpretation of German law. The guarantees of the ECHR are, however, not a direct constitutional standard of review in the German legal system; a complainant cannot, therefore, directly base a constitutional complaint upon an alleged violation of a human right contained in the ECHR. However, the guarantees of the ECHR impact upon the interpretation of the fundamental rights and constitutional principles of the *Grundgesetz* [i.e., the Basic Law, or constitution of Germany]. The ECHR and the case-law of the [ECtHR] serve as a guiding source in determining the content and scope of the fundamental rights and constitutional principles of the *Grundgesetz*, to the extent that this does not restrict or reduce the protection of a person's fundamental rights under the *Grundgesetz*.[64]

Of course, national legal systems usually are much more complicated than the broad monist and dualist approaches suggest, and one must look – as do

Covenant on Economic, Social and Cultural Rights or the International Covenant on Civil and Political Rights).

[63] *See supra* note 35; *see also* Francesco Francioni, *The Jurisprudence of International Human Rights Enforcement: Reflections on the Italian Experience*, in Enforcing International Human Rights in Domestic Courts 15, 17–18 (Benedetto Conforti & Francesco Francioni eds., 1997) (identifying obstacles in the form of the political question doctrine, deference to the executive's ability to breach international law, the doctrine of non-self-executing treaties, the later-in-time rule, the *forum non conveniens* principle, jurisdictional defects, or the act-of-state doctrine); Kälin, *supra* note 18, at 117 ("[T]he highest Swiss court, which in general shows a positive attitude vis-à-vis the application of international law, has been unwilling to accept the self-executing character of several important treaty provisions that most agree would be suitable for direct application.").

[64] Rainer Hofmann, *The German Federal Constitutional Court and Public International Law: New Decisions, New Approaches?* 47 Ger. Y.B. Int'l L. 9, 18–19 (2004) (footnotes omitted).

the remaining chapters in this volume – at each country's constitutional rules and judicial practice to fully understand how any given national legal system relates to international law.[65] Yet even accepting that there is a spectrum along which different countries achieve different levels of fusion between international and national law, it remains the case that the lack of uniformity in approach among national legal systems worldwide has precluded the emergence of a general principle of international law requiring states to allow individuals to invoke treaty norms in national courts.

The maxim *ubi jus, ibi remedium* may be regarded as a general principle of law that applies within the international legal system, but only in the sense that when a state violates the right of another state (or one of its nationals), that other state is entitled to demand reparation for the injury caused. In national legal systems, the maxim sometimes has been interpreted as entitling a right holder to have recourse to a court for enforcement of the right, on a theory that if there is no enforcement, then the right is not really legal in nature but rather a moral or natural right. Close analysis of national legal systems suggests that application of the maxim is far from absolute.[66] Yet whatever the maxim's meaning may be in national law, international law has

[65] *See* AUST, *supra* note 21, at 145 ("If one examines even a small selection of constitutions it soon becomes apparent that many contain both dualist and monist elements."); *see also* NATIONAL TREATY LAW AND PRACTICE (Duncan B. Hollis et al. eds., 2005).

[66] For a discussion of the right to a remedy in the context of U.S. law, *see, e.g.*, Donald H. Zeigler, *Rights, Rights of Action, and Remedies: An Integrated Approach*, 76 WASH. L. REV. 67, 95 (2001) (arguing "traditionally, courts were willing to make available all appropriate remedies to enforce rights. Most modern cases, by contrast, are ringed about with reservations."); Susan J. Stabile, *The Role of Congressional Intent in Determining the Existence of Implied Rights of Action*, 71 NOTRE DAME L. REV. 861, 862 (1996) (describing that since "1979, the Supreme Court has adopted a more passive view of the role of courts in determining implication issues, taking the position that whether to imply a cause of action from a federal statute depends solely on congressional intent."); David Schuman, *The Right to a Remedy*, 65 TEMP. L. REV. 1197, 1198–99 (1992) (finding that state law constitutional "remedy guarantees" that require "that the law furnish a remedy for specified types of injuries, have no federal counterpart, thus forcing courts and advocates to rely on their own skills of research, analysis, and creativity."); David Sloss, *Constitutional Remedies for Statutory Violations*, 89 IOWA L. REV. 355, 359 (2004) (analyzing the difficulties for private plaintiffs in suing state governments and state officers for violations of federal statutes, and noting that "in cases where plaintiffs sue to enjoin state executive action that allegedly violates a federal statute . . . , the Court will not address the merits of the claim unless plaintiffs can establish an express statutory cause of action."); Daryl J. Levinson, *Rights, Essentialism and Remedial Equilibration*, 99 COLUM. L. REV. 857, 861 (1999) (explaining a currently "pervasive theory" of constitutional rights "essentialism" whereby, "because courts have no special license or ability to make the types of policy decisions that remedies require, and because the political branches possess not only democratic legitimacy but also superior fact-finding and interest-balancing capacities, courts should defer to the political branches about issues of implementing or enforcing rights.").

never viewed the entitlement to a remedy as entailing a right to compulsory dispute settlement, at either the international or the national level. Indeed, to a large extent, this is why many persons are skeptical about referring to international law as law. Most rights that arise under international law – including some of the most fundamental, such as the right of a state not to be attacked by another in contravention of the UN Charter – cannot be vindicated by the right holder by compelling the transgressing state to appear before an international court or tribunal. While the right holder may be able to resort to an international tribunal if a specific treaty supports the tribunal's jurisdiction to adjudicate that right (e.g., a compromissory clause in a treaty of amity providing for jurisdiction of the ICJ over disputes arising under that treaty), most treaties do not provide for compulsory enforcement of treaty norms, and *ubi jus, ibi remedium* has never been viewed as establishing jurisdiction for an international court or tribunal simply because a treaty or nontreaty norm exists under international law. Even the VCLT provides only a nonbinding conciliation procedure for disputes about treaty violations, and a state party may file a reservation rejecting that procedure. Instead, to the extent that the principle of *ubi jus, ibi remedium* exists in international law, it appears to provide simply that, when a state breaches an international obligation, the state becomes obliged to provide reparation for that breach, which may consist of restitution, compensation, or some other form of reparation. The entitlement to that reparation does not carry with it a right to some form of compulsory dispute settlement before an international tribunal.

The situation does not change when the right holder is a nonstate actor. While the nonstate actor may be able to resort to an international tribunal if a specific treaty supports the tribunal's jurisdiction to adjudicate that right (e.g., investor-state arbitration under Chapter 11 of the North American Free Trade Agreement (NAFTA)), the nonstate actor cannot invoke *ubi jus, ibi remedium* alone as a means of supporting jurisdiction before some international court or tribunal.

Can *ubi jus, ibi remedium* support the proposition that when a nonstate actor is accorded a right under international law, then there is necessarily a right to compulsory dispute resolution before a national court? Given that the principle as it operates under general international law does not entail compulsory dispute resolution, it is doubtful that the principle should be so construed. Moreover, *ubi jus, ibi remedium* has never supported the proposition that a right created under one system of law (e.g., in the United States) entails a right to compulsory dispute settlement before the courts or tribunals of a different legal system (e.g., in the United Kingdom), so interpreting the principle as requiring national courts to adjudicate rights created under the system of international law is equally problematic. There does not appear to be any international case law construing the maxim in that fashion.

D. *Views of Publicists*

Scholars are in accord with the assessment that states are not generally obligated under international law to open their courts for such enforcement. As Professor Schachter stated in his lectures before the Hague Academy of International Law: "There is no general requirement in international law that States provide such remedies. By and large, international law leaves it to them to meet their obligations in such ways as the State determines. This is sometimes expressed as 'obligations of result' in contrast to 'obligations of means.'"[67] Similarly, the commentary to the *Restatement (Third) on the Foreign Relations Law of the United States* provides:

> International agreements, even those directly benefiting private persons, generally do not create private rights or provide for a private cause of action in domestic courts, but there are exceptions with respect to both rights and remedies. Whether an international agreement provides a right or requires that a remedy be made available to a private person is a matter of interpretation of the agreement.[68]

III. INVOCATION OF A TREATY NORM BY INDIVIDUALS IN NATIONAL COURTS PURSUANT TO AN EXPRESS TREATY OBLIGATION

Although the existence in a treaty of a benefit or right in favor of persons does not necessarily entail a right to invoke the treaty before national courts, a treaty might expressly provide for such a right as a part of the terms of the treaty. Express provision for access to national courts may be for the purpose of vindicating a substantive right contained in the treaty or it may be more procedural in nature, by simply creating a right of nondiscriminatory access to national courts.

At one time, international legal theory disputed whether it was possible for a treaty between two states to create rights or obligations for individuals

[67] SCHACHTER, *supra* note 57, at 240 (this volume is a revised version of the lectures).
[68] RESTATEMENT (THIRD) OF THE FOREIGN RELATIONS LAW OF THE UNITED STATES §907 cmt. a (1987) [hereinafter RESTATEMENT (THIRD)].

that could be vindicated in national courts. Some states and scholars contended that a treaty could only create rights and obligations as between states; if rights and obligations were to be created with respect to individuals, then it was asserted that a national law must be developed separate from the treaty. The Permanent Court of International Justice (PCIJ) laid that contention to rest in its advisory opinion on the *Jurisdiction of the Courts of Danzig*.[69]

In that case, a 1921 treaty had been concluded between Poland and the Free City of Danzig[70] by which Poland had taken into its railway service Danzig railway officials. In certain articles of the treaty referred to as the *Beamtenabkommen*, the treaty obligated Poland to accord various employment protections to the railway officials. When Poland failed to do so, the railway officials sued Poland (specifically, the Polish Railways Administration) in Danzig courts. After the League of Nations high commissioner for Danzig issued a decision that the treaty provisions could not serve as a basis for individuals to sue in the Danzig courts, the Danzig government succeeded in having the League Council request an advisory opinion from the PCIJ.

Before the PCIJ, Poland accepted that the 1921 treaty created rights and obligations as between Poland and Danzig, but not ones possessed by the employees on which they could sue in national courts, at least in the absence of an associated national law. If any violation of the treaty had occurred, Poland maintained that it was only the Free City of Danzig that might pursue a claim against Poland. By contrast, Danzig impressed on the Court that the treaty, in effect, created the terms for a services contract, and that what should be emphasized was not the form of the instrument but rather its substance. The PCIJ agreed and rejected Poland's position, stating:

> It may be readily admitted that, according to a well established principle of international law, the *Beamtenabkommen*, being an international agreement, cannot, as such create direct rights and obligations for private

[69] Jurisdiction of the Courts of Danzig, Advisory Opinion, 1928 P.C.I.J. (ser. B) No. 15 (Mar. 3).

[70] The Free City of Danzig was an autonomous city-state established in 1920, pursuant to the Treaty of Versailles, from territory that had been possessed by Germany. The city was placed under the protection of the League of Nations (represented by a high commissioner), though certain economic rights were maintained for Poland. The railway line connecting Danzig, a major port, with Poland was administered by Poland. After World War II, the city became a part of Poland and is now referred to as Gdańsk.

> individuals. But it cannot be disputed that the very object of an international agreement, according to the intention of the contracting Parties, may be the adoption by the Parties of some definite rules creating individual rights and obligations and enforceable by the national courts. That there is such an intention in the present case can be established by reference to the terms of the *Beamtenabkommen*....
>
> The wording and general tenor of the *Beamtenabkommen* show that its provisions are directly applicable as between the officials and the Administration. This is particularly the case in regard to Articles 6, *litt.* (*a*) and (*b*), 7, 11 and 12, which are of such a nature as to lead possibly to pecuniary claims. According to its contents, the object of the *Beamtenabkommen* is to create a special legal regime governing the relations between the Polish Railways Administration and the Danzig officials, workmen and employees who have passed into the permanent service of the Polish Administration.[71]

Although the Court recognized that Article 9 of the treaty contemplated that such labor matters would be addressed in accordance with Polish law, the Court stated that Article 9 "should not be construed in a manner which would make the applicability of the provisions of the *Beamtenabkommen* depend on their incorporation into a Polish Regulation."[72]

The Court's approach thereafter became accepted doctrine.[73] Consequently, as indicated in the *Restatement (Third)* provision quoted earlier, it is now commonly accepted that a treaty might, by its express terms, create rights for individuals separate from rights held by states. Moreover, many treaties expressly provide that the parties to the treaty must open their courts to individuals so that alleged violations of those rights may be litigated.[74]

[71] 1928 P.C.I.J. (ser. B) No. 15 at 17–18.

[72] *Id.*, at 20.

[73] In the same time frame, it also became accepted doctrine that individuals could be empowered by treaty to vindicate treaty norms before an international tribunal (even against their own government). *See, e.g.*, Steiner & Gross v. Poland, 4 ANN. DIG. PUB. INT'L L. CASES 291, 292 (1928) (international tribunal established under German-Polish treaty determined that an individual could invoke before the tribunal a treaty norm against his own government, finding that the treaty "conferred in unequivocal terms jurisdiction upon the tribunal irrespective of the nationality of the claimants").

[74] Of course, there are also treaties that open up national courts for enforcement of judgments from other national legal systems, such as exists in Europe under the Brussels and Lugano conventions. Brussels Convention on Jurisdiction and Enforcement of Judgments in Civil and Commercial Matters, Sept. 27, 1968, as amended, 1990 O.J. (C 189) 1 (harmonizing rules of jurisdiction and procedures for recognition and enforcement of judgments among EU states); Lugano Convention on Jurisdiction and Enforcement of Judgments in Civil and Commercial Matters, Sept. 16, 1988, 1988 O.J. (L 319) 9 (harmonizing such rules and procedures among EU States and European Free Trade Area States). In December 2000, the European Commission adopted a regulation that amends the terms of the Brussels and

For example, treaties of friendship, commerce, and navigation typically contain provisions that allow persons (including corporations) access to local courts to vindicate their rights, at least on terms no less favorable than are accorded to local nationals or nationals of third states. The 1948 United States–Italy Treaty on Friendship, Commerce, and Navigation provides that nationals of either party shall "enjoy freedom of access to the courts of justice and to administrative tribunals and agencies" of the other party "both in pursuit and in defense of their rights."[75] Bilateral investment treaties (BITs)[76] contain similar provisions, often allowing the affected

Lugano conventions and transforms them into a European Community legal instrument that is binding and directly applicable to the member states. *See* Council Regulation on Jurisdiction and the Recognition and Enforcement of Judgments in Civil and Commercial Matters, (EC) No. 44/2001 (Dec. 22, 2000), 2001 O.J. (L 12) 1.

[75] Treaty on Friendship, Commerce and Navigation, U.S.-Italy, art. V(4), Feb. 2, 1948, 63 Stat. 2255, 79 U.N.T.S. 171. The provision states in full:

> The nationals, corporations and associations of either High Contracting Party shall enjoy freedom of access to the courts of justice and to administrative tribunals and agencies in the territories of the other High Contracting Party, in all degrees of jurisdiction established by law, both in pursuit and in defense of their rights; shall be at liberty to choose and employ lawyers and representatives in the prosecution and defense of their rights before such courts, tribunals and agencies; and shall be permitted to exercise all these rights and privileges, in conformity with the applicable laws and regulations, upon terms no less favorable than the terms which are or may hereafter be accorded to the nationals, corporations and associations of the other High Contracting Party and no less favorable than are or may hereafter be accorded to the nationals, corporations and associations of any third country.

Treaties providing access to national courts for certain purposes have existed for a long time. For example, the Treaty of Peace between the United States and Great Britain that ended the U.S. Revolutionary War provided that British creditors were not to meet with any "lawful impediment" to the recovery of debts they had previously contracted, and that "all persons who have any interest in confiscated lands, either by debts, marriage settlements, or otherwise, shall meet with no lawful impediment in the prosecution of their just rights" – provisions designed to allow colonists who remained loyal to Britain to obtain recovery through U.S. courts. *See* Definitive Treaty of Peace, U.S.-Gr. Brit., arts. 4–5, Sept. 3, 1783, *reprinted in* 2 Treaties and Other International Acts of the United States of America 151 (Hunter Miller ed., 1931). More express reference to access to U.S. courts appeared in the 1795 amity treaty between the United States and Spain, which provided: "It is also agreed that the inhabitants of the territories of each Party shall respectively have free access to the Courts of Justice of the other, and they shall be permitted to prosecute suits for the recovery of their properties, the payment of their debts, and for obtaining satisfaction for the damages which they may have sustained...." Treaty of Friendship, Limits, and Navigation, U.S.-Spain, art. XX, Oct. 27, 1795, *reprinted in* 2 Treaties and Other International Acts of the United States of America 318, 334 (Hunter Miller ed., 1931). For a general discussion, see Robert R. Wilson, *Access-to-Courts Provisions in United States Commercial Treaties*, 47 Am. J. Int'l L. 20 (1953).

[76] As of 2003, there were 2,265 BITs involving 176 of the world's 191 countries. *See* U.N. Conference on Trade and Development, *UNCTAD Analysis of BITs* (Aug. 17, 2004), *at* www.unctadxi.org/templates/Page____1007.aspx.

person to choose either to pursue a dispute in the local courts or to take the matter to international arbitration. Thus, the 1985 China-Denmark BIT provides that when a dispute arises between an investor and the host country, and the complaint cannot be settled within six months, either party "shall be entitled to submit the dispute to the competent court" of the host country.[77] Contemporary BITs are becoming increasingly specific about the standards expected for the national processes. The 2004 model BIT developed by the United States sets forth various provisions on administrative procedures that a treaty party must establish or maintain to ensure protection of foreign investments,[78] and then provides:

> Each Party shall establish or maintain judicial, quasi-judicial, or administrative tribunals or procedures for the purpose of the prompt review and, where warranted, correction of final administrative actions regarding matters covered by this Treaty. Such tribunals shall be impartial and independent of the office or authority entrusted with administrative enforcement and shall not have any substantial interest in the outcome of the matter.[79]

Access to court provisions also have long appeared in treaties relating to patents, copyrights, and trademarks, thereby allowing foreign owners of intellectual property to have access to local courts to vindicate their rights.[80]

Such provisions are not limited to the field of international commerce. Various international environmental agreements expressly provide for suits in national legal systems as a means of vindicating treaty norms, usually in the context of transboundary environmental damage. For example, the

[77] Agreement on the Encouragement and the Reciprocal Protection of Investments, P.R.C.-Den., art. 8, Apr. 29, 1985, 1443 U.N.T.S. 69. The provision states in full:

1. In the event of a dispute between a national or company of one Contracting Party and the other Contracting Party in connection with an investment in the territory of the other Contracting Party, the national or company concerned may file [a] complaint with the competent authority of the other Contracting Party. Negotiations for settlement will then take place between the parties in dispute.
2. If such dispute cannot be thus settled within six months, either Party to the dispute shall be entitled to submit the dispute to the competent court of the Contracting Party accepting the investment.
3. If a dispute involving the amount of compensation resulting from expropriation . . . cannot be settled within six months after resorting to the procedure specified in Paragraph 1 of this Article by the national or company concerned it may be submitted to an international arbitral tribunal established by both parties.

[78] *See* Treaty between the Government of the United States of America and the Government of [Country] Concerning the Encouragement and Reciprocal Protection of Investment, art. 11(4) (Nov. 2004), *available at* http://www.state.gov/documents/organization/38710.pdf.

[79] *Id.*, art. 11(5)(a).

[80] *See, e.g.*, Paris Convention for the Protection of Industrial Property, arts. 2 & 3, Mar. 20, 1883, 25 Stat. 1372, as amended, *available at* http://www.wipo.int/treaties/en/ip/paris/.

1998 Aarhus Convention, which was developed by the UN Economic Commission for Europe, is designed to promote public access to information and participation in decision making on environmental matters. Article 9, titled "Access to Justice," provides in Paragraph 1:

> Each Party shall, within the framework of its national legislation, ensure that any person who considers that his or her request for information ... has been ignored, wrongfully refused, whether in part or in full, inadequately answered, or otherwise not dealt with in accordance with the provisions of that article, has access to a review procedure before a court of law or another independent and impartial body established by law.[81]

More commonly, environmental treaties speak to the ability to sue in national courts for damage caused to the environment. In 1974 the Nordic countries adopted the Convention on the Protection of the Environment, which provides:

> Any person who is affected or may be affected by a nuisance caused by environmentally harmful activities in another Contracting State shall have the right to bring before the appropriate Court or Administrative Authority of that State the question of the permissibility of such activities, including the question of measures to prevent damage, and to appeal against the decision of the Court or the Administrative Authority to the same extent and on the same terms as a legal entity of the State in which the activities are being carried out.[82]

Examples of treaties requiring access to courts also exist among European states for damage from carriage of dangerous goods by land,[83] from seabed exploitation,[84] at transport terminals engaged in international trade,[85] and in the field of nuclear energy.[86] Perhaps the most ambitious effort is the

[81] Convention on Access to Information, Public Participation in Decision-Making and Access to Justice in Environmental Matters, art. 9(1), June 25, 1998, 38 I.L.M. 517 (1999) (Aarhus Convention).

[82] Convention on the Protection of the Environment, Den.-Fin.-Nor.-Sweden, art. 3, Feb. 19, 1974, 1092 U.N.T.S. 279, 296, 13 I.L.M. 591.

[83] Convention on Civil Liability for Damage Caused during the Carriage of Dangerous Goods by Road, Rail and Inland Navigation Vessels, art. 5, U.N. Doc. ECE/TRANS/79 (Oct. 10, 1989).

[84] Convention on Civil Liability for Oil Pollution Damage from Offshore Operations, art. 11, Dec. 17, 1976, *reprinted in* 16 I.L.M. 1450 (1977).

[85] U.N. Convention on the Liability of Operators of Transport Terminals in International Trade, art. 5, U.N. Doc. A/CONF/152/13 (Apr. 19, 1991), *reprinted in* 30 I.L.M. 1503 (1991).

[86] Paris Convention on Third Party Liability in the Field of Nuclear Energy, art. 3, July 29, 1960, 956 U.N.T.S. 251, *reprinted in* 55 Am. J. Int'l L. 1082 (1960) (subsequently amended); Vienna Convention on Civil Liability for Nuclear Damage, art. 7, May 21, 1963, 1063 U.N.T.S.

1993 Convention on Civil Liability for Damage Resulting from Activities Dangerous to the Environment (Lugano Convention) addressing harm to human health and the environment from a range of "dangerous activities," although that convention has proved unpalatable to some European states.[87]

Environmental regimes establishing access to national courts also exist on the global level and, in some instances, are quite detailed regarding the scope of access to national courts. For example, the 1999 Basel Protocol on Liability and Compensation for Damage Resulting from Transboundary Movements of Hazardous Wastes and Their Disposal[88] seeks to establish a comprehensive regime for liability, and for adequate and prompt compensation, for damage resulting from transboundary movements of hazardous wastes, including illegal traffic in those wastes. Under the protocol, a person who notifies an importing state of a shipment shall be liable for damage until the disposer has taken possession of the hazardous wastes and other

265, *reprinted in* 2 I.L.M. 727 (1963). The two regimes were linked in the Joint Protocol Relating to the Application of the Vienna Convention and the Paris Convention, Sept. 21, 1988, *reprinted in* 42 NUCLEAR L. BULL. 56 (1988). On damage from ships carrying nuclear material, see Brussels Convention on the Liability of Operators of Nuclear Ships, May 25, 1962, *reprinted in* 57 AM. J. INT'L L. 268 (1963); Brussels Convention Relating to Civil Liability in the Field of Maritime Carriage of Nuclear Material, Dec. 17, 1971, 974 U.N.T.S. 255, *reprinted in* 11 I.L.M. 277 (1972).

87 Convention on Civil Liability for Damage Resulting from Activities Dangerous to the Environment, June 21, 1993, *reprinted in* 32 I.L.M. 1228 (1993). This convention channels liability to all persons and companies (and state and other agencies) exercising control over "dangerous activities" that cause damage, with no limitations on liability. The scope of damage extends to all deaths or bodily harm. Liability is not imposed if the activity was taken for the benefit of the person damaged. Since 1993, six European states have signed the convention, but others (including Denmark, Germany, and the United Kingdom) have indicated that they do not intend to join. Resistance to the convention from states and industry apparently turns on a belief that the scope of the convention is too wide and too vague in both its definitions and legal rules. *See* Commission of the European Communities, White Paper on Environmental Liability, at 25, COM(2000) 66 final (Feb. 9, 2000).

88 Basel Protocol on Liability and Compensation for Damage Resulting from Transboundary Movements of Hazardous Wastes and Their Disposal, U.N. Doc. UNEP-CHW.1-WG-1-9-2 (Dec. 10, 1999) [hereinafter Basel Protocol], *available at* http://www.basel.int/text/con-e.pdf. This instrument is a protocol to the Basel Convention on the Transboundary Movement of Hazardous Wastes and Their Disposal, Mar. 22, 1989, UN Doc. UNEP/IG.80/3 (1989) [hereinafter Basel Convention]. For information, *see* http://www.basel.int/convention/about.html. African states have developed their own convention banning the import into the region of hazardous wastes, which contains an article calling for a protocol on liability. Bamako Convention on the Ban of the Import into Africa and the Control of Transboundary Movement and Management of Hazardous Wastes within Africa, art. 12, Jan. 29, 1991, *reprinted in* 30 I.L.M. 790 (1991). While the Bamako Convention is in force, no liability protocol has yet been concluded.

wastes; thereafter, the disposer shall be liable for damage.[89] Further, any person shall be liable for damage caused or contributed by his or her lack of compliance with the 1989 Basel Convention or by his wrongful intentional, reckless, or negligent acts or omissions.[90] However, compensation may be reduced or disallowed "if the person who suffered the damage . . . has caused or contributed to the damage having regard to all circumstances."[91] Claims must be filed within certain time periods, and recovery is limited on the basis of the tonnage of the shipment.[92] Claims may be filed in the courts of the state where the damage was suffered, the state where the damage occurred, or the state where the defendant has his or her habitual residence or principal place of business.[93] Potentially liable persons are obligated to establish insurance, bonds, or other financial guarantees during the period of potential liability.[94] Final judgments issued by a competent court are enforceable in the courts of the other States who are party to the Basel Protocol, with certain limited exceptions.[95] Additional examples of global regimes providing for explicit access to national courts may be found in regimes concerning damage from carriage of dangerous goods by sea[96] and in the field of civil aviation.[97]

In the field of human rights, the standard approach in multilateral treaties is twofold. First, the treaty imposes a duty on the state to ensure that certain rights are accorded to individuals. Second, the treaty requires the state to adopt national measures, including sometimes judicial measures,

[89] Basel Protocol, *supra* note 88, art. 4.
[90] *Id.*, art. 5.
[91] *Id.*, art. 9.
[92] *Id.*, arts. 12, 13, & Annex B.
[93] *Id.*, art. 17.
[94] *Id.*, art. 14.
[95] *Id.*, art. 21.
[96] International Convention on Liability and Compensation for Damage in Connection with the Carriage of Hazardous and Noxious Substances by Sea, IMO Doc. LEG/CONF.10/8/2 (May 9, 1996), *reprinted in* 35 I.L.M. 1415 (1996).
[97] *See, e.g.*, Convention for the Unification of Certain Rules Relating to International Carriage by Air (Warsaw Convention), Oct. 12, 1929, 137 L.N.T.S. 11, 49 Stat. 3000 (subsequently amended). For example, art. 28(1) provides: "An action for damages must be brought, at the option of the plaintiff, in the territory of one of the High Contracting Parties, either before the Court having jurisdiction where the carrier is ordinarily resident, or has his principal place of business, or has an establishment by which the contract has been made or before the Court having jurisdiction at the place of destination." Some 120 states are parties to this convention, which places strict liability on civil airlines for harm to passengers up to certain limits. The treaty was designed in part to help the fledgling civil air industry of the 1920s to attract capital investment by limiting the potential liability of air carriers for accidents.

necessary to help prevent the abuse of rights from occurring, often by criminalizing certain conduct.[98] More specific to the issue of invocation of the treaty by individuals in national courts, several human rights treaties contain an express obligation to ensure access for persons to competent authorities, including judicial authorities, to secure an effective remedy for violation of rights held by the person under the treaty. For example, the International Covenant on Civil and Political Rights (ICCPR) provides in Article 2(3) that each party will ensure that any person whose ICCPR rights or freedoms are violated "shall have an effective remedy," "shall have his right thereto determined by competent judicial, administrative or legislative authorities," and shall "ensure that the competent authorities shall enforce such remedies when granted."[99] The International Convention on the Elimination of All Forms of Racial Discrimination (CERD) contains a similar provision that expressly contemplates access to national "tribunals" to vindicate an individual's treaty rights, both to secure injunctive relief for preventing the abuse and to obtain compensation if the abuse occurs.[100]

[98] A further dimension to this result-based and conduct-based dichotomy is the division between individual-oriented and collective-oriented duties of the state. *See* Tara J. Melish, *Rethinking the "Less as More" Thesis: Supranational Litigation of Economic, Social, and Cultural Rights in the Americas*, 39 N.Y.U. J. INT'L L. & POL. 171, 248 (2006).

[99] International Covenant on Civil and Political Rights, art. 2(3), Dec. 19, 1966, 999 U.N.T.S. 171 [hereinafter ICCPR]. The provision states in full:

Each State Party to the present Covenant undertakes:

(a) To ensure that any person whose rights or freedoms as herein recognized are violated shall have an effective remedy, notwithstanding that the violation has been committed by persons acting in an official capacity;

(b) To ensure that any person claiming such a remedy shall have his right thereto determined by competent judicial, administrative or legislative authorities, or by any other competent authority provided for by the legal system of the State, and to develop the possibilities of judicial remedy;

(c) To ensure that the competent authorities shall enforce such remedies when granted.

See Oscar Schachter, *The Obligation to Implement the Covenant in Domestic Law*, in THE INTERNATIONAL BILL OF RIGHTS 311 (Louis Henkin ed., 1981); *see also* International Convention on the Protection of the Rights of All Migrant Workers and Members of Their Families, art. 83, G.A. Res. 45/158, Annex, 45 U.N. GAOR Supp. at 262 (Dec. 18, 1990). Access to court provisions may also be seen in the context of rights for the alleged perpetrator of the abuse. Thus, in the context of criminal charges, the ICCPR provides: "In the determination of any criminal charge against him, or of his rights and obligations in a suit at law, everyone shall be entitled to a fair and public hearing by a competent, independent and impartial tribunal established by law." ICCPR, *supra*, art. 14(1).

[100] Convention on the Elimination of Racial Discrimination, art. 6, Dec. 21, 1965, 660 U.N.T.S. 195, 5 I.L.M. 350. Art. 6 states:

States Parties shall assure to everyone within their jurisdiction effective protection and remedies, through the competent national tribunals and other State

Other human rights treaties are less explicit in indicating that the access to courts is to vindicate treaty rights, as opposed to simply preventing or obtaining redress for a type of harm inflicted on the individual. Thus, rather than emphasize rights granted by treaty, the Convention against Torture[101] speaks of access by an individual to "competent authorities" both to have "his case" examined regarding an act of torture[102] and to obtain redress including "fair and adequate compensation."[103] Similarly, CEDAW obligates states "to ensure through competent national tribunals and other public institutions the effective protection of women against any act of discrimination."[104] The recently adopted convention on disabilities focuses on nondiscriminatory "access to justice" for disabled persons.[105]

On the regional level, the Council of Europe's Convention for the Protection of Human Rights and Fundamental Freedoms states that "[e]veryone whose rights and freedoms as set forth in this Convention are violated shall have an effective remedy before a national authority notwithstanding that the violation has been committed by persons acting in an official capacity."[106] Language to similar effect appears in the inter-American and

institutions, against any acts of racial discrimination which violate his human rights and fundamental freedoms contrary to this Convention, as well as the right to seek from such tribunals just and adequate reparation or satisfaction for any damage suffered as a result of such discrimination.

[101] Convention against Torture and Other Cruel, Inhuman, or Degrading Treatment or Punishment, Dec. 10, 1984, 1465 U.N.T.S. 85, S. Treaty Doc. No. 100–20 (1988) [hereinafter Convention Against Torture].

[102] *Id.*, art 13 ("Each State Party shall ensure that any individual who alleges he has been subjected to torture in any territory under its jurisdiction has the right to complain to, and to have his case promptly and impartially examined by, its competent authorities. Steps shall be taken to ensure that the complainant and witnesses are protected against all ill-treatment or intimidation as a consequence of his complaint or any evidence given.").

[103] *Id.*, art. 14(1) ("Each State Party shall ensure in its legal system that the victim of an act of torture obtains redress and has an enforceable right to fair and adequate compensation, including the means for as full rehabilitation as possible. In the event of the death of the victim as a result of an act of torture, his dependents shall be entitled to compensation.").

[104] CEDAW, *supra* note 44, art. 2(c).

[105] Convention on the Rights of Persons with Disabilities, art. 13(1), U.N. GAOR, 61st Sess., Annex, U.N. Doc. A/61/611 (Dec. 6, 2006) ("States Parties shall ensure effective access to justice for persons with disabilities on an equal basis with others, including through the provision of procedural and age-appropriate accommodations, in order to facilitate their effective role as direct and indirect participants, including as witnesses, in all legal proceedings, including at investigative and other preliminary stages.").

[106] European Convention for the Protection of Human Rights and Fundamental Freedoms, art. 13, Nov. 4, 1950, 213 U.N.T.S. 221, E.T.S. 5, as amended; *see also id.*, art. 6 (right to a fair trial).

African conventions on human rights.[107] Interestingly, the Banjul Charter appears to obligate states parties to provide access to their "competent national organs" for individuals to vindicate not just rights arising under the Banjul Charter but also fundamental rights arising under other conventions.[108] Nonbinding human rights instruments also speak of the right of access to national tribunals and courts, including the Universal Declaration of Human Rights[109] and the American Declaration of the Rights and Duties of Man.[110]

By contrast, other human rights treaties – such as the Convention on the Prevention and Punishment of the Crime of Genocide[111] – do not expressly contemplate the creation of individual rights that can be vindicated through resort to national tribunals. Moreover, when ratifying human rights treaties, it is entirely possible that a state may reject, modify, or interpret the obligation to allow access to national courts by means of a reservation or understanding to the treaty. For example, when New Zealand ratified the Convention against Torture, it reserved "the right to award compensation to torture victims referred to in article 14 of the Convention Against Torture only at the discretion of the Attorney-General of New Zealand."[112] The United States filed an understanding to Article 14 interpreting it as

[107] American Convention on Human Rights, arts. 8 & 25, Nov. 22, 1969, 1144 U.N.T.S. 123, 9 I.L.M. 673 (1970); African Charter on Human and Peoples' Rights, art. 7, June 27, 1981, 21 I.L.M. 58 (1982) (Banjul Charter).

[108] Banjul Charter, *supra* note 107, art. 7(1) ("Every individual shall have the right to have his cause heard. This comprises . . . the right to an appeal to competent national organs against acts of violating his fundamental rights as recognized and guaranteed by conventions, laws, regulations and customs in force."). For a discussion, however, of how the Banjul Charter has not featured significantly in African case law, in part because some national legal systems have not incorporated the treaty into their national law and in part because the local courts primarily interpret and apply local law, see Frans Viljoen, *Application of the African Charter on Human and Peoples' Rights by Domestic Courts in Africa*, 43 J. AFRICAN L. 1 (1999).

[109] Universal Declaration of Human Rights, G.A. Res. 217 (III), art. 10, U.N. Doc. A/810 (Dec. 10, 1948) ("Everyone is entitled in full equality to a fair and public hearing by an independent and impartial tribunal, in the determination of his rights and obligations and of any criminal charge against him.").

[110] American Declaration of the Rights and Duties of Man, OAS Res. 1591, art. XVIII (1948), *reprinted in* 43 AM. J. INT'L L. SUPP. 133, 136 (1949) ("Every person may resort to the courts to ensure respect for his legal rights. There should likewise be available to him a simple, brief procedure whereby the courts will protect him from acts of authority that, to his prejudice, violate any fundamental constitutional rights.").

[111] Convention on the Prevention and Punishment of the Crime of Genocide, Dec. 9, 1948, 78 U.N.T.S. 277.

[112] *See* Convention against Torture, Declarations, and Reservations, *available at* http://www.ohchr.org/english/countries/ratification/9.htm.

requiring "a State Party to provide a private right of action for damages only for acts of torture committed in territory under the jurisdiction of that State Party."[113] When a state takes such action, if other states do not object, the treaty obligation becomes conditioned for that state to the extent of the reservation or understanding.

Finally, it should be noted that express provisions within treaties may also accord rights for individuals to avoid suit in national courts, such as immunity from legal process accorded to diplomats, consular officials, heads of state, or officials of international organizations. In a 1999 advisory opinion, the ICJ considered Section 22(b) of the Convention on Privileges and Immunities of the United Nations, which provided that UN experts on mission shall be accorded "immunity from legal process of every kind" for words or acts done in the course of performing their mission.[114] In light of such language, the Court stated that national courts had a direct obligation to take action at an early stage in the proceedings to address the issue of immunity:

> By necessary implication, questions of immunity are therefore preliminary issues which must be expeditiously decided *in limine litis*. This is a generally recognized principle of procedural law, and Malaysia was under an obligation to respect it. The Malaysian courts did not rule *in limine litis* on the immunity of the Special Rapporteur . . . , thereby nullifying the essence of the immunity rule contained in Section 22(b). As indicated above, the conduct of an organ of a State – even an organ independent of executive power – must be regarded as an act of that State. Consequently, Malaysia did not act in accordance with its obligations under international law.[115]

IV. INVOCATION OF A TREATY NORM BY INDIVIDUALS IN NATIONAL COURTS PURSUANT TO AN IMPLIED TREATY OBLIGATION

Even if a treaty does not expressly require that access be provided to national courts in order to vindicate a treaty norm, a requirement of such access may

[113] *Id.*

[114] Convention on Privileges and Immunities of the United Nations, Sec. 22(b), Feb. 13, 1946, 1 U.N.T.S. 16, 21 U.S.T. 1418.

[115] Advisory Opinion on Difference Relating to Immunity from Legal Process of a Special Rapporteur of the Commission on Human Rights, 1999 I.C.J. 62, 88, ¶ 63 (Apr. 29). The Court ultimately advised that "the Malaysian courts had the obligation to deal with the question of immunity from legal process as a preliminary issue to be expeditiously decided *in limine litis*." *Id.*, at 90.

be implicit in the treaty. The PCIJ's advisory opinion on the *Jurisdiction of the Courts of Danzig* is an example of implying access to national courts; in that case, the 1921 treaty did not expressly indicate that railway officials were to be granted access to the national legal system of either party to the treaty. Determining whether a right of access is implicit in the treaty requires a careful analysis of the language of the treaty, in the context and in light of the treaty's object and purpose, as well as the practice of states parties subsequent to the treaty's entry into force, and possibly the treaty's negotiating history.

The ICJ engaged in such an analysis in the course of rendering its decisions in *LaGrand* and *Avena* with respect to VCCR Article 36.[116] In those cases, the Court found that the United States had violated its obligations under Article 36(1) by not informing aliens of their right of consular notification, by not notifying their consulates of their detentions, and by effectively depriving the consulates of their ability to communicate with and have access to the aliens. The further question that arose was whether the failure to provide judicial review in U.S. courts of the aliens' convictions and sentences, in light of the lack of notification, constituted an additional violation of the VCCR.

[116] VCCR, *supra* note 3, art. 36. Art. 36 provides:

1 With a view to facilitating the exercise of consular functions relating to nationals of the sending State:

(a) consular officers shall be free to communicate with nationals of the sending State and to have access to them. Nationals of the sending State shall have the same freedom with respect to communication with and access to consular officers of the sending State;

(b) if he so requests, the competent authorities of the receiving State shall, without delay, inform the consular post of the sending State if, within its consular district, a national of that State is arrested or committed to prison or to custody pending trial or is detained in any other manner. Any communication addressed to the consular post by the person arrested, in prison, custody or detention shall also be forwarded by the said authorities without delay. The said authorities shall inform the person concerned without delay of his rights under this sub-paragraph;

(c) consular officers shall have the right to visit a national of the sending State who is in prison, custody or detention, to converse and correspond with him and to arrange for his legal representation. They shall also have the right to visit any national of the sending State who is in prison, custody or detention in their district in pursuance of a judgment. Nevertheless, consular officers shall refrain from taking action on behalf of a national who is in prison, custody or detention if he expressly opposes such action.

2 The rights referred to in paragraph 1 of this Article shall be exercised in conformity with the laws and regulations of the receiving State, subject to the proviso, however, that the said laws and regulations must enable full effect to be given to the purposes for which the rights accorded under this Article are intended.

Article 36 does not expressly provide for judicial review in the national courts of a failure to provide consular notification. Yet Article 36(2) states that the rights expressed in Article 36 "shall be exercised in conformity with the laws and regulations of the receiving State, subject to the proviso, however, that the said laws and regulations must enable full effect to be given to the purposes for which the rights accorded under this Article are intended."[117] Germany argued that this proviso required that violations of the consular notification obligations of Article 36(1) be remedied through the criminal justice systems of parties to the convention.[118] The United States responded that the failure to provide consular notification did not trigger any such requirement. According to the United States, the purpose of Article 36(2) was simply to recognize that the ability of consular officials to communicate with and visit detainees was subject to local laws, so long as those laws did not defeat the purpose of Article 36.[119] The express language of Article 36 did not establish an "individual right" and certainly did not establish any remedy for criminal defendants in national legal systems.[120] Further,

> the language and structure of Article 36(1) do not support any claim that the receiving State must hold its criminal justice process in abeyance pending the provision of consular services. Because Article 36(1) does not link the justice process to consular notification, it cannot be read to require that receiving States provide remedies in the criminal justice process if Article 36(1) is not fully observed.[121]

In its judgment, the Court found that Article 36(1) did create individual rights. When reaching that conclusion, the Court found significant the language in Article 36(1)(b) that the "said authorities shall inform the person concerned without delay of *his rights* under this subparagraph," and in Article 36(1)(c) that consular assistance to the detained person may not be exercised "if he expressly opposes such action."[122] According to the Court:

> The clarity of these provisions, viewed in their context, admits of no doubt. It follows, as has been held on a number of occasions, that the Court must apply these as they stand.... Based on the text of these provisions, the Court concludes that Article 36, paragraph 1, creates individual rights,

[117] *Id.*, art. 36(2).
[118] Memorial of the Federal Republic of Germany, LaGrand Case (Ger. v. U.S.), ¶¶ 4.17–4.24 (Sept. 16, 1999).
[119] Counter-Memorial of the United States of America, LaGrand Case (Ger. v. U.S.), ¶ 79 (Mar. 27, 2000).
[120] *Id.*, ¶ 76.
[121] *Id.*, ¶ 87.
[122] LaGrand, *supra* note 1, ¶ 77 (emphasis in original).

> which, by virtue of Article I of the Optional Protocol, may be invoked in this Court by the national State of the detained person. These rights were violated in the present case.[123]

The Court did not find it necessary to determine, as Germany urged it to do, that the right at issue had the character of being a "human right."[124]

The Court then determined that Article 36(2) concerned not just the rights of the sending state but also the individual rights of the detained person, such that the local laws and regulations must "enable full effect" to be given to the purposes of those individual rights.[125] Although the United States argued that the language of Article 36(2) "does not require States Party to create a national law remedy permitting individuals to assert claims involving the Convention in criminal proceedings,"[126] the Court found that U.S. laws and regulations, principally the procedural default rule, could not be invoked so as to preclude review in U.S. courts of arguments that the detainees' convictions and sentences were flawed because of the lack of consular notification.[127] In other words, "the procedural default rule had the effect of preventing 'full effect [from being] given to the purposes for which the rights accorded under this article are intended', and thus violated paragraph 2 of Article 36."[128]

Looking to the future, Germany asked that the Court order the United States to issue assurances that it would "provide effective review of and remedies for criminal convictions impaired by the violation of the rights under Article 36."[129] The Court declined to order that such assurances be made, but it did find that if future violations of Article 36(1) were to occur, a mere apology from the United States would not be a sufficient response. Rather, the Court stated in *LaGrand* that, "should nationals of the Federal Republic of Germany . . . be sentenced to severe penalties" without their right to consular notification having been respected, the United States, "by means of its own choosing, shall allow the review and reconsideration of the conviction and sentence by taking account of the violation of the rights set forth" in the VCCR.[130] The choice of the means for such review and reconsideration, said the Court, must be left to the United States.

[123] *Id.*
[124] *Id.*, ¶ 78.
[125] *Id.*, ¶ 89.
[126] Counter-Memorial of the United States, *supra* note 119, ¶ 77.
[127] LaGrand, *supra* note 1, ¶¶ 90–91.
[128] *Id.*, ¶ 91.
[129] *Id.*, ¶ 12.
[130] *Id.*, ¶ 128(7); *see id.*, ¶ 125.

With respect to the some fifty Mexican nationals at issue in the *Avena* case, the Court reached similar findings. For three of the nationals who had already failed to get past the procedural default rule, the Court found that using the rule to preclude review and reconsideration of the effects of an Article 36(1) violation separately violated Article 36(2). According to the Court, the "*review and reconsideration* of conviction and sentence *required by Article 36, paragraph* 2, which is the appropriate remedy for breaches of Article 36, paragraph 1, has not been carried out."[131] As such, "by not permitting the review and reconsideration, in light of the rights set forth in the Convention, of the conviction and sentences [of the three individuals], after the violations [of Article 36(1)] had been established in respect of those individuals, the United States of America breached the obligations incumbent upon it under Article 36, paragraph 2, of the Convention."[132]

As was the case in *LaGrand*, the *Avena* court also found that there should be prospective "review and reconsideration" of the effects of violations of Article 36(1).[133] With an eye to the U.S. approach of relying on governors and parole boards to commute death sentences in light of the VCCR violations, the Court in *Avena* also stated that prospective "review and reconsideration" must entail "a procedure which guarantees that full weight is given to the violations of the rights set forth in the Vienna Convention" and "should occur within the overall *judicial* proceedings relating to the individual defendant concerned."[134] The Court specifically noted that "the clemency process, as currently practised within the United States criminal justice system, does not appear to meet the requirements."[135]

[131] Avena, *supra* note 2, ¶ 152 (emphasis added). Mexico had asked the Court to find that the United States had "violated its obligations under Article 36(2) of the Vienna Convention by failing to provide meaningful and effective review and reconsideration of convictions and sentences impaired by a violation of Article 36(1)." *Id.*, at 23.

[132] *Id.*, ¶ 153(8).

[133] *Id.*, ¶ 153(9).

[134] *Id.*, ¶¶ 138–39 (emphasis added).

[135] *Id.*, ¶ 143. The Court revisited the "review and reconsideration" obligation as a part of Mexico's 2008 request for an interpretation of the judgment. One of the Mexicans on death row in the United States, José Ernesto Medellín Rojas, was unsuccessful in obtaining "review and reconsideration" of his conviction and sentence in Texas courts. Consequently, he asked U.S. federal courts to regard as binding federal law either the *Avena* judgment itself or a February 2005 memorandum by President Bush stating that the United States would "discharge its international obligations" under *Avena* "by having State courts give effect to the decision." After the U.S. Supreme Court found that neither source constituted directly enforceable federal law, Medellin v. Texas, 128 S.Ct. 1346 (2008), Germany filed an application at the ICJ asking for an interpretation of ¶ 153(9) of the *Avena* judgment. In the course of issuing provisional measures of protection (calling for Medellín and four others not to be executed pending the ICJ's interpretation), the Court noted that both Mexico and

Four aspects of the Court's reasoning in *LaGrand* and *Avena* are worth emphasizing. First, the Court did not simply conclude that since persons benefited from obligations imposed on states under the VCCR, those persons consequently were entitled to invoke the VCCR in national courts in order to secure those benefits. Rather, the Court found it necessary to determine that the treaty created individual rights, which the Court said existed in this particular treaty by virtue of specific language referring to personal rights ("his rights") and assigning significance to the individual's personal preference regarding the operation of the treaty (consular assistance may not be exercised "if he expressly opposes such action"). By its language, the treaty expressly accorded to the individual an important role in the process by which consular notification was to be undertaken; the process was not one entailing simply conduct by representatives of states. By contrast, a treaty that did not contain such language – perhaps one that simply imposed constraints on governmental action – might not lead to the same result, even if the treaty was beneficial to the interests of third parties (individuals).

Second, in *LaGrand* the existence of those individual rights alone did *not* trigger a requirement that there be access to local courts to vindicate those rights. Indeed, the only consequence that flowed from a finding that there were "individual rights" was that Germany could invoke those rights before the ICJ, given that the United States had accepted the ICJ's jurisdiction over disputes arising under the VCCR.[136] Rather, the Court's scrutiny of the treatment of the individuals in U.S. courts arose because of the language of Article 36(2), which stated that national "laws and regulations must enable full effect to be given to the purposes for which the rights accorded under this Article are intended."[137] The Court explicitly characterized the process of "review and reconsideration" as "required by Article 36(2)" and characterized Article 36(2) as setting forth the "remedy" for violations of Article 36(1).[138] The application by U.S. courts of the procedural default rule so as to preclude an alien from challenging his or her conviction and

the United States regarded the Court's "review and reconsideration" finding as creating an "obligation of result," since there were various means by which the United States might accomplish such review and reconsideration. Request for Interpretation of the Judgment of 31 March 2004 in the Case Concerning *Avena and Other Mexican Nationals* (Mex. v. U.S.), 2008 I.C.J. 139 (July 16), *reprinted in* 47 I.L.M. 723 (2008).

[136] LaGrand, *supra* note 1, ¶ 77 ("the Court concludes that Article 36, paragraph 1, creates individual rights, which, by virtue of Article I of the Optional Protocol, may be invoked in this Court by the national State of the detained person.").

[137] VCCR, *supra* note 3, art. 36(2).

[138] Avena, *supra* note 2, ¶ 152.

sentence (a challenge based on violation of Article 36(1)) was a further violation of the treaty, this time arising under Article 36(2).

Hence, the Article 36(2) language directly linked the primary international obligation (concerning notification of the right to consular access) to the national legal system, transforming what might otherwise have been solely a protection accorded to individuals that was actionable before an international court into, instead, a protection for which the treaty provided a remedy in a national court. In essence, the Court viewed the United States as having agreed in Article 36(2) of the treaty that the individual rights arising under the treaty may be exercised in national law and that, while such exercise must be in accordance with national laws and regulations, those laws could not be applied or construed in a manner that precluded giving full effect to the purposes underlying the treaty rights. Had Article 36(2) not existed, it is not at all clear that the Court would have found an obligation for national courts to allow individuals to invoke VCCR rights; there is nothing express or implied in the Court's reasoning to suggest as much.[139] Instead, it is possible the Court would have found only that Germany or Mexico had an ability to bring a diplomatic claim against the United States to vindicate the individual rights of their nationals.

At the same time, the Court additionally ordered that, in the future, when U.S. courts are confronted with a claim that Article 36(1) has been violated, U.S. courts shall allow review and reconsideration of the conviction and sentence taking into account that violation. Here, the Court's finding is best regarded as a form of declaratory relief, similar to an order from the Court that the United States provide assurances of nonrepetition of Article 36(1) violations. However it may be characterized, the Court's issuance of such

[139] In their pleadings before the Court, neither Germany nor Mexico alleged that there was a general norm of international law requiring that nationals protected by VCCR art. 36(1) be accorded access to national courts to vindicate their rights. In particular, neither state argued that the general obligation of a state under international law to perform a treaty in good faith, *see* VCLT, *supra* note 5, art. 26, required the United States to open its courts for vindication of art. 36(1) rights (even though both states cited the VCLT for other reasons in other contexts, such as on how treaties should be interpreted). Neither state argued that such a general obligation under international law provided the legal basis for the Court to declare the barring of such claims in U.S. courts to be unlawful. Rather, Germany and Mexico both pleaded that the adjudication of art. 36(1) rights must be allowed in U.S. courts due to VCCR art. 36(2), with their arguments focusing in depth on the text of art. 36(2) and on its *travaux préparatoires*. *See* Memorial of Germany, LaGrand Case (Ger. v. U.S.), ¶¶ 4.17–4.24, 7.02(2) (Mar. 27, 2000); Memorial of Mexico, Avena Case (Mex. v. U.S.), ¶¶ 209–225 (June 20, 2003). The Court's reasoning followed suit, with no suggestion of any kind that a norm external to the VCCR required that U.S. courts adjudicate art. 36(1) claims.

reparation does not appear to arise from the simple existence of a provision in a treaty providing protection for an individual (i.e., Article 36(1)) or from some general principle of international law mandating enforcement of such rights in national courts. Rather, the issuance of the relief appears fully grounded in and exercised for the purpose of forestalling future violations of Article 36(2).

Third, there are important aspects relating to the posture of the *LaGrand* and *Avena* cases that suggest caution in reading the cases too broadly. The cases concerned criminal actions in which the individuals were exposed to the severest of penalties – death. Thus, the Court's finding of a U.S. violation by not allowing review and reconsideration in national courts, both retrospectively and prospectively, arose in the context of an inability of individuals to invoke the violation of a treaty as a potential means for avoiding execution. There is nothing in Article 36 that would preclude the Court's reasoning from being applied to criminal cases involving less severe penalties,[140] but it would not be surprising for an international court to adopt a wider margin of appreciation for national courts in circumstances where the stakes are much lower for the individual. Further, the *LaGrand* and *Avena* cases did not involve a civil action; indeed, Article 36 is exclusively concerned with the treatment of an individual in a criminal context. Therefore, the Court's decisions are not speaking directly to the ability of individuals to invoke treaties in national courts for the purpose of advancing civil claims against a government or against other individuals.

Fourth, in applying Article 36(2) so as to find an obligation that national courts take the effects of a treaty violation into account in their decision making, it should be borne in mind that the Court rendered a very circumscribed judgment. The obligation found to exist for U.S. courts was to review and reconsider the convictions and sentences in light of the treaty violation, not to alter them through any particular substantive response. Although Germany did not request that the convictions and sentences of the LaGrand brothers be annulled (which is not surprising, since the brothers had already been executed at the time the Court considered the case on the merits),[141] Mexico did request a finding that the United States was obligated "to restore the *status quo ante* by annulling or otherwise depriving

[140] In a separate declaration to the *LaGrand* judgment, the president of the Court indicated that the Court's reference to "severe penalties" did not necessarily mean that nonsevere penalties would not benefit from the same protection, LaGrand, *supra* note 1, at 517 (declaration of President Guillaume), but the reality is that the issue of less severe criminal penalties was simply not before the Court.

[141] *See* LaGrand, *supra* note 1, ¶ 12 (setting forth Germany's final submissions).

of full force or effect the convictions and sentences of all 52 Mexican nationals."[142] The Court refused to order any such remedy. Consequently, it presumably meets the obligation of the United States for U.S. courts, after review and reconsideration, to determine that the convictions and sentences should stand. If so, then the Court's conclusion that an individual must be entitled to raise a treaty violation before the national court left considerable discretion to the national court in determining what consequences flow from that violation.[143]

The willingness of the Court to find an implicit obligation within a treaty to permit litigation by individuals of treaty rights in national courts echoes the jurisprudence of the European Court of Justice (ECJ) concerning the direct effects of European Community (EC) treaty instruments. Successive EC treaties have been concluded among the EC member states; by their terms, those treaties impose obligations on the member states, without any express provision for redress by individuals in national courts when those obligations are unfulfilled. While EC regulations were to be directly applicable in national legal systems, EC member states originally did not view EC treaty provisions as creating directly enforceable individual rights. Only after the ECJ's 1963 decision in *Van Gend en Loos v. Nederlandse Administratie der Balanstingen*[144] did it become accepted that individuals could directly invoke certain EC treaty provisions as a source of individual rights in national courts. Interestingly, it is generally understood that the ECJ in *Van Gend en Loos* sought to distinguish the EC system from the traditional system of public international law – the ECJ saw the latter as "merely creat[ing] mutual obligations between the contracting states."[145] Instead, the ECJ said that the EC regime "constitutes *a new legal order* of international law for the benefit of which the states have limited their sovereign rights,

[142] *See* Avena, *supra* note 2, ¶ 14 (setting forth Mexico's final submissions).

[143] *See* Shany, *supra* note 47, at 935–36 (noting that the Court refused to resort to the traditional *Chorzów Factory* remedy of *status quo ex ante*). In the *Chorzów Factory* case, the PCIJ stated that "reparation must, as far as possible, wipe out all the consequences of the illegal act and re-establish the situation which would, in all probability, have existed if that act had not been committed." Factory at Chorzów (Ger. v. Pol.), 1928 P.C.I.J. (ser. A) No. 17, at 47.

[144] Van Gend en Loos v. Nederlandse Administratie der Balanstingen, Case 26/62, N.V. Algemene Transport–en Expeditie Onderneming Van Gend en Loos v. Nederlandse Administratie der Belastingen, 1963 E.C.R. 1, 25, 1963 C.M.L.R. 105, 130–31 (finding that it was necessary to interpret the treaty article in question "as to produce direct effect and to create individual rights which internal courts should protect"). For a discussion of subsequent EC practice, *see* Angela Ward, Judicial Review and the Rights of Private Parties in EC Law (2000).

[145] Van Gend en Loos, *supra* note 144, at 12. For a discussion, *see* Joseph H.H. Weiler, *The Transformation of Europe*, 100 Yale L.J. 2403, 2427–30 (1991).

albeit within limited fields, and the subjects of which comprise not only Member States but also their nationals."[146]

The approach of both the ICJ and the ECJ in viewing certain treaties as establishing rights for individuals that are actionable in national courts is consistent with the position expressed by Hersch Lauterpacht in his study of the status of the individual under international law: "The question [of] whether individuals in any given case are subjects of international law and whether that quality extends to the capacity of enforcement must be answered pragmatically by reference to the given situation and to the relevant international instrument. That instrument may make them subjects of the law without conferring upon them procedural capacity; it may aim at, and achieve, both these objects."[147]

V. WHEN SHOULD A RIGHT TO INVOKE THE TREATY IN NATIONAL COURTS NOT BE IMPLIED IN THE TREATY?

Although for some treaties there will be an implied right for individuals to invoke the treaty in national courts, a standard treaty interpretation analysis may lead to a conclusion that a right of access to national courts should not be implied. That analysis would focus on the ordinary meaning of the treaty provisions, in the context of and in light of the object and purpose of the treaty, as well as the practice of states under the treaty and possibly the *travaux préparatoires*. Four factors should be of particular relevance in rejecting an implied right of access to national courts.

First, where the treaty expresses a benefit or protection for individuals that is highly inchoate or aspirational in nature, and thus implicitly anticipates some further action by states to clarify and implement the treaty provision, then it is improper to imply an international obligation to accord access to national courts to vindicate the treaty provision. For example, the provisions on human rights set forth in Articles 55 and 56 of the UN Charter represent important pledges by UN members to pursue improvements in the economic well-being of individuals and the promotion of human rights, but they are precatory in nature; they require further elaboration by states for implementation either on the international or the national plane. That further elaboration has occurred in numerous global and regional treaties on human rights.

Yet even for those subsequent treaties, careful attention must be paid to the content of the rights that are established. For example, the International

[146] Van Gend en Loos, *supra* note 144, at 12 (emphasis added).
[147] Herschel Lauterpacht, International Law and Human Rights 27 (1950).

Covenant on Economic, Social, and Cultural Rights (ICESCR)[148] provides greater detail regarding the content and scope of economic, social, and cultural rights, but it contains several caveats that demonstrate that the parties have not accepted wholesale obligations to provide social security, employment, food, and shelter to their nationals. Thus, Article 2(1) recognizes that there can be a "progressive" realization of these rights over a period of time.[149] Given that the rights are contingent on further steps, there is no basis for implying into such a treaty a right to invoke these treaty rights in national courts.

Second, if the treaty is similar to certain other treaties in nature or scope, and if the other treaties expressly provide for a right of access for persons to national courts, then a right of access to national courts should not be implied with regard to the treaty that is silent on the matter. Thus, the 1989 UN Convention on the Rights of the Child[150] is similar to other UN human rights treaties in terms of setting forth certain normative standards, requiring state parties to report on their implementation, and creating a committee of experts to review that implementation. Unlike other UN human rights treaties, however, such as the treaties on civil and political rights, racial discrimination, and torture,[151] the Convention on the Rights of the Child contains no express, general provisions calling for access to national organs, including national courts, for vindication of personal rights.[152] The absence of such a provision, when it was included in earlier human rights treaties, weighs against implying such access to national courts on the basis of that convention. Obviously, this factor is strongest when a comparison is being made between treaties that have the same parties and that were concluded in the same temporal period.

[148] International Covenant on Economic, Social, and Cultural Rights, Dec. 16, 1966, 993 U.N.T.S. 3 [hereinafter ICESCR].

[149] *Id.*, art. 2(1). Art. 2(1) states: "Each State Party to the present Covenant undertakes to take steps, individually and through international assistance and co-operation, especially economic and technical, to the maximum extent of its available resources, with a view to achieving progressively the full realization of the rights recognized in the present Covenant by all appropriate means, including particularly the adoption of legislative measures."

[150] UN Convention on the Rights of the Child, Nov. 20, 1989, 1577 U.N.T.S. 3 [hereinafter Convention on the Rights of the Child].

[151] *See supra* notes 99–101.

[152] There are some provisions concerning access to courts that are more limited in nature than the provisions contained in other human rights treaties. *See* Convention on the Rights of the Child, *supra* note 150, art. 9(2) (opportunity to participate in proceedings on separation); *id.*, art. 12 (opportunity of child to be heard in any judicial proceedings that are held); *id.*, art. 37(d) (prompt access to court to challenge a detention); *id.*, art. 40(2)(b)(iii) (opportunity for speedy penal proceedings).

Third, if the treaty itself provides a mechanism for private individuals to vindicate private rights, then an alternative mechanism (access to national courts to vindicate a treaty norm) should not be implied. Certainly this is the case when the international agreement both creates an alternative mechanism and expressly precludes the pursuit of actions in national courts, as occurred under the 1981 Iran–United States Algiers Accords. In that instance, the two states created an international arbitral tribunal in the Hague for the resolution of commercial claims,[153] provided access to that tribunal for individuals with large claims, and expressly foreclosed U.S. nationals whose claims fell within the scope of that tribunal from pursuing actions in U.S. courts.[154] To imply that the agreements oblige the United States to allow individuals access to U.S. courts would fly in the face of the express terms of the agreements.

Yet even where actions in national courts are not expressly precluded by a treaty, an obligation under the treaty to provide access to national courts should not be implied if the treaty creates an alternative mechanism for individuals to vindicate their treaty rights. For example, a bilateral investment treaty that solely provides for reference of a dispute between the investor and the host state to international arbitration should not be read as implying a right of access to national courts as well.[155] When this occurs, the treaty regime is self-contained in nature; it reflects a package deal by the treaty parties whereby individual rights are created but only in the context of vindication by individuals through a forum with which the treaty parties are comfortable. For this factor to apply, the alternative mechanism should be one that permits invocation of treaty rights by individuals; a mechanism that only allows states to pursue those rights, such as before the ICJ, does not by itself indicate an intention by the parties to displace actions by individuals in national courts.

[153] *See* Declaration of the Government of the Democratic and Popular Republic of Algeria Concerning the Settlement of Claims, Jan. 19, 1981, arts. II(1) & VII (2), *reprinted in* 1 Iran-U.S. Cl. Trib. Rep. 9, 11 (1981–82).

[154] *See* Declaration of the Government of the Democratic and Popular Republic of Algeria, Jan. 19, 1981, ¶ 11, *reprinted in* 1 Iran-U.S. Cl. Trib. Rep. 3, 6–7 (1981–82).

[155] *See, e.g.*, Agreement Concerning the Mutual Promotion and Protection of Investments, Fr.-Isr., art. 8(2), June 9, 1983, 1410 U.N.T.S. 3 (providing that, if a dispute cannot be settled amicably within six months, either party may submit it for arbitration at the International Centre for Settlement of Investment Disputes); Protocol Amending the Convention for the Avoidance of Double Taxation and the Prevention of Fiscal Evasion with Respect to Taxes on Income and Capital and to Certain Other Taxes, Ger.-U.S., art. XIII, June 1, 2006, *available at* http://www.treas.gov/press/releases/reports/germanprotocol06.pdf (providing for arbitration of tax disputes).

In the field of human rights, the ICJ has suggested that "where human rights are protected by international conventions, that protection takes the form of such arrangements for monitoring or ensuring respect for human rights as are provided for in the conventions themselves."[156] As indicated herein, some human rights treaties contain obligations for states to enact national measures that punish human rights abusers and some oblige states to provide an effective remedy in the national legal system for victims. Where the treaty is silent on such matters, an important aspect when determining whether to imply a right to invoke the treaty before national courts is whether the treaty provides some other mechanism for vindication of individual rights, such as through a system of individual petition to a treaty monitoring committee. The presence of such a mechanism, even if it were triggered only on an optional basis, would weigh against implying any such right.

Finally, if when joining a treaty a state files an uncontested understanding, or in some other definitive way signals to its treaty partners that the treaty does not require the state to open up its national courts for vindication of treaty norms, then the state's interpretation as to the meaning of the treaty should weigh against implying any such right of access. (Implying such a right is even less compelling if numerous states have filed similar understandings.) For instance, as part of the statute by which the United States consented to ratification of the Uruguay Round Agreements of the World Trade Organization, the United States enacted statutory language stating that no person shall have any "cause of action or defense" based on those treaties.[157] This position of the United States was well known to its

[156] Military and Paramilitary Activities in and against Nicaragua (Nicar. v. U.S.), 1986 I.C.J. 14, 134 (June 27).

[157] 19 U.S.C. § 3512(c)(1) (2000) states:

> No person other than the United States (A) shall have any cause of action or defense under any of the Uruguay Round Agreements or by virtue of congressional approval of such an agreement, or (B) may challenge . . . any action or inaction by any department, agency, or other instrumentality of the United States, any State, or any political subdivision of a State on the ground that such action or inaction is inconsistent with such agreement.

See Bronco Wine Co. v. Bureau of Alcohol, Tobacco & Firearms, 168 F.3d 498 (9th Cir. 1999) (finding no cause of action based on the Uruguay Round Agreements for a private litigant).

The United States adopted similar statutory language when it entered into the North American Free Trade Agreement, U.S.-Can.-Mex., Dec. 17, 1992, 32 I.L.M. 289 & 605. *See* 19 U.S.C. § 3312(c) (2000) ("No person other than the United States . . . shall have any cause of action or defense under" NAFTA or "may challenge . . . any action or inaction by any department, agency or other instrumentality of the United States . . . on the ground that such action or inaction is inconsistent with" NAFTA).

treaty partners and elicited no adverse reactions. In such a situation, it is implausible to imply into the Uruguay Round Agreements an obligation on the United States to open its courts to claims or defenses based on those treaties.[158]

VI. EVOLVING INTERNATIONAL LAW?

Although the Court's decisions in *LaGrand* and *Avena* should not be read as broadly supporting a customary international law rule that states must allow individuals to invoke treaty norms in national courts, the decisions may nevertheless represent an important incremental step in that direction. As international law increasingly establishes treaty norms protective of the individual and increasingly develops avenues for individuals to invoke their rights (including before international tribunals), there may emerge a settled expectation that access to national courts is the logical consequence of embedding protections for individuals in treaty regimes. The exact contours of this right to invoke, however, are at present unclear, and there are reasons to think that the emergence of such a right would prove problematic.

A. *Trends in International Law*

The arc of the development of international law may point in the direction of a more general obligation to allow invocation of treaty norms by individuals in national courts in situations where the treaty contains provisions that are protective of individuals. For reasons stated subsequently, the same forces that motivated the ECJ to develop the direct effects doctrine in EC law may, over time, crystallize in general international law.

It is commonly said that when public international law first emerged, its principal focus was on the regulation of relations among states, not the regulation of persons. Yet that understanding of early international law was never quite accurate; international law from its inception concerned itself with individuals in various respects. There were crimes under international law for which persons could be prosecuted, such as for the slave trade or for piracy, and rules emerged holding states responsible for injuries inflicted on aliens present in their territories.

[158] *See* Mitsuo Matsushita, Thomas J. Schoenbaum & Petros C. Mavroidis, The World Trade Organization: Law, Practice and Policy 102 (2003) ("The United States has adopted virtually a purely dualistic approach to the WTO agreement. . . . No person may assert any cause of action or defence directly under any of the WTO agreements before a U.S. tribunal" (footnote omitted).

Moreover, international law has not viewed international and national legal systems as hermetically sealed spheres, especially when it comes to the treatment of persons. As the international law of state responsibility developed, an expectation emerged that host states must not deny aliens procedural justice in local courts. This denial-of-justice standard requires a host state to treat aliens with a minimum level of internal security and law and order, including police protection for the aliens and their property, and to provide aliens a minimally adequate system of justice for resolving disputes, including in national courts.[159] If a host state fails to accord the alien such treatment, the alien's state is empowered to pursue an international claim (derivative of the alien's claim) against the host state. The standard continues to operate today, notably in the context of claims brought for alleged mistreatment of foreign investors.[160]

By means of the rule of exhaustion of local remedies, customary international law also has accorded to national courts an important role both in clarifying whether a state has in fact breached a norm of international law as it relates to a person and in establishing the factual record on which international tribunals will operate in considering that alleged breach.[161] States advancing claims based on an injury to their national must show that the

[159] *See generally* JAN PAULSSON, DENIAL OF JUSTICE IN INTERNATIONAL LAW (2005); Andrea K. Bjorklund, *Reconciling State Sovereignty and Investor Protection in Denial of Justice Claims*, 45 VA. J. INT'L L. 809 (2005). For an example, *see Van Bokkelen Case*, 2 MOORE, INT'L. ARB. 1807 (1888).

[160] One NAFTA dispute resolution panel recently characterized the standard as follows:

> The test is not whether a particular result is surprising, but whether the shock or surprise occasioned to an impartial [international] tribunal leads, on reflection, to justified concerns as to the judicial propriety of the outcome [in the national court], bearing in mind on the one hand that international tribunals are not courts of appeal, and on the other hand that Chapter 11 of NAFTA (like other treaties for the protection of investments) is intended to provide a real measure of protection. In the end the question is whether, at an international level and having regard to generally accepted standards of the administration of justice, a [international] tribunal can conclude in the light of all the available facts that the impugned [national court] decision was clearly improper and discreditable, with the result that the investment has been subjected to unfair and inequitable treatment. This is admittedly a somewhat open-ended standard, but it may be that in practice no more precise formula can be offered to cover the range of possibilities.

Mondev Int'l v. United States, NAFTA Ch. 11 Arb. Trib., ¶ 127 (Oct. 11, 2002), *reprinted in* NAFTA ARBITRATION REPORTS (2003).

[161] *See generally* C.F. AMERASINGHE, LOCAL REMEDIES IN INTERNATIONAL LAW (2d ed. 2003); International Law Commission, Second Report on Diplomatic Protection, U.N. Doc. A/CN.4/5/514 (Feb. 28, 2001) (report of special rapporteur John Dugard); A.A. CANÇADO TRINDADE, THE APPLICATION OF THE RULE OF EXHAUSTION OF LOCAL REMEDIES IN INTERNATIONAL LAW (1983). For a recent example at the ICJ, *see* Ahmadou Sadio Diallo (Guinea v. Dem. Rep. Congo), Judgment, ¶¶ 68–75 (May 24, 2007), *available at* http://www.icj-cij.org.

national has exhausted remedies in the national legal system of the defendant state; failure to do so bars the claim as inadmissible before the international court or tribunal. According to Jiménez de Aréchaga, the basis for the rule is "the respect for the sovereignty and jurisdiction of the state competent to deal with the question through its judicial organs."[162]

Piercing through into the national legal system may be viewed as especially appropriate in situations where the gravest forms of human rights abuses are at issue. It is commonly accepted that international law contains within it *jus cogens* (peremptory norms), which may be defined as norms "accepted and recognised by the international community of States as a whole as [norms] from which no derogation is permitted and which can be modified only by a subsequent norm of general international law having the same character."[163] Some *jus cogens* norms relate to the rights of individuals; for example, the Inter-American Court of Human Rights has advised that the prohibition against racial discrimination is *jus cogens*[164] and the International Criminal Tribunal for the Former Yugoslavia (ICTY) has declared that the prohibition against state-sponsored torture "has evolved into a peremptory norm or *jus cogens*, that is, a norm that enjoys a higher rank in the international hierarchy than treaty law and even 'ordinary' customary rules."[165]

In the *Furundžia* case, the ICTY trial chamber stated that for such a norm, it was not sufficient to follow the normal approach of allowing states to reach the desired result by a means of their choosing; rather, states must affirmatively act in certain ways, such as through the adoption of national criminal laws, so as to forestall the egregious act from occurring. The failure to adopt such laws itself constituted a violation of international law.[166] The

For an arbitral example, *see* Loewen Group v. United States, NAFTA Ch. 11 Arb. Trib., ¶ 217 (June 26, 2003), *reprinted in* NAFTA ARBITRATION REPORTS (2003).

[162] Eduardo Jiménez de Aréchaga, *International Responsibility*, MANUAL OF PUBLIC INTERNATIONAL LAW 584 (Max Sørensen ed., 1968).

[163] VCLT, *supra* note 5, art. 53; *see* Alfred von Verdross, *Forbidden Treaties in International Law*, 31 AM. J. INT'L L. 571 (1937); *but see* Georg Schwarzenberger, *International Jus Cogens?* 43 TEX. L. REV. 455, 467 (1965).

[164] *See* Advisory Opinion on Juridical Condition and Rights of Undocumented Migrants, 2003 Inter-Am. Ct. Hum. Rts. (ser. A) No. 18, ¶¶ 98–101 (Sept. 17, 2003). Various decisions of the Inter-American Commission on Human Rights have also declared norms as *jus cogens. See, e.g.*, Domingues, Case 12.285, Inter-Am. C.H.R., Report No. 62/02, ¶¶ 45–46, 64 (2002) (regarding death penalty for juvenile offenders).

[165] Prosecutor v. Furundžia, Judgment, Case No. IT-95–17/1-T, ¶ 153 (Int'l Crim. Trib. Former Yugo. Dec. 10, 1998).

[166] The chamber stated:

> Normally States, when they undertake international obligations through treaties or customary rules, adopt all the legislative and administrative measures necessary for

chamber's decision should be seen in the context of treaties – such as the Convention against Torture – that contain an express obligation for parties to adopt "effective legislative, administrative, judicial or other measures to prevent acts of torture in any territory under its jurisdiction."[167] Nevertheless, the language of the decision suggests a wider sentiment, which is that in situations where a serious violation of human rights may be at issue, states are obligated to take certain measures internally to forestall violations. To the extent that such reasoning becomes prevalent in certain areas of international law, it may lead to an expectation that the international norm carries with it an obligation to allow invocation of treaty norms in national courts by individuals. Already there are voices calling for moving past traditional notions of sovereign immunity so as to ensure that fundamental protections are accorded to individuals,[168] and it seems likely that those voices will become more insistent.

An example of the evolution occurring in the international sphere may be seen in the 2006 *Basic Principles and Guidelines on the Right to a Remedy and Reparation for Victims of Gross Violations of International Human Rights Law and Serious Violations of International Humanitarian Law (Basic Guidelines)*. The *Basic Guidelines* originated in the UN Human Rights Commission,[169] were blessed by the UN Economic and Social Commission,[170] and then were adopted by consensus in the UN General Assembly.[171] Hailed by one of its drafters as an "international bill of rights

> implementing such obligations. However, subject to obvious exceptions, failure to pass the required implementing legislation has only a potential effect: the wrongful fact occurs only when administrative or judicial measures are taken which, being contrary to international rules due to the lack of implementing legislation, generate State responsibility. By contrast, in the case of torture, the requirement that States expeditiously institute national implementing measures is an integral part of the international obligation to prohibit this practice. Consequently, States must immediately set in motion all those procedures and measures that may make it possible, within their municipal legal system, to forestall any act of torture or expeditiously put an end to any torture that is occurring.

Id., ¶ 149.

[167] Convention against Torture, *supra* note 101, art. 2(1).

[168] *See generally* Kenneth C. Randall, *Universal Jurisdiction under International Law*, 66 Tex. L. Rev. 785 (1988); *see also* Arrest Warrant of 11 April 2000 (Congo v. Belg.), 2002 I.C.J. 3, 63 (Feb. 14) (joint separate opinion of Judges Higgins, Kooijmans & Buergenthal); *id.*, at 137 (dissenting opinion of Judge *ad hoc* Van den Wyngaert).

[169] U.N. Commission on Human Rights Res. 2005/35, Annex (Apr. 19, 2005).

[170] ECOSOC Res. 2005/30, Annex (July 25, 2005).

[171] G.A. Res. 60/147, Annex, U.N. Doc. A/RES/60/147 (Dec. 16, 2005) [hereinafter *Basic Guidelines*]. For a forerunner to these guidelines, one principally focused on remedies for victims of crimes committed by nonstate actors under national law, and on abuse of power by a

of victims,"[172] the non-legally-binding *Basic Guidelines* call on states to incorporate international human rights and humanitarian law into their national law and to adopt "measures that provide fair, effective and prompt access to justice" so as to vindicate those norms.[173] The premise of the *Basic Guidelines* is that the obligation to implement prohibitions on "gross violations of international human rights law and serious violations of international humanitarian law" necessarily entails a duty to "[p]rovide those who claim to be victims of a human rights or humanitarian law violation with equal and effective access to justice."[174] The victim's right of "access to justice" includes both a right to have the state criminally prosecute the offender[175] and a right to effective reparation. Consequently, whether or not a particular treaty expressly so provides, "[i]n accordance with its domestic laws and international legal obligations, a State shall provide reparation to victims for acts or omissions which can be attributed to the State and constitute gross violations of international human rights law or serious violations of international humanitarian law."[176] The forms of reparation contemplated are (1) restitution, (2) compensation, (3) rehabilitation, and (4) satisfaction and guarantees of nonrepetition.[177] This emphasis in the *Basic Principles* on an obligation of states to provide access to justice within their national legal systems, though arising in the context of serious violations of international human rights and humanitarian law, may reflect increased expectations that individuals must have resort to national courts to vindicate individual rights cognizable under treaties.

As international treaties contain increasingly detailed rights and obligations for individuals – not just in the context of treaties on international human rights but in other areas as well[178] – it seems plausible that there will be a growing expectation that national legal systems are indispensable for making those rights and obligations fully effective. Even a cursory perusal of the highly legislative treaties that have emerged to address contracts for

government, see Declaration of Basic Principles of Justice for Victims of Crime and Abuse of Power, G.A. Res. 40/34, Annex, U.N. Doc. A/RES/40/34 (Nov. 29, 1985).

[172] *See* M. Cherif Bassiouni, *International Recognition of Victims' Rights*, 6 HUM. RTS. L. REV. 203 (2006). Professor Bassiouni served as a special rapporteur on the topic for the Human Rights Commission, building on earlier work by Professor Theo van Boven.

[173] *Basic Guidelines*, *supra* note 171, art. 2(b).

[174] *Id.*, art. 3(c); *see id.*, art. 12.

[175] *See* Bassiouni, *supra* note 172, at 263.

[176] *Basic Guidelines*, *supra* note 171, art. 15.

[177] *Id.*, art. 18.

[178] *See generally* Symposium, *Global Governance and Global Administrative Law in the International Legal Order*, 17 EUR. J. INT'L L. 1 (2006).

the international sale of goods, abduction of children, regulation of pollution from marine vessels, or other matters makes clear that treaty regimes are becoming far too complex to be viewed as principally interstate regulation, such that deviations should only be hashed out through interstate negotiation and dispute settlement. Indeed, in many cases the treaty regime runs in tandem with extensive national laws and regulations that implement the treaty, often through incorporation by reference. Where national laws and regulations exist, the individual might be viewed as bringing an action nationally based on those laws and regulations, and not on the treaty, but that distinction is becoming increasingly blurred and artificial.

Moreover, there appears to be an increasing acceptance that the individual, rather than the state, should be in a position to vindicate, on the international plane, international rights possessed by the individual. Although before the mid-twentieth century, the state was the principal vehicle for vindicating those rights on the international plane,[179] there are now numerous examples of international mechanisms whereby the individual serves as the claimant, whether in the fields of human rights (e.g., ECHR or the Inter American Commission on Human Rights), investment (e.g., dispute resolution under NAFTA Chapter 11 or before the International Centre for the Settlement of Investment Disputes (ICSID)), other property rights (e.g., Iran–United States Claims Tribunal for large-value claims), or international organizations (e.g., UN Administrative Tribunal). To the extent that there is an increasing recognition that individuals have an important role to play in vindicating rights accorded to them under a treaty, and indeed a desire on the part of states that they do so without state involvement, a collateral expectation may emerge that individuals be able to do so through national legal systems.

This evolution, if it is occurring, may be yet another facet of the trend in globalization, whereby the once-monolithic nation-state is increasingly disaggregated and nonstate actors are increasingly challenging traditional state structures.[180] As Peter Spiro has noted, in the aftermath of the cold war, an "architectural change" may be occurring in the international legal system, whereby prior doctrines (e.g., deference by courts to political branches, concern with entanglement in foreign affairs) are no longer necessary or

[179] The main exceptions were the some sixty mixed claims commissions set up to address disputes arising from injury to the interests of aliens.

[180] *See generally* Janne Nijman & André Nollkaemper, *Beyond the Divide*, in New Perspectives on the Divide between National and International Law 341 (Janne Nijman & André Nollkaemper eds., 2007) Anne-Marie Slaughter, A New World Order (2004).

appropriate.[181] If so, national legal systems may need to find a way to adapt to those changes, and allowing persons to invoke treaty norms in national courts may be a step in that direction. National courts provide a ready-made and extensive infrastructure for interpretation and application of treaty law; as those treaties become more and more complex, regulating wide arrays of areas and wide arrays of actors, perhaps it is inevitable that national courts be called on in support. While there is potential for conflicting views among different fora, there is also considerable potential for coordination among international and national courts on interpretation and application of treaties, and one can postulate certain ground rules for doing so.[182]

B. *Concerns with the Emergence under General International Law of a Private Right to Invoke Treaties in National Courts*

The emergence under general international law of a right for individuals to invoke treaties in national courts may serve to help promote and protect the rights of individuals, and to force states to take more seriously the treaty commitments they make. Yet there are also reasons to be concerned about such a development.

First, if such a right emerges under general international law, there will likely be confusion about the contours of the right. Presumably the individual cannot invoke all the rights contained in treaties but only those rights that protect individuals. If so, some standards must be developed for differentiating between treaty norms that can be invoked only by states and those that can be invoked by individuals. Once the latter are determined, a further determination must be made concerning how those rights can be invoked in a national court. Does the right to invoke a treaty apply only in the context of enjoining state action against the individual or does it extend to other contexts, such as the pursuit of claims for damages? Is the right to invoke the treaty solely a procedural right, leaving the national court with the discretion to decide the merits as it sees fit, or does the right to invoke the treaty in some fashion narrow that discretion? The ICJ in *LaGrand* and *Avena* focused solely on the individual's ability to raise the treaty violation, and studiously avoided dictating to U.S. courts the consequences that should flow from judicial review and reconsideration of the treaty violation. Indeed, the review by U.S. courts could lead to an

[181] Peter J. Spiro, *Globalization and the (Foreign Affairs) Constitution*, 63 OHIO ST. L.J. 649 (2002).

[182] *See* Jenny S. Martinez, *Towards an International Judicial System*, 56 STAN. L. REV. 429 (2003).

annulling of the conviction but could equally lead to a conclusion that the treaty violation had no significant effect on the conviction and therefore was irrelevant. Providing national courts with such discretion is consistent with the margin-of-appreciation doctrine discussed earlier, and a nascent rule intruding on that discretion might elicit hostile reaction from states and perhaps widespread noncompliance with the rule.

Even if the right to invoke the treaty in national courts is principally a procedural right, what is the relationship between that procedural right and other procedural rules of the national court? In *LaGrand* and *Avena*, the ICJ stated that a particular national rule – the procedural default rule – could not be used to bar invocation of the treaty. Yet if a right emerges under general international law for individuals to invoke treaties in national courts, it might wreak havoc on national legal systems if that right trumps all national procedural rules, such as rules on personal and subject matter jurisdiction, statutes of limitations, *forum non conveniens*, or res judicata. Presumably some kind of balance would have to be reached, but drawing the line may prove quite difficult. Moreover, if the individual is invoking the treaty in a national court against a foreign sovereign, the nascent rule might be in competition with other elements of international law, such as rules on immunities accorded to governments and government officials, rules circumscribing the exercise of national jurisdiction extraterritorially, or notions of comity such as those reflected in the act-of-state doctrine.[183]

Second, if there emerges an implied right to invoke in national courts treaties that are protective of individuals, there might be collateral consequences for the creation and development of such treaty regimes. National courts might be powerful engines for treaty implementation, but the fact of that power may well chill governments from negotiating and ratifying robust treaties that are protective of individuals. Although it is conjectural whether a new rule would result in less enthusiasm for meaningful treaties, it is worth noting that many of the environmental treaties that expressly provide for civil jurisdiction in national courts[184] have elicited relatively low rates of adherence by states. Alternatively, if it is known that a right to litigate the treaty in national courts will be readily implied, states may be prompted to find ways of drafting around the new rule by expressly stating

[183] *See* RESTATEMENT (THIRD), *supra* note 68, § 907 cmt. a ("Where a remedy was intended [in an international agreement for private rights in national courts], suit against a foreign state (or the United States) might nonetheless be barred by principles of sovereign immunity, unless such immunity is found to have been waived.").

[184] *See, e.g.*, the treaties noted *supra* notes 81 to 97.

in the treaty that no such right should be implied or by crafting reservations or declarations to that effect when ratifying the treaty.[185]

Third, it is not entirely clear that the emergence under general international law of a private right to invoke treaties in national courts would help to promote and protect the rights of individuals. If the paradigmatic human rights case concerns the right of an individual to invoke a treaty against conduct by a government in that government's own national courts, then presumably that right is useful only in situations where the national courts are sufficiently independent of the political branches and capable of unbiased decisions in accordance with the rule of law. National courts of that caliber do exist, but they are lacking in many national legal systems, especially those where the most grievous human rights abuses occur. Even in well-developed national legal systems, national courts at times can be driven by extreme forms of nationalism, patriotism, or xenophobia, which is why many treaties in the commercial or tax law areas are designed to get disputes out of national courts and into international arbitration. Arguably, a better approach would be for alleged violations of a treaty first to be addressed in the context of an international proceeding, and then have the international forum's decision be enforced through whatever national means are appropriate. That approach could allow for a less biased or parochial adjudication of the alleged treaty violation. Indeed, although the prior section suggested that the increasing ability for individuals to litigate claims in international fora might concomitantly increase expectations that individuals should be able to litigate treaties in national fora, it might actually lead to the opposite result by promoting a sense that national fora are inferior to international fora.

Finally, to the extent that we are looking to national courts for implementation of treaties because those treaties have become complex regulators of relations between states and persons, one must ask whether national courts

[185] A Coasian analysis might suggest that, at least for new treaty regimes, it does not matter whether there emerges, under general international law, a ground rule favoring private rights to invoke treaties in national courts, so long as the ground rule is clear. If the ground rule recognizes the existence of an implied right to invoke treaties in national courts, then states can either allow it to operate or can bargain out of it through an express provision in the treaty or through reservations/declarations. Alternatively, if the rule does not recognize the existence of an implied right to invoke treaties in national courts, then states can expressly write into the treaty a right for access to national courts, if they wish there to be one. Such theorizing, however, breaks down if there are factors that impede the bargaining process. For example, the content of the ground rule does matter if it can be shown that politically it is much harder for states to expressly contract out of a rule favoring access for individuals to national courts than it is for states to simply remain silent in the face of a rule that does not favor such access.

are up to the task. As national legal systems have become more complex, techniques have developed for administrative remedies or other mechanisms for handling entitlements rather than traditional litigation. Further, judges in national courts typically are not trained in international law, are not familiar with the techniques of treaty interpretation, and are unaware of how to go about researching relevant background rules.[186] Even if a judge has such expertise, the complexity of a treaty regime may favor methods of dispute resolution other than traditional litigation in national courts. One of the most fertile areas of transnational dispute resolution today is the mass claims procedure that has been developed for use by institutions such as the UN Compensation Commission, the Bosnia Real Property Commission, the Claims Resolution Tribunal for Dormant Bank Accounts in Switzerland, and the International Commission for Holocaust Era Insurance Claims.[187] In some of those mass claims situations, removal of cases from national court proceedings to more streamlined international fora was a key objective for resolving the claims, as the prospect for multiple national courts, in multiple jurisdictions, addressing multiple claims all of a similar nature portended an extremely inefficient and costly approach to dispute resolution.[188]

VII. CONCLUSION

At present, there is no obligation under general international treaty law, customary international law, or general principles of international law for a state to open its courts for invocation by individuals of treaty norms. Various treaties, however, either expressly or by implication provide a right for individuals to invoke those treaties in national court systems. The ICJ's decisions in *LaGrand* and *Avena* indicate the circumstances in which a right of this kind may be implied in a treaty, but there are also various circumstances that can be postulated for when such a right should not be implied.

International law is changing, particularly under the pressures of globalization. It is possible that one aspect of that change will be the ultimate

[186] For an indication of the complexity of the issues that confront national courts in such situations, and some guidance on how to cope with it, see André Nollkaemper, *Internationally Wrongful Acts in Domestic Courts,* 101 Am. J. Int'l L. 760 (2007).

[187] *See* International Mass Claims Processes: Legal and Practical Perspectives (Howard M. Holtzmann & Edda Kristjánsdóttir eds., 2007); Permanent Court of Arbitration, Institutional and Procedural Aspects of Mass Claims Settlement Systems (2000).

[188] *See, e.g.*, Am. Ins. Assoc. v. Garamendi, 539 U.S. 396 (2003).

recognition of a general obligation under international law for states to make their national courts available to individuals seeking interpretation and application of treaty norms that are protective of the individual. While there are reasons to welcome a general obligation of that nature, there are also reasons to be wary of it. The caution evinced by the ICJ in the *LaGrand* and *Avena* cases should be heeded as states and nonstate actors contemplate whether such a general norm should be recognized.

3

Australia

Donald R. Rothwell*

Professor of International Law, ANU College of Law, Australian National University, Canberra, Australia

I. INTRODUCTION

The Commonwealth of Australia emerged as a federation of six states on January 1, 1901, formed under a constitution adopted by the Parliament at Westminster after extensive Australian debate and consultation during the preceding decade. Australia emerged as a new state in the then-international system very much under the umbrella of Britain and, just like the other emerging British colonies of Canada, New Zealand, and South Africa, took some time to find a truly independent voice in international affairs.[1] Indeed, it was not until the First World War and the conduct of significant military campaigns on European battlefields that Australia began to develop a stance approaching that of an independent state in international affairs. The Paris Peace Conference permitted Australia to take its place on the world diplomatic stage and, in the years between the First and the Second World Wars, a more independent Australia began to emerge. Various Empire Conferences gave greater voice to the British Dominions as a constitutional matter, culminating in the 1931 Statute of Westminster that recognized the true independence of the Dominions and their ability to play a role in international affairs, including the adoption of treaties. However, there was an ongoing reluctance on the part of Australia to take the final step onto the international stage and the Statute of Westminster was not adopted during the 1930s. The onset of the Second World War and especially the Japanese attack on Pearl Harbor ultimately proved to be the turning point

*The author acknowledges previous collaborative projects on international law within Australia with colleagues, on which part of this work is drawn, in particular works with Brian Opeskin, Jane McAdam, and Tim Stephens.

[1] For a general overview of the development of the international personality of former British colonies and Dominions, see, J.E.S. Fawcett, *The British Commonwealth in International Law* (1963).

in Australia's journey toward full international independence. The Statute of Westminster Adoption Act of 1942 was quickly passed with important provisions backdated to be operative from September 1939.[2] At the same time, diplomatic missions were established for the first time in some foreign capitals. Australia had finally come of age.[3]

The importance of this journey is that, in addition to Australia being a participant in both the First and the Second World Wars, Australia had established itself as an important player in world affairs by the time of the San Francisco Conference. Accordingly, Australia not only had a voice at San Francisco but also demonstrated its commitment to the new international system by fully engaging with the developing United Nations and its institutions. This was especially the case with international law and the contemporary multilateral treaty system that the United Nations spawned. As a former British colony in the Southern Hemisphere – geographically isolated from much of the rest of the developed world, but resource rich in minerals and agricultural products – Australia was keen to promote an international security system under the United Nations that gave prominence to the rule of law and respect for international rules. To that end, treaties and conventions dealing with subjects such as international trade,[4] the freedom of maritime navigation,[5] air transportation,[6] global[7] and regional security,[8] and communications[9] were all pivotal to Australia's economic and national security. Treaties played a crucial role for Australia at that time, and Australia has generally been an enthusiastic supporter of multilateral, regional, and bilateral treaty instruments and frameworks over the duration of the current UN system.

[2] Statute of Westminster Adoption Act 1942, s. 3 providing for ss. 2, 3, 4, 5, 6, to be operative as from 3 September 1939.

[3] For an overview of this process, *see* D.P. O'Connell, "The Evolution of Australia's International Personality" in D.P. O'Connell (ed.), *International Law in Australia* (1965) 1–34; Gareth Evans and Bruce Grant, *Australia's Foreign Relations* (2d ed., 1995) 15–21; Brian Galligan, Winsome Roberts, and Gabriella Trifiletti, *Australians and Globalisation: The Experience of Two Centuries* (2001) 86–111.

[4] Australia became a party to the 1947 General Agreement on Tariffs and Trade (GATT) on 1, January 1948: [1948] Australia Treaty Series [hereinafter ATS] No. 23.

[5] Australia became a party to the 1958 Geneva Convention on the High Seas on 13, June 1963: [1963] ATS No. 12.

[6] Australia became a party to the 1944 Chicago Convention on International Civil Aviation on 1 March 1947: [1957] ATS No 5.

[7] Australia became a party to the 1945 U.N. Charter on 1 November 1945: [1945] ATS No. 1.

[8] Australia became a party to the 1951 Security Treaty between Australia, New Zealand and the United States [ANZUS] on 29 April 1952: [1952] ATS No. 2.

[9] Australia became a party to the 1947 International Telecommunication Convention on 7, January 1949: [1949] ATS No. 1.

While Australia then grew and developed in the post–Second World War era into a significant player in international affairs, which places a heavy reliance on treaty frameworks and mechanisms,[10] the Australian courts have not been as enthusiastic to embrace international law and treaties. The Australian Constitution makes little reference to international affairs, let alone treaties. There is an acknowledgment that federal courts have original jurisdiction with respect to matters concerning treaties,[11] but for at least the first fifty years this provision was relatively dormant. Australian courts, however, have gradually become more engaged in reviewing the impact of treaties on Australian law since the commencement of the United Nations era and, in the past twenty years, have begun to consider claims by individuals seeking to assert international treaty rights. At times, this process has been fraught with controversy for both the courts and the national-level political branches.

This dynamic is perhaps no better illustrated than the public awareness of the consequences of international law for Australians, which was highlighted during the battle in the 1980s to halt the damming of the Franklin River in southwestern Tasmania. That battle, which eventually resulted in the Commonwealth Parliament relying on the provisions of the 1972 Convention for the Protection of the World Cultural and Natural Heritage (World Heritage Convention)[12] to enact the World Heritage Properties Conservation Act of 1983 (Cth), was finally resolved when, in 1983, the High Court of Australia in the *Tasmanian Dam Case*[13] upheld the validity of the legislation on the basis of the Commonwealth's Section 51(xxix) "external affairs" power under the Constitution. This decision set off a sequence of events that resulted in subsequent High Court judgments that gave further scope to the external-affairs power based principally on the treaty-implementation power of the federal executive.[14] In the two decades since that High Court decision, the growing influence of international law on Australian law has continued to

[10] This can be evidenced by a review of the Australian Treaties Library maintained by the Australian Department of Foreign Affairs and Trade, within which the Australian Treaty Series, the official record of all treaties to which Australia becomes a party, is located; *available at* http://www.austlii.edu.au/au/other/dfat/ (3 July 2007).

[11] Commonwealth of Australia Constitution, s. 75(i).

[12] 1037 U.N.T.S. 151, [1975] ATS No. 47.

[13] Commonwealth v. Tasmania (1983) 158 CLR 1.

[14] For the author's contribution to that debate, see Donald R. Rothwell, "The High Court and the External Affairs Power: A Consideration of Its Outer and Inner Limits" (1993) 15 *Adelaide L. Rev.* 209–40. *See also* Richard D. Lumb, "The External Affairs Power and Constitutional Reform" (1988) 62 *Australian L.J.* 679–89; Michael Coper, *The Franklin Dam Case* (1983).

result in substantial public debate regarding the role of international law in Australia.[15] Much of that debate has centered on the impact of treaties on Australian law, which have an ever-increasing influence through both direct and indirect incorporation.[16]

This chapter will seek to trace the development of the role of the Australian courts in the interpretation and application of treaties in Australia. Consideration will first be given to the constitutional framework within Australia and the judicial system that operates under the Commonwealth and state constitutions. A review will then be undertaken of important High Court jurisprudence concerning the treaty aspect of the external-affairs power in the Commonwealth Constitution and the role the Court has recognized for treaties in the legislative capacity of the Commonwealth Parliament. The ability to seek judicial remedies based on treaties before Australian courts will be considered, especially in the context of incorporated and unincorporated treaties. The role of treaties in statutory and constitutional interpretation will also be assessed, with particular attention given to the view of Justice Michael Kirby of the High Court. An analysis of the impact of statutory quasi incorporation and the tension that has emerged within the High Court over the weight to be given to treaties in Australian municipal law will also be undertaken.

II. THE CONSTITUTIONAL FRAMEWORK AND INTERNATIONAL LAW

Australia's Constitution, drafted during the 1890s, and operational as from 1901, contains very few direct references to matters that could be considered related to international law. This is perhaps unsurprising, because at the time of federation it was anticipated that much of the conduct of Australia's international relations, and hence issues arising from treaty making, would be under the control of Great Britain. Accordingly, there is no direct reference in the Constitution to a formal treaty-making power because it was

[15] *See, e.g.*, the following works: P. Alston and M. Chiam (eds.), *Treaty-Making and Australia: Globalisation versus Sovereignty?* (1995); Brian R. Opeskin and Donald R. Rothwell (eds.), *International Law and Australian Federalism* (1997); Hilary Charlesworth et al., *No Country Is an Island: Australia and International Law* (2006).

[16] For a broader analysis of the relationship between international and municipal law in Australia, *see* I.A. Shearer, "The Relationship between International Law and Domestic Law," in Opeskin and Rothwell, *supra* note 15, at 34–68; J. Crawford and W.R. Edeson, "International Law and Australian Law," in K.W. Ryan (ed.), *International Law in Australia* (2d ed., 1984) 71–135.

not contemplated that Australia would have this responsibility. In addition, international law was not as developed at that time as it is today. The Constitution was also drafted to ensure that the Australian states would retain considerable constitutional powers within the new federation, and accordingly the scope of the powers of the new Parliament of the Commonwealth was initially considered somewhat limited. This is particularly reflected in those heads of constitutional power dealing with treaties. The references in Section 51(xxix) to "external affairs" and in Section 51(xxx) to "relations of the Commonwealth with the islands of the Pacific" are the only two clear heads of power that, at the time of federation, could be viewed as linked with subjects dealt with by international law. The Constitution, however, did not completely ignore international law, as the newly created High Court of Australia was given original jurisdiction to deal with matters arising under any treaty in Section 75. Nevertheless, as Cheryl Saunders has noted: "The relative silence of the Constitution on what is now such a significant constitutional issue reflects both its age and the colonial status of Australia when the Constitution came into effect."[17] Notwithstanding this limited view of international law and treaties at federation, the history of Australian constitutional law has been one of ongoing expanded interpretation of Commonwealth powers by both the Parliament and the High Court so that the position today is far different from that in 1901.[18]

A. *The Judicial System*

The Australian judicial system revolves around federal courts vested with "judicial power of the Commonwealth"[19] and state and territorial courts vested with a range of jurisdiction and functions principally under state and territorial law but also in some instances conferred Commonwealth law. The most established of the federal courts and the highest appellate court in the country is the High Court of Australia, which is provided for under the Commonwealth Constitution and was established in 1903 following federation. The High Court has both original and appellate jurisdiction, which among a number of areas extends to matters:

[17] Cheryl Saunders, "Articles of Faith or Lucky Breaks? The Constitutional Law of International Agreements in Australia" (1995) 17 *Sydney L.R.* 150, at 150.

[18] This history of expanded High Court interpretation of the Constitution is perhaps best reflected in the work of Professor Leslie Zines, *The High Court and the Constitution* (4th ed., 1997).

[19] Commonwealth of Australia Constitution, s. 71.

- Arising under any treaty[20]
- Affecting consuls or the representatives of other countries[21]
- Arising under the Commonwealth Constitution[22]
- Arising under any laws of the Commonwealth Parliament.[23]

As a result, the High Court has principal jurisdiction with respect to matters directly arising under international law, such as a treaty, or any matters that may arise under the Constitution or a Commonwealth statute concerning international law, including treaties.[24] In 1977, a new court with federal jurisdiction was added with the creation of the Federal Court of Australia. This court is a superior court of law and equity with jurisdiction extending throughout Australia with respect to matters assigned it by the laws of the Commonwealth Parliament.[25] One feature of the Federal Court's jurisdiction has been as a court of appeal from decisions of the Refugee Review Tribunal (RRT) – and as a court of original jurisdiction in some instances in relation to migration decisions.[26] As a consequence, the Federal Court has developed a distinctive caseload in matters concerning migration and accordingly has been called on to develop considerable expertise in interpreting relevant provisions of the 1951 Convention Relating to the Status of Refugees (Refugees Convention).[27] Other federally established courts that may have occasion to consider matters dealing with international law include the Family Court of Australia[28] and the more recently created Federal Magistrates Court.[29]

All of the six Australian states[30] and the two internal territories[31] have established judicial systems including superior courts of record.[32] There is

[20] Commonwealth of Australia Constitution, s. 75(i).
[21] Commonwealth of Australia Constitution, s. 75(ii).
[22] Commonwealth of Australia Constitution, s. 76(i).
[23] Commonwealth of Australia Constitution, s. 76(ii).
[24] Judiciary Act 1903 (Cth) ss. 20, 38; *see generally* Brian Opeskin and Fiona Wheeler (eds.), *The Australian Federal, Judicial System* (2000).
[25] Judiciary Act 1903 (Cth) s. 39B; *see generally* Federal Court of Australia Act 1976 (Cth), and, James Crawford, *Australian Courts of Law* (3d ed., 1993) 149–72.
[26] Migration Act 1958 (Cth), s. 476A.
[27] Convention Relating to the Status of Refugees, [1954] ATS No. 5; for discussion of the Federal Court's jurisdiction in refugee matters, see Mary Crock, Ben Saul, and Azadeh Dastyari, *Future Seekers II: Refugees and Irregular Migration in Australia* (2006) 71–81.
[28] *See* Family Law Act 1975 (Cth).
[29] *See* Federal Magistrates Act 1999 (Cth).
[30] New South Wales, Queensland, South Australia, Tasmania, Western Australia, Victoria.
[31] Australian Capital Territory, Northern Territory.
[32] For details on the oldest of the state supreme courts – New South Wales – *see* Anne Twomey, *The Constitution of New South Wales* (2004).

also a superior court for Norfolk Island Territory, which sits on an occasional basis.[33] These courts exercise jurisdiction vested in them under relevant state and territorial laws, some of which give cause from time to time for consideration of international law matters.[34] Matters arising before the state and territorial courts, especially if addressing an issue of international law such as a treaty, are eligible for appeal to the High Court of Australia subject to the Court's special leave rules regarding appeals in civil and criminal matters. At federation, provision was made in the Constitution for appeals from the High Court of Australia to the Judicial Committee of the Privy Council in Britain, and similar appeal avenues were also open from State Supreme Courts; however, the Australia Act of 1986 (Cth) removed that right and Privy Council appeals are no longer available from Australian courts.

B. *The Constitution and Early Interpretation of International Law Matters*

Given the Constitution's ambiguity with respect to treaties and international law more generally, it is helpful to revisit the debates that took place in the 1890s, when the Constitution was being drafted. The 1891 draft of the Constitution clearly envisaged the Commonwealth Parliament having power with respect to treaties. This was reflected in covering clause 7 of the draft bill, which contemplated the Commonwealth having the ability to enter into treaties,[35] and Subclause 52(xxvi), which granted the Parliament power to make laws with respect to "[e]xternal affairs and treaties." In addition, it was proposed that federal jurisdiction with respect to treaties made by the Commonwealth with another country be vested in a superior federal

[33] *See* Norfolk Island Act 1979 (Cth) s. 52.

[34] For example, the Marine Pollution Act 1987 (NSW) is substantially based on provisions of the 1973 International Convention for the Prevention of Pollution from Ships (MARPOL), [1988] ATS No. 29; a matter of interpretation of the act and MARPOL arose before the Land and Environment Court of New South Wales (NSW), which went on appeal to the NSW Supreme Court: Morrison v. Peacock (2000) 50 NSWLR 178. This case eventually went on appeal to the High Court of Australia: Morrison v. Peacock [2002] HCA 44.

[35] Clause 7 provided:

> The Constitution established by this Act, and all laws made by the Parliament of the Commonwealth in pursuance of the powers conferred by the Constitution, and all Treaties made by the Commonwealth, shall, according to their tenor, be binding on the Courts, Judges, and people, of every State and of every part of the Commonwealth, anything in the laws of any State to the contrary notwithstanding.
>
> *Reprinted in* Australia, *Official Record of the Debates of the Australasian Federal Convention*, 3d Sess., Melbourne, 20, January to 17 March 1898, Appendix.

court.[36] These provisions of the draft Constitution did not generate much debate until 1897, when they came under the scrutiny of first the New South Wales Legislative Council and then again at the Second Session of the Constitutional Convention, held in Sydney. Concerns were first raised over the ability of the Commonwealth to negotiate treaties with other countries independently from Westminster.[37] As a result, the New South Wales Legislative Council proposed that Clause 7 be amended so as to remove any reference to "treaties made by the Commonwealth," and this was later accepted at the Sydney session of the Convention.[38] The Legislative Council also proposed that the words "and treaties" be removed from Subclause 52(xxvi), and this proposal was eventually adopted in 1898 during the Third Session of the Convention in Melbourne.[39] The Colonial Office in London, which took the view that the new Commonwealth of Australia would not be considered an independent state but would remain a part of the British Empire, was influential in the adoption of these amendments.[40] It remains uncertain, however, whether it was the intention of the Constitution's framers that the Commonwealth Parliament have no power with respect to international law. A review of the Convention debates on this issue does, however, clearly indicate that the amendments were made to the Constitution in the belief that postfederation Australia would lack the ability to enter into treaty obligations independently of Great Britain rather than from a desire to curtail the ability of the Parliament to legislate with respect to the subject matter of treaties.[41]

Notwithstanding this apparent failure to consider the extent of the power over external affairs, postfederation commentators were prepared to express a view on how far the power could extend. Harrison Moore adopted an expansive approach to the operation of the power and clearly contemplated that the power extended to the enactment of laws for the execution of treaties made by either the imperial government or the Commonwealth itself.[42] John Quick and Robert Garran were more circumspect and disagreed with Harrison Moore's "wide and far-reaching" construction even

[36] For comment, *see* Peter M. McDermott, "External Affairs and Treaties: The Founding Fathers' Perspective" (1990) 16 *Univ. Queensland L.J.* 123, at 123.

[37] John A. La Nauze, *The Making of the Australian Constitution* (1972) 173.

[38] McDermott, *supra* note 36, at 127–29.

[39] *Id.*, at 131; for a comment on these matters, *see also* H.B. Connell, "International Agreements and the Australian Treaty Power" (1968–69) *Australian Y.B. Int'l L.* 83–101.

[40] La Nauze, *supra* note 37, at 184.

[41] See the discussion on this point in Senate Legal and Constitutional References Committee (Australia), *Trick or Treaty? Commonwealth Power to Make and Implement Treaties* (1995) 56–57; *cf.* McDermott, *supra* note 36 at 136.

[42] W. Harrison Moore, *The Constitution of the Commonwealth of Australia* (1902) 143.

while acknowledging that the term was vague.[43] In their view, the power extended to external representation of the Commonwealth, the conduct of business and promotion of interests of the Commonwealth in outside countries, and the extradition of fugitives.[44] This narrow interpretation of the external affairs power was not, however, shared by Sir Isaac Isaacs, who played a role in the Convention debates and later served as attorney general, a justice of the High Court, and eventually chief justice. In a May 1906 opinion when acting as attorney general, Isaacs was of the view that the Commonwealth Parliament had power to enact a law relating to external affairs which gave effect to a Convention between the United States and Great Britain to which Australia had since acceded. However, Isaacs emphasized that such a law would be valid as an external affair of the Commonwealth rather than on the basis of a plenary power to legislate with respect to treaties.[45]

C. *Australian Courts and the Monism-Dualism Debate*

At this point it is helpful to make some observations regarding the manner in which Australian courts have traditionally viewed the impact of international law on Australian municipal law. This is a topic that will be given greater consideration herein; accordingly, at this stage only a brief outline of the position will be presented. Australia inherited much of its legal tradition from England, and since the establishment of a Western legal system in Australia following settlement in 1788, English law and legal tradition has had an enormous influence. While there is now only a minimal link between Australian and English law in a constitutional sense, none of which is currently relevant, the views of English courts on the role of international law upon municipal law have proved influential. This factor, in addition to the provisions of the Constitution that clearly confer distinctive roles on the executive in treaty making[46] and the Parliament in treaty implementation through the adoption of statutes,[47] has seen Australia adopt essentially a dualist approach toward international law.[48]

[43] John Quick & Robert R. Garran, *The Annotated Constitution of the Australian Commonwealth* (1901) 631.
[44] *Id.*, at 632.
[45] *See* Attorney-General's Department, *Opinions of Attorneys-General of the Commonwealth of Australia*, No. 244, pgs. 291–94; *see also* a June 1908 opinion of Attorney-General E. Littleton Groom that endorsed this view, *id.*, No. 312, at 386–89.
[46] Commonwealth of Australia Constitution, s. 61.
[47] Commonwealth of Australia Constitution, s. 51(xxix).
[48] These matters are thoroughly canvassed in Shearer, *supra* note 16, at 34–68.

In the case of customary international law, the High Court did not come to consider its potential impact on Australian law until as late as 1945, when it was called on to consider regulations adopted under the National Security Act of 1939 (Cth), which imposed on male Allied aliens an obligation to serve in the armed forces.[49] While noting the capacity of international law to be influential in the case of statutory interpretation, the High Court had no reservations as to the ability of the Parliament to enact a law that may have been contrary to customary international law at that time.[50] More recently, in the 1992 case of *Mabo v. Queensland [No. 2]*,[51] the landmark High Court decision on aboriginal land rights in Australia, Justice Gerard Brennan had occasion to refer to the way in which international law viewed the doctrine of terra nullius in light of the International Court of Justice decision in the *Western Sahara Case.*[52] Justice Brennan noted: "The common law does not necessarily conform with international law, but international law is a legitimate and important influence on the development of the common law, especially where international law declares the existence of universal human rights."[53] While Australian courts have had further occasion to consider the influence of customary international law on Australian law – both in terms of the common law and in terms of the interpretation of statutes – the position as stated previously remains the same.[54] The common law of Australia is therefore susceptible to influence by international law, and particularly customary international law, but ultimately this is a matter for the courts to determine on a case-by-case basis.

With respect to treaties, while the Australian courts have had considerably more experience in assessing their impact because of the debates over the extent of the Commonwealth constitutional power over treaties, the courts have nevertheless taken a fairly consistent dualist approach. To that end, the classic statement appears in the joint judgment of Chief Justice Anthony Mason and Justice Brennan in *Minister of State for Immigration and Ethnic Affairs v. Teoh*,[55] where they noted:

[49] Polities v. Commonwealth (1945) 70 CLR 60.
[50] Polities v. Commonwealth (1945) 70 CLR 60 at 77, per Dixon, J.
[51] Mabo v. Queensland [No. 2] (1992) 175 CLR 1.
[52] Western Sahara Case, [1975] ICJ Rep 12.
[53] Mabo v. Queensland [No. 2] (1992) 175 CLR 1 at 42.
[54] *See*, *e.g.*, the decisions in Nulyarimma v. Thompson (1999) 165 ALR 621, and discussion in Henry Burmester and Susan Reye, "The Place of Customary International Law in Australian Law: Unfinished Business" (2001) 21; *Austrl. Y.B. Int'l L.* 39–53, Kristen Walker and Andrew D Mitchell, "A Stronger Role for Customary International Law in Domestic Law?" in *The Fluid State: International Law and National Legal Systems* (Hilary Charlesworth et al. eds., 2005) 110–35.
[55] Minister of State for Immigration and Ethnic Affairs v. Teoh (1995) 128 ALR 353.

> It is well established that the provisions of an international treaty to which Australia is a party do not form part of Australian law unless those provisions have been validly incorporated into our municipal law by statute. This principle has the foundation in our constitutional system that the making and ratification of treaties fall within the province of the Executive in the exercise of its prerogative power whereas the making and alteration of the law fall within the province of Parliament, not the Executive. So, a treaty which has not been incorporated into our municipal law cannot operate as a direct source of individual rights and obligations under that law.[56]

Notwithstanding this position, treaties have the potential to influence the development or interpretation of Australian law irrespective of whether a statute giving effect to that treaty has been adopted by the Parliament. This is a matter considered further herein.

III. TREATIES, THE HIGH COURT, AND THE EXTERNAL-AFFAIRS POWER

The legislative powers of the Commonwealth Parliament are principally outlined in Sections 51 and 52 of the Constitution, of which Section 51 relevantly provides:

> The Parliament shall, subject to this Constitution, have power to make laws for the peace, order and good government of the Commonwealth with respect to:
>
> (xxix) External affairs.

In recent decades the legislative ability of the Parliament to give effect to the terms of treaties and conventions to which Australia is a party has become the most significant operational element of the so-called external-affairs power. These constitutional developments have also cast the spotlight onto the High Court of Australia's role in interpreting treaties to which Australia is a party. Although earlier interpretations of the Constitution's treaty-implementing power suggested that it provided only a basis for giving effect to treaties that clearly imposed international obligations, the modern view is that the power is sufficiently expansive to extend to the subject matter of the treaty, notwithstanding the absence of a clear international obligation

[56] Teoh (1995) 128 ALR 353 at 361–62.

to act.[57] This aspect of the power was clarified only in the 1980s, despite many previous opportunities for the High Court to conclusively deal with the issue.

Prior to 1983, very few judges were prepared to accept that a treaty, without any further evidence of international concern or an international obligation, could be relied on to enact a law under Section 51(xxix).[58] However, in the *Tasmanian Dam Case*, the majority judgments of Justices Mason, Lionel Murphy, Brennan, and Sir William Deane accepted that any international obligation imposed on Australia by a bona fide international treaty could form the basis for legislation enacted in reliance on Section 51(xxix). Some of the judges individually expressed wider views. Justice Mason believed that the mere entry into an international treaty by Australia demonstrated the judgment of the executive and of Parliament that the subject matter of the instrument was of international concern and that its implementation would benefit Australia. As such, "The Court should accept and act upon the decision of the executive government and upon the expression of the will of Parliament in giving legislative ratification to the treaty or convention."[59] Of the majority, only Justice Brennan believed that the mere existence of a treaty was not a sufficient basis for domestic legislation. The treaty had also to be one that imposed an international obligation on states to take action or deal with a subject matter of international concern.[60] Nevertheless, Justice Brennan did concede: "It is difficult to imagine a case where a failure by Australia to fulfil an express obligation owed to other countries to deal with the subject-matter of a treaty in accordance with the terms of the treaty would not be a matter of international concern, a matter capable of affecting Australia's external relations."[61]

Following the *Tasmanian Dam Case*, the minority in that case and some of the justices subsequently appointed to the Court accepted the expansive

[57] The distinction to be made here is between treaties that impose clear international duties and obligations on the parties and those that only confer rights on the parties or contain language that does not clearly impose an obligation; this was a matter of distinction between the majority and minority judges in both *Koowarta v. Bjelke-Petersen* and *Commonwealth v. Tasmania.*

[58] R. v. Burgess, *ex parte* Henry (1936) 55 CLR 608, at 681–82, per Evatt and McTiernan, JJ.

[59] Commonwealth v. Tasmania (1983) 158 CLR 1, at 125–26, also at 170–71, per Murphy, J.

[60] *Id.*, at 220. Here, reference was made to the test adopted in *Koowarta v. Bjelke-Petersen* by Stephen, J.

[61] *Id.*, at 219. See Geoffrey Sawer, "The External Affairs Power" (1984), 14 *Federal Law Review* 199 at 213, where Sawer notes that the "liberal view of what constitutes an international obligation" adopted by Justice Brennan would result in few occasions in which he would disagree with the other majority judges in *Commonwealth v. Tasmania.*

view of the external-affairs, treaty-implementing power.[62] Accordingly, the position is now that, irrespective of whether an international treaty is representative of international concern or contains international obligations, Australia's acceptance of a treaty is a sufficient basis for the Commonwealth to enact domestic legislation based on the treaty.[63]

Notwithstanding the adoption of this wide view of the power, the Court has also addressed limitations. In numerous cases, the Court has emphasized that the power extends only to bona fide treaties, and accordingly, "colourable" treaties, or those that raise the question of a "sham" or use of a "circuitous device to attract legislative power," are unacceptable.[64] The extent of such a limitation is, however, uncertain, and the Court has never clearly explained how such a determination of a mala fide treaty could be made.[65] The Court has also consistently held that a treaty relationship with other states does not confer on the Commonwealth a plenary power over the general subject matter of the treaty.[66] This was reaffirmed in 1996 by the High Court's decision in *Victoria v. Commonwealth*, when it noted:

> When a treaty is relied on under s 51(xxix) to support a law, it is not sufficient that the law prescribes one of a variety of means that might be thought appropriate and adapted to the achievement of an ideal. The law must prescribe a regime that the treaty has itself defined with sufficient specificity to direct the general course to be taken by the signatory states.[67]

[62] Richardson v. Forestry Commission (Tasmania) (1988) 164 CLR 261, at 321, per Dawson, J, at 343; per Gaudron, J, and at 332–33, per Toohey, J. *See also* Queensland v. Commonwealth (1989) 167 CLR 232, at 245–49, per Dawson, J. Justices McHugh, Gummow, and Kirby have all yet to express an individual opinion on this issue since their appointment to the High Court. However, Justice McHugh was a member of the unanimous court in *Queensland v. Commonwealth*, while Justice Gummow was a member of the majority in *Victoria v. Commonwealth* (1996) 138 ALR 129.

[63] James Crawford, "The Constitution and the Environment" (1991) 13 *Sydney L. Rev.* 11, at 23; *cf.* Richard D. Lumb, "The External Affairs Power and Constitutional Reform" (1988) 62 *Australian L.J.* 679 at 681.

[64] *See* Horta v. Commonwealth (1994) 181 CLR 183, at 195–97; Koowarta v. Bjelke-Petersen (1982) 153 CLR 168, at 231, per Mason, J; at 260, per Brennan, J; and *see also* R. v. Burgess; *ex parte* Henry (1936) 55 CLR 608, at 642, per Latham, CJ; at 687, per Evatt and McTiernan, JJ. See also the discussion in Hempel v. Attorney General (Cth) (1987) 77 ALR 641, at 671, per French, J.

[65] Geoffrey Sawer, "Execution of Treaties by Legislation in the Commonwealth of Australia" (1955) 2 *Univ. Queensland L.J.* 297 at 299. In note 13 Sawer has remarked that "this restriction seems largely academic"; *see also* George Winterton, "Limits on the Use of the 'Treaty Power'" in Alston and Chiam, *supra* note 15, 29 at 30–32; Saunders, *supra* note 17, at 160.

[66] Commonwealth v. Tasmania (1983) 158 CLR 1, at 131, per Mason, J; and 172, per Murphy, J.

[67] Victoria v. Commonwealth (1996) 138 ALR 129, at 146, per Brennan, CJ, and Toohey, Gaudron, McHugh, Gummow, JJ; this decision considered the status of certain International Labour Organization conventions under Australian law and reliance on those

Of all the limitations the High Court has considered with respect to the legislative power concerning treaties, the key test the Court has adopted in assessing the relationship between the treaty and a legislative instrument is that the legislation must be "appropriate and adapted" to the terms of the treaty.[68] This was a vital question in *Richardson*,[69] when the Commonwealth sought to establish a commission of inquiry to ascertain the suitability of certain areas in Tasmania for World Heritage listing and, until such time as the commission had handed down its findings, to protect those areas on an interim basis. While the Court unanimously upheld the creation of the commission as a legitimate exercise of the Commonwealth's power to implement the World Heritage Convention, the validity of the interim protection measures caused some division. Justices Deane and Gaudron wrote strong dissents against the majority view[70] that the measures adopted under the Lemonthyme and Southern Forests (Commission of Inquiry) Act of 1987 (Cth) were consistent with Australia's international obligations under the treaty. Both judges believed that, on the facts, the Commonwealth's legislation went beyond what the Convention prescribed. Justice Deane argued that the test in these cases should be whether there exists "a 'reasonable proportionality' between that purpose or object and the means which the law adopts to pursue it."[71] In this instance, Justice Deane was of the view that the Commonwealth had failed to demonstrate such a relationship because the protective measures implemented in reliance on the World Heritage Convention prohibited a range of activities beyond the commercial exploitation of the forests.[72] Justice Gaudron made a similar point, noting that the Commonwealth law prohibited activities that posed no threat to

conventions in adoption of the Industrial Relations Reform Act 1993 (Cth); see discussion in Richard Dalton and Richard Groom, "The Right to Strike in Australia: International Treaty Obligations and the External Affairs Power" (2001) 1 *Melbourne J. Int'l L.* 162–68.

[68] Airlines of NSW Pty v. New South Wales (No. 2) (1965) 113 CLR 54, at 87, per Barwick, CJ. This was accepted in later cases: *see* Commonwealth v. Tasmania (1983) 158 CLR 1, at 130, per Mason, J; at 259, per Deane, J; Richardson v. Forestry Commission (Tasmania) (1988) 164 CLR 261, at 289, per Mason, CJ and Brennan, J, and at 303, per Wilson, J. In *Victoria v. Commonwealth* (1996) 136 ALR 129, at 147, per Brennan, CJ, Toohey, Gaudron, McHugh and Gummow, JJ, reference is also made to an assessment of the "purpose or object" of the legislation in implementing the treaty.

[69] Richardson v. Forestry Commission (Tasmania) (1988) 164 CLR 261.

[70] Richardson v. Forestry Commission (Tasmania) (1988) 164 CLR 261, at 291, per Mason, CJ, and Brennan, J; at 303, per Wilson, J; at 327, per Dawson, J; and at 336, per Toohey, J.

[71] *Id.*, at 311–12. The view adopted by Gaudron, J, at 342, on this question was that a Commonwealth law will be "reasonably capable of being viewed as conducive to the purpose of the treaty if it is also reasonably capable of being viewed as appropriate, or adapted to, the circumstance which engages the power."

[72] Richardson v. Forestry Commission (Tasmania) (1988) 164 CLR 261, at 317–8.

those qualities of the identified property that were integral to its potential as a World Heritage area.[73] These dissenting views clearly indicate that every Commonwealth act that is based on a treaty will be carefully scrutinized by the High Court to ensure that there is appropriate conformity between the legislation and the treaty.

One issue that follows from the need for there to be an appropriate relationship between domestic legislation and a treaty is whether the Commonwealth must implement all provisions of the treaty. This was a matter that initially came before the Court in the 1936 decision of *R. v. Burgess; ex parte Henry (Burgess)*.[74] In that case, Justices Evatt and McTiernan, who had adopted a wide view of the Commonwealth's ability under Section 51(xxix) to implement treaties into domestic law, commented on the need for a proper relationship between the legislation and the treaty. They stated that:

> it must be possible to assert of any law . . . passed solely in pursuance of . . . the "external affairs" power, that it represents the fulfilment, so far as that is possible in the case of laws operating locally, of all the obligations assumed under the convention. Any departure from such a requirement would be completely destructive of the general scheme of the Commonwealth Constitution.[75]

While this strict view of the need to implement the terms of the treaty imposes limitations on the Commonwealth's ability to select what measures are most appropriate, it was conceded by these judges that much will depend on the terms of the treaty and the rights and duties that it confers or imposes.[76] Not all the judges in *Burgess*, though, adopted such a strict view of this limitation on the Commonwealth. Justice Sir Owen Dixon, in particular, referred to the need for a "faithful pursuit of the purpose" of the treaty rather than a strict implementation of its terms.[77] When this issue was next considered in *R. v. Poole; ex parte Henry*,[78] the question was not whether the legislation expressly implemented every term of the treaty but instead whether there had been a proper implementation of the treaty.

[73] *Id.*, at 346.

[74] R. v. Burgess; *ex parte* Henry (Burgess) (1936) 55 CLR 608.

[75] *Id.*, at 688.

[76] *Id.* For a comment, see A.R. Blackshield, "The Development of Commonwealth Powers: From Goya Henry to the Queensland Power Dispute," in *Human Rights: The Australian Debate* (L. Spender ed., 1987) 91, at 92–93.

[77] R. v. Burgess; *ex parte* Henry (1936) 55 CLR 608, at 674. However, at 674–75, it was warned: "But wide departure from the purpose is not permissible, because under colour of carrying out an external obligation the Commonwealth cannot undertake the general regulation of the subject matter to which it relates."

[78] R. v. Poole; *ex parte* Henry (1939) 61 CLR 634.

Accordingly, in the view of the majority, the Air Navigation Regulations implemented under the Air Navigation Act of 1920 (Cth) were a faithful implementation of the Convention for the Regulation of Aerial Navigation of 1919 under Australian conditions. Members of the Court emphasized that it was at the discretion of the Parliament to determine the best methods of implementing the Convention.[79] It was accepted, however, that the degree of discretion that the Parliament will have in these instances will very much depend on the language of the treaty.[80]

This approach has been confirmed in recent cases where the High Court has concentrated more on the exact relationship between the terms of the treaty and the domestic legislation than on the question of whether there has been a complete implementation of the treaty into Australian law.[81] In squarely addressing this point in the *Tasmanian Dam Case*,[82] Justice Brennan noted: "Where a treaty obligation gives rise to legislative power in the Commonwealth to perform the obligation fully and the Commonwealth chooses to exercise the power only to a limited extent, the validity of the law it chooses to make is not affected by its failure to exercise its powers and to perform Australia's obligations more fully."[83] The only question, therefore, is whether the domestic legislation seeks to carry out the purpose of the treaty in a manner that can be classified as appropriate and adapted to Australian conditions.[84]

IV. JUDICIAL REMEDIES AND TREATIES IN AUSTRALIAN COURTS

Because of this expansive interpretation of the Commonwealth Parliament's power with respect to treaties – thereby enlivening the ability of the Parliament to legislate on a greater range of subjects that directly relate to international law questions addressed in treaties – and the experience gained by the High Court in considering the issues raised by the constitutional challenges to that legislation, Australian courts have regularly become exposed to issues

[79] *Id.*, at 647, per Starke, J.

[80] *Id.*, at 644, per Rich, J; on this point, see C. M. Chinkin, "The Conclusion and Implementation of Treaties in Federal and Unitary States," in *Australian Law and Legal Thinking between the Decades* (A. Tay ed., 1990) 241, at 249.

[81] Victoria v. Commonwealth (1996) 138 ALR 129, at 194, per Brennan, CJ, Toohey, Gaudron, McHugh, Gummow, JJ.

[82] Commonwealth v. Tasmania (1983) 158 CLR 1, at 233, where it was accepted that the World Heritage (Western Tasmania Wilderness) regulations under the World Heritage Properties Conservation Act 1983 (Cth) implemented only part of the World Heritage Convention.

[83] *Id.*, at 234.

[84] This position has been followed in recent Federal Court of Australia decisions; see Toben v. Jones [2003] FCAFC 137, per Allsop, J [140–42].

arising from treaties from the 1980s. Setting aside the discrete issues arising from the constitutional challenges noted earlier, Australian courts have increasingly been asked to adjudge on matters that directly address rights conferred by treaty or that applicants before the Court have argued should be recognized under Australian law because of their basis in treaty law. To that end, the pivotal consideration is whether a remedy before the court is being sought from a statute that is either directly based on a treaty or that infers or imports certain treaty rights and obligations. In the absence of such a statute – be it an instrument of Commonwealth, state, or territorial law – an applicant will have a much-diminished chance of success in securing a treaty-based remedy. An alternate approach may be for a litigant to argue that a treaty-based right, while not directly or even indirectly imported into Australian law, is one that is reflected in customary international law and that the courts should accordingly give effect to that right. However, as has been noted, the most that can possibly be achieved from such an argument, given Australia's dualist legal system with respect to international law, is that the treaty, as reflected in customary international law, has the ability to influence the common law of Australia. Nevertheless, one clear trend is that the courts have become more open to hearing matters based on the existence not only of a treaty right recognized under Australian law but also of a right that exists entirely under international law by way of a treaty to which Australia is a party.[85]

The existence of a right and remedy under law is essential, then, for a plaintiff to pursue his or her claim in the Australian courts. This was a key issue in the *Toonen* case. In this case, Toonen, a gay man who resided in the state of Tasmania, alleged that his sexual privacy as recognized under the 1966 International Covenant on Civil and Political Rights (ICCPR)[86] was being infringed by the existence of Tasmanian law prohibiting homosexual sex.[87] Australia had become a party to the ICCPR in 1980, but the treaty had not been directly incorporated into either Commonwealth or state law by statute. Accordingly, because there was no legal remedy available

[85] In the case of *Baird v. Queensland*, [2005] FCA 1245, the applicants sought to argue that certain actions on the part of the government of the state of Queensland were not only contrary to the provisions of the Racial Discrimination Act 1975 (Cth) but also contrary to various treaties to which Australia was a party; while the applicants' claim was ultimately unsuccessful, the trial judge expressed some sympathy for the view that when a claim has been based on relief in connection with an international treaty to which Australia is a party, orders for costs should take into account whether the court should discourage such actions: [2005] FCA 1245 at [3], per Dowsett, J.

[86] International Covenant on Civil and Political Rights, 999 U.N.T.S. 171; [1980] ATS No. 23.

[87] In particular, Criminal Code Act 1924 (Tasmania), ss. 122, 123.

under either Tasmanian or Commonwealth law, Toonen had no ability to litigate the matter before Australian courts and therefore no ability to raise treaty law arguments. As an alternative, Toonen took his claim to the UN Human Rights Committee via the complaint mechanism available under the ICCPR Optional Protocol. The Human Rights Committee ruled on the communication and concluded that the Tasmanian law was in violation of Article 17 of the Covenant. In the Committee's finding, Toonen was entitled to a remedy and in its opinion "an effective remedy would be the repeal of Sections 122 (a), (c) and 123 of the Tasmanian Criminal Code."[88] The eventual response of the Commonwealth government and the Parliament was enactment of the Human Rights (Sexual Conduct) Act of 1994 (Cth), which sought to guarantee a right to sexual privacy under Australian law. However, the Commonwealth statute did not formally repeal the offending Tasmanian law, and it remained as a law on the books in that state. Under the terms of the Australian Constitution, a valid law of the Commonwealth will prevail over a law of a state, but that law is not as such repealed; rather, it becomes inoperative.[89] It was therefore constitutionally impossible for the Commonwealth Parliament to repeal a state law, though the Commonwealth government did seek to engage the Tasmanian government in discussions seeking repeal of the law.

When Tasmania continued to refuse to repeal the offending law, Toonen and his partner commenced litigation before the High Court to seek a declaration that the Tasmanian law was inconsistent with a law of the Commonwealth and therefore inoperative. This immediately raised an issue of constitutional standing before the High Court, because it was unclear whether the case presented a justiciable matter. The Court did determine that standing existed.[90] However, before a final judgment was rendered, the Tasmanian law was repealed by the Tasmanian Parliament and the litigation was discontinued.[91] Although this case is one of the most celebrated in Australian history with respect to the recognition of treaty-based international human rights, the fact that there had been no litigation before an Australian court directly addressing the ICCPR right to sexual privacy highlights the difficulty plaintiffs have in bringing these matters before the courts.

[88] Human Rights Committee, Views, Communication No. 488/1992 (CCPR/C/50/488/1992: 4 April 1994). For comment, *see* Wayne Morgan, "Sexuality and Human Rights: The First Communication by an Australian to the Human Rights Committee under the Optional Protocol to the International Covenant on Civil and Political Rights" (1993) 14 *Austrl. Y.B. Int'l L.* 277–92.

[89] Commonwealth of Australia Constitution, s. 109.

[90] Croome v. Tasmania [1997] HCA 5.

[91] Criminal Code Amendment Act 1997 (Tasmania), ss. 4, 5.

A. *Judicial Remedies and Treaties Incorporated under Australian Law*

In the case of treaties to which Australia is a party and in which there is implementing legislation giving effect to the terms of the treaty under Commonwealth, state, or territorial law, there may exist a range of remedies based on certain treaty rights and obligations. An important factor at play is the actual legislative scheme that has been adopted to give effect to the treaty under Australian law. In some instances, albeit rare ones, there may be full implementation of the treaty into Australian law, as has occurred with the Carriage of Goods by Sea Act of 1991 (Cth), giving effect to the so-called Hague Rules,[92] or the Civil Aviation (Carriers Liability) Act of 1959 (Cth), giving effect to the Warsaw Convention.[93] The more common situation, however, is where a statute seeks to give partial effect to a treaty provision such that the treaty has been adapted and adopted for the purposes of Australian law. In these instances, the treaty right may have been modified to reflect Australian circumstances, or a distinctive statutory scheme may have been developed around it. Consider some examples.

1. The Migration Act and the Refugee Convention. One clear example is the legislative program giving partial effect to Australia's obligations under the 1951 Refugee Convention through the Migration Act of 1958 (Cth), Section 36 of which creates a category of protection visas that may be granted to persons seeking asylum in Australia as refugees. During the past twenty years, Australian law and policy dealing with refugees has been the subject of considerable controversy, culminating in 2001 in the adoption of the so-called Pacific solution, whereby persons seeking asylum in Australia arriving by boat without having first been granted a visa were relocated to offshore processing facilities in adjacent Pacific states.[94] Both prior to and since the adoption of the Pacific solution there has been a significant upswing in litigation with respect to refugee matters, particularly before the Federal Court and on appeal to the High Court. An important issue in many of these cases is the extent to which the courts can, under the Migration Act and generally consistent with Australian law, have regard to the Refugee Convention. Ultimately, this is a question as to the status of the Convention in Australian law, and the High Court has generally taken a narrow view on

[92] *See* the decision of the High Court reviewing the predecessor act in Great China Metal Industries v. Malaysian International Shipping Corp. (1998) 196 CLR 161.

[93] *See* the decision of the High Court in Povey v. QANTAS Airways Ltd. (2005) 216 ALR 427.

[94] *See* generally the discussion in Crock, Saul, and Dastyari, note 27 at 115–17.

this question. As noted in 2002 by Justices Michael McHugh and William Gummow, in *Minister for Immigration and Multicultural Affairs v. Khawar*:

> [T]he Act is not concerned to enact in Australian municipal law the various protection obligations of the Contracting States found in Chs II, III and IV of the Convention. The scope of the Act is much narrower. In providing for protection visas whereby persons may either or both travel to and enter Australia, or remain in this country, the Act focuses upon the definition in Art 1 of the Convention as the criterion of operation of the protection visa system.[95]

Notwithstanding this view, there has been ongoing debate within the High Court as to the extent to which the Refugee Convention can inform the Court's reasoning. Justice Kirby, a member of the High Court since 1996 and a judge with a significant interest and passion for international law, has long argued that in refugee matters it is appropriate to refer extensively to the provisions of the Refugee Convention when interpreting the act.[96] This position is, however, a minority one, and the majority of judges on the Court adopt a narrower construction of the act and of the ability of the Convention to inform their views. The Court's 2006 judgment in the case of *QAAH* best illustrates this position. The majority noted:

> Australian courts will endeavour to adopt a construction of the Act and the Regulations, if that construction is available, which conforms to the Convention. And this Court would seek to adopt, if it were available, a construction of the definition in Art 1A of the Convention that conformed with any generally accepted construction in other countries subscribing to the Convention, as it would with any provision of an international instrument to which Australia is a party and which has been received into

[95] Minister for Immigration and Multicultural Affairs v. Khawar (2002) 210 CLR 1 at 16.

[96] *See, e.g.*, Justice Kirby's observations on these matters in the following High Court cases addressing matters relating to the status of refugees in Australia: "Applicant A" v. Minister for Immigration and Ethnic Affairs (1997) 142 ALR 331; R. v. Minister for Immigration and Multicultural Affairs & Anor; *Ex parte* Miah [2001] HCA 22; Minister for Immigration and Multicultural Affairs v. Singh [2002] HCA 7; Dranichnikov v. Minister for Immigration and Multicultural Affairs [2003] HCA 26; Minister for Immigration and Multicultural Affairs v. Respondents S152/2003 [2004] HCA 18; NAGV and NAGW of 2002 v. Minister for Immigration and Multicultural and Indigenous Affairs [2005] HCA 6, where at 89 Justice Kirby stated: "The Convention constitutes an important means of protection for the human rights and fundamental freedoms of refugees who claim such protection as non-citizens in Australia. The Parliament, by the terms of ss 36(2) and 65(1) of the Act, has given effect, in domestic law, to Australia's accession to the Convention. Ordinarily, this Court would give a meaning to such a provision so as to ensure that Australia's international obligations were thereby carried into full effect."

> domestic law. . . . But despite these respects in which the Convention may be used in construing the Act, it is the words of the Act which govern.[97]

Justice Kirby continues to view these matters differently, taking the position that it was the intention of the Parliament to give effect to the Convention definition of refugees. As a result, Justice Kirby concluded in *QAAH* that,

> [b]ecause, in this way, art 1 is incorporated into Australian law, it cannot be said that having recourse to the requirements, object, scope and purpose of that article amounts to a subordination of municipal law to the demands of the Convention, as the joint reasons of this Court would suggest. On the contrary, any other approach would involve a departure from the letter of Australian law.[98]

Much of this distinction revolves around one of incorporation or otherwise of the treaty into Australian law and ultimately statutory interpretation and ascertaining the intent of the parliament.

2. The World Heritage Convention. Parties have sought to rely on other treaties as the foundation of a remedy under Australian law. In a follow-on from the constitutional litigation before the High Court concerning the Commonwealth Parliament's powers with respect to sites placed on the World Heritage List under the 1972 World Heritage Convention, the Federal Court has been invited from time to time to consider whether certain activities taking place within World Heritage listed areas were consistent with both Australian law and the Convention. In *Friends of Hinchinbrook Society v. Minister for the Environment*,[99] the Federal Court reviewed whether a development proposal within the Great Barrier Reef World Heritage Area was consistent with the provisions of the World Heritage Properties Conservation Act of 1983 (Cth). While the declaratory relief and orders sought by the plaintiffs were denied both by the trial judge and on appeal, the Federal Court had no difficulty in reviewing the legitimacy of the development proposals under the Convention, the World Heritage Properties

[97] Minister for Immigration and Multicultural and Indigenous Affairs v. QAAH [2006] HCA 53 at [34], per Gummow ACJ, Callinan, Heydon, and Crennan, JJ.

[98] Minister for Immigration and Multicultural and Indigenous Affairs v. QAAH [2006] HCA 53 at [69], per Kirby, J. The debate within the High Court on this matter was continued in the case of *NBGM v. Minister for Immigration and Multicultural Affairs* [2006] HCA 54, a decision handed down on the same day as that in *QAAH* and where similar views by both the majority judges and Justice Kirby (in dissent) as to the role of the Refugee Convention in the interpretation of the Migration Act were repeated.

[99] Friends of Hinchinbrook Society v. Minister for the Environment (1997) 147 ALR 608; (1998) (Unreported – 13 March 1998).

Conservation Act of 1983 (Cth), and the Administrative Decisions (Judicial Review) Act of 1977 (Cth), which gave to the court the capacity for judicial review. In *Booth v. Bosworth*[100] the Federal Court was asked to grant an injunction against a private landowner who had erected aerial electric fences resulting in the electrocution of flying foxes, whose habitat included a World Heritage protected area and adjacent sites. In assessing the World Heritage values of the protected area, Justice Catherine Branson reviewed the provisions of the Convention, and "Operational Guidelines" adopted by the World Heritage Committee, as aids in interpreting the provisions of the Environment Protection and Biodiversity Conservation Act of 1999 (Cth), which sought to give effect to the Convention.[101] The Court, satisfied that the activities in question were likely to have a significant impact on the World Heritage values of the area, granted the injunction.[102]

3. Partial Incorporation of Treaties: *Project Blue Sky* Case.[103] Even where an act of parliament makes only indirect reference to the terms of a treaty or a related international law obligation, there may be a judicial remedy available. In 1998 this was explored fully in the *Project Blue Sky* case,[104] where the High Court was required to interpret the effect of the 1988 Protocol on Trade in Services to the Australian New Zealand Closer Economic Relations Trade Agreement (CER)[105] on the operation of the Australian Broadcasting Authority (ABA) under the provisions of the Broadcasting Services Act of 1992 (Cth) (BSA). The CER is one of Australia's longest-standing bilateral free-trade agreements and has played an important role in developing a trans–Tasman Sea integrated market between Australia and New Zealand. Here, the relevant statute, the BSA, directly provided that the ABA was to perform its functions in a manner consistent with "Australia's obligations under any convention to which Australia is a party or any agreement between Australia and a foreign country."[106] It was this direct application of international law to the operation of the ABA that was the focus of

[100] Booth v. Bosworth [2001] FCA 1453.
[101] Booth v. Bosworth [2001] FCA 1453 at [59], per Branson, J.
[102] Booth v. Bosworth [2001] FCA 1453 at [105], per Branson, J.
[103] This material is partly drawn from Donald R. Rothwell, "Quasi-Incorporation of International Law in Australia: Broadcasting Standards, Cultural Sovereignty and International Trade" (1999) 27 *Fed. L. Rev.* 527–45.
[104] Project Blue Sky Inc. v. Australian Broadcasting Authority (1998) 153 ALR 490.
[105] [1988] ATS No. 20; for the principal agreement, see Australia New Zealand Closer Economic Relations – Trade Agreement, [1983] ATS No. 2.
[106] Broadcasting Services Act 1992 (Cth), s. 160 (d).

the legal challenge launched by the New Zealand–based Project Blue Sky group.[107] The litigation was commenced against the ABA for failing to uphold the BSA and perform its functions consistent with Australia's obligations under international conventions.[108] Project Blue Sky argued that the ABA was bound to take into account the provisions of the Protocol to the CER, Article 4 of which provided: "Each Member State shall grant to persons of the other Member State and services provided by them access rights in its market no less favourable than those allowed to its own persons and services provided by them." In addition, Article 5 (1) also provided: "Each Member State shall accord to persons of the other Member State and services provided by them treatment no less favourable than that accorded in like circumstances to its persons and services provided by them." Pursuant to its statutory obligations,[109] the ABA had adopted a standard known as the Australian Content Standard, the principal purpose of which was to establish requirements for certain levels of Australian content in Australian television broadcasting. Project Blue Sky particularly objected to those provisions of the Australian Content Standard that had the following effect:

- Providing that until the end of 1997, Australian programs were to constitute at least 50 percent of all programming broadcast between 6 A.M. and midnight;
- Providing that from the beginning of 1998, Australian programs must be at least 55 percent of all programming broadcast between 6 A.M. and midnight.

It argued that the impact of the provisions was to impose a quota on foreign programs that could be broadcast during these periods, the effect of which was that New Zealand television programs were limited from being broadcast on Australian television.[110]

[107] Project Blue Sky comprised a group of like-minded individuals and associates who had the objective of encouraging the profitable growth of the New Zealand film and television industry.

[108] Other indicators under which the ABA were to operate included:
- The objects of the act and regulatory policy
- General policies of the government as notified by the minister
- Directions given by the minister in accordance with the act.

[109] Broadcasting Services Act 1992 (Cth), s. 122, outlines the obligation on the ABA to determine standards for commercial and community television, including commercial television standards for children and Australian content.

[110] The Australian Content Standard, cl. 7, provided a definition of an Australian program, of which factors taken into account included:
- If the program was produced under the creative control of Australians
- If the minister has issued a certificate

The case was originally heard before a single judge of the Federal Court, where Justice John Davies upheld Project Blue Sky's application and made a declaration that the ABA's Australian Content Standard was invalid and that it varied to the extent that it failed to be consistent with the CER Protocol.[111] This finding was reversed on appeal to a full bench of the Federal Court by a 2–1 majority. Justices Murray Wilcox and Paul Finn were of the view that the BSA contained within it two mutually inconsistent instructions: that the ABA provide preferential treatment for Australian programs and that the ABA do so evenhandedly as between Australia and New Zealand.[112] Taking the view that an irreconcilable conflict existed between the provisions of the BSA, it was found that Section 122 (2)(b) prevailed and that the ABA was not bound to take into account the operation of the CER.[113]

Before the High Court, the appeal by Project Blue Sky and others was unanimously upheld, though Chief Justice Brennan disagreed with his fellow judges as to the legal effect of their ruling. In a joint judgment, Justices McHugh, Gummow, Kirby, and Hayne gave particular attention to the Australian Content Standard and its provisions. The Court found that Clause 9 of the Australian Content Standard was in conflict with Articles 4 and 5 of the CER Protocol, with the result that there were two questions for determination:

1. Was the Australian Content Standard in breach of the provisions of the Broadcasting Services Act?
2. If so, was Clause 9 of the Australian Content Standard invalid?[114]

In addressing these issues, the judges spent some time assessing the effect of Section 122 of the BSA, which related to the Australian content of programs.

- If the program was made under an agreement between Australia and another country
- If the producers were Australian and a percentage of the cast were Australian

[111] For comment, *see* A. Henderson and M. Kelly, "Australia's Identity Crisis: The Cost of Closer International Relations" (1996) 15 (4) *Communications L. Bull.* 26–27.

[112] (1996) 141 ALR 397 at 414, per Wilcox and Finn, JJ.

[113] *Id.*; here Justices Wilcox and Finn relied on the principle of *generalia specialibus non derogant.* Justice Northrop was in dissent and was of the view that the provisions of s. 160(d) of the Broadcasting Services Act were mandatory with the result that if they were not complied with, a program statement that is inconsistent with that provision is invalid; *id.* at 406. However, it was noted: "This conclusion is reached without considering whether a domestic law which is inconsistent with an obligation of Australia under a convention or agreement with a foreign country is invalid by reason of that inconsistency."

[114] Project Blue Sky Inc. v. Australian Broadcasting Authority (1998) 153 ALR 490 at 508, per McHugh, Gummow, Kirby and Hayne, JJ.

It was found that the determination of Australian content under the BSA was one of the functions of the ABA and that in carrying out these functions the ABA was required to act in accordance with the directions given in Section 160 of the BSA – that being the section that directly refers to treaties and other agreements to which Australia is a party. In this respect the judges noted:

> If s 122 (1) and (2) were given their grammatical meaning, without regard to the provisions of s 160, they would authorise the making of standards which were inconsistent with Australia's obligations under international conventions or under its agreements with foreign countries.... When s 122 is read with s 160, the legal meaning of s 122 is that the ABA must determine standards relating to the Australian content of programs but only to the extent that those standards are consistent with the directions in s 160. If, by reason of an obligation under a convention or agreement with a foreign country, it is impossible to make an Australian content standard that is consistent with that obligation, the ABA is precluded by s 160 from making the standard notwithstanding the literal command of s 122 (1) and (2).[115]

It was found that the CER and the Protocol were agreements between Australia and a foreign country for the purposes of Section 160 of the BSA, with the result that the ABA was precluded from making a standard inconsistent with the CER or the Protocol.[116]

The judges then proceeded to consider the effect of their determination, in particular whether the Australian Content Standard was invalid or unlawful; the latter going directly to the actions of the ABA in determining a standard beyond the scope of its powers. In this instance, the Court found that the terms of Section 160 of the BSA were such that powers or functions not carried out in accordance with the policy was a question relating to the administration of a power or function rather than to its validity.[117] In this particular context, the following comment was made:

> Furthermore, while the obligations of Australia under some international conventions and agreements are relatively clear, many international conventions and agreements are expressed in indeterminate language as the

[115] *Id.*, at 512.

[116] In this regard the Court made reference to the explanatory memorandum that accompanied the bill that became the act, in which it was stated that cl. 160 "[r]equires the ABA to perform its functions in a manner consistent with various matters, including Australia's international obligations or agreements such as Closer Economic Relations with New Zealand." *Project Blue Sky* (1998) 153 ALR 490 at 512.

[117] *Id.*, at 517, per McHugh, Gummow, Kirby and Hayne, JJ.

> result of compromises between the contracting State parties. Often their provisions are more aptly described as goals to be achieved rather than rules to be obeyed. The problems that might arise if the performance of any functions of the ABA carried out in breach of Australia's international obligations was invalid are compounded by Australia being a party to about 900 treaties.[118]

It was subsequently determined that, while there was a legal duty on the ABA to act in accordance with the provisions of Section 160, an act done in breach of its provisions was not invalid. As such, the majority judges differed from Justice Davies in the Federal Court in finding that the Australian Content Standard was invalid by substituting the view that the standard had been unlawfully made.[119] It was at this point that Chief Justice Brennan diverged from the other members of the Court by instead finding that the standard adopted by the ABA was invalid and had no effect.[120] Consequently, the orders issued by Chief Justice Brennan on this point differed; however, the practical consequences in terms of the appeal remained the same.[121]

B. *Judicial Remedies and Treaties Not Yet Incorporated under Australian Law*

A feature of Australia's practice with respect to human rights treaties is that, while externally the country has been a strong supporter of the international human rights regime, municipal law does not mirror the nation's

[118] *Id.*, at 517–18, per McHugh, Gummow, Kirby and Hayne, JJ.

[119] *Id.*, at 518–19, per McHugh, Gummow, Kirby and Hayne, JJ; however, it was noted: "In a case like the present, however, the difference between holding an act done in breach of s 160 is invalid and holding it is valid is likely to be of significance only in respect of actions already carried out by, or done in reliance on the conduct of, the ABA. Although an act done in contravention of s 160 is not invalid, it is a breach of the Act and therefore unlawful." In this regard the Court made important comments as to whether the provisions were directory rather than mandatory. *See id.*, at 515–17 and comments in E. Campbell, "Waiver by Agencies of Government of Statutory Procedural Requirements" (1998) 21 *UNSW L.J.* 711 at 716–17.

[120] *Project Blue Sky* (1998) 153 ALR 490 at 504, per Brennan, CJ.

[121] For further discussion of this decision, *see* in M. Jacka, "Further Blue Sky Fall Out" (November 1998) 149 *Communications Update* 4; P.D. Mattina "When Blue Skies Aren't True Blue" (September 1998) 38 *Int'l L. News* 36; M. Leiboff "Football, Meat Pies, Kangaroos and Holden Cars? The Arts and Cultural Implications of Project Blue Sky v. Australian Broadcasting Authority" (1998) 3 *Media & Arts L. Rev.* 135; J. Brosnan, "True Blue v. Blue Sky: Australian Content Standards in Doubt" (1998) 17 *Communications L. Bull.* 1–2.

wide-ranging acceptance of international human rights treaties.[122] With the exception of the Racial Discrimination Act of 1975 (Cth)[123] and the Human Rights (Sexual Conduct) Act of 1994 (Cth) noted earlier,[124] there is little Commonwealth legislation giving effect to Australia's human rights treaty obligations. Indeed, this has been a distinctive feature of Australian law ever since the development of modern human rights during the UN era, and successive Australian governments have resisted efforts to introduce either a bill of rights or a more comprehensive domestic human rights regime.[125] Recent initiatives in the Australian states and territories have, however, seen the adoption of bill of rights statutes that broadly seek to give effect to human rights treaties to which Australia is a party,[126] and while these are welcome developments, the position still remains that Australia is without a comprehensive domestic human rights regime and is one of the few Western liberal democracies in such a position.[127]

This is not to suggest that human rights treaties have little influence on Australian law or that Australian courts have had little occasion to consider them.[128] As noted earlier, a significant Australian jurisprudence has developed around the Refugee Convention in the context of the Migration Act, and the ICCPR has influenced constitutional and statutory interpretation – an issue considered in more detail subsequently. In addition, a distinctive approach has been developed by the courts in the context of ratified treaties

[122] G.P.J. McGinley, "The Status of Treaties in Australian Municipal Law: The Principle of Walker v. Baird Reconsidered" (1989–90) 12 *Adelaide L. Rev.* 367 at 367, who notes: "Australia, like so many other nations, sometimes speaks with a forked tongue. It negotiates and is party to international instruments recognizing certain principles, rights and obligations which it then it fails to implement into Australian domestic law. Litigants relying on those instruments have generally received short shrift from the Australian courts."

[123] Seeking to give effect to the Convention for the Elimination of Racial Discrimination.

[124] Adopted by the Commonwealth Parliament in the wake of the UN Human Rights Commission finding in the *Toonen* case, which in any event only purports to give effect to art. 17 of the ICCPR and not the whole of the treaty.

[125] For a historical overview of Australia's engagement with international human rights, *see* Peter H. Bailey, *Human Rights: Australia in an International Context* (1990); Hilary Charlesworth, "The Australian Reluctance about Rights," in *Towards an Australian Bill of Rights* (P. Alston ed., 1994) 21–53; Hilary Charlesworth, "International Human Rights Law and Australian Federalism," in Opeskin and Rothwell, *supra* note 15, 280–305.

[126] *See* Human Rights Act 2004 (ACT); Charter of Human Rights and Responsibilities Act 2006 (Vic).

[127] For an overview and critique of the Australian practice in this regard, *see* Hilary Charlesworth et al., *No Country Is an Island: Australia and International Law* (2006) 64–105.

[128] For comment on this point, *see* Fleur E. Johns, "Human Rights in the High Court of Australia, 1976–2003: The Righting of Australian Law?" (2005) 33 *Fed. L. Rev.* 287, who at 318 describes the position in Australia as follows: "The trail blazed by international human rights principles through Australian law is meandering and inconclusive."

that have not yet been incorporated into Australian law but that are considered to form the basis of an administrative right under Australian law. This approach is known as the *Teoh* doctrine, based on the case of the same name.

In the 1995 case of *Minister of State for Immigration and Ethnic Affairs v. Teoh*,[129] the applicant was a Malaysian citizen who while living in Australia had married and children were born from that marriage. While an application for permanent resident status was pending, Teoh was convicted on drug-related offenses and proceedings were commenced for his deportation before the Immigration Review Panel. Teoh argued before the panel, and on appeal to the Federal Court, that due consideration should be given to his family circumstances, especially as at the time his spouse had six children all younger than the age of ten living with her. As this matter progressed through various appellate courts on its way to the High Court, the argument was further advanced that consideration should be given to the 1989 Convention on the Rights of the Child,[130] a treaty to which Australia was a party but that had yet to be given effect under municipal law.

By a majority judgment, the High Court was of the view that Australia's ratification of the Convention created a legitimate expectation for individuals whose matters were under review and that administrative decision makers would have some regard to the Convention when making their determinations. This was despite the fact that no direct or indirect reference had been made to the Convention in Australian law. The leading opinion was coauthored by Chief Justice Mason and Justice Brennan who commenced by noting:

> But the fact that the Convention has not been incorporated into Australian law does not mean that its ratification holds no significance for Australian law. Where a statute or subordinate legislation is ambiguous, the courts should favour that construction which accords with Australia's obligations under a treaty or international convention to which Australia is a party, at least in those cases in which the legislation is enacted after, or in contemplation of, entry into, or ratification of, the relevant international instrument. That is because Parliament, prima facie, intends to give effect to Australia's obligations under international law.[131]

However, the opinion noted that this was not a case in which an ambiguity in a statute was under consideration or with the development of an existing principle of the common law. Rather, the issue was the extent of

[129] (1995) 128 ALR 353.
[130] [1991] ATS No. 4; Australia had become a party to the treaty on 16 January, 1991.
[131] Teoh [26], per Mason, CJ, and Brennan, J.

the discretion held by an administrative decision maker, the ambit of the inquiries that could be undertaken when making determinations, and the level of expectation by persons impacted by such decisions as to how those determinations would be reached. To that end, the pivotal question was whether it was legitimate to give consideration to a treaty to which Australia was a party and under which Australia had assumed certain international obligations. In this regard, Chief Justice Mason and Justice Brennan were firmly of the view as to the role the Convention would play in that process:

> [R]atification by Australia of an international convention is not to be dismissed as a merely platitudinous or ineffectual act, particularly when the instrument evidences internationally accepted standards to be applied by courts and administrative authorities in dealing with basic human rights affecting the family and children. Rather, ratification of a convention is a positive statement by the executive government of this country to the world and to the Australian people that the executive government and its agencies will act in accordance with the Convention. The positive statement is an adequate foundation for a legitimate expectation, absent statutory or executive indications to the contrary, that administrative decision-makers will act in conformity with the Convention and treat the best interests of the children as a "primary consideration."[132]

In concluding that the minister's delegate had not taken Australia's treaty obligation into account, Chief Justice Mason and Justice Brennan stressed that the existence of a legitimate expectation "does not necessarily compel" the decision maker to act in a certain way. To do so, they said, would be, in effect, treating the legitimate expectation as a rule of law and would have the effect of incorporating the treaty "into our municipal law by the back door."[133] This view was broadly endorsed by Justices Toohey and Gaudron, with only Justice McHugh in dissent.

The decision in the *Teoh* case resulted in significant political, legal, and academic debate within Australia as to both the appropriateness of the decision and the impact of ratified but unimplemented treaties. Various Commonwealth governments of both political persuasions spent considerable energy through both executive action and proposed parliamentary legislation to counteract the effect of the decision,[134] though ultimately

[132] Teoh [34], per Mason, CJ, and Brennan, J.
[133] Teoh [36], per Mason, CJ, and Brennan, J.
[134] This action has taken the form of two executive statements by former governments, plus attempts to enact legislation designed to specifically counteract the decision in the *Teoh* case; see discussion in M. Allars, "International Law and Administrative Discretion," in Opeskin and Rothwell, *supra* note 15, 232 at 262–69; S. Browhuis, "International Law by the

without having much impact.[135] The Federal Court was confronted with an influx of cases in which applicants sought to rely on the *Teoh* case in arguing that administrative decision makers had failed to give appropriate consideration to the Convention on the Rights of the Child.[136] Eventually another case came before the High Court in which the principle addressed in *Teoh* was once again raised.

In the 2003 case of *Re Minister for Immigration and Multicultural Affairs; Ex parte Lam*,[137] the High Court was asked to consider the legitimate expectation doctrine. Justices McHugh and Gummow[138] doubted whether the mere ratification of an international convention was sufficient to give rise to a legitimate expectation. Consistently with their view that a legitimate expectation could arise only if a person in fact subjectively held that expectation, they observed that assessing whether a legitimate expectation might arise in respect of the ratification by Australia of a treaty required a consideration of the extent to which ratification had impinged on the popular consciousness.[139] They then noted that, "in general, ratification as an executive act, [does] not in the domestic constitutional structure thereby confer rights upon citizens or impose liabilities upon them."[140] However, Justices McHugh and Gummow were careful not to deny that unincorporated treaties could have any effect in the Australian domestic legal order. Thus, they observed:

> Nevertheless, in various respects, an unincorporated treaty, left in that state, may be invoked in various ways in the conduct of domestic affairs. For example, a peace treaty will, without legislation, change the status of enemy aliens in Australian courts. Further, the taking of a step by the

Back Door?" (1998) 72 *Austrl. L.J.* 794; L. Katz, "A Teoh FAQ" (March 1998) 16 *AIAL Forum* 1; A. Duxbury "The Anti-Teoh Bill Revisited" (July 1997) 35 *Int'l L. News* 28; R. Piotrowicz, "Unincorporated Treaties in Australian Law: The Official Response to the Teoh Decision" (1997) 71 *Austrl. L.J.* 503; Wendy Lacey "In the Wake of Teoh: Finding An Appropriate Government Response" (2001) 29 *Federal Law Review* 219.

[135] *See* the decisions in Department of Immigration and Ethnic Affairs v. Ram (1996) 69 FCR 431; Tien v. Minister for Immigration and Multicultural Affairs (1998) 159 ALR 405.

[136] *See* the decisions in Vaitaiki v. Minister for Immigration and Ethnic Affairs (1998) 150 ALR 608; Browne v. Minister for Immigration and Multicultural Affairs [1998] FCA 566; Minogue v. Human Rights and Equal Opportunity Commission [1999] FCA 85; Le v. Minister for Immigration and Multicultural and Indigenous Affairs [2004] FCA 875. For a decision that also considered the Convention on the Rights of the Child but not in a Teoh context of legitimate expectation, see Re O and P [2005] NSWSC 1297.

[137] Re Minister for Immigration and Multicultural Affairs; *Ex parte* Lam [2003] HCA 6.

[138] Justice McHugh was the dissenting judge in *Teoh*, while Justice Gummow was not a member of the Court at the time of the decision.

[139] [2003] HCA 6 [95], per McHugh and Gummow, JJ.

[140] [2003] HCA 6 [99].

> executive government in the conduct of external affairs, whilst of itself neither creating rights nor imposing liabilities, may supply a step in a broader process of resolution of justiciable disputes.... However, in the case law a line has been drawn which limits the normative effect of what are unenacted international obligations upon discretionary decision-making under powers conferred by statute and without specification of those obligations. The judgments in *Teoh* accepted the established doctrine that such obligations are not mandatory relevant considerations attracting judicial review for jurisdictional error. The curiosity is that, nevertheless, such matters are to be treated, if *Teoh* be taken as establishing any general proposition in this area, as mandatory relevant considerations for that species of judicial review concerned with procedural fairness.[141]

Thus, without actually overruling the decision in *Teoh*,[142] the High Court in *Lam* cast doubt on the doctrine of legitimate expectation, raising the specter of *Teoh* being overruled and discarded by a future High Court.[143]

In addition to the scenario that arose in *Teoh*, during the past decade, Australian courts have also faced a variety of actions in which litigants have sought to rely on treaties as a possible basis of claim, notwithstanding the absence of a statute giving effect to the treaty. In all instances, these cases have failed because of the inability of the applicants to make out their claim, because there was an insufficient legal basis to recognize the claim under Australian law, or because of adherence by the courts to a dualist approach to international and municipal law.[144] In one of the more ambitious of these cases, a prisoner alleged breach of various international human rights standards while incarcerated at a prison in South Australia. In the Supreme Court of South Australia, Justice Robin Millhouse was prepared to find that there had been a breach of Article 10 of the ICCPR;[145] however, as the treaty had not been given effect in South Australia or Australia generally, there was no remedy available under law and the applicant for relief was

[141] [2003] HCA 6 [100–101].

[142] *See also* the judgments in *Lam* of Hayne, J, [2003] HCA 6 [122], and Callinan, J [2003] HCA 6 [147].

[143] Wendy Lacey, "The Judicial Use of Unincorporated International Conventions in Administrative Law: Back-Doors, Platitudes and Window-Dressing" in Charlesworth et al. (eds.), note 127, 82 at 84.

[144] *See* Thorpe v. Commonwealth of Australia (No. 3) (1997) 144 ALR 677, where before Justice Kirby a claim was brought seeking a declaration that the Commonwealth of Australia request that the UN General Assembly seek an advisory opinion from the ICJ with respect to certain acts of genocide in Australia; in *Perry v. Howard* [2005] FCA 1702, an applicant sought to make out a claim against the Australian government of a failure to provide consular assistance under the Vienna Convention on Consular Relations.

[145] Collins v. South Australia [1999] SASC 257 at [30], per Millhouse, J.

refused.[146] These recent cases have followed the previous trend whereby Australian courts were not prepared to entertain the existence of rights or remedies founded on treaties to which Australia was a party in the absence of an implementing statute.[147]

C. *Interpretation of Treaties by Australian Courts*

Finally, in this section it is helpful to comment briefly on the approaches taken toward treaty interpretation in Australian courts. Under Australian law, the Acts Interpretation Act of 1901 (Cth) makes it clear that extrinsic materials can be relied on when interpreting a statute, including "any treaty or other international agreement that is referred to in the Act."[148] This approach is further supplemented by the fact that Australia is a party to the 1969 Vienna Convention on the Law of Treaties,[149] and the High Court has accepted the legitimacy of the Vienna Convention's provisions when confronted with the task of interpreting a treaty. In the 2002 case of *Morrison v. Peacock*,[150] when the Court was called on to consider the provisions of the 1973 MARPOL Convention, the Court, in a unanimous judgment, directly referred to Article 31 of the Vienna Convention and noted:

> The effect of Art 31 is that, although primacy must be given to the written text of the 1973 Convention, the context, objects and purpose of the treaty must also be considered. The need to give the text primacy in interpretation results from the tendency of multilateral treaties to be the product of compromises by the parties to such treaties. However, treaties should be interpreted in a more liberal manner than that ordinarily adopted by a court construing exclusively domestic legislation.[151]

While the status, then, of the Vienna Convention is not in doubt when Australian courts come to interpret treaties, the judicial approach toward this issue has remained the subject of some debate. In an authoritative discussion on the issue in the case of "*Applicant A*," Justice McHugh in

[146] Collins v. South Australia [1999] SASC 257 at [47], per Millhouse, J, noting, "[As] much as I regret it, as a single judge I am not able to give force to the basic human rights set out in these conventions."

[147] For a review of the case law prior to the 1990s, see McGinley, note 122.

[148] Acts Interpretation Act 1901 (Cth), s 15AB (2)(d).

[149] [1974] ATS No. 2; in force for Australia on 27 January, 1980.

[150] [2002] HCA 44.

[151] [2002] HCA 44 at [16], per the Court. This follows precedent of the High Court in this area, for example, in *"Applicant A" v. Minister for Immigration and Ethnic Affairs* (1997) 142 ALR 331 at 351, McHugh, J noted, "In Australia, treaties are interpreted in accordance with the requirements of the Vienna Convention on the Law of Treaties."

the High Court went to some lengths to outline the approach to be taken to treaty interpretation based on Vienna Convention rules and the practice of other international courts and tribunals.[152] The judge identified an approach based on the need to "examine both the 'ordinary meaning' and the context... [and] 'object and purpose' of a treaty" supported by:

- Article 31 of the Vienna Convention;
- The basic principle of interpretation of taking the text of the treaty as the starting point;
- Looking at both the context, object and purpose as well as the text as being consistent with the general principle that international instruments should be interpreted in a more liberal manner; and
- That because treaties lack the precision of domestic legislation, there is a need to adopt broad interpretative principles.[153]

These principles of treaty interpretation have been adopted and followed by various Australian courts,[154] especially the Federal Court, whose caseload regularly requires the Court to consider treaties.[155]

V. TREATY INFLUENCES ON AUSTRALIAN COURTS

Parallel with the increase in litigation before the courts in which treaty issues have been raised has been an upsurge in cases in which debate has

[152] Particular reference was made to the approaches of the European Court of Human Rights; this in the context of the High Court being asked to consider a case requiring interpretation of the provisions of the Refugee Convention.

[153] (1997) 142 ALR 331 at 351–352, per McHugh, J.

[154] *See* the Supreme Court of Victoria decision in Povey v. Civil Aviation Safety Authority [2002] VSC 580; the Vienna Convention was also noted in the Supreme Court of New South Wales in Application of O. and P. [2005] NSWSC 1297.

[155] *See* Federal Court decisions in Minister for Immigration and Multicultural Affairs v. Savvin [2002] FCA 478; Booth v. Bosworth [2001] FCA 1453; *see also* El Greco v. (Australia) Pty v. Mediterranean Shipping Co. [2004] FCAFC 202, where Justice Allsop gave particular attention to the provisions of art. 32 of the Vienna Convention on the Law of Treaties, noting at [146]: "An understanding of the circumstances of the conclusion of the convention or protocol in question is not reached merely by reading, literally, the text of either the convention or protocol or what was said and written by delegates at the various meetings and conferences leading up to the making of the relevant instrument. The relevant legal, practical and jurisprudential context and history must be understood in order that the compromises inherent in these international agreements be appreciated. Further, care must be taken not to accept too literally or overwhelmingly any particular words by one delegate (however eminent he or she may be or have been) without understanding the context of such words in the whole of the preparatory work and in the circumstances of the conclusion of the relevant agreement.... In the end, to the extent there were compromises, it was the text of the agreement that embodied such compromises."

arisen as to the extent to which consideration can be given to the terms of a treaty as influencing the interpretation of a domestic statute. This debate has been partly noted previously in the context of the refugee cases under the Migration Act, where the High Court has taken a strict view on these matters, with the majority being prepared only to take into account the provisions of the Refugee Convention when that is directly contemplated by statute. As was seen in that discussion, Justice Kirby favors a more liberal view.

However, there has long been acceptance within the High Court and other superior courts in Australia that treaties not only have the ability to influence the development of the common law in Australia but also may be legitimately relied on as an aid to statutory interpretation. This position is confirmed by the Acts Interpretation Act of 1901 (Cth),[156] and by Justice Brennan's comments in *Mabo v. Queensland [No. 2]* noted earlier.[157] Writing extrajudicially, the former chief justice of the High Court, Chief Justice Gleeson, endorsed this approach. With respect to the decision in *Mabo* and its impact on how international law is viewed in relation to Australian law, the then chief justice observed:

> There is no event in Australia's recent legal history that more vividly illustrates the effect on Australian law of developments in international human rights jurisprudence than the decision in *Mabo* and the subsequent legislative response to that decision. In resolving ambiguity in a statute, courts favour a construction which accords with Australia's obligations under a treaty, on the basis that they presume that parliament intends to legislate in accordance with, rather than contrary to, its international obligations.[158]

The key issue that arises from these exchanges is whether there exists an ambiguity in a statute.

A. *Resolving Statutory Ambiguity by Reference to a Treaty*

Justice Kirby has been at the forefront of attempts to develop within Australian courts a more ready acceptance of the value of referring to international law – especially international treaties to which Australia is a party,

[156] Acts Interpretation Act 1901 (Cth), s. 15 AB.
[157] Mabo v. Queensland (No. 2) (1992) 175 CLR 1 at 42, per Brennan, J.
[158] Murray Gleeson, "Global Influences on the Australian Judiciary" (2002) 22 *Austrl. B. Rev.* 184 at 187. The chief justice noted the *Teoh* decision as supportive of this view; with respect to the legislative response to *Mabo, see* Native Title Act 1993 (Cth).

not only when there exists statutory ambiguity, but also where the construction of a statute would result in an interpretation contrary to international human rights standards. This position, which Justice Kirby has long advocated since his appointment to the New South Wales Court of Appeal in the 1980s, has been partly influenced by the so-called Bangalore Principles adopted in 1988 at a judicial colloquium of senior Commonwealth jurists.[159] Presently, there does not seem to be disagreement among the High Court that it is entirely legitimate to refer to a treaty when the language of a statute so permits, or where there is statutory ambiguity,[160] and there are numerous examples during the past decade when, from time to time, the High Court has looked to various international treaties as such an interpretative aid.[161] This position has been broadly followed by the Federal Court[162] and within the State supreme courts.[163] However, it is clear that some members of the High Court are hostile to argument that suggests that it go further and import the provisions of the treaty into Australian law in the absence of ambiguity or a clear invitation within the statute to do so. This strict approach to the limited role of treaties in statutory interpretation is typically reflected in the position advanced by Justice Callinan in the 2002 case of *Western Australia v. Ward* as follows:[164]

> The task of this Court and other courts in Australia is to give effect to the will of Australian Parliaments as manifested in legislation. Courts may not flout the will of Australia's democratic representatives simply because they believe that, all things considered, the legislation would "be better" if it were read to cohere with the mass of (often ambiguous) international obligations and instruments. Consistency with, and subscription to, our international obligations are matters for Parliament and the Executive, who are in a better position to answer to the international community than tenured judges. Where legislation is not genuinely ambiguous, there is no warrant for adopting an artificial presumption as the basis for, in effect, rewriting it.[165]

[159] *See* the discussion in Allars, *supra* note 134, at 248–50.

[160] *See, e.g.*, AMS v. AIF; AIF v. AMS [1999] HCA 26, and particularly the views of Gleeson, CJ, McHugh, Gummow, Hayne, and Callinan, JJ.

[161] Coleman v. Power [2004] HCA 39; *Re* Woolley; *ex parte* Applicants M276/2003 [2004] HCA 49; Sinanovic v. R. [1998] HCA 40.

[162] Minogue v. Williams [1999] FCA 1585 at [35], per Williams, J; MIMIA v. Al Masri [2003] FCFCA 70; Tran v. Minister for Immigration and Multicultural and Indigenous Affairs [2005] FCFCA 143.

[163] Collins v. South Australia [1999] SASC 257; McGee v. Gilchrist-Humphrey [2005] SASC 254.

[164] [2002] HCA 28.

[165] [2002] HCA 28 at [956], per Callinan, J.

There can be no denying that the upward trend in reliance on treaties in submissions for relief made before the courts in Australia has created challenges for the judiciary. Many are not trained in international law and, because Australia remains legally remote from robust regional legal systems such as those of Europe, international law is still often viewed with suspicion and as "foreign" and inimical to the Australian legal system. Much of the debate has raged in particular over the interpretation of the Migration Act consistently not only with the Refugee Convention but also with other international human rights instruments. In this regard, it must be observed that recent Australian policy with respect to refugees and its interpretation of human rights standards generally has not only been a matter of legal debate but also one of significant political controversy that, on occasion, has been at the forefront of national political debate.[166] There has also been a separate but parallel reliance on the provisions of the ICCPR, notwithstanding that it has been given very limited effect under Australian law.

Notwithstanding the general position described here, advocates have not been dissuaded from arguing before the courts that Australia's treaty obligations should be taken into account when interpreting statutes. The division of views in the High Court on this matter is best represented by the 2006 case of *NBGM v. Minister for Immigration and Multicultural Affairs*,[167] where the Court was reviewing yet another refugee case on appeal in a matter in which Judge Allsop in the Federal Court had given particular regard to the Refugee Convention as an interpretative aid. A majority of the High Court rejected the legitimacy in this instance of any reference to the treaty. They sought, perhaps for the first time, to clearly articulate an approach to be taken in these matters:

> It is appropriate to point out at this stage that to approach the matter in that way was to invert the steps which an Australian court should take in situations in which international instruments have been referred to in, or adopted wholly or in part by, enactments. The first step is to ascertain, with precision, what the Australian law is, that is to say what and how much of an international instrument Australian law requires to be implemented, a process which will involve the ascertainment of the extent to which Australian law by constitutionally valid enactment adopts, qualifies or modifies the instrument. The subsequent step is the construction of so

[166] *See* the discussion in Charlesworth et al., *No Country Is an Island*, *supra* note 15, at 64–105; Crock, Saul, and Dastyari, *supra* note 27; Frank Brennan, *Tampering with Asylum: A Universal Humanitarian Problem* (2003).

[167] [2006] HCA 54.

> much only of the instrument, and any qualifications or modifications of it, as Australian law requires.[168]

Unsurprisingly, Justice Kirby directly rebuffed these views, suggesting that they:

> fly in the face of long established general principles for the construction of municipal legislation referring to treaty provisions which have been ratified by the nation concerned. They are contrary to the long-standing authority of this Court and of other courts of high authority throughout the common law world. They are inimical to the effective participation of this country in the growing body of international, regional and bilateral treaties which substantially depend, in Australia, on municipal law to bring them into local effect.[169]

In the alternative, Justice Kirby argued that there needed to be a greater facilitation of international law by the Australian courts:

> We in this Court, at this time, should not be hostile to the provisions of international law. After all, the treaty expressing the applicable obligations of international law has been ratified by this country in accordance with its Constitution and the requisite legal procedures and practices. . . . Hostility is entirely out of place. Facilitation and implementation constitute the correct legal approach.[170]

In light of some of these recent developments, it is clear that a majority of the current High Court members are not prepared to endorse a wider role for treaties in statutory interpretation other than where the legislature has clearly envisaged such a role or where there exists a clear ambiguity on the face of the statute. Justice Kirby and a small number of Federal Court judges take a more liberal view on these matters, but they are very clearly in the minority.

B. *Resolving Constitutional Ambiguity by Reference to a Treaty*

Parallel to Justice Kirby's support for greater reliance on treaties in statutory interpretation has been his support for appropriate reliance on treaties and international law more generally in the interpretation of the Australian Constitution. In a number of constitutional cases that have arisen since Justice Kirby's 1996 appointment to the High Court, he has taken the opportunity

[168] [2006] HCA 54 at [61], per Callinan, Heydon and Crennan, JJ, this view was also endorsed by Gummow ACJ.
[169] [2006] HCA 54 at [16], per Kirby, J.
[170] [2006] HCA 54 at [18], per Kirby, J.

to refer to the role of international law as an interpretative aid in construing the words of the Constitution. As has already been noted, there is a record of interaction between international law and the Australian Constitution, but primarily in the context of a treaty being a possible source of Commonwealth constitutional power under Section 51(xxix) of the Constitution. As a result, it cannot be said that there was any "coherent approach" to the use of treaties in constitutional interpretation up until the time of Justice Kirby's appointment to the High Court.[171]

In two cases in 1997 and 1998, Justice Kirby took the opportunity to develop his so-called interpretative principle of constitutional law interpretation by making reference where appropriate to principles of international law as found both in customary international law and treaties. This position was first fully articulated in the 1997 case of *Newcrest Mining v. Commonwealth*,[172] a matter dealing with the interpretation of Commonwealth Parliament's Section 51(xxxi) power concerning the acquisition of property. In this instance, the Court was called on to review the Commonwealth acquisition of certain mining leases. Justice Kirby was of the view that international law was an appropriate tool in constitutional interpretation in the case of ambiguity, and that this was especially the case when the issue at stake concerned fundamental rights. It was argued:

> [I]nternational law is a legitimate and important influence on the development of the common law and constitutional law, especially when international law declares the existence of universal and fundamental rights. To the full extent that its text permits, Australia's Constitution, as the fundamental law of government in this country, accommodates itself to international law, including insofar as the law expresses basic rights. The reason for this is that the Constitution not only speaks to the people of Australia who made it and accept it for their governance. It also speaks to the international community as the basic law of the Australian nation which is a member of that community.[173]

These views were repeated and clarified the next year in *Kartinyeri v. Commonwealth*,[174] a case examining the extent of the Section 51(xxvi) power with respect to races. Justice Kirby stressed that the approach he advanced in *Newcrest Mining* did not involve the application of international law to distort the meaning of the Constitution. Rather, if the Constitution is clear

[171] Kristen Walker, "International Law as a Tool of Constitutional Interpretation" (2002) 28 *Monash Univ. L. Rev.* 85 at 91.

[172] (1997) 147 ALR 42; see also the previous decision in Wilson v. Minister for Aboriginal and Torres Strait Islander Affairs (1996) 189 CLR 1.

[173] (1997) 147 ALR 42 at 148, per Kirby, J.

[174] [1998] HCA 22.

and the law under consideration is clearly within the power of the Commonwealth Parliament, then "no rule of international law, and no treaty (including one to which Australia is a party) may override the Constitution or any law validly made under it."[175] In the case of an ambiguity, however, Justice Kirby was of the view that it was legitimate to have regard to international law,[176] and accordingly he took these matters into account when interpreting Section 51(xxvi) of the Constitution.

This approach of Justice Kirby toward constitutional interpretation has been repeated in subsequent cases where he has felt that the circumstances allow for appropriate reference to international law principles, especially those reflecting basic human rights as found in treaties.[177] However, this approach has not won general support within the High Court, and in the 2004 case of *Al-Kateb v. Godwin*, Justice McHugh, for the majority, rejected any reference to international law in Australian constitutional interpretation, asserting that the "courts cannot read the Constitution by reference to the provisions of international law that have become accepted since the Constitution was enacted in 1900."[178] While accepting that statutes can, subject to limitations be read consistently with international law, Justice McHugh claimed that it would be "heretical" to say that the Constitution should be read in the same way, as it would operate as a restraint on the grants of power that it confers.[179] Further, to interpret the Constitution consistently with international law would be commensurate with "amending the Constitution in disregard" of the provisions with respect to amendment found in Section 128.[180] Therefore, Justice Kirby's international law interpretative approach toward the Constitution has even less support within the High Court than do his arguments in support of reliance on treaties as an aid to statutory interpretation.

VI. IMPACT OF TREATIES ON AUSTRALIAN LAW: THE QUASI INCORPORATION OF INTERNATIONAL LAW

The *Project Blue Sky* decision carries with it several important implications for the impact of treaties on Australian law. The most obvious is that, where municipal legislation imports international agreements, conventions, and

[175] (1998) 152 ALR 540 at 599, per Kirby, J.
[176] (1998) 152 ALR 540 at 600, per Kirby, J.
[177] Austin v. Commonwealth [2003] HCA 3.
[178] [2004] HCA 37 at [62], per McHugh, J.
[179] [2004] HCA 37 at [66], per McHugh, J.
[180] [2004] HCA 37 at [68], per McHugh, J.

treaties, those international instruments have operative effect. This is not a new principle. What is significant is the weight this ruling has given to the CER Protocol and the consequent spotlight that it has thrown on the impact of treaties on municipal law. To that end, there are two relevant categories of municipal laws. The first are laws that are based, either substantially or partly, on international instruments and are clearly designed to give effect to international obligations. These types of municipal laws are well known, and the courts have experience in dealing with them as a result of the growing impact international treaties have on the everyday business of citizens, corporations, and government.[181] However, as Bill Campbell has noted, the "language of most international agreements is not suited to simple transportation into Australian law," and often the Commonwealth and, where necessary, state legislation will seek to adapt the international instrument to Australian conditions.[182] In the case of Commonwealth statutes, however, this will raise a constitutional issue as to whether the legislation is appropriate and adapted or whether there is proportionality with the international instrument. If not, then the law may be beyond the reach of the Commonwealth's Section 51(xxix) treaty-implementing power over external affairs.[183]

The second category of municipal legislation is where statutory authorities, government departments, and administrative decision makers are given directions to take into account the provisions of named international instruments or the international instruments to which Australia is a party. This was the situation that arose in *Project Blue Sky* under the BSA. This is not, however, an isolated instance in Australian law, and there are other Commonwealth statutes that make reference to international instruments without directly incorporating those treaties into Australian law.[184] Within these examples, it is possible to isolate some important distinguishing features.

[181] Illustrations in Australia are the Civil Aviation (Civil Liability) Act 1959 (Cth); World Heritage Properties Conservation Act 1983 (Cth); Diplomatic Privileges and Immunities Act 1963 (Cth); Charter of the United Nations Act 1945 (Cth).

[182] Bill Campbell, "The Implementation of Treaties in Australia," in Opeskin/Rothwell, *supra* note 15, 132 at 145. This was an issue that particularly arose in R. v. Poole; *ex parte* Henry (1939) 61 CLR 634 when the High Court was required to consider whether adjustment of metric measurements to imperial was acceptable.

[183] *See* the discussion of these issues in Richardson v. Forestry Commission (Tasmania) (1988) 164 CLR 261; Victoria v. Commonwealth (1996) 138 ALR 129.

[184] These instruments include Australian Postal Corporation Act 1989 (Cth), s. 28; Civil Aviation Act 1988 (Cth), s. 11; Customs Act 1901 (Cth), s. 269SK; Nuclear Non-Proliferation (Safeguards) Act 1987 (Cth), s. 70; s. 70(4) and (5) make express reference to the 1967 Treaty on the Non-Proliferation of Nuclear Weapons (1967) 7 ILM 809, [1973] ATS No. 3, and the 1980 Convention on the Physical Protection of Nuclear Material (1980) 18 ILM 1419; [1987]

First, in some instances, a statutory body is directed to perform its functions in a manner that is consistent with Australia's international obligations by way of reference to instruments relating to a particular subject matter,[185] or generally under any convention.[186] Second, a statutory or administrative decision maker may be required to act or to issue permits under an act consistent with either named conventions or under the terms of conventions that deal with a specific subject matter.[187] A similar and related category are those acts that require the minister to act in conformity with certain international obligations or to direct persons under the act to do so.[188] These two subcategories are distinguished with respect to the level of specificity given to particular treaties or categories of treaties or conventions. Third, there are acts that allow for an extremely broad import for international law and provide that the act is to apply subject to international obligations.[189]

In *Project Blue Sky* it was the second category of incorporation of international law into domestic law that applied. However, it was not until the High Court's judgment that the potential impact of this type of reference to treaties and other international agreements on municipal law was fully understood.

What is the effect on municipal law of the type of reference made to international law in the preceding examples? Ivan Shearer has referred to quasi incorporation of international law by reference to the manner in which a number of human rights instruments are referred to in Australian law and then attached to legislation as a schedule.[190] It would seem appropriate to

ATS No. 16; Ozone Protection and Synthetic Greenhouse Gas Management Act 1989 (Cth), s. 45 (5); Sea Installations Act 1987 (Cth), s. 13; Telecommunications Act 1997 (Cth), s. 366.

[185] *See* Air Services Act 1995 (Cth), s. 9 (3) which provides:

AA [Airservices Australia] must perform its functions in a manner that is consistent with Australia's obligations under:

(a) the Chicago Convention

(b) any other agreement between Australia and any other country or countries relating to the safety of air navigation.

See also Civil Aviation Act 1988 (Cth), s. 11.

[186] *See* Australian Postal Corporation Act 1989 (Cth), s. 28, which provides:

Australia Post shall perform its functions in a way consistent with: ...

(c) Australia's obligations under any convention.

[187] *See* the Customs Act 1901 (Cth), s. 269 SK (referring to obligations between Australia and another country that attach a rate of duty to the importation of goods); Nuclear Non-Proliferation (Safeguards) Act 1987 (Cth), s. 70, which refers to named treaties and conventions; Chemical Weapons (Prohibition) Act 1994 (Cth), s. 22, which refers to the 1993 Convention on the Prohibition of the Development, Production, Stockpiling and Use of Chemical Weapons and on their Destruction (1993) 32 ILM 800.

[188] *See* Ozone Protection Act 1989 (Cth), s. 45; Telecommunications Act 1997 (Cth), s. 366.

[189] *See* Sea Installations 1987 (Cth), s. 13.

[190] Shearer, *supra* note 16 at 55–57; see the Human Rights and Equal Opportunity Commission Act 1986 (Cth).

also extend this characterization to Section 160 of the BSA dealt with in *Project Blue Sky*. This is not an instance where international law by way of a treaty or agreement has been directly incorporated into municipal law by expressly making its terms part of the statute. Nor is this an example of a legitimate expectation arising from the ratification of an international instrument and imposing an obligation on an administrative decision maker despite the instrument not having been directly incorporated into domestic law. The BSA illustration squarely falls between these two and broadly falls within Shearer's notion of quasi incorporation.

However, as *Project Blue Sky* demonstrates, while the international instrument may not have been directly incorporated into municipal law, it still has a substantial impact. Requiring a statutory instrumentality to act in accordance with a state's international obligations without giving any precise direction as to which international obligations in particular may be relevant will potentially open the door for a vast array of international instruments to be considered when the ABA or even Australia Post undertake their activities.[191] This task is made even more difficult because of the uncertainty that exists as to the full extent of the international obligations imposed on Australia by conventions, treaties, and other agreements.

In the third example of quasi incorporation, where the legislation indicates that it is to operate subject to international obligations under international law, it is much more difficult to assess the overall impact. In these instances, the legislature does not provide precise guidance as to how the legislation is to be interpreted consistently with international law obligations. Difficult questions will arise as to whether as a result of the language used in the statute the international legal instruments prevail and provide an operating framework for all actions taken under the statute, or rather if the intention is merely that the spirit of the international instrument broadly apply. Here, international law will have its greatest impact because of the broad reference made to international obligations in general.

A feature of the debate within Australian courts since the mid-1990s over the impact of treaties and international law more generally is the growing tension among the justices of the High Court. At one end of the spectrum has been Justice Kirby, who has continually argued for a more liberal use of international law not only in statutory interpretation but also when

[191] *See* Australian Postal Corporation Act 1989 (Cth), s. 28; the predecessor Commonwealth statutory authority responsible for postal services in Australia was involved in an incident concerning international law in Bradley v. Commonwealth (1973) 128 CLR 557, when postal services were denied to a representative of the government of Rhodesia pursuant to an UN Security Council Resolution.

considering the Constitution; at the other end are judges such as Justices McHugh and Callinan, who favor a more conservative approach that gives little attention to international law unless statutes make clear that a treaty has been directly adopted into Australian law. These divergent views within the High Court, while not ultimately having a significant impact on the Court's jurisprudence because of Justice Kirby's views having such little sympathy among his fellow judges, has nonetheless resulted in from time to time a robust exchange of judicial views in some High Court judgments. Perhaps the strongest of these exchanges in recent times occurred in *Al-Kateb v. Godwin.*[192]

In this case, the High Court considered whether it was lawful for a stateless person, with no prospect of removal in the reasonably foreseeable future, to remain indefinitely in immigration detention in Australia. The stateless appellant had applied unsuccessfully for refugee status and had subsequently requested that he be removed from Australia. However, because no other state would accept him, he could not be removed. The key question was whether the mandatory detention provisions of the Migration Act of 1958 (Cth) ceased to apply where it was not "reasonably practicable" to effect an unlawful noncitizen's removal. The minority found in favor of that proposition, holding that, without clear language authorizing indefinite detention, the provisions of the act did not sustain the applicant's continuing detention. By contrast, the majority found that the language of the relevant provisions of the Migration Act required that an unlawful noncitizen be kept in detention until removal became possible.

The decision reflects polarized understandings of the relationship between international and domestic law, exemplified by the judgments of Justices McHugh and Kirby. Justice Kirby endorsed Justice Gummow's view that there are limits on the executive's power under the Constitution to detain aliens for the purposes of deportation or expulsion,[193] noting that conclusion is also supported by the common law presumption in favor of personal liberty and by international law.[194] Drawing on comparative jurisprudence, Justice Kirby argued that the High Court of Australia "should be no less defensive of personal liberty" than courts in the United States, the United Kingdom, and Hong Kong, which had all withheld a power of

[192] (2004) 219 CLR 562. The discussion which follows is partly drawn from Jane McAdam, Deborah Roach, and Donald R. Rothwell, "Australian Cases before Australian Courts and Tribunals Involving Questions of Public International Law 2004" (2006) 25 *Austrl. Y.B. Int'l L.* 377 at 384–86.

[193] *Id.*, at [140], per Gummow, J.

[194] *Id.*, at [150], per Kirby, J.

unlimited detention from the executive.[195] This view was strongly disputed by Justice McHugh, whose views on this matter were partly noted earlier. A significant basis of Justice McHugh's objection to relying on international law as an aid in constitutional interpretation seems to have been "the widespread nature of the sources of international law," which, in his view, makes it "impossible to believe that, when the Parliament now legislates, it has in mind or is even aware of all the rules of international law."[196] By contrast, Justice McHugh accepted that political, social, and economic developments since 1900 could be taken into consideration in constitutional interpretation. He regarded these as different from rules of international law, as rules are specific and, when so applied, would necessarily have an amending effect on the Constitution rather than simply adding "context."[197]

Justice Kirby countered these arguments, stating that he did not accept Justice McHugh's use of the term *rules* to describe his application of international law; rather, he relied on international law principles. "They do not bind as other 'rules' do. But the principles they express can influence legal understanding."[198] Furthermore, no matter what the historical position in Australia:

> [T]he complete isolation of constitutional law from the dynamic impact of international law is neither possible nor desirable today. That is why national courts, and especially national constitutional courts such as this, have a duty, so far as possible, to interpret their constitutional texts in a way that is generally harmonious with the basic principles of international law, including as that law states human rights and fundamental freedoms.[199]

Justice Kirby argued that the use of international law as an interpretive principle of the Constitution was simply another step in the evolutionary process of constitutional law.[200] International law developments were another change requiring adaptation, in the same way that the High Court had adapted the Constitution to changing times before,[201] and Justice Kirby noted that the constitutional courts of many other states followed this interpretative approach.[202]

[195] *Id.*, at [149], [156]–[161].
[196] *Id.*, at [65].
[197] *Id.*, at [71].
[198] *Id.*, at [173].
[199] *Id.*, at [175].
[200] *Id.*, at [169]–[170].
[201] *Id.*, at [178].
[202] *Id.*, at [184]–[185].

This robust exchange between two leading members of the High Court starkly illustrates the diverse views among the Justices on the role and place of international law before the courts, and especially what role, if any, it should play in constitutional interpretation.[203] It also serves to highlight how Justice Kirby's views on the ability of international law to broaden the ability of Australian courts to bring different approaches to the judicial function remain relatively isolated and have yet to attract much judicial support.

VII. CONCLUDING REMARKS

The history of treaties before Australian courts has been one of cautious engagement, with some unresolved uncertainty as to how precisely to deal with the potential international law offers. While the *Tasmanian Dam* decision remains one of the most significant in Australian constitutional history for not only the High Court but also the federation, it did not represent a wholesale overthrow of constitutional doctrine. The High Court was at pains in its ruling and in subsequent decisions to reinforce that both express and implied constraints on Commonwealth constitutional powers remained in place. This has indeed proved to be the case, and notwithstanding some instances of expansive reliance on the external-affairs power by the Commonwealth Parliament, it is difficult to argue that the scope of the treaty-implementation aspect of the power has been abused. In a similar vein, while the *Teoh* decision attracted considerable controversy, and notwithstanding some of the doubts cast over the decision by the latter ruling in *Lam*, the actual scope for the consideration of treaties by administrative decision makers remains narrow in scope and was never intended to create a legal obligation to apply treaty rights.

Treaties in Australian law will no doubt continue to play an important role, especially as Australia becomes more integrated into the global economy and as the Asia-Pacific region begins to take on some of the characteristics of the American and European marketplaces. This will inevitably result in an ever-increasing reliance on treaty standards for trade and commerce, which will no doubt be reflected within Australian law, which will in turn see the courts have more frequent encounters with treaties. Much of this adjustment to the Australian legal landscape will, however, be driven by the Commonwealth and the state parliaments, presenting the courts with little

[203] For an overview of aspects of this decision, *see* James Allen, "'Do the Right Thing' Judging? The High Court of Australia in Al-Kateb" (2005) 24 *Univ. Queensland L.J.* 1–34.

option but to engage with the treaties on which new laws have been made. Whether the Australian courts will, however, go to the next step and more actively engage with treaties as an independent source of law remains to be seen. Much will depend on the legacy of Justice Kirby's engagement with international law and treaties and whether a new generation of Australian judges pursue the same cause.

4

Canada

Gib van Ert

Associate, Hunter Litigation Chambers, Vancouver

If asked whether Canadian courts enforce treaties binding on the state at international law, most Canadian judges and lawyers would say no. Some might hesitate a little or qualify their answers. Many would not. They would explain that treaties are not part of Canadian law unless given domestic effect by legislation, and even then a court interpreting or applying such legislation is not, in fact, enforcing the treaty but simply giving effect to domestic law. There is much truth in this depiction of the Canadian approach. But there is also some generalization, even some simplification. While the orthodox account of the place of treaties in Canadian law retains much of its force today, it was elaborated at a time when Canada's engagement with international law and international law's engagement with the domestic laws of Canada and other states were more narrowly circumscribed. An accurate account of treaty enforcement in Canadian courts today must pay due regard to received doctrines while also considering the contemporary practices of Canada's judicial, legislative, and executive branches of government. Seen in this light, Canadian courts play an increasingly important role in enforcing the state's treaty obligations, though largely through such indirect means as interpretive presumptions and implementing legislation.

I. THE STATUS OF TREATIES IN CANADIAN LAW

The status of international treaties[1] in Canadian law is complicated by Canada's constitutional structure, which blends written constitutional

[1] The phrase "international treaties" will appear redundant to most readers but is necessary, in the Canadian context, to distinguish treaties governed by international law from those legal agreements, also known as treaties, which govern relations between Canadian governments (both federal and provincial) and Canada's aboriginal peoples. Aboriginal treaties enjoy a measure of constitutional protection in Canadian law under sec. 35(1) of the Constitution Act 1982, being Schedule B to the Canada Act 1982 (UK) 1982 c. 11.

provisions with unwritten doctrines and interpretive practices. Canada's Constitution is partially codified in a series of statutes enacted by the British Imperial Parliament, most notably the Constitution Act 1867[2] (which established Canada as a federation of British North American colonies) and the Constitution Act 1982[3] (which entrenched judicially enforceable human rights protections in Canadian law and removed the need for British involvement in constitutional amendments). Together, these enactments form the written Constitution of Canada. But they do not comprehensively codify Canadian public law. In particular, the Canadian Constitution includes unwritten elements derived from the British Constitution, upon which Canada's Constitution is based.[4]

A. *Treaty Making Is an Executive Act*

One such unwritten element is the royal prerogative. In British constitutional tradition, certain functions are recognized as belonging entirely to the Crown (i.e., the executive branch of government). Such royal prerogatives may be exercised without the need for parliamentary approval or even parliamentary involvement.[5] Among these prerogatives is the conduct of foreign affairs, including the negotiation and conclusion of treaties. In the absence of any express written provisions concerning treaty making (or foreign affairs generally) in the Canadian Constitution, treaty making in Canada is recognized by the courts as an exclusively executive function. This is consistent with British constitutional tradition.

The fact that treaty making is characterized as a royal prerogative is very significant. In Canada, as in other British-derived constitutional democracies, domestic laws cannot be made by executive action alone. They must be made by legislatures.[6] This rule is rightly seen as a fundamental constitutional doctrine on which the structure of Canadian representative government rests. By contrast, the royal prerogative over foreign affairs means

[2] 30 & 31 Vict. c. 3 (UK), reprinted in RSC 1985 App. II No. 5.

[3] Schedule B to the Canada Act 1982 (UK) 1982 c. 11.

[4] The preamble to the Constitution Act 1867 records the desire of the founding provinces "to be federally united into One Dominion . . . with a Constitution similar in Principle to that of the United Kingdom."

[5] *See* G. van Ert, *Using International Law in Canadian Courts*, 2nd ed. (Toronto: Irwin Law, 2008) at 92–102; J. Harrington, "Scrutiny and Approval: the Role for Westminster-Style Parliaments in Treaty-Making" 55 ICLQ 121, 136–41 (2006).

[6] *Case of Proclamations* (1611) 12 Co. Rep. 75, 77 ER 1352; *Archbishop of York and Sedgwick's Case* (1612) Godbolt 201, 78 ER 122; Bill of Rights 1689 (UK) 1 Will. & Mary sess. 1 c. 6 art. 1. Delegated forms of legislation, such as regulations, are no exception. Delegated legislative power is created by statute and is invalid if it exceeds its authority.

that treaties in Canada can be made by unilateral executive action. For this reason, Canadian courts have repeatedly declared that a treaty is not, in itself, a source of law on which litigants may directly rely. The best-known statement of this principle occurred in the judgment of the Privy Council in a Canadian appeal known as the *Labour Conventions* case.[7] Lord Atkin for the board observed:

> Within the British Empire there is a well-established rule that the making of a treaty is an executive act, while the performance of its obligations, if they entail alteration of the existing domestic law, requires legislative action. Unlike some other countries the stipulations of a treaty duly ratified do not within the Empire, by virtue of the treaty alone, have the force of law. If the national executive, the government of the day, decide to incur the obligations of a treaty which involve alteration of law they have to run the risk of obtaining the assent of Parliament to the necessary statute or statutes.[8]

This doctrine is the basis for Canada's so-called dualist approach to international law: for a treaty to take direct effect in domestic law without legislative action would violate the fundamental constitutional principle that laws are made by legislatures and not by the Crown. Canadian dualism is qualified, however. It does not extend to rules of customary international law.[9] And as we will see, it does not prevent judicial notice of treaties or judicial interpretive practices to ensure conformity with treaty requirements.

The location of treaty making in the executive is unproblematic in a unitary state such as the United Kingdom. Canada, however, is a federation of ten provinces, all of which have their own executives. The instrument that created Canada's federal structure, the Constitution Act 1867, was drafted at a time when the foreign affairs of Britain's colonies were conducted by the imperial government in London. The Constitution Act 1867 is therefore silent on whether, or how, the treaty-making power is distributed among Canada's federal and provincial executives. This lacuna has not been remedied in subsequent constitutional amendments. In practice, however, treaty-making authority in Canada is vested in the federal executive, partly through the acquiescence of the majority of the provinces and partly (perhaps more importantly) through the de facto recognition by other states that Canada's federal government is the proper treaty partner. Nevertheless, the

[7] *Attorney-General for Canada v. Attorney-General for Ontario* [1937] AC 326 (PC) (*Labour Conventions*).

[8] *Labour Conventions*, at 347. *See also Francis v. The Queen* [1956] SCR 618 at 621.

[9] Customary international law is incorporated directly into Canadian common law. *See* R. v. Hape, 2007 SCC 26, at paras. 36–39.

province of Quebec has long maintained that the treaty-making power is in fact distributed between the federal and provincial governments according to their legislative jurisdictions under the Constitution Act 1867.[10]

B. *Treaties Lack Direct Effect without Legislation*

The constitutional prohibition on executive lawmaking means that treaties concluded by Canada cannot in themselves be regarded as sources of domestic law. In most cases this rule presents no difficulty, for even today most treaties concluded by Canada (and other states) do not address themselves to the domestic laws of the parties. For those treaties that operate purely on the international plane, without requiring any domestic legal effect from the parties, the Canadian implementation requirement is a nonissue. But treaty practice underwent a remarkable change in the twentieth century. The frequency with which states committed themselves, at international law, to observing treaty-based standards in their own internal legal systems increased dramatically. The state practice of concluding such inward-looking treaties, which address not only the international legal order but also the domestic legal systems of the parties, shows no signs of abating in the present century. In Canada, treaties of this nature must be implemented by legislative action in order to take direct effect in Canadian law.

There is no set rule governing what kind of legislative action constitutes treaty implementation. Canadian legislative practice reveals a variety – some would say a bewildering variety – of ways in which legislatures choose to give direct effect to the state's treaty obligations in domestic law. The most obvious way, of course, is for the legislature to declare that the treaty has the force of law and perhaps, for convenience, to include the treaty's text as a schedule to the enactment. There are many examples of this type of legislation.[11] Another way to implement a treaty in Canada is to amend domestic law to bring it into conformity with the treaty's requirements,

[10] *See* G. van Ert, "The Legal Character of Provincial Agreements with Foreign Governments," 42 Les Cahiers de Droit 1093 (2001).

[11] *See, e.g.*, United Nations Foreign Arbitral Awards Convention Act RSC 1985 c. 16 (2nd Supp.) (approving the New York Convention, declaring it to have the force of law in Canada, and scheduling it); Family Relations Act, RSBC 1996 c. 128 s. 55 (granting the Hague Convention on the Civil Aspects of International Child Abduction force of law and requiring its publication in the BC Gazette); Trusts Convention Implementation Act, S.S. 1994 c. T-23.1 (providing that the Convention on the Law Applicable to Trusts and on Their Recognition applies in Saskatchewan and scheduling it); Intercountry Adoption (Hague Convention) Act RSPEI 1988 c. I-4.1 (giving force in Prince Edward Island to the Convention on Protection of Children and Co-Operation in Respect of Intercountry Adoption and scheduling it).

without expressly mentioning the treaty in the amending legislation. The international effect of this approach is to achieve Canadian compliance with the treaty. The treaty is therefore implemented in domestic law, even if it is not expressly mentioned in the enactment. This is a very common legislative method of implementing treaties in Canada.[12] Another way of ensuring domestic conformity with treaty obligations, in many cases, is simply to retain laws that predate the treaty but that, as it happens, suffice to discharge the state's responsibilities under the supervening treaty. Under this approach, which is frequently relied on in Canada in respect of human rights treaties, the preexisting legislation effectively becomes implementing legislation, even though it began life with no connection to the treaty.[13] Treaties can also be implemented in Canada by means of delegated legislation (such as regulations), provided that the parent legislation confers on the delegate the power to make whatever changes are necessary to meet the treaty's requirements.[14]

In short, Canadian legislatures (led by their executives) take a functional, not a formal, approach to treaty implementation. If a given legislative action (or inaction) suffices to achieve Canada's compliance with the treaty's requirements, that action will be taken (or not taken), without any legal requirement to annex the treaty as a schedule to an enactment, or refer to it by name, or do anything else that makes explicit the legislature's intent to give the treaty domestic effect. In theory, this approach is entirely satisfactory. On the international plane, it secures Canadian compliance with the treaty. On the domestic plane, in the absence of any constitutional or other legal requirement that legislatures follow a set pattern or procedure for

[12] *See, e.g.*, references to the "best interests of the child" principle of art. 3(1) of the Convention on the Rights of the Child 1989 [1992] CanTS no. 3 in the following statutes (cited by McLachlin CJ in Canadian Foundation for Children, Youth and the Law v. Canada (Attorney General) 2004 SCC 4): Immigration and Refugee Protection Act SC 2001 c. 27 ss. 25, 28, 60, 67, 68, and 69; Youth Criminal Justice Act SC 2002 c. 1 ss 25(8), 27(1), 30(3) and 30(4); Divorce Act RSC 1985 c. 3 (2nd supp) ss. 16(8), 16(10), 17(5), and 17(9); Family Relations Act RSBC 1996 c. 128 s. 24(1); Child and Family Services Act RSO 1990 c. C.11 s. 1(a); Children's Law Reform Act RSO 1990 c. C.12 s. 19(a). *See also* Criminal Code RSC 1985 c. 10 (3rd Supp.) s. 2, enacting s. 269.1 (torture offences) in implementation of Canadian obligations under the Convention Against Torture 1984 [1987] CanTS no 36.

[13] *See* E. Eid and H. Hamboyan, "Implementation by Canada of Its International Human Rights Treaty Obligations: Making Sense Out of the Nonsensical" in O. Fitzgerald, ed., *The Globalized Rule of Law: Relationships between International and Domestic Law* 449, 450 (Toronto: Irwin Law, 2006).

[14] *See, e.g.*, Pan American World Airways v. The Queen [1981] 2 SCR 565, Schavernoch v. Foreign Claims Commission [1982] 1 SCR 1092 and Benin v. Whimster [1976] 1 QB 297 (Eng. CA).

implementing treaties, this somewhat haphazard approach to treaty implementation is legally unobjectionable. In practice, however, the functional approach to treaty implementation in Canada risks confusion about the status of a given treaty in domestic law. In recent years, Canadian courts have declared certain treaties to be unimplemented simply, it seems, because the treaties were not mentioned expressly in any statute.[15] One might say, with some truth, that these judgments reflect a lack of sophistication by courts and counsel. The realities of Canadian treaty implementation are now well documented in the literature.[16] Furthermore, for a court to conclude that an inward-looking treaty (i.e., one that requires its parties to adhere to stated international norms in its domestic law) is unimplemented is tantamount to finding the state in breach of the treaty, a conclusion that Canadian courts presumptively avoid. It must be acknowledged, however, that the absence of formal rules on how treaties are implemented can create uncertainty about whether treaties have been implemented at all.[17]

As noted above, the implementation requirement is an inheritance from British law. Britain is a unitary state, or at least it was in 1867. Transposing the implementation requirement into Canada's federal context has generated controversy. Section 132 of the Constitution Act 1867 expressly provides that the federal Parliament has "all Powers necessary or proper for performing the Obligations of Canada or of any Province thereof, as Part of the British Empire, towards Foreign Countries, arising under Treaties between the Empire and such Foreign Countries." Otherwise, the written constitution

[15] *See, e.g.*, Ahani v. Canada (Minister of Citizenship and Immigration) (2002) 58 OR (3d) 107 (Ont. CA).

[16] *See* J. Keyes and R. Sullivan, "A Legislative Perspective on the Interaction of International and Domestic Law," in O. Fitzgerald, ed., *The Globalized Rule of Law: Relationships between International and Domestic Law* 277 (Toronto: Irwin Law, 2006); E. Eid and H. Hamboyan, "Implementation by Canada of Its International Human Rights Treaty Obligations: Making Sense Out of the Nonsensical," in O. Fitzgerald, ed., *The Globalized Rule of Law: Relationships between International and Domestic Law* 449 (Toronto: Irwin Law, 2006); G. van Ert, "What Is Treaty Implementation?" in *Legitimacy and Accountability in International Law: Proceedings of the Canadian Council of International Law 2004* 165–74 (Ottawa: Canadian Council on International Law, 2005); G. van Ert, *Using International Law in Canadian Courts*, 2nd ed. at 234-52 (Toronto: Irwin Law, 2008). *See also* Pfizer Inc. v. Canada [1999] 4 FC 441 (FCTD) per Lemieux J. at paras. 29–31 (affirmed (1999) 250 NR 66 (Fed. CA)), in which the learned judge describes the variety of ways in which the WTO and TRIPS Agreements were implemented in Canadian law.

[17] This uncertainty is exacerbated by the federal government's inexplicable refusal, in spite of years of campaigning by members of Parliament and academics, to adopt the practice (now well established in other Commonwealth jurisdictions) of accompanying Canadian treaty action with an explanatory memorandum setting out what legislative changes, if any, are necessitated by new treaty obligations.

is silent on treaty implementation. Since empire treaties are a thing of the past, Section 132 no longer has any practical effect. The modern rule, decided by the Privy Council in the *Labour Conventions* case,[18] is that treaty implementation is subject to the ordinary division of legislative powers under Sections 91 and 92 of the Constitution Act 1867. Thus, if the subject matter of a treaty falls within federal legislative jurisdiction, Parliament may implement it alone. If, however, the treaty falls partly or entirely within provincial legislative jurisdiction, it must be implemented by each provincial legislature. The effect of this rule has sometimes been to frustrate Canadian participation in treaties as a result of provincial objections.[19]

C. *Indirect Effects of Treaties*

Some observers contend that the Canadian implementation requirement prevents unimplemented treaties from having any effect at all in Canadian law. However, decided cases make clear that treaties do influence Canadian law indirectly, even in cases where they are not implemented, or at least are not implemented by the statutory provisions at issue in a given dispute. Canadian courts generally take judicial notice of the state's treaty obligations.[20] Having done so, they usually seek to harmonize domestic law with the state's international obligations by means of an interpretive presumption of conformity between domestic and international law. This presumption is discussed at length below. The undeniable effect of the presumption of conformity is to grant some measure of legal significance to the purely executive act of concluding a treaty with another state.

No Canadian judgment has ever attempted (explicitly at least) to reconcile the tension between the indirect effect given to treaties by the presumption of conformity and the constitutional fundamentals informing the implementation requirement. It seems that at least two factors prevent the presumption of conformity from being regarded as wholly inconsistent with the implementation requirement. First, there is only so much an interpretive

[18] *See supra* note 7.

[19] One of the most notorious examples is the International Convention on the Settlement of Investment Disputes, 575 UNTS 159. Canadian participation in this treaty has been delayed for over forty years due to resistance from certain Canadian provinces. All provinces are now supporting the treaty and Canada signed it on December 15, 2006. Ratification is expected shortly, following the passage of implementing legislation in all Canadian jurisdictions.

[20] The scope of this doctrine remains uncertain. *See* G. van Ert, "The Admissibility of International Legal Evidence," 84 CBR 31 (2005); and F. Bachand, "The 'Proof' of Foreign Normative Facts Which Influence Domestic Rules," 43 Osgoode Hall LJ 269 (2005).

presumption can do. If the treaty requires Canada to achieve certain results in its domestic law, then construing a given legislative provision to conform with that treaty may avoid a breach in that single instance but will not, in most cases, wholly relieve the government of the need to seek implementation of the treaty by legislation. Second, the presumption of conformity is rebuttable. If the provision under consideration is simply not amenable to a conforming interpretation, the court may find the presumption rebutted and leave it to the legislature to rectify any resulting treaty breach. Likewise, if the court finds that application of the presumption in a given case comes too close to granting the treaty direct legal effect without implementation, it may seemingly refuse to do so.[21]

While the presumption of conformity is well established in Canadian law, another type of indirect means by which treaties might take effect in domestic law has so far gained no traction. Courts in other Commonwealth jurisdictions have occasionally held that the state's ratification of a treaty may give rise to a legitimate expectation that the government will conform to it, particularly in the exercise of discretionary powers.[22] The majority of the Supreme Court of Canada rejected this approach in *Baker v. Canada*,[23] finding on the facts that the treaty at issue (the Convention on the Rights of the Child of 1989[24]) did not give rise to a legitimate expectation of specific procedural rights. The decision purported to leave open the question whether an international instrument ratified by Canada could, in other circumstances, give rise to a legitimate expectation, but commentators tend to regard *Baker* as implicitly rejecting the doctrine. Even if a Canadian court were, one day, to recognize a treaty as the basis of a legitimate expectation to certain rights, those rights would likely be procedural only, not substantive. This is because in Canada, unlike in other jurisdictions, the doctrine of legitimate expectations can give rise only to procedural rights.[25] Regardless,

[21] This is one possible interpretation of the position taken by Iacobucci and Cory JJ, dissenting, in Baker v. Canada (Minister of Citizenship and Immigration) [1999] 2 SCR 817, discussed below. There is, however, no Canadian case in which the court expressly found the presumption rebutted for this reason.

[22] *See, e.g.*, Minister for Immigration and Ethnic Affairs v. Teoh (1994–5) 183 CLR 273 (High Court of Australia); Tavita v. Minister of Immigration [1994] 2 NZLR 257 (NZ CA); R. v. Secretary of State for the Home Department, *Ex parte* Ahmed [1999] Imm LR 22 (Eng. CA); Thomas v. Baptiste [1999] 3 WLR 249 (PC). *But see also* R. (European Roma Rights Centre) v. Immigration Officer at Prague Airport [2004] QB 811 (Eng CA), Re Minister for Immigration and Multicultural Affairs, *ex parte* Lam (2003) 195 CLR 502 (HCA).

[23] [1999] 2 SCR 817, at para. 29.

[24] [1992] CanTS no. 3.

[25] Mt. Sinai Hospital Center v. Quebec (Minister of Health and Social Services) [2001] 2 S.C.R. 281, at paras. 22–38.

the absence of an internationally informed doctrine of legitimate expectations in Canadian law is little barrier to the reception of international legal norms in domestic law. While the legitimate expectations doctrine differs in theory from the presumption of conformity, in practice the two approaches achieve similar results.

II. TREATY INTERPRETATION IN CANADIAN COURTS

The international law of treaty interpretation is codified in Articles 31 to 33 of the 1969 Vienna Convention on the Law of Treaties (VCLT).[26] These articles are well known, but it is helpful to restate them before considering the extent to which they are given effect by Canadian courts.

Article 31(1) states the "[g]eneral rule of interpretation" that a treaty "shall be interpreted in good faith in accordance with the ordinary meaning to be given to the terms of the treaty in their context and in the light of its object and purpose." Article 31(2) elaborates on this rule by providing that the context of a treaty comprises, in addition to its text, any related agreement or instrument accepted by the parties as related to the treaty. Article 31(3) requires to be "taken into account, together with the context" subsequent agreements between the parties, subsequent practice establishing the parties' agreement regarding its interpretation, and any relevant rules of international law applicable in the relations between the parties. Article 31(4) allows for special meanings to be given to treaty terms where the parties so intend.

Article 32 states that the interpreter of a treaty may have recourse to "supplementary means of interpretation," including the preparatory work of the treaty (the *travaux préparatoires*) and the circumstances of its conclusion, in order to confirm the meaning resulting from the application of Article 31 or to determine the meaning where the interpretation according to Article 31 is ambiguous or obscure, or leads to a manifestly absurd or unreasonable result.

Article 33 governs the interpretation of treaties authenticated in more than one language, establishing that each language text is equally authoritative and that conflicts between texts that cannot be resolved by applying Articles 31 and 32 are to be resolved in favor of the meaning that best reconciles the texts, having regard to the object and purpose of the treaty.

[26] While the VCLT has not been universally ratified, it tends to be treated as largely a codification of customary international law. *See* A. Aust, *Modern Treaty Law and Practice* (Cambridge: Cambridge University Press, 2000).

A. *The VCLT in Canada*

Canada is a party to the VCLT.[27] As discussed below, the interpretive rules set out in Articles 31 and 32 of that convention have been recognized and applied by the Supreme Court of Canada and other Canadian courts. By contrast, VCLT Article 33 (on the interpretation of treaties authenticated in two or more languages) has received very little attention from Canadian courts.[28] This is surprising given Canada's bilingual and bijuridical legal culture, in which the problem of applying equally authentic English and French texts of domestic statutes and regulations arises with some frequency.[29]

The leading case on the application of VCLT treaty interpretation rules by Canadian courts is *Pushpanathan v. Canada (Minister of Citizenship and Immigration)*.[30] In that case, the Supreme Court of Canada sought to interpret the term *refugee* in light of Article 1F(c) of the 1951 UN Convention Relating to the Status of Refugees,[31] as implemented in Canadian law by the Immigration Act.[32] The appellant was a permanent resident of Canada who had been convicted of conspiring to traffic in narcotics. He sought refugee status while on parole. The federal government subsequently issued a conditional deportation order against him, the condition being that he could not be deported if he were found to be a Convention refugee. The claim was heard by the Convention Refugee Determination Division of the Immigration and Refugee Board, which decided that the appellant was excluded from refugee status by Convention Article 1F(c): "The provisions of this Convention shall not apply to any person with respect to whom there are serious reasons for considering that . . . [h]e has been guilty of acts contrary to the purposes and principles of the United Nations." This finding was upheld on judicial review in the Federal Court, Trial Division, and the Federal Court of Appeal.

In the latter court, Justice Strayer began by considering the rules of interpretation applicable to determining the scope of Article 1F(c) as implemented in Canadian law. His comments merit lengthy quotation:

[27] [1980] CanTS no. 37.

[28] *But see* R. v. Vincent (1993) 12 OR (3d) 427 (Ont. CA) (noting, in the course of interpreting art. III of the 1794 Jay Treaty, that VCLT art. 33(2) requires that only authentic versions of treaties be used when interpreting them, unless the parties agree otherwise).

[29] One commentator has noted the similarity between VCLT art. 33 and Canadian practice in resolving disparities between equally authentic legal texts. *See* J.P. McEvoy, "The Charter as a Bilingual Instrument," 64 Can. Bar Rev. 155, 169–70 (1986).

[30] [1998] 1 SCR 982 (*Pushpanathan*).

[31] [1969] CanTS no. 6.

[32] RSC 1985 c. I-2 (since repealed). For the current statute, *see* Immigration and Refugee Protection Act SC 2001 c. 27.

> [W]hile Canadian courts must respect domestic law where it is clearly inconsistent with a treaty to which this country is a party, where there is no clear conflict a court should try to give domestic law a meaning which is consistent with Canada's international obligations. This may lead the court into using interpretative aids as to the meaning of the treaty being implemented even where such aids might not be available for the simple interpretation of a domestic statute. Where a statute incorporates a treaty, it is treaty interpretation rules which should apply.
>
> . . . It is also appropriate if necessary, in interpreting [Article 1F(c)] to look at other provisions of the Convention which, though not incorporated in the *Immigration Act*, may assist in the interpretation of section F of Article 1.
>
> It is also accepted that in interpreting a treaty-implementing statute one may have regard to the treaty and the means for its interpretation even if the implementing statute is not on its face ambiguous. But none of the rules of interpretation of statutes or treaties authorize a court to ignore completely the express terms of the language finally adopted in the treaty or the statute, in favour of vague expressions of intention derived from extrinsic sources which fail to demonstrate ambiguity in the text of the treaty or adopting statute. This has particular relevance to the lengthy invocation, by counsel on both sides of this case, of the *travaux préparatoires* of the Convention. Counsel for the appellant himself recognized that *travaux préparatoires* are normally far from determinative and he suggested this should be even more so [in] the situation where the interpretation of a human rights treaty is involved. In the present case I have read the *travaux préparatoires* referred to and I find them completely unhelpful. It is difficult to understand fully the committee discussions of the earlier drafts of section F of Article 1 because in the excerpts provided it is not clear what was the exact text under discussion. Further, much of the discussion appears to relate to the contents of what became Article 1F(b) without specific reference to Article 1F(c). Also it is hazardous to assume that the meaning attributed to a text by one or two delegations in a multilateral international negotiation necessarily reflects the collective intention, if indeed there was a common intention. I believe it would be wrong to conclude that paragraph (c) was thought to be of little consequence: it embraces some of the specific language of section 2 of Article 14 of the *Universal Declaration of Human Rights* [GA Res. 217 A (III), UN GAOR, December 10, 1948], which delegates were attempting to implement.
>
> In such circumstances it is far safer to place the most emphasis on the final text as approved. That is conspicuously true in this case.

> It must also be kept in mind, when one seeks to infer the meaning of one provision of a treaty by reference to other provisions in that same treaty, that the drafting of multilateral conventions by the United Nations often lacks the discipline and cohesion imposed on the drafters of domestic Canadian laws. Thus, for example, it is not surprising to find in such conventions overlapping provisions without internal guidance as to which, if either, is to have paramountcy. It must be assumed, however, that every provision was intended to have some distinct purpose and meaning unless it is impossible to ascribe one.[33]

Applying this approach to the interpretation of Article 1F(c), Justice Strayer for the court held that the appellant was not a Convention refugee.

The Supreme Court of Canada allowed the appeal, finding that conspiring to traffic in a narcotic is not a violation of Article 1F(c). Justice Bastarache for the majority held that, in the absence of clear indications that the international community recognizes drug trafficking as a sufficiently serious and sustained violation of fundamental human rights as to amount to persecution, individuals should not be deprived of the essential protections contained in the Convention for having committed those acts.[34] On the interpretation of the Convention, Justice Bastarache began by observing: "Since the purpose of the [Immigration] Act incorporating Article 1F(c) is to implement the underlying Convention, the Court must adopt an interpretation consistent with Canada's obligations under the Convention. The wording of the Convention and the rules of treaty interpretation will therefore be applied to determine the meaning of Article 1F(c) in domestic law."[35] Justice Bastarache then quoted VCLT Articles 31 and 32 in full, noting that they had been applied by the court in two recent cases.[36] He added that the court had made use of such interpretive devices as the drafting history and preparatory work of the Refugee Convention, the *UNHCR Handbook on Procedures and Criteria for Determining Refugee Status*, and previous judicial comments on the object and purpose of the treaty.[37] Justice Bastarache then reviewed and rejected Justice Strayer's interpretive approach to the Convention, finding that he "erred in dismissing the objects and purposes of the treaty, and in according virtually no weight to the indications provided

[33] Pushpanathan v. Canada (Minister of Citizenship and Immigration) [1996] 2 FC 49 (Fed. CA) at paras. 10–14.
[34] Pushpanathan, *supra* note 30, at para. 75.
[35] Pushpanathan, *supra* note 30, at para. 51.
[36] Thomson v. Thomson [1994] 3 SCR 551, and Canada (Attorney General) v. Ward [1993] 2 SCR 689.
[37] Pushpanathan, *supra* note 30, at para. 53.

in the *travaux préparatoires*," adding that the "extremely general words in Article 1F(c) are not so unambiguous as to foreclose examination of other indications of the proper scope of the provision."[38]

Justice Bastarache described the "starting point of the interpretive exercise" as "to define the purpose of the Convention as a whole and, second, the purpose and place of Article 1F(c) within that scheme."[39] Relying on previous jurisprudence, Justice Bastarache found that the background against which interpretation of the Convention's individual provisions must take place is its "human rights character."[40] The learned judge then turned to the definition of *refugee* in Article 1, relying at length on the debates surrounding that article during the treaty's negotiation in the Social Committee of the UN Economic and Social Council. From these *travaux*, Justice Bastarache concluded that Article 1F(c) was intended by the delegates who negotiated it to identify "non-war-related crimes against humanity . . . even if the acts falling into this category could not be clearly enumerated at that time."[41] Justice Bastarache therefore held that the purpose of Article 1F(c) was to exclude those individuals responsible for serious, sustained, or systemic violations of fundamental human rights which amount to persecution in a nonwar setting.[42]

Having established the purpose of Article 1F(c), Justice Bastarache turned to the meaning of the phrase "contrary to the purposes and principles of the United Nations." He described the "guiding principle" as "where there is consensus in international law that particular acts constitute sufficiently serious and sustained violations of fundamental human rights as to amount to persecution, or are explicitly recognized as contrary to the purposes of and principles of the United Nations, then Article 1F(c) will be applicable."[43] Justice Bastarache looked to UN resolutions and International Court of Justice jurisprudence for the purposes and principles of the United Nations,[44] finding there to be "no indication in international law that drug trafficking on any scale is to be considered contrary to the purposes and principles of the United Nations," in spite of evidence of UN activity to stop such trafficking.[45] Likewise, Justice Bastarache found no indication that drug trafficking "comes close to the core, or even forms a part of the

38 *Id.*, at para. 55.
39 *Id.*, at para. 56.
40 *Id.*, at para. 57.
41 *Id.*, at paras. 58–60.
42 *Id.*, at para. 64.
43 *Id.*, at para. 65.
44 *Id.*, at paras. 66–68.
45 *Id.*, at para. 69.

corpus of fundamental human rights."[46] Finally, Justice Bastarache relied on the possible overlap between Articles 1F(b) and (c) with regard to drug trafficking as a basis for excluding that activity from the latter.[47]

The *Pushpanathan* case establishes the centrality of the VCLT to the interpretation of treaties by Canadian courts and tribunals. One may question, however, whether the interpretive model *Pushpanathan* provides truly conforms to the VCLT's requirements. Justice Bastarache's judgment is arguably too quick to turn to the *travaux*, which, it must be remembered, are described in Article 32 as "supplementary means of interpretation" to be resorted to in order to confirm the meaning resulting from the application of Article 31 or to determine the meaning when the interpretation according to Article 31 is ambiguous or absurd. One can sympathize with Justice Strayer's hesitation to rely on the *travaux* in the court below, although even his judgment appears to put the cart before the horse by ruling out reference to the *travaux* based not on the clarity of the treaty's terms, as interpreted according to Article 31, but on the lack of clarity in the *travaux* themselves.

Another leading Canadian case on treaty interpretation arguably conforms more closely to the VCLT method of starting with the treaty's ordinary meaning, then confirming that meaning, as necessary, through extrinsic materials. In *Crown Forest Industries Ltd. v. Canada*,[48] the respondent company withheld 10 percent tax on certain rental payments to another company, N, pursuant to Article XII of the 1980 Canada–United States Income Tax Convention,[49] claiming that N was a "resident of a Contracting State" (the United States) within the meaning of Article IV of the treaty. The appellant argued that N was not a U.S. resident, in spite of the fact that N's sole office and place of business was located in the United States, because it was a Bahamas corporation. The amount of withholding tax under the treaty was therefore 25 percent, not 10 percent.

Justice Iacobucci for the Supreme Court of Canada allowed the appeal, finding that N was not a U.S. resident and that therefore the 25 percent withholding tax applied. He stated: "In interpreting a treaty, the paramount goal is to find the meaning of the words in question. This process involves looking to the language used and the intentions of the parties. Both upon the plain language reading of Article IV and through an interpretation of the goals and purposes of the [treaty], I reach the same destination: to allow

[46] *Id.*, at para. 72.
[47] *Id.*, at para. 73.
[48] [1995] 2 SCR 802 (*Crown Forest*).
[49] [1984] CanTS no. 15.

the appeal."[50] Immediately following this passage is a lengthy consideration of the plain language of the treaty, in which the court affirms that a trial judge's interpretation of a treaty is a question of law, not a finding of fact, and therefore subject to appellate review.[51] Having established the plain language meaning of Article IV of the treaty, Justice Iacobucci went on to find his conclusion confirmed by "the intention of the drafters of the Convention" and the "goals of international taxation treaties."[52] The learned judge quoted approvingly a well-known Canadian statement on the interpretation of tax treaties by Justice Addy in *J. N. Gladden Estate v. The Queen*: "Contrary to an ordinary taxing statute a tax treaty or convention must be given a liberal interpretation with a view to implementing the true intentions of the parties. A literal or legalistic interpretation must be avoided when the basic object of the treaty might be defeated or frustrated in so far as the particular item under consideration is concerned."[53]

Next, Justice Iacobucci considered the object and purpose of the treaty, noting in passing that "a court may refer to extrinsic materials which form part of the legal context . . . without the need first to find an ambiguity before turning to such materials."[54] Among the extrinsic materials considered by Justice Iacobucci was the Organisation for Economic Co-operation and Development's *Model Double Taxation Convention on Income and on Capital*, which "served as the basis for the [Canada–United States treaty] and also has world-wide recognition as a basic document of reference in the negotiation, application and interpretation of multilateral or bilateral tax conventions."[55] To ascertain the object and purpose of the treaty, Justice Iacobucci also considered a report of the U.S. Senate Foreign Relations Committee on the proposed Canada–United States treaty.[56] Justice Iacobucci cited VCLT Articles 31 and 32 as authority for referring to extrinsic materials, but without specifying which article or sub-article he relied on in specific cases.[57] Having reviewed these materials, Justice Iacobucci concluded that N was not a "U.S. resident" as that term is used in the Convention.

While *Crown Forest* makes fewer express references than *Pushpanathan* to the VCLT's interpretation provisions, the methodology actually applied by the court in the former case seems to follow more closely the VCLT scheme,

[50] Crown Forest, *supra* note 48, at para. 22.
[51] *Id.*, at paras. 23–41, especially para. 38 (stating that treaty interpretation is a finding of law).
[52] *Id.*, at para. 42.
[53] [1985] 1 CTC 163 (FCTD) at 166–67.
[54] *Id.*, at paras. 43–67. On extrinsic materials, *see especially* para. 44.
[55] *Id.*, at para. 55.
[56] *Id.*, at para. 46.
[57] *Id.*, at para. 54.

starting with the treaty's express terms, viewed in their context and in the light of the treaty's object and purpose, then resorting to supplementary means of interpretation to confirm the textual meaning or to resolve textual ambiguity.

A number of other Canadian decisions might be cited illustrating judicial resort to the VCLT to interpret Canadian treaty obligations. Many of these cases arise from the interpretation of statutes implementing international tax treaties.[58] Extradition,[59] human rights,[60] and investment treaties[61] are other areas in which the VCLT has been cited. In many of these cases, references to the VCLT rules are brief and consist largely of affirming the need to interpret the treaty's provisions in their entire context or in light of the treaty's object and purpose. More specific applications of the VCLT rules are found in some cases, however. In *Coblentz v. Canada*,[62] the Federal Court of Appeal considered the interpretive weight to be given to a technical explanation accompanying Article XVIII of the 1980 Canada–United States Income Tax Convention. The explanation was prepared by the U.S. Treasury Department four years after the convention was signed and was endorsed by the Canadian Department of Finance. The court was satisfied that the explanation did not fall within VCLT Article 32 but debated whether it fell within Article 31(2) or 31(3). In *Bouzari v. Iran*, the judge admitted expert evidence on state practice in the interpretation of Article 14 of the 1984 Convention Against Torture[63] in order to determine whether states parties to that treaty recognized it as creating an enforceable obligation on them to provide a civil right of redress for torture – whether committed at home or abroad.[64]

In summary, Canadian courts take judicial notice of the VCLT and purport to give effect to its interpretive rules in construing treaties. The authority for doing so is well established and uncontroversial. In particular, the practice of resorting to *travaux préparatoires* is accepted – possibly more

[58] *See, e.g.*, MIL (Investments) S.A. v. Canada 2006 TCC 460 (TCC); Beame v. Canada 2004 FCA 51 (Fed. CA); Edwards v. The Queen [2002] 4 CTC 2202 (TCC) (in which the court mistakenly states that Canada is not a party to the VCLT but applies it anyway, following *Crown Forest*); CUDD Pressure Control Inc. v. Canada [1999] 1 CTC 1 (Fed. CA).

[59] *See, e.g.*, R. v. Parisien [1988] 1 SCR 950.

[60] *See, e.g.*, Bouzari v. Iran [2002] OJ no. 1624 (Ont. SCJ), *affirmed* (2004) 71 O.R. (3d) 675 (Ont. CA); Quebec (Minister of Justice) v. Canada (Minister of Justice) (2003) 228 DLR (4th) 63 (Que. CA).

[61] *See, e.g.*, Canada (Attorney General) v. S.D. Myers, Inc. 2004 FC 38 (FCTD).

[62] [1997] 1 FC 368 (Fed. CA).

[63] Convention against Torture and Other Cruel, Inhuman or Degrading Treatment or Punishment 1984 [1987] CanTS no. 36.

[64] Bouzari (Ont. SCJ), *supra* note 60, at paras. 44–56. *See also* (2004) 71 O.R. (3d) 675 (Ont. CA), at paras. 72–79 (the appeal in the same case).

so than the VCLT itself envisions. Especially outside the specialized area of international taxation, Canadian judicial resort to the VCLT might be criticized as somewhat superficial. This seems likely to change, however, as Canadian courts become increasingly accustomed to hearing submissions based on the state's treaty obligations.

B. *VCLT and Domestic Interpretive Rules*

The *Pushpanathan* case does not expressly state that the VCLT treaty interpretation rules take precedence over domestic interpretive practices, but one can readily infer that conclusion from the strong reliance on VCLT Articles 31 and 32 in that decision. Furthermore, at least two leading Canadian decisions expressly prefer the international law of treaty interpretation over domestic interpretive rules. The first is *Gladden v. The Queen*,[65] from which Justice Iacobucci quoted approvingly in *Crown Forest*, reproduced above. That case approved a previous decision, *Cruikshank v. The Queen*,[66] in which the court noted the usual domestic rule of strict construction of taxing statutes but held that the rule did not apply where a tax treaty was involved.

The second case preferring international over domestic law in treaty interpretation is *Re Regina and Palacios*,[67] a decision of the Court of Appeal for Ontario in which Justice Blair for the court adopted the following statement from O'Connell's *International Law*:

> The rules of municipal law for interpretation are not to be utilised unless they can be regarded as "general principles of law recognised by civilised nations." Hence, the restrictive rule of common law relating to literal interpretation has no place in international law. The dictionary meaning of words, and the rules of syntax, may be departed from to produce an "effective" result, but only when this is necessary.[68]

After reviewing the international law of treaty interpretation as set out by O'Connell, Justice Blair concluded that the "rules of treaty interpretation make it clear that the court is not bound by the common law canon of literal construction of statutes upon which it appears [the trial judge] may have relied." Thus liberated from common law interpretive principles, Justice Blair went on to give a more liberal meaning to Article 39(2) of the 1961

65 [1985] 1 CTC 163 (FCTD).
66 [1978] 1 F.C. 256 (FCTD).
67 (1984) 45 OR (2d) 269 (Ont. CA).
68 D.P. O'Connell, *International Law*, 2d ed. (1970) vol. 1, at 257.

Vienna Convention on Diplomatic Relations[69] than the usual Canadian common law interpretive rules might otherwise have permitted.

There is therefore authority in Canada for the claim that international treaty interpretation rules supplant domestic interpretive rules where the two approaches differ. Notably, however, the Supreme Court of Canada observed in *Thomson v. Thomson*, "By and large, international treaties are interpreted in a manner similar to statutes. This is evident from a perusal of Article 31 of the [VCLT]."[70] It is certainly true that the contextual and purposive approach adopted in VCLT Article 31 resembles accepted Canadian interpretive practice.[71] The court in *Thomson* noted one "significant difference" between international and domestic interpretive practices, namely "the use that may be made of legislative history and other preparatory material" in international practice.[72] Yet even that does not seem to be an important difference, given the increasing reliance by Canadian courts on records of legislative proceedings and other extrinsic material in the interpretation of domestic statutes and regulations.

C. *Interpretation of Treaties in Light of International and Foreign Judicial Decisions*

Canadian courts have, on occasion, considered the state's treaty obligations in light of pronouncements by international and/or foreign judicial or quasi-judicial bodies. Certainly there is no rule against doing so, and the potential relevance of such decisions is obvious. Furthermore, Canadian judges and lawyers are very familiar with comparative legal materials, given the long history of reliance on English and, to a lesser extent, Commonwealth and U.S. authority in common law matters. At the risk of generalizing, it seems that Canadian judges and lawyers do not – consciously, at least – take a parochial view of legal problems. The controversy that has developed in the United States in recent years concerning the propriety of American courts having regard to the judgments of international and foreign courts, has no parallel – and seemingly no resonance – in Canada. Having said this, there is little authority on the extent to which Canadian courts may or must pay heed to the decisions of international or foreign tribunals in the interpretation

[69] [1966] CanTS no. 29.

[70] Thomson v. Thomson [1994] 3 SCR 551 at 577.

[71] *Compare, e.g.*, Interpretation Act RSC 1985 c. I-21 s. 12: "12. Every enactment is deemed remedial, and shall be given such fair, large and liberal construction and interpretation as best ensures the attainment of its objects."

[72] Thomson, *supra* note 70, at 577.

of Canadian treaty obligations. While Canadian courts have occasionally cited foreign and international interpretations of treaties to which Canada is a party, they have offered little guidance on when or how to use such sources.

Perhaps the most remarkable example of a Canadian court relying on the decisions of international tribunals is *Mugesera v. Canada (Minister of Citizenship and Immigration)*.[73] In that case, the Supreme Court of Canada overruled in part its own prior decision in *R. v. Finta*[74] to conform with later decisions by the International Criminal Tribunals for Rwanda and the former Yugoslavia involving the international law of incitement to genocide and crimes against humanity. In the words of the court: "In the face of certain unspeakable tragedies, the community of nations must provide a unified response. Crimes against humanity fall within this category. The interpretation and application of Canadian provisions regarding crimes against humanity must therefore accord with international law. Our nation's deeply held commitment to individual human dignity, freedom and fundamental rights requires nothing less."[75] But *Mugesera* concerned customary international law, not treaty. It is therefore not strictly on point, although it certainly suggests that the Supreme Court of Canada is interested in the judicial decisions of international courts concerning Canada's international legal obligations.

The Supreme Court has also paid heed, at times, to the views of quasi-judicial international bodies. In the *Canadian Foundation* case,[76] both the majority and the dissent relied on the reports of UN treaty-monitoring bodies established under the 1966 International Covenant on Civil and Political Rights (ICCPR)[77] and the 1989 Convention on the Rights of the Child.[78] Other recent Supreme Court judgments have likewise referred to the reports and comments of UN treaty bodies.[79] Similarly, in the recent

[73] [2005] 2 SCR 91 (*Mugesera*).
[74] [1994] 1 SCR 701.
[75] Mugesera, *supra* note 73, at para. 178.
[76] Canadian Foundation for Children, Youth and the Law v. Canada (Attorney General) [2004] 1 SCR 76.
[77] [1976] CanTS no. 47.
[78] [1992] CanTS no. 3.
[79] *See* Health Services and Support – Facilities Subsector Bargaining Association v. British Columbia 2007 SCC 27, at para. 74 (citing the Human Rights Committee's concluding observations on Canada (1999) in respect of ICCPR art. 22); Sauvé v. Canada (Chief Electoral Officer) [2003] 3 SCR 519, at para. 133 (Gonthier J, dissenting, relies on certain General Comments of the Human Rights Committee concerning prisoner voting rights); Suresh v. Canada (Minister of Citizenship and Immigration) [2002] 1 SCR 3, at paras. 66–67 (considering General Comment 20 of the Human Rights Committee).

Health Services case,[80] the court referred to the work of the International Labour Organization's (ILO) Committee on Freedom of Association, Committee of Experts, and Commissions of Inquiry, noting the court's reliance on the "jurisprudence" of the first two bodies in a previous decision, *Dunmore v. Ontario (Attorney General)*.[81] In this respect, the court appears to have been following the trail blazed twenty years earlier by Chief Justice Dickson (dissenting) in *Re Public Service Employee Relations Act (Alta.)*,[82] where the chief justice relied on ILO committee interpretations of the ILO Convention (No. 87) on the Freedom of Association and Protection of the Right to Organize.[83] It is notable, however, that these occasional references to the decisions of international bodies proceed from no legal requirement that such decisions be considered and have given rise to no such rule or practice. No Canadian decision sets out, in a general or authoritative way, the interpretive weight to be given to treaty interpretations advanced by such international tribunals as UN treaty bodies, World Trade Organization panels, or even international courts.

In the case of multilateral treaties, the views of courts from foreign states parties ought to be of especial interest. Yet Canadian precedent for having regard to foreign interpretations of the state's treaty obligations is scarce. In *N. V. Bocimar S. A. v. Century Insurance Co. of Canada*,[84] Justice Addy held that a maritime law principle enunciated by the U.S. Court of Appeals for the Fifth Circuit should be applied in Canadian courts; he quoted with approval two English authorities[85] to the effect that courts applying rules elaborated by international agreement should strive for uniformity in interpretation. Similarly, in *Canadian Pacific Ltd. v. Canada*,[86] Justice Walsh observed:

> While it is true that this Court has the right to interpret the Canada-U.S. Tax Convention and Protocol itself and is in no way bound by the interpretation given to it by the United States Treasury, the result would be unfortunate if it were interpreted differently in the two countries when this would lead to double taxation. Unless therefore it can be concluded that the interpretation given in the United States was manifestly erroneous it is not desirable to reach a different conclusion, and I find no compelling reason for doing so.

[80] Health Services and Support – Facilities Subsector Bargaining Association v. British Columbia 2007 SCC 27, at paras. 69–79.
[81] [2001] 3 SCR 1016.
[82] [1987] 1 SCR 313, at paras. 66–71.
[83] [1973] CanTS no. 14.
[84] [1981] FCJ no. 1033 (QL) (FCTD).
[85] Stag Line Ltd. v. Foscolo, Mango & Co. et al. [1932] AC 328; Scruttons v. Midland (1962) AC 446.
[86] [1976] 2 FC 563, at 596–97 (FCTD).

Justice Walsh referred here to the U.S. Treasury rather than a U.S. court, but the principle is the same.

Both these decisions are somewhat dated. More recently, decisions from Ontario and Quebec concerning international air carriage have had resort to foreign decisions interpreting the treaties that underlie Canadian legislation in this area.[87] Particularly notable is the *Connaught* case, in which Justice Molloy reviewed several Canadian and foreign authorities on the question of whether a subjective or objective test should be applied in determining whether damage to Connaught's cargo had been inflicted recklessly within the meaning of Article 25 of the International Convention for the Unification of Certain Rules relating to International Carriage by Air (the Warsaw Convention).[88] On concluding that no binding Canadian decision decided the point, she turned to foreign authorities. She observed that the treaty's "objective of having uniform regulations limiting the liability of carriers would be seriously weakened if the courts of every country interpreted the Convention without any regard to how it was being interpreted and applied elsewhere. This potential problem supports an approach favoring consistency of interpretation among nations, rather than one in which each country applies its own domestic principles."[89] Justice Molloy therefore reviewed a number of foreign decisions on point, together with the text of the convention, its drafting history, and its protocols, from which she concluded that a subjective test must be applied.

There is much to be said for cooperation between the judicial and other authorities of states in the interpretation of international agreements. Yet despite the previously cited cases, the practice of having regard for foreign interpretations of common treaty obligations is regrettably infrequent in Canada.

D. *Deference to the Executive in Treaty Matters*

Canadian constitutional and administrative law contain a variety of doctrines setting out when, and to what extent, the courts will defer to the federal and provincial executives on questions of policy or even, on occasion, questions of law. There is, however, no doctrine in Canadian law requiring courts to defer to the executive in questions of treaty interpretation.

[87] *See* Recchia v. K.L.M. Lignes Aériennes Royale Néerlandaises [1999] R.J.Q. 2024 (Que SC); Connaught Laboratories Ltd. v. British Airways (2002) 61 OR (3d) 2004 (Ont. SCJ); Plourde v. Service Aérien FBO Inc. (Skyservice) 2007 QCCA 739 (Que CA).

[88] [1947] Can TS no. 15 (as amended by subsequent protocols).

[89] Connaught, *supra* note 87, at para. 46.

To the contrary, the interpretation of treaties is regarded as a legal question within the scope of the judicial function.[90]

The courts will, however, defer to the executive on the question of whether a treaty exists at all or is in effect as against Canada. In *Ganis v. Canada (Minister of Justice)*,[91] the appellant, appealing his extradition, argued that the existence of a valid extradition treaty between Canada and the Czech Republic had not been established. He sought to exploit a typo in certain agreements between the two countries that erroneously referred to a previous extradition treaty between the United Kingdom and Czechoslovakia. In making the extradition order, the minister of justice had relied on advice from the Canadian Ministry of Foreign Affairs that a treaty existed. Chief Justice Finch, for the Court of Appeal for British Columbia, rejected the appellant's argument. He explained:

> Our courts are sometimes asked to interpret a treaty's provisions and determine its domestic effect; that task, involving legal questions, is within the judiciary's expertise. A treaty's existence, however, is not an ordinary question of law but a highly political matter as between the executive of two contracting states. The Supreme Court of Canada has recognized this distinction, holding that "whether a treaty is in force, as opposed to what its effect should be, [is] wholly within the province of the public authority."[92]

Similarly, in *Château-Gai Wines Ltd. v. Attorney General of Canada*,[93] President Jackett considered whether a 1933 trade agreement between Canada and France had ever come into force. To prove that it had, the attorney general relied on certificates from the secretary of state for external affairs. President Jackett found these certificates to be "conclusive that the agreement did come into force as a binding international agreement at that time" and explained that, where doubt existed on the point, it should be resolved by resort to certificates from the executive in the same manner as courts determine other disputed questions of foreign affairs (e.g., whether a person is a foreign sovereign, whether persons must be regarded as constituting the

[90] *See, e.g.*, Pushpanathan v. Canada [1998] 1 SCR 982 (judicial review of immigration board's decision subject to a correctness standard, i.e. no deference to the executive's decision on the meaning of the treaty and its implementing legislation); Crown Forest Industries Ltd. v. Canada [1995] 2 SCR 802, at para. 38 (treaty interpretation a finding of law and therefore subject to appellate review).

[91] 2006 BCCA 543 (*Ganis*).

[92] *Id.*, at para. 24 (quoting Institut National des Appellations d'Origine des Vins et Eaux-de-Vie v. Chateau-Gai Wines Ltd., [1975] 1 S.C.R. 190, per Pigeon J. at 199).

[93] [1970] Ex CR 366.

effective government of a foreign territory, whether a particular place must be regarded as being in Canada or as being under the authority of a foreign sovereign authority, whether Canada is at peace or at war with a foreign power, whether a person in Canada is entitled to diplomatic privileges).

E. *Interpretive Significance of Treaties in Canadian Law*

As has been noted, when construing domestic laws Canadian courts apply an interpretive presumption that those laws conform to the state's obligations under treaties and other sources of international law. This presumption of conformity with international law has long been present in Canadian law but appears to be growing stronger following a series of important Supreme Court of Canada decisions invoking the presumption to resolve interpretive problems in a variety of domestic laws including ordinary statutes,[94] the Criminal Code,[95] the Civil Code of Quebec,[96] and even the constitutionally entrenched Charter of Rights and Freedoms.[97] In the past, resort to international treaties and the presumption of conformity has tended to be the preserve of appellate courts and lawyers. But the Supreme Court of Canada's increasing reliance on the presumption to dispose of appeals seems likely eventually to filter down to the lower courts. If so, the importance of treaties for judicial decision making in Canada will likewise increase, further eroding support for the proposition that treaties always require legislative implementation before taking effect in domestic law.

There is no clearer statement of the presumption of conformity with international law as understood and applied in Canada than the following passage from Justice LeBel's majority judgment in *R. v. Hape*:

> It is a well-established principle of statutory interpretation that legislation will be presumed to conform to international law. The presumption of conformity is based on the rule of judicial policy that, as a matter of law, courts will strive to avoid constructions of domestic law pursuant to which the state would be in violation of its international obligations,

[94] *See, e.g.*, Ordon Estate v. Grail [1998] 3 SCR 437 (presumption applied to determine the applicable limitation period).

[95] *See, e.g.*, Canadian Foundation for Children, Youth and the Law v. Canada (Attorney General) [2004] 1 SCR 76 (presumption applied in construing the so-called spanking defense to child assault).

[96] *See, e.g.*, GreCon Dimter v. J.R. Normand Inc. [2005] 2 SCR 401 (presumption applied to determine whether the Quebec court had jurisdiction in light of a choice of forum clause).

[97] *See, e.g.*, Health Services and Support – Facilities Subsector Bargaining Association v. British Columbia 2007 SCC 27 (presumption invoked as one of four reasons for overturning previous decisions excluding collective bargaining as a right constitutionally protected by the freedom of association guarantee in Charter sec. 2(d)).

> unless the wording of the statute clearly compels that result. R. Sullivan, *Sullivan and Driedger on the Construction of Statutes* (4th ed. 2002), at pg. 422, explains that the presumption has two aspects. First, the legislature is presumed to act in compliance with Canada's obligations as a signatory of international treaties and as a member of the international community. In deciding between possible interpretations, courts will avoid a construction that would place Canada in breach of those obligations. The second aspect is that the legislature is presumed to comply with the values and principles of customary and conventional international law. Those values and principles form part of the context in which statutes are enacted, and courts will therefore prefer a construction that reflects them. The presumption is rebuttable, however. Parliamentary sovereignty requires courts to give effect to a statute that demonstrates an unequivocal legislative intent to default on an international obligation. See also P.-A. Côté, *The Interpretation of Legislation in Canada* (3rd ed. 2000), at pgs. 367–68.[98]

This far-reaching description of the presumption of conformity makes at least three significant points.

First, the presumption is described as a rule of judicial policy – as opposed to an interpretive rule founded in the actual or presumed intent of the lawmaker whose law is in question. Thus, the presumption does not depend on finding that the legislature actually possessed any historical intent to conform to or not to conform to the international norm at issue. The legislature need not be shown to have had international law in its contemplation at the time of the enactment for the presumption to apply. Rather, it applies because Canadian courts choose to interpret domestic laws in conformity with international law. This policy-based approach to the presumption explains its occasional application by Canadian courts to legislation that predates the treaty with which the law is presumed to conform.[99] The policy-based approach is consistent with earlier Canadian and English cases,[100] and with the well-known Bangalore Principles.[101]

[98] 2007 SCC 26, at para. 53.

[99] *See, e.g.*, Canadian Foundation for Children, Youth and the Law v. Canada (Attorney General) [2004] 1 SCR 76 (presumption applied to interpret a Criminal Code provision in conformity with treaties that postdated it). *See also* Health Services and Support – Facilities Subsector Bargaining Association v. British Columbia 2007 SCC 27 at para. 78 (Canada's current international law commitments and the current state of international thought on human rights provide a persuasive source for interpreting the scope of the Charter, that is, it may be interpreted in the light of treaties, etc., that postdate it).

[100] *See* Zingre v. The Queen [1981] 2 SCR 392 and Corocraft v. Pan American Airways [1968] 3 WLR 1273 (Eng. CA), both describing it as the court's duty to interpret domestic law consistently with international law.

[101] *See* "The Challenge of Bangalore: Making Human Rights a Practical Reality" in *Developing Human Rights Jurisprudence*, vol. 8 (London: INTERIGHTS & Commonwealth Secretariat, 2001) at 267–70.

Second, the values and principles of international law (including treaties) are said to form part of the context in which statutes are enacted. The significance of this lies in its consistency with the general Canadian law of statutory interpretation. There is perhaps no better-established Canadian legal doctrine than the so-called modern approach to statutory interpretation, according to which the words of an Act are to be read in their entire context and in their grammatical and ordinary sense harmoniously with the scheme of the Act, the object of the Act, and the intention of Parliament.[102] In *Hape*, Justice LeBel indicates that international treaties and custom form part of the entire context in which legislation is to be interpreted.

Third, the presumption of conformity with international law is rebuttable. As previously noted, the constitutional doctrine of parliamentary sovereignty makes this conclusion inescapable. Nothing in the written constitution of Canada prevents Canadian legislatures from enacting laws contrary to the state's obligations under treaties or rules of customary international law. While the Supreme Court of Canada has at times suggested that legislation may be judicially reviewed for inconsistency with certain unwritten constitutional principles,[103] the orthodoxy is that Canadian legislatures may do anything not expressly prohibited by the written constitution. While *Hape* and other cases affirm the sovereignty of Canadian legislatures to violate international law, they also insist on applying the presumption of conformity to avoid such interpretations where possible. The inevitable question is, How far will the courts go in asserting the presumption? In *Hape* the answer (in obiter, at least) is, "Very far." Justice LeBel says the presumption applies "unless the wording of the statute clearly compels" an internationally unlawful result, and that the legislature must demonstrate "an unequivocal legislative intent to default on an international obligation." It is notable that few Canadian decisions have ever found the presumption of conformity with international law to be rebutted.[104]

F. *Ambit of the Presumption*

Justice LeBel's description of the presumption of conformity in *Hape* suggests its broad application in a variety of instances. The presumption's wide

[102] Rizzo & Rizzo Shoes Ltd. (Re) [1998] 1 SCR 27, at para. 21.

[103] *See, e.g., Re Secession of Quebec* [1998] 2 SCR 217.

[104] *But see* Co-operative Committee on Japanese Canadians v. Attorney General for Canada [1947] AC 87 (PC) (Privy Council found that wartime conditions rebutted the presumption of conformity with principles of international law prohibiting the forcible removal of British subjects of Japanese descent to Japan).

ambit in Canadian law is confirmed by decided cases. There are a number of ways in which the presumption might theoretically be constrained. In almost every case, these theoretical restraints have been rejected, either implicitly or explicitly, in favor of a far-reaching application of the doctrine.

The presumption seemingly applies with respect to all treaties to which the state is bound. While this point has never been expressly made in a Canadian case, it surely goes without saying. All treaties to which the state is a party are equally binding as a matter of international law and should therefore equally benefit from the presumption of conformity in domestic law. No Canadian case has ever declined to apply the presumption of conformity in respect of a binding Canadian treaty obligation on the ground that the presumption does not or ought not apply to that particular treaty.

The presumption applies with respect to a wide variety of domestic laws. It applies not only to statutes enacted by legislatures but also to regulations promulgated by statutory authority.[105] In England, the presumption has also been applied to instruments made under the royal prerogative,[106] and there is no reason to think that it would not also do so in Canada. Whether the presumption applies to Canadian common law is less certain. To presume that the common law conforms to the state's treaty obligations may, in some cases, come perilously close to dispensing with the constitutional requirement that treaties be implemented before taking direct effect in domestic law. English courts have seemingly accepted that the presumption may apply both to statutes and to the common law.[107] Canadian courts have not yet gone that far. English and Canadian courts are agreed, however, that the presumption applies not only to legislation purporting to implement a treaty but also to other legislation, whether or not expressly stated as implementing a given treaty.[108] Finally, the presumption appears to apply equally to federal and provincial statutes, in spite of the fact that the treaty-making power is de facto federal.[109] No Canadian court has ever declined to apply the presumption of conformity on the ground that provincial legislation is not to be presumed to conform to federally made treaties. That

[105] *See supra* note 14.

[106] Post Office v. Estuary Radio [1968] 2 QB 740 (CA).

[107] See R. v Lyons [2002] UKHL 44, at para. 27.

[108] *See, e.g.*, Canadian Foundation for Children, Youth and the Law v. Canada (Attorney General) [2004] 1 SCR 76 (presumption applied to a Criminal Code provision adopted decades before the treaties in question were negotiated).

[109] Examples of the presumption applied to provincial laws include *Re* Foreign Legations [1943] SCR 209; 114957 Canada Ltée (Spraytech, Société d'arrosage) v. Hudson (Town) [2001] 2 SCR 241; and GreCon Dimter Inc. v. J.R. Normand Inc. [2005] 2 SCR 401.

is not to say, however, that no court will ever do so. The possibility of a treaty-compliant interpretation of a provincial statute being found objectionable on federalism grounds is remote but may nevertheless be real.

Perhaps the most important example of a Canadian court rejecting a supposed limitation on the ambit of the presumption of conformity is the *National Corn Growers* case.[110] The question before the court was whether an administrative tribunal had erred by having regard to a treaty, the General Agreement on Tariffs and Trade of 1947,[111] in interpreting a federal statute. Decided cases in Canada and England had, at times, held that courts could not invoke a treaty for interpretive purposes unless the statute under consideration was first determined to be ambiguous on its face.[112] Absent such ambiguity, the statute had to be interpreted literally, without resort to the treaty and without regard to the international consequences of the resulting interpretation. The majority of the court of appeal in *National Corn Growers* applied this supposed rule. Justice Gonthier, for the majority of the Supreme Court of Canada, rejected this approach, holding instead that a court or tribunal may make reference to an international agreement at the very outset of the inquiry to determine whether there is any ambiguity, patent or latent, in the domestic legislation. Justice Gonthier wrote:

> I share the appellants' view that in circumstances where the domestic legislation is unclear it is reasonable to examine any underlying international agreement. In interpreting legislation which has been enacted with a view towards implementing international obligations, as is the case here, it is reasonable for a tribunal to examine the domestic law in the context of the relevant agreement to clarify any uncertainty. Indeed where the text of the domestic law lends itself to it, one should also strive to expound an interpretation which is consonant with the relevant international obligations.
>
> . . . [M]ore specifically, it is reasonable to make reference to an international agreement at the very outset of the inquiry to determine if there is any ambiguity, even latent, in the domestic legislation. The Court of Appeal's suggestion that recourse to an international treaty is only available where the provision of the domestic legislation is ambiguous on its face is to be rejected.[113]

[110] National Corn Growers Association v Canada (Import Tribunal) [1990] 2 SCR 1324 (*National Corn Growers*).

[111] [1948] CanTS no. 31.

[112] *See, e.g.*, Capital Cities Communications Inc. v. Canadian Radio-Television Commission [1978] 2 SCR 141 (*Capital Cities*).

[113] *National Corn Growers, supra* note 110, at 1372–73.

The court then quoted at length from Ian Brownlie's treatise on international law to support this point:

> If the convention may be used on the correct principle that the statute is intended to implement the convention then, it follows, the latter becomes a proper aid to interpretation, and, more especially, may reveal a latent ambiguity in the text of the statute even if this was 'clear in itself'. Moreover, the principle or presumption that the Crown does not intend to break an international treaty must have the corollary that the text of the international instrument is a primary source of meaning or 'interpretation'. The courts have lately accepted the need to refer to the relevant treaty even in the absence of ambiguity in the legislative text when taken in isolation.[114]

Since *National Corn Growers*, the so-called ambiguity requirement has largely disappeared from Canadian law. Courts need not justify their resort to relevant treaties binding on the state by purporting to find some patent ambiguity on the face of the legislation, but may instead (as *R. v. Hape* confirms) regard international instruments as part of the legal context in which statutes are enacted.

G. *The Presumption and Discretionary Decision Making*

The foregoing discussion indicates the extent to which interpretive resort to treaties has become an accepted part of Canadian judicial practice. There remain, however, at least two areas of Canadian law in which the presumption of conformity remains uncertain, if not controversial. The first area is administrative law, and more particularly the application of the presumption in cases where an administrative decision maker exercises statutory discretion.

In principle, a statute that grants an administrative decision maker the power to make discretionary decisions ought to be construed, like other Canadian statutes, according to the presumption that it conforms to Canadian treaty obligations and other rules of international law binding on the state. There is a problem, however, in applying the presumption to such statutes: to do so introduces an additional ground for judicial review of discretionary decisions, one based on the conformity or lack of conformity of the decision with the state's treaty obligations. The effect, potentially at least, is to curtail the statutorily granted discretion in a significant way.

[114] *Id.*, at 1372–73 (quoting I. Brownlie, *Principles of Public International Law*, at 51 (3d ed. 1979)).

Furthermore, where the treaty relied on by the litigant challenging the discretionary decision is not expressly implemented by statute in Canadian law, the constitutional objection may arise that to supervise the decision maker's discretion by resort to that treaty is to give direct effect to the treaty without legislative action, contrary to the constitutional requirement that treaties be implemented in domestic law before changing the law or affecting private rights.

Two decisions of the Supreme Court of Canada have considered this problem, though in both cases somewhat obliquely. In *Capital Cities*,[115] petitioners sought judicial review of the decision of a licensing body to alter the license of a cable television provider. The altered license permitted the provider to replace advertisements on U.S.-based television channels with public service announcements. The regulator's power to alter the license in this way was based on a federal statute.[116] The treaty in question allegedly required states parties not to interfere with other states' broadcasts.[117] Whether the treaty was implemented in federal law was disputed. The majority of the court found that the treaty was not implemented in Canadian law and could not prevail against the express stipulations of the Act. Against this conclusion, Justice Pigeon, for himself and two other dissenting judges, argued that the licensing body could not grant licenses contrary to Canadian treaty commitments. Even if the treaty were not implemented, said the dissent, "It is an oversimplification to say that treaties are of no legal effect unless implemented by legislation."[118] The dissent would have accepted the appellants' argument that the presumption of conformity restrained the licensing body from acting inconsistently with Canada's treaty obligations.

Over twenty years later, the application of the presumption of conformity to discretionary decision-making powers arose again in *Baker v. Canada*.[119] The case concerned a Jamaican woman whom the federal government sought to deport for overstaying her visitor's visa by several years. She sought to apply for permanent residence in Canada but could not do so from within the country without an exemption from the minister, pursuant to a discretionary power exercisable on humanitarian and compassionate grounds. The minister declined to make the exemption. Baker challenged this decision arguing, among other things, that it unreasonably failed to

115 *Capital Cities*, *supra* note 112.
116 Broadcasting Act SC 1967–68 c. 25 s. 17(1).
117 Inter-American Radiocommunications Convention 1937 [1938] CanTS no. 18.
118 *Capital Cities*, *supra* note 112, at 188.
119 [1999] 2 SCR 817 (*Baker*).

give sufficient weight to the interests of her Canadian-born children, contrary to Canada's obligations under the 1989 Convention on the Rights of the Child.[120] The federal government argued (implausibly, given the legislative record)[121] that that treaty was not implemented in Canadian law. The majority of the Supreme Court of Canada accepted that conclusion but held nevertheless that the minister's decision was an unlawful exercise of discretion because, among other reasons, it unreasonably neglected certain considerations, including Canada's obligations under the Convention. While the majority did not depict this aspect of its decision as an application of the presumption of conformity with international law, that was its effect.[122]

In separate reasons, Justice Iacobucci (with Justice Cory concurring) agreed with the majority's disposition of the case but sounded the alarm about its resort to international law to control the minister's decision, saying in part:

> It is a matter of well-settled law that an international convention ratified by the executive branch of government is of no force or effect within the Canadian legal system until such time as its provisions have been incorporated into domestic law by way of implementing legislation: *Capital Cities Communications Inc. v. Canadian Radio-Television Commission*. . . . I do not agree with the approach adopted by my colleague, wherein reference is made to the underlying values of an unimplemented international treaty in the course of the contextual approach to statutory interpretation and administrative law, because such an approach is not in accordance with the Court's jurisprudence concerning the status of international law within the domestic legal system.
>
> In my view, one should proceed with caution in deciding matters of this nature, lest we adversely affect the balance maintained by our Parliamentary tradition, or inadvertently grant the executive the power to bind citizens without the necessity of involving the legislative branch. I do not share my colleague's confidence that the Court's precedent in *Capital Cities*

[120] [1992] CanTS no. 3.

[121] Numerous amendments were made to federal and provincial statutes as a result of Canada's accession to the Convention. In its *First Report on the Convention on the Rights of the Child* (1994) CRC/C/11/Add.3 at para. 27, the government of Canada reported to the Committee on the Rights of the Child (under the heading "Implementation by states: Article 4") that Canada had "taken measures of a constitutional, legislative, administrative and other nature to implement the rights set forth in the Convention."

[122] Subsequent Supreme Court of Canada decisions have depicted *Baker* as a presumption case. *See* R. v. Sharpe [2001] 1 SCR 45, at para. 175; and 114957 Canada Ltée (Spraytech, Société d'arrosage) v. Hudson (Town) [2001] 2 SCR 241, at para. 30.

> . . . survives intact following the adoption of a principle of law which permits reference to an unincorporated convention during the process of statutory interpretation. Instead, the result will be that the appellant is able to achieve indirectly what cannot be achieved directly, namely, to give force and effect within the domestic legal system to international obligations undertaken by the executive alone that have yet to be subject to the democratic will of Parliament.
>
> The primacy accorded to the rights of children in the Convention, assuming for the sake of argument that the factual circumstances of this appeal are included within the scope of the relevant provisions, is irrelevant unless and until such provisions are the subject of legislation enacted by Parliament.[123]

The basis of Justice Iacobucci's objection to the use of international law is not immediately clear. There was nothing new in "the adoption of a principle of law which permits reference to an unincorporated convention during the process of statutory interpretation." That is simply the presumption of conformity as it has been applied many times, including by Justice Iacobucci himself in *Ordon Estate v. Grail*.[124] There is a difference, however, between *Baker* and other cases: in *Baker*, as in *Capital Cities*, the application of the presumption introduces international law as a basis for judicial review of administrative decision making even in the absence of any statute permitting international law to control discretionary decisions in this way.[125] That appears to be Justice Iacobucci's real concern in *Baker*. Seen in this light, it is hard to disagree with him that the precedent in *Capital Cities* is undone by the majority's decision in *Baker*.

That may not be a bad thing. Subjecting administrative decisions to the requirement that they conform to the state's treaty obligations is consistent with the judicial policy in favor of conforming interpretations of domestic law and serves to prevent treaty breaches by administrative action. There may be some cases where applying the presumption of conformity in this way takes Canadian law too far away from its traditional constitutional position of requiring legislative implementation of treaties before giving them direct effect in domestic law. But instead of adopting an absolute rule on the point, Canadian law may be better served by considering the matter on a case-by-case basis. *Baker* dealt with the issue too abstractly to be

[123] *Baker*, *supra* note 119, at paras. 79–81.

[124] [1998] 3 SCR 437.

[125] The problem has arisen in other Commonwealth jurisdictions. *See*, *e.g.*, R. v. Secretary of State for the Home Department, *ex parte* Brind [1991] 1 AC 696 (HL); and Ashby v. Minister of Immigration [1981] 1 NZLR 222 (NZ CA).

considered the last word (or perhaps even binding authority) on the point. One must conclude that the application of the presumption of conformity to Canadian administrative decision making remains uncertain. Given the Supreme Court of Canada's resounding endorsement of the presumption in *R. v. Hape*, however, it seems likely that it applies in the interpretation of the powers granted by statute to administrative decision makers. Unless that presumption is rebutted in a given case, conformity with treaties and other sources of Canadian international legal obligations must be regarded as an implicit limit on the powers of administrative decision makers in this country.[126]

H. *The Presumption and the Charter*

The second area of Canadian law in which the presumption of conformity with treaties and other forms of international law is controversial (or perhaps was until very recently) is the Canadian Charter of Rights and Freedoms,[127] the country's leading human rights instrument. Ever since its adoption as part of the written constitution of Canada in 1982, academics and commentators have debated the extent to which the Charter can properly be regarded as implementing legislation for Canadian human rights treaties, chiefly the International Covenant on Civil and Political Rights (ICCPR).[128] As neither the Charter nor any other Canadian law expressly implements the ICCPR or Canada's other human rights treaties,[129] the question of how Canadian law discharges the state's international human rights commitments has often arisen.[130]

[126] For a recent case in which the presumption of conformity was applied to a statutory discretion to control its exercise consistently with the Convention on the Rights of the Child, *see* Munar v. Canada (Minister of Citizenship and Immigration) 2005 FC 1180 (FCTD).

[127] Constitution Act 1982 part I (Canadian charter of rights and freedoms), being Schedule B to the Canada Act 1982 (UK) 1982 c. 11.

[128] [1976] CanTS no. 47.

[129] Canada is a party to most UN human rights treaties, including the ICCPR, the International Covenant on Economic, Social, and Cultural Rights 1966 [1976] CanTS no. 46, the International Covenant on the Elimination of All Forms of Racial Discrimination 1965 [1970] CanTS no. 28, the Convention on the Elimination of All Forms of Discrimination against Women 1979 [1982] CanTS no. 31, the Convention against Torture and Other Cruel, Inhuman or Degrading Treatment or Punishment 1984 [1987] CanTS no. 36 and the Convention on the Rights of the Child 1989 [1992] CanTS no. 3.

[130] *See* M. Freeman and G. van Ert, *International Human Rights Law* (Toronto: Irwin Law, 2004), esp. chaps. 9–10; W. Schabas and S. Beaulac, *International Human Rights and Canadian Law: Legal Commitment, Implementation and the Charter* (Toronto: Thompson Carswell, 2007); E. Eid and H. Hamboyan, "Implementation by Canada of Its International

Until recently, it was uncertain whether the presumption of conformity applied to the Charter in the same way as it does to ordinary (i.e., non-constitutional) statutes. No majority judgment of the Supreme Court of Canada had clearly applied the presumption to the Charter. The reasons for not doing so have been speculated on, and in some cases shored up by, academics and other commentators.[131] They included the textual disparities between some Charter provisions and their treaty counterparts, the fact that some human rights treaties postdate the Charter, and the concern that to presume that the Charter conforms to international human rights treaties may effectively entrench those treaties in the constitution without formal constitutional amendment.

Opposition to presuming the Charter to be consistent with international human rights law was not uniform, however. The most important proponent of an internationally compliant Charter was Chief Justice Dickson, Canada's first chief justice of the Charter era. In his dissenting reasons in *Re Public Service Employee Relations Act (Alta.)*, Chief Justice Dickson wrote: "The content of Canada's international human rights obligations is, in my view, an important indicia of the meaning of the 'full benefit of the *Charter*'s protection.' I believe the *Charter* should generally be presumed to provide protection at least as great as that afforded by similar provisions in international human rights documents which Canada has ratified."[132] Read in isolation from the rest of his judgment, this passage seems like an unqualified endorsement of the application of the presumption of conformity to the Charter. In the context of Chief Justice Dickson's entire judgment, however, the passage is less clear. The chief justice invoked presumption-like language at some points. But in other passages he seemed to equate Canadian human rights treaties with foreign law and to regard all such sources as relevant and persuasive rather than presumptively conformed with by Canadian law. In a later decision, *Slaight Communications Inc. v. Davidson*,[133] Chief Justice

Human Rights Treaty Obligations: Making Sense out of the Nonsensical," in O. Fitzgerald, ed., *The Globalized Rule of Law: Relationships between International and Domestic Law* 449 (Toronto: Irwin Law, 2006); I. Weiser, "Effect in Domestic Law of International Human Rights Treaties Ratified without Implementing Legislation," in *The Impact of International Law on the Practice of Law in Canada. Proceedings of the 27th Annual Conference of the Canadian Council on International Law, Ottawa October 15–17, 1998* 132 (The Hague: Kluwer Law International, 1999).

[131] *See, e.g.*, A. Warner La Forest, "Domestic Application of International Law in Charter Cases: Are We There Yet?" 37 UBC LR 157 (2004); and I. Weiser, "Undressing the Window: Treating International Human Rights Law Meaningfully in the Canadian Commonwealth System," 37 UBC LR 113 (2004).

[132] [1987] 1 SCR 313 at 349.

[133] [1989] 1 SCR 1038 at 1056.

Dickson carefully lifted the presumption-friendly passages out from the earlier case, quoting them only. This time he spoke for the majority of the court, yet even this restatement of the presumption did not suffice to establish it as an accepted interpretive tool in Charter interpretation.[134]

Though it may be too early to say, two recent decisions of the Supreme Court of Canada, released one day apart, appear to establish the court's determination to subject the Charter to the same presumption of conformity that is applicable to the rest of Canadian law. In *R. v. Hape*, the majority of the court stated, under the heading "Conformity with International Law as an Interpretive Principle of Domestic Law":

> Wherever possible, [this court] has sought to ensure consistency between its interpretation of the *Charter*, on the one hand, and Canada's international obligations and the relevant principles of international law, on the other....
>
> In interpreting the scope of application of the *Charter*, the courts should seek to ensure compliance with Canada's binding obligations under international law where the express words are capable of supporting such a construction.[135]

The first part of this statement strains credulity. The case law since *Slaight Communications* tends to show that the Supreme Court of Canada did not, with some exceptions, concern itself very much with reaching internationally compliant interpretations of the Charter.[136] That being said, the *Hape* decision appears to show the court turning over a new interpretive leaf as regards the Charter and international law. But perhaps one cannot give too much weight to these comments, given the facts of *Hape*. The case concerned an RCMP money-laundering investigation in the Turks and Caicos Islands. The accused sought to have documentary evidence produced by the investigation excluded from his trial on the basis that it was obtained in violation of his Charter right to be secure against unreasonable search and seizure.[137] The majority held that the Charter does not generally apply to searches and seizures that take place in other countries. To find otherwise

[134] *See* M. Freeman and G. van Ert, *International Human Rights Law* 189–96 (Toronto: Irwin Law, 2004).

[135] 2007 SCC 26, at paras. 55–56.

[136] The most egregious example is Suresh v. Canada (Minister of Citizenship and Immigration) [2002] 1 SCR 3, in which the court contemplated (in obiter) the possibility that deporting a person to a place where he or she might be tortured, contrary to the 1984 Convention Against Torture, might be possible without violation of the Charter's guarantee of life, liberty and security of the person.

[137] Charter sec. 8.

(the majority held) would be to apply the Charter extraterritorially contrary to both international law[138] and the terms of Charter Section 32 (which sets out the extent of the Charter's application). Thus, the internationally conforming interpretation of the Charter advanced by the majority concerned the Charter's geographic scope of application – not a substantive Charter right.

A clearer signal of the Supreme Court of Canada's newfound determination to apply the presumption of conformity to the Charter's human rights protections came in *Health Services and Support – Facilities Subsector Bargaining Association v. British Columbia*,[139] released one day after *Hape*. In the *Health Services* case, the appellant unions and union members challenged the constitutionality of provincial labor legislation that effectively precluded collective bargaining in some areas. Previous Supreme Court decisions (including *Re Public Service Employee Relations Act (Alta.)*,[140] in which Chief Justice Dickson, dissenting, first advocated the application of the presumption of conformity to the Charter) had held that collective bargaining was not protected by the Charter's freedom of association guarantee. In *Health Services*, the court overruled those decisions and held that the Charter includes a procedural right to collective bargaining. In overruling its previous decisions, the court relied significantly on international human rights and labor law, including treaties to which Canada is a party. Chief Justice McLachlin and Justice LeBel, for the majority, wrote:

> Under Canada's federal system of government, the incorporation of international agreements into domestic law is properly the role of the federal Parliament or the provincial legislatures. However, Canada's international obligations can assist courts charged with interpreting the Charter's guarantees. . . . Applying this interpretive tool here supports recognizing a process of collective bargaining as part of the Charter's guarantee of freedom of association.
>
> Canada's adherence to international documents recognizing a right to collective bargaining supports recognition of the right in section 2(d) of the Charter. As Dickson C.J. observed in the *Alberta Reference*, at pg. 349, the *Charter* should be presumed to provide at least as great a level of protection as is found in the international human rights documents that Canada has ratified.

[138] One may question whether an extraterritorial application of Canadian human rights law in such circumstances would truly be contrary to international law. That question, however, is beyond the scope of this chapter.
[139] 2007 SCC 27 (*Health Services*).
[140] [1987] 1 SCR 313.

> The sources most important to the understanding of section 2(d) of the *Charter* are the *International Covenant on Economic, Social and Cultural Rights*, 993 U.N.T.S. 3 ("ICESCR"), the *International Covenant on Civil and Political Rights*, 999 U.N.T.S. 171 ("ICCPR"), and the International Labour Organization's (ILO's) *Convention (No. 87) Concerning Freedom of Association and Protection of the Right to Organize*, 68 U.N.T.S. 17 ("Convention No. 87"). Canada has endorsed all three of these documents, acceding to both the ICESCR and the ICCPR, and ratifying Convention No. 87 in 1972. This means that these documents reflect not only international consensus, but also principles that Canada has committed itself to uphold. . . .
>
> In summary, international conventions to which Canada is a party recognize the right of the members of unions to engage in collective bargaining, as part of the protection for freedom of association. It is reasonable to infer that section 2(d) of the Charter should be interpreted as recognizing at least the same level of protection: *Alberta Reference*.[141]

Unlike *Hape*, the *Health Services* decision is a clear case of the Supreme Court of Canada invoking and applying the presumption of conformity to a Charter right – with momentous results. Judging by *Health Services*, it appears that the presumption of conformity with international law has now been admitted into the one area of Canadian law in which it was previously prohibited.

III. JUDICIAL REMEDIES FOR BREACHES OF TREATY RIGHTS

The maxim "No right without a remedy" is well established in Canadian law. When it comes to rights guaranteed by international law, however, the maxim is in tension with the constitutional principles set out at the beginning of this chapter, namely that treaty making is a prerogative of the Crown and therefore rights established by treaty require legislative implementation before taking direct effect in domestic law.

The implementation requirement is not necessarily rights denying. It can also preserve rights. In *Miller v. Canada*,[142] an employee of the International Civil Aviation Organization in Montreal sued Canada for damage to his health allegedly caused by poor air quality in the organization's building. Canada was the lessor of the premises to the organization under a treaty. Canada contended that the effect of the treaty was to immunize it from the claim, even though the treaty was unimplemented in Quebec law. The Court

[141] Health Services, *supra* note 139, at paras. 69–71, 79.
[142] [2001] 1 SCR 407.

of Appeal for Quebec rejected this argument, affirming that if the Crown had committed a fault in Quebec that caused a person damage, the courts had jurisdiction unless removed by domestic law. An unimplemented treaty could not, without more, restrict the claimant's right to sue.[143] The Supreme Court of Canada agreed and dismissed the appeal.

While the implementation requirement can preserve rights, it also has the potential to frustrate attempts by individuals to vindicate rights promised to them by a treaty. The right may be insufficiently implemented or not implemented at all in domestic law. In such cases, the presumption of conformity may fill the legislative gap,[144] but interpretation can only reach so far. Other possible remedies, such as declaratory relief or arguments founded on legitimate expectations, are undeveloped in Canada. In short, the most certain way of vindicating treaty-based rights in Canadian law is to rely on domestic laws that implement them or can be said to implement them. In the absence of implementation, there may be little a claimant can do, within Canadian law at least, to vindicate a treaty-based right.

A. *Remedies for Breaches of Implemented Treaty Rights*

Where the treaty right on which a claimant seeks to rely is implemented in Canadian law, there may be no need to refer to the international aspect of the right at all. The right has descended from the lofty heights of international law to the solid ground of domestic law and will be applied in the same way as any other domestic provision. An example of this in Canada is the human right of equality before the law, as guaranteed internationally in Article 26 of the ICCPR and other provisions. That right is implemented in Canada by a number of constitutional, quasi-constitutional, and ordinary laws, chief among them Section 15 of the Charter. For the most part, Canadian equality jurisprudence has been found to meet international standards.[145] It seems clear that the international right to equality before the law is fully, or at least very satisfactorily, implemented in Canadian law. Yet Canadian equality jurisprudence rarely relies on, or even refers to, the international aspect of the right. Rightly or wrongly, the feeling seems to be that Canada

[143] *See also* The Parlement Belge [1878–9] 4 PD 129 (Eng.).

[144] Speaking in a different context, Justice Bouck in *Neonex Int'l Ltd. v Kolasa et al.* (1978) 84 DLR (3d) 446, 452–53 (BCSC) memorably observed: "If Parliament intends to deprive the minority of these common law rights then the law demands the statute say so in the most clear and unequivocal language. Otherwise, the common law will blossom through the cracks and crevices of the legislation and try to ensure that justice is done."

[145] Indeed, Canadian equality law clearly exceeds international standards in some areas, such as the protection of equality rights for gays, lesbians, and other sexual minorities.

has nothing to learn about equality from the international experience. The result is that a person seeking to vindicate his or her right to equality before the law in Canada may readily do so by means of a Charter challenge under Section 15 or reliance on other equality guarantees, without resorting (or even referring) to ICCPR Article 26. The same can be said about many of the less controversial civil and political rights that Canada is required to protect under international law. In short, the international right is implemented in Canadian law, yet the implementing nature of the provisions that serve that purpose often goes unnoticed.

Not every treaty right is as well protected in Canadian law as equality, of course. Where a treaty right is implemented domestically, but the right's full meaning or the sufficiency of its implementation is in question, resort to the treaty basis of the right is clearly permissible and may be helpful. As we have seen, the interpretative presumption of conformity with international law is well established in Canada and may assist rights claimants to ensure they obtain the full benefit of the right as provided for by international law. In the *Canadian Foundation* case,[146] a children's rights foundation challenged the constitutionality of Section 43 of the Criminal Code,[147] which justifies the use of force against children when done by parents or teachers by way of correction "if the force does not exceed what is reasonable under the circumstances." The foundation's constitutional challenge was unsuccessful before the Supreme Court of Canada, yet the majority of the court effectively read down the impugned provision by interpreting the phrase "reasonable under the circumstances" as implicitly limited by (among other things) Canadian treaty obligations under the Convention on the Rights of the Child and the ICCPR. Those obligations were found to prohibit violence against children and cruel, inhuman, or degrading treatment or punishment of children. Applying the presumption of conformity with international law, Chief Justice McLachlin interpreted Section 43 to exempt from criminal sanction only minor corrective force of a transitory and trifling nature. The chief justice observed, "From these international obligations, it follows that what is 'reasonable under the circumstances' will seek to avoid harm to the child and will never include cruel, inhuman or degrading treatment."[148]

Of course, argument by reference to the underlying international law can go both ways. If the opposing party (normally a government) can show that the domestic legislation on which the claimant relies was intended to

[146] Canadian Foundation for Children, Youth and the Law v. Canada (Attorney General) [2004] 1 SCR 76.
[147] RSC 1985 c. C-46.
[148] *Canadian Foundation, supra* note 146, at paras. 32 and 40.

implement a treaty, and that the right as established in the treaty is more circumscribed than the claimant suggests, this may be an argument for reading the implementing legislation more narrowly.

There is a great deal of federal and provincial legislation in Canada that gives domestic legal effect to rights established under Canadian treaty obligations. Human rights laws are the most obvious example. They may be found in all jurisdictions and in a variety of forms, from constitutional provisions to so-called quasi-constitutional laws to ordinary statutes. But rights-creating treaties exist in many other areas of international law, including family law, taxation, labor, international humanitarian law, commercial law, and beyond. It would be a huge task to attempt to identify all those federal and provincial laws that serve to implement rights established under Canadian treaty obligations in these and all other fields of law into which treaty making has expanded in the modern era.

B. *Remedies for Breaches of Unimplemented Treaty Rights*

In principle, all rights benefiting individuals and founded in Canadian treaty obligations ought to be implemented in domestic law. The usual Canadian practice is not to allow treaties requiring domestic implementation to enter into force for Canada until the federal government has ensured the treaty's implementation.[149] The reason for this is simply that, where a treaty requires domestic legal action by states parties, failure to take that action may breach the treaty. Usually, then, if a right-creating treaty is in force against Canada, there exists some legislative implementation of that right. If the right is one that falls to be implemented federally, the federal government will have ensured its implementation by Parliament. If the right falls within provincial jurisdiction, the federal government will normally hold off on ratifying or acceding to the treaty until it has persuaded all the provinces to ensure implementation of the right in their jurisdictions.

However, theory is not always matched by practice. Where a treaty right is not, for whatever reason, implemented in Canadian law, the orthodox rule is that judicial remedies will not be available. Failure to implement a treaty is not a cause of action against the government, and Canadian judges can apply only Canadian laws. Failure to implement a treaty right in domestic

[149] "Governments have come to take the position that they will normally only ratify a treaty after any necessary enabling legislation has been passed. . . . Today, on only rare occasions does Canada ratify a treaty prior to the enactment of enabling legislation": M. Copithorne, "National Treaty Law and Practice: Canada" in M. Leigh and others, eds., *National Treaty Law and Practice* (Washington, DC: American Society of International Law, 2003) at 5.

law may be a legal problem from the perspective of a foreign state party to the treaty in question (which may regard the failure as a breach of the treaty), but from the perspective of a Canadian judge the failure is not legal but political: the legislature has declined to make the law the claimant wants it to make.

This orthodox account is largely sound but is subject to some caveats, the most important of which is the presumption of conformity. As we have seen, Canadian courts are hesitant to conclude that Canada has failed to give legal effect in domestic law to those treaties that require it. To the contrary, the courts endeavor, as a matter of judicial policy, to interpret Canadian laws harmoniously with international requirements. In the *Health Services* case,[150] the Supreme Court of Canada revised its interpretation of the freedom of association right established by Section 2(d) of the Canadian Charter of Rights and Freedoms to conform to Canada's obligations under the 1966 International Covenant on Economic, Social, and Cultural Rights,[151] the ICCPR,[152] and ILO Convention (No. 87) Concerning Freedom of Association and Protection of the Right to Organize.[153] While the court observed that international law was only one of four considerations informing its decision,[154] it also made clear that it was applying the presumption of conformity with international law to the Charter.[155] The result was to establish collective bargaining as a constitutionally protected right in Canadian law. That right had clearly not existed, at least in constitutional form, prior to the court's decision. Indeed, the court had to overrule four of its own decisions[156] to reach this result. *Health Services* is a dramatic example of a court applying the presumption of conformity to vindicate an unimplemented treaty right in domestic law.

While *Health Services* is an example of a court applying the presumption of conformity to give effect to a treaty right unimplemented (or at least previously unimplemented) in Canadian law, the case is exceptional. The treaty right in question (collective bargaining) was one that lent itself to judicial vindication by means of constitutional interpretation. Furthermore,

[150] Health Services and Support – Facilities Subsector Bargaining Association v. British Columbia 2007 SCC 27.
[151] [1976] CanTS no. 46.
[152] [1976] CanTS no. 47.
[153] [1973] CanTS no. 14.
[154] Health Services, *supra* note 150, at para. 20.
[155] *Id.*, at paras. 70–79.
[156] Reference re Public Service Employee Relations Act (Alta.) [1987] 1 SCR 313; PSAC v. Canada [1987] 1 SCR 424; RWDSU v. Saskatchewan [1987] 1 SCR 460; Professional Institute of the Public Service of Canada v. Northwest Territories (Commissioner) [1990] 2 SCR 367.

the court presented with the problem was the only one in the country that could have reached an internationally conforming result, being the only Canadian court with the power to depart from Supreme Court of Canada precedent. In most cases, where a treaty right remains unimplemented in Canadian law, judicial interpretation will likely not suffice to provide the missing right. The right to compensation for wrongful conviction of a criminal offense provides an example. That right is established by Article 14(6) of the ICCPR. Yet compensation for wrongful conviction in Canada is made purely on an ex gratia basis, without any domestic legal entitlement to such payments.[157] In short, the treaty right is unimplemented in domestic law. A court faced with this stark example of non-implementation might very well be forced to conclude that it can provide no remedy.

There may, however, be another remedial option available to Canadian courts faced with unimplemented treaty rights: declaratory relief. Historically, declaratory relief has seemingly not been available against governments for legislative failures to implement treaties in domestic law.[158] Such relief was sought, however, by the Quebec government against the government of Canada in *Quebec (Minister of Justice) v. Canada (Minister of Justice)*.[159] Quebec brought a number of challenges to a federal law, the Youth Criminal Justice Act.[160] Most of the challenges were constitutional in nature, but Quebec also sought two declarations that the Act was incompatible with Canadian obligations under the ICCPR[161] and the 1989 Convention on the Rights of the Child.[162] The Court of Appeal for Quebec held that the declarations were available and that the compatibility of the Act with Canadian treaty obligations was a question properly before it. Whether this case constitutes a precedent for granting declaratory relief against governments for failure to implement treaty rights is by no means clear. The case arose as a reference by the Quebec government directly to the Court of Appeal and may not be authority for granting declaratory relief in litigation involving private parties.[163] Declaratory relief for non-implementation of treaty

[157] M. Freeman and G. van Ert, *International Human Rights Law* 373–75 (Toronto: Irwin Law, 2004).

[158] I am forced to say "seemingly" because I am not aware of any Canadian case in which the question has been put to the court. Declaratory relief is not, to my knowledge, a remedy that has ever been sought for failure to implement a treaty, except in the cases discussed previously.

[159] (2003) 228 DLR (4th) 63 (Que CA).

[160] SC 2002 c. 1.

[161] [1976] CanTS no. 47.

[162] [1992] CanTS no. 3.

[163] *But see* Montana Band of Indians v. Canada [1991] 2 FC 30 (Fed. CA).

rights or other legislative treaty breaches would offer litigants a powerful new means of ensuring that treaty obligations freely undertaken by the state are respected by the state's own domestic law. There is much to recommend such relief in theory but only modest authority for its existence in practice.

In the absence of any other remedy for non-implementation of a treaty right, Canadian claimants are left to assert the right, if possible, in international fora. Canadians have often had resort to mechanisms established under UN human rights treaties, ILO conventions, and other international agreements. Favorable decisions at the international level do not always prompt governmental or legislative action, however. For example, a number of decisions by the UN Human Rights Committee have found Canada in breach of its ICCPR obligations, yet without executive or legislative response.[164]

IV. CONCLUSION

Any consideration of judicial interpretation and enforcement of treaties, in Canada at least, must bear in mind certain essential, if indistinct, limits to judicial action in respect of treaties. As Canadian law currently stands, treaties can be subject to judicial interpretation and enforcement only in certain circumstances. These circumstances can be difficult to describe, and one hesitates to generalize at the risk of suggesting artificial or unnecessary exclusions. It is clear, however, that Canadian courts are not international courts and will not determine legal disputes between states occurring purely on the international plane. A treaty question put before a Canadian court must have some purchase in Canadian law. The observations of the Supreme Court of Canada in *Re Secession of Quebec*[165] are helpful. Faced with the objection that it did not have jurisdiction to answer an international legal question referred to it by the government of Canada,[166] the court replied:

164 *See, e.g.*, Waldman v. Canada (1999) Comm. no. 694/1996, in which the UN Human Rights Committee found a violation of Waldman's right to equal and effective protection against discrimination (ICCPR art. 26) resulting from Ontario legislation granting public funding to Roman Catholic schools but not to Jewish schools. The legislation gives effect to constitutional education guarantees under sec. 93 of the Constitution Act 1867. To remedy the breach found by the Committee would seemingly require constitutional amendment. No such amendment has been made.

165 [1998] 2 SCR 217.

166 The question was, "Does international law give the National Assembly, legislature or government of Quebec the right to effect the secession of Quebec from Canada unilaterally? In this regard, is there a right to self-determination under international law that would give the National Assembly, legislature or government of Quebec the right to effect the secession of Quebec from Canada unilaterally?"

> This concern is groundless. In a number of previous cases, it has been necessary for this Court to look to international law to determine the rights or obligations of some actor within the Canadian legal system. . . .
>
> More importantly, Question 2 of this Reference does not ask an abstract question of "pure" international law but seeks to determine the legal rights and obligations of the National Assembly, legislature or government of Quebec, institutions that clearly exist as part of the Canadian legal order. As will be seen, the amicus curiae himself submitted that the success of any initiative on the part of Quebec to secede from the Canadian federation would be governed by international law. In these circumstances, a consideration of international law in the context of this Reference about the legal aspects of the unilateral secession of Quebec is not only permissible but unavoidable.[167]

Related to this point is the constitutional doctrine, described at the beginning of this chapter, that foreign affairs is a prerogative of the Crown. That prerogative is, generally speaking, beyond judicial review.[168] The orthodoxy is that Canadian courts will not sit in judgment of government acts in the area of foreign affairs. An actual or potential treaty breach by Canada will seemingly not entitle a claimant to any relief from a Canadian court when granting such relief would interfere with the government's conduct of foreign relations without some substantial connection to domestic law. These statements are generalizations and made with some hesitation. As the cases reviewed in this chapter demonstrate, Canadian judicial engagement with treaties is increasing and expanding. The boundaries of judicial action in these areas have never been entirely clear and may grow more uncertain as the linkages between Canadian and international law continue to multiply.

[167] *Re* Secession of Quebec, *supra* note 165, at paras. 22–23.

[168] Black v. Chrétien (2001) 54 OR (3d) 215 (Ont CA). *But see* Operation Dismantle v. R. [1985] 1 SCR 441 re review of foreign affairs prerogative for compliance with the Charter.

5

Germany

Andreas L. Paulus*

Professor of Public and International Law; Director, Institute of International and European Law, University of Göttingen, Germany

I. INTRODUCTION: INTERNATIONAL TREATIES AND GERMAN PRACTICE

After the traumatic experience of German self-isolation from the democratic world in the Nazi era and World War II, the founders of the new (West) German Constitution, the Grundgesetz, regarded integration into the world community as a primary goal, perhaps the primary goal, for the establishment of a democratic and federal Germany. Accordingly, the Grundgesetz became famous for its "friendliness" toward international legal relations.[1]

Under the prevailing interpretation of Article 59 of the Grundgesetz,[2] duly ratified treaties are part of German law and enjoy the same status as federal statutes, similar to the Supremacy Clause of the U.S. Constitution. Under the prevailing canons of interpretation, however, this is only part of the story: German courts are also bound to interpret domestic law, as far as possible, in a way that avoids the breach of international legal obligations.[3] Cases of

*I am particularly indebted to Giulia Conte, Anne Dienelt, Mareike Krug, and Johann Ruben Leiss for their invaluable research assistance in the different stages of this article. The responsibility for all mistakes and omissions rests, of course, alone with the author.

[1] Decisions of the Federal Constitutional Court [hereinafter: BVerfGE], 112, 1 at 26; 92, 26 at 48; 6, 309 at 362; C. Tomuschat, "Die staatsrechtliche Entscheidung für die internationale Offenheit" in J. Isensee and P. Kirchhof (eds.), 7 *Handbuch des Staatsrechts der Bundesrepublik Deutschland* (2d ed., CF Müller, Heidelberg 1992) 483 at 485, paras. 3, 8. For the related terms of *offener Verfassungsstaat* (open constitutional state), *see* K. Vogel, *Verfassungsentscheidung für eine internationale Zusammenarbeit* (Mohr, Tübingen 1964).

[2] *See* BVerfGE 74, 358 at 370; BVerfGE 82, 106, at 120.

[3] BVerfGE 74, 358 at 370, trans. in *Decisions of the Bundesverfassungsgericht – Federal Constitutional Court – Federal Republic of Germany* (Nomos, Baden-Baden 1992) vol. 1, pt. II, at 634.

open and intentional conflict between an international treaty and domestic legislation are extremely rare.[4] Thus, the role of German courts in the domestic implementation of international treaties appears to be considerable but straightforward: their task is to allow Germany to fulfill its international obligations by faithfully interpreting German law in accordance with Germany's international obligations, in particular treaty obligations.

If it was ever so simple, this is no longer true. As a member of the United Nations and the European Union, Germany has become a state party to a great number of international treaties so that potential conflicts become increasingly frequent. In European Community law, what used to be considered the exception became the rule: if it is detailed enough, EC law claims both direct effect and supremacy over domestic law.[5] Classical international law left the choice of whether to recognize the direct applicability of international treaties in the domestic legal order to domestic law itself. However, the case law of the European Court of Justice (ECJ) – which enjoys, under Article 220 of the Treaty on the European Community (TEC), the prerogative to ensure the observance of the treaty[6] – establishes that European law requires the direct effect of community law in the domestic legal order. Moreover, the ECJ demands supremacy of European over domestic law, including domestic constitutional law.[7] Thus, compared to classical international law, the permanently expanding European law has a much greater potential for generating conflicts with domestic law.

Similarly, there is an increasing potential for conflict between general international law and domestic law. Like European law, general international law deals increasingly with issues that are not limited to interstate affairs, but that regulate daily life and, in particular, the relationship between states and individuals. In the *LaGrand* and *Avena* cases,[8] the International Court of Justice (ICJ) interpreted international law to require a minimum standard of protection for the right to consular information; it also derived individual

[4] For the treaty override in international tax law, *see* A. Rust and E. Reimer, "Treaty Override im deutschen Internationalen Steuerrecht," *Internationales Steuerrecht* (2005) 843–49; for examples of open violation in German law *see id.*, pg. 844.

[5] *See* Van Gend & Loos, Case 26/62, [1963] ECR 1 (direct effect); Costa/ENEL, Case 6/64 [1964] ECR 585 (supremacy over domestic law).

[6] Art. 220, para. 1, of the TEC states: "The Court of Justice and the Court of First Instance, each within its jurisdiction, shall ensure that in the interpretation and application of this Treaty the law is observed."

[7] Internationale Handelsgesellschaft, Case 11/70, [1970] ECR 1125, para. 3.

[8] LaGrand (Ger. v. U.S.) [2001] 466; Avena (Mex. v. U.S.), Judgment [2004] ICJ Rep 12. In the *LaGrand* case, the author served as counsel for Germany.

rights of foreigners from Article 36 of the Vienna Convention on Consular Relations,[9] a multilateral treaty otherwise limited to interstate affairs. That was not quite the same as according direct effect to the treaty in the domestic legal order. The Court directed its provisional measures in the *LaGrand* case, however, not only to the United States as a state but also to the governor of Arizona.[10] As an organ of the United States, she was considered bound by the United States' treaty commitments, even though she was the governor of a state rather than the union.

In Europe, the European Court of Human Rights interprets the European Convention on Human Rights as implying a duty of the state to give effect to the rights enshrined in the Convention by way of legislation or other means of its own choosing,[11] whereas the text of the Convention provides for compensation in cases in which the internal law allows only for partial reparation.[12]

Another reason for the increasing potential for conflict between domestic and international law lies in the changing substance of international legal obligations. Traditional international law consisted mainly – but not exclusively – of reciprocal obligations between states that were not directly binding on private parties. And even in cases in which some provisions were considered self-executing, that is, applicable within the domestic legal order, this was not considered controversial as long as they created rights and obligations in the relationship between the state and its citizens only. In other words, when individual citizens claimed rights against the state on the basis of international law, it was quite natural that the state that had given its word to other states could be regarded also bound toward its own citizens. However, in contemporary European and human rights law, many rights – and respective obligations – apply in the relationships between citizens, the state only intervening by its Courts to delimit, define, and implement these

[9] Convention on Consular Relations of 24 April 1963, 596 UNTS 261.

[10] LaGrand (Ger. v. U.S.), *Provisional Measures, Order of 3 March 1999* [1999] 9, at 26, para. 28.

[11] In one case, the Court indicated specific measures to be taken for remedying a systemic failure of human rights protection, *see* Broniowski v. Poland, ECHR 2004-V, at 2, paras. 193–94; *see also* Assanidze v. Georgia, ECHR 2004-II, at 223, paras. 202–03, ordering the release of a detained person independent of damages due to him.

[12] Convention for the Protection of Human Rights and Fundamental Freedoms [hereinafter ECHR], Council of Europe Treaty Series (CETS) No. 5, last amended by Additional Protocol No. 11, ETS No. 155, entry into force on 1 Nov. 1998, art. 41; *see also* Additional Protocols 12, CETS No. 177 (nondiscrimination), and 13, CETS No. 187 (abolition of the death penalty in war time). Additional Protocol 14, which amends the Convention to allow, inter alia, for accession of the European Union to the Convention, awaits ratification by Russia to enter into force.

rights and obligations.[13] Thus, the individual citizen not only gains rights against the state through international and European law but also may incur additional responsibilities toward his or her fellow citizens. In these cases, the interventions of international courts may strike the balance between the rights and obligations of citizens involved differently from domestic courts – an intervention that is not always welcome and may at times be regarded as patronizing. Certainly, to account for the legitimate differences between member states, the European Court of Human Rights has developed the doctrine of the margin of appreciation. But it is the Court, not the individual country, who decides on the limits of this margin.[14]

In many cases in which international or European law has direct consequences in the domestic legal order, the task of determining the precise content and application of international obligations falls to the courts. However, with the increasing judicialization of international law,[15] international courts and tribunals may interpret international rules differently than domestic courts. In fact, one might expect that international courts and tribunals would tend to extend the role of international law, whereas domestic courts would tend to limit it. The picture is more complicated than that,[16] but the potential for conflict remains. If international and European law means what the ICJ, ECJ, or European Court of Human Rights say it means, then domestic courts would become mere executioners of their decisions. This sits badly, however, with the traditional prerogatives of domestic courts, such as the U.S. Supreme Court[17] and the German Federal Constitutional Court, the Bundesverfassungsgericht (BVerfG).

This chapter analyses the way German courts have dealt with these questions in several steps. First, it will parse the text of the German Constitution with regard to international affairs. The German text is far more detailed than Article VI of the U.S. Constitution, for example. Second, the chapter will examine recent conflicts between German laws and court decisions, on the one hand, and international ones, on the other hand. The analysis shows

[13] For a recent example, *see I.A. v. Turkey*, ECHR 2005-VIII 251, para. 27 (freedom of expression vs. freedom of religion).

[14] *See I.A. v. Turkey, supra* note 13, para. 25.

[15] Regarding the debate on legalization and judicialization, *see* J. Goldstein, "Legalization and World Politics: A Special Issue of International Organization," 54 *International Organization* (2000) 385 ff.

[16] *See* J.H.H. Weiler, *Constitution of Europe* (Cambridge UP, Cambridge 1999) 39–63 (explaining how the system of the communities strengthened rather than weakened member-state courts).

[17] For the vigorous, if polite, reaction by the Supreme Court, *see Sanchez-Llamas v. Oregon*, 126 S.Ct. 2669, 2686–87 (2006).

that the German Constitutional Court does not accept each and every international claim for primacy over domestic law, but it attempts to interpret German law in conformity with German treaty obligations and decisions of international courts and tribunals.

However, such conformity has its limits. The German Constitutional Court drew a line in the sand when it suggested, in its famous *Maastricht* judgment, that EU law that oversteps EU competencies (as determined by the German court) may be nonbinding on Germany.[18] Again, in its recent *Görgülü* decision,[19] the German Court followed the European Court of Human Rights in the result only but denied simple automaticity. Finally, in the most recent of these cases, namely the *Waldschlösschen* case,[20] the Federal Constitutional Court suggested that domestic referenda might override an international treaty if the treaty had been concluded by the executive branch but had not been approved by the domestic legislature.[21] While this part of the judgment was an obiter dictum, it suggests that German courts are increasingly assuming a different role than they did in the past: they are playing the role of a "gatekeeper"[22] or border guard who decides which international rules may cross the bridge into domestic law.

Thus, the German Constitutional Court has made clear that the role of German courts is not limited to a mere rubber stamp for the decisions of international courts applying international treaties. In contrast, as its recent decision involving the Vienna Convention on Consular Relations suggests,[23] the Court has shown great respect for international jurisprudence, and its decisions have promoted a large measure of compliance with Germany's treaty obligations.[24] The proactive attitude of the Federal

[18] BVerfGE 89, 155 at 188, Engl. transl. as Brunner v. European Union Treaty (Cases 2 BvR 2134/92 & 2159/92) [1994] 31 CMLR 57 at 89.

[19] *Görgülü*, BVerfGE 111, 307, Engl. transl. provided by the Court, BVerfG, 2 BvR 1481/04 of 14 October 2004, *available at* http://www.bverfg.de/entscheidungen/rs20041014_2bvr148104en.html (last accessed 22 April 2009).

[20] BVerfG (Federal Constitutional Court), 2 BvR 695/07 of 29 May 2007, *available at* http://www.bverfg.de/entscheidungen/rk20070529_2bvr069507.html (last accessed 22 April 2009).

[21] *Id.*, para. 35.

[22] The gatekeeper metaphor is taken from P. Kirchhof, "Der deutsche Staat im Prozeß der Europäischen Integration" in J. Isensee and P. Kirchhof (eds.), 7 *Handbuch des Staatsrechts* (C.F. Müller, Heidelberg 1992) 855 § 183, para. 65.

[23] BVerfG, 2 BvR 2115/01 of 19 Sept. 2006, *available at* http://www.bverfg.de/entscheidungen/rk20060919_2bvr211501.html. (last accessed 22 April 2009).

[24] In its final decision in the *Görgülü* affair, a Constitutional Court chamber even suggested that the local court had misled the Court on purpose and vigorously ordered the court to implement its judgment giving effect to the decision of the European Court of Human Rights. *See* BVerfG, 1 BvR 2790/04 of 10 June 2005, *available*

Constitutional Court is further evidence of a pluralism of legal systems, in which no court or tribunal can claim to have exclusive jurisdiction over a particular territory or a single subject matter.[25] In this respect, German courts may indeed become forerunners of their international brethren.

II. CONSTITUTIONAL TEXT AND THE ROLE OF DOMESTIC COURTS

Section II analyzes the text of the German Constitution (the Grundgesetz, or Basic Law) as it relates to treaties and the role of courts. This analysis provides the foundation for the subsequent analysis of recent case law in Section III.

A. *Treaties in the German Basic Law*

The text of the German Constitution contains several provisions regarding international law but little on the role of courts. According to Article 59, Paragraph 1, Section 2, of the Basic Law [hereinafter GG, for Grundgesetz], international treaties are to be concluded by the federal president. He or she must obtain the countersignature of the federal chancellor or of the competent federal minister.[26] In addition, Article 59, Paragraph 2, Section 1, provides: "[t]reaties that regulate the political relations of the Federation or relate to subjects of federal legislation shall require the consent or participation, in the form of a federal law, of the bodies responsible in such a case for the enactment of federal law."[27] Thus, while ratification is performed by the federal president together with the chancellor or cabinet minister, such ratification requires the prior consent of Parliament if the treaty deals with the political relations of the federation or relates to matters that would require legislation when regulated domestically.

at http://www.bverfg.de/entscheidungen/rk20050610_1bvr279004.html (last accessed 22 April 2009), para. 32.

[25] On pluralism, *cf.* A. Fischer-Lescano and G. Teubner, "Regime-Collisions: The Vain Search for Legal Unity in the Fragmentation of Global Law," 25 *Mich. J. Int'l L.* 999 (2004); A. Paulus, "The Emergence of the International Community and the Divide between International and Domestic Law," in A. Nollkaemper and J.E. Nijman (eds.), *New Perspectives on the Divide between International Law and National Law* (Oxford UP, Oxford 2007) 216; N. Walker, "The Idea of Constitutional Pluralism," 65 *Mod. L. Rev.* 317 (2002).

[26] Art. 58, GG.

[27] Translation provided by the German Bundestag (2008), *available at* http://www.bundestag.de/interakt/infomat/fremdsprachiges_material/downloads/ggEn_download.pdf (last accessed 22 April 2009).

The political relations are those that "directly affect the existence of the state, its territorial integrity, its independence and its position or prominent weight within the community of states."[28] This category includes, for example, alliances, treaties of peace and disarmament, as well as arbitration agreements. The wording of Article 59, Paragraph 2, relates to the way in which parliament provides its consent for the conclusion of a treaty by the executive branch. The distinction between "consent" and "participation" refers to the distinction between the Bundestag as the federal parliament and the Bundesrat (Federal Council) as the participatory body of the German Länder,[29] and thus does not imply two different modi operandi.[30] Recently, in the *Waldschlösschen* case, the question arose as to what extent treaties ratified without legislative consent are legally binding within the domestic legal order.[31]

As to the subjects requiring legislation, this relates to the separation of powers within the federal government between the legislative and executive branches. Whenever a single provision of a treaty touches on a matter that would require legislation when regulated domestically, the treaty itself is subject to legislative consent prior to ratification.

The more difficult question concerns the matters domestically falling under the competences of the Länder, in other words, all matters that are not explicitly within federal jurisdiction pursuant to federal constitutional law.[32] Some writers maintain that Article 59, Paragraph 2, does not apply to them.[33] The textual reference to "federal legislation" supports this view. However, the dominant doctrine holds that, with respect to treaties, the federal legislature is empowered to regulate matters that would domestically be regulated exclusively by Länder legislatures, because Article 32, Paragraph 1, of the Constitution vests responsibility for the conclusion of treaties in the

[28] BVerfGE 1, 372 at 382; 90, 286 at 359; transl. in *Decisions of the BVerfG* 1 I at 27. For a doctrinal view, *see* C. Calliess, "Auswärtige Gewalt," in J. Isensee and P. Kirchhof (eds.), 4 *Handbuch des Staatsrechts* (3d ed., Heidelberg 2006) 589 at 605, para. 30, with further references.

[29] *Cf.* art. 50, GG: "The Länder shall participate through the Bundesrat in the legislation and administration of the Federation and in matters concerning the European Union."

[30] Streinz, art. 59, para. 34, in M. Sachs (ed.), *Grundgesetz. Kommentar* (4th ed., Beck, München 2007). *But see* Pernice, art. 59, para. 48, in 2 H.H. Dreier (ed.), *Grundgesetz-Kommentar* (2d ed., Mohr Siebeck, Tübingen 2006) (who regards participation as an indication of the possibility of anticipated consent). However, this distinction appears artificial: if consent is required for ratification, it will always happen before ratification.

[31] *See supra* note 20 and accompanying text.

[32] *See* arts. 30, 70, 83 GG.

[33] Pernice, art. 59, para. 34, in Dreier (ed), *GG, supra* note 30.

federation.[34] If one does not find Article 59, Paragraph 2, applicable as such, one should at least consider an application *per analogiam* to preserve the rights of the legislature to protect the freedom of the citizens.

Taken literally, Article 59, Paragraph 2 does not say anything about the rank accorded to treaties in domestic law. However, the Bundesverfassungsgericht has consistently maintained that the legal form of consent by legislation also determines the legal rank of the respective treaty provisions.[35] The doctrine also speaks of the double function of the law providing prior consent for treaty ratification, namely the function of empowering the federal president to ratify and that of determining the domestic rank of the treaty ratified on the basis of legislative consent.[36] The requirement of legislative consent guarantees democratic decision making by preserving parliamentary control over legislative matters. It also ensures the implementation of international obligations through future legislation, if necessary;[37] that is, it leads to a kind of self-binding of the parliament to pass further implementing legislation, if necessary.

Treaties not falling under Article 59, Paragraph 2, Section 1, can be ratified without prior legislative consent. These are so-called executive agreements. Under Article 59, Paragraph 2, Section 2, the competence for domestic implementation of these agreements is the same as the domestic provisions on domestic administrative matters.[38] These provisions divide power between the federation and the Länder. In case executive agreements contain norms directly applicable to individuals, Article 80 of the Constitution narrowly circumscribes the competences of the executive branch. According to most writers, this provision applies by analogy to executive agreements.[39] Otherwise, their implementation in the domestic legal order follows the common provisions for administrative acts,[40] particularly with regard to the division of competences between the executive branch and the Federal Council,

[34] *See, e.g.*, Streinz, art. 32 para. 42, in Sachs (ed.), *GG, supra* note 30; *id.*, art. 59, para. 49. On the difficult matter of the division of competences regarding the jurisdiction to conclude treaties in the areas left to the Länder, *see* Calliess, "Auswärtige Gewalt," *supra* note 28, at 621–24; *Streinz*, art. 32, paras. 31–42, in Sachs (ed.), *GG, supra* note 30.

[35] BVerfGE 1, 396 at 410–11; 99, 145 at 158.

[36] *See, e.g.*, Jarass, art. 59, paras. 16–17, in H.D. Jarass and B. Pieroth (eds.), *Grundgesetz für die Bundesrepublik Deutschland. Kommentar* (9th ed., Beck, München 2007), with further references; Streinz, art. 32, paras. 59–70, in Sachs (ed.), *GG, supra* note 30.

[37] Calliess, "Auswärtige Gewalt", *supra* note 28, at 603, para. 26.

[38] Art. 59, para. 2, sec. 2, states: "In the case of executive agreements the provisions concerning the federal administration shall apply mutatis mutandis."

[39] *Cf.* Kempen, art. 59, para. 104, in H. von Mangoldt, F. Klein, and C. Starck (eds.), *Kommentar zum Grundgesetz* (5th ed., Vahlen, München 2005).

[40] Art. 83 ff., GG.

which represents the interests of the Länder, who administer the bulk of German public law.

B. *The Incorporation of Treaties in Domestic Law*

The domestic rank of treaties concluded with legislative consent is equal to that of domestic legislation. This result can be explained by the incorporation of treaties through an act of legislation. There exists, however, no agreement within German doctrine on the question of how this effect comes about. The complete incorporation (adoption) of the treaty, as such, into domestic law is usually rejected as too radical and disrespectful of the distinction between international and domestic law.[41] According to the traditional view, the theory of transformation, the legislative act of approval not only provides legislative consent for the international act of ratification but also transforms the treaty from the international into the domestic sphere. In contrast, the more progressive view, the theory of execution, regards the legislative act as an order to follow this particular treaty as international law within the domestic legal order.[42]

The BVerfG first followed the transformation theory, and later it leaned toward the theory of execution.[43] Lately, it has cited both theories without clarifying which one it follows.[44] While this is theoretically unsatisfactory, there does not appear to be much of a practical difference between the two theories.[45] Inasmuch as the theory of transformation maintains a rather artificial separation of domestic from international law, it also suggests that the legislative act that transforms the treaty, qua domestic law, can be interpreted differently from the international treaty from which it derives its content. The transformation theory thus creates the illusion that, by its incorporation into domestic law, international law somehow loses its international character and can therefore be interpreted independently of the other state parties. Moderate supporters of the theory of transformation

[41] *See, e.g.*, Streinz, art. 25, paras. 15–16, in Sachs (ed.), *GG, supra* note 30; Herdegen, art. 25, para. 36, in T. Maunz and G. Dürig (eds.), *Grundgesetz: Kommentar* (Beck, München 2007).

[42] Pernice, art. 59, para. 47, in Dreier (ed.), *GG, supra* note 30; Streinz, art. 25 para. 15, in Sachs (ed.), *GG, supra* note 30; *id.*, art. 59, para. 65; M. Schweitzer, *Staatsrecht III* (9th ed., CF Müller, Heidelberg 2008) paras. 420 ff.

[43] *Compare* BVerfGE 46, 342 at 363, 403–04; 75, 223, at 245–46 *with* BVerfGE 1, 372 at 389; 6, 309 at 332–33. For general discussion of the issue, *see* I. Seidl-Hohenveldern, "Transformation or Adoption of International Law into Municipal Law," 12 *Int'l & Comp. L.Q.* 88 (1963).

[44] *Görgülü*, BVerfGE 111, 307. *See, e.g.*, E. Klein, "Urteilsanmerkung," *Juristenzeitung* 1176 (2004) (attacking this return to earlier terminology).

[45] Pernice, art. 59, para. 47, in Dreier (ed.), *GG, supra* note 30; Klein, *supra* note 44, at 1176.

thus loosen its requirements in a way that makes it hardly distinguishable from the theory of execution.[46] The theory of execution, in contrast, properly identifies the object of the law of consent, and thus better accords with the wording of Article 59, Paragraph 2, which provides for legislative consent or participation in treaty-making rather than a domestic doubling of international law. It is thus hardly surprising that most academic writers tend to the latter view.[47]

For all its apparent innocuousness, the recent double speak of the BVerfG maintains an unfortunate ambiguity regarding the role of domestic courts in the interpretation of international law: the Court's reluctance to abandon the transformation theory suggests that the domestic mirror image of international law is interpreted exclusively by national courts, without regard to its special international or interstate character. It is thus no accident that the theory of transformation reappears in circumstances where the BVerfG strives to set limits on the incorporation of treaties into the domestic legal order.

C. *Treaties of Integration and the Special Role of Europe*

One overarching goal of the drafters of the Grundgesetz was the reintegration of Germany into Europe and the world community. In its second paragraph, the preamble explains that, in drafting the Grundgesetz, the German people were "[i]nspired by the determination to promote world peace as an equal partner in a united Europe." This clause was initially added in 1949; it was maintained when the preamble was amended in 1990 to accommodate the changes brought about by German reunification. The preambular language gives a strong indication that the Constitution treats German integration into the world community as an implementation of the constitutional writ.

In the earliest version of the Basic Law, adopted in 1949, the drafters included Article 24, which provides, inter alia, that "[t]he Federation may by a law transfer sovereign powers to international organizations." Thus, there is no doubt that treaties made under Article 59 may provide for the direct intervention of international organizations in domestic affairs without implementing legislation. This distinguishes the Grundgesetz from

[46] *See, e.g.*, Schweitzer, *supra* note 42 paras. 423, 435 (defending a moderate theory of transformation that can hardly be distinguished from the theory of execution).

[47] In addition to the writers in note 42, *see* Kempen, art. 59, para. 90, in von Mangoldt, Klein, and Starck (eds.), *GG*, *supra* note 39; R. Geiger, *GG und VR* (3d ed., Beck, München 2002) at 164, 172.

the U.S. Constitution.[48] Despite the wording of this provision, however, the transfer of sovereign powers should not be taken literally. What is implied, rather, is the opening of the German legal space to regulation by international organizations, not a transfer of sovereignty to international organizations in the proper sense of the term.[49] Thus, for any particular treaty, the degree to which the German legal space is opened can be regulated by the act of parliamentary approval under Article 59, Paragraph 2, Section 1.

Article 24 does not state expressly that the transfer of sovereign powers is constrained by the other provisions of the Constitution. Consequently, it was once contested whether the transfer of powers was subject to the observance of the constitutional rights of individuals, or at least to the provisions for which Article 79, Paragraph 3, of the Constitution prohibits constitutional amendments.[50] These principles are very broad – human dignity, democracy, rule of law – and the respective constitutional case law is extensive. Thus, making international regulation subject to the interpretation of these principles by the Constitutional Court would be akin to putting international organizations under the supervision of the BVerfG.[51] In contrast, Article 24, Paragraph 1, was hardly meant to imply an unconditional surrender of the most basic principles of German democracy to international organizations.

Whereas traditional international law would usually not conflict with the grand principles of the Constitution, this was much less clear with respect to German integration into the European Union. The breadth and depth of European regulation was bound to lead to conflicts of European case law with judgments of the BVerfG. Moreover, the principles of supremacy and

[48] *See*, in particular, the Supreme Court opinion in *Sanchez-Llamas*, *supra* note 17, at 2684–85 (arguing that international courts do not take away Supreme Court prerogatives of interpretation and application of domestic law), but *see also Medellín v Texas*, 128 S.Ct. 1346, 1365 (2008) (opining that delegation of judicial power is possible in the confines of the constitution).

[49] *See As long as... Decision I*, BVerfGE 37, 271 at 279; Decision of the Bundesverfassungsgericht 1 I pg. 270 at 275. *See also* Geiger, *supra* note 47, at 138 ff.; Streinz, art. 24, in Sachs (ed.), *GG*, *supra* note 30, para. 18; *id.*, art. 23, para. 57; Randelzhofer, art. 24, abs. 1, para. 55, in Maunz and Dürig (eds.), *GG*, *supra* note 41; Classen, art. 24, abs. 1, para. 11, in Mangoldt, Klein and Starck (eds.), *GG*, *supra* note 39.

[50] Art. 79, para. 3, states: "Amendments to this Basic Law affecting the division of the Federation into Länder, their participation on principle in the legislative process, or the principles laid down in Articles 1 [human dignity, AP] and 20 [democracy, rule of law, separation of powers, federalism, AP] shall be inadmissible."

[51] *Cf.* C. Tomuschat, "Die Europäische Union unter der Aufsicht des Bundesverfassungsgerichts" *Europäische Grundrechtezeitschrift* 489 (1993).

direct effect of European Community law over domestic law, combined with the prerogative of the European Court of Justice to interpret the treaties of integration under Article 220 of the TEC,[52] appeared to require absolute compliance.

Before ratifying the 1992 Maastricht Treaty, which provides for economic and monetary union, however, the German legislature added a special provision to the Constitution to deal with European integration, namely Article 23.[53] The provision clarified that the transfer of powers to the European Union was not unconditional, but subject to the limits for constitutional amendments as contained in Article 79, Paragraph 3. Moreover, Article 23 explicitly requires a European commitment "to democratic, social, and federal principles, to the rule of law and to the principle of subsidiarity," and it promises "a level of protection of basic rights essentially comparable to that afforded by this Basic Law." Thus, Article 23 provided an opening for domestic courts to play a much greater role in enforcing compliance with constitutional guarantees.[54]

Article 24 was not amended in the same way. However, the fact that the new Article 23 conditions a transfer of sovereign powers on respect for the unmodifiable core of the German Constitution, as codified in Article 79, Paragraph 3, strongly suggests that the Article 23 limitations apply, with even greater vigor, to general international law.[55] The precise scope of these limitations has remained in dispute.[56] The abundant literature is, however, remarkably short of concrete examples of a violation of basic constitutional

[52] For the text of art. 220 of the TEC, *see supra* note 6.

[53] Art. 23 (1) states, inter alia, "With a view to establishing a united Europe, the Federal Republic of Germany shall participate in the development of the European Union that is committed to democratic, social, and federal principles, to the rule of law and to the principle of subsidiarity, and that guarantees a level of protection of basic rights essentially comparable to that afforded by this Basic Law. To this end the Federation may transfer sovereign powers by a law with the consent of the Bundesrat. The establishment of the European Union, as well as changes in its treaty foundations and comparable regulations that amend or supplement this Basic Law, or make such amendments or supplements possible, shall be subject to paragraphs (2) and (3) of Article 79." The further paragraphs contain procedural provisions broadening the participation of the federal parliament and the Federal Council. On this point, *see, e.g.*, Calliess, "Auswärtige Gewalt," *supra* note 28, at 626–30.

[54] *See infra* note 80 and accompanying text.

[55] *See, e.g.*, BVerfGE 73, 339 at 375–76; 58, 1 at 40 ff.; Jarass, art. 24, paras. 9–11, in Jarass and Pieroth (eds.), *GG, supra* note 36.

[56] *Cf.* Classen, art. 24, paras. 24–32, in von Mangoldt, Klein and Starck (eds.), *GG, supra* note 39 (contending that art. 24, like art. 23, is also subject to the restrictions in art. 79, para. 3); Pernice, art. 24, paras. 32–38, in Dreier (ed.) *GG, supra* note 30 (contending that art. 24 is subject to greater limitations than art. 23). Both papers contain further references to an abundant literature.

principles by an international organization. This is hardly surprising because any treaty transferring sovereign rights of intervention is itself subject to parliamentary approval under Article 59, Paragraph 2, and it is difficult to imagine that Parliament would approve a treaty openly defying basic constitutional principles. This does not exclude, however, the infringement of individual rights that were not foreseeable at the time of the conclusion of the treaty.

D. *The Role of Domestic Courts*

With regard to treaties, the Grundgesetz is silent as to the role of courts. However, Article 100, Paragraph 2, addresses the related question of which rules of general international law (i.e., custom and general principles of law)[57] are incorporated by Article 25 of the Basic Law[58] and which of these rules create rights and duties for individuals. Article 100, Paragraph 2, provides that, in cases of doubt, courts must refer the matter to the Federal Constitutional Court, which thereby enjoys an almost exclusive prerogative to decide on the domestic effect of general international law not enshrined in a treaty.[59] The BVerfG has emphasized, however, that this provision does not extend to treaty law.[60] Rather, claims regarding the applicability of a treaty provision can be brought before regular courts or before the BVerfG, pursuant to the same rules as domestic legal issues. Thus, in principle, the role of courts in enforcing treaties is no different from the judicial role in enforcing domestic laws.

In practice, however, the Federal Constitutional Court accords greater latitude to the federal government in matters involving international affairs,

[57] *See* art. 38 of the ICJ Statute. On their incorporation by art. 25 GG, *see* BVerfG, 2 BvM 1/03 of 8 May 2007, para. 31, *available at* http://www.bverfg.de/entscheidungen/ms20070508_2bvm000103.html (last accessed 5 Sept 2007); Koenig, art. 25, para. 35, in Mangoldt, Klein, and Starck (eds.), *GG, supra* note 39; Herdegen, art. 25 paras. 19ff., 23ff., in Maunz-Dürig (eds.), *GG, supra* note 41; Streinz, art. 25, paras. 32ff., 34 ff., in Sachs (ed.), *GG, supra* note 30.

[58] Art. 25, GG, states: "The general rules of international law shall be an integral part of federal law. They shall take precedence over the laws and directly create rights and duties for the inhabitants of the federal territory."

[59] Art. 100, para. 2, GG, states: "If, in the course of litigation, doubt exists whether a rule of international law is an integral part of federal law and whether it directly creates rights and duties for the individual (Article 25), the court shall obtain a decision from the Federal Constitutional Court."

[60] BVerfG-K (chamber of the BVerfG), Europäische Grundrechtezeitschrift 2001, pg. 76 at 77; BVerfGE 94, 315 at 328.

including international human rights.[61] This approach has met with vigorous criticism among some scholars in Germany.[62] Indeed, the Grundgesetz does not distinguish between the judicial role in the interpretation of treaties and its role in the application of domestic legislation. It is thus doubtful whether it is appropriate for the Court to apply this approach, which was developed with regard to treaties involving the primordial goal of German unification, to other, more pedestrian matters as well.

German courts play a significant role in the enforcement of treaties. Tensions between the transformation theory and the execution theory are largely irrelevant to the concrete analysis of the impact of international treaties on domestic affairs. Whether a treaty creates directly applicable provisions – in other words, whether it is self-executing – or whether it creates directly enforceable rights and obligations for individuals[63] largely depends on its interpretation by domestic courts. For example, in the case of recently introduced student fees, German administrative courts analyzed their compliance with Article 13, para. 2, of the International Covenant for Economic, Social, and Cultural Rights regarding the right of access to a university education.[64] The Federal Administrative Court held that the Covenant is directly applicable to individual students but does not prohibit the reintroduction of student fees when accompanied by social measures guaranteeing equal access.[65]

Recently, in the *Görgülü* decision, the Constitutional Court pointed out that it has a special role to play in ensuring the observance of international

[61] BVerfGE 94, 12 at 35; 68, 1 at 97.

[62] *See, e.g.*, Pernice, art. 59 paras. 52–53, in Dreier (ed.), *GG, supra* note 30 (with further references); Kempen, art. 59 paras. 71ff., in von Mangoldt, Klein, and Starck (eds.), *GG, supra* note 39. For a more measured view, *see* Calliess, "Auswärtige Gewalt," *supra* note 28, at 608.

[63] Kempen, art. 59, abs. 2, para. 95, in Mangoldt, Klein, and Starck (eds.), *GG, supra* note 39; Pernice, art. 59 para. 8, in Dreier (ed.), *GG, supra* note 30; Geiger, *supra* note 47, at 159 ff.; Schweitzer, *supra* note 42, paras. 436 ff.

[64] International Covenant on Economic, Social, and Cultural Rights, 993 UNTS 3, BGBl. (Federal Gazette) II 428 (1976). For a decision of a lower court, see OVG NRW (Higher Administrative Court), Deutsches Verwaltungsblatt 1442–48 (2007), paras. 44 ff. By wrongly holding that the German translation of the Covenant, and not its authentic wording in the official UN languages, was applicable to the interpretation of the treaty, *id.*, para. 42, the decision also shows the pitfalls of the theory of transformation; *cf.* art. 33 Vienna Convention on the Law of Treaties, 1155 UNTS 331, requiring an interpretation in the official languages, that entered into force in Germany on 26 Nov. 1987, BGBl. (Fed. Gaz.) II 757 (1987), and thus governs the interpretation of the treaty in Germany under both theories.

[65] Federal Administrative Court (Bundesverwaltungsgericht, BVerwG), Judgment of 29 Apr. 2009, press release No. 24/2009, available at http://www bverwg.de (last visited 6 May 2009).

law by the Federal Republic of Germany. Thus, the Constitutional Court will also supervise lower courts in a way not appropriate in domestic cases:

> [A]s part of its competence the Federal Constitutional Court is also competent to prevent and remove, if possible, violations of public international law that consist in the incorrect application or non-observance by German courts of international law obligations and may give rise to an international law responsibility on the part of Germany (see BVerfGE 58, 1 (34); 59, 63 (89); 109, 13 (23)). In this, the Federal Constitutional Court is indirectly in the service of enforcing international law and in this way reduces the risk of failing to comply with international law. For this reason it may be necessary, deviating from the customary standard, to review the application and interpretation of international law treaties by the ordinary courts.[66]

Thus, in the view of the Court itself, the Constitutional Court fulfils a special role in the service not only of the domestic Constitution but also "in the service of enforcing international law."

III. TOWARD AN INTERNATIONAL COMMUNITY OF COURTS? THE GERMAN BVerfG AND ITS INTERNATIONAL INTERLOCUTORS

Viewed against this background of the constitutional text, the recent case law of the BVerfG has generated discussions on the cooperation between national and international courts and tribunals. When the Court first used this terminology in its famous judgment on the compatibility of the Maastricht Treaty on European Economic and Monetary Union with the Grundgesetz (the *Brunner* case),[67] the rather innocent formula was a hardly veiled threat of domestic resistance to an ECJ whose decisions were regarded as biased in favor of European competences.[68] More recently, a divergence of views between the BVerfG and the European Court of Human Rights on the relationship between privacy and freedom of the press has created a similar

[66] *Görgülü*, BVerfGE 111, 307 at 328; Engl. transl., *supra* note 19, para. 61.

[67] This is the denomination in the most commonly used translation, *Brunner v. European Union Treaty, supra* note 18.

[68] See, in particular, the debate regarding the power of small amendments under art. 235 TEC of the time. *Id.*, BVerfGE 89, 155 at 210, 31 CMLR 57, para. 99. Against the false citation to a commentary by the German ECJ judge of the time, *see* J.H.H. Weiler, "The State "über alles": Demos, Telos and the German Maastricht Decision," in O. Due, M. Lutter and J. Schwarze (eds.), *Festschrift für Ulrich Everling* (Nomos, Baden-Baden 1995) 1651, at 1655 ff., and former ECJ judge M. Zuleeg, "Die Rolle der rechtsprechenden Gewalt in der europäischen Integration," *Juristenzeitung* (1994) 1 at 3 ff.

confrontation.[69] Many influential writers, such as Anne-Marie Slaughter, have transformed the veiled threat, more amicably, into a theory of a "global community of courts."[70]

Indeed, at least as far as the relationship between European and German courts is concerned, cooperation by far exceeds confrontation. The following sections discuss, in chronological order, the recent case law of the highest German court, the BVerfG, with regard to the implementation of decisions by international courts. The analysis shows that the attitude of German courts toward international treaties, especially those of a quasi-constitutional character, such as the Treaty on European Union[71] and the European Convention on Human Rights,[72] is indeed correctly described

[69] *See* von Hannover v. Germany, Application no. 59320/00, judgment of 24 June 2004, European Court of Human Rights [hereinafter ECtHR], ECHR 2004-VI, 1. For the original case in Germany, called the *Caroline* case, *see* BVerfGE 101, 361. For criticism of the ECtHR decision, *see*, *e.g.*, the former BVerfG judge and rapporteur in the respective BVerfG decision, D. Grimm, "Discussion Statement," 66 *Veröffentlichungen der Vereinigung der Deutschen Staatsrechtslehrer* 427–28 (2007). For an extensive treatment, see S. Mückl, "Kooperation oder Konfrontation? – Das Verhältnis zwischen Bundesverfassungsgericht und Europäischem Gerichtshof für Menschenrechte," 44 *Der Staat* 403 (2005) (with ample references).

[70] A. Slaughter, "A Global Community of Courts," 44 *Harv. Int'l L.J.* 191 (2003).

[71] On its constitutional character, *see* Les Verts, Case 294/83, [1986] ECR 1357 at 1365; *EEA I*, Opinion 1/91, [1991] ECR I-6079, at 6102. On the boundaries of its competences, *see*, *e.g.*, ECJ Judgement on the New Tobacco Directive [2000] ECR I-8419. *See also* I. Pernice, "Europäisches und nationales Verfassungsrecht," 60 *Veröffentlichungen der Vereinigung der Deutschen Staatsrechtslehrer* 149, 155 (2001) (postnational notion of a constitution); A. Peters, *Elemente einer Theorie der Verfassung Europas* (Duncker & Humblot, Berlin 2001) 93 ff.; Weiler, *supra* note 16, pg. 221 ff.; and A. von Bogdandy and J. Bast (eds.), *Principles of European Constitutional Law* (Hart, Oxford, Portland 2006). For the role of European courts in this process, *see* E. Stein, "Lawyers, Judges and the Making of a Transnational Constitution," 75 *Am. J. Int'l L.* 1 (1981). Distinguish the functional use of the term *constitution* by the ECJ, however, from the debate on the constitutional character of the (failed) European Constitutional Treaty. On this point, *see* Calliess, in C. Calliess and M. Ruffert (eds.), *Verfassung der Europäischen Union. Kommentar der Grundlagenbestimmungen* (Beck und Manz, München; Wien 2006), Art. I-1, paras. 1–24. For the renaming of the former Constitutional Treaty into Reform Treaty, *see* Brussels European Council, 21/22 June 2007, *available at* http://www.consilium.europa.eu/ueDocs/cms_Data/docs/pressData/en/ec/94932.pdf (last accessed 22 April 2009) pg. 15. However, the constitutional character of the European treaties relates not to their contents but to their constitutional form and authority. For opponents of any application of the term *constitution* to international bodies, *see*, *e.g.*, D. Grimm, "Ursprung und Wandel der Verfassung," in J. Isensee and P. Kirchhof (eds.), 1 *Handbuch des Staatsrechts* (3d ed., CF Müller, Heidelberg 2003) 3 at 41–42 (constitution implies exclusivity); U. Haltern, "Internationales Verfassungsrecht? Anmerkungen zu einer kopernikanischen Wende," 128 *Archiv des öffentlichen Rechts* 511 (2003); J. Isensee, "Staat und Verfassung," in J. Isensee and P. Kirchhof (eds.), 2 *Handbuch des Staatsrechts* (3d ed., CF Müller, Heidelberg 2004) 3 at 4, 14–15 (no constitution without popular consent).

[72] *See* Mückl, "Kooperation oder Konfrontation," *supra* note 69, at 407 ff.

as cooperative. Neither the BVerfG nor the ECJ nor the European Court of Human Rights has been successful in maintaining supremacy. Rather, all three courts need to find an accommodation of views. Confrontation cannot last for long; dialogue is inevitable.

A. *Between Dialogue and Confrontation: The German Courts and the ECJ after the* Maastricht *Case*

The most important relationship is the one between the Federal Constitutional Court and the ECJ. If one examines the constituent documents, their confrontation appears inevitable. However, and remarkably so, despite the considerable potential for a clash, it has yet to happen. The basic propositions are contradictory. The ECJ, relying on Article 220 of the TEC, claims the prerogative to "ensure that in the interpretation and application of this Treaty the law is observed."[73] The BVerfG maintains that it controls the act of transformation, and therefore the opening of German legal space to European law.[74] The dialogue at times resembles a shouting match, even warning shots are fired, but both courts have thus far avoided giving contradictory commands to national courts in a concrete case.

In fact, the Constitutional Court has taken considerable steps to ensure that ordinary courts are meeting their obligation under Article 234 of the TEC to refer to the ECJ cases involving European law. The BVerfG has accorded the ECJ the status of a "lawful judge" under Article 101, Paragraph 1, Section 2 of the GG, thus allowing individuals to raise a constitutional claim before the BVerfG against a lower court accused of disregarding its obligations under the TEC.[75] In contrast, the ECJ has adapted its case law to the demands of the Constitutional Court by incorporating human rights principles into European law, even before those principles were mentioned explicitly in what is now Articles 6 and 7 of the European Union treaty.[76] Of

[73] Art. 220, TEC, para. 1. *See Foto Frost*, [1987] ECR 4199. On the boundaries of the competences, *see, e.g., Tabakwerberichtlinie* [2000] ECR I-8419; F. Mayer, "The European Constitution and the Courts," in von Bogdandy and Bast (eds.), *Principles of European Constitutional Law, supra* note 71, pg. 281 at 291 ff. For a comprehensive treatment of the relationship between the ECJ and domestic courts, see the contributions to A. Slaughter, A. Stone Sweet, and J.H.H. Weiler (eds.), *The European Court and National Courts – Doctrine and Jurisprudence* (Hart, Oxford 1998).

[74] Brunner v. European Union Treaty, BVerfGE 89, 155 at 188, 31 CMLR 57 at 89. See also the present BVerfG president, H.-J. Papier, "Interview" *Frankfurter Allgemeine Zeitung* (Frankfurt 24 Jul. 2007) pg. 5.

[75] *As long as... Decision II*, BVerfGE 73, 339 at 366, *Decisions of the BVerfG* 1 II, pg. 613 at 618.

[76] For the *Solange* (German for "as long as") saga, in which the BVerfG threatened to apply domestic fundamental rights without approval by the ECJ but backed off when the ECJ

course, controversy continues to exist, in particular regarding the ECJ's expansive view of EC and EU competences,[77] but recent amendments to the treaty – and those still to come in the Treaty of Lisbon[78] – may further reduce the potential for conflict.

Nevertheless, the Federal Constitutional Court continues to maintain, in principle, its prerogative, first pointed out in the *Maastricht* decision, to overrule the ECJ in two types of cases:

1. If human rights protection in the European Union breaks down, the BVerfG reserves the right to step in and ensure that basic human rights are respected. Note, however, that the BVerfG does not require the ECJ to satisfy the German standard for constitutional rights but only to uphold a minimum standard for the preservation of human dignity and protection of the rights enshrined in the European Convention on Human Rights (ECHR) and its additional protocols. This is the standard the ECJ has vowed to guarantee anyway.[79] At one time, there was a debate about whether the Constitutional Court's threat to overrule the ECJ was applicable in each case where the European Union disrespected the minimum standard of the BVerfG, or whether the reservation of BVerfG jurisdiction was meant to apply only in the unlikely case of a general break down of European human rights jurisprudence. The most recent case suggests a trend in the latter direction, particularly as the European human rights case law has matured to provide effective protection.[80] Although the BVerfG has called its relationship with the ECJ one of "cooperation," it still claims for itself the right to overrule the ECJ, however.[81]

introduced human rights into Community law, *see* Mayer, *supra* note 73, at 295; J. Kokott, "Report on Germany," in A. Slaughter, A. Stone Sweet, and J.H.H. Weiler (eds.), *The European Court and National Courts – Doctrine and Jurisprudence* (Hart, Oxford 1998) 77 at 82–92.

[77] *See, in particular,* FCC president Papier, "Interview," *supra* note 74.

[78] Treaty of Lisbon amending the Treaty on European Union and the Treaty Establishing the European Community, signed at Lisbon, 13 December 2007, Official Journal C 306 of 17 December 2007 at 01, *available at* http://eur-lex.europa.eu/JOHtml.do?uri=OJ:C:2007:306:SOM:en:HTML (not yet in force) (last accessed 22 April 2009).

[79] *See* Treaty on the European Union, art. 6.

[80] *See* Bananenmarktordnung [Banana Market Regulation], BVerfGE 102, 147, at 164, Engl. transl BVerfG, 2 BvL 1/97 of 06/07/2000, para. 39, *available at* http://www.bverfg.de/entscheidungen/ls20000607_2bvl000197en.html (last accessed 22 April 2009): ("[C]onstitutional complaints and submissions by courts are . . . inadmissible from the outset if their grounds do not state that the evolution of European law, including the rulings of the Court of Justice of the European Communities, has resulted in a decline below the required standard of fundamental rights after the 'Solange II' decision.")

[81] *Id. See also* Papier, "Interview," *supra* note 74.

2. In cases where European organs act beyond the scope of their legitimate authority, the Federal Constitutional Court maintains that it may decide that such an act does not have effect on German territory.[82] This could have implied a complete control of the ECJ case law on EU competences by German courts. However, this reading of the relevant passage in the *Maastricht* judgment has not been confirmed in practice. Despite some criticism by the Court's president of the European practice of adopting an expansive reading of European competences,[83] the BVerfG has never declared a European act inapplicable in the German legal order. It continues to respect the legislative authority of the Council and the European Parliament.

The conclusion to be drawn is relatively clear: the dialogue between the BVerfG and the ECJ may, at times, resemble a *dialogue des sourds*, but so far they have found an accommodation with each other. The introduction of human rights standards into European law may count as the greatest success of the BVerfG in its dialogue with its brethren. It also appears that the ECJ has adopted a more cautious approach toward matters of European competences; this may also be connected to the position of the German constitutional court. However, the German court remains in an important position: while maintaining a very liberal customs regime, it still appears to be sitting on the fence, or in the gatehouse,[84] and it may yet decide to prevent the crossing of a particular European legal act into Germany's domestic legal order. Meanwhile, the BVerfG ensures that lower courts observe their obligation to refer matters involving European law to the ECJ.

It would thus amount to a profound misunderstanding of the role of domestic courts to regard them as irrelevant. Rather, in most cases, it is the task of domestic courts to apply European law or refer a case to the ECJ. Indeed, it may well be the empowering of domestic courts – including the lower courts who may, but need not always, refer matters to the ECJ – rather than their disenfranchising that has made this two-tier system one of the greatest success stories of European integration.[85]

[82] Brunner v. European Union Treaty, BVerfGE 89, 155 at 188, [1994] 31 CMLR 57 at 89.
[83] Papier, "Interview," *supra* note 74.
[84] *See* Kirchhof, *supra* note 22.
[85] *See* K. Alter, "Explaining National Court Acceptance of European Court Jurisprudence: A Critical Evaluation of Theories of Legal Integration," in A. Slaughter, A. Stone Sweet, and J.H.H. Weiler (eds.), *The European Court and National Courts – Doctrine and Jurisprudence* (Hart, Oxford 1998) 227; Weiler, W. Mattli and A.-M. Slaughter, "The Role of National Courts in the Process of European Integration," in A.-M. Slaughter, A. Stone Sweet, and

B. *From Cooperation to Confrontation?*[86] *The ECHR before German Courts*

Whereas the relationship between the Federal Constitutional Court and the ECJ seems to have developed into a mature relationship of reciprocal respect and accommodation, the corresponding relationship between German courts and the European Court of Human Rights (ECtHR) – which sits in Strasbourg, France, and has jurisdiction over the observance of the ECHR[87] – seems to have soured lately. Until recently, the two courts worked hand in hand. However, two recent cases have endangered the earlier camaraderie between the courts, despite the fact that one former BVerfG judge, Renate Jaeger, now sits on the ECtHR in Strasbourg. In one case, the BVerfG and the ECtHR reached opposite conclusions about the relationship between freedom of speech and the protection of privacy. In the second case, the ECtHR and the BVerfG appear to have joined forces against the unwillingness of a regional court to implement a Strasbourg judgment. Nevertheless, the position of the Constitutional Court in the latter affair is more ambiguous than it appears at first sight.

1. The Special Role of the Convention in the German Legal Order. Until recently, there was a remarkable accord between German courts and the ECtHR. While the ECHR itself enjoys the status of normal legislation – that is, it is subject only to the constitution and to later or more specialized legislation (*lex superior, lex posterior*, and *lex specialis*)[88] – German courts generally interpret national law in a way that renders it compatible, as far as possible, with international law, including treaty law.[89] This principle is known in

J.H.H. Weiler (eds.), *The European Court and National Courts – Doctrine and Jurisprudence* (Hart, Oxford 1998) 253 at 39–63.

86 *See* Mückl, "Kooperation oder Konfrontation, *supra* note 69.

87 *See* ECHR, art. 19 ("To ensure the observance of the engagements undertaken by the High Contracting Parties in the Convention and the Protocols thereto, there shall be set up a European Court of Human Rights.").

88 BVerfGE 79, 358 at 370; *Görgülü*, BVerfGE 111, 307 at 317; Mückl, "Kooperation oder Konfrontation," *supra* note 69, at 407–08. *But see* C. Walter, "Die Europäische Menschenrechtskonvention als Konstitutionalisierungsprozeß," 59 *Zeitschrift für ausländisches öffentliches Recht und Völkerrecht* 961, 977 (1999); J.A. Frowein, "Die Europäisierung des Verfassungsrechts," in P. Badura and H. Dreier (eds.), *Festschrift 50 Jahre Bundesverfassungsgericht* (Mohr Siebeck, Tübingen 2002) 209 at 218 (arguing for a quasi-constitutional rank of the Convention).

89 BVerfGE 74, 358 at 370, with further references; Engl. trans. in *Decisions of the Bundesverfassungsgericht* vol. 1, pt. II, pg. 634 at 637.

the United States as the *Charming Betsy* canon of interpretation;[90] it also applies to the application of the ECHR in the German legal order.

However, and importantly, courts apply the canon differently in Germany than they do in the United States. For example, in the *Breard* case,[91] which dealt with the right of foreign detainees to receive information and to consult with a consular officer, the Supreme Court held that the Antiterrorism and Effective Death Penalty Act (AEDPA)[92] had overruled the Vienna Convention on Consular Relations, particularly with regard to the applicability of procedural default rules. However, there is no indication whatsoever that the drafters of AEDPA had the Vienna Convention – or any other conflict with international law – in mind when drafting an act that was designed to accelerate the domestic administration of justice. In the practice of German courts, this would normally result in a preference for the treaty as *lex specialis.* German courts assume that the legislature, had it anticipated a conflict between a treaty and a statute, would have provided a legislative exception to accommodate the treaty. In the words of the BVerfG:

> laws . . . are to be interpreted and applied in harmony with . . . international law, even when such laws have been enacted [after] an applicable international treaty; it cannot be assumed that the legislature, insofar as it has not clearly declared otherwise, wishes to deviate from the Federal Republic of Germany's international treaty commitments or to facilitate violation of such commitments.[93]

Indeed, in one case, the Court modified its case law to comply with a ruling of the ECtHR.[94]

Of course, this argument does not pertain to the arguably higher rank of procedural default as a constitutional principle stemming from federalism, which would be superior to a treaty, such as the Vienna Convention. But in *Breard* the U.S. Supreme Court did not even contemplate this discussion.

[90] *See* Murray v. Charming Betsy, 6 U.S. (2 Cranch) 64, 118 (1804). On the different emphasis in application of this principle, *see, e.g.*, A.L. Paulus, "From Neglect to Defiance? The United States and International Adjudication," 15 *Eur. J. Int'l L.* 783, 803–04 (2004) (with further references).

[91] *See* Breard v. Greene, 523 U.S. 371 (1998).

[92] Pub. L. No. 104–132, 110 Stat 1214 (1996).

[93] BVerfGE 74, 358 at 370, Engl. trans. in *Decisions of the Bundesverfassungsgericht* vol. 1, pt. II, pg. 634 at 638. The translation falsely renders "wenn sie zeitlich *später* erlassen worden sind als ein geltender Völkerrechtlicher Vertrag" by "enacted *prior to* an applicable international treaty" (my emphasis), a mistake that has been corrected above.

[94] Feuerwehrabgabe [fire service levy], BVerfGE 92, 91; *see* Karlheinz Schmidt v. Germany, judgment of 18 July 1994, [ECHR] Series A, no. 291-B.

Instead, the Court limited itself to the statement that AEDPA conflicted with the Convention; therefore, the later-in-time statute prevailed.[95]

By also interpreting the basic rights enshrined in the GG in light of the guarantees of the ECHR and the decisions of the ECtHR,[96] the BVerfG makes clear that it accepts the European Court as an equal, which deserves respect and should be followed whenever possible. The BVerfG also endeavors to harmonize domestic and European human rights law as far as possible. This harmonization is facilitated by the European Court's margin-of-appreciation doctrine, which leaves member states some discretion in choosing how to implement the rights enshrined in the Convention.[97]

2. *Caroline* and the Rise of the Conflict. However, there is one situation where the effort to harmonize domestic and European human rights law does not work: that is when the duty corresponding to an individual right belongs to another individual citizen rather than the state. In such a case, the right of one citizen will be the obligation of the other, and any enhancement of one person's right will increase the burden on the other. In the *Caroline von Monaco* case decided by the ECtHR, there was a conflict between Caroline's right to privacy, as enshrined in Article 8, Paragraph 1, of the Convention, and the right to freedom of expression of the Burda and Heinz Bauer publishing companies (who published the German magazines *Bunte*, *Freizeit Revue*, and *Neue Post*), which is protected by Article 10, Paragraph 1, of the GG. The German courts had resolved the conflict largely in favor of freedom of expression. However, the ECtHR, in a decision not appealed by the German government, decided in favor of the princess's privacy.[98] The clash was there.

Although the lower Courts have, in practice, largely followed the ECtHR, there was fierce opposition against the ruling, especially from previous members of the bench and the current president of the German Constitutional Court.[99] However, German opinion on the issue was divided. Thus, there were also voices in Germany supporting the substance of the European Court decision.[100] The thrust of the opposition by the Court president, Hans-Jürgen Papier, was that the European Court had not left enough

[95] See *supra* note 91 and accompanying text.

[96] BVerfGE 57, 358 at 370; *Decisions of the Bundesverfassungsgericht*, vol. 1, pt. II, pg. 638; confirmed in *Görgülü*, BVerfGE 111, 307 at 329, Engl. trans., *supra* note 19, para. 62.

[97] Lawless v. Ireland, judgment of 14 November 1961, Series A, no. 1, para. 28; *Kokkinakis v. Greece*, judgment of 25 May 1993, Series A, no. 260-A, para. 47.

[98] Von Hannover, *supra* note 69.

[99] *See supra* note 69.

[100] *See, e.g.*, R. Stürner, "Urteilsanmerkung," *Juristenzeitung* 1018 (2004).

discretion to the domestic court. Indeed, he argued that the European Court should guarantee only a minimum standard, leaving the remainder to national jurisdictions.[101] The debate is ongoing. But it is remarkable that the president of the BVerfG leads an effort to limit the rise of a common European standard in favor of national prerogatives of treaty implementation. Regardless, two factors may limit the significance of the case:

1. The federal government, apparently advised by the Constitutional Court itself,[102] chose not to appeal the *Caroline* ruling to the Grand Chamber of the ECtHR, as it was entitled to do under Article 43, Paragraph 2, of the Convention. The motives for this decision are unclear. Institutional fairness would have required going before the Grand Chamber if the execution of the judgment had appeared impossible.[103] However, the government's decision not to appeal may indicate a willingness to comply, notwithstanding its vocal protest against the ruling.
2. Given that most of the rights accorded under the Convention protect individuals against the government, so-called three-polar cases, in which Courts are requested to protect individuals against one another, will be fairly rare.

Finally, as the following discussion shows, the Federal Constitutional Court remains willing to respect the rulings of the ECtHR.

3. *Görgülü* and the Protection of ECHR Law by the Constitutional Court. If lower courts might have believed that the *Caroline* controversy gave them a free pass to disregard adverse rulings of the ECtHR, the *Görgülü* case serves as a strong reminder that the *Caroline* case is an exception to the rule of compliance and cooperation between the highest German and European Courts.

In 2005, for the third time in six months, the Constitutional Court admonished the Regional Court (Oberlandesgericht) Naumburg to implement a judgment of the ECtHR regarding a father's right of access to his son, whom the regional Court had assigned to foster parents.[104] According to a

[101] Papier, "Interview," *supra* note 74.
[102] *See* M. Hanfeld, FAZ of 25 June 2004, pg. 46.
[103] *See* A.L. Paulus, "Discussion Statement," 66 *Veröffentlichungen der Vereinigung der Deutschen Staatsrechtslehrer* 449 (2007).
[104] BVerfG, 1 BvR 1664/04, Entscheidung vom 5 April 2005 (Decision of 5 Apr. 2005), *available at* http://www.bverfg.de/entscheidungen/rk20050405_1bvr166404.html (last accessed 22 April 2009).

newspaper report, both the court in the German Land of Saxonia-Anhalt and the regional officials prevented the father from seeing his son, despite rulings by the ECtHR and the BVerfG to establish visitation rights.[105]

In the first of its three decisions in this case,[106] the Federal Constitutional Court emphasized that only the "violation of fundamental principles of the constitution" may justify the violation of international law.[107] As to the effect of judgments of international courts and tribunals, the highest German court held: "[s]ince the European Convention on Human Rights – *as interpreted by the ECtHR* – has the status of a formal federal statute, it shares the primacy of statute law and must therefore be complied with by the judiciary."[108] With respect to the European Court's interpretation of the Convention and its relationship to German law, the Constitutional Court added:

> As long as applicable methodological standards leave scope for interpretation and weighing of interests, German courts must give precedence to interpretation in accordance with the Convention. The situation is different only if observing the decision of the ECtHR . . . clearly violates statute law to the contrary or German constitutional provisions, in particular also the fundamental rights of third parties. "Take into account" means taking notice of the Convention provision as interpreted by the ECtHR and applying it to the case, provided the application does not violate prior-ranking law, in particular constitutional law.[109]

Thus, international law and decisions of international courts are subordinated to constitutional law, but the deference due to the rulings of the ECtHR is considerable. In particular, the German Constitutional Court accepts that not only the Convention itself, but also its interpretation by the ECtHR is authoritative.

However, some passages in the latter part of the judgment suggest that some members of the Court may also regard structures of simple German law as bars to following international judgments. In a convoluted paragraph, the Court seems to regard international law and decisions of competent

[105] Bernd Fritz, "Vater ohne Sohn," FAZ of 14 April 2005, pg. 7.
[106] BVerfGE 111, 307 (2004, in German). The following citations are to the English translation provided by the Court, BVerfG, 2 BvR 1481/04 of 14 October 2004, *available at* http://www.bverfg.de/entscheidungen/rs20041014_2bvr148104en.html (last accessed 22 April 2009).
[107] *Id.*, para. 35.
[108] *Id.*, para. 53 (emphasis added).
[109] *Id.*, para. 62.

international courts as binding, provided that they can be incorporated into domestic law without destroying its basic structure:

> "Take into account" means taking notice of the Convention provision as interpreted by the EC[t]HR and applying it to the case, provided the application does not violate prior-ranking law, in particular constitutional law. . . . Here, it will always be important how taking account of the decision takes [place] in the [legal sub]system . . . in question. On the level of federal law too, the Convention does not automatically have priority over other federal law, in particular if in this connection it has not already been the object of a decision of the EC[t]HR.[110]

What emerges from the decision is that German courts are usually bound by the ECtHR's interpretation of the European Convention. However, this is not true in a case where a decision to follow the ECtHR may violate the German Constitution itself, because the Constitution is superior in rank to the Convention. In the case at hand, there was an arguable case of contradictory constitutional interpretations between the German court and the ECtHR. The Constitutional Court sent the case back to the lower court, and when that court did not comply, it issued a provisional measure putting the judgment of the ECtHR into effect.[111] It remains unclear, however, how far the respect for basic structures of Germany's domestic legal system may thwart the execution of a judgment. (The "in particular" clause at the end of the cited passage suggests that a decision of the Court may clarify the matter but not necessarily in all cases). The most appropriate understanding of the BVerfG decision limits the impact of nonconstitutional law on the implementation of international judgments to cases where a collision of individual rights takes place and the European Court has failed to take all rights in question into account[112] or has failed to account for the balance struck by the legislature between the rights involved.

The confusion created by the convoluted language of parts of the *Görgülü* decision, however, should not obscure its main message: German courts must "take account" of international treaty law through the lens of the competent international court or tribunal, and they need to cross a high threshold if they wish to disregard decisions by international courts and tribunals acting within their jurisdiction.

[110] BVerfG 111, 307 at 329 (Engl. transl., *supra* note 19, para. 62.)

[111] BVerfG, Decision 1 BvR 2790/04 of 28 Dec. 2004, *available at* http://www.bverfg.de/entscheidungen/rk20041228_1bvr279004.html (no English translation available) (last accessed 22 April 2009).

[112] *See* Klein, "Urteilsanmerkung," *supra* note 44, at 1177–78.

C. *From Ignorance to Implementation? German Courts and the ICJ*

In the *LaGrand* case, in response to a German application, the ICJ decided that Article 36, Paragraph 1, of the Vienna Convention on Consular Relations (VCCR) grants individuals a right to consular notification.[113] Moreover, under Article 36, Paragraph 2, of the same Convention, state parties are required to provide remedies within their domestic legal systems for individuals whose rights under Article 36(1) have been violated, at least in cases involving severe penalties.[114] Since the ICJ decision in *LaGrand*, three cases regarding the VCCR reached the German Bundesgerichtshof[115] (Federal Supreme Court) and later the BVerfG.

In a 2006 chamber decision, the Federal Constitutional Court applied the reasoning of the *Görgülü* decisions to the relationship between the ICJ and the Federal Constitutional Court.[116] Accordingly, the principle of friendliness to international law enshrined in the German Constitution, and the judiciary's obligation to respect law and justice (*Gesetz* and *Recht*) pursuant to Article 20, Paragraph 3 of the German Basic Law, require domestic courts to "take into account" decisions of the ICJ that are binding on Germany.[117] In line with the *Görgülü* decisions, however, "taking into account" means "taking notice of the Convention provision as interpreted by [the international court] and applying it to the case, provided the application does not violate higher-ranking law, in particular constitutional law."[118] But even when ICJ decisions are not technically binding, the decision accords them a "function as normative guideline" ("normative *Leitfunktion*") for the parties that German courts must respect and apply when interpreting an international treaty.[119] In addition,

[113] LaGrand (Ger. v. U.S.), ICJ Reports 2001, pg. 466, at 515, referring to the Vienna Convention on Consular Relations of 24 April 1963, 596 UNTS, pg. 261.

[114] LaGrand (Ger. v. US), ICJ Reports 2001, pg. 466, at 515–16.

[115] BGH, Beschluss v. 7.11.2001 (Decision of 7 November 2001), 5 StR 116/01, (2003) *Strafverteidiger* 57 (with comment Paulus), (2002) *Neue Zeitschrift für Strafrecht* 168.

[116] BVerfG, 2 BvR 2115/01 of 19 Sept. 2006, *supra* note 23. For a comparison of this decision with the Supreme Court's decision in *Sanchez-Llamas, supra* note 17, *see* J. Gogolin, "Avena and Sanchez-Llamas Come to Germany – The German Constitutional Court Upholds Rights under the Vienna Convention on Consular Relations," 8 *German L.J.* 261 (2007); C. Hoppe, "Implementation of LaGrand and Avena in Germany and the United States: Exploring a Transatlantic Divide in Search of a Uniform Interpretation of Consular Rights," 18 *Eur. J. Int'l L.* 317 (2007).

[117] BVerfG, 2 BvR 2115/01 of 19 Sept. 2006, para. 58.

[118] *See supra* note 110 and accompanying text.

[119] BVerfG, 2 BvR 2115/01 of 19 Sept. 2006, *supra* note 23, para. 62; *see also Görgülü*, BVerfGE 111, 102 at 128; BVerwGE [Decisions of the Federal Administrative Court] 110, 203 at 210.

in a remarkable display of comparativism, the Constitutional Court analyzed the U.S. Supreme Court judgment in *Sanchez-Llamas* and agreed with the dissenters rather than the Supreme Court majority.[120] Because of the failure of the Federal Supreme Court to properly consider the ICJ decisions, the chamber of the Constitutional Court quashed two of the three decisions in question and referred them back to the Federal Supreme Court. At the time of writing in May 2009, the implementing decisions of the Federal Supreme Court[121] that were rather reluctant to implement the Constitutional Court ruling are pending at the Federal Constitutional Court.

The German Court's decision does not follow a path of complete subservience to international courts and tribunals. It preserves the supremacy of the German Constitution, but it emphasizes that international integration is also a constitutional value and may thus require a considerable measure of respect and accommodation toward competent international courts. In an ideal case, this procedure will result in a meaningful dialogue between international and domestic courts.[122]

IV. DEMOCRACY AND THE IMPLEMENTATION OF INTERNATIONAL LAW BY DOMESTIC COURTS

The ideal of dialogue does not deny the possibility of clashes between the domestic legal order and international treaties or judgments interpreting and applying those treaties. German courts tend to interpret constitutional provisions in harmony with treaties and international court decisions. Clear conflicts of wording will be extremely rare, particularly with regard to treaties that have passed parliamentary approval procedures. However, one might ask whether such a nonconflictual view accommodates too much. In other words, how do German courts square their practice with democracy? Some U.S. writers maintain that domestic democracy should always take precedence over international legal strictures, and, as we shall see, Art. 23 GG and some passages in the relevant German case law seem to agree.[123]

This section analyzes the *Maastricht* decision, with particular emphasis on the question of democracy. In addition, it briefly touches on a recent case that raises the question of whether direct democracy at the local level can

[120] BVerfG, 2 BvR 2115/01 of 19 Sept. 2006, *supra* note 23, para. 61.
[121] BGH, Neue Juristische Wochenschrift, 2008, pg. 307 ff.
[122] *See* Mückl, "Kooperation oder Konfrontation," *supra* note 69, at 418–19.
[123] J.L. Goldsmith and E.A. Posner, *Limits of International Law* (Oxford UP, Oxford 2005) at 205 ff.

override international agreements. The analysis sheds light on the attitude of German courts toward the relationship among democracy, federalism, and international integration.

A. Maastricht *and the Consequences: Limits to International Legal Integration*

The decision of the BVerfG in the *Maastricht* case remains the most important yardstick for a discussion of German views about the relationship between democracy and international integration by treaty. European integration is by far the most ambitious project of integration by treaty. Although the project of a constitutional treaty has failed, the ECJ used the term *constitution* in its early case law to describe the huge impact of the founding treaties of the European Union.[124] Indeed, given the supranational character of the TEC, the term *constitutional treaty* provides an apt description, especially because the TEC is directly applicable in the domestic legal order and enjoys supremacy over domestic law.[125] The Lisbon Treaty that is expected to replace the failed constitutional treaty will, if ratified, further strengthen the quasi-constitutional features of the EU legal order, regardless of the change of name.[126]

Democracy is enshrined in Article 20 and Article 79, Paragraph 3, of the GG as one of the central tenets of the German constitutional order that cannot be removed by means of a constitutional amendment, let alone by an international treaty. Article 23, Paragraph 1, lists respect for democratic principles and human rights among the conditions for German participation in the development of the European Union.[127] Its second sentence also makes clear that the transfer of powers to the union is conditioned on respect for these basic principles. Nevertheless, in the absence of a democratic world state, the democratic deficit is an inherent feature of any international organization, particularly the European Union, with its broad powers and its institutionalized intervention in the previously sovereign affairs

[124] *See supra* note 71.

[125] See the famous ECJ judgments in *van Gend & Loos* and *Costa/E.N.E.L.*, *supra* note 5.

[126] See *supra* note 78 and accompanying text.

[127] Art. 23, para. 1, secs. 1 and 2 state: "With a view to establishing a united Europe, the Federal Republic of Germany shall participate in the development of the European Union that is committed to democratic, social, and federal principles, to the rule of law, and to the principle of subsidiarity, and that guarantees a level of protection of basic rights essentially comparable to that afforded by this Basic Law. To this end the Federation may transfer sovereign powers by a law with the consent of the Bundesrat."

of its member states.[128] In a special legal order that claims, unlike most other international law, direct effect and supremacy, the question arises as to how these immediately legally binding and effective decisions are legitimated.

Faced with this problem, the BVerfG emphasized that it was willing to supervise the democratic legitimacy of the European institutions. First, it transformed the objective principle of democracy into an individual right of citizens by reinterpreting the principles of free and fair elections in Article 38 of the Constitution[129] to provide for an individual right to democracy.[130] Second, the Court maintained that the democratic legitimacy of the European Union depended primarily on national democratic processes, reducing the European Parliament to a "supporting function."[131] Third, it emphasized that the national legislatures needed to maintain competences of substantial weight to fulfill the requirements of the principle of democracy.[132]

> If the peoples of the individual States provide democratic legitimation through the agency of their national parliaments (as at present) limits are then set by virtue of the democratic principle to the extension of the European Communities' functions and powers. . . . The States need sufficiently important spheres of activity of their own in which the people of each can develop and articulate itself in a process of political will-formation which it legitimates and controls, in order thus to give legal expression to what binds the people together (to a greater or lesser degree of homogeneity) spiritually, socially and politically. . . . From all that it follows that functions of substantial importance must remain for the German Bundestag [federal parliament].[133]

Finally, the BVerfG deduced from these holdings a requirement of determinacy for the delegation of powers to the European Union: "There is accordingly a breach of Article 38 of the Constitution if an Act that opens

[128] *See, e.g.*, Calliess, "Auswärtige Gewalt," *supra* note 28, at 616–17. On the democratic deficit of the European Union, *see* Weiler, *supra* note 16, 264 ff. with further references.

[129] Art. 38 provides that "(1) Members of the German Bundestag shall be elected in general, direct, free, equal, and secret elections. They shall be representatives of the whole people, not bound by orders or instructions, and responsible only to their conscience. (2) Any person who has attained the age of eighteen shall be entitled to vote; any person who has attained the age of majority may be elected. (3) Details shall be regulated by a federal law."

[130] Brunner v. European Union Treaty, BVerfGE 89, 155 at 187; [1994] 1 CMLR 76, para. 3 ff.

[131] BVerfGE 89, 155 at 189; [1994] 1 CMLR 87.

[132] BVerfGE 89, 155 at 190; [1994] 1 CMLR 88.

[133] BVerfGE 89, 155 at 207, [1994] 1 CMLR 88. For criticism regarding the citation to the homogeneity argument, *see* Weiler, *supra* note 16, at 1655 ff.

up the German legal system to the direct validity and application of the law of the (supra-national) European Communities does not establish with sufficient certainty the powers that are transferred and the intended programme of integration."[134] Accordingly, if the European Union oversteps the limits contained in the treaty transferring sovereign powers to it, such an action by the European Union would not be legally binding within the domestic legal sphere.[135] With this line of argument, the German Court derived from the principle of democracy the requirement of determinacy and the principle that German court(s) exercise supervisory powers. With these qualifications, the Court decided that the act ratifying the Maastricht Treaty passed constitutional scrutiny.

However, this argument may prove too much. The very purpose of international and regional integration is to solve problems that cannot be tackled efficiently or effectively at the domestic level. A failure to solve these problems would not contribute to domestic democracy. Thus, the Court took into account the benefits that accrue from the pooling of sovereignty.

> The conferring of sovereign powers has the consequence that their exercise no longer depends solely on the will of one member-State all the time. To see that as a breach of the constitutional principle of democracy would not only contradict the openness of the Constitution to integration . . . ; it would also entail a conception of democracy that would make every democratic state incapable of any integration going beyond the principle of unanimity. Unanimity as a universal requirement would inevitably set the wills of the particular States above that of the community of States itself and would put the very structure of such a community in doubt. The wording and sense of Articles 23 and 24 show that such a result is not intended.[136]

What is required, then, is the striking of a balance between domestic democracy and international integration. National parliaments protect democracy by approving the legal basis of any act of integration. After parliamentary approval, though, it is the task of domestic courts to ensure that international institutions remain within the confines of the powers delegated to them.

In theory, therefore, the conflict between national courts and international courts is unavoidable:[137] whereas the latter must determine the

[134] Brunner v. European Union Treaty, BVerfGE 89, 155 at 187, [1994] 1 CMLR 88–89.

[135] *Id.*, BVerfGE 89, 155 at 188, [1994] 1 CMLR 89.

[136] *Id.*, BVerfGE 89, 155 at 183, [1994] CMLR 85–86.

[137] On this point, *see* the two rapporteurs of the German Association of Constitutional Lawyers on this topic in 2006. F. Merli, "Rechtsprechungskonkurrenz zwischen nationalen

extent of the competences delegated to an international organization in the process of interpreting and applying the constituent treaty of that organization,[138] national courts claim a right to form an independent judgment to ensure that international institutions and their courts remain within the bounds of powers delegated to them.[139] Whereas, at times, the cooperation between international and domestic courts may become strained, confrontation is hardly unavoidable. Rather, reciprocal respect and accommodation are preferable. Indeed, while neither the ECJ nor the BVerfG has compromised on their respective claims of exclusivity, there has not been a single case of direct confrontation between the two courts, and to date, only one such case has occurred before a lower court.[140] Although the potential for conflict remains, it is up to the courts involved to avoid such a situation by applying generally accepted principles of legal interpretation to guide their decisions.

B. *Democracy versus International Treaties? Some Remarks on the* Waldschlösschen *Case*

The recent *Waldschlösschen* case has shown that the potential for conflict between treaty law and democracy is not limited to treaties of integration. Rather, the exercise of regional democracy may lead to violations of international treaties because of a discrepancy between the obligations assumed internationally and the status accorded to treaties domestically.

The people of the German city of Dresden decided by popular referendum to build a bridge in the Elbe Valley, the so-called Waldschlösschenbrücke, despite the valley's status as a World Cultural Heritage site. After this decision, the World Heritage Committee, an intergovernmental committee established under the UNESCO Convention concerning the Protection of

Verfassungsgerichten, Europäischem Gerichtshof und Europäischem Gerichtshof für Menschenrechte," 66 *Veröffentlichungen der Vereinigung der Deutschen Staatsrechtslehrer* (2007) 392 ff.; S. Oeter, "Rechtsprechungskonkurrenz zwischen nationalen Verfassungsgerichten, Europäischem Gerichtshof und Europäischem Gerichtshof für Menschenrechte," 66 *Veröffentlichungen der Vereinigung der Deutschen Staatsrechtslehrer* (2006) 361.

[138] *See, e.g.*, art. 220 of the TEC, *supra* note 6. For the equivalent provision regarding the ECtHR, *see* art. 19 ECHR, *supra* note 87.

[139] For an extensive analysis, *see* Mayer, in von Bogdandy and Bast (eds.), *Principles of European Constitutional Law, supra* note 71, at 281 ff.

[140] Finanzgericht Rheinland-Pfalz, Entscheidungen des Finanzgerichte [Decisions of Financial Courts] 378 (1995). The next instance, the Federal Court of Finance, did base its identical result in the case on other grounds. *See* Entscheidungen des Bundesfinanzhofs [Decisions of the Federal Court of Finance] 180, 231 at 236. For details, *see* Mayer, in von Bogdandy and Bast (eds.), *Principles of European Constitutional Law, supra* note 71, at 299 (with further references).

the World Cultural and Natural Heritage,[141] added the Elbe Valley to its List of World Heritage in Danger, pursuant to Article 11, Paragraph 4, of the Convention. The committee determined that the Elbe Valley would lose its status as a World Heritage site if the bridge was built.[142] Despite an apparent shift of public opinion after the committee's decision, the referendum was legally binding for three years,[143] and a new referendum within this period would have required a two-thirds majority in the city council. That majority did not exist.

Germany had ratified the UNESCO Convention under Article 59, Paragraph 2, of the GG without the approval of Parliament, because the federal government at that time had determined that the Convention was neither of a political character nor contradicted existing domestic law. The federal states were apparently involved in the ratification decision, but the Convention contains a federal clause in Article 34(b) that exempts regional authorities from the duty to enact legislation.

The Higher Administrative Court decided that it was not relevant whether the Convention contained concrete obligations that were directly applicable. Rather, in the absence of federal ratification legislation, and in the absence of a clear international obligation to protect the Elbe Valley, specifically, popular sovereignty trumped the more general duty to protect World Heritage sites.[144] A chamber of the Federal Constitutional Court rejected a complaint filed by city authorities who were opposed to building the bridge. On the one hand, the chamber pointed out that the Convention was not self-executing. On the other hand, it agreed that

> [i]n consequence of this international legal framework it is possible that, pursuant to constitutional law, the will of the citizens in a formal vote, as an authentic expression of democracy, prevails in a conflict over the development of a cultural landscape.... As a consequence, the possible detriments of such a decision – for example the loss of the status as a world heritage site and of the reputation attached to it – must be tolerated.[145]

Two aspects of this decision help explain the attitude of German courts toward the enforcement of international treaties. First, both courts avoided

[141] Convention Concerning the Protection of the World Cultural and Natural Heritage of 16 Nov. 1972, 1037 UNTS 153.

[142] UNESCO, World Heritage Committee, 30th Sess., 13 July 2006. *See* SächsOVG, decision of 9 March 2007, Az.: 4 BS 216/06, pg. 10, no. 8.

[143] § 24 Abs. 4 Saxonian Local Government Ordinance.

[144] SächsOVG, *supra* note 142, at 19.

[145] BVerfG (Federal Constitutional Court), 2 BvR 695/07 of 29 May 2007, para. 35, *available at* http://www.bverfg.de/entscheidungen/rk20070529_2bvr069507.html (last accessed 22 April 2009) (my translation).

a clear break with the Convention. Rather, the courts argued that the clash between the Convention and the local vote was more apparent than real, because the Convention defined the obligations of Germany very broadly, their bindingness on the local government was doubtful, and the application of the Convention by the World Heritage Committee was neither persuasive nor binding on the city of Dresden. This enabled the courts to avoid the charge of violating Germany's international legal obligations. Second, it is remarkable that both courts took the Convention extremely seriously: they did not simply hold the Convention to be non-self-executing and therefore irrelevant, and they did not claim that local democracy prevailed over international treaties. Rather, they attempted to strike a balance between the degree of international obligation and the constitutional value of democracy.

One may certainly reach a different conclusion as to the balance finally struck. For example, the German courts did not weigh the interests of other German World Heritage sites in the balance. Regardless, one cannot charge the courts with neglecting international obligations, as weak as they may have been. It is also remarkable that, in both the *Maastricht* and the *Waldschlösschen* cases, German courts regarded international integration and international treaties as values deserving respect and demanding implementation, even when measured against a foundational principle such as democracy. This is possible only because the constitution explicitly hails international integration as a constitutional value. Thus, international integration is not antithetical to democracy because integration itself is considered the will of the people.

V. CONCLUSION: TOWARD PLURALISM?

The German Constitutional Court does not recognize any inherent hierarchical authority of international courts but usually regards its relationship with international courts, such as the ECJ, as "cooperative."[146] It will thus integrate international legal pronouncements into German domestic law, not as a matter of hierarchy, but because integration into the international community is a value enshrined in the German Constitution. However, in practice, integration may entail some derogation from international standards. In the consular information cases, the Constitutional Court overruled the Federal Supreme Court, which had paid lip service to the international decision without actually following it. In the *Görgülü* case, the

[146] This was famously the description of the relationship between BVerfG and ECJ in the *Maastricht* decision, Brunner v. European Union Treaty, BVerfGE 89, 155 at 175, [1994] 1 CMLR 79 ("Kooperationsverhältnis" – relationship of cooperation between the ECJ and BVerfG regarding the protection of human rights).

local authorities were deaf both to the ECtHR and their own Constitutional Court, and the Constitutional Court, before ordering compliance with the ECtHR's decision, considered whether domestic legislation might be a bar to implementation of that decision. Nevertheless, the general practice is one of compliance with international decisions.

Thus, the role of German courts in the implementation of international treaties is twofold. On the one hand, they have a constitutional obligation to implement international treaties – especially treaties ratified with parliamentary consent, which are equivalent in rank to a domestic statute – provided that the treaty is self-executing in character. With regard to EU law, Article 234 of the TEC requires domestic courts to refer cases to the ECJ when unsettled questions of European law are involved in the decision. Also, with regard to international law, the Constitutional Court has emphasized the duty of domestic courts to implement international law, a role that German courts have regularly undertaken. Courts may have to recognize a certain executive prerogative, but this may cut both ways: either by giving the executive branch the option of not fulfilling non-self-executing obligations, or by allowing the executive branch to bring domestic law into compliance with international rights and obligations.

On the other hand, domestic courts may also, in rare cases, have to fulfill a gatekeeping[147] role to safeguard constitutional values against encroachments by international institutions that may interfere with vested rights of Germany and its citizens. But this is a role of last resort. Since the drafting of the German Constitution in the aftermath of World War II, international integration has been one of Germany's central goals, not only because of the dreadful Nazi past but also in recognition of the fact that a medium-size power needs friends, and because Germany benefits from the pooling of resources in a globalized world. It is likely that these basic characteristics of the attitude of German courts will continue for the foreseeable future.[148]

[147] *See* Kirchhof, *supra* note 22.

[148] This chapter was written before the Federal Constitutional Court issued its judgment of 30 June 2009, BVerfG, 2 BvE 2/08 vom 30.6.2009, on the Treaty of Lisbon on the European Union and the Treaty on the Functioning of the European Union, Official Journal C 115 of 9 May 2008. While upholding the constitutionality of the Treaty itself, the Federal Constitutional Court set aside the part of the implementing legislation demanding additional legislative rights for the Bundestag in European affairs before allowing a further transfer of competences to the EU. The judgment confirms the previous judgments of the Court, while emphasizing the residual rights of the Constitutional Court and Parliament to check on the exercise of competences by the EU itself and the federal government in the EU organs for the protection of Germany's constitutional identity and democracy.

6

India

Nihal Jayawickrama

Formerly Ariel F. Sallows Professor of Human Rights at the University of Saskatchewan and Associate Professor of Law at the University of Hong Kong

I. THE STATUS OF TREATIES IN THE DOMESTIC LEGAL SYSTEM

A. *The Nature of the State*

India is a Union of States. The Constitution of India, which was adopted by a constituent assembly in 1949, defines the distribution of power in the Union List, a State List and a Concurrent List.[1] Parliament (i.e., the President and the two Houses, known as the Council of States and the House of the People[2]) may make laws for the whole or any part of the territory of India, while a state legislature may make laws for the whole or any part of that state.[3] Parliament alone has exclusive power to make laws with respect to any of the matters enumerated in the Union List. Among these is "[e]ntering into treaties and agreements with foreign countries and implementing of treaties, agreements and conventions with foreign countries."[4] The executive power of the Union is vested in the President and is exercised by the President either directly or through officers subordinate to him or her.[5] This power extends to "the matters with respect to which Parliament has power to make laws, and to the exercise of such rights, authority and jurisdiction as are exercisable by the Government of

[1] "The Constitution is not only the paramount law of the land but it is the source and sustenance of all laws." Tellis v. Bombay Municipal Corp., [1987] LRC (Const) 351 at 366 (Chandrachud, CJ).

[2] INDIA CONST. art. 79.

[3] *Id.*, art. 245.

[4] Other items include foreign affairs; UN organization; and participation in international conferences, associations, and other bodies and implementation of decisions made by such bodies.

[5] INDIA CONST. art. 53.

India by virtue of any treaty or agreement."[6] In the exercise of functions, the President acts on the advice of the Council of Ministers, headed by the Prime Minister.[7] Treaties are entered into in the exercise of the executive power of the Union. The Constitution has empowered Parliament "to make any law for the whole of any part of the territory of India for implementing any treaty, agreement or convention with any other country or countries or any decision made at any international conference, association or other body."[8]

B. *Treaties Not Self-Executing*

According to the government of India, treaties are not self-executing and therefore "require enabling legislation, or constitutional and legal amendments in cases where existing provisions of law and the Constitution are not in consonance with the obligations arising from the treaty."[9] In other words, if a treaty merely replicates existing law, no legislative action is required and the existing law will continue to be applied; but if a treaty covers new ground or is inconsistent with existing law, new legislation is necessary to give effect to the terms of the treaty. Therefore, until municipal law is changed to accommodate a treaty, what binds a court is the former, not the latter.[10] This view is based on the dualist theory, which regards international law and municipal law as two separate systems of law that regulate different subject matter. They are mutually exclusive, and the former has no effect on the latter unless and until international law is transformed into municipal law through domestic legislation. One reason for this negative view is because "the making of a treaty is an executive act, while the performance of its obligations, if they entail alteration of the existing domestic law, requires legislative action."[11] It is, however, an accepted proposition of law in India that the rules of customary international law that are not

[6] *Id.*, art. 73.
[7] *Id.*, art. 74.
[8] *Id.*, art. 253.
[9] Third Periodic Report of India submitted under Article 40 of the International Covenant on Civil and Political Rights, U.N. Doc. CCPR/C/76/Add.6, 17 June 1996, para. 8.
[10] Jolly George Verghese v. Bank of Cochin, [1980] 2 SCR 913. See Sheela Barse v. Secretary, Children's Aid Society, (1987) SCC 469, per Bhagwati J: "India as a party to these international conventions, having ratified them, it is an obligation of the Government of India as also the State machinery to implement the same in the proper way."
[11] Attorney General for Canada v. Attorney General for Ontario, Privy Council on appeal from the Supreme Court of Canada, [1937] AC 326 at 347, per Lord Atkin.

contrary to the municipal law are deemed to be incorporated in the domestic law.[12]

In 1984 the Supreme Court of India addressed the question of whether international law was, of its own force, drawn into the law of India without the aid of a municipal statute, and if so, whether it then overrides municipal law in the event of conflict.[13] Having examined decisions of English courts on the doctrines of incorporation and transformation, Justice Chinnappa Reddy explained:

> There can be no question that nations must march with the international community, and the municipal law must respect rules of international law even as nations respect international opinion. The comity of nations requires that rules of international law may be accommodated in the municipal law even without express legislative sanction, provided they do not run into conflict with Acts of Parliament. But when they do run into such conflict, the sovereignty and the integrity of the Republic and the supremacy of the constituted legislatures in making the laws may not be subjected to external rules except to the extent legitimately accepted by the constituted legislatures themselves. The doctrine of incorporation also recognizes the position that the rules of international law are incorporated into national law and considered to be part of the national law, unless they are in conflict with Acts of Parliament. Comity of nations or no, municipal law must prevail in case of conflict. National courts cannot say yes if Parliament has said no to a principle of international law. National courts will endorse international law but not if it conflicts with national law. National courts being organs of the National State and not organs of international law must perforce apply national law if international law conflicts with it.[14]

II. THE APPLICATION OF TREATIES

A. *Directive Principles of State Policy*

Part IV of the Constitution contains the statement "Directive Principles of State Policy." Unlike the statement of fundamental rights that precedes it, this statement is not directly enforceable by any court. But the Constitution

[12] People's Union for Civil Liberties v. Union of India, [1999] 2 LRC 1 at 12. Domestic law would include statute law and judicial decisions.
[13] Gramophone Company of India v. Birendra Bahadur Pandey, [1984] 2 SCR 664.
[14] Gramophone Company, [1984] 2 SCR 673.

provides that "the principles therein laid down are nevertheless fundamental in the governance of the country and it shall be the duty of the State to apply these principles in making laws."[15] The last of these principles is titled "Promotion of International Peace and Security," and reads thus:

> 51 The State shall endeavour to –
>
> (a) promote international peace and security;
> (b) maintain just and honourable relations between nations;
> (c) foster respect for international law and treaty obligations in the dealings of organised peoples with one another; and
> (d) encourage settlement of international disputes by arbitration.

The directive principles, in the view of the Supreme Court, "form the fundamental feature and the social conscience of the Constitution and the Constitution enjoins upon the State to implement these directive principles. The directives thus provide the policy, the guidelines and the end of socio-economic freedom."[16] The Court has also held that the provisions of Parts III (Fundamental Rights) and IV (Directive Principles of State policy) are supplementary and complementary to each other, and that the fundamental rights must be construed in light of the directive principles.[17] Moreover, "[i]nternational law today is not confined to regulating the relations between the states. Its scope continues to extend. Today matters of social concern, such as health, education, and economics apart from human rights fall within the ambit of international regulations. International law is more than ever aimed at individuals."[18] The Supreme Court has observed that, in view of Article 51 of the directive principles, "this Court must interpret the language of the Constitution, if not intractable, which is after all a municipal law, in the light of the United Nations Charter and the solemn declaration subscribed to by India."[19] In the more recent case of *Visaka v. State of Rajasthan*,[20] Chief Justice Verma considered it to be "implicit from article 51(c)" that any international convention not inconsistent with the fundamental rights provisions in the Constitution and in harmony with its spirit must be read into those provisions to enlarge the meaning and content thereof. Indeed, Article 51 has been considered not only relevant but also

[15] Art. 37.
[16] State of Kerala v. Thomas, [1976] 1 SCR 906 (Fazal Ali, J).
[17] Krishnan v. State of Andhra Pradesh, [1993] 4 LRC 234 at 297.
[18] People's Union for Civil Liberties v. Union of India, [1999] 2 LRC 1 at 12 (Kuldip Singh, J).
[19] Kesavananda Bharati v. State of Kerala, (1973) 4 SCC 225 at 333.
[20] Visaka v. State of Rajasthan, [1997] 3 LRC 361.

highly influential in determining the impact of treaties on the domestic legal system.

B. *Treaties That Have Not Been Transformed into Municipal Law*

With respect to treaties that, though signed and ratified, have not been legislated into municipal law, the Supreme Court has, in a series of very innovative decisions, applied the following principles:

Principle One – Domestic Law Must be Interpreted in Accordance with the State's International Obligations. If two constructions of municipal law are possible, the court will lean in favour of adopting such construction as will bring the provisions of municipal law into harmony with international law or treaty obligations. Accordingly, a statute will be interpreted, so far as its language permits, so as not to be inconsistent with the comity of nations or the established rules of international law, and the court will avoid a construction which would give rise to such inconsistency, unless compelled to do so by plain and unambiguous language.[21]

In *Jolly George Verghese v. Bank of Cochin*,[22] the Supreme Court examined the validity of Section 51 of the Civil Procedure Code, which enabled a court, on the application of a decree holder, to order execution of the decree "by arrest and detention in prison" of the judgment-debtor if the court was satisfied that the latter "has, or has had since the date of the decree, the means to pay the amount of the decree or some substantial part thereof and refuses or neglects or has refused or neglected to pay the same." It was argued that this section was inconsistent with Article 11 of the International Covenant on Civil and Political Rights (ICCPR), which provides that "[n]o one shall be imprisoned merely on the ground of inability to fulfil a contractual obligation." Noting that India was a signatory to the Covenant, and that Article 51(c) of the Constitution "obligates the State to 'foster respect for international law and treaty obligations,'" the Court held that Section 51 of the Civil Procedure Code should be interpreted in accordance with the state's international obligations. Justice Krishna Iyer explained:

> The words which hurt are "or has had since the date of the decree, the means to pay the amount of the decree." This implies, superficially read, that if at any time after the passing of an old decree the judgment-debtor had come by some resources and had not discharged the decree, he could

[21] ADM v. Shivakant Shukla, (1976) 2 SCC 521 at 754.
[22] Jolly George Verghese, [1980] 2 SCR 913.

> be detained in prison even though at that later point of time he was found to be penniless. This is not a sound position apart from being inhuman going by the standards of article 11 of the Covenant and article 21 of the Constitution.[23] The simple default to discharge is not enough. There must be some element of bad faith beyond mere indifference to pay, some deliberate or recusant disposition in the past or, alternatively, current means to pay the decree or a substantial part of it. The provision emphasizes the need to establish not mere omission to pay but an attitude of refusal on demand verging on dishonest disowning of the obligation under the decree. Here, considerations of the debtor's other pressing needs and straitened circumstances will play prominently. We would have, by this construction, sauced law with justice, harmonised section 51 with the Covenant and the Constitution.[24]

Transmission Corporation of Andhra Pradesh v. Ch. Prabhakar[25] involved a person charged before an Andhra Pradesh metropolitan magistrate with theft of electrical energy. In this case, the Supreme Court examined the validity of an amendment to the Indian Electricity Act that was enacted by the Andhra Pradesh legislature after the trial had commenced and that purported to make several changes to the procedure and mode of trial of offenses under that act, including permitting the imposition of higher or more severe punishments and curtailing the right of appeal. Consequent to that amendment, the case was transferred to a special tribunal. It was argued that the amending act could not have any retroactive operation; that is, it could not affect the proceedings that had already commenced and were pending before court. Article 20(1) of the Constitution provided that "[n]o person shall be convicted of any offence except for violation of a law in force at the time of the commission of the act charged as an offence, nor be subjected to a penalty greater than that which might have been inflicted under the law in force at the time of the commission of the offence." A literal interpretation of this provision would mean that the protection available was only against a conviction for an act or omission that was not an offense under the law in force when the same was committed and against infliction of a greater penalty than what was provided under the law in force when

[23] Art. 21 reads: "No person shall be deprived of his life or personal liberty except according to procedure established by law." The Court observed that it could be inferred from art. 11 of the ICCPR that the "procedure" would be unreasonable or unfair in the absence of proof of willful failure to pay despite his sufficient means and the absence of more terribly pressing claims on his means such as medical bills to treat cancer or other grave illness.

[24] Jolly George Verghese, [1980] 2 SCR 913 at 922.

[25] Supreme Court of India, Civil Appeal 6131 of 2002, 26 May 2004, Judgments of the Supreme Court of India, *available at* http://www.judis.nic.in/supremecourt/.

the offense was committed. But, as the Court observed: "The Constitution, being a living organic document, needs to be construed in a broad and liberal sense. A construction most beneficial to the widest possible amplitude of its powers may have to be adopted. Of all the instruments, the constitution has the greatest claim to be construed broadly and liberally."[26] The Court cited both Article 11(2) of the Universal Declaration of Human Rights and Article 15 of the ICCPR,[27] and it noted that India was a state party to the Covenant and a member state of the United Nations. The Court said that, concerned as it was with the liberty of the person, a liberal construction, not a narrow one, had to be given to the language used in Article 20(1) of the Constitution. Accordingly, it was a moot point to debate

> whether the constitutional guarantee in article 20(1) is confined only to prohibition against conviction for any offence except for violation of a law in force at the time of the commission of the act charged as an offence and subjection to a penalty greater than that which might have been inflicted under the law in force at the time of the commission of the offence, or it also prohibits legislation which aggravates the degree of crime or makes it possible for an accused person to receive greater punishment even though it is also possible for him to receive the same punishment under the new law as could have been imposed under the prior law, or deprives the accused of any substantial right or immunity possessed at the time of the commission of the offence charged.[28]

The Court referred the question of the interpretation of Article 20(1) as to its scope and ambit to a larger bench for consideration.

Principle Two – In Construing Any Provision in Domestic Law Which is Ambiguous, the Meaning Which Conforms Most Closely to the Provisions of Any International Instrument Will be Preferred. Where a statute or subordinate legislation is ambiguous, the court will favor the construction that accords with India's obligations under a treaty or international convention

[26] *Id.*, para. 13.

[27] In his judgment, Justice Mathur erroneously but repeatedly cites art. 7 of the European Convention for the Protection of Human Rights and Fundamental Freedoms, to which, he says, India is a signatory state. It is obvious that he intended to refer to art. 15(1) of the ICCPR, which is in identical terms. Art. 15(1) provides: "No one shall be held guilty of any criminal offence on account of any act or omission which did not constitute a criminal offence, under national or international law, at the time when it was committed. Nor shall a heavier penalty be imposed than the one that was applicable at the time when the criminal offence was committed."

[28] Supreme Court of India, Civil Appeal 6131 of 2002, 26 May 2004, Judgments of the Supreme Court of India, *available at* http://www.judis.nic.in/supremecourt/, para. 15.

to which India is a party. This is because Parliament, prima facie, intends to give effect to India's obligations under international law.[29]

In *People's Union for Civil Liberties v. Union of India*,[30] the Supreme Court was required to determine whether a police officer who had retired as director of the Central Bureau of Investigations was eligible to be appointed as a member of the National Human Rights Commission. The relevant statutory provision stipulated that the Commission shall consist of (1) a chairperson who shall have been a chief justice of the Supreme Court; (2) one member who is, or has been, a judge of the Supreme Court; (3) one member who is, or has been, the chief justice of a High Court; and (4) two members to be appointed from among persons having "knowledge of, or practical experience in, matters relating to human rights." The question that arose was whether a retired police officer would fall in the category stipulated under (4). In examining that question, the Court took account of the powers and functions of the Commission, which included reviewing the safeguards provided by or under the law for the protection of human rights, studying treaties and other international instruments on human rights, and recommending measures for their effective implementation. The Court noted that the Commission was also empowered to investigate and prosecute offenses arising out of the violation of human rights, but that many of these offenses related to custodial deaths and other alleged excesses by members of the police force.

> Assuming two constructions of section 3(2)(d) are reasonably possible, the construction which promotes public confidence, advances the cause of human rights, and seeks to fulfil the purpose of international instruments has to be preferred than the one which nullifies it. Ambiguity, if any, in the statutory provision is required to be removed by judicial process to advance the cause of protection of human rights.[31]

The Court considered it relevant to note first the developments at the international level that led to the enactment of the Protection of Human Rights Act of 1993 (under which the National Human Rights Commission was constituted), including the two international human rights covenants which India had ratified, and next, the Paris Principles on the Status of National Human Rights Institutions formulated under the auspices of the

[29] See Minister of State for Immigration and Ethnic Affairs v. Teoh, High Court of Australia, [1995] 3 LRC 1, cited with approval by Justice Jeevan Reddy in People's Union for Civil Liberties v. Union of India, 5 February 1997, [1999] 2 LRC 19.

[30] Supreme Court of India, Writ Petition (Civil), 18 January 2005, Judgments of the Supreme Court of India, *available at* http://www.judis.nic.in/supremecourt/.

[31] *Id.*

United Nations and endorsed by the Commission on Human Rights and the UN General Assembly. The Paris Principles set out the principles relating to the status and functioning of national institutions for the protection and promotion of human rights, including their composition and guarantees of independence and pluralism.

> We have to consider the eligibility of a person who has to become a part of the decision making process of the National Human Rights Commission and not the process of investigation which the commission may direct to be conducted. The exclusion of the category under consideration seems evident when seen as to who are included in the light of the Paris Principles, namely, representatives of non-governmental organizations responsible for human rights and efforts to combat racial discrimination, trade unions, concerned social and professional organizations, for example, associations of lawyers, doctors, journalists, eminent scientists; trends in philosophical or religious thought; universities and qualified experts; and parliament.[32]

The Court accordingly held that a police officer was ineligible to be appointed as a member of the Commission. As the Court explained:

> International treaties have influenced the interpretation of Indian law in several ways. This court has relied upon them for statutory interpretation where the terms of any legislation are not clear or are reasonably capable of more than one meaning. In such cases, the courts have relied upon the meaning which is in consonance with the treaties, for there is a prima facie presumption that Parliament did not intend to act in breach of international law, including State treaty obligations. It is also well accepted that in construing any provision in domestic legislation which is ambiguous, in the sense that it is capable of more than one meaning, the meaning which conforms most closely to the provisions of any international instrument is to be preferred, in the absence of any domestic law to the contrary. In this view, section 3(2)(d) is to be read keeping in view the Paris Principles.[33]

Principle Three – In Exercising Discretionary Powers, Regard Must be had to the Government's International Obligations. *Chinnappa v. Union of India*[34] was a public-interest interlocutory application in which it was argued

[32] *Id.*

[33] *Id.*

[34] Supreme Court of India, Interlocutory Application No.670 of 2001 in Writ Petition (Civil) No. 202 of 1995, 30 October 2002, Judgments of the Supreme Court of India, *available at* http://www.judis.nic.in/supremecourt/

that certain orders made by a state government were in violation of the provisions of the Wild Life (Protection) Act of 1972. In 1987, the government of India had declared Kudremukh National Park in the Western Ghats to be a national park in terms of Section 35(1) of the act. The forests in the area were among eighteen internationally recognized hotspots for biodiversity conservation in the world. Under the Forest (Conservation) Act 1980, no forestland or any portion thereof could be used for a nonforest purpose except with the approval of the central government. However, a state government, purporting to act under the Mineral Concession Rules made under the Mines and Minerals (Regulation and Development) Act 1957, had permitted a mining company to carry out mining activity in a portion of the national park. Affirming an injunction previously issued in a related proceeding prohibiting the removal of certain trees from the national park, the Supreme Court clarified the potential liabilities for noncompliance with environmental legislation. The Supreme Court observed that the government was enjoined under Article 48A (Directive Principles) of the Constitution "to protect and improve the environment and to safeguard the forests and wild life of the country," and that the two salutary principles which governed the law of the environment were: (i) the principle of sustainable development, and (ii) the precautionary principle. Accordingly, when exercising discretionary powers under the Conservation Act, regard must be had to the Convention on Biological Diversity 1992 to which the government of India had acceded.

In the course of a lengthy judgment in which he referred to several international initiatives, including the Stockholm Declaration of the United Nations Conference on Human Environment in 1972 and the World Charter for Nature adopted by the UN General Assembly in 1982,[35] Justice Arijit Pasayat explained:

> It needs to be highlighted that the Convention on Biological Diversity has been acceded to by our country and, therefore, it has to implement the same.... In the absence of any inconsistency between the domestic law and the international conventions, the rule of judicial construction is that regard must be had to international conventions and norms even in construing the domestic law. It is, therefore, necessary for the Government to keep in view the international obligations while exercising discretionary

[35] Also reproduced in full in the judgment was the reply of the "wise Indian Chief of Seattle" to "the offer of the great White Chief in Washington to buy their land." It was quoted because "The reply is profound. It is beautiful. It is timeless. It contains the wisdom of the ages. It is the first ever and most understanding statement on environment."

powers under the Conservation Act unless there are compelling reasons to depart therefrom.[36]

Principle Four – Domestic Law Must be Interpreted to Avoid Conflict With Well-Established Principles of International Law. The courts are under an obligation, within legitimate limits, to interpret a statute so as to avoid confrontation with the comity of nations or the well-established principles of international law. But if conflict is inevitable, the latter must yield.[37]

In *Gramophone Company of India Ltd. v. Birendra Bahadur Pandey*,[38] the issue before the Supreme Court was the meaning to be attributed to the word *import* in Section 53 of the Copyright Act. A company based in Nepal, a landlocked country bordering India, ordered a consignment of prerecorded cassettes from Singapore. The appellant company, having received information that the consignment had arrived in the port of Calcutta in India by ship and was awaiting its dispatch to Nepal, and suspecting the cassettes to be unauthorized reproductions of its own records and cassettes, moved the registrar of copyrights for action under Section 53 of the Copyright Act. That section enables the registrar to order that copies made out of India, of a work that if made in India would infringe copyright, shall not be imported. Because Nepal's only access to the sea is across India, a principal question that arose was whether the right of innocent passage necessary to facilitate Nepal's international trade extended to the transit of goods that may not be imported into India but whose importation into Nepal was not prohibited.

The Court noted that divergent views existed among the leading authorities on the question of whether there was a well-established principle of international law on the right of landlocked states to innocent passage of goods across the soil of another state. Consequently, it was necessary to rely on

[36] Supreme Court of India, Interlocutory Application No. 670 of 2001 in Writ Petition (Civil) No. 202 of 1995, 30 October 2002, Judgments of the Supreme Court of India, *available at* http://www.judis.nic.in/supremecourt/, para. 42.

[37] Gramophone Company, [1984] 2 SCR 664. A similar view was earlier expressed by the Supreme Court in Tractorexport Moscow v. Messrs Tarapore & Co., [1970] 3 SCR 53 at 70: "There is a presumption that Parliament does not assert or assume jurisdiction which goes beyond the limits established by the common consent of nations and statutes are to be interpreted, provided that their language permits, so as not to be inconsistent with the comity of nations or with the established principles of international law. But this principle applies only where there is an ambiguity and must give way before a clearly expressed intention. If statutory enactments are clear in meaning, they must be construed according to their meaning even though they are contrary to the comity of nations or international law."

[38] Gramophone Company, [1984] 2 SCR 664.

bilateral, regional, or multilateral treaties. India and Nepal had both signed the 1965 Convention on Transit Trade of Land-locked Countries.[39] That Convention, while providing for freedom of transit for the passage of goods between a landlocked state and the sea across the territory of a transit state, emphasized the need for agreement between the two states and specified certain exceptions. The bilateral transit treaty contracted between India and Nepal was based on the 1965 Convention and contained exceptions to protect "industrial, literary or artistic property." The 1952 Universal Copyright Convention (revised in 1971), to which India was a signatory, called on each contracting state to undertake "to provide for the adequate and effective protection of the right of authors and other copyright proprietors in literary, scientific and artistic works, including writings, musical, dramatic and cinematograph works and paintings, engravings and sculpture."[40]

In evaluating the tension between the Copyright Convention and the bilateral transit treaty, the Court observed: "So great is the concern of the international community for industrial, literary or artistic property that the Convention on Transit Trade of Land-locked Countries views traffic in this kind of property with the same gravity as it views traffic in narcotics, dangerous drugs and arms."[41] Accordingly, Justice Chinnappa Reddy concluded:

> In interpreting the word "import" in the Copyright Act, we must take note that while the positive requirement of the Copyright Conventions is to protect copyright, negatively also, the Transit Trade Convention and the bilateral Treaty make exceptions enabling the Transit State to take measures to protect copyright. If this much is borne in mind, it becomes clear that the word "import" in section 53 of the Copyright Act cannot bear the narrow interpretation sought to be placed upon it to limit it to import for commerce. It must be interpreted in a sense which will fit the Copyright Act into the setting of the International Conventions.[42] . . . We have, therefore, no hesitation in coming to the conclusion that the word "import" in sections 51 and 53 of the Copyright Act means "bringing into India from outside India", and that it is not limited to importation for commerce only but includes importation for transit across the country. Our interpretation, far from being inconsistent with any principle of international law, is

[39] Convention on Transit Trade of Land-locked Countries, New York, 8 July 1965 (entry into force 9 July 1967), 597 U.N.T.S. 3.

[40] Universal Copyright Convention, UNESCO Geneva, 6 September 1952 (entry into force 16 September 1955) 943 U.N.T.S. 178, registered at the United Nations, 27 September 1955, No. 2937.

[41] Gramophone Company, [1984] 2 SCR 664 at 684.

[42] [1984] 2 SCR 664 at 690.

> entirely in accord with International Conventions and the Treaties between India and Nepal. And, that we think is as it should be.[43]

Principle Five – An International Convention May Play a Part in the Development by the Courts of the Common Law. Where the provisions of a treaty, being the result of international harmonization and development of the laws on a subject, can be regarded as the international common law or transnational law rooted in the general principles of national laws, such provisions may, in the absence of specific statutory provisions, be adopted and adapted by courts to supplement and complement national statutes on the subject.[44]

In *M. V. Elisabeth v. Harwan Investment and Trading Pvt. Ltd.*,[45] a foreign shipping company that did not have a place of residence or business in India appealed against the assumption of jurisdiction by a High Court in an in rem action against one of its ships for a breach of obligation arising from the carriage of goods from an Indian port to a foreign port. The vessel had been arrested when it entered an Indian port. The Supreme Court held that it was within the competence of the appropriate Indian courts, in accordance with the general principles of maritime law and the applicable provisions of statutory law, to adjudicate claims involving all persons and things found within their jurisdiction. The Court observed that it was well recognized in international law that a merchant ship, though generally governed by the laws of the flag state, subjected itself to the jurisdiction of a foreign state as it entered its waters. The Geneva Convention on the Territorial Sea and the Contiguous Zone of 1958 and the Law of the Sea Convention of 1982 affirmed that the sovereignty of a state extended over its internal and territorial waters.

On the power of a state to arrest a foreign vessel, the Court noted that, while such power was recognized in several international conventions, India was not a party to many of them, including the International Convention Relating to the Arrest of Seagoing Ships of 1952. However, Justice Thommen was of this view:

> Although many of these Convention [*sic*] have yet to be ratified by India, they embody principles of law recognized by the generality of maritime States, and can therefore be regarded as part of our common law. The want of ratification of these Conventions is apparently not because of

[43] [1984] 2 SCR 664 at 691–92.
[44] M.V. Elisabeth v. Harwan Investment and Trading Pvt., [1992] 1 SCR 1003.
[45] M.V. Elisabeth, [1992] 1 SCR 1003.

for Action."[55] The Court had no hesitation in relying on these international initiatives for the purpose of construing the nature and ambit of the constitutional guarantee of gender equality in the Constitution.

> The meaning and content of the fundamental rights guaranteed in the Constitution are of sufficient amplitude to encompass all the facets of gender equality including prevention of sexual harassment or abuse. The independence of the judiciary forms a part of our constitutional scheme. The international Conventions and norms are to be read into them in the absence of enacted domestic law occupying a field when there is no inconsistency between them. It is now an accepted rule of judicial construction that regard must be had to international Conventions and norms for construing domestic law when there is no inconsistency between them and there is a void in the domestic law.[56]

Noting the absence of enacted law to provide for the effective enforcement of the basic human right of gender equality and guarantee against sexual harassment at workplaces, the Court proceeded to lay down specific guidelines and norms for due observance at all workplaces and other institutions, until legislation was enacted for the purpose. The Court directed that the guidelines and norms be strictly observed; they would be binding and enforceable in law.[57]

Apparel Export Promotion Council v. Chopra[58] also arose out of a complaint of sexual harassment in the workplace. A female clerk-typist, Miss X, made a complaint to the council's personnel director alleging sexual harassment by the secretary to the chairman of the council. The matter was referred to an inquiry officer, who concluded that the secretary had molested Miss X and had tried to touch her person with ulterior motives, despite her objections. The personnel director agreed with the inquiry officer's report and dismissed the secretary. The secretary appealed to the staff committee, an internal appellate body, which concluded that the order terminating the secretary's employment was legal, proper, and valid. The secretary thereupon commenced proceedings in the High Court by way of

[55] Visaka, [1997] 3 LRC 361 at 367.

[56] Visaka, [1997] 3 LRC 361 at 367. In this regard, the Court referred to the decision of the High Court of Australia in *Minister for Immigration and Ethnic Affairs v. Teoh*, [1995] 3 LRC 1, which had recognized the concept of legitimate expectation of the observance of international Conventions in the absence of a contrary legislative provision, even in the absence of a Bill of Rights in the Constitution of Australia.

[57] Visaka, [1997] 3 LRC 361 at 368–70. Among the matters addressed by the Court were preventive steps, criminal proceedings, disciplinary action, complaint mechanism, complaints committee, workers' initiative, awareness, and third-party harassment.

[58] Apparel Export Promotion Council v. Chopra, [2000] 1 LRC 563.

a writ petition for judicial review of the staff committee's decision. A single judge granted the petition, finding that the secretary had tried to molest but had not in fact molested Miss X and made an order directing reinstatement of the secretary. Affirming that decision, the Divisional Bench of the High Court found that, on the evidence, it was not even possible to conclude that there was an attempt to molest, as there had been no physical contact.

The Supreme Court reversed the High Court decision that the punishment of removal from service was not justified where a superior officer had not "actually molested" the complainant but had only "tried to molest" her and had "not managed" to make physical contact with her. "It appears that the High Court re-appreciated the evidence while exercising the power of judicial review and gave meaning to the expression 'molestation' as if it was dealing with a finding in a criminal trial," noted Chief Justice Anand.[59] He added that each incident of sexual harassment at the place of work resulted in a violation of the fundamental right to gender equality. He referred to a 1993 International Labour Organization seminar held in Manila, where it was recognized that sexual harassment of women at the workplace was a form of gender discrimination against women.

> In our opinion, the contents of the fundamental rights guaranteed in our Constitution are of sufficient amplitude to encompass all facets of gender equality, including prevention of sexual harassment and abuse, and the courts are under a constitutional obligation to protect and preserve those fundamental rights. That sexual harassment of a female at the place of work is incompatible with the dignity and honour of a female and needs to be eliminated and that there can be no compromise with such violations admits of no debate.[60]

Chief Justice Anand observed that the "message of international instruments such as the Convention on the Elimination of All Forms of Discrimination against Women 1979 and the Beijing Declaration which directs all state parties to take appropriate measures to prevent discrimination of all forms against women, besides taking steps to protect the honour and dignity of women, is loud and clear."[61] He referred also to Article 7 of the International Covenant on Economic, Social, and Cultural Rights, and he expressed the view that the international instruments cast an obligation on the Indian state to gender sensitize its laws. He emphasized:

[59] Apparel Export, [2000] 1 LRC 563 at 574.
[60] Apparel Export, [2000] 1 LRC 563 at 576.
[61] Apparel Export, [2000] 1 LRC 563 at 576.

> The courts are under an obligation to see that the message of the international instruments is not allowed to be drowned out. This court has in numerous cases emphasized that while discussing constitutional requirements, court and counsel must never forget the core principle embodied in the international conventions and instruments and as far as possible give effect to the principles contained in those international instruments. The courts are under an obligation to give due regard to international conventions and norms for construing domestic laws, more so when there is no inconsistency between them and there is a void in domestic law. . . . In cases involving violation of human rights, the courts must forever remain alive to the international instruments and conventions and apply the same to a given case when there is no inconsistency between the international norms and the domestic law occupying the field.[62]

People's Union for Civil Liberties v. Union of India[63] arose out of the publication of the report "Tapping of Politicians' Phones" by the Central Bureau of Investigation in the exercise of powers conferred by Section 5(2)(b) of the Indian Telegraph Act of 1885.[64] The report highlighted several deficiencies in the application of Section 5(2)(b). These included not properly maintaining authorization records, incomplete lists of interception of telephones, interception continuing beyond authorized periods, and so on. The People's Union for Civil Liberties challenged the constitutional validity of Section 5(2)(b), contending, inter alia, that the right to privacy (which was not expressly mentioned in the Constitution) was a fundamental right, and that to save Section 5(2)(b) from being declared unconstitutional, it was necessary to read it down to provide procedural safeguards to protect the right to privacy.

The Supreme Court held that Article 17 of the ICCPR, which recognizes the right of the individual to the protection of the law against any arbitrary or unlawful interference with his or her privacy, family, home or correspondence, and unlawful attacks on his or her honor or reputation, "does not go contrary to any part of our municipal law." Accordingly, although the

[62] Apparel Export, [2000] 1 LRC 563 at 576–77. See also Hariharan v. Reserve Bank of India, [2000] 3 LRC 71, in which the Supreme Court construed the Guardian and Wards Act 1890 in a manner that was consistent with the Convention on the Elimination of All Forms of Discrimination against Women 1979.

[63] People's Union for Civil Liberties, [1999] 2 LRC 1.

[64] Sec. 5(2) provided that, in the event of the occurrence of a public emergency or in the interest of public safety, the central government or a state government or any officer specially authorized, could intercept telegraphed messages if satisfied that it was necessary or expedient to do so in the interest of (1) the sovereignty and integrity of India, (2) the security of the state, (3) friendly relations with foreign states, (4) public order, and (5) to prevent inciting the commission of a crime.

right to privacy, as such, had not been identified under the Constitution, it was a part of the right to life and personal liberty enshrined under Article 21 of the Constitution, and it could not be curtailed "except according to procedure established by law." Justice Kuldip Singh observed that, while as a concept the right to privacy might be "too broad and moralistic for judicial definition," so that whether it could be invoked or infringed in a given case would depend on the facts, the right to conduct a telephone conversation in the privacy of one's home or office without interference could certainly be claimed as falling within the right to privacy.[65] Noting that the statute had been in existence for more than a century but that successive governments had not thought it proper to frame the necessary rules, the Court proceeded to prescribe procedural safeguards for the exercise of the power under Section 5(2)(b) so that the right to privacy of a person was protected, and it ordered and directed that they be observed.[66]

Basu v. State of West Bengal[67] commenced with the receipt by the chief justice of a letter from the executive chairman of Legal Aid Services of the state of West Bengal to draw his attention to certain newspaper items regarding deaths in police lockups and custody. The letter submitted that it was imperative that the issue be examined in depth, custody jurisprudence developed, and modalities formulated for awarding compensation to the victim and/or his family for atrocities and death in police custody and that provision be made for the accountability of the officers concerned. The letter stated that efforts were often made to hush up the deaths, and thus such crimes went unpunished and flourished. The letter was treated as a writ petition and notices issued to all state governments and to the Law Commission. Among the issues raised at the hearing was whether monetary compensation should be awarded for established infringements of the fundamental rights guaranteed by Articles 21 (the right to life and personal liberty) and 22 (protection against arrest and detention) of the Constitution.

The Supreme Court noted that there was no provision in the Constitution similar to Article 9(5) of the ICCPR, which provides that "[a]nyone who has been the victim of unlawful arrest or detention shall have an enforceable right to compensation." In fact, the government of India, when ratifying the Covenant in 1979, had made a specific reservation to the effect that the Indian legal system did not recognize such a right to compensation. However, the Court was of the view that that reservation had lost its relevance in view

[65] People's Union for Civil Liberties, [1999] 2 LRC 1 at 11. *See also* Kharak Singh v. State of Uttar Pradesh, [1964] 1 SCR 332.
[66] People's Union for Civil Liberties, [1999] 2 LRC 1 at 16–18.
[67] Basu v. State of West Bengal, [1997] 2 LRC 1.

of the law laid down in a number of cases awarding compensation for the infringement of the fundamental right to life of a citizen.[68] Although there was indeed no express provision in the Constitution for grant of compensation for violation of a fundamental right to life; nonetheless, the Court had judicially evolved a right to compensation in cases of established unconstitutional deprivation of personal liberty or life.[69] Justice Anand concluded:

> It is now a well-accepted proposition in most of the jurisdictions that monetary or pecuniary compensation is an appropriate and indeed an effective and sometimes the only suitable remedy for redressal of the established infringement of the fundamental right to life of a citizen by the public servants, and the state is vicariously liable for their acts. The claim of the citizen is based on the principle of strict liability to which the defence of sovereign immunity is not available and the citizen must receive the amount of compensation from the state, which shall have the right to be indemnified by the wrongdoer. In the assessment of compensation, the emphasis has to be on the compensatory and not on the punitive element. The objective is to apply balm to the wounds and not to punish the transgressor or the offender, as awarding appropriate punishment for the offence (irrespective of compensation) must be left to the criminal courts in which the offender is prosecuted, which the state, in law, is duty bound to do. The award of compensation in the public law jurisdiction is also without prejudice to any other action like civil suit for damages which is lawfully available to the victim or the heirs of the deceased victim with respect to the same matter for the tortuous act committed by the functionaries of the state. The quantum of compensation will, of course, depend upon the peculiar facts of each case and no strait jacket formula can be evolved in that behalf. The relief to redress the wrong for the established invasion of the fundamental rights of the citizen, under the public law jurisdiction is, thus, in addition to the traditional remedies and not in derogation of them. The amount of compensation as awarded by the court and paid by the state to redress the wrong done may, in a given case, be adjusted against any amount which may be awarded to the claimant by way of damages in a civil suit.[70]

[68] *See, e.g.*, Rudul Sah v. State of Bihar, (1983) 4 SCC 141; Hongray v. Union of India, [1984] 1 SCR 904; Bhim Singh v. State of Jammu and Kashmir, (1984) Supp. SCC 504, (1985) 4 SCC 677; and Saheli v. Commissioner of Prisons, (1990) 1 SCC 422.

[69] In Nilibati Behera v. State of Orissa, (1994) 2 LRC 99, the Court cited the International Covenant on Civil and Political Rights to support the view that "an enforceable right to compensation is not alien to the concept of enforcement of a guaranteed right" as a public law remedy under art. 32 of the Constitution, distinct from the private law remedy in torts.

[70] Basu, [1997] 2 LRC 1 at 25–26. In the following year, in People's Union for Civil Liberties, [1999] 2 LRC 19 at 28, the Supreme Court, in ordering the payment of compensation to the

The Court also considered it appropriate to issue requirements to be followed in all cases of arrest or detention until legal provisions were made on that behalf. The Court stated that failure to comply with the requirements would, apart from rendering the official concerned liable for departmental action, also render him or her liable to be punished for contempt of court.[71]

Chairman, Railway Board v. Chandrima Das[72] began with a petition filed in the Calcutta High Court by an advocate practicing in that court against the chairman of the Railway Board and several other railway and police officials, claiming compensation for a Bangladeshi national who had been gang-raped by several railway employees in a room at a railway station and later in a rented flat. The respondents argued, inter alia, that the Railway Board was not liable to pay compensation to the victim because she was a foreigner and not an Indian national. The Supreme Court referred to the Universal Declaration of Human Rights for the purpose of determining whether the right to life in Article 21 of the Constitution[73] could be invoked by a noncitizen. Noting that Article 3 of the Declaration recognized the right of "everyone" to life, liberty, and security of person, and that Article 2 required that no distinction shall be made on the basis of the political, jurisdictional, or international status of the country or territory to which a person belongs, Justice Saghir Ahmad held:

> On this principle, even those who are not citizens of this country and come here merely as tourists or in any other capacity will be entitled to the protection of their lives in accordance with the constitutional provisions. They also have a right to "life" in this country. Thus, they also have the right to live, so long as they are here, with human dignity. Just as the State is under an obligation to protect the life of every citizen in this country, so also the State is under an obligation to protect the life of the persons who are not citizens.[74]

families of two persons who had died in custody, reiterated that "it would suffice to state that the provisions of the Covenant, which elucidate and go to effectuate the fundamental rights guaranteed by our Constitution, can certainly be relied upon by the courts as facets of those fundamental rights and, hence, enforceable as such."

[71] Basu, [1997] 2 LRC 1 at 18–20.

[72] Chairman, Railway Board v. Chandrima Das, [2000] 1 SCR 480.

[73] Art. 21 provides: "No person shall be deprived of his life or personal liberty except according to procedure established by law."

[74] Chairman, Railway Board, [2000] 1 SCR 480 at 501. While he noted that India had ratified the International Covenant on Civil and Political Rights, the judge did not specifically refer to art. 6(1) of that Covenant, which reads: "Every human being has the inherent right to life. This right shall be protected by law. No one shall be arbitrarily deprived of his life."

In *Andhra Pradesh Pollution Control Board v. Nayudu (No. 2)*,[75] the question at issue was the location of a hazardous industry within ten kilometers of a reservoir. Affirming the refusal of the Pollution Control Board to provide a no-objection certificate to a company that had purchased twelve acres of land within the prohibited zone to establish a factory for the production of "vegetable oils including solvent extracted oils," the Supreme Court recognized that the right to a healthy environment and to sustainable development were fundamental rights implicit in the right to life. Indeed, the Supreme Court of India had been one of the first courts to develop the concept of a right to healthy environment as part of the right to life under Article 21 of the Constitution.[76] Noting that water was a basic need for the survival of human beings,[77] the Court invoked a resolution adopted at the UN Water Conference in 1977, which stated, inter alia, "All people, whatever their stage of development and their social and economic conditions, have the right to have access to drinking water in quantum and of a quality equal to their basic needs."[78] Justice Jagannadha Rao concluded that the right of access to drinking water was fundamental to life; therefore, there was a duty on the state under Article 21 of the Constitution to provide clean drinking water to its citizens.

C. *Treaties That Have Been Transformed into Municipal Law*

Recent jurisprudence records at least two instances when the Supreme Court had recourse to the original treaty in order to satisfy itself that the treaty provisions had been faithfully transformed into municipal law.

In *Dadu alias Tulsidas v. State of Maharashtra*,[79] the Supreme Court addressed the question of the constitutional validity of Section 32A of the Narcotic Drugs and Psychotropic Substances Act of 1985. That section read as follows: "Notwithstanding anything contained in the Code of Criminal Procedure, 1973 or any other law for the time being in force but subject to the provisions of section 33, no sentence awarded under this Act (other than section 27) shall be suspended or remitted or commuted." It was argued that the section, by purporting to take away the judicial function of

[75] Andhra Pradesh Pollution Control Board v. Nayudu (No. 2), [2002] 3 LRC 275.

[76] *See* Bandhua Mukti Morcha v. Union of India, [1984] 2 SCR 67.

[77] In Narmada Bachao Andolan v. Union of India, (1999) 8 SCC 308, Justice Kirpal observed that "[w]ater is the basic need for the survival of human beings and is part of right to life and human rights as enshrined in article 21 of the Constitution of India."

[78] Andhra Pradesh Pollution Control, [2002] 3 LRC 275 at 279.

[79] Supreme Court of India, Writ Petition (Criminal) 169 of 1999, 12 October 2000, Judgments of the Supreme Court of India, *available at* http://www.judis.nic.in/supremecourt/.

the court in the matter of deciding whether, after conviction, the sentence could be suspended, created an unreasonable distinction between prisoners convicted under that act and prisoners convicted under other statutes. It was further argued that the taking away of that judicial function rendered the substantive right of appeal illusory and ineffective. The vires of the section was defended on the ground that it was enacted to fulfill the international obligations imposed on the state by the International Convention of Psychotropic Substances of 1971. Justice Sethi examined in detail the provisions of the Convention and of the UN Convention against Illicit Traffic in Narcotic Drugs and Psychotropic Substances of 1988, to which India was a party, and concluded that this submission was without substance.

> A perusal of the [1988] Convention clearly and unambiguously shows that the court's jurisdiction with respect to the offences relating to narcotic drugs and psychotropic substances was never intended to be ousted, taken away or curtailed.... There was no international agreement to put a blanket ban on the power of the court to suspend the sentence awarded to a criminal under the Act notwithstanding the constitutional principles and basic concepts of its legal system.[80]

The Court held that Section 32A, insofar as it completely debarred the appellate courts from suspending a sentence imposed on a person convicted under the act, could not stand the test of constitutionality.

In *Indian Handicrafts Emporium v. Union of India*,[81] a group of persons engaged in the business of manufacture and sale of ivory-based articles challenged the validity of a 1991 amendment to the Wild Life (Protection) Act of 1972, which imposed a total prohibition on trade in imported ivory. The amending law was made operational six months after enactment to enable traders to dispose of their stocks of ivory. It was argued that the law violated, *inter alia*, the constitutional right of a citizen to carry on any occupation, trade, or business. The Supreme Court referred to the Convention on International Trade in Endangered Species of Wild Fauna and Flora, which India had ratified, and to Appendix 1 of that Convention. The appendix came into effect in 1990; it provided, *inter alia*, for the complete prohibition of internal and transborder trade in ivory. The amending act had been enacted to give effect to the Convention. Referring to a statement made in Parliament by the minister of state for the environment and forests that, although the trade in Indian ivory had been banned in 1986, the trade

[80] *Id.*

[81] Supreme Court of India, Civil Appeal 7533 of 1997, 27 August 2003, Judgments of the Supreme Court of India, *available at* http://www.judis.nic.in/supremecourt/.

in imported ivory provided an opportunity for unscrupulous ivory traders to legalize poached ivory in the name of imported ivory, the Court held that the law constituted a reasonable restriction on the exercise of the right relied on.[82]

III. DOMESTIC LEGAL PRINCIPLES GOVERNING JUDICIAL REMEDIES

A. *Violation of Treaty-Protected Rights*

The answer to the question of whether a person, natural or corporate, could obtain a remedy from a domestic court for a violation of a treaty-protected right is to be found in the following passage from a judgment of the High Court of Kerala, which was cited with approval by the Supreme Court.[83] The High Court was referring to the ICCPR:

> The remedy for breaches of International Law in general is not to be found in the law courts of the State because International Law per se or proprio vigore has not the force or authority of civil law, till under its inspirational impact actual legislation is undertaken. I agree that the Declaration of Human Rights merely sets out a common standard of achievement for all peoples and all nations but cannot create a binding set of rules. Member States may seek, through appropriate agencies, to initiate action when these basic rights are violated; but individual citizens cannot complain about their breach in the municipal courts even if the country concerned has adopted the Covenant and ratified the Optional Protocol. The individual cannot come to Court but may complain to the Human Rights Committee which, in turn, will set in motion other procedures. In short, the basic human rights enshrined in the International Covenants above referred to may at best inform judicial institutions and inspire legislative action within Member States; but apart from such deep reverence, remedial action at the instance of an aggrieved individual is beyond the area of judicial authority.[84]

B. *Violation of Constitutionally Protected Rights*

The right to move the Supreme Court by appropriate proceedings for the enforcement of the fundamental rights recognized in the Constitution is

[82] *Id.*
[83] Jolly George Verghese, [1980] 2 SCR 913.
[84] Jolly George Verghese, [1980] 2 SCR 913 at 919–20.

guaranteed.[85] The jurisdiction of the Supreme Court includes the power to issue, in appropriate cases, directions, orders, or writs in the nature of habeas corpus, mandamus, prohibition, quo warranto, and certiorari.[86] The Supreme Court, in the exercise of its jurisdiction, may also pass such a decree or make such an order as is necessary "for doing complete justice to any cause or matter pending before it."[87] The law declared by the Supreme Court is binding on all courts within the territory of India,[88] and any decree passed or order made is also enforceable throughout the territory of India.[89]

The nature and extent of the relief which the Supreme Court is empowered to grant has been described by Justice Pathak: "Article 32 confers the widest amplitude of power on this Court in the matter of granting relief. It has power to issue 'directions or orders or writs', and there is no specific indication, no express language, limiting or circumscribing that power."[90] Yet the power is limited by its very nature: that it is judicial power. Justice Pathak explained:

> It is power that pertains to the judicial organ of the State, identified by the very nature of the judicial institution. There are certain fundamental constitutional concepts which, although elementary, need to be recalled at times. The Constitution envisages a broad division of the power of the State between the legislature, the executive and the judiciary. Although the division is not precisely demarcated, there is general acknowledgment of its limits. The limits can be gathered from the written text of the Constitution, from convention and constitutional practice, and from an entire array of judicial decisions. The constitutional lawyer concedes a certain measure of overlapping in functional action among the three organs of the State. But there is no warrant for assuming a geometrical congruence. It is commonplace that while the Legislature enacts the law, the Executive implements it and the Court interprets it and, in doing so, adjudicates on

[85] In Ujjam Bai v. State of Uttar Pradesh, [1963] 1 SCR 778, the Supreme Court held that the question of enforcement of the fundamental rights would arise in three classes of cases: (1) where action is taken under a statute that is ultra vires the Constitution; (2) where the statute is intra vires but the action taken is without jurisdiction; and (3) an authority under an obligation to act judicially passes an order in violation of the principles of natural justice. In Naresh Shridhar Mirajkar v. State of Maharashtra, [1966] 3 SCR 744, a special bench of nine judges held that when the action taken against a citizen is procedurally ultra vires, the aggrieved party can move the Supreme Court for enforcement of a fundamental right.

[86] India Const. art. 32.

[87] *Id.*, art. 142.

[88] *Id.*, art. 141.

[89] *Id.*, art. 142.

[90] Bandhua Mukti Morcha v. Union of India, [1984] 2 SCR 67 at 161.

the validity of executive action and, under our constitution, even judges the validity of the legislation itself. And yet it is well recognized that in a certain sphere the Legislature is possessed of judicial power, the Executive possesses a measure of both legislative and judicial functions, and the Court, in its duty of interpreting the law, accomplishes in its perfected action a marginal degree of legislative exercise. Nonetheless, a fine and delicate balance is envisaged under our Constitution between these primary institutions of the State. . . .

Where the court embarks upon affirmative action in an attempt to remedy a constitutional imbalance within the social order, few critics will find fault with it so long as it confines itself to the scope of its legitimate authority. But there is always the possibility, in public interest litigation, of succumbing to the temptation of crossing into territory which properly pertains to the Legislature or the executive Government. For in most cases the jurisdiction of the Court is invoked when a default occurs in executive administration, and sometimes where a void in community life remains unfilled by legislative action. The resulting public grievance finds expression through social action groups, which consider the court an appropriate forum for removing the deficiencies. Indeed, the citizen seems to find it more convenient to apply to the Court for the vindication of constitutional rights than appeal to the executive or legislative organs of the State. In the process of correcting executive error or removing legislative omission the court can so easily find itself involved in policy making of a quality and to a degree characteristic of political authority, and indeed run the risk of being mistaken for one. An excessively political role identifiable with political governance betrays the Court into functions alien to its fundamental character and tends to destroy the delicate balance envisaged in our constitutional system between its three basic institutions. The Judge, conceived in the true classical mould, is an impartial arbiter, beyond and above political bias and prejudice, functioning silently in accordance with the constitution and his judicial conscience. Thus does he maintain the legitimacy of the institution he serves and honour the trust which his office has reposed in him.[91]

Despite this cautionary statement delivered by a senior judge, the Supreme Court has, in recent years, boldly and profitably, ventured into executive and legislative territory on numerous occasions.

For example, in *Basu v. State of West Bengal*,[92] the Supreme Court observed that it was "a sacred duty of the court, as the custodian and protector of the fundamental and the basic human rights of the citizens"

[91] Bandhua Mukt Morcha, [1984] 2 SCR 67 at 161–62.
[92] Basu, [1997] 2 LRC 1.

to "deter breaches of the affirmed rights of every human being." It then proceeded to issue eleven requirements to be followed in all cases of arrest or detention "till legal provisions are made in that behalf as preventive measures." The Court directed:

> The requirements mentioned above shall be forwarded to the Director General of Police and the Home Secretary of every state/union territory and it shall be their obligation to circulate the same to every police station under their charge and get the same notified at every police station at a conspicuous place. It would also be useful and serve larger interests to broadcast the requirements on All India Radio besides being shown on the National Network of Doordashan and by publishing and distributing pamphlets in the local language containing these requirements for information of the general public.[93]

In *People's Union for Civil Liberties v. Union of India*,[94] the Supreme Court noted that Section 5(2) of the Indian Telegraph Act of 1885 set out the conditions under which the power to order the interception of messages could be exercised. Section 7(2)(b) empowered the government to make rules providing the "precautions to be taken for preventing the improper interception or disclosure of messages." Observing that the central government had not thought it proper to frame the necessary rules despite severe criticism of the manner in which the power under Section 5(2) had been exercised, the Court held that, to safeguard the right to privacy of an individual by ruling out arbitrariness in the exercise of that power, and until the central government laid down a just, fair, and reasonable procedure, the Court would prescribe the procedural safeguards. Accordingly, the Court formulated nine rules, in the form of orders and directions, including one under which review committees were to be established both at the central and at the state levels of government.[95]

In *Visaka v. State of Rajasthan*,[96] the Supreme Court observed that the obligation to enforce fundamental rights under Article 32 of the Constitution must, in the absence of legislation, be viewed "along with the role of the judiciary envisaged in the Beijing Statement of Principles of the Independence of the Judiciary in the LAWASIA region."[97] The Court referred,

[93] Basu, [1997] 2 LRC 1 at 20.
[94] People's Union for Civil Liberties, [1999] 2 LRC 1.
[95] Basu, [1997] 2 LRC 1 at 17–18.
[96] Visaka, [1997] 3 LRC 361.
[97] These principles were accepted by the chief justices of Asia and the Pacific at Beijing in 1995 as those representing the minimum standards to be observed to maintain the independence and effective functioning of the judiciary.

in particular, to the objectives of the judiciary as declared in Paragraph 10 of the Beijing Statement:

> The objectives and functions of the judiciary include the following: (a) to ensure that all persons are able to live securely under the Rule of Law; (b) to promote, within the proper limits of the judicial function, the observance and the attainment of human rights; and (c) to administer the law impartially among persons and between persons and the State.[98]

The Court noted the absence of enacted law to provide for the effective enforcement of the basic human right of gender equality and the guarantee against sexual harassment and abuse, more particularly against sexual harassment at workplaces. Accordingly, the Court proceeded to lay down guidelines and norms for due observance at all workplaces or other institutions, until legislation is enacted for the purpose. The Court emphasized that this was done in the exercise of the power available under Article 32 of the Constitution for enforcement of the fundamental rights, and further emphasized that this would be treated as the law declared by the Supreme Court under Article 141 of the Constitution.[99]

C. *Public-Interest Litigation*

The Supreme Court has waived some of its old, well-established procedural rules and practices to facilitate public-interest litigation, which now can be initiated not only by filing formal petitions in Court but also by writing letters and telegrams or when the Court takes notice of articles in newspapers. In *Bandhua Mukti Morcha v. Union of India*,[100] an organization dedicated to the cause of the release of bonded laborers in the country, addressed a letter to Justice Bhagwati. The letter alleged that there were a large number of laborers from different parts of the country who were working in some of the stone quarries in the state of Haryana under "inhuman and intolerable conditions"; that many of them were bonded laborers; and that the provisions of the Constitution and of various other social welfare laws passed for the benefit of these workers were not being implemented in regard to them.

[98] Visaka, [1997] 3 LRC 361 at 366.

[99] In Apparel Export Promotion Council, [2000] 1 LRC 563, also a case involving sexual harassment in the workplace, Chief Justice Anand described the guidelines as "a rather innovative judicial law-making process" that was resorted to "after taking note of the fact that the present civil and penal laws in the country do not adequately provide for specific protection of women from sexual harassment at places of work and that the enactment of such legislation would take a considerable time."

[100] Bandhua Mukti Morcha, [1984] 2 SCR 67.

The Court treated the letter as a writ petition and appointed a commission to inquire into the allegations. The commission confirmed the allegations, and the Court issued several directions to the central government and the state governments for implementing a host of social welfare laws then in force. Justice Bhagwati explained the rationale for the Court's intervention:

> [W]here a person or class of persons to whom legal injury is caused by reason of violation of a fundamental right is unable to approach the court for judicial redress on account of poverty or disability or socially or economically disadvantaged position, any member of the public acting *bona fide* can move the court for relief... so that the fundamental rights may become meaningful not only for the rich and well-to-do who have the means to approach the Court but also for large masses of people who are living a life of want and destitution and who are by reason of lack of awareness, assertiveness and resources unable to seek judicial redress.[101]

Recognizing that the poor and the disadvantaged cannot possibly produce relevant material before the court in support of their case, or even when an action is brought on their behalf by a citizen acting pro bono publico, Justice Bhagwati asked what the Supreme Court should do in such a case:

> Would the Supreme Court not be failing in the discharge of its constitutional duty of enforcing a fundamental right if it refuses to intervene because the petitioner belonging to the under-privileged segment of society or a public spirited citizen espousing his cause is unable to produce the relevant material before the Court? If the Supreme Court were to adopt a passive approach and decline to intervene in such a case because relevant material has not been produced before it by the party seeking its intervention, the fundamental rights would remain merely a teasing illusion so far as the poor and disadvantaged sections of the community are concerned. It is for this reason that the Supreme Court has evolved the practice of appointing commissioners for the purpose of gathering facts and data in regard to a complaint of breach of a fundamental right made on behalf of the weaker sections of society. The report of the commissioner would furnish *prima facie* evidence of the facts and data gathered by the commissioner... and the Court then considers the report of the commissioner and the affidavits which may have been filed and proceeds to adjudicate upon the issue arising in the writ petition. It would be entirely for the Court to consider what weight to attach to the facts and data stated in the report of the commissioner and to what extent to act upon such facts and data.[102]

[101] Bandhua Mukti Morcha, [1984] 2 SCR 67 at 105.
[102] Bandhua Mukti Morcha, [1984] 2 SCR 67 at 111–12.

Through such public interest litigation and the judicial activism for which it is now justly renowned, the Supreme Court of India has been able to extend the frontiers of human rights protection well beyond those that the UN General Assembly had in mind when the principal human rights treaties were adopted forty years ago.

IV. CONCLUSION

India is a country in which international law and municipal law are regarded as mutually exclusive systems, the former having no effect on the latter unless and until transformed through an act of parliament. However, by developing a body of interpretive jurisprudence, the Supreme Court has succeeded in incorporating into municipal law several important principles of international law encapsulated in recent multilateral treaties, of which some India is not even a signatory. Through this technique the Court has refashioned and adapted, and supplied deficiencies in, several Indian statutes to enable their application to meet the imperatives of contemporary life. In a significant departure from the conventional, straitlaced approach of many of the superior courts of the region, the Supreme Court of India, through its now legendary activism, continues to provide to those subject to its jurisdiction the obvious benefits of the expanding body of law of the international community.

7

Israel

David Kretzmer

Bruce W. Wayne Professor Emeritus of International Law, Hebrew University of Jerusalem; Professor of Law, Transitional Justice Institute, University of Ulster, and Academic Center of Law and Business, Ramat Gan

I. THE STATUS OF INTERNATIONAL LAW IN THE DOMESTIC LEGAL SYSTEM

A. *Introduction: The Constitutional and Legal System of Israel*

It is impossible to discuss the role of international law in the jurisprudence of Israel's courts without some understanding of the country's constitutional and legal system. This introduction will be devoted to a short description of that system.

Israel's Declaration of Independence of 14 May 1948, stated that the new state, established as the state of the Jewish people, would have a formal constitution to be drawn up by an elected constituent assembly. This reflected the demands of the international community, which in UN General Assembly Resolution 181 on the partition of Palestine and the establishment there of two states – a Jewish state and an Arab state – had demanded that the states each have a formal constitution that would protect the rights of minorities.[1] It did not, however, reflect a real commitment of the dominant political parties at the time of independence. A constituent assembly was indeed elected, but it transformed itself into the Knesset, Israel's Parliament, and the adoption of a formal constitution was postponed.

Under a Knesset resolution adopted in 1950, the formal constitution was to be drawn up in a piecemeal fashion. A series of Basic Laws were to be adopted, and when these were complete, they would become the country's formal constitution. The Basic Law: The Knesset was enacted in 1958, and since then Basic Laws dealing with all aspects of Israel's system of government have been enacted.

[1] UNGA Resolution 181, A/RES/181(II)(A+B), 29 November 1947.

The Supreme Court of Israel originally refused to attribute any special status to the Basic Laws, holding that they were no different from other parliamentary legislation, which may be changed at the will of Parliament.[2] The only exception related to a few clauses in the Basic Laws that require support of an absolute majority of Knesset members for their amendment.[3]

In 1992 the Knesset adopted two Basic Laws relating to protection of fundamental rights – the Basic Law: Human Dignity and Liberty and the Basic Law: Freedom of Occupation.[4] These Basic Laws contain a limitations clause under which protected rights may not be curtailed except by, or under, a law that is consistent with the values of Israel as a Jewish and democratic state, that was passed for a proper purpose, and that does not infringe on the protected right disproportionately. Following enactment of these Basic Laws, the Supreme Court of Israel revised its position on the status of Basic Laws. It held that all Basic Laws have constitutional status and may not be amended by ordinary legislation.[5] Adopting the approach of *Marbury v. Madison*,[6] the Court decided that even though the Basic Laws contained no express provision on the matter, the courts have the power to review legislation and to declare it unconstitutional if it was passed after the Basic Laws came into force and was incompatible with those laws. On a few occasions it has exercised this power and declared provisions in Knesset legislation unconstitutional because they curtailed protected rights in a manner that was not compatible with the Basic Laws.[7]

In the absence of a formal written constitution in the formative years of the state, it was left to the Supreme Court to create what may be called a common law material constitution. The British authorities, who conquered Palestine from the Ottoman Empire in 1917 and ruled the country under a mandate from the League of Nations until 1948, had established a modern

[2] *See* HCJ 148/73 Kaniel v. Minister of Justice, 29 P.D. (1) 794; HCJ 60/77, Ressler v. Central Elections Committee, 31 P.D. (2) 566.

[3] *See* HCJ 98/69, Bergman v. Minister of Finance, 23 P.D. (1) 693; HCJ 141/82, Rubinstein v. Knesset Speaker, 37 P.D. (3) 141. The absolute majority must be 61 of the 120 Knesset members, not a simple majority of those voting, as is required in ordinary legislation.

[4] I have discussed the constitutional status of these Basic Laws elsewhere: see D. Kretzmer, "The New Basic Laws on Human Rights: A Mini-Revolution in Israeli Constitutional Law?" (1996) 14 *Neth. Q. Hum. Rts.* 173. *See also* Daphna Barak-Erez, "From an Unwritten to a Written Constitution: The Israeli Challenge in American Perspective," *26 Colum. Hum. Rts. L. Rev.* 309 (1995).

[5] *See* C.A. 6821/93, United Mizrachi Bank v. Migdal, 49 P.D. (4) 221.

[6] Marbury v. Madison, 5 U.S. 137 (1803).

[7] *See, e.g.*, HCJ 1715/97, Bureau of Investment Advisors v. Minister of Finance, 97 Takdin-Elyon (3) 791; HCJ 6055/95, Sagui Zemach v. Minister of Defence, 99 Takdin-Elyon (3) 1400; Gaza Shore Regional Council v. Knesset, 59 P.D. (2) 481.

legal system and imposed a layer of English common law on the existing system of Ottoman law. After independence, the Supreme Court continued the British tradition; largely by developing principles of English law relating to judicial review of administrative action, it began establishing constitutional principles. These were especially important in the field of individual rights. The Court held that, as a democratic country, fundamental rights recognized in other democratic regimes were part and parcel of Israeli common law. No public authority is empowered to infringe on these rights without clear statutory authority; statutes, whether enacted during the mandate or after independence, are to be interpreted so as to give effect to the rights of the individual; and when exercising statutory powers that authorize curtailment of individual liberties the authorities are bound to give appropriate weight to those liberties, and the Court may interfere if they fail to do so.[8]

The lack of a formal constitution defining the recognized rights of the individual, alongside the jurisprudence of the Supreme Court recognizing the legal standing of individual rights, meant that the Court was forced to look to other systems for inspiration in defining the protected rights and their scope of protection. As the legal system inherited from the British mandate period was a mixed system, incorporating elements of Ottoman law on which principles of English common law and equity had been imposed, the courts were used to looking to a variety of sources in interpreting the law and forging legal principles. It was therefore only natural that in developing its human rights jurisprudence the Supreme Court and other courts looked not only to other domestic legal systems but also to human rights conventions and to decisions of international judicial bodies and treaty bodies. In the *Foguel* case, decided before adoption of the Basic Laws on human rights, Justice Landau addressed the question of the identification of the rights that are part of Israel's material constitution. He stated: "In defining the liberties of the individual we will draw inspiration from fundamental ideas of a liberal-democratic regime as reflected in classic declarations on human rights, beginning with the 1789 French Declaration on the Rights of Man and the Citizen and ending with the 1948 UN General Assembly Universal Declaration of Human Rights."[9] In turning to international documents and treaties as a source of inspiration and interpretation the courts do not

[8] For fuller treatment of the Court's jurisprudence on protection of human rights before introduction of the Basic Laws, *see* David Kretzmer, "Constitutional Law," in A. Shapira and K.C. Delwitt-Arar (eds.), *Introduction to the Law of Israel* (The Hague: Kluwer International, 1995), pg. 39.

[9] HCJ 112/77, Foguel v. Broadcasting Authority, 31 P.D. (3) 657, 664.

confine themselves to those international treaties to which Israel is a party. The courts refer frequently to the European Convention for the Protection of Human Rights and Fundamental Freedoms (ECHR), even though Israel is not a party to that convention.[10]

To this day the courts retain a liberal attitude toward citing decisions of foreign courts, international tribunals, and other international decision-making bodies such as treaty bodies. These decisions are never regarded as binding and are referred to only as a source of inspiration or guidance.

B. *International Law in the Domestic Legal System*

Neither the Basic Laws nor ordinary statutes of the Knesset contain provisions relating to the status of international law in the domestic legal system. It was therefore left to the courts, and primarily the Supreme Court, whose precedents bind the lower courts, to solve this question. The question arose soon after the state was established. In the absence of domestic legislative provisions, the Supreme Court looked to the approach of the English legal system.

The English approach rests on three principles. First, Parliament is supreme in the field of legislation. Hence, any law enacted by parliament is valid, even if it is incompatible with the state's international law obligations. Second, norms of customary international law are part and parcel of the common law of the land, and the domestic courts will enforce them unless they are incompatible with parliamentary legislation. Third, the domestic courts will not enforce international treaties that were duly ratified by the state and bind it in international law unless their provisions have been incorporated in domestic law through parliamentary legislation. The Supreme Court of Israel adopted all three principles.

1. **Primacy of Parliamentary Legislation.** In the *Steinberg* case,[11] the defendant, a resident of Jerusalem, had been conscripted under the Defence Service Law and was prosecuted for failing to appear for army duty. He argued that Jerusalem should be regarded as occupied territory under international law, and that customary international law prohibits conscription of residents of occupied territory. The Court held that even if it were to accept that his conscription was incompatible with a norm of international law, the clear language of a Knesset statute would prevail over that

[10] See decisions cited *infra* note 108.

[11] Cr. A. 5/51, Steinberg v. Attorney General, 5 P.D. 1061.

norm.[12] In the *Eichmann* case,[13] the accused, who had been responsible for implementation of the Nazi plan to annihilate the Jews in Europe, was kidnapped in Argentina by Israeli agents and brought to Israel to stand trial under the Nazi and Nazi-Collaborators Punishment Law, 1950. He argued, inter alia, that under norms of customary international law Israel could not try him on the basis of a statute that had been enacted after the commission of the crimes he was accused of committing. The Supreme Court dismissed this argument on a number of grounds. For present purposes, the important grounds were that even if the Israeli statute granting the courts jurisdiction to try persons accused of committing crimes against the Jewish people during the Nazi regime had been incompatible with international law, the Israeli statute would have taken precedence.[14]

While the principle in relation to parliamentary legislation is quite clear, there is some doubt as to the position when there is a clash between customary international law and delegated legislation (i.e., subordinate legislation promulgated by statutory bodies on the strength of clear statutory authority). In one case, it was argued that regulations promulgated by a minister were ultra vires because they were incompatible with norms of international law relating to freedom of religion. The Court rejected the argument that the regulations violated freedom of religion, and it therefore did not have to rule on the argument. Nevertheless, Justice Haim Cohn opined that subsidiary legislation that was incompatible with customary international law would be invalid.[15] This would indeed seem to be the case unless the enabling legislation grants the subsidiary authority clear and unequivocal authority to promulgate norms that are incompatible with the state's international obligations.[16]

[12] *See also* HCJ 256/01 Rabakh v. Jerusalem Municipal Court 52 P.D. (2) 930. In this case, it was argued that application of Israeli law in the whole of Jerusalem following the 1967 War was contrary to international law and that the Jerusalem municipal court had no jurisdiction over matters in East Jerusalem. The Supreme Court held that, even if the application of Israeli law was incompatible with international law, the Knesset statute granting the executive express authority to apply Israeli law in parts of the Land of Israel that were held by Israeli forces prevailed.

[13] Cr. A. 366/61, Eichmann v. Attorney General 16 P.D. 2033.

[14] The other grounds were that as the accused was charged with crimes against humanity, which constituted offences under international criminal law, there was universal jurisdiction.

[15] HCJ 103/67, The American-European Beth-El Mission v. Minister of Welfare, 21 P.D. (2) 325.

[16] On this issue, *see* A. Reich, "Globalization and Law: The Influence of International Law on Commercial Law in Israel in the Next Fifty Years" (in Hebrew) 17 *Mechkarei Mishpat* (2001) 17.

2. Place of Customary International Law. In two cases decided shortly after independence, the Supreme Court held that the fundamental rules of international law accepted as binding by all "civilized" nations were incorporated in the domestic legal system. In the *Shimshon* case,[17] the reason given was the tradition of English common law, which had been incorporated in the law of the land during the British Mandate and remained in force after the state was established by virtue of Article 11 of the Law and Administration Ordinance, 1948. A short while later, in the *Stampfer* case,[18] the Court stated that there was no need to enlist English common law as a basis for the role of fundamental principles of the law of nations in the law of the state. This status was a direct consequence of Israel's standing as an independent sovereign state.[19] The Court failed to explain why this status implied not only that the state itself was bound by these fundamental principles but also that the principles should be regarded as part and parcel of the domestic legal system.[20]

The foregoing two cases were accepted as precedents for the automatic incorporation of customary international law in the domestic legal system.[21] This principle became highly relevant when issues relating to the Occupied Territories began to reach the Supreme Court. It also becomes important in relation to other issues that arise concerning the place of international humanitarian law (IHL) in the domestic legal system. Thus, the Supreme Court has held that whether an Israeli soldier who kills a person will be entitled to the defense of "authorization by law"[22] will be determined by the lawfulness of the killing under customary IHL.[23]

[17] C.M. 41/49, Shimshon v. Attorney General, 9 P'sakim 16.

[18] Cr.A. 174/54, Stampfer v. Attorney General, 21 P'sakim 298.

[19] *See id.*, at 309, where the court declared: "The Declaration of Independence opened up for the new state a window to international laws and customs, which all states enjoy by virtue of their sovereignty, and enriched its system of laws with the principles accepted in the law of nations."

[20] *See* Ruth Lapidot, "International Law within the Israel Legal System" 24 *Isr. L. Rev.* 451, 453 (1990).

[21] *See, e.g.*, HCJ 69/81, Abu Ita v. IDF Commander, 37 P.D. (2) 197 (the *VAT case*); HCJ 785/87, Afu v. IDF Commander, 42(2) P.D. 4 (for an English translation see 29 *Int'l Legal Materials* 139 (1990)).

[22] Under art. 34m(1) of the Penal Code, 5737–1977, a person shall not be criminally liable for an act that he or she "has a duty, or is authorized, by law, to do."

[23] HCJ 769/02, Public Committee against Torture v. Government of Israel (*Targeted Killings* case), 80 Dinim-Elyon 683, para. 19. Chief Justice Barak stated: "When soldiers of the Israel Defense Forces act pursuant to the laws of armed conflict, they are acting 'by law,' and they have a good justification defense. However, if they act contrary to the laws of armed conflict they may be, *inter alia*, criminally liable for their actions. Indeed, the "geometric location" of our issue is in customary international law dealing with armed conflict. It is

Given the place of customary international law in the domestic legal system, the issue of proof becomes relevant. How is the customary status of a norm of international law established in court? The Supreme Court addressed this question in the *VAT* case.[24] Accepting the definition of customary law in Article 38, Paragraph 1, of the Statute of the International Court of Justice as "international custom, as evidence of a general practice accepted as law," the President of the Court, Justice Shamgar, ruled that the existence of a customary norm must be proved by the party that pleads its existence. That party must prove that the custom is accepted at least by an overwhelming majority of states.[25]

While this remains the theory of the Court regarding proof of customary law, in practice the Court sometimes relies on academic writers and judgments of other tribunals who have opined or ruled on the customary status of given norms. Thus, as shall be explained here, in ruling that the Regulations annexed to the *Hague Convention (IV) Respecting the Laws and Customs of War on Land, 1907* (Hague Regulations) are part of customary international law, the Supreme Court relied on an article by an Israeli academic and the sources presented in that article.[26] In contrast, in the *Targeted Killings* case,[27] the Court followed its own jurisprudence on the need to prove the existence of custom when it rejected the argument that customary IHL recognizes a third category of unlawful combatants, in addition to combatants and civilians. It stated, "[W]e were not presented with data sufficient to allow us to say, at the present time, that such a third category has been recognized in customary international law."[28]

3. Nonincorporation of International Treaties. In the *Samara* case,[29] the resident of a village that had been ceded to Israel under the terms of the Rhodes Armistice Agreement between Israel and Jordan challenged expropriation of his land under the authority granted to the executive in a Knesset statute. He argued that the expropriation was incompatible with Israel's obligations under the Rhodes Agreement. The Supreme Court stated:

from that law that additional law which may be relevant will be derived according to our domestic law. International treaty law which has no customary force is not part of our internal law."

[24] *Supra* note 21.
[25] *Id.*, at 241.
[26] *See* HCJ 606/78, Ayyub v. Minister of Defence, 33 P.D. (2) 113 (the *Beth El* case).
[27] *Supra* note 23.
[28] *Id.*, para. 28.
[29] C.A. 22/55, Custodian of Absentee Property v. Samara, 10 P.D. 1825.

> The Rhodes Agreement is a treaty between the State of Israel and another state. Whatever the power and validity of such a treaty from the point of view of international law, it is not a statute to which the courts will resort or give any force. The rights which it grants and the obligations that it imposes are the rights and obligations of the states that made the agreement and their enforcement is only in their hands in the special ways that exist for achieving performance of international treaties.[30]

This judgment is regarded as the main precedent for the undisputed principle that domestic courts in Israel may not enforce treaties that bind the state in international law unless the provisions of such treaties have been incorporated by parliamentary legislation.[31] It should be noted that the rationale provided in this case for the status (or lack thereof) of the specific treaty under consideration was that it imposed contractual duties only on the states parties themselves, giving no rights to private individuals.[32] It has been argued that a different rule should apply to treaties, such as human rights conventions, whose very purpose is to guarantee rights to individuals.[33] However, when faced with the argument that the courts should enforce the latter type of treaty, the Supreme Court provided another rationale for non-enforcement of international treaties that have not been incorporated by Knesset legislation.[34] This rationale relies on the division of powers in the state. More specifically, it relies on the treaty-making power of the executive.

C. *Treaty-Making Power*

Neither the Basic Laws nor any other legislation in Israel expressly regulates the treaty-making power of the state.[35] Following the English tradition, after the state was established the executive branch of government assumed the power both to sign and to ratify international treaties on behalf of the state.

[30] *Id.*, at 1828.
[31] *See* Lapidot, *supra* note 20, at 459.
[32] This rationale was repeated by the Court in HCJ 337/71, Christian Society v. Minister of Defence, 26 P.D. (1) 574.
[33] *See* B. Rubin, "Adoption of International Treaties in Domestic Law by the Courts," 13 *Mishpatim* (1984) 210.
[34] Afu v. IDF Commander, *supra* note 21; HCJ 253/88, Sejdiah et al. v. Minister of Defence, 42 P.D. (3) 801.
[35] Art. 11(a)(5) of the Basic Law: The State President, which enumerates the functions of the largely titular state president, states that the president "shall sign treaties with foreign countries that have been approved by the *Knesset.*" The Supreme Court rejected the view that this implies that all treaties require Knesset approval. It ruled that the provision applies to those treaties for which the government chooses to request Knesset approval: Cr.A 131/67, Kamiar v. State of Israel, 22 P.D. (2) 85.

No approval of the legislative branch of government was requested either before or after ratification of a treaty. In 1951 the Minister for Foreign Affairs informed the secretary-general of the United Nations of this practice.[36]

In the *Kamiar* case,[37] a defendant in an extradition proceeding challenged the validity of an extradition treaty between the State of Israel and the requesting state on the grounds that the treaty had not been confirmed by the Knesset. The Supreme Court rejected the argument and upheld the existing practice according to which the treaty-making power is in the hands of the executive, not the legislature. Justice Haim Cohn stated:

> Forming and maintaining international relations generally, and entering into international agreements specifically, is clearly a matter for the executive branch of government, and not at all a matter for the legislative branch. In this matter our constitutional position is different from the position in those countries in which international treaties have the status or validity of a law, or even of a preferred law; ratifying a treaty is anyhow a legislative act. This is not the situation in our country, where no international treaty has legislative status until it has been given such status through an express law passed by the *Knesset*.[38]

Hence, the Court drew a connection between two principles: the treaty-making power of the executive branch of government and the lack of status in domestic law of international treaties that have not been incorporated by parliamentary legislation. One could obviously argue that the issue is one of the chicken and the egg. Does the lack of domestic status flow from the treaty-making power of the executive, or does the exclusive authority of the executive to ratify treaties flow from the lack of domestic legal status of treaties? In the *Kamiar* case, the Court adopted the latter approach. Later, however, when explaining why the domestic courts could not enforce the Geneva Convention (IV) Relative to the Protection of Civilians in Time of War, 1949 (GCIV), the Court accepted the former approach.[39]

Whichever way one looks at it, the two principles are well-entrenched in the jurisprudence of the Supreme Court. In his monumental decision

[36] The summary of the Israeli memorandum sent to the Secretary General summarizes the legal situation as follows: "the legal power to negotiate, sign and ratify international treaties on behalf of Israel is vested exclusively in the Government of Israel and is in the charge of the minister for foreign affairs"; Memorandum of Government of Israel, cited in Kamiar v. State of Israel, *id.*, at 104. *And see* Lapidot, *supra* note 20, at 452, n. 2.

[37] Kamiar v. State of Israel, *supra* note 35.

[38] *Id.*, at 97.

[39] *See, e.g.*, Afu v. IDF Commander, *supra* note 21; Sejdia v. Minister of Defence, *supra* note 34.

in the *VAT* case,[40] the President of the Court, Justice Shamgar, referred at length to the relationship between domestic law and international norms. He explained the position in relation to international treaties as follows:

> the rules of conventional international law are not automatically incorporated, and they do not become part of the law that applies in Israel until they have been adopted or incorporated by the process of legislation, and thereby become part of the law which applies in Israel on the strength of the provisions of statutes or subsidiary legislation that derives its validity from the enabling legislation *praeter legem*.[41]

While the executive retains the power to sign and ratify international treaties on behalf of the state, according to a cabinet decision passed in 1983 all international conventions are tabled in the Knesset at least two weeks before ratification.[42] The government has also adopted the practice of presenting peace agreements to the Knesset for debate and approval before ratification.[43] It has been argued that this practice has become a binding constitutional custom.[44] During the negotiations between the Barak government and the Palestinians, after Prime Minister Barak had resigned and the government had become a transitional government,[45] a petition was submitted to the Supreme Court in which it was argued that the government was bound to obtain Knesset approval before signing any agreement with the Palestinians. The Supreme Court held that it had not been proved that there was a constitutional custom to present such agreements for Knesset approval before they were signed.[46] Since the government declared that any

[40] *Supra* note 21.

[41] *Id.*, at 234.

[42] *See* Lapidot, *supra* note 20, 480–81. This decision is now incorporated in art. 6 of the Government Rules of Procedures. Art. 6(c) states that the government may decide to present a treaty for approval or ratification by the Knesset.

[43] *See* S. Shetreet, "The Role of the Knesset in Making Treaties" (in Hebrew) 36 *HaPraklit* (1985) 349; Y. Zilbershatz, "International Law in Constitutional Law" (in Hebrew) 4 *Mishpat Umemshal* 47 (1997).

[44] *See* S. Shetreet, *id.*

[45] According to Israel's constitutional law, when the prime minister resigns or the Knesset passes a vote of no confidence in the government, the government remains in power as a transitional government until a new government has been formed that has gained the confidence of the Knesset.

[46] HCJ, 01/5167 Weiss v. Prime Minister, 55 P.D. (2) 455. The government accepted that after an agreement had been reached it would be presented to the Knesset for its approval. *See also* H.C.J. 5934/95, Shilansky v. Prime Minister (unreported), in which the Court rejected the argument that there was a constitutional custom that required prior approval of the Knesset for political agreements such as the agreement between Israel and the PLO, stating that such a custom had not been proved and that, in previous cases, Knesset approval was sought after the agreement had been signed. According to a legal opinion

agreement signed would thereafter be presented to the Knesset for discussion and approval, the Court refused to decide whether the government was bound by constitutional custom to do so.

D. *Incorporation Techniques*

Many treaties that have been ratified by the government and are consequently binding on Israel in international law have not been incorporated by domestic legislation.[47] In those cases in which the provisions of treaties are incorporated, various techniques of incorporation are employed.[48]

1. Adoption of Substantive Provisions in Special Legislation. In some cases, the substantive provisions of a treaty are simply included in a Knesset statute. Thus, for example, the Crime of Genocide (Prevention and Punishment) Law, 1950 incorporates the provisions of the Convention on the Prevention and Punishment of the Crime of Genocide, 1948. Article 10 states expressly that the law was enacted following adoption of the Convention and its ratification by Israel. Following this approach, special legislation was enacted to give effect to the agreements between Israel and the Palestinian Liberation Organization (PLO) that established the Palestinian Authority and granted it control over parts of the West Bank and Gaza.[49]

of the Attorney General of Israel, dated 6 July 2005 (*available at* http://209.85.129.104/search?q=cache:s54t_eaB8WcJ:www.justice.gov.il/NR/rdonlyres/), the existing practice is to present all "important political agreements" for Knesset approval. The Attorney General did not regard the agreement between Israel and Egypt regarding deployment of Egyptian police on the border of Gaza after the Israeli withdrawal ("Agreed Arrangements Regarding the Deployment of a Designated Force of Border Guards along the Border in the Rafah Area") as such an agreement.

[47] Possibly the most glaring of these treaties are the four 1949 Geneva Conventions and various human rights conventions to which Israel is a party, including the International Covenant on Civil and Political Rights, 1966 and the International Covenant on Economic, Social, and Cultural Rights 1966. For a strong argument regarding Israel's obligation to incorporate such conventions, *see* Ruth Lapidot, Yuval Shany, and Orna Ben-Naftali, *The Duty to Incorporate Human Rights Conventions in Israeli Law* (Concord Institute for Research on the Interaction of International Law and Israeli Law, 2004). The *Designation of Information Regarding the Influence of Legislation on the Rights of the Child Law, 2002* requires that information on the likely effects of new legislation on the rights of the child be expressly mentioned in the explanatory notes of draft legislation. Sec. 2 of the law states that its purpose is to oblige members of the Knesset and the government to consider the effects of legislation on the rights of the child, "in the spirit of the principles" in the Convention on the Rights of the Child.

[48] *See* Lapidot, *supra* note 20, 460–64.

[49] *See* Implementation of Agreement Relating to Preparatory Transfer of Powers to the Palestinian Authority (Amendments of Legislation and Miscellaneous Provisions) Law, 1995.

2. Express Application of Convention. In other cases, the Knesset legislation expressly refers to a specific international convention and provides that it will apply in certain defined circumstances. This was the approach adopted in the Air Carriage Law, 1980, which applies the Warsaw Convention for the Unification of Certain Rules Relating to International Carriage by Air, 1929 and its protocols to air carriage between Israel and other parties to the Convention; the Sales (International Sales of Goods) Law, 1999, which incorporates the UN Convention on Contracts for the International Sale of Goods, 1980; and the Hague Convention (Return of Abducted Children) Law, 1991 which gives the force of law to the Hague Convention on the Civil Aspects of International Child Abduction, 1980, explicitly stating that the provisions of that Convention shall apply notwithstanding any law.

3. Statutory Reference to Treaty Obligations. The third method of incorporation is by reference in Knesset legislation to international treaty obligations of the state. Thus, for example, Article 16 of the Penal Code Law, 1977 provides that Israeli courts shall have jurisdiction to try persons for crimes committed outside Israeli territory if the State of Israel undertook in multilateral international treaties to punish persons for those crimes. This is the statutory basis in domestic law for Israel's courts to exercise universal jurisdiction for grave breaches of the four Geneva Conventions and for torture, as required under the UN Convention against Torture and Other Forms of Cruel, Inhuman or Degrading Treatment or Punishment.

4. Reference to Any Treaty in a Defined Area. In some areas of activity, provision of services depends on international cooperation. The clearest example is that of postal services. The Postal Law, 1986 includes many references to the "*Universal Postal Convention* which is in force at the particular time."

5. Authorization to Promulgate Regulations. No organ other than the Knesset has power to promulgate legislation unless expressly empowered to do so in a Knesset statute. In some cases, administrative bodies have been given the statutory power to promulgate regulations giving force to the provisions of international agreements.[50] In other cases, administrative authorities have relied on the power granted to them in a particular

[50] *See, e.g.*, sec. 13, Legal Assistance between States Law, 1998, which states that if an international agreement to which Israel is a party makes provisions on certain defined matters, and regulations have been promulgated for their implementation, those regulations shall have the force of law and shall apply notwithstanding any other provisions in the law.

statute to promulgate regulations in a certain field in order to incorporate an international treaty in the field. Under the National Parks, Nature Reserves, National Sites and Memorial Sites Law, 1998 the minister of environmental protection has the power to declare natural species as protected species. According to a declaration published in 2004, the minister adopted the Convention on International Trade in Endangered Species of Wild Fauna and Flora, declaring that all species mentioned in the annexes to the Convention were protected species.[51]

E. *The Occupied Territories*

During the course of the 1967 Six-Day War, Israel gained control over the West Bank and Gaza, both parts of the former British Mandate territory, which since 1948 had been ruled by Jordan and Egypt, respectively. With the exception of East Jerusalem, Israel did not apply its domestic laws in these territories and they are ruled under a regime of belligerent occupation.[52] The executive branch of government adopted an ambiguous attitude toward the territories, and on the political level, it refused for a long time to acknowledge their status as occupied territory. However, there are now dozens of Supreme Court decisions confirming that the West Bank and Gaza are subject to a regime of belligerent occupation.[53] In defending a challenge to the legislation and government decision that required all Israelis to leave settlements in Gaza as part of the Sharon government's disengagement plan, the government itself argued that because Gaza was occupied territory, the settlements were only temporary.[54]

The first military order promulgated in the territories occupied in 1967 expressly stated that the military courts established to try residents accused

[51] National Parks, Nature Reserves, National Sites and Memorial Sites (Application of Convention on International Trade in Endangered Species of Wild Fauna and Flora) (Protected Natural Species) Declaration, 2004.

[52] Some doubt has arisen concerning the status of the Occupied Territories after the Oslo Accords, and more specifically since Israel withdrew its forces and settlements from Gaza in August 2005. I shall not be discussing these issues here.

[53] The leading judgment in which the Court ruled unequivocally on this issue is HCJ 393/82, Ja'amait Ascan v. IDF Commander, 37 P.D. (4) 785. The most interesting recent decision is the Court's decision in HCJ 1661/05, Gaza Shore Regional Council v. Knesset, *supra* note 7. In this case, Israeli settlers who were forced, under the government's disengagement plan, to leave their homes in Gaza settlements challenged the legality of that plan. The Court ruled that since the settlements had been established in occupied territory, they were by nature temporary and the settlers could therefore be required to leave when the government decided to withdraw Israeli forces from the area.

[54] The government's arguments are presented in the Court decision in Gaza Shore Regional Council, *id.*

of security offences would apply GCIV. Nevertheless, a short while after the war ended, the government claimed that because the West Bank and Gaza had not been the sovereign territory of Jordan and Egypt when taken from those states during their armed conflict with Israel in 1967, it was doubtful whether GCIV formally applied to these territories.[55] The reference to GCIV in the military order was subsequently abrogated, and the government adopted the line that while Israel was not bound de jure to apply GCIV, the Israel Defence Forces (IDF) would respect its humanitarian provisions.[56] It was never made clear which provisions would be regarded as humanitarian provisions.

Soon after the 1967 war ended, Palestinian residents of the Occupied Territories (OT) submitted petitions to the Supreme Court, sitting as a High Court of Justice, in which they challenged the legality of acts or decisions of the IDF. While it was not self-evident that the Court had jurisdiction over petitions relating to territory in which Israeli law did not apply, the government's legal advisers made a policy decision not to contest the jurisdiction of the Court. Later the Court ruled that it had legal jurisdiction over such petitions, under its statutory jurisdiction to grant writs to "bodies fulfilling public functions under law."[57] The Court reasoned that all branches of the government, including the military, were exercising such functions, wherever they operated, and were therefore subject to its jurisdiction.[58]

Since 1967 the Supreme Court has ruled on hundred of petitions relating to the OT, in issues ranging from changes in local law, deportations, house demolitions, land requisition, and establishment of settlements to the building of the separation barrier on the West Bank. In its decisions in these cases, international law has played a prominent role. In fact, it is mainly in relation to the OT that international law has gained prominence in the Court's jurisprudence. Section III of this essay will be devoted to the place of international law in this jurisprudence.

[55] *See* M. Shamgar, "The Observance of International Law in the Administered Territories," 1 *Isr YHR* (1971) 262.

[56] For discussion of the government's position, *see* Nissim Bar-Yaacov, "The Applicability of the Laws of War to Judea and Samaria (The West Bank) and to the Gaza Strip," 24 *Isr. L. Rev.* (1990) 485.

[57] *See* Ja'amait Ascan v. IDF Commander, *supra* note 53. The competence of the Supreme Court, sitting as a High Court of Justice, to review governmental action is defined in secs. 15(c) and (d) of the Basic Law: Judicature.

[58] The Court's jurisprudence on this question is discussed in D. Kretzmer, *The Occupation of Justice: The Supreme Court of Israel and the Occupied Territories* (SUNY Press, 2002) [hereinafter *Occupation of Justice*].

II. INTERNATIONAL LAW IN INTERPRETATION

A. *The Presumption of Compatibility*

In principle, the courts in Israel are required to interpret domestic legislation so as to avoid noncompliance with Israel's international obligations. If the legislation is open to more than one interpretation, the courts must choose that interpretation which is compatible with those obligations, whether customary or conventional. In contrast, if primary legislation (i.e., legislation of the Knesset itself or Mandatory legislation that remains in force in Israel) clashes head-on with the norms of international law, customary or conventional, leaving no room for an interpretation that will make the legislation compatible with those norms, then the legislation prevails. The Supreme Court first articulated this principle in the *Steinberg* case,[59] mentioned earlier. The Court stated: "It is a well-known rule that in interpreting the law the court will try if possible to avoid a clash between the national law and norms of international law that bind the state, but this is only one of the rules of interpretation."[60] Similarly, in another case the Court declared: "It is a well-known rule that a local statute should be interpreted – unless its contents demand another interpretation – according to the norms of public international law."[61] The presumption of compatibility has been addressed and applied by the courts on numerous occasions. In the *Yated* case,[62] parents of Downs syndrome children petitioned the Court to order the state to pay for special education for their children who had been integrated in ordinary schools rather than special education schools. The provisions in the Special Education Law, which regulates education of children with special needs, seemed to imply that the state had no obligation to finance special education for children who were integrated in regular classrooms. Among the factors cited by the Court in interpreting the law so as to require the state to finance the special education of such children were Israel's obligations under the International Covenant on Economic, Social and Cultural Rights (ICESCR) and the Convention on the Rights of the Child. Justice Dorner stated: "Another rule of interpretation expresses the presumption of compatibility between the laws of the state and the norms of international law with which Israel is bound to comply. According to this presumption, the

[59] *Supra* note 11.
[60] *Id.*
[61] HCJ 279/51, Amsterdam v. Minister of Finance, 6 P.D. 945, 966.
[62] HCJ 2599/00, Yated – Friendly Society of Downs Syndrome Children's Parents v. Ministry of Education, 56 P.D. (5) 834.

laws will be interpreted, as far as possible, as being compatible with these norms."[63]

In another case dealing with the time required under a statute to submit objections under the *Planning and Building Law*, one of the judges in the Supreme Court cited the presumption of compatibility to support an interpretation of the law that would be compatible with conventions protecting the environment.[64] In the *Shalom* case,[65] the plaintiff attempted to bring a tort action against the ambassador of a foreign country. The Torts Ordinance contains no provision exempting a diplomat from liability in torts, and the plaintiff argued that there was therefore no place for diplomatic immunity, even if the rules of immunity in the Vienna Convention on Diplomatic Immunity were part of customary international law. The district court rejected the argument, stating that the presumption of compatibility required it to find an interpretation of the Torts Ordinance that would not involve breach of Israel's international obligations. This meant holding that there was no inevitable clash between the right of action recognized in the Torts Ordinance and diplomatic immunity from tort actions recognized in customary international law.[66]

The presumption of compatibility itself is not controversial, and the Supreme Court and other courts have cited it on numerous occasions, sometimes, as in the cases mentioned here, to support an interpretation of legislation that would meet the presumption.[67] It should not be assumed,

[63] *Id.*, at 846. Also see HCJ 4542/02, *Kav La'oved* v. *Government of Israel*, 2006 Takdin-Elyon (1) 4336, para. 37, (in considering the legality of government policy to tie migrant workers to a specific employer, the Court stated that the statutory power of the minister of interior to subject entry visas to conditions should be interpreted so as to be compatible with article 6 of the International Covenant on Economic, Social and Cultural Rights that recognizes "the right of everyone to the opportunity to gain his living by work which he freely chooses or accepts".)

[64] See the opinion of Justice Dorner in HCJ 4128/02, Adam, Teva VeDin, Israeli Association for Protection of the Environment v. Prime Minister, 58 P.D. (3) 503, 527–28.

[65] C.A. 4289/98 (T.A.) Shulamit Shalom v. Attorney-General et al., P.M. 5758 (3) 1.

[66] *Id.*

[67] For other cases citing the presumption, *see, e.g.*, V.A. 1545/97, Attorney General v. Ploni, 5758 P.M. (2) 145 (interpreting the meaning of the term *citizen* in the Extradition Law in accordance with international law); Cr.A. 3112/94, Abu Hassan v. State of Israel, 53 P.D. (1) 422 (narrowing discretion of a judge to impose a life sentence on a minor convicted of premeditative murder so as to avoid incompatibility with art. 37(a) of the Convention on the Rights of the Child); V.C.M (TA) 10408/01, L.S. v. L.A. (unreported) (where a husband moved to dismiss a divorce action from the family court on the grounds that he had the right to choose the jurisdiction of the rabbinical court in all matters connected with a divorce dispute, the family court refused to dismiss the action, holding that the husband's position was incompatible with art. 16 of the Convention for the Elimination of All Forms of Discrimination against Women); Cr. A. 6659/06, Ploni v. State of Israel,

however, that in all cases the courts actually do rule on the basis of the presumption. One of the glaring examples of a clear diversion from the presumption was a case regarding administrative detention of persons held as bargaining chips for return of Israeli soldiers captured by Hezbollah and other armed groups in Lebanon. The Emergency Powers (Detention) Law, 1979 allows detention of persons if the minister of defense is of the opinion that "state or public security demands their detention." The question was whether this term could be interpreted so as to allow detention of a person, even if he or she did not personally threaten state or public security. The detainees argued against an affirmative answer to this question because it would allow holding "hostages," in clear contravention of international law. At the first hearing of the case, a majority rejected their argument.[68] In a most peculiar judgment, the President of the Court, Justice Barak, stated that once the statute was clear, international law was irrelevant. No mention was made of the duty to consider international law when interpreting the statute itself, a point made forcefully by the dissenting judge.[69] To Justice Barak's credit, he later conceded his mistake. In a further hearing of the case before an expanded bench, he retracted and held that the administrative detention law should indeed be interpreted so as to avoid incompatibility with international law, and that an interpretation which allowed holding of persons as bargaining chips was therefore to be rejected.[70]

In the *Shinbein* case,[71] there was an interesting division of opinion in the Supreme Court. The issue related to a provision in the Extradition Law, 1954, according to which an Israeli citizen shall not be extradited to another state. This provision was introduced into the law after Israel had concluded an extradition treaty with the United States that made no mention of this restriction on extradition. In a dissenting opinion, Chief Justice Barak argued that the term *Israeli citizen* should be given a narrow interpretation, so as to exclude persons who have formal citizenship but no real connection to the country. While he did not explicitly mention the presumption of

2008 Takdin-Elyon (2) 3270 (interpreting the Detention of Unlawful Combatants Law, 2002, so as to be compatible with provisions of GCIV that allow internment of civilians on security grounds. This law states that its purpose is to allow detention of persons "in a manner that is compatible with the State of Israel's obligations under the norms of international humanitarian law."); C.A. (Jm) 6184/05, Zarihen v. Amidar, Israel National Housing Company Ltd., 2007 Takdin-Mechozi (1) 11443 (interpreting the Public Housing Law, 1998 so as to avoid incompatibility with the International Covenant on Economic, Social and Cultural Rights).

[68] *See* A.D.A. 10/94, Plonim v. Minister of Defence, 53 P.D. (1) 97.

[69] *See* the opinion of Justice Dorner, *id.*

[70] *See* F.C.H. 7048/97, Plonim v. Minister of Defence, 54 P.D. (1) 721.

[71] Cr. A. 6182/98, Shinbein v. Attorney General, 63 P.D. (1) 625.

compatibility, one of the reasons Chief Justice Barak provided in favor of this interpretation was to narrow the discrepancy between the Israeli statute and Israel's obligations under the extradition treaty with the United States. The majority rejected this view. It held that when the Knesset introduced the amendment into the Extradition Law, Knesset members were well aware of the disparity between the amended law and Israel's extradition treaties, including the treaty with the United States, and they rejected attempts to narrow the citizenship exemption. The amended Extradition Law was clear in excluding citizens from extradition, and there was no justification for subjecting citizens to further conditions, such as residence or another connection to the country. Writing for the majority, Justice Orr added:

> It is hard to escape the impression that the thesis presented to us, according to which a requirement of residence, not mentioned in section 1A of the Extradition Law, be read into that section, was born principally out of concern for the undesirable consequence likely to flow from Israel's refusal to extradite the appellant. I do not want to belittle the difficulties that flow from the disparity between section 1A of the Extradition Law and binding extradition treaties, which Israel has signed. However, it seems to me that from the point of view of proper judicial policy, these difficulties must be solved by the King's Highway of amending the Extradition Law by the *Knesset*, and not by way of judicial interpretation of the existing law.[72]

B. *Interpretation of Incorporating Legislation*

How do the courts interpret legislation that incorporates the terms of an international treaty under one of the foregoing described techniques? In the *Teichner* case,[73] the Supreme Court was split on this question. The issue related to interpretation of the Air Carriage Law, according to which the Warsaw Convention for the Unification of Certain Rules Relating to International Carriage by Air, 1929 applies to civil actions for damages against air carriers. Under the Convention, causes of action against carriers expire after two years. The specific question was whether this provision should be read as subject to the provisions of the domestic Limitations of

[72] *Id.*, at 661. Following this judgment, the Extradition Law was indeed amended. It no longer prevents extradition of an Israeli citizen. However, it provides that a person who is both a citizen and a resident of Israel may not be extradited to stand trial in another country unless the requesting country undertakes in advance to return the person to serve his or her sentence in Israel, if he or she is convicted and sentenced to imprisonment.

[73] F.H. 36/84, Teichner v. Air France, 41 P.D. (1) 589.

Actions Law, which allows extension of the time for submitting a civil action in certain circumstances. The dissenting judge gave a positive answer to this question. However, the majority held that the policy behind the unqualified provision on expiry of actions in the Convention should prevail. They held that as the particular purpose of the statute had been incorporation of the treaty, its terms should be interpreted according to the specific purpose of that treaty. In summarizing his opinion, Justice Dov Levin declared:

> as long as the Convention remains in force, according to its present text, we must give section 29 [of the Air Carriage Law] the interpretation according to which a cause of action expires after two years and may not be extended on the basis of the rules of domestic law. This interpretation reflects . . . the purposes of the Convention, the intention of those who drew it up and the reasonable, desirable and fair balance between the carrier and its passengers that they wished to achieve.[74]

The view of the majority in this case, according to which an attempt is made to interpret legislation that incorporates international treaties so as to achieve conformity with the interpretation adopted internationally, generally reflects the policy of the courts. Whichever incorporation technique is employed, the courts will try to interpret the legislation according to the terms of the convention.[75] In one case, the Court regarded the accepted treaty interpretation as incompatible with the special circumstances in Israel and adopted a different interpretation. It was careful to state, however, that after examining the views of leading jurists, it was satisfied that the interpretation that it had adopted for the Israeli statute that incorporated the particular Convention was not incompatible with that Convention.[76]

In interpreting a convention that has been incorporated into Israeli law, the courts refer extensively to decisions of courts in other jurisdictions relating to the convention. Thus, for example, in cases dealing with the Warsaw Convention the courts have frequently cited decisions of foreign courts relating to the Convention and have interpreted the Convention according to these decisions.[77] In the *Hakstatter* case,[78] the question before the Court was whether the European Extradition Convention applied to crimes committed before Israel had acceded to it. The Supreme Court stated

[74] *Id.*, at 638.

[75] *See* Lapidot, *supra* note 20, 464–65.

[76] C.A. 200/52, Attorney General v. Cane, 7 P.D. 107 (considering the UN Convention on the Declaration of Death of Missing Persons, 1950).

[77] *See* Teichner v. Air France, *supra* note 73, and the first round of this case, C.A. 20/83, Solomon v. Air France, 38 P.D. (3) 785; V.M. 1818/03 (Naz), El Al v. David, P.M. 5763 (1) 737.

[78] Cr.A. 557/71, Hakstatter v. State of Israel, 26 P.D. (1) 241.

that the Convention should be interpreted "according to international law and custom as were valid and published at the time it was drawn up; and according to these it is clear, that even in the absence of an express provision, it should be interpreted so as to apply even to crimes committed before the Convention came into force in respect to a given state."[79]

C. *Adopting Executive Interpretation of Treaties*

The Court has never officially subscribed to the view that it must accept the executive branch of government's interpretation of a treaty. On the contrary, it regards interpretation of all legal instruments, including international conventions, as the task of the courts, whose interpretation must be established according to accepted principles of interpretation. Nevertheless, in cases relating to the OT, for a long time, the Supreme Court in fact adopted the interpretation of the GCIV favored by the authorities, even when this meant changing the theory of interpretation from case to case.[80] In one case, the Court even intimated that if there were two possible interpretations of a convention, the Court should adopt that interpretation which is least restrictive of state sovereignty.[81]

In a series of cases, the Supreme Court considered petitions submitted by Palestinian residents of the OT against whom deportation orders had been issued by the military commander. The main argument of the petitioners was that Article 49, Paragraph 1, of GCIV prohibits all deportations of protected persons from occupied territory to the territory of the occupying power, or that of any other country, regardless of the motive. The Court held that the asserted absolute prohibition on all deportations in Article 49 is not part of customary international law.[82] It could therefore have simply avoided interpreting Article 49. However, the Court did not follow this path, and in a number of decisions it referred to the interpretation of the provision, only to conclude that it does not apply to deportation of individuals on security grounds.[83] The Court based this interpretation, which is totally inconsistent with the clear language of Article 49, Paragraph 1, on the supposed background to the provision, namely, the mass deportations to concentration and annihilation camps of persons in territories occupied by

[79] *Id.*
[80] For a discussion of this attitude of the Supreme Court, see *The Occupation of Justice*, chap. 3.
[81] See *Afu* case, *supra* note 21.
[82] HCJ 698/80, Kawasme v. Minister of Defence, 35 P.D. (1) 617.
[83] For a detailed discussion of these cases, see *Occupation of Justice*, chaps. 3 and 10.

the Nazis in World War II.[84] The Court argued that it should not simply take the text of Article 49, Paragraph 1, at face value and should interpret it in light of the purpose that lay behind inclusion of the provision in the Convention.[85] This led it to accept the view of the authorities that the provision does not apply to deportation of individual residents on security grounds.

As mentioned previously, the Government of Israel has argued that the GCIV does not apply de jure to the situation on the West Bank. This argument is based on a reading of Article 2, which provides:

> Art. 2. In addition to the provisions which shall be implemented in peacetime, the present Convention shall apply to all cases of declared war or of any other armed conflict which may arise between two or more of the High Contracting Parties, even if the state of war is not recognized by one of them.
>
> The Convention shall also apply to all cases of partial or total occupation of the territory of a High Contracting Party, even if the said occupation meets with no armed resistance.

The government's argument is that Paragraph 2 refers to "occupation of the territory of a High Contracting Party" and that, because the West Bank was not sovereign territory of Jordan when it was occupied by Israel in 1967, the Convention does not apply. The answer to this argument, accepted in 2004 by the International Court of Justice in its Advisory Opinion on Legal Consequences of Construction of the Wall,[86] is that Paragraph 2 does not apply to territory that is occupied in the course of an armed conflict between two high contracting parties. In such a case, Paragraph 1 applies and there is no need to resort to Paragraph 2, which was introduced into the Convention solely to cover cases when occupation meets with no armed resistance and consequently is not the outcome of an armed conflict between high contracting parties. This argument, which is supported in the Pictet Commentary on the Convention,[87] was presented before the Court

[84] An initial draft of art. 49, para. 1, prohibiting all deportations from occupied territories, appeared in the Tokyo Draft of GCIV, which was submitted to the Diplomatic Conference of the Red Cross in 1934. The Court was therefore mistaken in assuming that the prohibition was a lesson of World War II.

[85] *See Afu* case, *supra* note 21. And see the discussion herein of interpretation according to the Vienna Convention on the Law of Treaties.

[86] *Legal Consequences of the Construction of a Wall in the Occupied Palestinian Territory*, Advisory Opinion (Int'l Ct. Justice July 9, 2004), 43 ILM 1009 (2004).

[87] *See Commentary on IV Geneva Convention Relative to the Protection of Civilian Persons in Time of War*, ed. J.S. Pictet (Geneva: ICRC, 1958), 18.

in one case. In reply, the Court stated: "Even if we are prepared to make the drastic assumption that this was indeed the intention, the question still arises whether adequate expression was given to this intention in the text of the convention."[88] The interesting point here is that, since the text is ambiguous, according to Article 32 of the Vienna Convention on the Law of Treaties, the Court should have had recourse to the preparatory work of GCIV and the circumstances of its conclusion, to determine its meaning. However, the Court refused to look at the circumstances behind adoption of Article 2, Paragraph 2, even though the text is ambiguous. In contrast, in the deportation cases, the Court did look at the supposed circumstances that led to adoption of Article 49, even though the meaning of that provision is abundantly clear and is in no way ambiguous. In both cases, the interpretation adopted by the Court was that favored by the government.

It must be stressed that this approach of the Court in relation to the GCIV does not characterize its approach in all cases. Thus, for example, in the Court's decision relating to targeted killings, the Court expressly rejected the government's view as to the interpretation of Article 51(3) of Additional Protocol I to the Geneva Conventions.[89]

Although the Court has never adopted the theory that in interpreting international treaties it must accept the interpretation of the executive branch of government, it has held that on questions of fact relating to the relationship with other states it will accept the government's position as stated in a certificate issued by the minister of foreign affairs.[90] In a number of cases, the district courts have been asked to rule whether the Palestinian Authority, established under the interim agreement between Israel and the PLO signed following the Oslo Accords, has the status of a state in

[88] *See* Shahin v. IDF Commander in Judea and Samaria, (1986) 41 (1) P.D. 197.

[89] *See Targeted Killings* case, *supra* note 23.

[90] *See* H.C.J. 2717/96, Wafa v. Minister of Defence, 50 P.D. (2) 848, 855: "The government is authorized to determine what the factual position is relating to certain matters in the foreign relations sphere of the state, such as whether a certain person enjoys diplomatic immunity." In the famous *Elon Moreh* case, Justice Witkon expressed the opinion that had "serious doubt" arisen regarding the status of the West Bank, the Court would have had to ask for a certificate from the minister of foreign affairs, whose opinion on the question would have been determinative: HCJ 390/79, Dweikat v. Government of Israel, 34 P.D. (1) 1, 28. Justice Witkon had no doubt that the West Bank was occupied territory under international law and held that the military commander had acted on the understanding that he could exercise the powers of a military commander in occupied territory. Since this case, the government has never asked the court to reconsider its view on this. On the contrary, it has argued hundreds of cases relating to the West Bank and Gaza on the basis of the law of belligerent occupation.

international law. They have refrained from deciding the question.[91] In one case, the Jerusalem District Court was split over the issue of whether the answer to this question was one for the court or for the executive branch of government.[92] The majority said that, had the court been forced to decide the question, it would have requested a certificate from the minister for foreign affairs, since the question was a factual-political rather than a legal one. That certificate would have been the final word on the issue of the status of the Palestinian Authority. The dissenting judge took the view that the status in international law of the Palestinian Authority is a legal question that must be decided by the court itself.[93]

D. *Interpretation According to the Vienna Convention on Treaties*

Israel is not a party to the Vienna Convention on the Law of Treaties. Nevertheless, the Supreme Court and other courts have on occasion referred to the Convention, which is generally regarded as reflective of customary international law. In one of the cases previously referred to regarding interpretation of Article 49, Paragraph 1, of GCIV, two judges on the bench were split on the interpretation of this provision, which prohibits deportation of protected persons from occupied territory, regardless of the motive. Interestingly, both of these judges referred to Articles 31 and 32 of the Vienna Convention in support of their favored interpretation. Writing for the majority on the Court, its President, Justice Shamgar, refrained from declaring that the rules of interpretation in these articles are part of customary international law. Rather, he simply stated that since Israel had not ratified the Vienna Convention, he was referring to its provisions "for the purposes of comparison."[94] Justice Shamgar proceeded to set out his view on the proper rules of interpretation of international treaties. He stated:

> It would seem that from the provisions in the first part of article 31 (1) one could have thought that the intention in the Convention was to lend some support to that line of interpretation which places emphasis on the written text, as opposed to the alternative interpretative approach, which

[91] *See* C.A. (J-m) 2538/00, Norwich v. Palestinian Authority, 2003 Takdin-Mechozi (1) 4968; V.C.M. (J-m) 1008/06, Agudat Midreshet Elon Moreh v. State of Israel, 2006 Takdin-Mechozi (2) 1718.

[92] Norwich v. Palestinian Authority, *id.*

[93] He came to the conclusion that the Palestinian Authority is not a state in international law and does not enjoy immunity from action before Israel's courts. See judgment of Judge M. Drori in Norwich v. Palestinian Authority, *id.*

[94] *Afu* case, *supra* note 21, at 16.

> is no less accepted, which focuses on the intention of those who drafted the treaty. . . . However, the last part of article 31 and article 32 forge the bridge to other theories of interpretation, which are familiar to us from the examination we made of our own municipal law.
>
> This means that the provisions in the [Vienna] Convention leave room and wide space for examining the purpose behind the treaty [being interpreted]. It is also permissible to examine the preparatory works which describe the background to making the treaty, as material which complements understanding the plain text, as well as its aim and scope of application.
>
> The generally accepted view is, as stated, that one of the contributions of the Vienna Convention in this matter was drawing together the alternative systems of interpretation. In any event, examining the legislative purpose, which is one of the applicable systems of interpretation . . . is in all cases one of the recognized systems of interpretation.[95]

Having laid out this philosophy of interpretation, Justice Shamgar proceeded to interpret Article 49, Paragraph 1, in a manner that is totally incompatible with its clear language. Rather than accept that Article 49 means exactly what it says – namely, that all deportations of protected persons from occupied territory are forbidden – Justice Shamgar held that the provision does not apply to deportation of individuals on security grounds. While the dissenting judge, Justice Bach, declared that he did not disagree with the principles of interpretation laid out by Justice Shamgar or with the assumption that it was the experience with Nazi deportations that led to inclusion of Article 49, Paragraph 1, in GCIV, he was of the view that there was absolutely no justification for departing from the clear text of the provision. In the words of Justice Bach:

> The text of article [49], even in the context and in light of the background of the whole [Geneva] Convention, does not in my mind suffer an interpretation according to which it was intended only to prevent acts such as those committed by the Nazis for racial, ethnic or national reasons.
>
> We must not depart, through interpretation, from the clear and simple meaning of the words of a legislative act, when the language of the provision is unambiguous and the textual interpretation does not stand in contradiction to the purpose of the legislative act, and does not lead to an illogical or absurd result.[96]

[95] *Id.*, at 17–18.
[96] *Id.*, at 70.

It is hardly surprising that the theory of interpretation adopted by Justice Shamgar in this case was harshly criticized.[97] There is no support either in international law or in Israeli domestic law for narrowing the scope of application of a clear and unequivocal provision restricting the powers of governmental authorities, so as to limit it only to those cases which the court assumes led to adoption of the provision. Be this as it may, while the Supreme Court has never repeated the view adopted by Justice Shamgar in the *Afu* case, it has also never disassociated itself from this view.

Other references in court decisions to the Vienna Convention on the Law of Treaties are few and far between. In the *Shalom* case, mentioned earlier,[98] the Tel Aviv District Court referred to Article 31 of the Convention when considering interpretation of the Vienna Convention on Diplomatic Immunity. However, the reference to this provision was quite general in nature; the provision was mentioned more by way of passing than as a guide for the court in interpreting the specific treaty it was called on to interpret in that case. After citing Article 31 and a number of authorities who comment on this article, the Court adopted the view that it should give a narrow interpretation to the exceptions to diplomatic immunity included in the Convention on Diplomatic Immunity. It did not attempt to base this view on Article 31.[99]

Other judicial references to the Vienna Convention on the Law of Treaties are not of much consequence. In the case dealing with the government plan to withdraw Israeli settlements from Gaza, the one dissenting judge cited Article 70(1)(b) of the Convention to support his view that the right of Jews to settle in all parts of the Land of Israel that was recognized in the Mandate over Palestine survived after the Mandate ended.[100] In another case, the Supreme Court mentioned Article 59 of the Convention, according to which states parties to a convention may abrogate that convention in a later convention.[101]

[97] *See* Y. Dinstein, "Deportations from Occupied Territories" (in Hebrew) 13 *Tel Aviv U L Rev* (1988) 403.

[98] *Supra* note 65.

[99] A similar general reference to art. 31 appears in the Supreme Court's decision in Cr.A. 7569/00, Yagudeev v. State of Israel, 56 P.D. (4) 529. In this decision, the Court also mentioned the presumption in art. 28 of the Convention that treaties do not have retroactive application. *See also* V.C.M. 5663/07, Yanko-Weiss Holdings (1996) Ltd. v. Holon Assessment Officer, 2007 Takin-Mechozi (4) 15289 (when considering the power of tax authorities to avoid treaty abuse of a double taxation treaty, the court cites article 31 of the Vienna Convention according to which a treaty must be interpreted in good faith).

[100] Gaza Shore Regional Council v. Knesset, *supra* note 7.

[101] HCJ 852/86, Aloni v. Minister of Justice, 41 P.D. (2) 1.

In summary, the courts do occasionally refer to the Vienna Convention on the Law of Treaties. However, one can hardly say that the provisions of this Convention guide the courts in interpretation of treaties. As revealed by reliance of both the majority and the minority on Article 31 in the *Afu* case, the general tendency seems to be to use the provisions of the Convention to support that interpretation that the Court favors on other grounds.

E. *Citing Nonincorporated Treaties and Decisions of International Courts and Decision-Making Bodies*

As mentioned in the introduction to this chapter, Israeli courts have always adopted an extremely liberal approach toward the sources to which they refer in their decisions. In interpreting Basic Laws and ordinary legislation, as well as in discussing principles of Israel's common law, the courts regularly refer to conventions that have not been incorporated in domestic law. They also frequently cite decisions of international tribunals and treaty bodies, and of foreign courts. Such decisions are never regarded as binding; they are simply employed as part of the courts' reasoning, generally, of course, to support the interpretation they favor in the particular case.

The issue in the *Kidum* case[102] pertained to protection of commercial speech. Writing for the majority, Justice Dorner referred to Article 19 of the International Covenant on Civil and Political Rights (ICCPR), mentioned that the Covenant had been ratified by Israel, and quoted from the Views of the Human Rights Committee in a communication in which the Committee rejected the view that commercial speech was less protected than other forms of speech.[103]

Reference to the ICCPR in the *Kidum* case should not be considered direct enforcement of the ICCPR by the Court. In its jurisprudence on issues relating to human rights, the Supreme Court often refers to international treaties and other international instruments as a source for interpretation of local statutory or common law.[104] In one case the Supreme Court referred

[102] HCJ 606/93, Kidum Yazmut u'Molut (1981) Ltd. v. Broadcasting Authority, 48 P.D. (2) 1.

[103] The quotation was from the Views of the Committee in McIntyre et al. v. Canada (1993), 14 *Hum. Rts. L.J.* 171, 176.

[104] *See, e.g.*, HCJ 2376/01, Centre of Local Government in Israel v. Minister of Science, 56 P.D. (6) 803 (mentioning the ICESCR in support of the importance of public libraries); HCJ 4363/00, Poriah Elite Committee v. Minister of Education, 56 P.D. (4) 203 (mentioning the ICESCR and the Convention on the Rights of the Child (CRC) in relation to the right to education); Cr.A. 4596/98, Plonit v. State of Israel, 54 P.D. (1) 145 (mentioning the CRC in ruling against the legality of corporal punishment by parents).

to a provision in the ICCPR before it had entered into force;[105] in another case it mentioned the standards in the ICCPR before the State of Israel had ratified it.[106] In yet another case, in interpreting a domestic provision defining a criminal offence, the Court relied on a treaty that had been signed but not yet ratified by Israel.[107] On more than one occasion the Supreme Court has referred to the European Convention for the Protection of Human Rights and Fundamental Freedoms, although Israel is not a party to the Convention.[108]

Israel has a separate system of labor courts that deal with both individual and collective labor disputes. In interpreting labor legislation, as well as forging fundamental principles of common law that apply to labor disputes, these courts regularly refer to International Labour Organization (ILO) conventions to which Israel is a party. In the *Ben-Shimon* case,[109] the parties were divided over the question of whether the definition of "work hours" in the Hours of Work and Rest Law, 1951 refers to hours of actual work or the hours during which the employee is at the disposal of the employer. The Tel Aviv Labour Court stated that the definition in the law was not original and was derived from the definition in an ILO convention that had been

[105] *See* HCJ 103/67, American-European Beth-El Mission v. Minister of Welfare, *supra* note 15 (citing art. 18 of the ICCPR on freedom of thought, conscience, and religion).

[106] *See* HCJ 87/85, Arjuv v. IDF Commander, 42 P.D. (1) 353 (mentioning art. 14 of the Covenant on the right of a person convicted of a criminal offence to an appeal).

[107] Cr.A. 11196/02, Freudental v. State of Israel, 57 P.D. (6) 40 (interpreting crime of trafficking in persons in light of the UN Convention on International Organized Crime and the attached Protocol on Prevention, Elimination and Punishment of Trafficking in Persons). The Court explained: "In amending the criminal code the Israeli legislature wished to take part in the international struggle against trafficking in persons – and at this stage trafficking for purposes of prostitution – since this phenomenon has already reached Israel. The purposes of the legislation are therefore identical to the purposes of the above Convention and Protocol. We must therefore interpret the provisions of the Israeli law also according to the spirit of the Convention, which aimed to prevent exploitation of power in transferring and trafficking persons for purposes of prostitution and slavery. Hence we must adopt an interpretation of the law that accords with its purpose and does not allow frustration of the aim of the legislation."

[108] *See, e.g.*, Kidum v. Broadcasting Authority, *supra* note 102; HCJ 721/94, El Al v. Danilowitz, 48 P.D. (5) 749; HJC 4769/95, Menachem v. Minister of Transport, 40 P.D. (1) 235; HCJ 7052/03, Adala et al. v. Minister of Interior, 80 Dinim-Elyon 771; HCJ 3648/97, Stamka v. Minister of Interior, 53 P.D. (2) 728; HCJ 2080/05, Amutat B'Tzedek v. Chief of Police, 81 Dinim-Elyon 194; C.L.A. 10520/03, Ben Gevir v. Dankner, 80 Dinim-Elyon 159; HCJ 2245/06, Dovrin v. Prisons Service, 77 Dinim-Elyon 563; F.A.M. 377/05, Ploni and Plonit v. Biological Parents, 72 Dinim-Elyon 286; V.M.Cr. 2043/05, State of Israel v. Ze'evi, 74 Dinim-Elyon 533; HCJ 1661/05, Gaza Shore Regional Council v. Knesset, *supra* note 7; C.A. 10280/01, Yaros-Hakak v. Attorney General, 59 P.D. (5) 64; HCJ 4370/01, Lipka v. Ministry of Interior, 57 P.D. (4) 920.

[109] D.M. (T.A.) 6917/04, Ben Shimon v. Ben Ishay, unpublished decision of 7 November 2006.

ratified by Israel. There was therefore "no reason why the Court should not resort to the definition of 'work hours' in two ILO conventions, the *Hours of Work (Industry) Convention, 1919* and the *Hours of Work (Commerce and Offices) Convention, 1930.*"[110] The latter Convention expressly refers to the hours that the employee is at the disposal of his or her employer, and the Court interpreted the domestic statute accordingly. Similarly, in a number of cases a question arose relating to the meaning of the term *wages* in Israeli legislation. As there is no general definition of the term in Israeli legislation, the Labour Court referred to the wide definition in the ILO Protection of Wages Convention, 1949.[111]

In *El Al v. Hazin*,[112] the issue was the alleged discrimination between male and female air stewards in the collective agreement between the El Al airline and its staff. In deciding that different routes of promotion amounted to discrimination, the National Labour Court referred, inter alia, to an ILO convention and stated:

> According to the *International Discrimination (Employment and Occupation) Convention, 1958*, "discrimination" is any distinction, exclusion or preference made on the basis of race, colour, sex, religion, political opinion, national extraction or social origin, which has the effect of nullifying or impairing equality of opportunity or treatment in employment or occupation. This definition reflects the view of experts, theoreticians and practitioners, and seeing that we are not talking of a "technical" legal definition, there is no reason why the Court should not adopt it.[113]

As mentioned in the introduction to this chapter, in the absence of a formal constitution defining the recognized rights of the individual, the courts have filled the gap with a "material common law constitution." Courts often refer to international human rights declarations or treaties when locating and interpreting rights that are part of this constitution. In one leading case, the Supreme Court explained the status of the right of association in the following way:

> The right to freedom of association – in all its components – does not appear in the statute book. This right was entrenched in two ILO conventions: the first is the 1948 *Convention (no. 87) on Freedom of Association and*

[110] *Id.*

[111] DABA 32/3–21, Margalit v. Igud Bank, 4 P.D.A 7 (1972); DM 002350/05, Almaliach v. State of Israel, Pador 06 (4) 738.

[112] Labour Court 3–25/33, Committee of Air-Flight Staff and El Al v. Edna Hazin, 4 P.D.A 365 (1973).

[113] *Id. See also* L.A. 001849/03, Turjeman v. JNF, unpublished judgment of 30 November 2005; L.A. (National) 480/05, Ben Ami v. Plonit, 2008 Takdin-Artzi (2) 68.

> *Protection of the Right to Organize* (which entered into force on 4.7.50), and the second, the 1949 *Convention (no. 98) Relating to Implementation of the Principles of the Right to Organize and Collective Bargaining* (which entered into force in Israel on 28.1.58). While these conventions did not receive the status of law in Israel, the tendency of making domestic law compatible with obligations which the state has undertaken in treaties, necessarily leads to recognition that "according to international labour law which binds Israel, workers are guaranteed the right to organize." ... In light of the nature of this right there is place for the view that "the freedom of workers in Israel to professional organization is a fundamental feature of our democratic society ... and this court has taken care in the past, and will continue to take care in the future, to protect this freedom and to give it maximal meaning and effect."[114]

As mentioned earlier, the Supreme Court expressly stated that it would look to documents "such as" the Universal Declaration of Human Rights, when defining rights recognized in Israel's material constitution.[115] In the *Shtreit* case,[116] the Court referred to the Universal Declaration when discussing discrimination; in another case it referred to the Universal Declaration in relation to freedom of religion.[117] As will be seen in the next section, the Court also refers to international treaties when interpreting Israel's Basic Laws on human rights.

F. *Remedies*

The willingness of Israel's courts to grant a remedy for violation of a person's rights under international law is a function of the foregoing described principles. The original theory of the Supreme Court, that international treaties to which Israel is a party do not grant rights to individuals, is still cited by the courts as authority for their refusal to grant a remedy for violation of an individual's rights under a human rights convention ratified by the state. Thus, for example, in the *Amutat Shocharei Gilat* case,[118] the issue was the right to early education. While the Court rejected the argument

[114] HCJ 7029/95, New General Labor Federation v. National Labor Court, 51 P.D. (2) 63, 157, citing decisions of National Labor Court in NLC 1-5/48, Mizrachi Bank Workers' Union v. Hapoel Hamizrachi Federation, 21 P.D.A. 283 (1990) and NLC 18-4/740, General Labor Federation v. Tel Aviv Municipality, 12 P.D.A. 52 (1980).

[115] See *Foguel* case, *supra* note 9.

[116] HCJ 301/63, Shtreit v. Chief Rabbi, 18 P.D. (1) 598.

[117] American-European Beth El Mission v. Minister of Welfare, *supra* note 15.

[118] HCJ 1554/95, Amutat Shocharei Gilat v. Minister of Education, Culture and Sport, 50 P.D. (3) 2.

that the Convention on the Rights of the Child includes such a right, it saw fit to add:

> I will also note that the provisions of the Convention "are not part of the law that applies in the State of Israel, but norms on the international level". . . . And as such
>
> "the affected individuals do not acquire any real right for themselves on the basis of the agreement, and they are not able to enforce such a right in a court, as those who benefit from the agreement or in any other way" (. . . *Custodian of Absentee Property v. Samara*).
>
> For this reason too the petitioners may not derive the concrete rights they claim from the Convention on the Rights of the Child.[119]

Unless the particular right recognized in international law is part of domestic law, its violation will not be the basis for a judicial remedy. This means, in essence, that a remedy will be granted only when the international norm violated is either a norm of customary international law or is recognized as a norm in Israeli common law, Basic Laws, or statutory law.

As to the right to a remedy when the violated norm is part of customary international law, the main example is the *Elon Moreh* case.[120] In this case, the military commander on the West Bank had requisitioned the petitioners' land in order to establish an Israeli settlement. The petitioners argued that under the norms of customary international law, a military commander in occupied territory may requisition land only for military purposes, and as the purpose in this case had been political, rather than military, the commander had exceeded his authority. The Supreme Court accepted the argument, ruled that the requisition order was invalid, and ordered the authorities to return the land to the petitioners. Similarly, in the *Electricity Company* case, the military commander in the West Bank had terminated the concession of the Palestinian East Jerusalem Electricity Company to supply electricity on the West Bank. The Court ruled that the commander had exceeded his authority under customary international law and ordered him to allow the company to continue to supply electricity.[121]

As domestic courts do not enforce international treaties, persons whose rights are purely a function of international treaties are not entitled to a remedy. In other words, the mere argument that an individual has a right

[119] *Id.*, at 30.
[120] Dweikat v. Government of Israel, *supra* note 90.
[121] HCJ 351/80, East Jerusalem Electricity Company v. Minister of Energy and IDF Commander, 35 P.D. (2) 673.

under a human rights treaty ratified by Israel does not imply that he or she is entitled to a remedy for a violation of that right. However, given the tendency of the Supreme Court to define the common law rights recognized in the domestic system according to internationally accepted norms, in many cases the rights recognized in human rights treaties ratified by Israel are in fact recognized as common law rights. Furthermore, since 1992, Israel has had two Basic Laws that grant formal constitutional status to some of the rights recognized in international conventions. The consistent approach of the Supreme Court has been to give a broad interpretation to these rights, often on the basis of the rights accepted in international treaties.

A few examples will illustrate the policy of the Supreme Court. In the *Mara'ab* case,[122] the question related to the detention powers of the military commander in occupied territory. During the Defensive Shield campaign of the IDF in April 2002, the military had detained a large number of Palestinians and held them for up to eighteen days without judicial supervision. The petitioners argued that the detainees were not being held either for criminal investigation or as administrative detainees. They were therefore being held under a system of detention unrecognized in international law. Furthermore, they argued that the length of time before being brought before a judicial authority exceeded that permitted under international law.

Before dealing with the situation under a regime of belligerent occupation, Justice Barak discussed the position under international human rights law. Referring extensively both to the ICCPR and the ECHR, he accepted the argument that the only types of detention allowed under international law were detention as part of the criminal process or administrative detention in emergency situations. He further relied on international standards as to the right of a person arrested on a criminal charge to be brought before a judicial authority promptly. Justice Barak proceeded to examine the standards of promptness adopted by the European Court of Human Rights and the Human Rights Committee and declared that these standards were consistent with the Israeli legal system. He therefore held that they must be respected both in Israel itself and in the West Bank. Accordingly, he ruled that the time frame adopted by the military did not meet these standards and had to be changed.[123]

In the *Public Committee against Torture v. State of Israel*,[124] the petitioners attacked the interrogation practices of the General Security Service (GSS),

[122] HCJ 3239/02, Marab v. IDF Commander, 57 P.D. (2) 349.

[123] The formal basis for this ruling is not entirely clear, but it appears to be based on "the fundamentals of both international and Israeli law" (*id.*, para. 32).

[124] HCJ 5100/94, 53 P.D. (4) 817.

which allowed use of moderate physical force and other forms of pressure in interrogation of persons suspected of involvement in hostile activities. The Supreme Court ruled that, under domestic law, the GSS lacked legal authority to use any type of force in interrogations.[125] The Court was careful to add that this was compatible with

> international treaties, to which Israel is a signatory, which prohibit the use of torture, "cruel, inhuman treatment" and "degrading treatment." . . . These prohibitions are "absolute." There are no exceptions to them and there is no room for balancing. Indeed, violence directed at a suspect's body or spirit does not constitute a reasonable investigation practice. The use of violence during investigations can lead to the investigator being held criminally liable.[126]

The Basic Law: Human Dignity and Liberty does not expressly mention some of the rights we would expect to find in a modern bill of rights, such as equality, freedom of conscience and religion, and freedom of expression. Although omission of these rights reflects the reality of Israeli parliamentary politics, in a long list of cases judges on the Supreme Court have interpreted the enumerated rights in the Basic Law, especially the right to human dignity, as all-encompassing rights that include most aspects of the nonenumerated rights. Thus, it has ruled that the right to equality is a constitutionally protected right, and that all deviations from equality must therefore meet the demands of the limitations clause in the Basic Law.[127] In defining the meaning of equality and its implications the Court has referred to the protection of equality in international human rights conventions.[128]

While most civil and political rights included in international human rights conventions to which Israel is a party will be regarded as protected under common law principles, or under the Basic Laws, the same situation does not apply to economic, social, and cultural rights. Israel is a party to the ICESCR, but the Covenant's provisions have not been incorporated in domestic legislation and there is no express Basic Law on the rights protected in the Covenant.

[125] Under an undisputed principle of Israeli public law, no governmental authority has the power to interfere with the liberties of the individual without clear statutory authority.

[126] HCJ 5100/94, *supra* note 124, para. 23. Also see HCJ 4634/04, Physicians for Human Rights v. Minister for Internal Security, 2007 Takdin-Elyon (1) 1999 (referring to article 7 of the ICCPR and other international instruments relating to prisoner's rights in holding that the right to human dignity protected in the Basic Law: Human Dignity and Liberty entitles each prisoner to a bed).

[127] *See, e.g.*, HCJ 4541/94, Alice Miller v. Minister of Defence, 49 P.D. (4) 94; HCJ 7052/03, Adala v. Minister of Interior, 80 Dinim Elyon 771.

[128] *See* HCJ 6698/95, Kaadan v. Israel Lands Authority, 55 P.D. (1) 258.

In interpreting the right to human dignity, which is expressly protected in the Basic Law: Human Dignity and Liberty, some judges have attempted to include social and economic rights, thereby giving effect to Israel's commitments under the Covenant. In *Society for Commitment to Peace and Social Justice v. Minister of Finance*,[129] a number of human rights nongovernmental organizations (NGOs) attempted to challenge the constitutionality of legislative changes that reduced payments to a few categories of social security beneficiaries. They argued that this reduction violated the right of such persons to live in dignity. Justice Levi was of the opinion that the right to a living with dignity is indeed a constitutionally protected right in Israel. He declared: "The right to human existence in dignity is not recognized only in our domestic law. It is also recognized in international law, where it is defined as the right to an 'adequate standard of living': article 11 (1) of the International Covenant on Economic, Social and Cultural Rights, . . . which Israel joined on 3 October, 1991."[130] The majority did not accept Justice Levi's view. While acknowledging that the core of economic and social rights, which guarantee persons an economic safety net, are a function of the right to dignity, the majority held that "one cannot say that the existing Basic Laws provide full and complete protection to social rights."[131] Thus, clearly there will be many cases in which persons whose economic, social, or cultural rights protected under the ICESCR have not been respected, but they will not be entitled to a judicial remedy.

III. INTERNATIONAL LAW IN CASES RELATING TO THE OCCUPIED TERRITORIES

A. *Distinction between Customary Law and Conventional Law*

The first reported decision of the Court dealing with a petition by Palestinian residents of the OT, the *Christian Society* case, related to an order promulgated by the military commander that amended the local labor law in the West Bank.[132] The petitioners argued that this amendment was incompatible both with the Regulations annexed to the Hague Convention (IV) Respecting the Laws and Customs of War on Land, 1907 (the Hague Regulations) and GCIV. Without distinguishing between the two instruments, the Court expressed doubts as to whether it could enforce conventions

[129] HCJ 366/03, 75 Dinim-Elyon 512.
[130] *Id.*, para. 1 in judgment of Justice Edmond Levi.
[131] *Id.*, para. 15 in judgment of Justice Barak.
[132] Christian Society for the Holy Places v. Minister of Defense, *supra* note 32.

"that are a commitment between the signatory nations and are part of international law that binds the states in their mutual relations."[133] Counsel for the minister of defense declared that "it was not his intention to put this issue before the Court, as the commander of the area acts in accordance with the conventions, and his defense rests on the argument that he adhered to the conventions."[134] The Court therefore stated that it would reserve its doubts and refrain from deciding whether the conventions could be enforced in the domestic courts.

For a few years after the *Christian Society* case, the government followed the line taken in that case: asking the Court to rule on the merits of the case on the basis of the Hague Regulations and GCIV, without affirming that those instruments were both legally binding and enforceable before a domestic court. In the *Rafah Approach* case,[135] Justice Landau voiced reservations about the Court following this line. He obviously thought that he should provide some legal basis for the Court's willingness to base its decisions on international law, and he offered the following rationale:

> While our courts derive their jurisdiction from the laws of the state and not from international law . . . it is a well-accepted rule, following the English rule, that a court in Israel "will interpret a local statute, if its contents do not demand otherwise, according to the rules of public international law." . . . One may argue that it surely follows that the court will judge the validity of an administrative act in the areas of military government according to public international law, when there is no Israeli statute that applies and there is therefore no possibility of a clash between international law and the national Israeli law.[136]

The issue that bothered Justice Landau here was the legal basis for judging the acts of the military government in the OT according to the norms of international law. Given the ambiguous attitude of the government toward the very idea that the West Bank and Gaza should be regarded as occupied territory, he was reluctant to state explicitly that the relevant law that applied in these territories was the international law of belligerent occupation. Instead, he referred to the rule of interpretation adopted from English law that parliamentary legislation should, where possible, be interpreted according to the rules of public international law, and he drew the conclusion that in areas under Israeli military control, in which Israeli law had not

[133] *Id.*, at 580.
[134] *Id.*, at 581–82.
[135] HCJ 302/72, Khelou v. Government of Israel, (1972) 27 (2) P.D. 169.
[136] *Id.*, at 177.

been applied, the validity of the acts of the military government should be judged according to public international law. The catch was, of course, that despite Justice Landau's reluctance to call the baby by its name, the public international law to which he was referring was the law of belligerent occupation, as codified in the Hague Regulations and GCIV.

Another judge in the same case, Justice Witkon, was prepared neither to accept government consent as grounds for basing a judicial decision on law that was not formally applicable nor to adopt Justice Landau's approach. Justice Witkon assumed that neither the Hague Regulations nor GCIV had gained the status of customary international law, and he concluded that as international conventions that had not been incorporated by parliamentary legislation they could not be enforced by a domestic court.

In response to the Court's decision in the *Rafah Approach* case, Israel's leading academic scholar on the law of armed conflict, Professor Yoram Dinstein, published an article in a local law review in which he pointed out that the Nuremburg Tribunal had held that, by the time of World War II, the Hague Regulations had become part of customary law.[137] Justice Witkon appreciated the point, and subsequently in his judgment in the *Beth El* case, he admitted that he had been mistaken in lumping the Hague Regulations and GCIV together.[138] He accepted that the Hague Regulations were now indeed part of customary international law, and that, as such, they could be enforced by the domestic courts. This became the accepted jurisprudence of the Supreme Court.

As far as the GCIV goes, the matter is more complicated. The Court was prepared to accept that some of the provisions of the Convention were reflective of customary law. It was not prepared, however, to acknowledge that all its provisions had achieved this status. The issue arose in respect to two provisions: Paragraph 1 of Article 49, which prohibits deportation or forcible transfer of protected persons from the occupied territory to the territory of the occupying power or that of any other country, and Paragraph 6 of Article 49, which prohibits an occupying power from transferring part of its own civilian population into the occupied territory.

In a number of cases, the Court was faced with petitions by Palestinian residents of the OT, against whom deportation orders had been served on security grounds. In a forceful minority opinion in one case, Justice Haim Cohn argued that the prohibition on deporting persons from their own

[137] *See* Y. Dinstein, "The Judgment in the *Rafah Approach* Case," (in Hebrew) 3 *Tel Aviv U.L. Rev.* (1974) 934.

[138] *Beth El* case, *supra* note 26.

country was part of customary international law, and that this prohibition applied both in times of peace and during armed conflict.[139] The majority on the Supreme Court rejected this view. The Court ruled that the absolute prohibition on deportations, including of persons who were a threat to the security of the occupying power, was not part of customary law and could therefore not be enforced by the Court.[140]

Paragraph 6 of Article 49 provides the main basis for arguing that establishment of Israeli settlements on the West Bank and in Gaza is a violation of international law.[141] Given the strong commitment of the major political parties in Israel to the settlement policies of various governments that have held power since 1967, the Supreme Court was obviously highly reluctant to rule on the legality of these settlements. It evaded the issue by holding that Paragraph 6 was not part of customary law.[142] In one case, counsel for the government actually "invited the Court to confirm to the authorities that from the point of view of the Geneva Convention, there was nothing wrong with giving land to the settlers for their settlement."[143] The Court would have none of it, however. It refused the invitation, repeating that since Paragraph 6 was not part of customary law, the Court would not rule on the issue.[144]

When it comes to the domestic legal system, resort to the distinction between customary and conventional law would seem to be well founded.[145] Unless the legislature is involved in some way in the ratification process for conventions, automatic implementation of conventions ratified on behalf of the state by the executive branch would indeed grant that branch a way of circumventing the legislative authority of the legislature. It is far from self-evident, however, that the distinction should be applied in relation to matters that are in the sole domain of the executive branch, when treaties relating to such matters do not involve any change in the domestic legal system. Indeed, there is support for the view that, under English law, the rule that domestic courts will not enforce international conventions does not apply to conventions relating to the laws of war, as the waging of war is part of the royal prerogative and does not relate to the rights of citizens

[139] Kawasme v. Minister of Defence, *supra* note 82.

[140] *Id.*

[141] This is not the only basis for this argument. For a succinct presentation of the other arguments, see International Humanitarian Law Research Initiative, The Legal Status of Israeli Settlements under IHL: Policy Brief (Jan. 2004), *available at* http://www.ihlresearch.org.

[142] *Beth El* case, *supra* note 26.

[143] *Elon Moreh* case, *supra* note 90, at 28.

[144] *Id.*

[145] Cf. Y. Zilbershatz, *supra* note 43, for an argument against the distinction.

of the realm.[146] In two cases, petitioners tried to persuade the Supreme Court of Israel that, in light of this view, the distinction between customary and conventional international law was misplaced when it came to the OT, which were managed by the executive branch of government and were not subject to the legislative power of the Knesset.[147] The Supreme Court of Israel rejected the argument. The distinction between customary and conventional international law remains entrenched in Supreme Court jurisprudence relating to the OT to this day.

B. *Applying Geneva Convention IV De Facto*

While the government formally challenged the de jure application of GCIV to the situation in the OT, it declared that the IDF would respect the humanitarian provisions of the Convention.[148] When the argument was first raised that the government should be held to this commitment, Justice Landau opined that the commitment was purely political in nature and had no legal force.[149] This view was later rejected by two judges, who stated that the commitment could place legal obligations on the government.[150] The logic behind this view is not clear. If the Court cannot enforce the Convention because it was ratified by the executive and was not incorporated in parliamentary legislation, it is difficult to understand why a commitment by the very same executive that the armed forces would abide by the obligations imposed on the state by the Convention should be enforced. It would seem that the Court confused two issues: application of GCIV to the OT and domestic enforcement of international treaties. The government's commitment to abide by the Convention was made because it challenged its formal application. The Court latched onto the commitment to overcome the problem of nonenforcement of binding international treaties that have not been incorporated in parliamentary legislation. Whatever the merits of the Court's reasoning, it has now become standard practice for the Supreme

[146] I have presented these sources elsewhere. See D. Kretzmer, "The Application and Interpretation of Geneva Convention IV- Domestic Enforcement and Interpretation," (in Hebrew) 26 *Mishpatim* (1995) 49.

[147] *Afu* case, *supra* note 21; HCJ 323/88, Sejdia v. Minister of Defence, *supra* note 34.

[148] For detailed discussion of the government's view, *see* Nissim Bar-Yaacov, "The Applicability of the Laws of War to Judea and Samaria (The West Bank) and to the Gaza Strip," 24 *Isr. L. Rev.* (1990) 485.

[149] *Kawasme* case, *supra* note 82, 628.

[150] *See* the decision of Justice Barak in HCJ 393/82, Ja'amait Ascan v. IDF Commander, *supra* note 53, and the opinions of Justice Bach in *Afu* case, *supra* note 21, and *Sejdiah* case, *supra* note 34.

Court to cite the government commitment as a basis for the Court to rely on the humanitarian provisions of GCIV.[151] In many cases, the Court has even gone further in relying on provisions of the Convention, without necessarily giving the basis for its stand. This tendency can be discerned in two groups of cases: cases relating to construction of a separation barrier on the West Bank and cases relating to active hostilities in the OT.

1. **Separation Barrier.** Following a spate of suicide bombings and other attacks on civilians in Israel, the government decided to construct a separation barrier on the West Bank, which would make it more difficult for potential terrorists from the West Bank to enter Israel. While the initial grounds for construction of the barrier were security grounds, there can be little doubt that, in determining the course of the barrier, political considerations played a major role.[152] The legality of the barrier and its route was the subject of an advisory opinion of the International Court of Justice (ICJ)[153] and of dozens of judgments of the Supreme Court of Israel. The advisory opinion and the judgments have been widely discussed,[154] and further detailed discussion is beyond the scope of this essay. In this section, I discuss the role of GCIV in the Supreme Court's judgments; below I shall review the approach of the Supreme Court to the Advisory Opinion itself.

The *Beit Sourik* decision,[155] the first major judgment relating to the barrier, was delivered shortly before the ICJ issued its advisory opinion. In this case,

[151] *See, e.g.*, HCJ 3278/02, Hamoked, The Center for the Defense of the Individual v. IDF Commander, 57 P.D. (1) 385; HCJ 7862/04, Abu Dahar v. IDF Commander, 59 P.D. (5) 368, and separation barrier cases reviewed herein.

[152] *See, e.g.*, the interview with cabinet minister Zipi Livni published in the daily *Ha'aretz*. Gideon Alon, "I'll take existence," Ha'aretz, 20 September 2004. Livni stated that "construction of the fence is meant, in the future security policy of Israel, to transfer 85–90 percent of the territory to the Palestinians living on the other side of the fence. If Israel places itself around the fence to grant security to the blocs of settlements, this is meant to ease the lives of the Palestinians, even though the price is harm to the villagers who live close to the fence. When the dilemma is between the life of an Israeli citizen living in the settlement and the difficulty which we create by constructing the fence for Palestinian villagers in working their land, my value choice is clear." Also see Uzi Dayan, "In Defense of a Fence," Speech to Washington Institute's Special Policy Forum, 19 December 2003, *available at* http://www.washingtoninstitute.org/templateC05.php?CID=2128. Dayan is a former deputy chief of staff of the IDF and was head of the National Security Council of Israel when it submitted the initial proposal for the barrier to the government.

[153] Legal Consequences of the Construction of a Wall in the Occupied Palestinian Territory, *supra* note 86.

[154] *See, e.g.*, Agora: ICJ Opinion on Construction of a Wall in the Occupied Territory in 99 *AJIL* 1 et seq. (2005); Special Double Issue: Domestic and International Judicial Review of the Construction of the Separation Barrier, 38 Isr. L, Rev, Nos. 1-2 (2005).

[155] HCJ 2056/04, Beit Sourik Village Council v. Government of Israel, 58 P.D. (5) 807.

the Court discussed the legality both of the decision to build the barrier and of a forty-kilometer section of the barrier being built northwest of Jerusalem. In setting out the legal framework for analysis of these issues, the Court declared:

> The authority of the military commander flows from the provisions of public international law regarding belligerent occupation. These rules are established principally in the Regulations Concerning the Laws and Customs of War on Land, The Hague, 18 October 1907. . . .
>
> These regulations reflect customary international law. The military commander's authority is also anchored in IV Geneva Convention Relative to the Protection of Civilian Persons in Time of War 1949. . . . The question of the application of the Fourth Geneva Convention has come up more than once in this Court. . . . The question is not before us now, since the parties agree that the humanitarian rules of the Fourth Geneva Convention apply to the issue under review.[156]

The notion that, as the state had conceded that the humanitarian rules of GCIV applied there was no need for the Court to rule either on their formal applicability, or their enforceability by a domestic court, has been repeated in many cases relating to segments of the separation barrier.[157] In one of these cases, the *Alphei Menashe* case,[158] which was heard a short time after publication of the ICJ's advisory opinion, the Court requested that government counsel submit a brief presenting the government's attitude to that opinion. In its judgment in the case, the Supreme Court discussed the opinion at length, including the unequivocal statement of the ICJ that GCIV applies to the actions of Israel on the West Bank. On the latter question, the Court said:

> The law of belligerent occupation is also laid out in IV Geneva Convention Relative to the Protection of Civilian Persons in Time of War 1949. . . .
>
> The State of Israel has declared that it practices the humanitarian parts of this convention. In light of that declaration on the part of the government of Israel, we see no need to reexamine the government's position. We are aware that the Advisory Opinion of the International Court of Justice determined that *The Fourth Geneva Convention* applies in the Judea and

[156] *Id.*, para. 23.

[157] *See, e.g.*, HCJ 1748/06, Mayor of Dahriya v. IDF Commander, 2006 Takdin-Elyon (4) 4074; HCJ 5488/04, Elram Local Council v. Government of Israel, 2006 Takdin-Elyon (4) 3878.

[158] HCJ 7957/04, Mara'abe v. Prime Minister of Israel, 74 Dinim-Elyon 528.

> Samaria area, and that its application is not conditional upon the willingness of the State of Israel to uphold its provisions. As mentioned, as the government of Israel accepts that the humanitarian aspects of *The Fourth Geneva Convention* apply in the *area*, we are not of the opinion that we must take a stand on that issue in the petition before us.[159]

This pragmatic approach of the Court, which allows it to apply the Geneva Convention, without ruling that it applies de jure to the actions of Israel on the West Bank or that its provisions are all part of customary law that may be enforced by a domestic court, may obviously be criticized.[160] Be that as it may, the Court's approach was politically astute. It avoided pushing the government into the position in which it was forced either to abandon its formal position on the issue or to defend that position before its own Supreme Court.[161] At the same time, it allowed the Court to avoid either undermining a position adopted by the government of Israel for forty years or taking a stand that differs from the internationally accepted position, now authoritatively confirmed by the ICJ.

Notwithstanding the fact that the Court has not positively ruled that the GCIV applies de jure to the actions of the IDF on the West Bank, after actually relying on GCIV in so many cases, it is inconceivable that government counsel could in future cases successfully contest either its application or its domestic enforceability. This would seem to be borne out by the fact that, in more recent cases dealing with the barrier, the Court has simply relied on GCIV without repeating that it is doing so because the government agreed that its humanitarian provisions apply. Thus, for example, in the *Dir Kadis* case, the Court referred to the powers of the military commander in occupied territory and stated:

> These [powers] are entrenched mainly in the Hague Regulations Respecting the Laws and Customs of War on Land, 1907 which are annexed to the Fourth Hague Convention of 1907. . . . These Regulations reflect customary international law. The military commanders authority is also entrenched

[159] *Id.*, para. 14.

[160] *See* Geoffrey R. Watson, "The "Wall" Decisions in Legal and Political Context," 99 *AJIL* 6 (2005).

[161] In HCJ 7015/02, Ajuri v. IDF Commander, 56 P.D. (6) 352, the Court mentions that government counsel reargued the government position that GC IV does not apply to the West Bank. However, counsel also repeated the long-standing commitment of the government to abide by the humanitarian provisions of the Convention. The Court declared that in light of this declaration it need not "examine the legal arguments concerning this matter, which are not simple, and we may leave these to be decided at a later date." *Id.*, para. 13.

in the Fourth Geneva Convention Relative to the Protection of Civilians in Time of War, 1949 . . .[162]

While the Court is careful to state that the Hague Regulations are part of customary international law, nothing at all is said about the status of GCIV or the basis for relying on it. De facto, the provisions of GCIV have become a source of norms on which the Court relies in cases dealing with the separation barrier. This has also been carried over to other cases relating to the powers of the military commander in occupied territory.[163]

2. **Active Hostilities.** In September 2000 violence erupted in the OT and there was a widescale resort to armed force, both by Palestinian armed groups and by the IDF. Soon after the violence erupted, the legal advisers of the IDF declared that the situation in the OT was now one of "armed conflict short of war." The Government of Israel adopted this position in its brief to the Mitchell Commission, which was established to examine the causes of the violence.[164]

After the violence started, the Supreme Court was faced with numerous petitions relating to military operations of the IDF rather than to the exercise of its authority as an occupying force.[165] In these cases, the Supreme Court simply relied on provisions of GCIV, without any reservation or statement of its standing. One may assume that it did so for two reasons. First, the government's reservation about application of the GCIV relates specifically to the issue of occupation of the West Bank and Gaza. It does not relate to its application in cases of hostilities. Second, there seems to be little doubt today that the provisions of GCIV relating to protection of civilians who find themselves in the hands of a party to an armed conflict have become part of customary law.

A typical example of the Court's reliance on GCIV in situations of military operations is provided in the Court's decision in the *Rafah* case.[166] In that case, a human rights NGO requested that the Court intervene so as to

[162] HCJ 2645/04, Naaser v. Prime Minister, 83 Dinim-Elyon 14.

[163] *See, e.g.*, HCJ 7862/04, Abu Daher v. IDF Commander, 59 P.D. (5) 368; HCJ 10356/02, Hess v. IDF Commander, 58 P.D. (3) 443; HCJ 7607/05, Hussein v. IDF Commander, 75 Dinim-Elyon 644.

[164] *Sharm el Sheikk Fact-Finding Committee Report* (the *Mitchell Report*), citing statements submitted by the Government of Israel, *available at* http://www.mideastweb.org/mitchell_report.htm.

[165] For a review of the Supreme Court's approach in these cases, *see* D. Kretzmer, "The Supreme Court of Israel: Judicial Review during Armed Conflict," 47 *German Y.B. Int'l L.* (2005) 392.

[166] HCJ 4764/04, Physicians for Human Rights v. IDF Commander, 68 Dinim-Elyon 20.

ensure protection of civilians during an IDF military operation in Rafah. In describing the legal framework for its decision the Court stated: "The military operations of the IDF in Rafah, to the extent they affect local residents, are governed by Hague Convention IV Respecting the Laws and Customs of War on Land 1907 . . . and the Geneva Convention Relative to the Protection of Civilian Persons in Time of War 1949."[167] The Court has followed this position in other cases relating to military operations.[168]

C. *International Law in Decisions on OT: Recent Trends*

In hundreds of cases relating to actions of the authorities in the OT, petitioners before the Supreme Court have based their arguments on principles and norms of international law, especially international humanitarian law. It should not be thought that the Court has always been receptive to arguments based on international law; nor has the manner in which it has interpreted this law always been compatible with accepted modes of interpretation – far from it. In some cases, the Court has simply ignored norms of international law, preferring to rely solely on the local law that applied in the OT at the time it was occupied in 1967.[169] In other cases, such as those relating to the legality of Israeli settlements, the Court has leaned over backward to avoid having to rule on the issue. It has managed to do this by regarding the provision in Article 49, Paragraph 6, of GCIV, as an innovative provision that has not achieved the status of customary international law;[170] by denying the standing of individual Palestinians to challenge the use of public land for settlements;[171] by holding that a petition against the settlements submitted by an NGO was nonjusticiable;[172] and by ruling that whether or not the settlements are lawful under international law is irrelevant in examining segments of the separation barrier whose object is to provide protection for settlers.[173] As seen earlier in the discussion of modes of interpretation,

[167] *Id.*, para. 10.

[168] *See, e.g.*, HCJ 3451/02, Almandi v. Minister of Defence, 56 P.D. (3) 30.

[169] The most glaring case in which the Court has acted in this manner has been in relation to punitive demolition of houses of the families of persons who were involved in terrorist attacks. I have dealt with this issue at length elsewhere. *See Occupation of Justice*, chap. 9; "The Supreme Court of Israel: Judicial Review during Armed Conflict," *supra* note 165. *See also* Yoram Dinstein, "The Israel Supreme Court and the Law of Belligerent Occupation: Demolitions and Sealing Off of Houses," 29 *Isr YHR* (2000) 285.

[170] *Beth El* case, *supra* note 26.

[171] Ayreib v. Appeals Committee, (1984) 40 (2) P.D. 57.

[172] Bargil v. Government of Israel, (1991) 47 (4) P.D. 210 (*Peace Now* case). *See also* I'ad v. IDF Commander in Judea and Samaria, 1999 (3) Takdin-Elyon 1771.

[173] *Mara'abe* case, *supra* note 158.

while never explicitly adopting the theory that the courts should accept the interpretation of international law favored by the executive branch of government, in some cases relating to the OT, the Court has in practice implemented this theory.

For a long time it seemed that the main function of the Court in petitions relating to the OT, including those in which issues of international law arose, had been to legitimize almost everything that the authorities wished to do.[174] In recent years, however, there has been a change in the Court's approach; it has made a sincere effort to interpret international law in a credible fashion. I shall discuss this approach by reviewing the Court's judgments in three cases. The first deals with the issue of assigned residence; the second, with the advisory opinion of the ICJ in the Legal Consequences of the Wall; and the third, with the policy of targeted killings of suspected terrorists.

1. **Assigned Residence.** In the course of 2002, there was a series of suicide bombings of civilian targets in Israel and the OT. Tens of civilians were killed and wounded in these bombings. In an attempt to find a measure that would deter potential suicide bombers, the suggestion was raised that family members of persons involved in such bombings should be deported from the West Bank to Gaza. The Attorney General opined that no action could be taken against an individual unless he or she had been personally involved in the activities of the suicide bomber.

New military legislation was required to remove West Bank residents to Gaza. The lawyers who drafted the military order were well aware of the limitations on the powers of a military commander in occupied territory. They therefore tried to draft legislation that would fit into the confines of Article 78 of GCIV, which allows internment or assigned residence of protected persons for "imperative reasons of security." Accordingly a new military order was promulgated that dealt with "special supervision and assigning a place of residence." The order stated that if the military commander of the West Bank considered it imperative to do so for decisive reasons of security, he could issue an order placing an individual under special supervision. Such an order could include the provision that the said person "be required to live within the bounds of a certain place in Judea and Samaria or in Gaza, as specified by the military commander in the order." Soon after the order was promulgated, individual orders were issued against three residents of the West Bank whose family members had been involved in serious terrorist

[174] *See The Occupation of Justice.*

attacks. There was evidence that all of these residents had been involved in the activities of their family members. The order required each of the individuals to live in Gaza for an indefinite period.

In a petition to the Supreme Court challenging the legality of the orders, it was argued that the individuals subject to the orders were in fact being deported, in contravention of Article 49, Paragraph 1, of GCIV.[175] For their part, the authorities argued that the measure was a form of assigned residence, expressly allowed under Article 78 of GCIV. While repeating their claim that GCIV does not formally apply to the West Bank, the authorities declared that they would nevertheless respect the humanitarian provisions of this Convention. The Supreme Court therefore decided once again that it would assume that GCIV applied and would rule on the basis of that assumption.

Since the authorities had attempted to justify their action on the basis of Article 78, the Court decided that it would confine itself to this argument: the only questions being whether the measure was indeed a form of assigned residence, permitted under that provision, and if so, whether it had been taken for reasons of imperative security.

The parties agreed that assigned residence must take place within the occupied territory. While the authorities argued, however, that the West Bank and Gaza were part of one unit, the petitioners argued that they should be regarded as two separate occupied territories. The Court preferred the view of the authorities on this question. In doing so, it relied on a provision in the Israeli-Palestinian Interim Agreement on the West Bank and the Gaza Strip signed by Israel and the PLO, which states: "The two sides view the West Bank and the Gaza Strip as a single territorial unit, the integrity and status of which shall be preserved during the interim agreement." The Court accepted the petitioners' argument that the measure could not be used merely to deter others. It held, however, that where it was justified to take a measure against a given individual on security grounds, in choosing between different available measures, it was legitimate for the authorities to consider the deterrent effect of those measures.

Having established that the measure itself was a form of assigned residence, and that it could be used against an individual on the basis of a combination of preventive and deterrent factors, the Court proceeded to examine whether it had been justified in all three cases before it. In two of the cases, the Court held that the evidence of the connection between the individual petitioner concerned and the family member who had been

[175] *Ajuri* V. *IDF Commander, supra* note 161.

involved in terrorist activities was strong enough to justify use of the measure. In the third case, it held that the evidence of such a connection was not strong enough and that the assignment order should therefore be revoked.

The view taken by the Court is certainly not free of difficulties, but it does seem that the Court made an effort to take the Geneva Convention seriously, and to interpret Article 78 in a credible fashion. It was apparently aware that in using the measure of assigned residence of West Bank residents to Gaza, the authorities were scraping the bottom of the barrel in an attempt to find a measure that could be effective in deterring terrorist attacks by suicide bombers. The Court stretched credulity in accepting that the main purpose of each assignment order was to cope with an imperative security risk from the individual concerned that could not be handled by a less invasive measure (e.g., internment in the West Bank) rather than an attempt to deter potential suicide bombers. It obviously realized that, in ruling that general deterrence was a legitimate secondary aim, it was going beyond the language of Article 78. Probably for this reason the Court saw fit to add the following declaration at the end of its judgment:

> Before we conclude, we would like to make two closing remarks. *First*, we have interpreted to the best of our ability the provisions of art. 78 of the Fourth Geneva Convention. According to all the accepted interpretive approaches, we have sought to give them a meaning that can contend with the new reality that the State of Israel is facing. We doubt whether the drafters of the provisions of art. 78 of the Fourth Geneva Convention anticipated protected persons who collaborated with terrorists and "living bombs." This new reality requires a dynamic interpretive approach to the provisions of art. 78 of the Fourth Geneva Convention, so that it can deal with the new reality.[176]

This notion of a new reality that requires a dynamic interpretive approach to the Geneva Convention was repeated in another case that will be discussed subsequently.

2. The Separation Barrier Cases. In the *Beit Sourik* case,[177] the petitioners challenged the legality of a segment of the separation barrier being built on the West Bank. In deciding the case, the Supreme Court examined the legality both of the decision to build the barrier and of the implementation of that decision in the specific segment under review.

[176] *Id.*, para. 40.
[177] *Supra* note 155.

A number of features of this decision merit attention in the present context. In the first place, the Court accepted that the legality of the barrier itself would be determined first and foremost by international law. As the Court stated:

> The general point of departure of all parties – which is also our point of departure – is that Israel holds the area in belligerent occupation (*occupatio bellica*).... In the areas relevant to this petition, military administration, headed by the military commander, continues to apply.... The authority of the military commander flows from the provisions of public international law regarding belligerent occupation. These rules are established principally in the Regulations Concerning the Laws and Customs of War on Land, The Hague, 18 October 1907.... These regulations reflect customary international law. The military commander's authority is also anchored in IV Geneva Convention Relative to the Protection of Civilian Persons in Time of War 1949.... The question of the application of the Fourth Geneva Convention has come up more than once in this Court.... The question is not before us now, since the parties agree that the humanitarian rules of the Fourth Geneva Convention apply to the issue under review.[178]

In the second place, the Court accepted that, under the law of belligerent occupation, it would not be lawful for the occupying power to build a wall or barrier if its purpose were political. As the Court put it: "The separation fence cannot be motivated by a desire to 'annex' territories to the state of Israel. The purpose of the separation fence cannot be to draw a political border."[179] In contrast, such a barrier would not necessarily be unlawful if its purpose were security, namely protecting Israel and Israeli citizens against attacks emanating from the West Bank. In such a case its legality would depend on whether the decision to build the barrier on a specific route met the test of proportionality. This could be examined only by looking at each segment of the barrier.

The Court held that, on the evidence presented, it was convinced that the purpose of the barrier was security and not political considerations. It therefore proceeded to examine the lawfulness of the segment under review in the instant case – forty kilometers of the barrier being constructed northwest of Jerusalem.

Under traditional rules of IHL, security measures such as seizure of property may be justified on grounds of military necessity. Thus, for example,

[178] *Id.*, para. 23.
[179] *Id.*, para. 27.

Article 23(g) of the Hague Regulations prohibits destruction or seizure of enemy property during hostilities "unless such destruction or seizure be imperatively demanded by the necessities of war." The contribution of the Supreme Court in the *Beit Sourik* case was importation into international humanitarian law of the three-pronged test of proportionality developed in German constitutional law.[180] When employed to assess military necessity, the test involves inquiring whether there is a rational connection between the measure adopted and military needs; whether that measure is the least invasive measure capable of meeting the military needs; and what is termed *narrow proportionality*, namely whether the harm caused is not excessive in relation to the security benefits gained by employing the particular measure. In the case before it, the Court held that while the segment under review met the first two prongs of the test, most of it failed to meet the narrow proportionality test.

Ten days after the Court handed down its decision in this case, the ICJ delivered its advisory opinion. This opinion was radically different from the *Beit Sourik* decision of the Supreme Court in a number of respects. First and foremost, while the Supreme Court had examined the specific facts on the ground, analysis of the facts is conspicuous by its absence from the advisory opinion. The opinion rests on very general principles, so that it is extremely difficult to determine on what legal basis the ICJ opined that the whole barrier on the West Bank was being built in contravention of international law. Second, while the Supreme Court had held that parts of the barrier could be lawful and parts not, the ICJ opined that construction of the whole barrier constituted a violation of international law. Behind this view was the implied assumption that an occupying power may not build a structure in occupied territory to defend persons in its own territory from attacks emanating from the occupied territory.[181]

[180] In German constitutional law, this principle is known as *Verhältnismäßigkeit*. The principle has become well entrenched both in Canadian constitutional law and in Israeli constitutional law. To the best of my knowledge, the only document in which it has been expressly employed by an international body is *Human Rights Committee*, General Comment No. 27 on Art. 12 of the Covenant, para. 14, CPR/C/21/Rev.1/Add.9 of 2 November 1999. In discussing permissible restrictions to freedom of movement, the Committee states:

> Art. 12 para. 3 clearly indicates that it is not sufficient that the restrictions serve the permissible purposes; they must also be necessary to protect them. Restrictive measures must conform to the principle of proportionality; they must be appropriate to achieve their protective function; they must be the least intrusive instrument amongst those which might achieve the desired result; and they must be proportionate to the interest to be protected.

[181] *See* D. Kretzmer, "The Advisory Opinion: The Light Treatment of International Humanitarian Law," 99 *AJIL* 88 (2005).

Given the status of the ICJ as the judicial body with the authority to pronounce on international law, the Supreme Court of Israel could hardly have ignored the opinion in subsequent cases. Hence, in the *Alphei Menashe* case,[182] the first major case to be heard after publication of the advisory opinion, the Supreme Court requested that the state submit a brief on its attitude toward the advisory opinion. In its judgment in that case, the Court itself subsequently discussed the opinion. Its approach is revealing.

While the advisory opinion had been subject to harsh academic criticism,[183] the Supreme Court was careful to tread a different path. Rather than take issue with the opinion, the Court chose to show it due deference and to stress the similarities between its position and that of the ICJ. The Court mentioned that, as the ICJ itself had stated, the advisory opinion was not binding: "However, the opinion of the International Court of Justice is an interpretation of international law, performed by the highest judicial body in international law (S. Rosenne 3 *The Law and Practice of the International Court, 1920–1996* 1754 (3rd ed. 1997)). The ICJ's interpretation of international law should be given its full appropriate weight."[184] The manner in which the Court gave the ICJ interpretation "full appropriate weight" was to declare that there were no significant differences in the way the two judicial bodies interpreted international law. Thus, in a rather remarkable dictum, the Supreme Court declared:

> The basic normative foundation upon which the ICJ and the Supreme Court in *The Beit Sourik Case* based their decisions was a common one.... The ICJ held that Israel holds the West Bank (Judea and Samaria) pursuant to the law of belligerent occupation. That is also the legal view at the base of *The Beit Sourik Case.* The ICJ held that an occupier state is not permitted to annex the occupied territory. That was also the position of the Court in *The Beit Sourik Case.* The ICJ held that in an occupied territory, the occupier state must act according to *The Hague Regulations* and *The Fourth Geneva Convention.* That too was the assumption of the Court in *The Beit Sourik Case*, although the question of the force of *The Fourth Geneva Convention* was not decided, in light of the State's declaration that it shall act in accordance with the humanitarian part of that convention. The ICJ determined that in addition to the humanitarian law, the conventions on human rights apply in the occupied territory. This question

[182] HCJ 7957/04, Mara'abe v. Prime Minister of Israel, *supra* note 158.

[183] *See, e.g.*, articles in Agora: ICJ Opinion on Construction of a Wall in the Occupied Territory, and in Special Double Issue: Domestic and International Judicial Review of the Construction of the Separation Barrier, *supra* note 154.

[184] Mara'abe v. Prime Minister, *supra* note 158, para. 56.

> did not arise in *The Beit Sourik Case.* For the purposes of our judgment in this case, we assume that these conventions indeed apply. The ICJ held that the legality of the "wall" (the "fence" in our nomenclature) shall be determined, *inter alia*, by regulations 46 and 52 of *The Hague Regulations* and §53 of *The Fourth Geneva Convention.* This was also the position of the Supreme Court in *The Beit Sourik Case.* The ICJ held that as a result of the building of the "wall," a number of rights of the Palestinian residents were impeded. The Supreme Court in *The Beit Sourik Case* also held that a number of human rights of the Palestinian residents had been impeded by the building of the fence. Finally, the ICJ held that the harm to the Palestinian residents would not violate international law if the harm was caused as a result of military necessity, national security requirements, or public order. That was also the approach of the Court in *The Beit Sourik Case.*[185]

As the legal framework of the two courts was a common one, the difference in outcome between the decision of the Supreme Court, according to which it was not necessarily illegal to build a barrier in occupied territory, and the opinion of the ICJ, according to which the whole barrier was constructed in violation of international law, was to be explained by the different factual bases available to the two bodies. And it was here that the Supreme Court had the relative advantage. For while the ICJ had relied on "the material before it," which did not include presentation of the concrete facts by the State of Israel, the Supreme Court had been presented with affidavits relating to the concrete facts of each segment of the barrier that had been challenged. The Court held that this evidence justified its finding that the purpose of the barrier was security rather than political factors. It also ruled that, in most cases, the route chosen met the demands of proportionality.

It is not my intention here to analyze the different areas in which there is a clear disparity between the approaches of the two judicial bodies to the applicable law and its interpretation. Possibly the most glaring example is the attitude to the legality of Israeli settlements on the West Bank. The ICJ ruled that the settlements were established in violation of Article 49, Paragraph 6, of GCIV, and that drawing the route of the barrier to protect those settlements was therefore illegal.[186] The Supreme Court refused to

[185] *Id.*, para 57.

[186] The most extreme expression of this view is to be found in the declaration of Judge Thomas Buergenthal, who dissented from the decision of the Court to deliver the advisory opinion. "Paragraph 6 of Article 49 of the Fourth Geneva Convention also does not admit for exceptions on grounds of military or security exigencies. It provides that 'the Occupying Power shall not deport or transfer parts of its own civilian population into the territory it occupies.' I agree that this provision applies to the Israeli settlements in the West Bank and that their existence violates Article 49, paragraph 6. It follows that

express an opinion on the legality of the settlements. It held that even if they were illegal the military commander still had the power and duty to protect the civilians living in the settlements, and that the barrier could be a legitimate means to fulfill that aim. The Court attempted to base this power and duty of the commander on his duty under Article 43 of the Hague Regulations to "restore and ensure public order and public life" in the occupied territory. It did not consider whether, on the assumption that the settlements were established in contravention of international law, the proper way to restore public order and public life should have been to remove the settlements.

For the purposes of the present essay, the important issue is not the substantive differences between the approaches of the two judicial bodies but the attitude of the Israel Supreme Court toward the advisory opinion of the ICJ. As has been stressed, that attitude involved trying to show that the domestic court was in fact adopting the same approach to the law as the international court.

3. ***Targeted Killings* Case.** In the *Targeted Killings* case,[187] a number of human rights NGOs challenged the government policy of targeted killings of Palestinians suspected of involvement in terrorist activities against Israel and Israelis. In support of their argument that it is unlawful in international law to target persons who are not at the time directly participating in hostilities, they submitted an opinion written by Professor Antonio Casesse, the well-known expert in IHL, who had served as first president of the International Criminal Tribunal for the Former Yugoslavia.

In its decision in this case, the Supreme Court was forced to consider a number of extremely complicated questions of international law. These included whether the armed conflict in the OT between Israeli forces and organized Palestinian armed groups is of an international or noninternational character; whether members of such groups may be regarded as unlawful combatants; whether the protection of civilians, under Article 51, Paragraph 3, of Additional Protocol I, "unless and for such time as they take a direct part in hostilities," is part of customary law; what constitutes direct participation in hostilities; and how one assesses the time element of direct participation encapsulated in the words "for such time."

the segments of the wall being built by Israel to protect the settlements are *ipso facto* in violation of international humanitarian law." Para. 9 of Declaration of Judge Thomas Buergenthal, *Legal Consequences of the Wall, supra* note 86.

[187] HCJ 769/02, Public Committee against Torture v. Government of Israel, *supra* note 23.

In the separation barrier case mentioned previously, the Supreme Court attempted to present its legal position as one that was similar to that of the ICJ. Even though some of the views presented by Professor Casesse in his opinion in the *Targeted Killings* case were quite controversial, the Court attempted to follow his line of reasoning.[188] Thus, it accepted Casesse's view that, because the armed conflict was taking part in occupied territory, it should be governed by the legal regime that applies to armed conflicts of an international character.[189] It rejected the state's argument that alongside civilians and combatants a separate category of unlawful combatants is recognized in international law.[190] It also refused to accept the state's argument that the element of time in Article 51, according to which civilians only lose their immunity from attack "for such time as they take a direct part in hostilities," is not part of customary law.[191]

While accepting the basic framework for analysis set out by Professor Casesse, the Court repeated what it had said in the assigned residence case, that the "new reality at times requires new interpretation." It declared: "The rules developed against the background of a reality which has changed must take on dynamic interpretation which adapts them, in the framework of accepted interpretational rules, to the new reality. . . . In the spirit of such interpretation, we shall now proceed to the customary international law dealing with the status of civilians who constitute unlawful combatants."[192] It was here that the Court subtly parted ways from Casesse's framework of analysis. Having dismissed the state's argument that the loss of immunity from attack of civilians who take a direct part in hostilities is not confined to such time as they are taking such part, the Court extended the time frame implied in the words "for such time." After pointing out

[188] Besides citing the opinion of Casesse submitted to the Court, on a number of occasions the Court also cited with approval A. Casesse, *International Law* (2d ed., 2005).

[189] The problem with this view is that the Palestinian armed groups are not acting on behalf of a state. For this reason, others have questioned whether the armed conflict can be regarded as an international armed conflict. *See, e.g.*, Commission on Human Rights, *Question of the Violation of Human Rights in the Occupied Arab Territories, including Palestine, Report of the human rights inquiry commission*, (E/CN.4/2001/121), 16 March 2001, para. 62.

[190] Public Committee against Torture v. Government of Israel, *supra* note 23, para. 28. As seen earlier, it based rejection of the state's argument on the fact that it was not presented "with data sufficient to allow us to say, at the present time, that such a third category has been recognized in customary international law."

[191] Thus the Court stated: "In respondents' opinion, that part of article 51(3) of *The First Protocol* is not of customary character, and the State of Israel is not obligated to act according to it. We cannot accept that approach. As we have seen, all of the parts of article 51(3) of *The First Protocol* reflect customary international law, including the time requirement." *Id.*, para. 30.

[192] *Id.*, para. 28.

that there was disagreement on the parameters of this time frame, the Court stated:

> With no consensus regarding the interpretation of the wording "for such time," there is no choice but to proceed from case to case. Again, it is helpful to examine the extreme cases. On the one hand, a civilian taking a direct part in hostilities one single time, or sporadically, who later detaches himself from that activity, is a civilian who, starting from the time he detached himself from that activity, is entitled to protection from attack. He is not to be attacked for the hostilities which he committed in the past. On the other hand, a civilian who has joined a terrorist organization which has become his "home," and in the framework of his role in that organization he commits a chain of hostilities, with short periods of rest between them, loses his immunity from attack "for such time" as he is committing the chain of acts. Indeed, regarding such a civilian, the rest between hostilities is nothing other than preparation for the next hostility.[193]

This interpretation allowed the Court to rule that targeted killings carried out by the Israeli authorities were not necessarily unlawful under IHL. The Court provided no criteria for determining whether a person who carried out attacks in the past had "detached himself from that activity" or was merely resting between hostilities in "preparation for the next hostility." It did, however, subject use of targeted killings even in such circumstances to a number of conditions, taken, it would seem, from international human rights law rather than from IHL.[194]

The foregoing three cases are indicative of recent trends in the attitude of the Supreme Court of Israel toward international humanitarian law in petitions relating to the OT. While still maintaining the formal distinction between customary and conventional international law, and not positively ruling that the provisions of GCIV have become part of customary law, the Court regularly relies on provisions of that Convention. The Court is mindful of the way international humanitarian law has been interpreted by the ICJ and by well-recognized jurists, and it attempts to place its decisions within internationally accepted interpretations rather than take issue

[193] *Id.*, para. 39.

[194] These conditions are that well-based information is required before action is taken; that an individual may be targeted only as a last resort if less harmful means, such as arrest and prosecution, are unavailable; there must be an independent investigation into use of the measure every time a person is targeted; and finally, that if civilians who do not participate in hostilities are likely to be harmed, the lawfulness of targeting the person who does take part in hostilities is to be judged by the rule of proportionality.

with them. In contrast, the Court has, on a number of occasions, given expression to its view that the provisions of the Geneva Convention were not drawn up with the problems created by suicide bombings in mind and that they therefore require a dynamic interpretation. As opposed to the Court's jurisprudence in the first thirty years after the occupation began, the Court no longer uses international law as a mechanism for legitimizing almost everything the authorities wish to do. The legitimizing function is still there, but on a number of occasions the Court has ruled against the government on highly sensitive issues. Perhaps one can demand more from domestic courts; can one realistically expect more?

8

The Netherlands

André Nollkaemper

Professor of Public International Law
Faculty of Law of the Universiteit van Amsterdam

I. INTRODUCTION

This chapter discusses the application of treaties in the domestic legal order of the Kingdom of the Netherlands.[1] The term *treaties* is used here, in accordance with the definition that is used officially in the Netherlands, to refer to any agreement, irrespective of its name or form, that binds the Netherlands under international law.[2] I use the term *application* in a broad sense to cover supplementary legal or material action taken by the Netherlands in its domestic legal order to ensure the full effect of a given provision of a treaty. *Application* also covers judicial rulings (whether by administrative or judicial bodies) that give effect to a treaty provision in a particular case.[3] The term *application* thus includes *performance*, as that term is used in the Vienna Convention on the Law of Treaties.[4]

[1] What is commonly referred to as the Netherlands is in fact part of the Kingdom of the Netherlands, which consists of the Netherlands in Europe, the Netherlands Antilles, and Aruba (both located in the Caribbean). It is the Kingdom, as a subject of international law, that enters into treaties (though in some treaties it is stipulated that the territorial scope is limited to the Kingdom in Europe or the Kingdom in the Caribbean) and that is responsible for a breach of a treaty obligation. Specific questions related to the international constitutional order of the Kingdom are not discussed in this chapter. Whenever the chapter refers to the Netherlands, this is a reference to the Kingdom. For earlier discussions of subjects addressed in this chapter, *see, e.g.*, E.A. Alkema, *Foreign Relations in the 1983 Dutch Constitution*, 3 NETH. INT'L L. REV. 307 (1984); J.G. Brouwer, *The Netherlands*, *in* NATIONAL TREATY LAW AND PRACTICE: DEDICATED TO THE MEMORY OF MONROE LEIGH 483 (Duncan B. Hollis ed., 2005); H.H.M. Sondaal, *Dutch Treaty Practice*, NYIL. 1988, 179.

[2] K. II, 1979–1980, 15049 (R 1100), No. 3, at 6; Brouwer, *supra* note 1, at 486. This chapter does not discuss the binding nature or treaty status of administrative agreements or memoranda of understanding, nor does it address particular problems that may be raised by the domestic application of such agreements.

[3] Paul Reuter, INTRODUCTION TO THE LAW OF TREATIES (2d ed. 1995) nr. 137*, pgs. 148–49.

[4] Vienna Convention on the Law of Treaties, 1155 U.N.T.S. 331, art. 26 ("Every treaty in force is binding upon the parties to it and must be performed by them in good faith.").

This chapter demonstrates that the Netherlands is very open to the application of international law in its domestic legal order. However, it also shows that, like most or perhaps all other states, the Netherlands resorts to evasion strategies that may insulate the domestic legal order from the consequences of international legal obligations that are not considered sufficiently transparent or legitimate, that may conflict with existing law, or that may collide with political interests of the Netherlands.[5]

The chapter starts by discussing some aspects of treaty making in the Netherlands that are relevant to the subsequent phase of application of treaties (Section II). It then proceeds to discuss the general position of international law in the legal order of the Netherlands (Section III), and the application of treaties by the legislature (Section IV), the executive (Section V), and the courts (Section VI). Section VII discusses the practice of treaty interpretation in the Netherlands. Section VIII briefly discusses the influence of EC law on the application of treaties in the Netherlands. Section IX contains some conclusions.

II. SOME RELEVANT ASPECTS OF INTERNATIONAL LAWMAKING

The negotiation of treaties in the Netherlands is a task for the government. Once the text of a treaty is finalized, the Council of Ministers will consider it for approval and, if approved by the cabinet, the treaty will be signed. Parliament, in principle, is not involved in the process of negotiation. However, to ensure that Parliament is not confronted with a fait accompli after the negotiations are finalized, Article 1 of the Law on the Approval and Promulgation of Treaties (*Rijkswet Goedkeuring en bekendmaking verdragen*)[6] provides that Parliament must be informed regularly about treaties that are in the process of being negotiated. Although the government is not obliged to provide information about the contents of such treaties, this provision ensures that Parliament is informed of the treaties that are being negotiated and that it can seek further information in appropriate circumstances. But obviously, given the nature of the treaty-making process, the possibility for Parliament to exert any meaningful influence over the contents of a treaty is extremely limited.

Parliament has one additional way in which it can exercise some influence on the international obligations that are binding on the Netherlands.

[5] Eyal Benvenisti, *Judicial Misgivings Regarding the Application of International Law: An Analysis of Attitudes of National Courts*," 4 EUR. J. INT'L L. 159 (1993).

[6] Stb. 1994, 542 [hereinafter Law on Treaties]. An English translation is contained in Brouwer, *supra* note 1, Annex C.

It can add interpretive declarations or reservations to the bill of approval of the treaty. The government then will make such interpretive declarations or reservations at the stage of treaty ratification, potentially excluding or limiting the effect of treaty provisions in their application to the Netherlands.[7]

Whereas the executive negotiates and signs a treaty, it does not have the power to bind the Netherlands under international law. A treaty negotiated by the executive will become binding on the Netherlands only after it has been submitted to Parliament and Parliament has given its approval for that treaty. Article 91 of the Constitution provides: "The Kingdom shall not be bound by treaties, nor shall such treaties be denounced without the prior approval of the Parliament." It is this requirement of prior approval of the Parliament that explains to a large extent the relative openness of the legal system of the Netherlands to the application of treaties. It makes it at least somewhat acceptable, from a perspective of democratic legitimacy, that a rule stemming from an international source finds full application in the domestic sphere and, in particular circumstances, can trump domestic law.

The aforementioned Law on the Approval and Promulgation of Treaties[8] provides several exceptions to the general requirement that all treaties require parliamentary approval. No approval is required for treaties that execute treaties approved earlier, for short-term treaties, for secret treaties, or for changes to execution annexes that are an integral part of a treaty.[9] This last exception contains a potentially significant loophole in the democratic legitimacy of treaties.[10] It would, for example, exclude from parliamentary approval changes in annexes to environmental treaties detailing prohibited or restricted substances, unless parliament has made a reservation to preclude such unapproved changes. The Law also allows for provisional application of treaties.[11]

Treaties are approved by a simple majority vote in both Chambers of Parliament. The requirement of a simple majority is similar to what is

[7] Vienna Convention on the Law of Treaties, *supra* note 4, art. 19. For an example of a discussion of reservations during the discussion of the Bill of Approval in Parliament, see K. II 2000–2001, 27 509 (R 1671), nr. 7 (discussion on reservation to the Criminal Law Convention on Terrorism (Trb. 2000, 130)).

[8] *Supra* note 6. *See also* Jan Klabbers, *The New Dutch Law on the Approval of Treaties*, 44 Int'l & Comp. L.Q. 629 (1995).

[9] Law on Treaties, *supra* note 6, art. 7.

[10] Klabbers, *supra* note 8, at 634–35.

[11] Law on Treaties, *supra* note 6, art. 15.

required for the enactment of legislation; this requirement helps justify the rule that a treaty can trump a conflicting provision of domestic law.[12]

A more demanding requirement applies for provisions of a treaty that conflict with the Constitution or that lead to conflicts with it. As will be explained herein, the Netherlands is one of the few states in which provisions of treaties that conflict with the Constitution may override the Constitution.[13] Given the demanding parliamentary procedures for amending the Constitution,[14] it would be odd, and indeed unacceptable, if a treaty adopted by a simple majority could override the Constitution. Article 91(3) of the Constitution provides some assurances, though less demanding than those that apply to amendment of the Constitution, by stipulating that any provisions of a treaty that conflict with the Constitution or that lead to conflicts with it must be approved by a two-thirds majority in both Chambers of the Parliament. In a limited number of cases, either the government or Parliament was of the opinion that a conflict might occur and that, therefore, Article 91(3) was applicable. A relatively recent example is the approval of the Statute of the International Criminal Court.[15] It was thought that Article 27 of the Statute (providing that official capacity as a head of state or government, a member of a government or parliament, an elected representative, or a government official shall in no case exempt a person from criminal responsibility under the statute) might conflict with Article 42 of the Dutch Constitution (providing that the King is not responsible for acts of government).[16] In this case, the Statute was indeed approved by a two-thirds majority.

The controlling power of Parliament over the approval of treaties does not apply to decisions of international organizations. Article 92 of the Constitution provides that legislative, executive, and judicial powers may be conferred on international institutions by or pursuant to a treaty. If an international organization is given and exercises the power to legislate, such legislation subsequently will be part of domestic law. Although the constituent treaty will be approved by Parliament, that will not be the case for individual decisions taken by the organization. A (somewhat controversial)[17] example concerns the effect of Security Council Resolution 1688 (2006), by which

[12] *See infra* Sections III.C and VI.D.

[13] *See infra* Sections III.C and VI.D.

[14] Arts. 137–38 of the Constitution.

[15] Rome Statute of the International Criminal Court, 2187 U.N.T.S. 90. The statute approving the Rome Statute is published in Stb. 2001, 343.

[16] *See, e.g.*, K. II 2000–2001, nr. 27 848 (R 1699) pg. 4.

[17] Security Council Resolution 1688 was controversial not because of its status in Dutch law, but because of the question whether it had direct effect, as was argued by the government

the Security Council approved the transfer of Charles Taylor to the Netherlands. The Government indicated that, because of time pressures, it was not feasible to utilize the regular process (which had been followed, for example, in the Lockerbie trial)[18] consisting of a treaty with implementing legislation. Instead, the government chose to rely on the Security Council Resolution to provide the proper legal basis in domestic law for the arrest and detention of Charles Taylor.[19] The requirement of parliamentary approval of treaties under Article 91 does not apply to such decisions. However, parliamentary approval is needed for decisions of international organizations that amend treaties concluded under the auspices of that organization.[20] In all cases, decisions of international organizations must be published in the treaty series of the Netherlands (Tractatenblad).[21]

The absence of a role for Parliament in the negotiation or approval of acts of international organizations has been felt to be particularly problematic in the third pillar of the European Union (justice and home affairs), where the role of the European Court of Justice (ECJ) and the European Parliament has been much weaker than in other areas of European law. As in some other states (e.g., Denmark), Dutch parliaments have wished to retain some form of control. The Act of Approval of the 1992 Treaty of Maastricht provides that the draft of a decision that is intended to bind the Kingdom must be made public and submitted to Parliament before the Council of Ministers makes a final decision.[22] Approval of Parliament is required before the representative of the Netherlands can give consent to the adoption of the decision. Consequently, when the Council of Ministers seeks to take a decision but Parliament has not yet seen the text, the representative of the Netherlands will have to make a so-called parliamentary reservation to block further decision making by the Council. Such parliamentary reservations have been used frequently, in the context of the third pillar of the

but disputed by some members of Parliament. *See* discussion in the First Chamber, H. I 3 July 2006, EK 35–1681.

[18] In this case, U.N. Security Council Resolution 1192 (1998), calling on the Netherlands, the United Kingdom, and the United States to make arrangement for the trial of the Lockerbie suspects by a Scottish court in the Netherlands, was followed by a bilateral treaty between the Netherlands and the United Kingdom (Trb. 1998, 237) and by a statute making such arrangements under Dutch law (see Stb. 1998, 628).

[19] K. II 2005–2006, 30 610, nr 3, pg. 2.

[20] Brouwer, *supra* note 1, 487.

[21] *See* Law on Treaties, *supra* note 6, arts. 16 & 18.

[22] The Council of Ministers (or just the Council) forms, together with the European Parliament, the highest legislative body in the European Union. Each member state has one representative.

European Union, to ensure that the relevant preparatory documents are sent to Parliament well in advance to allow for a meaningful discussion.

It has been suggested that a similar practice would be desirable for decisions taken by other organizations. However, no such proposals have actually been adopted. The legislation approving the Statute of the International Criminal Court goes some way to involving Parliament in decision making by providing that the Minister for Foreign Affairs will send to Parliament the agenda of a meeting of the Assembly of States no later than two weeks prior to such a meeting.[23]

III. APPLICATION OF TREATIES: GENERAL ASPECTS

There are three distinct issues that govern the status of treaties in the Netherlands and their mode of application: (1) the validity of treaties, (2) their direct effect, and (3) their supremacy.

A. *Validity*

All treaties that are binding on the Netherlands as a matter of international law are automatically incorporated and thus have the force of law in the domestic legal order. Their validity in the national legal order is not dependent on any further implementing legislation. This principle is not expressly formulated in the Dutch Constitution but is based on unwritten constitutional law. The two provisions of the Dutch Constitution that are often quoted in this context, Articles 93 and 94, in fact concern the narrower issues of direct effect and supremacy, which are discussed subsequently.

The customary rule of the automatic validity of treaties in domestic law can be traced to a decision of the Supreme Court of 3 March 1919. The Court had to consider the legal status and effect of an 1816 agreement determining the boundary between Prussia and the Netherlands. The agreement provided that farmers who owned land on both sides of the border were allowed to transport their products across the border without needing any documents. A landowner was nonetheless convicted for bringing products across the border without transport documents. The Supreme Court held that the agreement had the double effect that the Netherlands was bound towards Prussia and that the treaty provided the landowner with the right to transport his products from the part of his property located in the Netherlands to the part of his property located across the border.[24] The Court thus

[23] Stb. 2001, 343, art. 5(1).
[24] Supreme Court, 3 March 1919, NJ 1919, 371.

accepted that the landowner could rely on the treaty to enforce his treaty rights in the domestic legal order and before a domestic court. Since then, the automatic incorporation of treaties and all rules of international law is undisputed and has frequently been confirmed by the courts.

The explanation and justification for the automatic incorporation of international law in the legal order of the Netherlands cannot be found, at least not exclusively, in the fact that treaties have been approved by Parliament. All international law is automatically incorporated, including customary international law, which obviously lacks the democratic quality of treaties. Rather, automatic incorporation is a reflection of the traditional international orientation of the Netherlands. This explains both the fact that the Constitution provides that the Netherlands will actively promote the development of the international legal order[25] and the fact that the Netherlands has opened its domestic legal order for all rules of international law that are binding on the Netherlands.[26]

B. *Direct Effect*

Although all treaty rules that are binding on the Netherlands are part of domestic law, there may be substantial differences in the actual legal consequences of particular treaties and their provisions. The concept of direct effect is key in explaining such differences. This concept is in particular relevant for determining which treaty rules can be applied to limit the rights of private persons and which rules may be invoked by private persons.[27]

The direct effect of treaty provisions is governed by Article 93 of the Constitution, which provides: "Provisions of treaties and of resolutions by international institutions that are *binding on all persons by virtue of their contents* shall become binding after they have been published" (emphasis added). Article 93 thus indicates that only certain treaty provisions, by virtue of their contents, may be binding on everyone and on that basis can be applied directly by the state organs vis-à-vis private persons. It adds the requirement that such provisions can only be applied directly if they have been properly published. Although Article 93 refers only to the binding of individuals, the courts have accepted that the same test applies to the question whether individuals can rely on treaty provisions.

[25] *See generally* L. Besselink, *The Constitutional Duty to Promote the Development of the International Legal Order: The Significance and Meaning of Article 90 of the Netherlands Constitution*, NYIL 2003, 89.

[26] *See* Brouwer, *supra* note 1, 498–99 (providing references to other scholars).

[27] *See generally* A. Nollkaemper, *The Direct Effect of Public International Law*, *in* Jolande Prinssen & Annette Schrauwen (eds.), DIRECT EFFECT: RETHINKING A CLASSIC OF EC LEGAL DOCTRINE 157 (Europa Law Publishers, 2002).

The requirement "binding on everyone" has been interpreted in case law to mean that a treaty provision has to be sufficiently clear to function as "objective law" in the domestic legal order.[28] This test essentially fulfils two functions. First, it limits the power of the courts to review governmental policy. The courts, in principle, will review governmental policy only against treaty provisions that are sufficiently clear and need no further implementation by the legislative branch. The foundation for this restriction is the separation of powers. Allowing courts to enforce vaguely formulated treaty provisions would give them a quasi-legislative role. The limitation to provisions that are binding on everyone limits judicial power.

Second, the doctrine of direct effect is based on the principles of notice and legal certainty. Treaty provisions can be applied to regulate private conduct only when the provisions are sufficiently clear, by virtue of their contents, that private parties can ascertain what conduct is permitted or prohibited. Also, as indicated, the treaty must be published to give notice to private parties.

The concept of direct effect is particularly relevant in the context of the application of treaties by the courts and will be discussed further in that context.[29]

C. *Supremacy*

The automatic incorporation of treaties into the domestic legal order inevitably raises the possibility that treaty provisions may collide with rules of domestic law. If such a conflict cannot be avoided by consistent interpretation,[30] Dutch law recognizes, under certain conditions, the supremacy of international law. Recall that the international law principle of the supremacy of international law itself does not and cannot force such supremacy at the domestic level. This principle, as contained, for instance, in Article 27 of the Vienna Convention on the Law of Treaties, applies only within the international legal order; by itself, it is not decisive in domestic law.[31] Article 94 of the Dutch Constitution accepts, however, to some extent,

[28] *See infra* Section VI.A.
[29] *See infra* Section VI.A.
[30] *See infra* Section VI.C.
[31] *But see Judgment of the Constitutional Court of the Republic of Latvia on a Request for Constitutional Review*, ILDC 189 (LV 2004) (in which a domestic court expressly referred to the international principle of supremacy as a basis for domestic reparation). The court had to consider whether the Latvian Code of Administrative Penalties was compatible with the International Convention on Facilitation of International Maritime Traffic, which provides that states shall not impose any penalty on ship owners if their passengers possess inadequate control documents. The Court derived from the obligations of Latvia under the

the consequences of international law's claim to supremacy. It provides: "Statutory regulations in force within the Kingdom shall not be applicable if such application is in conflict with provisions of treaties that are binding on all persons or of resolutions by international institutions."

Not only does Article 94 require the application of a treaty rule that conflicts with previously enacted rules of domestic law – a conflict rule that could be justified by the authority of the will of parliament[32] – Article 94 also provides that a treaty takes precedence over a later-enacted statute. Even though later-enacted statutes are a more recent reflection of the will of Parliament, they still will have to yield to conflicting requirements of treaties. This fact shows that the supremacy of international law under Article 94 is indeed based on the recognition of international law as higher law.

The recognition of a higher position of international law is also evident from the fact that different rules apply for a conflict between statutes and the Constitution, on the one hand, and statutes and treaties, on the other. Under Article 120 of the Constitution, the courts are not allowed to review the conformity of legislation with the Constitution, based on the idea that only Parliament can assess the existence and desirability of such conflicts. However, the courts are empowered to review the conformity of legislation with treaties.

The clearest evidence for the recognition of international as higher law is that the supremacy of treaties over domestic law applies even to the Constitution itself, at least in those cases where a treaty has been adopted pursuant to Article 91(3) of the Constitution, which requires a two-thirds majority vote in both Chambers of Parliament.[33]

The supremacy of treaties under Article 94 of the Constitution is subject to one limitation: it applies only to treaty provisions that are "binding on everyone." The language is confusing, but it really means that a treaty provision is supreme over domestic legislation only if it is sufficiently clear that it can function by itself in the domestic legal order, without additional implementing legislation being required. The rationale for this limitation is the separation of powers. It was considered undesirable, and would have

Vienna Convention on the Law of Treaties (VCLT), in particular the obligation to perform treaties in good faith, that in a case of contradiction between rules of international law and national legislation, the provisions of international law must be applied. Hence, the court set aside the domestic law.

[32] This commonly is accepted as the justification for the so-called later-in-time rule, as that applies in the United States. *See* Edye v. Robertson, 112 U.S. 580 (1884). *See also* Julian Ku, *Treaties as Laws: A Defense of the Last in Time Rule for Treaties and Federal Statutes*, 80 Ind. L.J. 319 (2005).

[33] See *supra* Section II.

granted the courts too much power, if the courts could set aside a law adopted by the legislature on the basis of a vaguely worded treaty provision that would leave too much room for judgment.

The supremacy of international law under Article 94 does not extend to customary international law. The Supreme Court had already determined this in 1959.[34] In the various subsequent revisions of the Constitution, this principle was left intact, particularly in view of the fact that the contents of customary law would be too uncertain. Moreover, the supremacy of customary law would conflict with the constitutional power of the government and of the legislative branch.[35]

Although Article 94 does not grant supremacy to customary international law, there are limited circumstances in which specific statutes provide for the supremacy of customary law. Specifically, these allow for the application of customary law to protect the jurisdictional immunities of foreign states and their organs. In the absence of legislation on immunities, or of directly applicable treaty law on the matter, the only basis for protection of the immunity of other states is the application of customary law, if necessary over domestic law.[36]

IV. APPLICATION OF TREATIES BY THE LEGISLATURE

Notwithstanding the automatic incorporation of treaties into the domestic legal order of the Netherlands, and the possibility of direct effect and supremacy, the usual way in which the Netherlands performs its treaty obligations is by introducing legislation that transforms them into national law. The executive and the courts then apply Dutch law rather than the international legal rules underlying that law.

This approach is followed when the international obligations require further elaboration. Whether national legislation is required to give effect to a treaty depends primarily on how the terms of the treaty are formulated. Treaty provisions obliging states to "permit," "regulate," "prohibit," or "recognize" will generally need implementing legislation.

However, even if the provisions of a treaty could in principle be applied directly, the Netherlands usually chooses to convert them into national legislation to harmonize Dutch law with the requirements of international law.

[34] Supreme Court, 6 March 1959, NJ 1962, 2.

[35] Kamerstukken II 1977/78, 15 049 (R 1100), nr. 3, pg. 11 e.v.

[36] *See, e.g.*, art. 8 of the Criminal Code (providing that the application of the jurisdictional provisions of the Criminal Code is restricted by the exceptions recognized in international law).

Indeed, the Netherlands generally does not join a treaty until after national law has been harmonized with the treaty. This approach ensures that an international obligation can be observed and enforced within the national legal order from the moment the obligation becomes binding. In practice, this means that, before it ratifies a treaty, the Dutch government investigates the impact of the treaty on existing national legislation and decides what legislative changes may be required to apply the treaty domestically. Typically, the government will table actual proposals for amendments or for new laws.[37]

Sometimes, however, the importance of adhering to a treaty as quickly as possible outweighs the desire for prior legislative harmonization. Doing so, for example, may allow the Netherlands to exercise influence over the establishment of treaty institutions. In such cases, national laws are modified in line with the treaty as soon as possible after the Netherlands has joined. For example, consider the procedure for approval of the Rome Statute establishing the International Criminal Court. After the Act of Accession (Goedkeuringswet) was adopted on July 5, 2001,[38] the Netherlands ratified the Rome Statute on July 17, 2001. However, Parliament did not pass the International Criminal Court Implementation Act (Uitvoeringswet Internationaal Strafhof), providing arrangements for cooperation with the Court, until June 20, 2002,[39] and its material provisions did not take effect until October 1, 2003.[40]

Depending on the nature and content of a treaty, its translation into national law may require either new legislation or the amendment of one or more existing statutes. The Rome Statute provides an example of the latter approach, with its ratification prompting a series of legislative amendments, as well as the new statutes mentioned previously. To implement the treaty, Netherlands amended the Penal Code (Wetboek van Strafrecht), the Code of Criminal Procedure (Wetboek van Strafvordering), the Pardons Act (Gratiewet), and the Police Records Act (Wet politieregisters).[41]

To bring domestic law in line with a treaty, Parliament frequently uses rules of reference as an alternative to the translation of treaty provisions into national law. Such rules refer to and ascribe legal force to particular

[37] Aanwijzingen voor de Regelgeving, Aanwijzing 311, Stcrt. 1992, 130, zoals gewijzigd bij de vierde wijziging, Stcrt. 2000, 191.

[38] Stb. 2001, 343.

[39] Stb. 2002, 315.

[40] Wet internationale misdrijven, Stb. 2003, 270 en Stb. 2003, 340. An English translation is published in NYIL 2003, 426.

[41] Wet van 20 June 2002 tot aanpassing van het Wetboek van Strafrecht, het Wetboek van Strafvordering en enige andere wetten aan de Uitvoeringswet Internationaal StrafCourt of Appeals, Stb. 2002, 316.

international legal standards. Although the organs of state apply such rules as if they are part of national law, their actual substance is enshrined in international law. For example, Section 29 of the 2000 Aliens Act (Vreemdelingenwet) states that a residence permit may be awarded to a "Convention refugee" ("verdragsvluchteling"). The Act does not define this term, but it refers to a person covered by the provisions of the 1951 Convention Relating to the Status of Refugees.[42] An organ of state applying this rule will therefore have to consult both national legislation (Section 29 of the Aliens Act) and Article 1A of the Convention.

Rules of reference are particularly important in cases where international law is subject to rapid change; their use avoids the need to repeatedly amend national legislation. This approach is therefore used with respect to treaties that are revised regularly and is also applied to customary law. Section 7, Clause 1, of the International Crimes Act (Wet internationale misdrijven) states: "Anyone who, in the case of an international or non-international armed conflict, commits a violation of the laws and customs of war other than as referred to in sections 5 or 6 shall be liable to a term of imprisonment not exceeding ten years or a fifth category fine."[43] Here, the phrase "laws and customs of war" is derived from customary international humanitarian law. Therefore, the content of the statutory rule develops in tandem with the development of customary international law.

To avoid a situation wherein every amendment to a treaty would give rise to a complete formal legislative process, which would substantially delay treaty implementation, the Netherlands usually applies simplified procedures for the implementation of treaty obligations. In particular, national law can be brought into line with a new treaty provision by means of an order in council or a ministerial regulation, which do not involve a full parliamentary process but are forms of delegated governmental power. For example, Section 30 of the Port State Control Act (Wet havenstaatcontrole) states that additional rules pertaining to the matters it covers may be adopted by ministerial regulation when such rules implement international agreements or resolutions of international organizations.[44]

V. APPLICATION OF TREATIES BY THE EXECUTIVE

Regardless of whether Parliament enacts legislation to transform treaty provisions into domestic law, they are, as indicated previously, incorporated into and part of the domestic legal order of the Netherlands. This implies

[42] Convention Relating to the Status of Refugees, 189 U.N.T.S. 137 (1951).
[43] *Supra* note 40.
[44] Stb. 2004, 117.

that the executive branch and local governments are required to apply treaty obligations on an equal footing with domestic law.

One consequence is that treaty provisions can limit the exercise of powers that executive organs may have under domestic law. For example, in 2005 the State Secretary for Transport, Public Works, and Water Management, after the discovery of safety lapses, suspended the permission he had previously granted for Thailand's Phuket Airlines to use Dutch airspace and to land at Amsterdam Schiphol Airport. The airline claimed that the State Secretary had exceeded his authority. A Dutch district court rejected the airline's claim, but in so doing the court acknowledged that a bilateral agreement between the Netherlands and Thailand did limit the State Secretary's authority so that he could only suspend, not withdraw, the airline's overflying and landing rights. A treaty provision thus directly curtailed the scope of the Secretary's powers under domestic law.[45]

In principle, treaty provisions that grant a power to the state rather than limit that power are also part of domestic law and can provide a basis for exercising executive power.[46] In this respect, however, two points should be noted. First, state organs should strictly confine their application of international law to the domain in which they enjoy national executive powers. State organs are required to apply treaty obligations within the limits of their own powers as defined under domestic law. If there is a conflict between a broad power defined by a treaty and a narrow power determined by domestic public law, the latter will prevail. Theoretically, it is possible that a directly effective provision, which under Article 94 of the Constitution can set aside domestic law, could expand the powers of the executive as defined under domestic law. Some other states, such as Belgium,[47] indeed adopt the view that not only the courts but also the government can and must set aside a provision of domestic law conflicting with a treaty. However, in the Netherlands it is generally accepted that Article 94 is primarily, and perhaps even exclusively, directed to the courts.[48] However, it should be noted that no case law exists on this point.

[45] District Court, The Hague, 23 March 2007, LJN BA2577, para. 2.2.

[46] *See* Council of State, 7 November 2007, LJN nr. BB7298 (discussing whether a bilateral treaty between the Netherlands and Suriname on air services (Trb. 1990,163) provided a basis for the Dutch minister to act against increases in tariffs by the Dutch and Suriname airline companies KLM and SLM. Though it could not find such a basis in the text of the agreement, the Council of State implicitly recognized that, had the treaty contained proper wording, it could have provided such a basis).

[47] Brussels Court of Appeal, Gruyez and Rolland v. Municipality of Sint-Genesius-Rode, ILDC 51 (BE 2003).

[48] L. Besselink, *Internationaal Recht en Nationaal Recht*, in Handboek Internationaal Recht 76 (R. Lefeber et al. eds., 2007).

Second, treaties do not specify which national organ is empowered to exercise the authority that the treaty bestows on the state in principle. Therefore, to determine which branch or department of government is authorized to exercise treaty-based powers, in addition to consulting the treaty, it is generally necessary to look at how authority is distributed at the domestic level. For example, in a case concerning the landing rights of Phuket Airlines, the court decided that the power derived from international law to prohibit access to Dutch airspace rested with the State Secretary for Transport "because that authority is contiguous with the powers he is assigned under the Aviation Act [Wet Luchtvaart]."[49]

The domestic legal consequences of treaties for the executive are not contingent on the doctrine of direct effect. All treaty obligations can be relevant to the exercise of executive power. This proposition can be illustrated by a ruling of the Rotterdam District Court. After a Rotterdam city borough issued a permit to Zestienhoven Airport to fell a number of trees that were endangering safety at the airport, local residents sought an injunction. In its defense, the airport claimed that it was required to fell the trees in view of its obligations under the Convention on International Civil Aviation,[50] and more particularly a resolution adopted by the Council of the International Civil Aviation Organisation. Since that resolution had not been published in the Netherlands, the Court concluded that it had no "direct effect," presumably referring to Article 93 of the Constitution. Nevertheless, the Court held that the resolution was binding on the local government. The Court said: "Dutch legislative and executive organs, regardless of whether they are organs of the State or other (sub-national) levels of government, are required to comply with Article 4.2.23 of Annex 14 of the Convention. Where there exists a discretionary power, this requirement implies that (the power must) be exercised in accordance with the said provision."[51] Likewise, in 1993, the Crown, under the then-applicable procedures of administrative law, held that even though Article 48 of the Ems-Dollart Treaty of 1960[52] did not have direct effect in the law of the Netherlands, it was nonetheless binding on the State of the Netherlands and hence on subnational government units.[53]

[49] *Id.* This judgment was confirmed by the Council of State on 6 February 2008, LJN nr. BC3585, para. 2.3.1.

[50] Convention on International Civil Aviation, 15 U.N.T.S. 295.

[51] District Court of Rotterdam, The Residents Association for Action against Aircraft Nuisance v. The Executive of Hillegersberg-Schiebroek Sub-Municipality, 27 June 2000, 33 NYIL 2002, 344.

[52] Ems-Dollart Treaty of 1960, 509 U.N.T.S. 1.

[53] Council of the Municipality of Delfzijl v. Provincial Executive of Groningen, KB 19 February 1993, 36 NYIL 2005, 336. *See also* KB of 11 September 2007, Stb 2007 No. 347 (holding that as the provisions of the 1975 Ramsar Convention on Wetlands, 996 U.N.T.S. 245, did not

The fact that Article 93 of the Constitution, as such, does not limit the application of treaty obligations by the executive also follows from the fact that Article 93 contains a requirement for publication of treaties as a precondition for direct application. If the legal effects of treaties on the executive were contingent on prior publication, the state could avoid its legal obligations simply by not publishing a provision. This would, in effect, undo the well-established principle that all international law is part of domestic law.

However, in at least one respect, the doctrine of direct effect, including the requirement of publication, is relevant to the exercise of executive power. This is when the executive exercises a power that encroaches directly on the rights of individuals – as it would if, for example, the government were to invoke an environmental treaty as grounds for withdrawing a license to carry out an activity damaging to the environment. In such a case, it is important for the public to be aware of the restrictions in question. It is precisely this form of protection that Article 93 of the Constitution is designed to provide. Thus, while a treaty could provide a basis for criminal investigations in theory, like searches of premises, seizure of documents, and transfer of such documents to authorities of another state, where these investigations would infringe on fundamental rights of the person in question,[54] it could only extend the powers of the executive if the provisions are self-executing. A mutual assistance treaty that creates obligations only between states and does not contain a directly applicable arrangement for search and seizure cannot provide a basis for infringements of fundamental rights of citizens.[55] It was also for this reason that the government had to argue that Security Council Resolution 1688 (2006), by which the Security Council approved the transfer of Charles Taylor to the Netherlands, had direct effect in terms of Article 93 of the Constitution, for it was that Resolution that, prior to the adoption of domestic legislation, was to provide the legal basis for the limitation of Taylor's right to personal liberty under Article 15 of the Constitution of the Netherlands and Article 5 of the European Convention on Human Rights (ECHR).[56]

have direct effect did not mean that the Convention was not binding for the Netherlands Antilles; see *infra* text accompanying notes 128–30).

[54] Supreme Court, H. v. Aruba, 9 January 1998, 31 NYIL 2000, 254.

[55] *Id.*, para. 3.5.

[56] European Convention on Human Rights, 213 U.N.T.S. 221; *supra* notes 17–19. Resolution 1688 (2006) was published in accordance with the requirements of art. 93 of the Constitution (Trb. 2006, 130), but there was some room for discussion as to whether this resolution regulated the rights only of states or also of individuals, notably Taylor.

VI. APPLICATION OF TREATIES BY THE COURTS

To analyze the application of treaties by courts in the Netherlands, it is helpful to divide the broader topic into four related subissues: (1) direct effect, (2) invocation, (3) consistent interpretation, and (4) legal consequences of a conflict between a treaty and domestic law. The subsequent sections address these issues primarily in the context of civil and administrative cases in which the government is a party. Section VI.E addresses some special questions that arise in cases involving claims between private persons and in criminal law cases.

A. *Direct Effect before the Courts*

The doctrine of direct effect finds its practical relevance in cases litigated before the courts. In principle, a Dutch court can honor an appeal to a treaty only when its content lends itself to application as the basis for a judicial ruling or when the standard has direct effect.[57]

The Supreme Court has indicated several times that the first step in analyzing the question of whether a treaty provision has direct effect is to examine the intention of the parties.[58] If no such intention can be determined, the question of whether provisions should have direct effect must be decided "exclusively by reference to the contents of these provisions."[59] As indicated earlier, this means that a provision can be applied only if it is sufficiently clear from its content that it can serve as objective law, without requiring adaptation to fall into line with the national legal order. This interpretation was set out in the Supreme Court's so-called strike judgment of 1986. The labor unions, seeking to protect a strike, relied on Article 6, Paragraph 4, of the European Social Charter.[60] The Court said that, in the absence of a clear intention that the provision be applied by the courts:

> Only the content of the provision itself [is] decisive: does it require the Dutch legislature to adopt a national regulation with a particular content or purpose, or is its nature such that it can serve in its own right as objective law within the national legal order? Article 6, Clause 4 [of the European Social Charter], is not drafted in such a way that it requires the signatory states to introduce legislation; rather, it confirms the absolute entitlement

[57] *See supra* Section III.B.
[58] *See, e.g.*, Supreme Court, E.O. v. Public Prosecutor, 18 April 1995, 28 NYIL 1997, 336.
[59] *Id.*, para. 6.2.
[60] European Social Charter, 529 U.N.T.S. 89.

> of workers and employers to take advantage of recognized rights in law under the national legal order, within certain boundaries.[61]

In *E. O. v Public Prosecutor*, the Supreme Court applied the same test to Article 1 of the International Labour Organization Convention Concerning Forced or Compulsory Labour of 1930.[62] The Court said that the article "merely contains a declaration that the members of the International Labour Organization that have ratified the Convention . . . undertake to suppress the use of forced or compulsory labour within the shortest possible period" and that it did not contain norms that are so precisely defined "as to be eligible by virtue of their contents for direct application and hence to be capable of being binding on all persons." It follows "that these provisions cannot function as objectively applicable law in the Netherlands."[63]

This test of direct effect is usually applied to treaty provisions and to resolutions adopted by international institutions, since Article 93 of the Constitution applies expressly only to them. It can be assumed, however, that the test criteria apply in equal measure to customary law. The most important differences between treaties and resolutions, on the one hand, and customary law on the other hand, concern the rules of precedence in the event of conflicts, not direct application by the courts.

The principal basis for the requirement that the content of a treaty provision must be clear for it to have direct effect lies in the boundaries of judicial competence. If a court were to enforce a treaty provision that is formulated too openly, it would effectively be taking over the task of the legislature.

For a variety of treaty provisions, the courts have accepted that they are clear enough to serve as objective law. This is the case, for example, with all the substantive provisions of the ECHR and most of the substantive provisions of the International Covenant on Civil and Political Rights (ICCPR).[64] The Central Appeals Tribunal (Centrale Raad van Beroep) has held that Article 5(1) of the Convention Concerning Equality of Treatment of Nationals and Non-Nationals in Social Security (ILO No. 118)[65] is directly effective in terms of Article 93. Article 5(1) provides that states shall guarantee specified social security benefits both to their own nationals, and to

[61] Supreme Court, 30 May 1986, NJ 1986, 688. *See also* Administrative Law Division of the Council of State, 15 September 2004, LJN AR2181, para. 2.2.6.

[62] International Labour Organization Convention Concerning Forced or Compulsory Labour of 1930, 39 U.N.T.S. 56.

[63] Supreme Court, E.O. v Public Prosecutor, 18 April 1995, 28 NYIL 1997, 336, para. 6.2.

[64] International Covenant on Civil and Political Rights, 999 U.N.T.S. 171.

[65] Convention Concerning Equality of Treatment of Nationals and Non-Nationals in Social Security (ILO No. 118), 494 U.N.T.S. 271.

nationals of other states parties, when they are resident abroad, subject to provisions contained in further agreements between the parties. The Tribunal did not consider this latter condition to be an obstacle to direct effect.[66] The Supreme Court held that the European Convention on Social and Medical Assistance has direct effect.[67] The Administrative Law Division of the Council of State held that Article 41(4) of the Ems-Dollart Treaty is binding on all persons as referred to in Article 93 of the Constitution. Article 41(4) provides that permits for fishing in a common fishing area of the disputed Ems-Dollart region will be granted to all fishermen who have resided in that area for at least one year. The Netherlands had refused a permit because a fisherman did not possess a license under national fisheries legislation, but the Administrative Law Division held that the treaty did not allow the government to refuse a permit on that basis and that the refusal was therefore a breach of the treaty.[68]

In contrast, the Dutch courts have generally ruled that the provisions of the International Covenant on Economic, Social and Cultural Rights (ICESCR)[69] and the European Social Charter (apart from Article 6, Clause 4, as cited in the railway strike judgment)[70] do not satisfy the criteria for direct effect. This is true, for example, with respect to Article 13 of the Charter, in which the parties undertake "to ensure that any person who is without adequate resources and who is unable to secure such resources either by his own efforts or from other sources, in particular by benefits under a social security scheme, be granted adequate assistance, and, in case of sickness, the care necessitated by his condition."[71] When a health insurer refused to register a person who was required by law to have medical insurance, that

[66] Central Appeals Tribunal, Management Board of the Employee Insurance Benefits Agency v. X., 14 March 2003, 36 NYIL 2006, 466.

[67] Supreme Court, Z.A. and the Foundation Known as the Committee for the Support of Illegal Workers v. The Netherlands, 1 February 2002, 34 NYIL 2003, 340.

[68] Administrative Law Division of the Council of State, X. v. State Secretary for Agriculture, Nature Management and Fisheries, 8 May 2002, 36 NYIL 2005, 477.

[69] International Covenant on Economic, Social and Cultural Rights, 993 U.N.T.S. 3. *See, e.g.*, Supreme Court, 14 April 1989, NJ 1989, 469 (no direct effect of art. 13(2) of the Covenant); Supreme Court, 30 January 2004, LJN nr. LJN: AM2312, para. 3.5.9 (no direct effect of art. 7 of the Covenant); Court of Appeal of The Hague, 3 April 2008, LJN nr. BC8719 (no direct effect of arts. 12 and 2(2) of the Covenant); Central Appeals Tribunal, 11 October 2007, LJN nr. BB5687 (no direct effect of arts. 9, 11, & 13). In the latter judgment, the Central Appeals Tribunal did indicate, with reference to the General Comment 3 (1990) of the Committee on Social, Economic and Cultural Rights, but in contrast to the aforementioned judgment of the Supreme Court of 30 January 2004, that this may be different for art. 7 (a)(i) of the Covenant.

[70] *Supra* note 61.

[71] *Supra* note 60, art. 13.

person invoked Article 13. But the Central Appeals Tribunal said: "Given the wording and tenor of [that article], it refers to a social objective formulated in general terms, one which the party states have undertaken to pursue and implement in their national regulations, rather than a right which those states recognize that citizens may invoke directly within the national legal order."[72]

The Dutch courts have also declined to enforce treaty provisions that would give the courts greater powers than they are afforded under national law, reasoning that any enhancement of judicial power would require further legislation with respect to judicial organization. For example, this is the case with respect to Article 14(5) of the ICCPR, which grants everyone convicted of a crime the right to appeal to a higher tribunal. Until 2005, for fiscal cases in the Netherlands, the court of appeal (gerechtshof) was both the tribunal of first instance and that of final resort. Although this situation had been held to contravene Article 14(5), the provisions of the ICCPR itself do not prevail. Without a legislative change to the organization of the judicial system, neither the Supreme Court nor any other body can act as an appellate tribunal for fiscal cases.[73]

Another illustration of the principle that a treaty provision cannot create judicial authority where none is provided under national law, and in that respect cannot have direct effect, is a case in which the Central Appeals Tribunal, after confirming a breach of Article 6 of the ECHR, ruled that the administrative court concerned did not have the authority to provide the remedy required by the Convention. The plaintiff would have to pursue a case in the civil courts in order to establish his entitlement to compensation. "In the absence of a statutory facility in this matter . . . in the Dutch legal system a judgement on the damage allegedly incurred – and its indemnification by the State – falls to the civil court."[74]

Whereas a treaty cannot create judicial authority where none exists under domestic law, it can limit the exercise of judicial authority that does exist under domestic law. If a treaty expressly creates an international dispute settlement procedure that is intended to foreclose resort to the courts of the Netherlands, the courts will honor such an intention. Also, resolutions of international organizations can limit the power of domestic courts (or the access of plaintiffs to such courts). For example, the aforementioned Security Council Resolution 1688 (2006) provides: "the Special Court shall

[72] Central Appeals Tribunal, 21 January 1994, RSV 1994, 192.
[73] Supreme Court, 11 October 1989, NJ 1990, 812, r.o. 4.9. In 2005 new legislation was enacted that changed this situation. Appeal (and cassation) are now possible.
[74] Central Appeals Tribunal, 4 July 2003, LJN AI01040.

retain exclusive jurisdiction over former President Taylor during his transfer to and presence in the Netherlands in respect of matters within the Statute of the Special Court, and that the Netherlands shall not exercise its jurisdiction over former President Taylor except by express agreement with the Special Court."[75]

Although the question of whether a treaty provision has direct effect is in principle one of national law, in certain cases an international tribunal may deliver a ruling that is relevant to a determination as to whether a provision is sufficiently well defined to be directly applied. That ruling may then be relevant to the provision's direct effect at the national level. For example, in one case the Central Appeals Tribunal ruled that Article 28(d) of ILO Convention No. 128 has no direct effect; this ruling was based in part on an interpretation of Article 28(d) issued by the ILO's own Committee of Experts.[76] In another case, the Central Appeals Tribunal held that Article 5(1) of ILO Convention No. 118 is directly effective; this ruling was also based in part on the views of the same Committee of Experts.[77]

B. *Invocation*

In principle, national courts will consider the application of a treaty provision only if a litigant in an administrative, civil, or criminal case has invoked it and has standing to invoke that provision. Ex officio review of the application of treaties is an interesting theoretical option, but it is of little practical significance because neither national nor international law provides for such review.

A key question in assessing the actual and potential role of Dutch courts in applying international law, therefore, is whether a private individual or company is entitled to invoke such a rule in a case against the state and, if so, under what circumstances. This can be a major hurdle because it is still widely (but perhaps mistakenly) assumed that the provisions of most treaties are primarily concerned with the legal relations between nation-states.

Whether a private party is allowed to invoke a treaty provision in a domestic court is governed by both domestic law and international law. The starting point in domestic law is the aforementioned Article 93 of

[75] U.N.S.C. Res. 1688 (2006). *See also supra* notes 17–19 and accompanying text.

[76] Central Appeals Tribunal, 4 April 2003, LJN AF7506.

[77] Central Appeals Tribunal, Management Board of the Employee Insurance Benefits Agency v. X., 14 March 2003, 36 NYIL 2006, 466. *See also supra* text accompanying notes 65–66.

the Constitution. It states: "Provisions of treaties and of resolutions by international institutions, which may be binding on all persons by virtue of their contents, shall become binding after they have been published." Taken literally, this text covers only provisions binding on persons. The goal is to protect legal certainty by ensuring that persons are not bound by laws that are not published. In practice, though, Article 93 is also interpreted and applied in such a way that individuals may invoke a rule of international law only if it is "binding on all persons by virtue of [its] contents."

There is a great deal of uncertainty surrounding the meaning and application of the clause "binding on all persons by virtue of their contents," as it relates to the invocation of international obligations by private parties. In the literature and in practice, the provision is generally interpreted in two rather different ways. The first interpretation (discussed in Section VI.A) concerns whether such a provision is sufficiently precise for a court to be able to apply it. The second interpretation relates to the standing of a private party to invoke a treaty provision. In many cases, the two interpretations will coincide because, if a private party raises a matter of international law, a court will have to decide both whether that party is entitled to do so and whether the provision lends itself to a judicial ruling. Moreover, the court may derive an answer to the first of these questions by considering how the provision in question is formulated: it may well conclude that a provision that is formulated in general terms is unlikely to be intended to be invoked by private parties or, conversely, that because a treaty is formulated in sufficiently specific terms it can be invoked by private persons. For example, in one case the Central Appeals Court for the Public Service and for Social Security Matters held that two provisions of ILO Convention No. 102 (concerning minimum standards of social security) were binding on all persons, within the meaning of Articles 93 and 94 of the Constitution, because "the description of the benefits to be granted and the imperative wording of the provisions in relation to the minimum nature both of the Convention as a whole and of these provisions in particular mean that they can be invoked by the protected persons to review the entitlement granted pursuant to national law by reference to the standards of the Convention."[78] Nevertheless, the two issues (precision and standing) are quite different in nature, and so it is preferable to consider them separately.

Whether a treaty provision can be invoked by private parties is regarded by the Dutch courts as a matter of treaty interpretation. If a treaty does

[78] Central Appeals Court for the Public Service and for Social Security Matters, X, Y & Z v. B.O.Z. Regional Compulsory Insurance Fund, 29 May 1996, 30 NYIL 1998, 241.

confer rights on private parties, then, as a matter of Dutch law and practice, those parties can invoke the treaty before a domestic court. What is relevant above all in regard to the process of treaty interpretation is the intent of the parties to that treaty, insofar as that can be determined. Dutch law recognizes the fact that states may agree by treaty to grant certain rights to individuals, which they are then entitled to enforce before national courts. In its Advisory Opinion of 1928 on the Danzig case, the Permanent Court of International Justice stated that "the very object of an international agreement, according to the intention of the contracting Parties, may be the adoption by the Parties of some definite rules creating individual rights and obligations and enforceable by the national courts."[79] Similarly, in Dutch case law, courts ask whether the parties intended to grant rights to individuals, and this is the first element in determining the invocability of a treaty provision by a private party. The fact that the ECHR is clearly intended to create individual rights that are enforceable before the courts is thus the primary reason why the courts now apply that treaty on an almost-daily basis.

If the intention of the parties is not clear from the treaty or its negotiating history, the court will analyze the nature and content of the treaty to ascertain whether its provisions are designed to protect the interests of individuals. In practice, the courts have identified a large number of international treaties and agreements that create individual rights that are invocable in domestic courts. These include all the conventions on human rights, the Convention relating to the Status of Refugees, various treaties covering social security and labor law, and numerous other agreements.

However, there remain many treaties that, according to Dutch courts, remain the province of relations between states, do not protect individual rights, and so are not invocable by private parties in the courts of the Netherlands. One example is a case brought by a group of Serbian citizens who alleged Dutch liability arising out of the government's support for the bombing of Yugoslavia during the Kosovo crisis of 1999. The plaintiffs based their argument in part on Article 2(4) of the UN Charter. However, the Supreme Court of the Netherlands held that the plaintiffs could not invoke Article 2(4): "By general acceptance, the prohibition on the use of force contained in Article 2, Clause 4, of the United Nations Charter applies only to states and so only states may invoke compliance with it."[80] Also, the Administrative Law Division of the Council of State held that two articles of

[79] Jurisdiction of the Courts of Danzig, 1928 P.C.I.J. (ser. B) No. 15, pgs. 17–18.
[80] Supreme Court, 29 November 2002, NJ 2003, 35, r.o. 30. *See also* Supreme Court, Association of Lawyers for Peace v. The Netherlands, 6 February 2004, 36 NYIL 2005, 509, para. 3.4.

the 1960 Ems-Dollart Treaty "were drafted in the interest of the Contracting Parties and create rights and duties only for the Contracting Parties. Private individuals cannot invoke these provisions."[81]

The case law in this area is far from consistent. Much depends on which branch of the law is concerned – civil or administrative – and the political significance of the case. Administrative law has its own rules of standing because the administrative courts have to ascertain that the government complies with the applicable public law, including international law. In administrative courts, standing is determined primarily by considering whether the interests of a person are affected by an administrative order.[82] There need not be a separate requirement that the treaty provision that is invoked grants a right to such a person. In a dispute over the widening of the A2 motorway, during which the width of the carriageway would be reduced to less than 3.5 meters, the private complainants invoked the 1975 European Agreement on Main International Traffic Arteries,[83] which defines a minimum width for traffic lanes. The Council of State (Raad van State) assessed the claim solely on the content of the provision concerned – which was specific enough – and ruled that the fact that the agreement imposes obligations only on states was irrelevant when assessing whether that provision was "binding on all persons."[84]

C. *Consistent Interpretation*

When a Dutch court is presented with a claim based on a treaty, it need not necessarily apply the treaty provision directly. Another option is to use the treaty to help elucidate the relevant national legislation. In this case, the court's ruling will formally be based on national law, but national law will be interpreted so that the outcome is consistent with the treaty.

As in most other states, such indirect application of international law is an accepted way of interpreting national law in the Netherlands. The Supreme Court has ruled that "Dutch courts should, as far as is possible,

[81] Administrative Law Division of the Council of State, Dutch Society for the Protection of the Waddenzee v. Minister of Agriculture, Nature Management and Fisheries, 29 September 1998, 31 NYIL 2000, 292, at 297.

[82] Section 1:2 of the General Administrative Law Act; an English translation is available at http://www.juradmin.eu/colloquia/1998/netherlands_annex.pdf.

[83] European Agreement on Main International Traffic Arteries, 1302 U.N.T.S. 91; 1388 U.N.T.S. 372.

[84] Council of State, 15 September 2004, LJN AR2181, para. 2.2.6. *See also* Council of the Municipality of Delfzijl v. Provincial Executive of Groningen, KB 19 February 1993, 26 NYIL 1995, 336, and KB of 11 September 2007, Stb 2007 No. 347, both of which can be explained in these terms.

interpret and apply Dutch law in such a way that the State meets its treaty obligations."[85]

One example of consistent interpretation is a ruling by the Supreme Court on Article 1:252 of the Civil Code, which states that parents who are not and have never been married, and have never shared custody of their minor children, may exercise parental authority jointly if they both so request. In this case, the mother was awarded custody of a child born from a relationship that had subsequently ended. The father then applied for parental authority as well. A lower court rejected the father's application on the grounds that Article 1:252 refers only to a joint request. But the Supreme Court reversed, ruling that the limitations inherent in Article 1:252 represent an unacceptable restriction of the father's right – guaranteed under Article 6, Clause 1, of the ECHR – to appeal to the courts to secure his entitlement to "the exercise of parental rights" under Article 8, Clause 1, of the ECHR. "In accordance with Article 6, Clause 1, of the ECHR," the court continued, "Article 1:252 of the Civil Code must be interpreted in such a way that the father may request the award of joint parental authority over the child as well as sole authority."[86]

The Dutch courts opt for treaty consistent interpretation for a number of reasons. First, it allows them to apply a treaty provision that is relevant to the settlement of the dispute in question, but that cannot be invoked directly by a party because it does not grant individual rights. Second, it enables them to apply a rule that lacks direct effect because it is not sufficiently precise. Third, courts may prefer this approach in cases where the direct application of international law would conflict with national law and would require a choice for one and a violation of the other. Courts usually prefer a conciliatory solution over the acknowledgment and resolution of a conflict of law. In many cases, the choice for a conciliatory interpretation means that courts opt for an indirect application of international legal rules that could actually have direct effect.

In the Netherlands, the principle of consistent interpretation applies both to rules of domestic law adopted prior to entry into force of an international obligation and to rules of domestic law enacted after (and with respect to) such obligations. In many states, consistent interpretation is justified by presuming that the legislature did not want to deviate from existing international obligations. That rationale applies only to legislation adopted after the effective date of an international obligation. However, this is not the

[85] Supreme Court, 16 November 1990, NJ 1992, 107.
[86] Supreme Court, 27 May 2005, LJN AS 7054, paras. 3.4–3.5.

rationale for judicial practice in the Netherlands, where legislation predating the conclusion of a treaty is also interpreted to be consistent with that treaty. The justification relies less on the presumed will of the legislature and more on a recognition that it is necessary or desirable to harmonize national and international law.

Treaty-consistent interpretation can have far-reaching consequences. A court adopting this approach may extend or alter a provision of national law to ensure that it complies with the requirements of international law. In particular cases, treaty-consistent interpretation can straddle into direct application and lawmaking by the judiciary. One example of far-reaching effects involves a case in which a German national was prosecuted in the Netherlands for a violation of the Road Traffic Act (Wegenverkeerswet). The summons was written in Dutch and was not served on the suspect in German, which contravened Article 6(3) of the ECHR. The lower courts had therefore either declared the case inadmissible or nullified the summons. But the Supreme Court ruled that a stay of prosecution was the correct approach, to allow the prosecution to provide the summons in the proper language. The Court issued this ruling despite the fact that the exhaustive list of grounds for such a stay in the Code of Criminal Procedure (Wetboek van Strafvordering) did not include violation of an international treaty. In issuing this verdict, then, the Supreme Court added a new rule to Dutch criminal procedure.[87]

The opportunities for courts to use treaty-consistent interpretation as a method of applying treaty provisions are not limitless, though. First and foremost, a rule in national law must be interpreted in a way that is consistent with the language of the rule. It has to be assumed that interpretation *contra legem* – contrary to the meaning of the rule – is unacceptable in principle.

A special form of treaty-consistent interpretation is the use of treaty provisions in the judicial review of an exercise of discretionary powers by the government. Since the executive is required to apply international law within the bounds of its authority, its discretionary powers must be exercised in harmony with the Netherlands' international obligations. Administrative courts may consider those international obligations when they engage in the administrative review procedures codified in the General Administrative Law Act (Algemene wet bestuursrecht).[88] For example, courts can draw on treaty provisions to help determine whether it was appropriate for the body that granted a license to pay little or no regard to treaty obligations in so

[87] Supreme Court, 23 April 1974, NJ 1974, 272.
[88] *See supra* text at note 51.

doing or to determine whether the government has properly balanced the interests at stake.

In a dispute concerning a change to planning regulations that would have allowed the construction of a hotel in a nature reserve, the Administrative Disputes Division (Afdeling Geschillen van Bestuur) of the Council of State ruled that the proposed development would contravene the Berne Convention on the Conservation of European Wildlife and Natural Habitats.[89] In light of that treaty, the court said, the "respondents, had they fairly weighed up all the interests concerned, could not have come to their contested decision."[90] It is noteworthy that the treaty provisions in question did not provide for individual rights and their direct effect was not an issue before the court – the government simply should have taken that treaty into account in its decision making.

In a number of states, courts have cited the doctrine of legitimate expectations to justify the enforcement of treaty provisions that have not actually been incorporated into national law. Those courts assume that the fact that the government has ratified a treaty gives a country's citizens a legitimate expectation that the government will behave in accordance with its international obligations.[91] In the Netherlands, there is no case law on this issue.

D. *Legal Consequences*

The consequences of the direct or indirect application of international law by the national courts depend on the context. If, for example, an executive order contravenes a treaty provision, the courts can simply quash it to bring the national situation back into harmony with international requirements.

The situation is more complex when a court establishes that a treaty provision conflicts with a domestic statute. If the conflict cannot be resolved through consistent interpretation, the court must decide which regulation takes precedence. As indicated previously, Article 94 of the Constitution states that courts must set aside domestic law that conflicts with a directly effective treaty provision.[92] The rationale for restricting this rule to directly effective provisions lies first and foremost in the separation of powers: it is regarded as undesirable for courts to be granted powers to overrule a law enacted by the legislature on grounds derived from a treaty provision that

[89] ETS No. 104.
[90] KB 30 December 1993, AB 1995, 24.
[91] High Court of Australia, Minister for Immigration and Ethnic Affairs v. Teoh (1995) 183 C.L.R. 273.
[92] *See supra* Section III.C.

is formulated in very general terms. As far as other treaty provisions – those without direct effect – and customary law are concerned, both the courts and Parliament have accepted that a court would be acting too much in the capacity of a lawmaker if it were to allow such provisions to prevail over laws duly adopted by the legislature.

Article 94 provides for concrete review. The courts have to determine whether application of a statute in a particular case contravenes the provisions of a treaty. If it does, that specific case must be exempted from the statutory regulations and the law must be set aside in that case. However, Article 94 does not require the court to determine whether a national law is reconcilable with the provisions of a treaty in general terms, nor does it allow the court to nullify the national law in its entirety if a conflict is identified.

If a court sets aside provisions of national law in accordance with Article 94 on the grounds that they conflict with a treaty – the prohibition of discrimination under Article 26 of the ICCPR, for example – the treaty will not always fill the gap left by nonapplication of the statute. Treaties, in particular those on human rights, tend to state only what is not allowed, without indicating in an affirmative manner what the situation should be when a conflicting domestic law is set aside. The court may then face the question of whether to establish new law to fill the gap. In Dutch law, a judgment issued by the Fiscal Chamber (Belastingkamer) of the Supreme Court in 1999 provides an authoritative formulation of the role of the courts in these circumstances.[93] The case in question concerned the compatibility of a particular rule in national tax law with the principle of nondiscrimination enshrined in Article 26 of the ICCPR and Article 14 of the ECHR in conjunction with Article 1 of Protocol 1 to the ECHR. After the Supreme Court concluded that the statute was incompatible with those treaty obligations, the question was whether and, if so, how the court could provide effective legal protection.[94] The Court provided an answer consisting of several steps.

First, the Court must consider whether simple nonapplication of the disputed statute will rectify the problem. If it does not, the question arises as to whether the Court itself can reverse the legal deficiency arising out of the discrimination by establishing new law or whether it must leave that responsibility to the legislature. The Supreme Court ruled that the answer to that question depends on a weighing of interests. "In favour of the court

[93] Supreme Court, State Secretary for Finance v. X., 12 May 1999, 33 NYIL 2003, 318.
[94] *Id.*, para. 3.13.

itself resolving the legal deficiency," it said, "is the fact that that can provide the [wronged] party with immediate and effective protection; against is the fact that, in our system of constitutional relationships, the courts should act with restraint when making such interventions affecting a statute."[95]

The Court also formulated a number of additional factors to be considered when weighing the interests concerned. To begin, the Court should rectify the legal deficiency itself when it can do so without usurping the policy-making responsibility of the legislature. But if there exists a choice among a number of possible solutions, each of which is linked to general policy considerations or other important issues of a political nature, then the Court should in the first instance defer to the legislature to make that choice.[96] However, the Court should itself step in and provide legal redress if the legislature, despite knowing that its rule violates one or more fundamental rights, fails to eliminate that conflict within a reasonable time period.

This approach implies that the individual party to a particular case might not obtain personal redress during the period when a court is waiting for the legislature to resolve the issue. This, in itself, can create a conflict between the restrictions on the lawmaking role of the national courts and the right to legal redress found in Article 13 of the ECHR. In the *Auerbach* case, the European Court of Human Rights (ECtHR) ruled, however, that judicial reticence is not automatically at odds with the "effective remedy" required under Article 13. The Court accepted "that the [Dutch] Supreme Court's finding of a violation of the applicant's rights under Article 14 of the Convention in conjunction with the cost orders issued in the applicant's favour, and its instruction to the legislator to enact new legislation, which has in fact occurred, may be regarded as adequate redress."[97]

In cases where an (alleged) violation of international law constitutes the basis of a tort claim, a determination by the Court that the treaty has indeed been violated may result in a determination of liability. General international law, unlike EC law, does not provide that an individual who suffers loss or harm resulting from a state's failure to comply with an international obligation is automatically entitled to seek monetary compensation through the state's legal system.[98] Although certain treaty provisions, such

[95] *Id.*, para. 3.15.

[96] Supreme Court, 4 May 1984, NJ 1985, 510.

[97] ECtHR, Auerbach v. The Netherlands, A. 45600/99, Decision on Admissibility, 29 January 2001, pgs. 12–13.

[98] In Andrea Francovich v. Italian Republic, Joined Cases C-6/90 and C-9/90 [1991] ECR I-5357, the European Court of Justice held that if a state failed to comply with its obligations

as article 5(5) of the ECHR, provide explicitly for monetary compensation for treaty violations, general international law usually allows states to decide for themselves the specific remedial consequences that flow from treaty violations. In the Netherlands, the violation of a duty under international law can create a civil liability. Specifically, government action in contravention of an international obligation may be deemed an unlawful act and thus engender a corresponding compensatory liability.[99]

Special questions arise when Dutch courts are called upon to enforce a previous ruling by an international tribunal that the Netherlands has contravened one of its international obligations. Most such cases involve judgments of the ECtHR. The Netherlands is then required to provide redress through the national legal system; in so doing, the form that it will take depends very much upon the nature of the violation and whether the case is a criminal, civil or administrative one.

When the ECtHR rules that the Netherlands has breached an individual's rights under the ECHR, and therefore is responsible under international law, the courts may find on that basis that the state has committed a wrongful act against that person. In criminal cases, a conviction resulting from proceedings deemed by the ECtHR to have breached the ECHR is considered wrongful and may give rise to an entitlement to compensation.[100] Depending on the nature of the case, however, other forms of redress are also possible. They include early release from prison in the event that the ECtHR has found a violation of Article 3 of the ECHR (inhuman or degrading punishment).[101] A few years ago, the legislature created a new statutory procedure for revising a final criminal sentence if the ECtHR subsequently rules that the proceedings leading to the conviction contravened the ECHR.[102] In administrative law, revisions would already be possible under the General Administrative Law Act.[103] For civil law cases, the government has taken the view that revisions are undesirable, as that would undermine the legal certainty of (third) parties.[104]

under EC law, under certain circumstances, affected individuals could bring a claim before their national courts for compensation for the damage they suffered due to this failure. State liability is enforced through national courts, but the ECJ has formulated requirements that national procedures must satisfy.

[99] *See, e.g.*, Supreme Court, 15 September 2006, NJ 2007, 277 m. nt. A.H. Klip.

[100] Supreme Court, 18 March 2005, LJN AR3144, paras. 3.4–3.8.

[101] Supreme Court, 31 October 2003, LJN AI0351, paras. 3.3.

[102] Art. 457 lid 1 sub 3^{e} of the Code of Criminal Procedure.

[103] Art. 4(6) of the Administrative Law Act provides "1. If a new application is made after an administrative decision has been made rejecting all or part of an application, the applicant shall state any new facts that have emerged or circumstances that have altered."

[104] K. II 2004/05 29 279, nr. 28

E. *Special Legal Relationships*

The principles described hitherto apply primarily to situations in which a private person invokes a treaty provision in a dispute with the state. But such a provision can also be relevant to a horizontal relationship (between private persons) or one under criminal law. In both cases, the treaty provision is used against a person rather than against the state. Such application is quite compatible with Article 93 of the Constitution, as it explicitly refers to provisions of international law that create obligations "binding on . . . persons." It is to this legal relationship that the publication requirement pertains: if treaty provisions have not been published, they cannot be used to the detriment of private individuals.

1. Horizontal Application. In broad terms, what has already been said about direct effect, the ability to invoke a provision, and treaty-consistent interpretation also applies to the horizontal application of treaties – that is, their application to legal relationships between private persons. If it is established that a provision is "binding on all persons," as stated in Article 93 of the Constitution, then that effect will, in principle, extend to the interactions between private persons. Certainly, this generally applies to treaties in the domain of private international law, as most of them are specifically intended to govern such relationships and, as a rule, meet the Article 93 criterion. For instance, the basic terms of a purchase agreement between two individuals in the Netherlands can be related directly to the UN Convention on Contracts for the International Sale of Goods.[105] There is also substantial case law applying other private law treaties, such as the Convention on the Contract for the International Carriage of Goods by Road (CMR)[106] and the Convention for the Unification of Certain Rules Relating to International Carriage by Air (Warsaw Convention).[107]

The Supreme Court in the *Second Cognac* case denied horizontal (direct) effect of treaty provisions. It held that the provisions entailed obligations only for the state, lacking effect in a horizontal context. According to the Supreme Court, Article 11 of the Netherlands-France Commercial Treaty of 1935 did not make clear that by the entry into force of that article, a situation would have come into existence carrying an obligation for everyone.

[105] Convention on Contracts for the International Sale of Goods, 1489 U.N.T.S. 3. *See, e.g.*, Supreme Court, 26 September 1997, NJ 1998, 691.

[106] Convention on the Contract for the International Carriage of Goods by Road, 399 U.N.T.S. 189. *See, e.g.*, Supreme Court, 22 February 2002, NJ 2002, 388.

[107] Convention for the Unification of Certain Rules Relating to International Carriage by Air, 137 L.N.T.S. 11. *See, e.g.*, Supreme Court, 19 April 2002, NJ 2002, 412.

The article contained obligations for the contracting parties only. Therefore, treaty provisions lacking direct effect were denied to have effect in a horizontal context.[108] Likewise, the Court of Appeal of the Hague held that the 1954 Convention for the Protection of Cultural Property in the Event of Armed Conflict did not establish obligations binding on private persons. The court had to decide on an application by the Autocephalous Greek Orthodox Church in Cyprus, which claimed that a person in possession of four religious icons should return them to the church. The Court found that the Convention imposes obligations only on states and thus could not be the basis for a claim against a citizen to return (allegedly stolen) property.[109]

Under certain circumstances, treaties of a public law nature (i.e., treaties imposing obligations on states rather than on private persons) can be applied indirectly to horizontal relationships. Private individuals can infringe the rights enshrined in the ECHR, for example, giving rise to an "unlawful act" as defined in Article 6:162 of the Dutch Civil Code. However, in such cases, courts have reasoned that, if the individual rights are infringed, it is the court as a state organ that is required to apply the ECHR. If the court fails to protect the individual, then it is the court, not the private individual, that breaches the Convention.[110] This is commonly referred to as indirect horizontal application – indirect, because the application of the treaty is linked to the court. This construction fits within the traditional perspective that international law binds states, not private parties.

In cases of this kind, the question arises as to whether treaty provisions that are not binding on all persons and are not intended to regulate private law relationships can nonetheless be applied through treaty-consistent interpretation of national statutes – for example, the "general duty of care" described in Article 6:162(2) of the Civil Code.[111] Courts have answered this question in the negative. This position seems to be informed mainly by separation-of-powers concerns and by the doctrine of legal

[108] Supreme Court, 1 June 1956, NJ 1958, 424. The Institut National des Appellations d'Origine des Vins et Eaux-de-Vie originally applied for an order declaring the unlawfulness of the introduction by Mettes into commerce, of alcoholic beverages not produced in France, under the name of *cognac*. The claim was based on art. 11 of the Netherlands-French Commercial Treaty of 1935 (protecting the denomination *cognac* for France). Both the District Court and the Court of Appeals dismissed the claim. Mettes appealed to the Supreme Court, asking the Court whether art. 11 is directly binding on Netherlands citizens by its very wording.

[109] Autocephalous Greek Orthodox Church in Cyprus v. W.O.A. Lams, 7 March 2002, 34 NYIL 2003, 394.

[110] Supreme Court, 15 April 1994, NJ 1994, 576; Supreme Court, 6 January 1995, NJ 1995, 422.

[111] Under this article, a tort is committed when an act or omission violates a right or a statutory duty, or violates a rule of unwritten law pertaining to proper social conduct.

certainty – provisions that are not binding on all persons by virtue of their nature and content should first be detailed by the legislature before they can be used against private individuals. In 1942 the Court of Appeal of the Hague ruled that the 1925 Hague Agreement Concerning the International Deposit of Industrial Designs did not apply to private individuals "now that the Dutch legislature has still failed to express any definite conviction as to the desirability of another fitting measure by establishing the Agreement's arrangements in law."[112]

2. Criminal Justice. Dutch courts have started to play an active role in the prosecution of persons accused of international crimes. As to the question of whether national courts can give effect to treaties in criminal proceedings, a distinction needs to be made between those situations in which the state prosecutes on the basis of international law and those in which the defendant invokes international law in his or her own defense.

In the first of these situations, criminal provisions of treaties are not excluded from the general regime on the effect of international law in Dutch law, and so, in principle, they can be applied by the Dutch courts. Pursuant to Article 93 of the Constitution, however, those provisions must conform to the principle of legality in criminal law. Article 1, Clause 1, of the Penal Code (Wetboek van Strafrecht) and Article 16 of the Constitution both affirm that no offence shall be punishable "unless it was an offence under the law at the time it was committed." The Supreme Court has said that the phrase "an offence under the law" refers to "Dutch law,"[113] a term that should be interpreted to include directly effective provisions of treaties.[114]

While the direct application of treaty-based international criminal law is theoretically possible, it is extremely rare in practice. One of the rare exceptions is found in the international regime governing Rhine shipping: ships' masters can be prosecuted directly under Article 32 of the Revised Convention for the Navigation of the Rhine.[115] The absence of any other significant judicial practice on this point may be due in part to the characteristics of treaty provisions in this domain; they are often formulated in terms too general to be used against individuals without first being specified in legislation. Accordingly, in most cases, the Dutch legislature chooses to translate criminal law treaties into the idiom of national criminal law.

[112] Court of Appeals of The Hague, 9 February 1942, NJ 1942, 371.
[113] Supreme Court, 18 September 2001, NJ 2002, 559, r.o. 4.3.1.
[114] After all, according to art. 93 of the Constitution, these are binding on everyone.
[115] Trb. 1955, 161. *See, e.g.*, Supreme Court, 9 June 1981, NJ 1981, 472; Supreme Court, 10 December 1996, NJ 1997, 223.

Prosecution and punishment are thus based on domestic legislation, even though the content of that legislation may have been informed – in whole or in part – by international law.

The principle of legality also hinders the direct effect of criminal provisions under customary law, as such provisions often fail to meet the requirement that the law defining the offence must have existed before the crime was committed. Because customary law cannot take precedence over the principle of legality, an individual in the Netherlands cannot be convicted for a breach of customary law. In the *Bouterse* case, the Supreme Court was required to consider whether unwritten international law – specifically, the prohibition of torture – prevailed over the principle of legality as contained in Article 16 of the Constitution and Article 1 of the Penal Code. As the alleged acts of torture took place in 1982 in Suriname, and the domestic law criminalizing torture took effect only in 1989, and as neither this law nor the Torture Convention provided for retroactive application, the only possible basis for prosecution would have been customary international law. However, the Supreme Court ruled that even if customary law would provide for an obligation to criminalize with retroactive effect, the courts are not free to disregard the Torture Convention Implementation Act [Uitvoeringswet folteringverdrag], which does not provide for retroactive effect, because it conflicts with unwritten international law: "From the . . . history of the compilation of Article 94 of the Constitution, it seems apparent that the authors did not want to accept the enforcement of unwritten international law if that clashed with national statutes."[116]

Because prosecution and conviction directly under customary international law are not possible, the state must ensure that national legislation implements the provisions of international criminal law. In the Netherlands, that has been done through the International Crimes Act (Wet Internationale Misdrijven).[117] An alternative is to prosecute under normal criminal law – classifying genocide as murder, for example – although it is disputed whether that practice accords with the requirements and expectations of international law.[118]

The application of treaties in criminal proceedings is different when the accused relies on a treaty provision as a defense. In principle, the invocation of a treaty by a criminal defendant is no different from the invocation of a

[116] Supreme Court, Appeal in Cassation in the interest of the law, 18 September 2001, 31 NYIL 2001, 282, para. 4.6.

[117] *Supra* note 40.

[118] *See, e.g.*, Michael A. Newton, Comparative Complementarity: Domestic Jurisdiction Consistent with the Rome Statute, 167 Mil. L. Rev. 20, 70–71 (2001).

treaty by a plaintiff in a civil or administrative case who invokes international law against the state. If, for example, a defendant claims that the prosecution violates his or her rights under international law, then it is necessary to establish whether the provisions cited are "binding on all persons," as stated in Article 93 of the Constitution. Provisions from the ECHR, for example, are used with great regularity to protect the rights of criminal defendants. From the case law, it seems that the direct-effect requirement is interpreted quite liberally in such situations. Treaties that, read literally, provide individuals with no specific rights are interpreted so that their effect does extend to protecting the interests of criminal suspects. For example, it is accepted in the Netherlands that individuals may invoke the provisions of extradition treaties to preclude prosecution for offences that were not listed in the extradition request. Article VII of the Treaty between the United Kingdom and the Netherlands for the Mutual Surrender of Fugitive Criminals, signed on September 26, 1898, prohibits a surrendered person from being "kept in prison or . . . brought to trial in the State to which the surrender has been made, for any other crime or on account of any other matters than those for which the extradition shall have taken place, until he has . . . had an opportunity . . . of returning to the State by which he has been surrendered."[119] However, the Dutch Supreme Court has held that this provision can be invoked by a criminal defendant because the provision "also protects his rights" and so requires the court to "review the indictment against the extradition order."[120]

There are also a few cases in which a suspect has successfully invoked the doctrine of sovereignty – which is generally thought to apply only to states – by persuading the court that the interests of the defendant demanded a broad interpretation of that principle. The International Criminal Tribunal for the Former Yugoslavia (ICTY) has said:

> An accused, being entitled to a full defence, cannot be deprived of a plea so intimately connected with, and grounded in, international law as a defence based on [a] violation of State sovereignty. To bar an accused from raising such a plea is tantamount to deciding that, in this day and age, an international court could not, in a criminal matter where the liberty of an accused is at stake, examine a plea raising the issue of [a] violation of

[119] United Kingdom of Great Britain and Northern Ireland and Netherlands: Treaty for the Mutual Surrender of Fugitive Criminals, signed at London on 26 September 1898; 186 CTS, 448.

[120] Supreme Court, 27 September 1983, NJ 1984, 96, r.o. 6.1.

> State sovereignty. Such a startling conclusion would imply a contradiction in terms which this Chamber feels it is its duty to refute and lay to rest.[121]

This argument also seems relevant to national jurisprudence, but the case law in the Netherlands contains conflicting decisions on this issue. In one case, a Dutch prosecutor exercised prosecutorial powers in the state of Colombia without the consent of that state. The Court of Appeal in The Hague concluded that the evidence obtained by the prosecution should be excluded. The Court said that the fact that the principle of state sovereignty is not intended to protect individual defendants is irrelevant given "the fundamental nature of the violation under international law."[122] In another case, though, Dutch detectives observed a truck in Belgium and France before the eventual arrest of a suspect in the United Kingdom. The High Court upheld a Court of Appeal ruling that, although the arrest and the subsequent seizure of a consignment of hashish were the result of an unlawful international surveillance operation, "it is not apparent what legally protectable interest on the part of the suspect was served by this unlawful cross-border observation."[123]

VII. TREATY INTERPRETATION[124]

In the many cases of treaty application by courts in the Netherlands, a large number of treaty interpretation questions inevitably arise. I will consider four aspects of the practice of treaty interpretation: (1) the application of the principles of the Vienna Convention, (2) the role of the position of the executive, (3) the weight given to judgments of international courts and tribunals, and (4) the weight given to interpretations by foreign courts.

The courts of the Netherlands have accepted that when they engage in the interpretation of a treaty provision, they may approach the issue on the basis of the principles of interpretation contained the Vienna Convention on the Law of Treaties. In a judgment of February 21, 2003, the Supreme Court had to interpret the term *reside* in a bilateral taxation treaty between the Netherlands and Nigeria. The Court noted that the treaty does not define the term *reside*: therefore, the meaning of the term must be determined by reference to the interpretive rules contained in the Vienna Convention,

[121] ICTY, Prosecutor v. Tadic, Case No. IT-94–1, Decision on the Defence Motion for Interlocutory Appeal on Jurisdiction, Appeals Chamber, 2 October 1995, para. 55.
[122] Court of Appeals of The Hague, 3 March 1998, NJ 1998, 923.
[123] Supreme Court, 7 March 2000, NJ 2000, 539, r.o. 3.4.
[124] I thank Bert Barnhoorn of the TMC Asser Institute for his input in this section.

in particular, Article 31(1) (which requires interpretation in good faith in accordance with the ordinary meaning to be given to the terms of the treaty in their context and in the light of its object and purpose).[125]

Another example of the application of the Vienna Convention is a judgment of the Supreme Court of February 21, 1997, in which the Court had to interpret Article 8 of the 1973 Hague Convention on the Law Applicable to Maintenance Obligations.[126] This provides that maintenance obligations between divorced spouses are governed by the law applicable to the divorce. The question arose as to whether this provision precluded the parties from choosing a different law. The court said that this question should be answered by reference to Articles 31 and 32 of the Vienna Convention on the Law of Treaties. It determined that the text of the treaty is ambiguous and therefore the question must be answered with the help of supplementary means of interpretation, including the preparatory work and the circumstances surrounding the conclusion of the convention.[127]

A third example involves an appeal from a decision of the Governor of the Netherlands Antilles. The local administration in Bonaire had allowed building in areas protected by the 1971 Ramsar Convention on Wetlands.[128] The governor had annulled this decision. The local authorities appealed to the Crown.[129] In interpreting the relevant provisions of the Ramsar Convention, the Crown noted that, under Article 31(3)(a) of the Vienna Convention, it is relevant to consider "any subsequent agreement between the parties regarding the interpretation of the treaty or the application of its provisions." The Crown found resolutions and other decisions adopted by the contracting parties to the Ramsar Convention, though not binding as such, relevant to the interpretation of the Convention and upheld the decision of the Governor.[130]

On the basis of these and similar examples, one can infer that the courts, including the Supreme Court, accept that the Vienna Convention on the Law of Treaties can be relevant to the interpretation of a treaty. Moreover,

[125] Supreme Court, State Secretary for Finance v. X., 21 February 2003, 36 NYIL 2005, 475. *See also* Supreme Court, State Secretary for Finance v. X. BV, 1 November 2000, 33 NYIL 2002, 356. para. 3.4; Supreme Court, Hansa Chemie v. Bechem Chemie, 16 May 1997, 30 NYIL 1999, 307, para. 3.4.3.

[126] Hague Convention on the Law Applicable to Maintenance Obligations, 1021 UNTS pg. 209.

[127] Supreme Court, R.H. v. S.K., 21 February 1997, 29 NYIL 1998, 283.

[128] Ramsar Convention on Wetlands, 996 U.N.T.S. 245.

[129] This was based on a rarely used provision of a royal decree governing the Netherlands Antilles (Stb. 1951, 64) that still allowed for appeal to the Crown. In almost all other parts of Dutch law, such procedures have been replaced by appeal to the Administrative Law Division of the Council of State.

[130] KB of 11 September 2007, Stb 2007 No. 347.

the courts are empowered to consider and apply the international rules of interpretation. However, among the cases where Dutch courts engage in treaty interpretation, express references to the Vienna Convention are extremely rare. Given the many cases in which courts do not refer to the Vienna Convention, it can be inferred that courts do not consider themselves obliged to interpret a treaty provision expressly on the basis of the Vienna Convention. In general, courts approach questions of treaty interpretation in a manner that is similar to the way they approach questions of statutory interpretation. In many, if not most cases, that need not lead to a discernable difference in outcome. In domestic law, as in the Vienna Convention, the ordinary meaning of a term is the normal starting point for interpretation. Moreover, the rules of the Vienna Convention that apply in cases where the ordinary meaning is unclear are open to a wide variety of interpretations, so that a decision to apply the Vienna Convention framework is often compatible with more than one outcome.

As to the second point, the Dutch courts are not bound by interpretations adopted by the executive or legislative branch. In some cases, courts do take into account the position espoused by one of the other branches on the interpretation of a treaty. When the Supreme Court had to examine whether the 1990 Convention implementing the Schengen Agreement of June 14, 1985, on the gradual abolition of checks at common borders,[131] provided for police cooperation, it confined itself to noting that the text of the convention provided for such cooperation and that this was affirmed by the implementing legislation and the legislative history thereof.[132] However, the final interpretation requires an independent judgment by the courts. An illustrative example is a decision of the Central Appeals Tribunal on the legal effect of views of the Human Rights Committee. In a case where the Committee adopted the view that the Netherlands had acted in contravention of Article 26 of the ICCPR,[133] the Government took the position that it did not agree with the view of the Committee.[134] The Central Appeals Tribunal adopted an independent position and held that, even though views of the Human Rights Committee are not legally binding, the state should only deviate from them if there are compelling reasons to do so. As no such

[131] 1990 Convention implementing the Schengen Agreement of 14 June 1985 among the governments of the states of the Benelux Economic Union, the Federal Republic of Germany, and the French Republic on the gradual abolition of checks at their common borders, Trb. 1990, 145.

[132] Supreme Court, 13 March 2007, LJN nr. AZ6671.

[133] Derksen and Bakker v. Netherlands (976/01).

[134] Stcrt, 30 August 2004, nr. 165.

reasons were found, the Tribunal ordered in line with the Human Rights Committee.[135]

The question of what weight should be attached to views of the executive arises quite often when a court has to determine whether a treaty has direct effect and/or is invocable by private parties. As indicated previously, such determinations depend on an interpretation of the treaty, generally involving an attempt to determine the intent of the parties.[136] As part of that exercise, it is quite common that courts examine the position taken by the executive, for instance in the legislative history of the bill of approval.[137]

It is quite common for the Netherlands courts to consider and give weight to an interpretation of a particular treaty provision that has been adopted by an international court or tribunal. Perhaps the acceptance of the legal relevance of such interpretations has been enhanced by the fact that courts have become accustomed to the use of the preliminary ruling procedure in the ECJ and, to a lesser extent, the Benelux Court of Justice.[138] It is routine practice that in interpretations of an article of the ECHR, the courts of the Netherlands refer to interpretations of that article adopted by the ECtHR. Thus, in a case where the Supreme Court held that Article 8 of the ECHR does not support a child's claim for maintenance against the former (female) partner of the mother, the Court based its decision in part on the fact that the case law of the ECtHR has not recognized that there is a "family life," within the meaning of Article 8, between a child and a former female partner of the mother.[139] Interpretations adopted by the ECtHR are not part of the Dutch legal order; the generally accepted view is that they are part of the interpretation of the ECHR itself.[140] If an interpretation of the ECHR is not followed, the courts make sure that the case can be distinguished on the facts.[141] The practice of following interpretations of the ECtHR is such that, in practice, they have almost a dispositive effect.

[135] Central Appeals Tribunal, 21 July 2006, LJN No. AY5560. For another example of the independent position of the courts in regard to interpretations of the executive, see Supreme Court, 29 September 1999, 32 NYIL (2001) 301.

[136] *Supra* text accompanying note 58.

[137] *See, e.g.*, District Court of the Hague, 25 July 2007, LJN No. BB0334.

[138] *See, e.g.*, Supreme Court, A.M. v. The Netherlands, 11 June 1993, 26 NYIL 1995, 341.

[139] Supreme Court, B. v. H., 10 August 2001, 35 NYIL 2004, 442. *See also* Supreme Court, Dairy Commodity Board v. C. van Eijk, 23 January 1998, 30 NYIL 329; Administrative Law Division of the Council of State, X. v. Minister for the Interior, 9 June 1994, 28 NYIL 1997, 326.

[140] Supreme Court, 10 November 1989, NJ 1990, 628.

[141] *See, e.g.*, H. v. Public Prosecutor, Court of Appeal of The Hague, ILDC 636 (NL 2007), para. 6.2.7.

Earlier, reference was made to several decisions where Dutch courts accorded significant weight to interpretations given by the ILO Committee of Experts, even though such interpretations in themselves are not legally binding.[142]

Dutch courts are rarely confronted with a question of treaty interpretation on which other courts, such as the International Court of Justice (ICJ) or the ICTY have shed light. The relatively few cases in which Dutch courts have referred to a judgment of the ICJ typically concerned questions of customary international law. For instance, the Supreme Court cited the ICJ's Advisory Opinion on the Legality of the Threat or Use of Nuclear Weapons[143] in support of its conclusion that the use of nuclear weapons is not necessarily unlawful in an extreme circumstance of self-defense, in which the very survival of a state is at stake. Therefore, the court said, a declaratory judgment that did not take account of specific facts and circumstances was insufficiently specific.[144] In 2007 the Court of Appeals of the Hague cited the ICJ's judgment in *Nicaragua*[145] in support of the proposition that minimum norms of international humanitarian law apply to both international and internal armed conflicts.[146]

Another illustration of this type of reference (and deference) to judgments of international courts is a judgment of the District Court of the Hague, ruling on an application by Slobodan Milošević for an interim injunction directing the state of the Netherlands to release him. The Court rebutted his claim that the ICTY was not validly established by noting that the ICTY itself had already rejected this argument in the *Tadic* case. Moreover, Milošević failed to establish that the decision of the ICTY was incorrect.[147]

Occasionally, the courts of the Netherlands resort to case law of other states for guidance in interpreting treaty provisions. Decisions of foreign courts are often cited as additional authority for interpretations reached on other grounds. An example is a decision of the Administrative Law

[142] Central Appeals Tribunal, Management Board of the Employee Insurance Benefits Agency v. X., 14 March 2003, 36 NYIL 2006, 466; Central Appeals Court for the Public Service and for Social Security Matters, X, Y and Z v. B.O.Z. Regional Compulsory Insurance Fund, 29 May 1996, 30 NYIL 1998, 241.

[143] ICJ Rep. 1996, pgs. 261–63.

[144] Supreme Court, Association of Lawyers for Peace v. The Netherlands, 21 December 2001, 34 NYIL 2003, 383, par. 3.7.1.

[145] Military and Paramilitary Activities in and against Nicaragua (Nicar. v U.S.) (Judgment–Merits) [1986] ICJ Rep. 70.

[146] H. v. Public Prosecutor, Court of Appeal of The Hague, ILDC 636 (NL 2007), para. 5.2.2.

[147] District Court of the Hague, S. Milosevic v. The Netherlands, 31 August 2001, 33 NYIL 2002, pg. 373.

Division of the Council of State, in which the tribunal had to interpret the term *persecution* as used in Article 1(A)(2) of the 1951 Convention relating to the Status of Refugees. After noting that it was the Division's consistent interpretation that *persecution* referred to persecution by government bodies and persecution by third parties that the authorities are unable or unwilling to prevent, it noted that persecution cannot be said to exist if there are no government authorities in the alien's country of origin (in this case, Somalia). The tribunal continued: "[T]his view is also in keeping with the case law of the central administrative bodies in France and Germany."[148]

VIII. THE IMPACT OF EUROPEAN LAW

The position of international law in the national legal order is quite different from the position of European law. In all of the areas discussed herein – validity, precedence, treaty-consistent interpretation, direct effect, and so on – Community law goes considerably further than general international law. For instance, EC law is automatically valid in domestic law, the ECJ requires consistent interpretation, and large sections of EC law have direct effect in the member states, taking precedence over contradictory rules in national law.

Although the European legal order is a relatively autonomous system within the wider international context, for the member states, including the Netherlands, these systems cannot strictly be separated and there are important mutual influences. The ECJ has ruled that international regulations in areas where the European Union exercises jurisdiction are automatically part of the EU legal order.[149] In this respect, the status of international law at the European level is comparable with its position in the Dutch legal order. That applies not only to EU treaties with non–member states but also to those treaties agreed to jointly by the European Union and its members with third nations. It applies, also, to international law in areas that fall within EU jurisdiction. Insofar as international law forms part of the European Union's legal order, it is subject to the EU Treaty: in the event of a conflict between the EU Treaty and other rules of international law, the EU Treaty prevails. But international law does take precedence over secondary Community law: the directives, regulations, and other legal instruments issued by European institutions.

[148] Administrative Law Division of the Council of State, M.E.D. v. State Secretary for Justice, 6 November 1995, 28 NYIL 1997, 353.

[149] Court of Justice EC, Haegeman, T-181/73, 30 April 1974, pg. 449.

This situation has direct consequences for the national legal orders of the member states. It means that member states receive international law into their domestic legal systems not only directly (as independent members of the international community) but also indirectly, as members of the European Union, because international obligations that form part of the European legal order are binding on member states as an element of core Community law.[150]

The Europeanization of international law is primarily expressed through the implementation rules established by the European Union. Just as individual states, including the Netherlands, generally endeavor to translate their international obligations into domestic legislation, so the European Union uses those rules to effectuate its own international obligations. Once the implementing rules are in place, national courts enforce those rules rather than the underlying treaty provisions.

In one case, the Administrative Jurisdiction Division (Afdeling bestuursrechtspraak) of the Council of State adjudicated a dispute over the compatibility of a local zoning plan with the Berne Convention on the Conservation of European Wildlife and Natural Habitats. The European Union is a party to that Convention, which is implemented by means of the so-called Habitats Directive. In its judgment, the division stated:

> In so far as the Convention falls within the cognisance of the Community, there exists no place for a review in the context of Article 94 of the [Dutch] Constitution. In so far as it [the Convention] is in accordance with the Habitat Directive, through that Directive the Convention has force in law and its legal consequences are governed by the Directive within the Community. Given the importance of consistent interpretation of Community law, there are no grounds as such for the direct testing of the plan against the Convention.[151]

Insofar as all or part of a treaty that forms part of the European Union's legal order has not been translated into Community law, a national court may apply its provisions directly. However, in these circumstances, the criteria for direct application are those of European law rather than national law, and the ECJ is the tribunal of last resort. In its settled case law, the Court of Justice has ruled that

[150] This phenomenon is discussed in Jan Wouters, André Nollkaemper & Erika de Wet, The Europeanization of International Law (TMC Asser Press, 2008).

[151] ABRvS, 11 June 2003, LJN AF9740, para. 2.15.6. *See also* Administrative Law Division of the Council of State, Limburg Badger Working Group v. State Secretary for Agriculture, Nature Management and Fisheries, 27 April 2000, 32 NYIL 2001, 234, para. 2.7.2.

> a provision of an agreement entered into by the Community with non-member countries must be regarded as being directly applicable when, regard being had to the wording, purpose and nature of the agreement, it may be concluded that the provision contains a clear, precise and unconditional obligation which is not subject, in its implementation or effects, to the adoption of any subsequent measure.[152]

In these matters, then, the controlling function of national constitutions is overridden. The result is that, as member states transfer more and more powers to the European Union, they are increasingly incorporating international law into their own legal orders as a part of European law. In its ruling concerning the Berne Convention, the Administrative Jurisdiction Division stated that the question of whether the Convention has direct effect should be answered using the criteria formulated by the ECJ.[153]

For the Netherlands, however, the practical significance of this implementation of international law through European channels is relatively limited. The domestic criteria for validity, direct effect (Article 93 of the Constitution), and precedence are broadly the same – although not identical – to the Community criteria. One key difference is that the provisions of treaties and of resolutions by international institutions that form part of the EU legal order ultimately fall within the jurisdiction of the Court of Justice. This means that a Dutch court can request an ECJ ruling on a question concerning the interpretation and enforcement of such provisions – a possibility that does not exist outside the European legal order.[154]

For states with very different domestic principles regarding validity, direct effect, and precedence, such as the United Kingdom, the repercussions of the triangular relationship among international, European, and national law can be far more critical. In the case of international legal rules that form part of the EU legal order, those states are forced to acknowledge a validity, direct effect, and precedence that would not apply in national law.

The opposite situation can also arise. With respect to some treaties, the Court of Justice has adopted a more restrictive approach than was the case in certain member states. That applies particularly to agreements related to the World Trade Organization (WTO). Given their character, in particular the fact that they allow member states a wide range of possible means of

[152] HvJ EG, Meryem Demirel v. Stadt Schwäbisch Gmünd, Zaak T-12/86, 30 September 1987, NJ 1989, 727, para. 14; HvJ EG, Racke v. Hauptzollamt Mainz, 16 June 1988, NJ 1999, 362, para. 31.

[153] ABRvS, 11 June 2003, LJN AF9740, para. 2.15.6.

[154] HvJ EG, Christian Dior, Zaak C-300 en 392/98, 14 December 2000, NJ 2001, 403, para. 33.

settling disputes – the ECJ considers that they do not have direct effect.[155] If a treaty forms part of Community law, states have no freedom to choose a more liberal approach by ascribing direct effect to agreements reached under the auspices of the WTO.

However, member states can apply their own criteria for direct effect with respect to elements of WTO law that are not part of EU law. These criteria may be less restrictive than those applied by the ECJ. Although the ECJ has ruled that certain sections of the Trade-Related Aspects of Intellectual Property Rights (TRIPs) Agreement[156] fall under its jurisdiction, that ruling does not apply to the entire TRIPs regime. For example, the Dutch Supreme Court has ruled that interpretation of Article 45, Clause 1, which concerns damages for infringement of intellectual property rights, does not fall to the Court of Justice and so that provision has direct effect in Dutch law. According to the Dutch Supreme Court,

> The provisions of Article 45, Clause 1, of the TRIPs Agreement – the interpretation of which in respect of the section on copyright . . . is not assigned to the Court of Justice of the European Communities – should, given the wording thereof, which makes it applicable within the Dutch legal order without need of further elaboration, be regarded as . . . binding on all persons, so that, pursuant to Article 94 of the Constitution, the provisions of Article 43, Clause 2, of the 1910 Patents Act [Rijksoctrooiwet, ROW] must yield to those of Article 45, Clause 1, in so far as they are not reconcilable.[157]

In this case, then, the national criteria for direct effect and precedence govern the application of international law in the national legal order.

IX. CONCLUSIONS

The Netherlands continues to be a state with a legal system that is very open to international law. The fact that the Europeanization of international law, discussed in Section VIII, has only a modest influence on Dutch practice underlines the fact that the Netherlands is quite close to the relatively open (compared to general international law) system of the European Community.

Although the possibility of direct application of international law should not detract from the fact that in most areas, international law is given effect

[155] HvJ EG, Portugal v. Raad, Zaak C-149/96, 23 November 1999, para. 86.
[156] Trade-Related Aspects of Intellectual Property Rights Agreement, 1869 U.N.T.S. 299.
[157] Supreme Court, 19 December 2003, LJN AF9714, para. 5.2.3.

through legislation, perhaps the most remarkable aspects of the Dutch system remain the relatively large possibility of direct application by the executive and the courts, and the supremacy of directly effective provisions over statutes and even the Constitution.

However, several legal doctrines mediate and may limit the entry of treaties in the Netherlands. This is particularly true for the doctrine of direct effect, which often has a significant limiting effect on the application of treaties by the courts and the executive.

The formal features of the Dutch system for domestic application of treaties provide only a partial explanation of the practice of the organs (legislature, executive, and courts). The attitude of courts themselves may be as important as the formal features of the constitutional system. For instance, the role of international human rights treaties in Dutch courts, for a long time, was rather marginal. In the early 1980s, however, the courts began to take a different, more open approach and proceeded to apply many provisions of human rights treaties.[158] The constitutional background was stable – what changed was the attitude of courts toward the treaties. That may also happen in other fields, such as with international environmental treaties, where judicial application is still modest and where courts rely more on legislative implementation.

The open nature of the constitution means the Netherlands has given up safety valves that most other states still have in their possession. In cases such as the direct application of Security Council Resolution 1192 (1998),[159] where decisions of international organizations that themselves are not subject to effective control or even proper political accountability directly determine the rights and obligations of private persons, the drawbacks of that decision become clear. It will require a cautious handling of the various tools that are at the disposal of the courts, such as direct effect, if in the long run the open nature of the constitution is to be maintained.

[158] P. van Dijk, *De houding van de Hoge Raad jegens de verdragen inzake de Rechten van de Mens*, *in* De plaats van de Hoge Raad in het huidige staatsbestel: de veranderingen in de rol van de Hoge Raad als rechtsvormer 171–209 (Zwolle 1988).

[159] *Supra* note 18.

9

Poland

Lech Garlicki

Judge of the European Court of Human Rights, Former Judge of the Constitutional Court of Poland

Małgorzata Masternak-Kubiak

Professor of the University of Wrocław, Judge of the Regional Administrative Court

Krzysztof Wójtowicz

Professor of the University of Wrocław, Former Vice President of the University

I. STATUS OF TREATIES IN THE DOMESTIC LEGAL SYSTEM

A. *Introduction*

1. Early History, 1921–1952. Until 1997, constitutional regulation of the position of international law in the Polish domestic legal order was rather scarce. The Constitution of March 17, 1921 (adopted after Poland had regained its independence in 1918) provided that international treaties are concluded (i.e., ratified) by the president of the republic. However, ratification of certain categories of treaties required a prior authorization of the parliament;[1] in practice, this authorization was given in the form of a statute.[2] A similar framework was adopted in the Constitution of April 23, 1935[3] – Article 52,

[1] "Commercial and customs treaties as well as treaties imposing permanent financial burdens on the State or containing legal dispositions binding on citizens or providing for changes in the frontiers of the State, and alliances – require the consent of the Sejm." (The Polish Parliament is traditionally composed of two chambers: the Sejm and the Senate.)

[2] A. Wyrozumska, *Umowy międzynarodowe. Teoria i praktyka* [International Treaties. Theory and Practice], Warsaw 2006, pg. 538.

[3] "Treaties with other countries: commercial, customs tariff, permanently burdening the State Treasury, containing obligations to impose new burdens upon the citizens or evoking changes in the frontiers of the State – require before ratification the consent of the Legislative Chambers expressed in form of a law." Constitution of the Republic of Poland, London 1967.

Section 1, clearly established that parliamentary authorization had to be given in the form of a statute.

This system was understood – in both the legal commentary and judicial case law – as based on the concept of transformation: the presidential ratification and the official publication of a treaty in the *Journal of Laws* transformed its provisions into provisions of domestic law. As indicated by the Supreme Court, "a treaty, when ratified and duly published . . . becomes a statutory instrument and gains a binding force in the domestic legal relations."[4] Thus, the date of publication determined the date from which a treaty entered into the domestic legal system. Because ratification required a prior parliamentary authorization and because that authorization took the form of a statute, such treaties were considered to have a statutory rank within the domestic legal order. This meant that a subsequent treaty prevailed over legislative acts earlier in date according to the general principle *lex posterior derogat legi priori*.[5] However, the same logic dictated that a later statute of parliament had to prevail over treaties concluded at an earlier date,[6] a constitutional law conclusion that was hardly compatible with international law. Despite this position of relative primacy in domestic law, direct judicial application of international treaties did not occur often during this period because most of the international treaties concluded at this time were not drafted in self-executing language.

2. The 1952 Constitution. The first post–World War II Constitution (July 22, 1952) reflected the model developed in the Soviet Union and imposed on all countries of Central and Eastern Europe. Under this model, norms of international law were not directly binding on actors within the domestic legal order. The new Constitution remained silent as to the status of international law in the domestic legal system. However, and this represented a major difference in comparison to the previous system, the new Constitution did not require parliamentary authorization prior to international ratification of treaties; instead, the power of ratification was vested in the Council of State.[7]

[4] Judgment of Dec. 14, 1928. See also A. Wyrozumska, *supra* note 2, pg. 539.

[5] *See* R. Kwiecień, *Miejsce umów międzynarodowych w porządku prawnym państwa polskiego* [Place of International Treaties in the Legal Order of the Polish State], Warsaw 2000, pg. 101 (quoting judgments).

[6] *See id.*

[7] The Council of State was a kind of collective presidential body, vested also with legislative powers and, at least in the 1950s, assuming most of the powers formally granted to the parliament.

The lack of parliamentary authorization precluded further application of the doctrine of transformation. Since there was no statute introducing a treaty into the domestic legal system, it would hardly have been possible to claim that the provisions of such a treaty have a statutory rank. Scholars never developed a consensus about the status of international treaties in domestic law. Some prominent authors advanced the idea that ratified international treaties entered the domestic legal system and should be applied ex proprio vigore.[8] Others denied any direct applicability of international treaties until their provisions had been reproduced in domestic law or until a domestic statute referred to a specific treaty.

During this period, the courts remained uncertain about the effect of international treaties in the domestic legal system. As it was later summarized by one of the most distinguished scholars: "Polish courts always avoided any general discussion and resolution of the matter. Nevertheless, courts, the Supreme Court included, sometimes applied international treaties, sometimes showed readiness to apply them, and sometimes at least invoked them as an auxiliary argument (next to the analysis of Polish law) in deciding a particular case."[9] According to the Supreme Court, it was the act of ratification (and the subsequent act of official publication) that allowed the judicial application of treaty provisions. Thus, nonratified treaties could not be invoked before the courts and could not be regarded as a sufficient basis for individual claims.[10] Whereas ratified treaties might be regarded as directly applicable, the courts remained very reluctant to go beyond the provisions of domestic law. Except for the areas where domestic statutes clearly referred to a particular treaty, Polish judges rarely invoked provisions of international law.[11] This found its apex in the 1987 decision of the Supreme Court:

> [U]nder the Polish Constitution, there are no grounds to recognise that ratification of a treaty results in its transformation into domestic

[8] *See especially* S. Rozmaryn, *Skuteczność umów międzynarodowych PRL w stosunkach wewnętrznych* [Effectiveness of International Treaties in Poland's Internal Relations], Państwo i Prawo (State and Law Monthly) [hereinafter PiP] 1962, no. 12.

[9] K. Skubiszewski, *Umowy międzynarodowe w porządku prawnym PRL* [International Treaties in the Legal Order of Poland], PiP 1989, np. 6, pg. 143.

[10] *See, e.g.*, Judgment of the Supreme Court of June 12, 1961 (2 CZ 70/61, PiP 1962, no. 12; "Bug-River claims"); Judgment of the Supreme Court of October 5, 1974 (III CZP 71/73, Orzecznictwo Sądu Najwyższego. Izba Cywilna i Izba Pracy i Ubezpieczeń Społecznych [Jurisprudence of the Supreme Court, Civil Chamber and Labour and Social Insurances Chamber, hereinafter OSNCP] 1975, item 72 *Panonia* case).

[11] One of the most daring attempts was the judgment of Olsztyn Military Court applying art. 15, sec. 1, of the ICCPR to exclude retroactive application of the 1981 Martial Law Decree. *See infra* notes 130-31 and accompanying text.

law. . . . Ratification means only that the State takes an obligation to introduce provisions of a ratified treaty into the domestic legal order. However, as long as provisions of international law have not been introduced, in the manner provided by [the Constitution], into the domestic legal order, they cannot enter into that order and, in consequence, they cannot become binding on the courts. . . . This also deprives the Supreme Court of any power to assess whether there may be a contradiction between domestic legal norms and international legal norms.[12]

It can be concluded that, "the courts under communist rule, for manifestly political reasons, did not accept the possibility of direct application and effectiveness of international law within the Polish legal order. Individuals could not claim any rights granted under human rights treaties."[13] In other words, the position of the Supreme Court meant that the Polish system embodied an extreme version of the dualistic approach.[14]

3. From 1989 to 1997. The so-called Round Table Agreement and the constitutional amendment of April 7, 1989, opened the process of democratic transformation. The proponents of democratic reforms understood the importance of Poland opening up toward international law, particularly international instruments on protection of human rights. The constitutional amendment restored traditional, pre–World War II, regulation concerning international treaties. According to Article 32g, Section 1, of the 1989 Constitution, the power to ratify and denounce international treaties was vested in the (newly established) president of the republic. Section 2 restored the requirement of prior parliamentary authorization for ratification of those treaties that either impose serious financial obligations on the state or require changes in domestic legislation. In parliamentary practice, it was agreed that authorization should be given in the form of a statute.[15] The 1992 "Small Constitution"[16] adopted the same arrangement while expanding

[12] Decision of Aug. 25, 1987 (I PRZ 8/87, OSNCP 1997 nr 12). The Supreme Court refused to apply the provisions of ILO Convention No. 87 (ratified by Poland) to the legalisation request of the Solidarity trade union and refused to assess whether the domestic legislation on exclusion of trade union pluralism was consistent with the international obligations of Poland. *See* M. Masternak-Kubiak, *Umowa międzynarodowa w prawie konstytucyjnym* [International Treaty in the Constitutional Law], Warsaw 1997, pgs. 148–50.

[13] W. Czapliński, International Law and the Polish Constitution, in *Constitutional Essays*, ed. M. Wyrzykowski, Warsaw 1999, pg. 291.

[14] A. Wyrozumska, *supra* note 2, pg. 546.

[15] W. Sokolewicz, Ustawa ratyfikacyjna [Law on Ratification], in *Prawo międzynarodowe i wspólnotowe w wewnętrznym porządku prawnym* [International Law and Community Law in the Domestic Legal Order], ed. M. Kruk, Warsaw 1997, pgs. 99–100.

[16] *See* M. F. Brzezinski & L. Garlicki, Polish Constitutional Law, in *Legal Reforms in Post-Communist Europe*, ed. S. Frankowski & P. B. Stephan, Kluwer 1995, pgs. 39–49.

the list of treaties requiring parliamentary authorization[17] and clearly providing that authorization must be given in the form of a statute.

The new constitutional provisions suggested a return to the transformation approach of the pre–World War II constitutions, at least in regard to treaties ratified on parliamentary authorization. This view has been accepted, without particular troubles, by scholars of constitutional law.[18] Courts also understood that it was necessary to revise the prior case law and to clarify (1) whether particular provisions of international law have direct application in the domestic legal order, and (2) how to resolve potential conflicts between international and domestic legal norms.

As to the first question, the courts accepted that provisions of ratified treaties can and should be applied. Some judgments adopted the traditional theory of transformation.[19] Others gave preference to the concept that "treaties ratified and duly published in the Journal of Laws do not require any further transformation or incorporation, and are binding, ex proprio vigore, in the domestic legal order."[20] These doctrinal differences notwithstanding, the courts soon recognized that provisions of international treaties (if ratified on the basis of statutory authorization) form a part of the domestic legal order and may serve as a legal basis for individual claims. Thus, the principle of domestic applicability of international treaties had already become established in the Polish constitutional order before the 1997 Constitution came into force.

However, the courts were not ready to accept that applicability of treaties also meant that, in case of conflict, a treaty provision had priority over domestic statutes. Even in cases involving apparent conflicts, courts preferred to construe domestic statutes in a way that allowed their joint application with the relevant treaty provisions. This left a considerable margin

[17] Treaties relating to "the borders of the State, to defensive alliances, treaties which would burden the State with financial liabilities, or which would involve changes in legislation."

[18] M. Masternak-Kubiak, *supra* note 12, pg. 100.

[19] "The adoption of the statute authorizing ratification of a treaty means transformation of that treaty into domestic law of statutory rank. . . . Therefore, [the treaty in question] enjoys a statutory rank and may be applied by the courts like a statute." Resolution of the Supreme Court of June 12, 1992, III CZP 48/92, OSNCP 1992, no. 10, item 179).

[20] Judgment of the High Administrative Court of November 20, 1990 (II SA 759/90, Orzecznictwo Naczelnego Sądu Administracyjnego (Jurisprudence of the High Administrative Court, hereinafter ONSA); since 2006, Orzecznictwo Naczelnego Sądu Administracyjnego i wojewódzkich sądów administracyjnych (ONSA-WSA, Jurisprudence of the High Administrative Court and Regional Administrative Courts), 1991, no. 1, item. 4). Also the judgment of the Constitutional Court of January 7, 1992 (K 8/91, Orzecznictwo Trybunału Konstytucyjnego (Jurisprudence of the Constitutional Court [hereinafter OTK]), 1992, item 5).

of uncertainty[21] that had to be addressed by the drafters of the 1997 Constitution.

B. *The 1997 Constitution: Position of International Law*

The Constitution of April 2, 1997,[22] reiterated the traditional approach: the power of international ratification remains with the president of the republic (Article 133), but international ratification of important treaties requires prior parliamentary approval (Article 89). At the same time, the Constitution – for the first time in the history of Polish constitutionalism – went beyond the regulation of ratification procedure and adopted some general rules as to the position of international law and supranational law in the domestic legal order.

Article 9 declared generally that "the Republic of Poland shall respect international law binding on it." This provision has a universal scope and refers not only to treaties but also to all other sources of international law, in particular to generally recognized principles of international law, other norms arising from customary law, unilateral obligations, and binding norms adopted by international organizations.[23] As noted in the legal scholarship, Article 9 "expresses the principle of... Polish legal order in respect to the norms of international law and establishes a presumption of automatic, even if only indirect, incorporation of those norms into that order."[24] It also means that all Polish authorities (including the judicial branch) should give full effect to international law (particularly international treaties): that is, they should develop a friendly interpretation of international law. A similar interpretation of Article 9 was recently confirmed by the Constitutional Court.[25]

[21] *See* A. Wyrozumska, *supra* note 2, pgs. 548–49.

[22] For an overview of the 1997 Constitution, *see The Principles of Basic Institutions of the System of Government in Poland*, ed. P. Sarnecki, A. Szmyt, & Z. Witkowski, Warsaw 1999; L. Garlicki, Constitutional Law, in *Introduction to Polish Law*, ed. S. Frankowski, Zakamycze-Kluwer 2005. For the (semiofficial) translation of the Constitution, *see* Constitution of the Republic of Poland, Sejm Publishing Office, Warsaw 1999.

[23] W. Czapliński, *supra* note 13, pg. 298.

[24] R. Szafarz, Międzynarodowy porządek prawny i jego odbicie w polskim prawie konstytucyjnym [International Legal Order and Its Reflection in the Polish Constitutional Law], in *Prawo międzynarodowe*, *supra* note 15, pg. 19.

[25] Judgment of May 11, 2005, K 18/04, OTK 2005, no. 5A, item 49, III.2.1: "Article 9 expresses an assumption of the Constitution that, on the territory of Poland, a binding effect should be given not only to the acts (norms) enacted by the national legislature, but also to the acts (norms) created outside the framework of national law-making authorities. The Constitution accepts that the Polish legal system consists of multiple components/elements."

The regulation of the position of international treaties is also addressed in Article 87 of the 1997 Constitution, which enumerates all sources of law of a universally binding nature (i.e., laws that determine the rights, claims, and obligations of individual persons).[26] These sources include the Constitution, statutes, regulations, and ratified international treaties.

Therefore, the act of international ratification constitutes a necessary precondition to the inclusion of a treaty in the domestic legal order (or, more precisely – in the system of the domestic sources of law of a universally binding nature). The Constitution indirectly recognizes the existence of other (nonratified) categories of international agreements, but those agreements – even when covered by the general declaration of Article 9 – remain outside the system of "universally binding [domestic] law" and cannot address rights, claims, and/or obligations of individual persons.[27]

The modalities of the procedure for conclusion and ratification of international treaties and agreements are now provided in the International Treaties Act of April 14, 2000.[28] All international treaties and agreements are concluded by the Council of Ministers or – if concluded at the departmental level – have to be accepted by the Council of Ministers (Article 146, Section 4.10, of the Constitution). No ratification is required for agreements of a purely administrative nature. However, as already mentioned, such agreements cannot belong to the system of universally binding sources of law. All other treaties and agreements require ratification.

The power of international ratification belongs to the president of the republic. However, in regard to certain important treaties, ratification, as well as denunciation, requires prior statutory authorization. Hence, there is a distinction between so-called full ratification (i.e., ratification authorized by statute) and small ratification (i.e., ratification without statutory authorization). Article 89, Section 1, of the Constitution requires that the procedure of full ratification must be followed with respect to all treaties that concern: "1) peace, alliances, political or military treaties; 2) freedoms, rights or obligations of citizens, as specified in the Constitution; 3) the

See Summaries of Selected Judgments of the Polish Constitutional Tribunal Concerning EU Law, Warsaw 2006.

[26] *See* K. Działocha, Law and Its Sources in the Constitution, in *The Principles of Basic Institutions of the System of Government in Poland*, *supra* note 22, pgs. 80–81.

[27] In effect, this means that if Poland joins a treaty by means of accession, or by any means other than ratification, separate legislative action is needed to incorporate the treaty into the domestic legal order.

[28] The International Treaties Act is an ordinary statute adopted by Parliament pursuant to its general legislative powers under the Constitution.

Republic of Poland's membership in an international organization; 4) considerable financial responsibilities imposed on the State; 5) matters regulated by statute or those in respect of which the Constitution requires the form of statute." This is a rather comprehensive list. Practically speaking, all international treaties that are meant to be directly applicable in domestic courts must be adopted through the procedure of full ratification.

The authorizing statute has to be enacted in a regular legislative procedure (i.e., adopted by the Sejm; confirmed by the Senate; and promulgated by the president of the republic, who may also exercise veto power, as provided in Article 122, Section 5, of the Constitution). The constitutionality of the statute may be reviewed by the Constitutional Court.[29]

Article 90 of the Constitution establishes a particular authorization procedure for treaties that "delegate to an international organization or international institution the competence of organs of State authority in certain matters." The authorization shall be granted either in the form of a statute adopted separately in both Chambers of Parliament by a two-thirds majority vote (a greater majority than that required for a constitutional amendment) or – if the Sejm so decrees – in a national referendum.[30]

If the subject matter of a particular treaty does not require full ratification, the prime minister submits it directly to the president of the republic with a ratification request. The prime minister must simultaneously inform the Sejm about each ratification request submitted to the president.[31] In practice, the Foreign Affairs Committee of the Sejm examines each request to assess the applicability of the small ratification procedure for a particular treaty.[32] In those few cases where the Sejm has expressed reservations about the use of the small ratification procedure, the problem has always been resolved through informal negotiations.[33] If no friendly solution were found, the last word belongs to the judicial branch: the Constitutional Court may declare that a treaty ratified without statutory authorization had not

[29] This review extends, indirectly, also to the constitutionality of the treaty in question. *See especially* Resolution of the Constitutional Court of Nov. 30, 1994, W 10/94, OTK 1994, item 48.

[30] For the interpretation of art. 90, *see* Judgment of the Constitutional Court of May 27, 2003, K 11/03, OTK 2003, no. 5A, item 43. *See also* Summaries, *supra* note 25, pgs. 238–49.

[31] Art. 89, sec. 2, of the Constitution.

[32] *See* J. Jaskiernia, Charakter prawny i funkcje Komisji Spraw Zagranicznych Sejmu RP [Legal Nature and Functions of the Foreign Affaires Committee of the Sejm], 4 *Polski Przegląd Dyplomatyczny* [Polish Diplomatic Review] 2004, no. 6, pgs. 84–87.

[33] *See id.*, pgs. 87–91.

acquired validity in domestic law, and/or ordinary courts may refuse its application in individual cases.[34]

The act of international ratification is taken by the president of the republic, but it also requires the countersignature of the prime minister.[35] Neither the authorization statute nor the prime minister's ratification request is binding on the president, who may refuse ratification, postpone its date, or challenge the constitutionality of a treaty before the Constitutional Court.[36] However, if – in the particular procedure of Article 90 – authorization is given in a national referendum, the president is bound to ratify without delay. All ratified treaties have to be officially published in the *Journal of Laws*[37] and cannot become effective in the domestic legal order before the date of publication.

The position of international treaties and agreements in the domestic legal order depends on which of the previously mentioned procedures has been applied. A ratified treaty becomes, by virtue of its ratification, a "part of the domestic legal order and shall be applied directly, unless its application depends on the enactment of a statute."[38] In other words, the act of ratification "does not transform such a treaty into an act of domestic law, but only includes it into that system."[39] While it may suggest that the 1997 Constitution adopted the system of incorporation, other scholars support the traditional approach of adoption.[40] Differences in opinions are also present in the judicial case law.[41]

Article 91, Section 1, clearly establishes the principle of direct applicability of all ratified treaties. One of the consequences of that principle is

[34] This is the author's opinion. There is no case directly on point.

[35] Art. 144 of the Constitution.

[36] Art. 133, sec. 2, of the Constitution.

[37] Art. 88, sec. 3, of the Constitution.

[38] Art. 91, sec. 1 of the Constitution.

[39] K. Działocha, Uwaga 2 do art. 91 [Note 2 to Article 91], in *Konstytucja Rzeczypospolitej Polskiej. Komentarz* [A Commentary to the Constitution of the Republic of Poland], ed. L. Garlicki, Warsaw 1999, pg. 2.

[40] Under the adoption system, international treaties become part of domestic law as a consequence of international ratification and (usually) domestic publication only; no separate legislative measure is needed. Under the incorporation system, a separate domestic enactment is approved for the purpose of giving all or part of the treaty provisions domestic legal validity, without repeating the material contents of the provisions in the text of the enactment. *See, e.g.*, M. Scheinin, General Introduction, in *International Human Rights Norms in the Nordic and Baltic Countries*, ed. M. Scheinin, The Hague 1996, pg. 13.

[41] *See* A. Wyrozumska, *Umowa międzynarodowa*, *supra* note 2, pgs. 592–99; R. Kwiecień, *supra* note 5, pgs. 118–19; M. Masternak-Kubiak, *Przestrzeganie prawa międzynarodowego w świetle Konstytucji RP* [The Observation of International Law in the Perspective of the Constitution of Poland], Zakamycze 2003, pg. 199.

that treaty provisions are regarded as conferring rights on individuals and, consequently, may (and should) be applied by the courts as an independent legal basis for judicial decisions. However, if a treaty provision has not been formulated in a self-executing manner, courts (as well as other state authorities) must wait for its reformulation by the legislature.[42]

The position of a ratified treaty within the domestic legal order depends on the procedure of ratification. Treaties ratified on statutory authorization enjoy a suprastatutory rank. Article 91, Section 2, provides that such a treaty "shall have precedence over statutes if [it] cannot be reconciled with the provisions of such statutes." This is, probably, the most important part of the new constitutional arrangement. While parliamentary approval is necessary to incorporate such a treaty into the domestic legal order, the Constitution itself determines its position within that order. This constitutional arrangement places the rank of treaties on a higher level than the rank of the authorizing statutes.

Thus, full ratification situates a treaty above ordinary statutes. As a consequence, the courts not only are invited to apply directly the provisions of such treaties but also are obliged to grant them priority over a conflicting statutory norm, whether prior or subsequent to the treaty. The courts should, at first, endeavor to interpret the statute so as to avoid a conflict with the treaty and find a way to apply both simultaneously. However, if such interpretation is logically impossible, the conflict must be resolved in favor of the treaty. There are two procedural ways for the courts to address such a conflict. On the one hand, Article 188, Section 2, of the Constitution establishes the jurisdiction of the Constitutional Court to review "the conformity of a statute to ratified international treaties whose ratification requires prior consent given by statute." Each and every court may refer such a question to the Constitutional Court, if the question is relevant for the outcome of a pending case.[43] If the Constitutional Court finds that a statutory provision conflicts with a treaty, it annuls that statutory provision

[42] The very nature of a non-self-executing treaty is that it is written in a language that does not permit any direct application of its provisions in individual cases. For example, a treaty may stipulate that both parties will adopt legislation introducing reciprocal tax benefits for their companies or citizens. Such a provision is addresed only to the legislature, and until legislation is adopted, it is not possible to apply that provision in individual cases to claim a tax benefit. Thus, there is no difference whether we are talking about courts or administrative authorities – both must wait for implementation of the treaty provision by the national legislature.

[43] *See* art. 193 of the Constitution. The conformity of a statute to a treaty can also be assessed in the so-called abstract procedure (i.e., on request of authorities enumerated in art. 191 of the Constitution).

with immediate effect.[44] In practice, such challenges are regularly submitted to the Constitutional Court, particularly in reference to international human rights treaties.[45] On the other hand, some suggest that courts other than the Constitutional Court also have an independent power to refuse application of those statutory provisions that conflict with a treaty.[46] As discussed herein, the courts are, indeed, vested with such power when they apply provisions of EU law.[47] The same logic may, perhaps, apply to the process of applying regular international norms.[48] However, judicial practice in this area remains rather cautious.

The Constitution is less explicit as to the position of treaties ratified without statutory authorization. It is obvious (a contrario from Article 91, Section 2) that such treaties cannot take precedence over statutes. As to the rest, the views of legal scholars remain divided: some authors accept that such treaties have a rank equal to ordinary statutes; others assign them a substatutory position. In any case, under Article 89, Section 1.5, of the Constitution, a treaty ratified without statutory authorization cannot concern "matters regulated by statute." If such a treaty intervenes into the area of matière réservé à la loi, it would not be applied by courts and may be declared unconstitutional by the Constitutional Court.

An exception to the requirement of parliamentary authorization was provided in the transitory provisions of the 1997 Constitution. Under Article 241, Section 1, "international treaties, previously ratified upon the basis of

[44] However, art. 190, sec. 3, of the Constitution allows the Constitutional Court to postpone the annulment of an unconstitutional norm for a period not exceeding twelve or eighteen months. *See infra* note 56 and accompanying text.

[45] *See*, as one of the most recent examples, the 2007 judgment of the Constitutional Court, in which several dispositions of the 2007 Lustration Act were invalidated as contrary to both, the 1997 Constitution of Poland and the European Convention on Human Rights (judgment of May 11, 2007, K 2/07, OTK ZU 2007, no. 5, item 48). However, since many provisions of those treaties (in particular, the European Convention on Human Rights) were reproduced almost verbatim in the text of the Constitution, applications to the Constitutional Court usually raise simultaneously questions of a statute's constitutionality and of its conformity with the Convention. Not surprisingly, the Constitutional Court often prefers to focus on the former, striking down the statute as unconstitutional and finding it not necessary to examine separately its conformity to the Convention.

[46] *See, e.g.*, L. Garlicki, Konstytucja a "sprawy zewnętrzne" (Constitution and "External Affairs"), XV *Przegląd Sejmowy* (Sejm Review), no. 4, pgs. 205–06.

[47] *See infra* notes 62–63 and accompanying text.

[48] *See, e.g.*, L. Garlicki & M. Masternak-Kubiak, Władza sądownicza RP a stosowanie prawa międzynarodowego i prawa UE [Poland's Judicial Branch and the Application of International Law and EU Law], in *Otwarcie Konstytucji RP na prawo międzynarodowe i procesy integracyjne* [The Opening of the Constitution of Poland toward International Law and Processes of Integration], ed. K. Wójtowicz, Warsaw 2006, pg. 181.

constitutional provisions valid at the time of their ratification and promulgated in the Journal of Laws, shall be considered as treaties ratified with prior authorization granted by statute, and shall be subject to the provisions of Article 91 of the Constitution" if they pertain to matters in which Article 89, Section 1, requires statutory authorization. This provision saves the internal validity of many treaties ratified between 1952 and 1989, when no procedure of statutory authorization had been required by the Constitution.

Finally, there are nonratified agreements of an executive nature. While the Council of Ministers (and administrative departments) is allowed to conclude such agreements, they remain outside the system of the sources of universally binding law. Accordingly, such agreements only bind organizational units subordinated to the Council of Ministers (or to a particular minister) and cannot have any direct effect on relations outside the system of public administration. In particular, nonratified agreements cannot create any rights, claims, or obligations of individuals and, in principle, cannot be directly enforced by the courts.[49] That is why the implementation of those agreements may often require the enactment of statutes reproducing their provisions and introducing them into the system of "universally binding [domestic] law." But, "a risk is present that the Parliament does not adopt the statute required in time or that it changes its content comparing to the agreement."[50]

As previously mentioned, international treaties, if ratified on statutory authorization, "shall have precedence over statutes."[51] This means that treaties also take precedence over all substatutory instruments (in particular, regulations issued by the Council of Ministers and other administrative bodies). But this provision also implies that international treaties (whatever the procedure for their ratification) do not have precedence over the Constitution. In other words, provisions of international treaties must remain in conformity with the provisions of the national Constitution.

This conclusion finds a clear confirmation in Article 188 of the Constitution, which establishes the competence of the Constitutional Court to "adjudicate the matters of the conformity of... international treaties to the Constitution." This is the procedure of ex post review, in which the Constitutional Court assesses the constitutionality of a treaty that has already been

[49] See the Bug River and *Panonia* judgments of the Supreme Court, *supra*, note 10, later confirmed in the Bug River judgment of the Constitutional Court (December 19, 2002, K 33/02, OTK 2002, no. 7A, item 97, III.C.6).

[50] W. Czapliński, *supra* note 13, pg. 301. The same author observes that "the position of [nonratified] agreements in the Polish domestic legal order is unclear." *Id.*, pg. 300.

[51] Art. 91, sec. 2, of the Constitution.

ratified, has been published, and has become a part of the domestic legal order.[52] If the Constitutional Court finds that a treaty is, indeed, unconstitutional, it cannot invalidate that treaty as such, but its judgment would bar application of that treaty in domestic relations. Such a ruling would also impose an obligation on the competent authorities to take necessary steps to amend or renounce the treaty. A judicial ruling that a treaty is unconstitutional could produce a situation incompatible with the requirements of international law, particularly Article 27 of the Vienna Convention on the Law of Treaties. Because States may not invoke provisions of their internal law, even constitutional law, as an excuse for violating a treaty, a judicial finding that a treaty is unconstitutional may engage the international responsibility of the Republic of Poland. However, from the perspective of constitutional law, the national Constitution cannot yield to an international treaty. A kind of safety valve is provided in Article 190, Section 3, of the Constitution, which allows the Constitutional Court to retain the validity of an unconstitutional provision for a period not exceeding twelve months. This safety valve should offer enough time to resolve constitutional infirmities in a manner compatible with the requirements of international law. A judgment on unconstitutionality should be regarded, however, as an ultima ratio. Since both Article 9 of the Constitution and general principles of international law require respect for international treaties, domestic law (including the Constitution) should be interpreted in a manner that is friendly toward obligations resulting from international law and European law.[53]

In practice, there has been only one case in which the Constitutional Court undertook a full review of the constitutionality of a treaty. This case was of a very high importance, since the Court dealt with the constitutionality of the Treaty on Poland's Accession to the European Union. In the judgment of May 11, 2005 (K 18/04), the Court confirmed the constitutionality of the treaty. The position of the Court, however, cannot be understood as an unconditional surrender to the authority of international law. The Court emphasized that in case of "an irreconcilable inconsistency between a constitutional norm and a Community [i.e., also an international] norm . . . such collision may in no event be resolved by assuming the supremacy of the latter over the constitutional norm."[54] Thus, the Court

[52] The president of the republic also has a power to submit a treaty to the Constitutional Court before taking a decision about ratification. Art. 133, sec. 2, of the Constitution. This procedure has not found any practical application as yet.

[53] *See* Judgment of the Constitutional Court of May 11, 2005 (K 18/04), III.6.4.

[54] *Id.*, III.6.3–4.

confirmed its potential to declare a treaty (or any of its provisions) unconstitutional and, hence – inoperative in the domestic legal order.[55]

Another controversy of constitutional dimension may arise when a domestic statute faithfully implementing provisions of a treaty is incompatible with a provision of the Constitution. Even if, in such a case, it is a statute (and not a treaty) that is in conflict with the Constitution, the resolution of that conflict affects directly the implementation of the treaty by domestic authorities. The Constitutional Court examined this problem in the context of the so-called European arrest warrant. The Court made clear that, should such a conflict arise, unconstitutional statutory provisions would be annulled and the treaty would not be implemented until a constitutional amendment had been adopted.[56]

C. *The 1997 Constitution: Position of Supranational Law*

The Constitution addresses separately several questions concerning Poland's integration into the European structures. While the relevant provisions were drafted in general language, "there can be no doubt that they were meant to refer primarily to future integration within the European Union."[57] Formal accession to the European Union took place in 2004, giving rise to numerous political and constitutional controversies, many of which have to be resolved by the Constitutional Court.[58]

While it is not necessary to discuss all constitutional problems resulting from the accession, it is noteworthy that the system of EU law is based on the distinction between primary and secondary instruments. The former

[55] It should also be observed that the Accession Treaty was ratified using the particular procedure of Art. 90 of the Constitution and the authorization for ratification was granted in a national referendum. However, the Constitutional Court did not regard the referendum component as putting a bar on its jurisdiction. *Id.*, III.1.3.

[56] The 2002 EU Framework Decision on the European Arrest Warrant was implemented in 2004 by an amendment to the Polish Code of Criminal Procedure. The amendment provided for immediate extradition of every person demanded under the EAW procedure by another EU country. However, art. 55, sec. 1, of the 1997 Constitution forbade any extradition of Polish citizens. The Constitutional Court, in the judgment of April 27, 2005 (P 1/05), invalidated the amended provisions of the Code. However, the Court allowed the application of the EAW procedure for the following eighteen months and indicated that, during this period, Parliament should adopt a constitutional amendment. Such an amendment was, indeed, adopted at the end of 2006. While the case dealt with EU law, it seems obvious that the same logic would apply to a conflict arising under an international treaty sensu stricto.

[57] S. Biernat, Constitutional Aspects of Poland's Future Membership in the E.U., 36 *Archiv des Volkerrechts* (1998), H. 4, pg. 400.

[58] *See* Summaries, *supra* note 25, passim.

are composed of the establishment treaties, including the 2004 Treaty of Athens allowing the recent enlargement of the European Union. Thus, even if the subject matter of those instruments is a specific one, their legal status in Polish constitutional law is not different from the status of other international treaties. Consequently, EU treaties:

- Require, like all other important treaties, presidential ratification based on prior authorization. However, since those treaties may affect the sovereignty of Poland, the procedure of authorization is shaped in a manner offering a particular democratic legitimacy to that decision. Article 90 of the Constitution provides that the authorization is given either by a two-thirds majority vote in each of the Chambers of Parliament or – if the Sejm so decrees – by a national referendum;
- Acquire (on ratification and publication in the *Journal of Laws*) precedence over domestic statutes and shall be applied directly, unless their application depends on the enactment of a statute;[59]
- Remain, like all other treaties, below the national Constitution and, in case of an irreconcilable conflict, must yield to the provisions of the Constitution. Even if the procedure of authorization, as provided in Article 90, shows several similarities to the procedure for a constitutional amendment, it does not grant to the EU treaties a constitutional rank. This interpretation was confirmed by the Constitutional Court, in the judgment of May 18, 2005 (K 18/04). The Court observed that, while conflicts between EU law and the national Constitution may arise only exceptionally (since both legal orders are based on common premises and values), "such collision may in no event be resolved by assuming the supremacy of the Community norm over the constitutional norm."[60] In such a situation, the Polish legislature would have "either to amend the Constitution or to demand revision of the

[59] Art. 91, secs. 1–2, of the Constitution.

[60] *See supra* notes 54-55 and accompanying text. In the same judgment, the Court indicated limitations imposed by the Constitution on the process of integration. In particular, the Court observed that since art. 90, sec. 1, allows delegation to an international organization only "competencies in relation to certain matters," it implies a prohibition on the delegation of all competences (i.e., of "competencies concerning the entirety of matters within a certain field"), Art. 90, sec. 1, 1997 Constitution. Consequently, the Constitution does not authorize "the delegation of competencies to such extent that it would signify the inability of the Republic of Poland to continue functioning as a sovereign and democratic State." "Constitutional provisions on individual rights and liberties set minimal standards that cannot be negated or limited once Community law has entered into effect." Summaries, *supra* note 25, pg. 287.

Community regulations and – as an ultima ratio – to withdraw from the European Union."[61]

The position of the secondary sources of European law is addressed separately in Article 91, Section 3, of the Constitution, which provides that "if a treaty, ratified by the Republic of Poland, establishing an international organization, so provides, the laws established by it shall be applied directly and have precedence in the event of a conflict with statutes."

Thus, Article 91, Section 3, constitutes a legal basis for immediate and direct inclusion of some EU legal instruments into the domestic legal order. Once such an instrument has been adopted by a competent EU body,[62] it does not need any further approval of the national authorities. It becomes automatically incorporated into the system of law binding on the national level and must be enforced by all national authorities, in particular by the national courts. This is one of the most important consequences of EU membership, and – as is well known – the problems of authority and effect of secondary legislation were solved long ago by both the case law of the European Court of Justice (ECJ) and decisions of national constitutional and supreme courts. Poland, like all new member states, has no alternative but to follow the established rules.

The EU secondary legislation cannot be, because of its particular nature, assimilated with international treaties. Therefore, it is not necessary to discuss here at length the problems that may arise in the Polish constitutional discussions on that matter. Three general remarks seem sufficient. First, European Community law, because of its volume and nature, plays a paramount role in the reality of the Polish legal system. In many areas it has replaced (or will soon replace) preexisting national legislation. Its provisions, if appropriately drafted, create rights, claims, and obligations for individual persons. That is why national judges are more often invited to apply EU law than other regular international treaties. There are also more areas of potential conflict between national legislation and EU law.

[61] *Id.*, III.6.4.

[62] It should not be forgotten that those bodies are, to a considerable extent, composed of representatives of national governments and, in many areas, apply the principle of unanimity. Hence, national governments are still vested with quite important powers, and it may open another field of constitutional controversies, namely controversies related to the distribution of those powers between national Parliament (or its chambers) and the executive branch. *See especially* Judgment of the Constitutional Court of Jan. 2005, K 24/04, OTK 2005, no. 1A, item 3 (unconstitutionality of limitations imposed on the Senate's competencies).

Second, the national courts, as well as other national authorities, are bound by the provisions of Community law. They must apply, whenever possible, the technique of an interpretation that is friendly toward the idea of European integration. In other words, the provisions of domestic law should be construed in a way that assures effective implementation of Community law and, whenever possible, avoids conflicts with that law.[63]

Third, should such a conflict nevertheless arise, national statutes yield to Community law. This principle applies not only to provisions contained in the relevant treaties (or to other norms constituting the primary law) but also to the provisions contained in the secondary instruments of Community law. Each and every judge, when deciding a particular case or controversy, has a power to assess the compatibility of national legislation with a Community norm and, eventually, to refuse application of a conflicting national statute. Hence, compared to the centralized system of constitutional review of statutes exercised exclusively by the Constitutional Court, there is a diffuse system of community review of statutes exercised by all courts and judges. As recently decided by the Constitutional Court,

> domestic courts have a power, and also an obligation, to refuse application of a domestic norm if in conflict with any norm of Community law. A court does not decide on an annulment of the domestic norm, but only refuses its application.... This norm retains its validity and can be applied in all areas which are not covered by the conflicting disposition of Community law.... Therefore in such situations, it is not necessary [for the ordinary courts] to refer the question to the Constitutional Court.... Collisions between domestic statutes [and Community law] remain, in principle, outside the interest of the Constitutional Court.[64]

This position of the Constitutional Court refers to all types of European legislation, primary and secondary. While it corresponds with the approach elaborated by the ECJ in the 1970s, it remains to be seen to what extent ordinary and administrative courts will be ready to follow the Constitutional Court's invitation to take the law in their hands.

[63] The principle of interpretation of statutes in a manner "friendly towards European law" emerged in the case law of the Constitutional Court immediately after the enactment of the 1997 Constitution (Judgment of October 17, 1997, K 15/97, OTK 1997, no. 3–4, item 39) and later was confirmed in the Judgment of May 11, 2005, K 18/04. The same friendly approach applies – under art. 9 of the Constitution – to other international law instruments, but, in both the legal doctrine and judicial opinions, it is the interpretation of European law that evokes particular interest.

[64] Decision of Dec. 19, 2006, P 37/05, OTK 2006 nr 11A, item 176.

II. TREATY INTERPRETATION

A. *Principles Embodied in the Vienna Convention*

The role of Polish courts in the process of interpreting international law is defined by the Polish Constitution of 1997. Under Article 87, Section 1, and Article 241, Section 1, of the Constitution, the Vienna Convention on the Law of Treaties is part of the domestic legal order and constitutes a source of law of a universally binding nature. Consequently, Polish judges should follow principles governing treaty interpretation embodied in the Vienna Convention.

Article 31 of the Vienna Convention provides that "a treaty shall be interpreted in good faith in accordance with the ordinary meaning to be given to the terms of the treaty in their context and in the light of its object and purpose." This provision gives no greater weight to one particular method, such as the textual (literal) or teleological (effective) approach.[65] Any true interpretation of a treaty in international law will have to take into account all aspects of the agreement, and it is not possible to exclude completely any of its components.[66] Certainly, the teleological interpretation emphasizes the role of the judge, as the judge will be called on to define the object and purpose of the treaty.

Polish courts do not directly invoke Article 31 of the Vienna Convention, but in practice they first try to give the ordinary meaning to the terms of the treaty when interpreting it. The Supreme Court in the judgment of March 9, 2004, observed:

> [I]t results from the literal meaning of Article 11, Section 1[,] of the Customs Convention on the International Transport of Goods under Cover of TIR Carnets (TIR Convention), of November 14, 1975 that, where a TIR operation has not been discharged, the customs authorities shall not have the right to claim payment of the sums due from the guaranteeing association unless, within a period of one year from the date of acceptance of the TIR Carnet by those authorities, they have notified the association in writing of the non-discharge.[67]

In the ruling of July 14, 2004,[68] the Supreme Court indicated that commentators disagree about the meaning of Article 40 of the Lugano Convention on Jurisdiction and the Enforcement of Judgments in Civil and

[65] A. Aust, *Handbook of International Law*, Cambridge 2005, pg. 89.
[66] M. N. Shaw, *International Law*, Cambridge 1997, pg. 656.
[67] I CK 410/03 (not published Lex 182080).
[68] IV CK 495/03 (OSNC 2005, nr 4, item 73).

Commercial Matters, of September 16, 1988, to which Poland made a reservation. That is why the Court accepted the meaning of Article 40, which "results directly from the wording of this provision."

Sometimes, when a treaty lacks a precise and express definition of a term, courts refer to the relevant provisions of another treaty. In the ruling of March 31, 1999,[69] the Supreme Court took the position that, when interpreting Article 13 of the Hague Convention on the Civil Aspects of International Child Abduction, of October 25, 1980, it is necessary to resort to the general notion of the well-being of the child, as defined in the Convention on the Rights of the Child, adopted by the UN General Assembly on November 20, 1989.

Courts also take into account the purpose of the treaty in the course of interpreting and applying it. In the ruling of December 19, 2000,[70] the Supreme Court stated that when Poland adhered to the Hague Convention of October 25, 1980, mentioned earlier, it assumed an obligation to respect the main purpose of the Convention, which is to secure the prompt return of children wrongfully removed to or retained in any contracting state. The Court's decision explicitly referred to the purpose of the Convention.

In the judgment of March 9, 2004, quoted earlier, the Supreme Court took into account the purpose of the TIR Convention, indicating that "the periods defined in Article 11 of the Convention, on the one hand, should facilitate the trade and speed of transport under TIR carnets, and on the other, have a positive impact on the efficiency of the procedure concerning customs duties."[71]

To establish the purpose of a treaty, the courts often refer to its preamble. The Supreme Court, in the ruling of January 16, 1998,[72] observed that it results from the preamble and Article 3 of the Convention on the Rights of the Child that the well-being of the child constitutes the "general directive" to be followed when settling a conflict between parents concerning the custody of the child.

Polish commentators have discussed the obligation under Article 31 of the Vienna Convention to interpret the terms of a treaty in their context in connection with the declaration of the Polish Government relating to the interpretation of the concordat between the Holy See and Republic of Poland, signed on July 28, 1993. A. Kozłowski points out that the declaration (accepted by the Holy See) constitutes an element of the context

[69] I CKN 23/99 (OSNC 1999 nr 11, item 188).
[70] III CKN 1254/00 (not published Lex 51867).
[71] *See supra* note 67.
[72] II CKN 855/97 (OSNC 1998 nr 9, item 142).

of the concordat and should be taken into account by Polish courts when interpreting the latter. The court would break the law if it gave the provision of the concordat a meaning different from that which results from the declaration.

In the process of interpreting international agreements, Polish courts do not restrict themselves to the methods of interpretation embodied in the Vienna Convention. They also refer to rules of interpretation normally applied to acts of domestic law. One example is the decision of the Supreme Court in an extradition case where, after having confirmed its competence to interpret a bilateral treaty on extradition, the Court made direct reference to methods of interpretation utilized in the Polish criminal procedural law.[73] Academic literature suggests that Polish courts utilize international rules of interpretation in parallel with domestic methods of interpretation when interpreting provisions of international agreements.[74]

B. *Decisions of International Tribunals*

Decisions of international tribunals are a subsidiary source of international law,[75] but in some instances they are regarded as authoritative evidence of the law.[76] In practice, decisions of the European Court of Human Rights (ECtHR) and the ECJ have considerable influence on domestic courts in Poland.

In light of Article 9 of the Polish Constitution, the interpretation of international treaties by Polish courts must be consistent with international law. For the purpose of interpreting a treaty, it may not be sufficient to refer only to the text published in the Polish *Journal of Laws* (*Dziennik Ustaw*). Professor Wyrozumska, when discussing the European Convention on Human Rights (ECHR), indicates that Polish judges should refer to the case law of the ECtHR whenever it defines the scope and substance of the provisions of the Convention. Only after taking into account that interpretation may a court decide, for example, what is the meaning of the right to receive a fair trial under Article 6 of the Convention.[77]

1. The European Court of Human Rights. Poland has been a party to the ECHR since 1993. Polish commentators have expressed the view that the

[73] *See* Decision of 19.02.2003, I KZP 47/02.
[74] *See* A. Wyrozumska, *supra* note 2, pg. 366.
[75] A. Aust, *supra* note 65, pg. 10.
[76] I. Brownlie, *Public International Law*, 6th ed., Oxford 2003, pg. 19.
[77] A. Wyrozumska, *supra* note 2, pg. 565.

Convention is based on the solidarity principle, according to which the case law of the ECtHR is a binding part of the Convention.[78] On this view, the judgments of the ECtHR have legal effect for all states party to the Convention, regardless of the state to which the particular decision was addressed.[79]

Definitions and clarifications of the Convention rights and freedoms, as developed in the case law of the ECtHR, also play an important role in the interpretation of Polish law concerning the protection of individual rights. While this view is generally accepted by the judicial branch, judges often avoid making explicit statements that they are unconditionally bound by the case law of the ECtHR. Instead, judges constantly confirm in their verdicts that the ECtHR's case law should be taken into account in the process of interpretation and application of the Convention and the relevant provisions of domestic law.

In the ruling of January 11, 1995, the Supreme Court held that "from the moment of accession to the Council of Europe the case law of the ECtHR may and should be taken into account in the process of interpretation of the provisions of Polish law."[80] In the judgment of March 28, 1995, an appellate court stated that judicial practice may contradict neither the provisions of the Convention nor the permanent line of interpretation established by the ECtHR.[81] In the judgment of November 28, 2001, the Supreme Court observed that,

> in the interpretation of Article 451 of the Code of criminal procedure in conformity with the wording of Article 6, Section 3(c)[,] of the European Convention, and in the light of the relevant stable case law of the ECtHR in Strasbourg, the appellate court should first of all consider that it bears obligation to secure the effective right to defense.[82]

In the judgment of June 2, 2003, the Supreme Court noted that "Article 10 of the Convention, which guarantees the right to freedom of expression, is construed in the case-law of the ECtHR as guaranteeing freedom of all kinds of expression of opinions, ideas or information, irrespective of their content or the person expressing his or her opinion.... [T]he case-law of

[78] L. Garlicki & M. Masternak-Kubiak, *supra* note 48, pgs. 171–72.

[79] J. Jaskiernia, *Uwarunkowania skuteczności wykonywania orzeczeń Europejskiego Trybunału Praw Człowieka* [Conditions of Effectiveness in the Implementation of the ECtHR's Judgments], "Prawa Człowieka. Humanistyczne Zeszyty Naukowe," nr 8, Katowice 2002, pg. 50.

[80] III ARN 75/94 (OSNP 1995 nr 9, item 106).

[81] II AKR 28/95 (OSP 1996 1996/97 nr 7–8, item 150).

[82] KKN 565/99 (Lex nr 51620).

the ECtHR confirms that the freedom of a journalist includes the possibility to use an exaggeration and even a provocation."[83]

The Constitutional Court, in the judgment of October 30, 2006,[84] was asked to resolve an alleged conflict between, on the one hand, the constitutional freedom of the press and other means of social communication (Article 14 of the Constitution), taken jointly with the freedom to express opinions, and to acquire and to disseminate information (Article 54, Section 1, of the Constitution) and, on the other hand, the right to legal protection of one's private and family life, honor, and reputation (Article 47 of the Constitution). The question before the constitutional tribunal was the constitutionality of Article 212 of the Criminal Code, which imposes criminal penalties on journalists for acts of defamation. The Court decided that Article 212 was constitutional. In reaching this decision, the Court took into consideration not only its own case law (as well as that of the Polish Supreme Court) but also the case law of the ECtHR. The ECtHR case law supports the proposition that, even though freedom of expression is the fundamental principle of a democratic society, that freedom may be restricted to protect other constitutional goods like dignity, private and family life, honor, and reputation.

Polish courts also take account of the jurisprudence of the ECtHR in many other similar areas. However, Polish courts sometimes decide cases in accordance with general equitable principles rather than carry out specific analysis of the international instruments or decisions of international tribunals.[85]

2. The ECJ: The Preaccession Period. With respect to the case law of the ECJ in Luxembourg, it is necessary to distinguish the preaccession period from the period after Poland's accession to the European Union. In the period preceding accession, the Republic of Poland was bound by the 1994 Association Agreement, but Polish courts were not under an unconditional obligation to follow standards established in the ECJ's case law. Nevertheless, the Constitutional Court in the judgment of September 29, 1997, confirmed that Poland bears an obligation "to take all necessary efforts in order to ensure conformity of its future legislation with Community legislation.... The consequence of this responsibility (resting above all with the

[83] KK 161/03 (Lex nr 78847).

[84] P 10/06 (OTK 2006 nr 9A, item 128).

[85] J. Chlebny, Stosowanie Konwencji praw człowieka w sprawach o nadanie statusu uchodźcy [Application of the European Court of Human Rights (hereinafter ECHR) in Cases Concerning the Refugee Status], in *Sądownictwo administracyjne gwarantem wolności i praw obywatelskich 1980–2005* [Administrative Courts as Guarantors of Individual Rights and Freedoms], Warsaw 2005, pg. 69.

Parliament and the Government) is the obligation to give the legislation in force such an understanding that will fully ensure this conformity."[86] Commentators drew the conclusion from this judgment that the obligation to adjust Polish law to Community law was extended by the Constitutional Court to the judicial application of domestic statutes.[87]

This position was confirmed by the Supreme Court in the judgment of May 29, 2001,[88] where it was observed that "the functional approach to Polish law will make it possible to get a result consistent with European Union law. This conformity is ensured not only by referral to the letter of the law, but also by resort to Community judicial practice."[89]

Similarly, in the judgment of January 18, 2002, the Supreme Court accepted that national courts could refer to the ECJ's case law in the field of Community law as authority. However, the Supreme Court also emphasized that each such referral must be accompanied by an elaborated and sufficient legal argumentation based on the provisions of Polish law.[90]

The High Administrative Court (HAC), in the judgment of November 24, 2003, at first noted the convergence of the Polish regulation concerning the exemption from taxation imposed on goods with the EU founding treaties and directives, and then strengthened its argument by the statement that "also the ECJ case law categorically excludes the possibility of tax differentiation of goods based on the country of their origin."[91] The HAC made explicit reference to its earlier judgment of February 12, 2001,[92] in which it confirmed that the consequence of Poland signing the 1994 agreement is not only the adjustment of national law to European Union legal standards but also the harmonization of the standard of legal behavior, including practice and interpretation of law. This approach was again confirmed by the HAC in the judgment of January 21, 2004: "in the light of ECJ case law, the national court is obliged, when it applies internal law provisions, to interpret those provisions, as far as possible, in the light of the wording and purpose of the directive."[93]

[86] K 15/97 (OTK 1997 nr 3–4, item 37).

[87] M. Górka, C. Mik, *Sądy polskie jako sądy Unii Europejskiej (na tle doświadczeń przedakcesyjnych)* [Polish Courts as Courts of the European Union (the Pre-Accession Experience)], Kwartalnik Prawa Publicznego, nr 4/2005, pg. 14.

[88] I CKN 1217/98 (OSNC 2002 nr 1, item 13).

[89] *See* M. Górka, C. Mik, *supra* note 87, pg. 15.

[90] III RN 54/01 (OSNAPiUS 2002, nr 14, item 321). *See* L. Garlicki & M. Masternak-Kubiak, *supra* note 48, pg. 183.

[91] FSA 3/03 (ONSA 2004 nr 2, item 44).

[92] V SA 305/00 (LEX 51327).

[93] I S.A./Łd 128/03 (ONSA/WSA 2004 nr 2, item 40).

In summary, during the preaccession period, Polish courts applied EU law indirectly to produce interpretations of Polish law that would conform fully to EU law.[94]

3. The ECJ: The Postaccession Period. Following full accession to the European Union on May 1, 2004, Poland, in accordance with Article 2 of the Accession Treaty, became bound by EU law as well as by the *acquis communautaire*. All organs of public authority, including courts and tribunals, were thereafter in a new situation.

The obligation to follow EU law, including the case law of both Luxembourg courts,[95] resulted not only from the international legal obligations embodied in the Accession Treaty but also from the domestic Constitution, which clearly provided that international treaties, as well as EU secondary law, must be respected. This dual obligation was confirmed by the Constitutional Court in its landmark judgment of May 11, 2005.[96] The Court indicated that because, by virtue of the ratification decision, the Accession Treaty is included in the system of international law binding on Poland, it must be respected under the provisions of Article 9 of the Constitution. The same logic establishes the ECJ's competence under both domestic and international law to establish a binding interpretation of Community law (particularly via the procedure of preliminary rulings), since that competence is provided in Article 234 of the EC Treaty.[97]

Article 234 enables any question of Community law to be referred to the ECJ at the motion of any national court before which such a question arises. The ruling given by the Court is an interlocutory one. It constitutes a step in proceedings before the national court, which must apply the ruling to the facts of the case.[98]

According to the dominant view expressed by Polish commentators, the courts of member states have limited interpretive discretion as far as

[94] M. Górka & C. Mik, *supra* note 87, pg. 20.

[95] European Court of Justice (ECJ) and Court of First Instance (CFI).

[96] K 18/04 (OTK 2005 nr 5A, item 49). *See supra* notes 25 and 53 and accompanying text.

[97] Art. 234 of the EC Treaty provides: "The Court of Justice shall have jurisdiction to give preliminary rulings concerning: a) the interpretation of the Treaty; b) the validity and interpretation of the acts of the institutions of the Community . . . ; c) the interpretation of the statutes of bodies established by an act of the Council, where those statutes so provide. Where such a question is raised before any court or tribunal of a Member State, that court or tribunal may, if it considers that a decision on the question is necessary to enable it to give judgment, request the Court of Justice to give a ruling thereon. Where any such question is raised in a case pending before a court or tribunal of a Member State, against whose decisions there is no judicial remedy under national law, that court or tribunal shall bring the matter before the Court of Justice."

[98] *See* A. Arnull, *The European Union and Its Court of Justice*, 2d ed., Oxford 2006, pg. 95.

Community law is concerned. Their freedom of action is limited by the competence of the ECJ, which has a mandate to ensure the uniform interpretation of Community law by the courts of all member states.[99] In particular, the ECJ's preliminary rulings concerning the interpretation and validity of Community laws are regarded as having binding authority.[100] Moreover, given the member states' obligation under Article 10 of the EC Treaty to "take all appropriate measures... to ensure fulfilment of the obligations arising out of this Treaty or resulting from action taken by the institutions of the Community," a ruling from the ECJ adopted under Article 234 should also be applied in all subsequent cases.[101]

The Supreme Court, in the judgment of August 12, 2004,[102] stated that "when interpreting law, Polish courts must take into account the interpretation of the ECJ in Luxembourg and directives in force in the European Union."

Assessing effects of the Council Regulation (EC) 44/2001 on the jurisdiction and recognition of judicial decisions in civil and commercial matters, the Supreme Court, in its ruling of January 11, 2007,[103] referred to the interpretation adopted by the ECJ relating to the Brussels Convention of September 27, 1968, on the jurisdiction and recognition of judicial decisions in civil and commercial matters.[104]

In an earlier judgment,[105] the HAC acknowledged that the clarification of the meaning of provisions of the Polish law on the protection of personal data requires taking into account provisions of relevant EU directives. The Court observed that, according to the ECJ, national courts are required to interpret national law, as far as possible, in light of the wording and the purpose of the directive, in order to achieve the result sought by the European Union. Consequently, the HAC referred to the ECJ's interpretation of Article 7/f of Directive 95/46/EC on the protection of individuals with regard to the

[99] A. Wróbel, *Stosowanie prawa międzynarodowego i prawa Unii Europejskiej przez sądy RP* [Application of International Law and the Law of the European Union by the Polish Courts], in *Otwarcie, supra* note 48, pg. 231.

[100] P. Dąbrowska, *Skutki orzeczenia wstępnego Europejskiego Trybunału Sprawiedliwości* [Effects of the Preliminary Ruling of the Court of Justice], Warsaw 2004, pg. 87.

[101] J. Steiner & L. Woods, *Textbook on EC Law*, 9th ed., Oxford 2005, pg. 217.

[102] III PK 38/04 (OSNP 2005 nr 4, item 55).

[103] II CSK 343/06 (unpublished).

[104] The Brussels Convention of 1968 has now been transformed into Regulation 44/2001. However, the ECJ case law established under the Brussels Convention is still relevant when it is not contrary to provisions of the regulation. That is why national courts, including the Polish Supreme Court, refer to this case law.

[105] June 6, 2005 – I OPS 2/05 (ONSA/WSA 2006 nr 2, item 38).

processing of personal data and on the free movement of such data (OJ 1995 L 281, pg. 31).[106]

In the judgment of February 8, 2006,[107] the HAC determined the scope of application of the Agreement on Trade Related Aspects of Intellectual Property Rights (TRIPs Agreement), which is a part of Community law, to situations that had occurred before Poland's accession to the European Union. The Court held that, before the date of accession (May 1, 2004), the TRIPs Agreement occupied in the Polish legal order the status of a regular international treaty, and not the status of Community law.

> It may be added [observed the Court] that a similar attitude was assumed by the ECJ in the judgment of January 10, 2006 (C-302/04), in which the ECJ held that when the facts of the dispute in the main proceedings occurred prior to the accession of the State to the European Union, the ECJ did not have jurisdiction to interpret Community law by means of a preliminary ruling.[108]

It should be explained here that the Community itself and EU member states, including Poland after its accession to the European Union, are all members of the World Trade Organization (WTO). Some matters within the scope of the WTO fall within the competence of the member states. For example, the General Agreement on Trade in Services (GATS) and the TRIPs Agreement fall within the competence of member states. In contrast, other issues related to the WTO fall within the exclusive competence of the Community.[109] Polish courts can apply directly effective provisions of WTO law. For example, Article 50 of the TRIPs Agreement, which contains rules on provisional legal protection through the courts, has direct effect. The norm is directly addressed to the courts, and it does not require further normative implementation.[110]

With respect to the Community obligations resulting from the WTO agreements, the ECJ found that Community courts may review the legality

[106] *See* The Queen v. Minister of Agriculture, Fisheries and Food, *ex parte* Trevor Robert Fisher and Penny Fisher (C-369/98). In that case, the ECJ held that because the purpose of the directive is the protection of privacy, it is necessary, when adjudicating the legality of measures for processing personal data, to balance individual rights and freedoms on the one hand and the legitimate interests pursued by a third party, on the other.

[107] II GSK 54/05 ONSA/WSA 2006 nr 4, item 96.

[108] *Id.*

[109] *See* K. Lenaerts & P. van Nuffel, *Constitutional Law of the European Union*, ed. R. Bray, 2nd ed., London 2005, pg. 842.

[110] *See* R. Uerpmann-Wittzack, The Constitutional Role of Multilateral Treaty Systems, in *Principles of European Constitutional Law*, ed. A. von Bogdandy & J. Bast, Oxford 2006, pg. 153.

of Community measures under WTO rules only where the Community intended to implement a particular obligation assumed in the WTO agreements, or where the Community measure refers expressly to the precise provisions of those WTO rules.[111] Accordingly, a measure adopted by the Community to comply with reports adopted under the WTO dispute settlement machinery cannot be reviewed in light of those reports if the measure does not refer expressly to specific obligations ensuing from those reports.[112]

Polish courts must comply with the ECJ's judgments reviewing the conformity of a Community act with WTO rules. They must also apply the principle, confirmed by the ECJ, that EC law should be interpreted in light of binding international accords, including WTO agreements.

Similarly, in the resolution of October 16, 2006,[113] a panel of seven judges of the HAC held that "the judgment of the ECJ of January 10, 2006 (C-302/04) corresponds to the view expressed by the HAC."

The Regional Administrative Court (RAC), in the judgment of May 24, 2006,[114] pointed out that because the petitioner was ignorant as to the relevant provisions of Community law, it was impossible for him to uncover the error committed by the customs authority receiving the customs declaration. However, that ignorance was the result of the lack of official Polish translation of Council Regulation No. 1430/79 and, therefore, must not negatively affect the petitioner's legal position. The RAC added that "it is worth invoking here the judgment of the ECJ of May 15, 1986 (C-160/84), where the lack of access to the official translation of the Community act to the Greek language was considered to be one of the highly exceptional factors which constitute 'special circumstances' within the meaning of article 13 of Regulation No. 1430/79."[115]

In the resolution of January 8, 2007,[116] a panel of seven judges of the HAC interpreted the definition of the "supply of goods" contained in the Polish law on taxation imposed on goods and services. The Court established a correct meaning of that definition by invoking the case law of the ECJ interpreting the phrase "supply of goods," which appears in the Sixth Council Directive (77/388/EEC). The HAC concluded from this interpretation that the purpose of the directive could be endangered if the understanding of the "supply of goods" subjected to taxation would depend on fulfillment

[111] *See* Case C-93/02 P, *Biret International v Council* [2003] ECR I-10497.
[112] *See* Lenaerts, van Nuffel, *supra* note 109, pg. 746.
[113] I FSP 2/06 (ONSA/WSA 2007 nr, item 3).
[114] III S.A./Gd 45/06 (ONSA/WSA 2007 nr 1, item 18).
[115] *Id.*
[116] I FPS 1/06 (ONSA/WSA 2007 nr 2, item 27).

of conditions varying from one national law system to another. Similarly, in the judgment of December 13, 2005,[117] the HAC explained its position concerning the possibility of deducting a tax calculated on the purchase of goods and services if they serve the future taxable sales. The court observed that a "similar view is established in the ECJ case law interpreting the Sixth Directive." The same approach has been followed by one of the RACs. The RAC, in the judgment of August 2, 2005,[118] referred to the ECJ's interpretation of provisions of the Sixth Council Directive and pointed out that the Polish law on taxation imposed on goods and services "fully accomplishes the aim defined in Article 17 of that Directive."

The obligation to follow the interpretation established on the EC level is, however, not unlimited. As explained by the Constitutional Court, the principle that domestic law should be interpreted in a manner

> sympathetic to European law . . . in no event may lead to results contradicting the explicit wording of constitutional norms or being irreconcilable with the minimum guarantee functions realised by the Constitution. In particular, the norms of the Constitution within the field of individual rights and freedoms indicate a minimum and unsurpassable threshold which may not be lowered or questioned as a result of the introduction of Community provisions.[119]

The Constitutional Court indicated that the interpretation of Community law, as established by the ECJ, should remain within the area of functions and competences delegated to the Community by its member states. The Court also concluded that this division of interpretive authority should be understood in accordance with the principle of subsidiarity.

In the decision of December 19, 2006,[120] the Constitutional Court observed that the principal aim of the preliminary ruling procedure is to ensure uniform application of Community law by national courts of all member states. This procedure constitutes a fundamental mechanism of legal cooperation between national courts and the ECJ. Its very idea is based on a subtle difference between the interpretation and the application of law: while the power of interpretation is vested in the ECJ, the power of application of Community law belongs to national courts. This division of authority recognizes that a ruling issued by the ECJ represents an important factor in the settlement of a dispute, but it does not fully resolve a particular case. The

[117] I FSK 384/05 (ONSA/WSA 2006 nr 4, item 107).
[118] I SA/Bd 337/05 (ONSA/WSA 2006 nr 2, item 61).
[119] Judgment of May 11, 2005, K 18/04.
[120] P 37/05.

ECJ has often emphasized that the procedure for preliminary rulings should be regarded as a form of judicial cooperation, by means of which the national court and the ECJ, in accordance with the competencies vested in each of them, directly and mutually contribute to reaching a particular decision.

The ECJ, in a preliminary ruling delivered as a result of a question asked by the Polish administrative court, directed the attention of the Polish court to the settled case law to clarify the meaning of Articles 23, 25, and 90 of the EC treaty. The ECJ pointed out:

> [A]ccording to settled case law, the interpretation which the Court, in the exercise of the jurisdiction conferred upon it by Article 234, gives to a rule of Community law clarifies and where necessary defines the meaning and scope of that rule as it must be, or ought to have been, understood and applied from the time of its coming into force. It follows that the rule as thus interpreted can, and must, be applied by the courts even to legal relationships arising and established before the judgment ruling on the request for interpretation, provided that in other respects the conditions for bringing before the courts having jurisdiction an action relating to the application of that rule are satisfied.[121]

C. *Decisions of Foreign Courts*

Polish courts refer only occasionally to treaty interpretations embodied in the published decisions of the courts of other nations. Foreign jurisprudence is considered persuasive.

For example, the HAC, in the judgment of January 29, 2003,[122] concerning the refusal to grant refugee status to a foreign national, referred to the decision of the English Court of Appeal (Civil Division) in *Omoruyi v. Secretary of State for the Home Department*[123] – in order to demonstrate that judicial application of the 1951 Convention Relating to the Status of Refugees is not uniform.

D. *Interpretation Provided by the Executive Branch*

Under the Polish legal system, any court may request the Ministry of Justice to provide information related to the text of a foreign law or to the judicial practice of foreign countries.[124] Such information has no binding authority but in judicial practice is helpful to Polish courts.[125]

[121] Case-313/05, Maciej Brzeziński v. Dyrektor Izby Celnej w Warszawie.
[122] V S.A. 1494/02 (ONSA 2004 nr 2, item 57).
[123] (2001) Imm AR 175.
[124] Art. 1113 of the Code of Civil Procedure.
[125] Particularly in extradition cases, *see* A. Wyrozumska, *supra* note 2, pg. 369.

However, this procedure does not apply in any direct way to the interpretation of international treaties. Because all ratified international treaties enter into the domestic legal order, there is a presumption that they are known to the domestic courts and judges.[126] In any case, opinions and information submitted by the executive branch cannot have dispositive effects. For a court to treat executive branch views as dispositive would be incompatible with the principle of independence of the judicial branch, as understood under the Polish Constitution (Articles 173 and 175) and the ECHR.[127]

The recent case of *K. Galstyan*[128] demonstrates this point. By diplomatic note dated June 30, 1997, the Armenian embassy informed the Polish government that the Republic of Armenia did not consider itself a successor to a prior agreement between Poland and the former Soviet Union concerning exemptions from visa requirements. The Polish government accepted this note and informed Armenia that the prior agreement ceased to be in force as between Poland and Armenia. For the Polish Ministry of Foreign Affairs, this exchange of notes was sufficient to conclude that the agreement could not be applied internally. As a result, the Polish Ministry of Interior decided that an Armenian citizen, Karine Galstyan, should be expelled from Poland because she did not possess a valid visa. The HAC rejected this reasoning. For the HAC, the exchange of notes, as such, could not have any effect in the internal legal order because it did not meet the requirement of official publication in prescribed form. The Foreign Ministry's declaration was not published and, as a consequence, not binding for Polish courts adjudicating on the legal status of the Armenian citizen in Poland.

In practice, the courts rarely ask the executive branch to provide them with information concerning international treaties. In contrast, though, in the area of Community law, domestic courts frequently refer preliminary questions to the ECJ.

[126] Only exceptionally, the law invites courts to request information from the Executive branch on the effects of international law (e.g., when the scope and substance of diplomatic immunities is involved). See art. 1116 of the Code of Civil Procedure.

[127] *See, e.g.*, Beaumartin v. France (ECtHR, Nov. 24, 1994) (holding that a system under which an administrative court had to refer to a representative of the executive when difficulties arose in the interpretation of an international agreement, which was decisive for the outcome of the legal proceedings, was incompatible with guarantees provided for in art. 6 of the ECHR); Chevrol v. France (ECtHR, February 13, 2003) (holding that the Council of State, by having based its decision solely on the opinion of the minister for foreign affairs concerning reciprocity, voluntarily deprived itself of the power to examine the dispute before it).

[128] V SA 726/99.

III. TREATY APPLICATION

A. *Treaties and Rights for Private Parties*

Polish scholarship and judicial practice adhere to the position that, in light of the 1997 Constitution, international treaties are directly applicable in the Polish domestic legal order. However, under Article 91, Section 1, of the Constitution, a treaty is not directly applicable if the application of that treaty "depends on the enactment of a statute." This means that only those provisions of international treaties that are self-executing may be invoked by individuals before national courts. It is generally recognized that self-executing provisions create rights (and obligations) for private parties, even if those rights and obligations have no direct equivalent in domestic legislation. It is also recognized that, since there is a general obligation to interpret international treaties in good faith, domestic courts should, whenever possible, adopt the interpretation that best corresponds with the nature and goal of the treaty in question. Hence, the domestic courts should base their interpretation on a presumption in favor of broader protection for private rights where the protection of such rights is a goal of the treaty, as is the case with human rights treaties.

The determination of whether a particular treaty provision is self-executing constitutes the first step in the process of judicial application of international law. This determination remains, in principle, within the province of a court (or another public authority) invited to apply a particular treaty provision. The court must examine whether the treaty provision has been drafted in a complete manner (i.e., in a manner allowing its use as an exclusive legal basis for resolving an individual case or controversy). In other words, the legal norm can be drawn from the text of the treaty, and it is not necessary to enact domestic legislation to implement or concretize the treaty provisions.[129]

The case law of Polish courts has shown, at least since about 1988, a considerable readiness to accept the self-executing nature of treaty provisions and to apply them in a direct manner. This trend is particularly visible in regard to treaties establishing rights of individual persons.

One early example was the judgment of the Olsztyn military tribunal of June 8, 1982, adopted under the 1981 martial law. In that case, the military tribunal gave direct effect to Article 15(1) of the International Covenant on

[129] Resolution of the Supreme Court of October 5, 1974, III CZP 71/73, OSN CP 1975, no 5, item 72.

Civil and Political Rights (ratified by Poland in 1977), which establishes the principle of nonretroactivity. The Olsztyn tribunal rejected the position of the Prosecutor's Office that penal provisions of the martial law decrees had entered into force with immediate effect, even before the decree was duly published in the *Journal of Laws*. The court observed that such interpretation of the decree would be "contrary to provisions of the Covenant. Article 4 (2) of the Covenant renders impossible – even during the emergency periods – to derogate the application of its Article 15 establishing the principle *lex retro non agit*."[130] However, this judgment was later quashed by the Supreme Court.[131]

It was only in the end of the decade when courts began to accept the concept of self-executing norms. In 1988, the Supreme Court adopted the *Interagra* Judgment. The controversy was related to the protection of the trade name of a French company; a dispute arose when a Polish foreign enterprise later registered under that name. The French company invoked Article 8 of the Paris Convention for the Protection of Industrial Property (ratified by Poland in 1975). The Supreme Court held that the "discussed provision as straightforwardly deciding on the rights and obligations of private parties is directly enforceable in the domestic legal system. Since the coming into force of the Stockholm text of that Convention, its art. 8 is effective in Poland and might be a basis for protecting the commercial name."[132]

In the judgment of June 28, 1989, the Supreme Court observed that "international agreements in civil law and family relations might be a basis for judicial decision, parallel with provisions of internal law."[133]

The concept of self-executing treaties had become well established in judicial practice even before the 1997 Constitution entered into force. In the resolution of February 19, 1997, the Supreme Court noted:

> [T]here are no . . . obstacles to recognize that the provisions of ratified international treaties could be, and even should be, directly applied in the Polish internal legal order – particularly in the area of individual rights and freedoms. This assertion concerns all treaty norms that, due to their nature, are suitable for direct application. In the legal writings,

[130] Not published.

[131] Ten years later, the Supreme Court clearly confirmed that "the prohibition provided for in Article 15 of the Covenant belongs to those international norms that can be directly applied in the domestic legal order of the Member-States (so-called self-executing norms)." Judgment of October 17, 1991, II KRN 274/91, OSNKW 1992, no. 3–4.

[132] Judgment of June 14, 1988 (II CR 367/87), OSP 1990, nr 9, item 705.

[133] II CR 200/89, OSP 1990, no. 10, item 361.

these international provisions are qualified as self-executing, i.e. creating immediate entitlements for citizens and apt to be applied by the State bodies, especially by the courts and administrative organs.[134]

The Warsaw Appellate Court, in a decision of September 10, 1997, held: "International agreements are obligatory both to the ratifying States and to the individuals whose spheres of activity are regulated. Therefore, it is not necessary that the parties – in the private contract – recall the provisions of the binding international agreement as a basis for resolving the disputes and satisfying the judicial decision."[135] The Supreme Court, in the judgment of November 21, 2003, ruled:

> [I]nternational agreement provisions are effective not only with regard to the States, but may provide an independent ground of claims for damages raised before domestic courts (so-called self-executing norms). A particular provision of an international treaty could be regarded as a self-executing norm if it meets two conditions. The so-called formal condition is that the treaty must be duly ratified and published in the Journal of Laws. The substantive condition requires the completeness of the treaty provision that enables its operation without any additional implementation [in domestic legislation].[136]

The same approach is accepted in the jurisprudence of the HAC.[137]

In the area of penal law, some treaty provisions can become directly applicable because of their self-executing nature. However, the principle *nullum crimen sine lege* requires such provisions to be drafted in a precise manner. The Supreme Court addressed this problem in the judgment of April 19, 2004.[138] The Court examined the penal provisions of the 1949 Convention for the Suppression of the Traffic in Persons and of the Exploitation of the Prostitution of Others. The Court noted that the prohibitions ensuing from that Convention are identical to those provided in the Polish Criminal Code. However, the provisions of the Convention cannot be applied directly because the Convention only establishes the list of prohibited acts but does not specify any sanctions. Thus, the regulation of the Convention is not complete, and its provisions cannot be recognized as self-executing. Consequently, those provisions require incorporation into the domestic

[134] I KZP 37/96, OSNKW 1997 nr 3–4, item 21.
[135] I ACz 813/97, "Prawo Gospodarcze" 1998, no. 3, item 97.
[136] I CK 323/02, OSNC 2004 nr 6, item 103.
[137] *See, e.g.*, Judgment of February 8, 2006, in which the HAC recognized the direct applicability of provisions contained in Annex 1C to the agreement establishing the World Trade Organization (II GSK 54/05, ONSA 2006 nr 4, item 96).
[138] V KKN 353/00 (not published Lex 56863).

legal system by legislation providing penal sanctions for their violation. The Court observed:

> [T]here would not be any [constitutional] obstacles to the direct application by the courts of the principle established in Article 1 of the Convention. That provision requires punishment of any person who, to gratify the passions of another procures, entices or leads away, for the purposes of prostitution, another person, even with his/her consent, or exploits the prostitution of another person, even with the consent of that person. However, Article 1 was drafted in a manner that excludes its direct application by the criminal courts. The wording of that provision indicates that it was directly addressed only to the State, establishing its obligation to adopt a corresponding penal norm.[139]

The Court held that, under Article 91, Section 2, of the 1997 Constitution, direct application of an international penal norm is only possible when that norm, in addition to defining the crime, also determines the penalty.[140]

Limitations on the self-executing effect of international treaties in the area of penal law result from the particular characteristics of that branch of law. Poland requires that every penal law norm (domestic as well as international) must be drafted in a precise and complete manner. In particular, judges must not be accorded broad interpretive discretion in that area. The situation is different in regard to other branches of law. For example, in the area of civil law, Article 77 of the Constitution establishes the principle of state liability for illegal actions and omissions of public officials. While *illegality* is usually understood as a violation of a provision of domestic law, it may be argued that the same illegality emerges from acts violating provisions of international or European law and, as a consequence, that such acts may also entitle the affected persons to bring a suit against the State Treasury.

Once it is determined that the application of an international treaty or a provision thereof does not "depend on the enactment of a statute," the courts are allowed and required to use the treaty as an independent norm of reference.[141] The techniques of judicial application of international treaties can be compared, in many respects, to the techniques used in the application of constitutional norms. This is particularly true with respect to human rights treaties, since their content is, to a considerable extent, similar,

[139] V KKN 353/00, Lex 56863.
[140] *Id.*
[141] Art. 91, sec. 2, of the Constitution.

if not identical, with the provisions of the 1997 Constitution. In the doctrine, three principal techniques of such application have been distinguished:[142]

1. Autonomous application, wherein the court applies an international norm as the exclusive or essential legal basis for resolving an individual case. In these circumstances, domestic law is not the basis of judicial decision.
2. Coapplication, wherein the court applies an international norm concurrently with a domestic constitutional or statutory norm. In most situations, the international norm is used only as a subsidiary tool to establish the correct interpretation of the domestic norm. Sometimes, however, both provisions are used as components to construct the principle or norm governing the outcome of an individual case.
3. Remedial application, wherein a court resolves a conflict between an international norm and domestic law by giving priority to the former. This can result in the annulment of the domestic norm, or in a refusal to apply that norm in deciding individual cases.

Examples of autonomous application are rather rare because there are only a few areas in which regulations adopted in international treaties do not coexist with provisions of domestic legislation. This is why the most typical technique is that of coapplication of an international norm and a domestic norm.

The autonomous role of international law becomes particularly significant in regard to human rights treaties.[143] In comparison, cases of direct application of classic international treaties are less frequent. Even if they contain provisions of a directly applicable nature, courts usually apply them as background for the interpretation of domestic legislation. In regard to human rights treaties, though, and in particular to the ECHR, there is a clear case of "parallelism" between their provisions and constitutional norms.[144] In these cases, the courts often have a choice of using an international norm or a constitutional norm as the legal basis for their rulings. Judicial practice in this regard is varied.

[142] *See* L. Garlicki & M. Masternak-Kubiak, *supra* note 48, pg. 175.

[143] The courts routinely invoke the provisions of the European Convention for the Protection of Human Rights and Fundamental Freedoms (1950), the Convention on the Rights of the Child (1989), the International Covenant on Civil and Political Rights (1966), and various conventions of the International Labour Organization.

[144] It should not be forgotten that, in the drafting process of the 1997 Constitution, the provisions of the ECHR (ratified by Poland in 1992) constituted an important point of reference, and the authors of the Constitution attempted to ensure full consistency of those instruments.

The Constitutional Court, because of the very nature of its mission, gives clear preference to the provisions of the Constitution. On many occasions, the Court – after having held that the statute under review was unconstitutional – decided that it was no longer necessary to assess separately the conformity of that statute with the ECHR. The provisions of the Convention (and, in particular, the case law of the ECtHR) are usually invoked as additional arguments in establishing the scope and meaning of relevant constitutional provisions.[145] However, in some difficult cases, the Constitutional Court preferred to administer a double kill and to declare that the statute was contrary to both the Constitution and the Convention.[146]

Other courts give more independent meaning to the Convention. Particularly in the case law of the Penal Chamber of the Supreme Court, references to the ECHR seem to be more frequent than references to similar provisions of the Polish Constitution. There are, probably, several reasons for this approach. On the one hand, the ECtHR case law related to criminal procedure has always been quite abundant. Polish courts began applying that case law[147] almost immediately after the ECHR entered into the domestic legal realm in 1992.[148] On the other hand, the jurisprudence of the Polish Constitutional Court remains less developed in the area of criminal procedure. Indeed, the constitutional regulation of criminal procedure emerged only in the 1997 Constitution, that is, five years after the ECHR entered the domestic legal order. The direct applicability of the Convention seems so evident that the Supreme Court has simply assumed that the ECHR is directly applicable without ever deciding that question explicitly.

Whereas the case law of the Supreme Court has always focused on Articles 5 and 6 of the ECHR,[149] it is not limited to those two provisions. In

[145] *See, e.g.*, Judgment of the Constitutional Court of March 20, 2006 (K 17/05); Judgment of the Constitutional Court of October 11, 2006 (P 3/06).

[146] *See especially* the Lustration Case (Judgment of May 10, 2007, K 2/07), in which the Constitutional Court invalidated most of the provisions of the 2006 Lustration Act, as, inter alia, contrary to arts. 6(1), 8, and 10 of the Convention. *See supra* note 45.

[147] *See generally* R. Wieruszewski, Oddziaływanie prawa międzynarodowego i prawa Unii Europejskiej na konstytucyjny status jednostki w RP [The Influence of International Law and the Law of the European Union on the Constitutional Position of the Individual], in *Otwarcie*, ed. K. Wójtowicz, *supra* note 48, pg. 189.

[148] *See* P. Hofmański, *Ochrona praw człowieka* [Protection of Human Rights], Białystok 1994, pg. 136ff.

[149] The judgment of November 28, 2001 (V KKN 565/99, Lex nr 51620) may serve as an example. The Supreme Court addressed the right of the accused (and detained) person to be present, next to his or her lawyer, during the appeal hearing. The Court observed that "interpretation of the [appropriate provisions] of the Code of Criminal Procedure must be carried out in accordance with the text of Article 6 (3c) of the ECHR and also in light of the established jurisprudence of the ECtHR on this matter. Therefore, the Appellate Court

the decision of July 29, 1997,[150] the Supreme Court refused to allow extradition of two Chinese citizens, invoking directly Article 3 of the Convention and indicating that extradition could place the applicants at risk of being subjected to torture or to inhuman or degrading treatment or punishment. Article 3 was also discussed in the judgment of February 28, 2007, where the Supreme Court found that overpopulation of prison cells may give rise to civil claims and invoked the relevant case law of the ECtHR.[151] In the judgment of June 2, 2003, the Supreme Court referred to Article 10 of the Convention and noted:

> [I]n the case law of the ECtHR, freedom of expression encompasses all kinds of expression and/or communication of opinions, ideas and information, irrespective of their content. At the same time, it is worth stressing that the main component of free expression is the freedom of the press that constitutes a prerequisite of public scrutiny, as an essential element of democracy. For that reason, the case law of the European Court of Human Rights assumes that the freedom of journalistic action encompasses also the possibility of using an exaggeration, and even a provocation.[152]

The ECHR is also constantly present in the judicial practice of lower courts. As early as 1995, the Warsaw Appellate Court held:

> "[I]t is contrary to the presumption of innocence to include in the description of the imputed crime the name of an accomplice who neither was indicted in the proceedings, nor convicted in another trial. Such statement violates not only Article 3 of the Code of Criminal Procedure, but also Article 6 (2) of the ECHR as an international instrument duly ratified by Poland and applicable concurrently with the provisions of domestic law. It also contravenes the established and continuous case-law of the European Court of Human Rights."[153]

The 1980 Hague Convention on the Civil Aspects of International Child Abduction is another treaty that is directly applied quite frequently by the Polish courts. On many occasions, the Supreme Court has held that nonobservation of the provisions of that Convention constitutes sufficient

should have in mind that it has the duty to pay attention to the effectiveness of the right to defence. . . . [It must be taken in consideration] that the participation solely of the defence counsel in the appeal hearing cannot be regarded as an equal alternative to the personal attendance of the accused in it, especially when examination of evidence is envisaged."

[150] II KKN 313/97 (OSNKW 1997 nr 11–12, item 85), *Madugequi* case. See M. Masternak-Kubiak, *Przestrzeganie prawa międzynarodowego w świetle Konstytucji RP*, Zakamycze 2003, pg. 242.

[151] V CSK 431/06 (unpublished).

[152] III KK 161/03 (Lex nr 78 847).

[153] Judgment of March 28, 1995 (II AKR 28/95), OSP 1996/97, nr 7–8, item 150.

ground to quash rulings adopted by a lower court.[154] In the judgment of November 18, 1999, the Supreme Court referred to Article 12 of the Hague Convention and held that the separation from the mother could not, as such, impede the return of an illegally abducted child to the state of his lawful residence.[155]

The judicial interpretation of bilateral agreements on legal assistance in legal relations in civil, family and criminal matters is similar. The courts regard those agreements as directly applicable to legal relations among private persons.[156]

However, when national (particularly constitutional) law offers broader protection for the individual than international instruments, the court may base its decision on provisions of domestic law. In the ruling of September 9, 1998,[157] the Supreme Court, when allowing access to court for a foreign national who was seeking refugee status, based its decision on Article 45, Section 1, of the 1997 Constitution and chose not to refer to Article 14 of the International Covenant on Civil and Political Rights or to Article 6(1) of the ECHR. The Court explained that the constitutional access-to-court guarantee applies to all disputes, whereas both international instruments are limited only to civil and penal cases.[158]

B. *Treaties and Judicial Remedies*

The scope and nature of judicial remedies is determined by the position of international law within the domestic legal order. Since ratified international treaties become part of the domestic legal order, and since those treaties may give rise to rights and obligations of private parties, their legal effects are no different from the effects of other domestic norms. In other words, the violation of a treaty constitutes an unlawful act and triggers such legal consequences as, within a given area of law, are provided for violation of domestic law.

In the area of private law, natural persons as well as corporations can claim that their rights, and others' obligations, arise from the provisions

[154] *See, e.g.*, Judgment of Jan. 16, 1998 (II CKN 855/97, OSNC 1998 nr 9, item 142).

[155] I CKN 992/99 (OSNC 2000 nr 6, item 111). *See also* A. Wyrozumska, *Direct Application of the Polish Constitution and International Treaties to Private Conduct*, in *Poland's Way to the European Union: Legal Aspects*, ed. W. Czaplinski, Warsaw 2002, pg. 29.

[156] *See, e.g.*, Judgment of Dec. 12, 1997 (II CKN 512/97 OSNC 1998 nr 6, item 105), in which the Supreme Court decided on the scope of its jurisdiction and based its ruling on provisions of the agreement between Poland and Bulgaria. *See also* A. Wyrozumska, *supra* note 2, pg. 572.

[157] III RN 73/98 (OSNP 1999 nr 10, item 326)

[158] *See also* A. Wyrozumska, *supra* note 2, pg. 571.

of international or supranational law. When these treaty-based rules are violated, the aggrieved parties are entitled to vindicate their rights before domestic courts. The court must establish whether the invoked norm has an adequate legal rank – that is, whether it is contained in a duly ratified international treaty (or, in the case of secondary Community law, in a binding Community instrument) and whether it is drafted in a manner allowing its direct applicability. Once those two questions are answered in the affirmative, the court would not differentiate between the legal effects of international and domestic norms. The nature of available remedies as well as the type of relief depends not on the international or domestic nature of the norm in question but on the general regulation of procedural and substantive matters concerning different types of cases and controversies.

In the area of administrative law, the situation is similar. Provisions of international treaties can serve as a legal basis for claiming individual rights against public authorities and as a legal basis for enforcing the obligations of private parties. Community law plays a particularly significant role here, as several important areas of administrative law fall within the competence of the European lawmaker.

In the area of criminal law, domestic regulations play a more independent (which is not to say traditional) role. Nevertheless, international law is present in both the substantive and the procedural law. As to the former, there are a growing number of international agreements defining different types of crimes. If such an agreement is drafted in a self-executing manner, if it meets the requirements of precision and foreseeability, and if its provisions have not been reproduced in domestic legislation, the domestic courts will see no constitutional obstacles to apply a treaty as a sufficient basis for criminal responsibility. In the area of criminal procedure, a significant role is played by international human rights instruments, and particularly by the written provisions of the ECHR and the case law of the ECtHR. Any violation of those provisions that destroys the "fair nature" of a criminal trial constitutes a sufficient ground to quash a conviction.[159]

The absorption of ratified international treaties, as well as secondary Community law, into the domestic legal order results in harmonization of the system of judicial remedies. This phenomenon applies to specific remedies provided within particular branches of law and to general remedies of a civil or constitutional nature. Two types of general remedies are of particular importance.

[159] *See* the Constitutional Tribunal decision of Oct. 15 1997, K 15/97, OTK ZU no 3–4, pgs. 330–31.

The 1997 Constitution (Article 77, Section 1) and the 2004 Amendment to the Civil Code (Articles 417–421) extend the scope of the state's civil liability for unlawful actions or omissions of public authorities or agents. Such liability is borne by the State Treasury if it can be proved that an action or omission has been unlawful (i.e., contrary to the law). The notion of law encompasses all types of generally binding legal regulations, including ratified international treaties and secondary instruments of Community law. This means that, if it can be demonstrated that a public authority has acted in violation of provisions of international or supranational law, an affected person can sue for damages.

Another general remedy is the procedure for constitutional review. As has been already mentioned, the Constitutional Court and other courts have the power to examine the conformity of statutes and substatutory instruments not only with the Constitution but also with international treaties (if ratified on parliamentary authorization) and other instruments of Community law.[160] The procedure is, generally speaking, identical to the procedure of constitutional review. In practice, there have been some cases in which the Constitutional Court has declared that a statutory provision is contrary to an international treaty.[161] There have also been several cases in which civil or administrative courts found that statutory provisions were in collision with Community law and refused their application.[162]

Finally, certain international treaties establish their own system of remedies. A particularly developed procedural protection is provided under the ECHR. As is well known, the Convention guarantees a wide range of personal and political rights and provides that everyone whose rights and/or freedoms have been violated by any public authority can lodge an application with the ECtHR. The Court can award a pecuniary just satisfaction to the victim of the violation and order other remedial measures to be taken by the respondent state. All final judgments of the Court are binding and their execution is supervised by the Council of Ministers of the Council of Europe. Between 1999 and 2006, the Court adopted 318 judgments in which it found that Poland had violated different provisions of the Convention.[163]

[160] *See* A. Wróbel, *supra* note 99.

[161] Compare the decisions by the Constitutional Tribunal of Mar. 12, 2002 (P 9/01, OTK ZU 2002, no 2A, item 14) and Nov. 18, 2002 (K 37/01, OTK ZU 2002, no 6A, item 87).

[162] *See* C. Mik, *supra* note 87 and accompanying text.

[163] European Court of Human Rights, Annual Report 2006 (Strasbourg 2007, pg. 122). Most of those violations related to two issues: 210 judgments involving the length of judicial proceedings and 108 judgments involving the length of pretrial detention.

10

Russian Federation

William E. Butler

John Edward Fowler Distinguished Professor of Law, Dickinson School of Law, Pennsylvania State University

To a degree absolutely without precedent in a millennium of Russian history, international treaties are being used by the Russian state as a means of integrating with the world political, economic, and cultural order. Multilateral and bilateral treaties to which the Russian Federation is a party number in the thousands and regulate all areas of transnational life and activity. Few areas of the law are untouched by treaties. Of those areas regulated by treaty, fewer still have not been affected by treaty enforcement in the Russian judicial and arbitral systems. One may state unequivocally that Russia is among those states that use their legal system to advantage in order to enforce treaties.

The role of Russian domestic courts has been veritably revolutionary in this respect during the past fifteen years. Individuals and juridical persons may invoke treaty rights directly in Russian courts pursuant to Article 15(4) of the Russian Constitution. Judges are encouraged as part of their training to draw on international legal acts when appropriate (and are not necessarily dependent on counsel directing their attention to them).

Treaties occupy a central place in the legal system of the Russian Federation even more so than was the case in the former Soviet Union.[1] The reason is to be found in Article 15(4) of the 1993 Russian Constitution, which provides:[2] "Generally-recognized principles and norms of international law and international treaties of the Russian Federation shall be an integral part of its legal system. If other rules have been established by an international

[1] Although individual Soviet legislative acts recognized the supremacy of treaties in principle, it was controversial in doctrinal writings as to whether the rule was of general application or pertained only to the specific branch of law where such provision was made. For discussion of this, see W. E. Butler, *Soviet Law* (2d ed., 1988).

[2] Trans. in W. E. Butler, *Russian Public Law* (2005), pg. 7; W. E. Butler, *Russia and the Republics: Legal Materials* (loose-leaf service, 2006).

treaty of the Russian Federation than provided for by a law, the rules of the international treaty shall apply."

The meaning and scope of Article 15(4) have been the subject of substantial commentary. The Supreme Court of the Russian Federation (hereinafter, Supreme Court) and Supreme Arbitrazh Court of the Russian Federation (hereinafter, Supreme Arbitrazh Court) have each adopted a decree that glosses the constitutional provision for courts of ordinary jurisdiction and *arbitrazh* courts respectively. Published decisions of Russian courts include a significant number that cite treaties and other international acts. The Russian judicial system has become a central arena in which issues involving the application and enforcement of treaty rules are resolved.

Treaty rules are not solely a matter for the Russian courts, however. Insofar as they are an integral part of the Russian legal system, they are binding on state agencies and officials, juridical persons, citizens, foreigners, and stateless persons and international organizations that are subjects of Russian law. Enforcement responsibilities accordingly rest on state agencies and officials as well as the judicial system.[3]

I. DOMESTIC REGULATION OF TREATIES

For reasons not entirely explicable, the Independent States that continued or succeeded to the Soviet legal tradition have emulated and extended a practice that dates back to 1925 in the Soviet Union: the enactment of special laws to regulate the procedure for the conclusion, ratification, and denunciation of international treaties. The most comprehensive enactment of the Soviet period was the 1978 Law on the Procedure for the Conclusion, Performance, and Denunciation of International Treaties of the USSR.[4] Although treaty-making powers were within the jurisdiction of the fifteen union republics of the Soviet Union and some did actually conclude treaties (including, it should be said, the Treaty of the Union of December 30, 1922, which formed

[3] See [L. B. Arkhipova], ≪Применение судами общепризнанных принципов международного права и международных договоров Российской Федерации при осуществления гражданского и уголовного судопроизводства≫ [Application by Courts of Generally Recognized Principles of International Law and International Treaties of the Russian Federation When Effectuating Civil and Criminal Proceedings], *Российское правосудие* [Russian Justice], no. 6 (2007), pgs. 71–81.

[4] Trans. by W. E. Butler in ILM, XVII (1978), 1115–22; W. E. Butler, *Basic Documents on the Soviet Legal System* (1983), pgs. 285–92; and W. E. Butler, *The Law of Treaties in Russia and the Commonwealth of Independent States: Text and Commentary* (2002), pgs. 218–32. This law was never amended and continued to operate in the Independent States after the Soviet Union was dissolved until each enacted its own law on the subject.

the Soviet Union), none of the union republics had its own legislation on the procedure for treaty making. All the more interesting, therefore, that each felt the need on achieving independence to move reasonably promptly to introduce a law to replace the 1978 USSR law. On the level of comparative foreign relations law, the existence in each Independent State of laws modeled on the 1978 USSR law comprises part of the common core of the Soviet legal legacy that they continue to share and pursue.[5]

In the Russian Federation, the 1978 USSR law was replaced by the Federal Law of the Russian Federation on International Treaties of the Russian Federation of July 15, 1995 (hereinafter, 1995 Federal Law).[6] Articles 5(1) and (2) reproduce verbatim the language of Article 15(4) of the 1993 Russian Constitution quoted earlier. Each component of the formulation has been the subject of detailed gloss in doctrinal writings: international treaties, generally recognized principles, generally recognized norms. This chapter focuses on the judicial enforcement of international treaties, although passing attention will be accorded to general principles and norms and to international acts that do not enjoy the stature of an international treaty.

A number of government decrees and other subordinate normative-legal acts have been adopted in furtherance of the 1995 Federal Law: together, these comprise part of the Russian foreign relations law of treaties.[7] Insofar as an individual treaty is ratified by the Federal Assembly of the Russian Federation or confirmed by decree of the government of the Russian Federation, there are thousands of laws of ratification or decrees of confirmation with respect to individual treaties, together with considerably smaller numbers of enactments that introduce or remove reservations to treaties, denounce treaties, confirm the operation of Soviet treaties for the Russian Federation, empower the signature of or accession to treaties, and the like.

[5] A comparative analysis of and commentary on all the CIS enactments, together with the text of each, is to be found in Butler, *The Law of Treaties*, *supra* note 4. So far as the present writer can determine, these laws were adopted without the benefit of a CIS model law on the subject. On Russian treaty legislation, see also W. E. Butler, "Russia," in D. B. Hollis, M. R. Blakeslee, and L. B. Ederington (eds.), *National Treaty Law and Practice* (2005), pgs. 537–80.

[6] This 1995 law forms the basis for the comparative commentary in Butler, *The Law of Treaties*, *supra* note 4, and appears in its entirety in that volume. It also appears in Butler, *Russian Public Law*, *supra* note 2, pgs. 41–57, and, as amended on December 1, 2007, in Butler, *Russia and the Republics*, *supra* note 2. For a discussion of the amendments, see W. E. Butler, "Treaty Capacity and the Russian State Corporation," 102 Am. J. Int'l L. 310 (2008).

[7] These are discussed and to a considerable extent translated in Butler, *The Law of Treaties*, *supra* note 4.

II. THE JUDICIAL SETTING

The Russian judicial system consists of four components, all of which have responsibility for the application and enforcement of international treaties of the Russian Federation. They are the Constitutional Court of the Russian Federation and equivalent judicial institutions at the level of subjects of the Russian Federation, the Supreme Court and inferior courts of ordinary jurisdiction, the Supreme Arbitrazh Court and inferior arbitrazh courts, and justices of the peace of the Russian Federation. International arbitral tribunals in the Russian Federation, whether permanent or ad hoc, apply international treaties of the Russian Federation insofar as they are applicable to a particular dispute.

All courts of the Russian Federation apply, inter alia, "international treaties of the Russian Federation."[8] The phrase "all courts" embraces the Constitutional Court of the Russian Federation; the Supreme Court of the Russian Federation, supreme courts of the republics, territory and regional courts, courts of cities of Federal significance (Moscow and St. Petersburg), courts of the autonomous region and autonomous national areas, district courts, military and specialized courts comprising the system of courts of general jurisdiction; the Supreme Arbitrazh Court of the Russian Federation, federal arbitrazh courts of precincts, arbitrazh appellate courts, and arbitrazh courts of subjects of the Russian Federation comprising the system of federal arbitrazh courts; the constitutional or charter courts of subjects of the Russian Federation; and justices of the peace.[9]

The Constitutional Court of the Russian Federation is empowered to settle, inter alia, cases concerning the conformity to the Constitution of the Russian Federation of international treaties of the Russian Federation that have not entered into legal force. Both the Supreme Court and the Supreme Arbitrazh Court[10] may request the Constitutional Court to rule on whether treaties that have not entered into force do or do not conform to the 1993 Russian Constitution.

Most cases involving treaties, however, arise in connection with the Court's power to consider: (1) appeals against an alleged violation of constitutional rights and freedoms of citizens or (2) inquiries of courts concerning

[8] Article 3, Federal Constitutional Law on the Judicial System of the Russian Federation of 31 December 1996, as amended; trans. in Butler, *Russian Public Law*, *supra* note 2, pg. 361.
[9] Article 4(3) and (4), id., pg. 362.
[10] Article 10(1)(4), Federal Constitutional Law on Arbitrazh Courts in the Russian Federation of 28 April 1995, as amended; trans. in Butler, *Russian Public Law*, *supra* note 2, pg. 545.

verification of the constitutionality of a law applied or subject to application in a specific case.[11]

The United Nations itself and various UN documents have been mentioned or cited by the Constitutional Court in more than fifty cases. Individual treaties have been cited during the past decade alone in more than twenty-five cases. As an example, in one instance the Constitutional Court observed that, according to the 1993 Russian Constitution, human rights and freedoms have the highest value in the Russian Federation in its capacity as a rule-of-law state. The recognition, compliance with, and defense of the rights and freedoms of man and citizen are the duty of the state and are recognized and guaranteed according to generally recognized principles and norms of international law. Under the Constitution, these principles and norms determine the meaning, content, and application of laws and are enforced by the courts. The right to defend oneself in a court is among the basic inalienable rights and freedoms of man and acts simultaneously as a guarantee of all other rights and freedoms (Article 46(1) and (2), Constitution).

The Constitutional Court said that in pursuance of the said provisions of the Constitution and analogous provisions of the Universal Declaration of Human Rights (Articles 7, 8, and 10), the International Covenant on Civil and Political Rights (Article 14), the Convention on the Protection of Human Rights and Fundamental Freedoms (Article 6, and Article 3 and Article 4(2) of Protocol No. 7 to the Convention in the version of Protocol No. 11), all of which by virtue of Article 15(4) of the Constitution of the Russian Federation are an integral part of the legal system of Russia, it follows that justice is rendered only when it meets the criterion of justness and guarantees effective restoration of the claimant in his or her rights. In the sense of the provisions cited, a judicial decision is subject to review if a newly discovered circumstance or material violations permitted during an earlier consideration incontestably show the existence of judicial error. A materially erroneous decision does not meet the requirements of justness.

The Constitutional Court further held that an essential guarantee of judicial defense is that the parties have the real possibility to bring to the

[11] Article 3(1)(d) and (3), Federal Constitutional Law on the Constitutional Court of the Russian Federation of 21 July 1994, as amended; trans. in Butler, *Russian Public Law*, *supra* note 2, pgs. 454–55. It should be noted that individual cases referred to in this chapter originate in a variety of sources, including archival ones; that they are unofficial reports or excerpts whose authorship is unattributed in the sources themselves and may or may not represent a full statement of the courts concerned. The exception is the Constitutional Court of the Russian Federation, all of whose decisions and rulings are published officially in full.

information of the court their position relative to all aspects of the case. The right to judicial defense can be realized in a judicial session only on this basis, which in the meaning of Article 46(1) and (2) of the Constitution of the Russian Federation and Article 6 of the Convention on the Protection of Human Rights and Fundamental Freedoms should be just, comprehensive, and effective.

It followed in the Court's view that Article 405 of the Code of Criminal Procedure of the Russian Federation was unconstitutional to the extent that it does not allow material violations that lead to the incorrect resolution of the case to be eliminated during the review of a judicial decision by way of supervision on the appeal of the victim or representative thereof or on the submission of a procurator. The Court added that "material violations" are those violations that fall under the criteria provided for by Article 4(2) of Protocol No. 7 to the Convention on the Protection of Human Rights and Fundamental Freedoms (in the version of Protocol No. 11).[12]

Military courts outside the territorial limits of the Russian Federation have subject-matter jurisdiction over civil, administrative, and criminal cases that are subject to consideration by federal courts of general jurisdiction unless established otherwise by an international treaty of the Russian Federation.[13]

As part of their Soviet legal heritage, the Supreme Court and the Supreme Arbitrazh Court have each adopted decrees that are binding on all lower courts within their respective branches of the judicial system addressing the application of treaties. We consider each in turn.

A. *Supreme Court*

On October 10, 2003, the plenum of the Supreme Court adopted Decree No. 5 "On the Application by Courts of General Jurisdiction of Generally-Recognized Principles and Norms of International Law and International

[12] Extracted from the Decree of the Constitutional Court of the Russian Federation Regarding the Case Concerning the Verification of the Constitutionality of Article 405 of the Code of Criminal Procedure of the Russian Federation in Connection with the Request of the Kurgan Regional Court, Appeals of the Plenipotentiary for Human Rights in the Russian Federation, Production-Technical Cooperative "Sodeistvie," Limited Responsibility Society "Karelia," and a Number of Citizens, 11 May 2005, No. 5-П. *СЗ РФ* (2005), no. 22, item 2194; V. G. Strekozov (ed.), *Конституционный Суд Российской Федерации. Постановления. Определения. 2005* [Constitutional Court of the Russian Federation. Decrees. Rulings. 2005] (2006), pgs. 85, 93.

[13] Article 7(4), Federal Constitutional Law on Military Courts of the Russian Federation of 23 June 1999; trans. in Butler, *Russian Public Law*, *supra* note 2, pg. 574.

Treaties of the Russian Federation"[14] for "the purposes of ensuring the correct and uniform application of international law by courts when effectuating justice" (preamble). Decrees of this nature replicate provisions of Russian legislation, as a rule, sometimes with additional gloss and sometimes in a context that appears to lend additional gloss or emphasis.

The plenum of the Supreme Court addressed the following issues of relevance to this analysis. It reiterated that international treaties of the Russian Federation are an integral part of its legal system pursuant to Article 15(4) of the 1993 Russian Constitution and Article 5(1) of the Federal Law on International Treaties of the Russian Federation (1995 Federal Law). Courts were reminded that international treaties in force concluded by the USSR with respect to which the Russian Federation continues to effectuate international rights and obligations of the USSR in its capacity as the state-continuer of the USSR also are part of the legal system of the Russian Federation. The plenum then drew attention to the definition of an "international treaty" contained in Article 2(a) of the 1995 Federal Law (which in essence reproduces the definition contained in the 1969 Vienna Convention on the Law of Treaties). The 1995 Federal Law and Decree No. 5 (point 2), just as the 1969 Vienna Convention, address only treaties "in written form."

The plenum further observes, consistently with the 1978 USSR Law on treaties and the 1995 Federal Law, that there are three categories of international treaties: (1) interstate (concluded in the name of the Russian Federation), (2) intergovernmental (concluded in the name of the government of the Russian Federation), and (3) interdepartmental (concluded in the name of federal agencies of executive power). This classification, which originated in Soviet international legal doctrine and Soviet state practice, plays a crucial role in the Russian approach to the law of treaties, to which we shall return later.

The plenum reminds courts that pursuant to Article 5(3) of the 1995 Federal Law, the provisions of officially published international treaties that do not require the enactment of Russian legislation for application operate directly in the Russian Federation. Whether a treaty is of direct operation or not, the plenum says, can be determined, inter alia, by whether there are indications in the treaty text that the treaty obliges state parties to make changes in their domestic legislation.

[14] Trans. in Butler, *Russian Public Law*, *supra* note 2, pgs. 58–65. This decree replaced that of October 31, 1995, adopted by the same body. See *Бюллетень Верховного Совета Российской Федерации* [Bulletin of the Supreme Court of the Russian Federation], no. 11 (1995).

When deciding whether a treaty may be applied or not, the Russian court is instructed to determine whether the treaty is in force for the Russian Federation and as of what date. Reference is made in this connection to the 1969 Vienna Convention (Article 24). Whether the Russian Federation has expressed consent to be bound by a treaty depends on the competence of the agency expressing such consent and the performance of the actions necessary to give consent (ratification, confirmation, accession, and so on). In this connection the plenum offers a specific example to the lower courts: "the Convention on the Protection of Fundamental Rights and Freedoms was ratified by the Russian Federation by a Federal Law of 30 March 1998 . . . and entered into force for the Russian Federation on 5 May 1998 – the day on which the instrument of ratification was transferred to the Secretary-General of the Council of Europe in accordance with Article 59 of that Convention."[15]

Entry into force, moreover, is not sufficient. Official publication is also required: "those international treaties which have entered into force and which have been published officially in the Собрание законодательства Российской Федерации [Collection of Legislation of the Russian Federation] or in the Бюллетень международных договоров [Bulletin of International Treaties] in the procedure established by Article 30 of the said Federal Law may be applied by courts directly."[16] Courts accept that interdepartmental treaties are published in the official publications of the respective agencies, although in practice these can be exceedingly difficult to obtain. With respect to treaties of the former Soviet Union,

> International treaties of the USSR which are binding upon the Russian Federation as the State-continuer of the USSR have been published in official publications of the Supreme Soviet of the USSR and Council of Ministers (or Cabinet of Ministers) of the USSR. The texts of the said treaties also have been published in the collections of international treaties of the USSR, but this publication was not official.[17]

There is every reason to believe that substantial numbers of USSR treaties were never gazetted and, on the basis of this criterion, not subject to application by Russian courts.

The courts of ordinary jurisdiction and military courts deal primarily with civil, criminal, and administrative cases (as distinct from so-called economic disputes, which are within the jurisdiction of arbitrazh courts).

[15] *Id.*
[16] *Id.*
[17] *Id.*

Accordingly, the plenum of the Supreme Court drew the attention of courts of ordinary jurisdiction and military courts to a number of specific instances when treaties of the Russian Federation would be of express and direct operation, as follows:

> when considering civil cases, if other rules of procedure have been established by an international treaty of the Russian Federation than those by a law of the Russian Federation that regulates relations which have become the subject of judicial examination;
>
> when considering civil and criminal cases, if other rules of procedure have been established by an international treaty of the Russian Federation than by a civil procedure or criminal procedure law of the Russian Federation;
>
> when considering civil or criminal cases, if relations are regulated by an international treaty of the Russian Federation, including relations with foreign persons, which have become the subject of judicial examination (for example, when considering cases provided for in Article 402 of the Code of Civil Procedure of the Russian Federation, petitions concerning the execution of decisions of foreign courts, appeals against decisions concerning the extradition of persons accused of the commission of a crime or convicted by the court of a foreign State);
>
> when considering cases concerning administrative violations, if other rules have been established by an international treaty of the Russian Federation than those provided for by legislation on administrative violations.[18]

The failure to comply with treaty provisions, or the incorrect application of treaty provisions, the plenum cautioned, may be grounds for vacating or changing a judicial act: the incorrect application of a treaty norm may arise when a court failed to apply the norm, or a norm was applied that should not have been applied, or the court incorrectly interpreted the norm. In matters of treaty interpretation the courts were instructed to comply with the 1969 Vienna Convention (Articles 31–33). With respect to the European Convention on Human Rights, the courts must take into account both the text of the Convention and the practice of the European Court for Human Rights.

When international treaties require states parties to enact domestic legislation in order to give effect to the introduction of criminally punishable acts at the international level, in the Russian Federation, such enactments must be incorporated into the Criminal Code of the Russian Federation. Only when the Criminal Code expressly refers a Russian court to the treaty

[18] *Id.*

that contains the indicia of the constituent elements of a crime may the court look to the treaty for the indicia of the offense. Examples of relevant treaties cited by the plenum of the Supreme Court include the 1961 Single Convention on Narcotics, the 1979 International Convention on the Struggle against the Seizure of Hostages, and the 1970 Convention on the Struggle against the Illegal Hijacking of Aircraft; Articles 355 and 356 of the Criminal Code of the Russian Federation are examples of instances when the Criminal Code makes such express references.[19]

Russian courts of ordinary jurisdiction are specifically instructed to resolve issues of the criminal responsibility of diplomatic and consular officials in accordance with international treaties. This direction of the Supreme Court is based on the Criminal Code (Article 11(4)), which provides that persons who enjoy immunity in the event of their committing a crime on the territory of the Russian Federation shall be dealt with in accordance with norms of international law. In short, the Criminal Code was invoked first and international law second. However, the plenum of the Supreme Court then specified some of the relevant applicable treaties: the 1946 Convention on the Privileges and Immunities of the United Nations, the 1947 Convention on the Privileges and Immunities of Specialized Organizations, the 1961 Vienna Convention on Diplomatic Relations, and the 1963 Vienna Convention on Consular Relations.

In a decision rendered in February 2005, the Supreme Court considered a paternity suit filed in Ukraine.[20] O had filed suit to establish that L was the father of Anna, O's daughter. The district court in Ukraine ruled in favor of O and directed L to pay child support. O filed suit in Moscow to request enforcement of the foreign Ukrainian decision. L claimed that the foreign decision was unenforceable because he enjoyed diplomatic immunity at the time when the baby was born and when the Ukrainian court issued its decision. The Moscow City Court decided in favor of O and authorized enforcement of the Ukrainian decision in Russia. L appealed to the Supreme Court, which granted the appeal and vacated the lower court's ruling.

[19] Article 355 of the Criminal Code provides: "The development, production, accumulation, acquisition, or sale of a chemical, biological, toxic, and also other type of mass strike weapon prohibited by an international treaty of the Russian Federation" is punishable. See W. E. Butler, *Criminal Code of the Russian Federation* (4th ed.; 2004), pg. 271. Also see Butler, *Russia and the Republics*, *supra* note 2.

[20] Ruling of Judicial Division for Civil Cases of Supreme Court of Russian Federation, February 1, 2005, No. 5-Г05-1. *Бюллетень Верховного Судв Российской Федерации* [Bulletin of the Supreme Court of the Russian Federation], no. 10 (2005), pgs. 2–4. The Bulletin of the Supreme Court is considered an official publication, but it publishes only case excerpts, not the entire decision.

The Supreme Court said that, in satisfying the petition filed by O concerning enforcement of the decision of a foreign court, the judge of the Moscow City Court came to the conclusion that there were no grounds for refusal provided for by Article 412 of the Code of Civil Procedure of the Russian Federation and Article 55 of the Convention on Legal Assistance and Legal Relations with Regard to Civil, Family, and Criminal Cases of January 22, 1993.

The Supreme Court did not concur with this conclusion. In objecting to satisfaction of the petition filed, L referred in court and in the special appeal to the fact that during the period from December 8, 2000, until December 8, 2004, he was on an extended business trip at the embassy of Russia in Ukraine in the diplomatic post of second secretary of the embassy of Russia and at the time of rendering of the decision by the foreign court on March 16, 2004, enjoyed diplomatic immunity.

In accordance with Ukrainian legislation, the decision of a court concerning the establishment of the paternity of L with respect to a child born of O was not subject to execution at the moment of the entry of the decision into force because it was directed against a person officially having at that moment immunity from civil responsibility in accordance with the 1961 Vienna Convention on Diplomatic Relations, and for the reason that at the moment of his official sojourn in Ukraine in the diplomatic post (including the period from February to March 2004) any consideration of a case with respect to him was relegated to the exclusive jurisdiction of courts of the Russian Federation.

The Supreme Court said that the foregoing arguments, which have material significance for the consideration of the case, were not taken into account by the lower court and received no legal assessment. The reasons for which they were rejected were not cited in the ruling. Moreover, as is evident from the materials of the file of the case, it was established by the court and not contested by the persons participating in the case that L, at the moment of consideration of the case with respect to him concerning the establishment of paternity and recovery of alimony and rendering by the Solomensk District Court, City of Kiev, of the decision, was a member of the diplomatic personnel of the representation of Russia in Ukraine and relegated to the persons specified as diplomatic agents in the Vienna Convention on Diplomatic Relations. This circumstance was confirmed by evidence available in the file of the case, in particular by a reference of the embassy of December 7, 2004, and a copy of the diplomatic card.[21]

[21] *Id.*

The Supreme Court then quoted Article 31 of the Vienna Convention on Diplomatic Relations in its entirety and concluded that the initial suit in Ukraine was not within the jurisdiction of the Ukrainian court, because under Article 31 the case was "relegated to the exclusive jurisdiction of the courts in the Russian Federation." The Supreme Court then added:

> According to Article 412(1)(3) of the Code of Civil Procedure of the Russian Federation a refusal to enforce a decision of a foreign court is permitted if consideration of the case is relegated to the exclusive jurisdiction of courts in the Russian Federation.
>
> Having regard to the above, the conclusion of the court that the petition of O for enforcement of the decision of a foreign court is subject to satisfaction [cannot] be deemed to be legal and substantiated.[22]

Accordingly, the Supreme Court vacated the ruling of the Moscow City Court and refused to satisfy the petition.

In the view of the plenum of the Supreme Court, not all treaties are of equal stature within the Russian legal system. If an international treaty of the Russian Federation establishes rules other than those provided by a federal law, such rules have priority in application with respect to laws of the Russian Federation only if consent to the treaty being binding on Russia was given in the form of a federal law, that is, was ratified by a federal law of the Russian Federation. If consent to a treaty was not given by way of ratification in the form of a federal law, the treaty rules concerned have priority only with respect to subordinate normative-legal acts issued by the agency of state power that concluded the said treaty.[23]

B. *Supreme Arbitrazh Court*

On June 11, 1999, the plenum of the Supreme Arbitrazh Court adopted Decree No. 8 "On the Operation of International Treaties of the Russian Federation with Regard to Questions of Arbitrazh Procedure."[24] There are differences of formulation and emphasis between Decree No. 8 and its counterpart Decree No. 5 of the plenum of the Supreme Court discussed previously. The particular occasion for Decree No. 8 is the provision of

[22] *Id.* (author's translation).

[23] Decree No. 5, *supra* note 14.

[24] The text published in the legal database Consultant Plus has been used. *See also Хозяйство и право* [Economy and Law], no. 11 (1999). The decree has not been revised to take into account the enactment of the Code of Arbitrazh Procedure of 24 July 2002 and was drafted when the Code of Arbitrazh Procedure of 5 May 1995 was in force.

the Code of Arbitrazh Procedure, which stipulated that "if other rules of court proceedings have been established by an international treaty of the Russian Federation than those which have been provided by legislation of the Russian Federation, the rules of the international treaty shall apply."[25]

In April 2000 the Supreme Arbitrazh Court had occasion to apply this provision of the Code of Arbitrazh Procedure when a British juridical person alleged that a tax had been levied in contravention of a bilateral tax treaty. The Supreme Arbitrazh Court stated that when "rendering a decision, the tax inspectorate, in particular, was guided by the Instruction of the State Tax Service of Russia of 16 June 1995, No. 34 'On Taxation of Profit and Revenues of Foreign Juridical Persons.'"[26] According to this instruction, the "withholding of amounts of taxes from revenues of foreign juridical persons is made from sources in the Russian Federation with regard to all types of revenues in all instances of the payment of such revenues, and when there exists an international treaty that establishes lower rates of taxes or complete exemption from taxation in the Russian Federation, the refund of the excess withheld is made in accordance with point 6.2 of the Instruction."[27] Thus, the instruction established the duty to pay taxes in all instances.

However, by virtue of Article 11(1) of the Convention between the Government of the Russian Federation and the Government of the United Kingdom of Great Britain and Northern Ireland of February 15, 1994, for the Avoidance of Double Taxation and the Prevention of Fiscal Evasion with Respect to Taxes on Income and Capital Gains, which entered into force on April 18, 1997, "interest arising in a Contracting State and paid to a resident of the other Contracting State shall be taxable only in that other State if such resident is the beneficial owner of the interest."[28] Thus, in contrast to the aforesaid instruction, the provisions of the international treaty provided for the right of a private person not to pay determined taxes on revenues in the Russian Federation. Accordingly, the Russian Federation did not have the right to recover such taxes from a private person.

Having regard to the fact that the court of first instance did not take into account, in particular, the provisions of this international treaty, the

[25] СЗ РФ (2002), no. 30, item 3012, as amended.

[26] *Вестник Высшего Арбитражного Суда Российской Федерации* [Herald of the Supreme Arbitrazh Court of the Russian Federation], no. 8 (2000) (author's translation).

[27] Id. (quoting the Instruction of the State Tax Service).

[28] Convention between the Government of the Russian Federation and the Government of the United Kingdom of Great Britain and Northern Ireland of 15 February 1994 for the Avoidance of Double Taxation and the Prevention of Fiscal Evasion with Respect to Taxes on Income and Capital Gains

Supreme Arbitrazh Court of the Russian Federation by a decree of April 25, 2000, in Case No. 5029/99 vacated the judicial acts of inferior instances and sent the case for consideration to the court of first instance.[29]

In Decree No. 8, the Supreme Arbitrazh Court also underscored the requirement of publication of a treaty. Decree No. 8 contains the following formulation: "International treaties of the USSR binding upon the Russian Federation by virtue of *legal succession* have been published in collections of international treaties of the USSR"[30] (point 2). The reference to legal succession is an error of law; Russian doctrine holds that the Russian Federation is the legal continuer of the former USSR, and no legal succession occurred. With regard to USSR collections of treaties, which were unofficial, the Supreme Arbitrazh Court has both authorized their use and perhaps been more realistic in recognizing that the collections contain treaty texts otherwise ungazetted. Moreover, the Supreme Arbitrazh Court also recognizes the gazette in which treaties and documents equated thereto concluded within the framework of the Commonwealth of Independent States (CIS) are published: Содружество [Commonwealth].

The Supreme Arbitrazh Court has instructed arbitrazh courts that the operation of treaty rules in time and space is to be determined in accordance with the 1969 Vienna Convention on the Law of Treaties. However, the plenum takes the view that bilateral treaties are *lex specialis* with respect to multilateral treaties of a regional or universal character, a position that contains the embryo of a hierarchy of sources of international law. (Russian doctrine would require that any bilateral arrangements that constituted a form of side agreement with respect to a multilateral treaty must be consistent with the multilateral treaty; Russian courts are not known to have encountered the issue.)

The Russian Federation is party in its capacity of legal continuer and as a member of the CIS to a considerable number of multilateral and bilateral legal assistance treaties that affect the jurisdiction of arbitrazh courts. Among the multilateral treaties named by Decree No. 8 are the Minsk Convention on Legal Assistance and Legal Relations with Regard to Civil, Family, and Criminal Cases of January 22, 1993, and the Kiev Agreement on the Procedure for the Settlement of Disputes Connected with the Effectuation of Economic Activity of March 20, 1992 (which is in the process of being supplanted by the Kishinev Agreement).

[29] *Вестник Высшего Арбитражного Суда Российской Федерации* [Herald of the Supreme Arbitrazh Court of the Russian Federation], no. 8 (2000).

[30] Decree No. 8, *supra* note 24.

In matters of sovereign immunity, an *arbitrazh* court is instructed in Decree No. 8 that when accepting a suit with regard to a commercial dispute in which a foreign state is a defendant in its capacity as a sovereign, or a case involving an interstate organization that has immunities according to an international treaty, the suit may proceed only when the defendant has clearly expressed consent to consideration of the dispute in an arbitrazh court of the Russian Federation. The consent to consideration of the dispute in an arbitrazh court must be signed by persons empowered by legislation of the foreign state or empowered by the internal rules of the international organization to waive immunity.

Arbitrazh courts are directed to take into account that the parties to a foreign economic contract have the right to make provision for referral of disputes to an arbitration court, either ad hoc or permanently operating. In support of the proposition that an arbitrazh court has the right to consider a dispute within its jurisdiction with the participation of a foreign person, provided that the defendant does not petition to transfer the dispute to an arbitration court before its first statement with regard to the essence of the dispute, Decree No. 8 cites Article VI(1) of the 1961 European Convention on Foreign Trade Arbitration. Furthermore, arbitrazh courts, pursuant to the 1958 New York Convention on the Recognition and Enforcement of Arbitration Awards (Article 2(3)), are advised that they may accept a suit for consideration even when there is an arbitration clause in the relevant contract if the arbitration agreement has lost force or cannot be executed. And if the dispute arose from legal relations that are not within the competence of arbitration tribunals, the arbitrazh court may accept the suit for consideration, also citing the 1961 European Convention on Foreign Trade Arbitration.

The principle of national regime operates with respect to the payment of court costs in Russian arbitrazh courts. Foreign natural and juridical persons are required to comply with procedural duties, including court costs, on the same basis as Russian organizations and citizens. Foreign persons from states that are parties to the 1993 Ashkhabad Agreement[31] on the Amount of State Duty and Procedure for the Recovery Thereof When Considering Economic Disputes between Subjects of Economic Management of Different States pay state duty in the procedure provided by that agreement. However, costs connected with converting national currencies when paying state duty in rubles for the consideration of economic disputes between persons from member countries of the CIS are to be regarded as losses arising additionally

[31] Available on Consultant Plus.

because of the defendant's failure to perform its principal obligation – a conclusion whose origin lies in a Decision of the Economic Court of the CIS of February 7, 1996, No. 10/95 C1/3–96.[32]

Judicial commissions within the CIS framework are subject to a special procedure under the 1992 Kiev Agreement, which does not, however, extend to Georgia. Mongolia, which is not part of the CIS, has a special bilateral agreement dating from the former Soviet Union: the Treaty on the Mutual Rendering of Legal Assistance of September 23, 1988 (Article 3(4)).

Legalization of documents in the case of the Russian Federation is dealt with on the basis of the 1961 Hague Convention and, in the case of numerous other countries, mostly former socialist legal systems, without consular legalization on the basis of bilateral legal assistance treaties. Arbitrazh courts may refuse to render legal assistance and to enforce foreign court decisions when treaties are in force only on the grounds set out in the respective treaty.

The courts of ordinary jurisdiction and arbitrazh courts in the Russian judicial system together consider more than 99 percent of all cases in Russian courts. By virtue of the decrees of the Supreme Court and Supreme Arbitrazh Court, the inferior courts are specifically informed about the status of international treaties as an integral part of the Russian legal system. They are also instructed how to interpret and apply particular treaty provisions.

III. THE DOCTRINAL SETTING

The Russian language imposes a constraint on discussions of the law of treaties that is not necessarily found in other languages, certainly not in English. The word in Russian for *treaty* (since the tenth century at least) is also the same word for *contract* [договор]. Whether someone is speaking of one or the other is usually determined on the basis of context, for even introducing the word *international* as an adjective is not conclusive. There are international treaties and international contracts. The Supreme Arbitrazh Court of the Russian Federation faced this issue in a Decree of December 24, 2002,[33] noting that the: "court of cassational instance lawfully pointed out that a contract for the international carriage of goods may not be regarded as carriage provided for by an international treaty (or agreement), the definition of the concept of which is given in

[32] Available on Consultant Plus.

[33] Case No. 6018/02 (available on Consultant Plus).

Article 2(a) of the Federal Law 'On International Treaties of the Russian Federation.'"[34]

The issue is more complicated, however, for even when the meaning of the word is plainly "treaty," there are under Russian law treaties that fall into the classical international legal model governed by the 1969 Vienna Convention on the Law of Treaties and treaties that are not regulated by international law. We leave aside from this discussion arrangements between states that are by common consent between them not treaties.

The 1995 Federal Law replicates and Russian state practice follows the provision of the 1969 Vienna Convention that provides that when determining whether a particular agreement is an international treaty the specific name of the legal act is not decisive. The repertoire of appellations for treaties is as vast in Russian state practice as in the practice of other states. Oral treaties also are known in Russian state practice.[35]

As noted previously, the Russian Federation has incorporated the definition of a treaty contained in the 1969 Vienna Convention (Article 2) into the 1995 Federal Law (Article 2). In doing so, the 1995 Federal Law followed the Vienna Convention by confining itself to an "agreement in written form." During the very late years of the former Soviet Union and the early months in 1992 of the formation of the Russian Federation, a number of entities began to emphasize their independence, autonomy, and international legal personality in various international acts and in local doctrinal writings. Politically, there was genuine apprehension that these centrifugal forces might actually make the Russian Federation unviable. A number of measures were introduced to accommodate these considerations, the most tangible being a set of three documents known in the singular as the Treaty of the Federation or in the plural as the Treaties of the Federation.[36] They are an integral part of the 1993 Russian Constitution. Debate continues as to whether they are true international treaties under the 1969 Vienna

[34] *Бюллетень Высшего Арбитражного Суда Российской Федерации,* [Herald of Supreme Arbitrazh Court of Russian Federation] no. 5 (2003), pg. 6 [hereinafter *Вестник ВАС РФ*].

[35] A favorite example in Russian doctrinal writings is the so-called London Gentleman's Agreement among the Soviet Union, the United States, the United Kingdom and other states concerning the geographical distribution of seats for nonpermanent members of the UN Security Council. Talalaev considered this a legally binding treaty. See Talalaev, *Венская конвенция о праве международных договоров. Комментарий* [Vienna Convention on the Law of International Treaties. Commentary] (1997), pg. 97. Lukashuk believed that this agreement had moral and political, but not legally binding, force. See Lukashuk, *Современное право международных договоров* [Contemporary Law of International Treaties] (2004), vol. 1, pg. 540.

[36] They are translated in Butler, *Russian Public Law, supra* note 2, pgs. 627–44.

Convention or constitutional treaties. In addition, it remains unclear what position they occupy in the hierarchy of sources of Russian law.[37] Zimnenko argues, for example, that "neither a subject of the Federation, nor a natural or juridical person, may be a party to an international treaty."[38] This view makes assumptions about the international legal status of subjects of the Russian Federation that those subjects do not necessarily share. However, in Russian state practice, specific exceptions have been made to consolidate the position. A number of subjects of the Federation have concluded international and foreign economic links with entities in other countries pursuant to the Federal Law on the Coordination of International and Foreign Economic Relations of Subjects of the Russian Federation of January 4, 1999.[39] Certain treaties of the Russian Federation actually address relations between the respective foreign state and subjects of the Federation. Under the Agreement between the Government of the Russian Federation and the Government of Canada on the Principles and Foundations of Cooperation between Subjects of the Russian Federation and Provinces and Territories of Canada of December 18, 2000, "arrangements concluded between subjects of the Russian Federation and provinces and territories of Canada shall not be international treaties."[40]

Because the classification of treaties that eventually found recognition in the 1978 USSR law on treaties and the 1995 Federal Law on treaties had its origins in doctrinal writings, it is not surprising that there continues to be considerable doctrinal discussion of the issue. Article 15(4) of the 1993 Russian Constitution refers to "international treaties" of the Russian Federation without any further qualification. A literal interpretation of this phrase or provision requires that it extend to all treaties of the Russian Federation, including interdepartmental treaties. Some Russian jurists have taken the view, shared by the plenum of the Supreme Court of the Russian Federation,[41] that Article 15(4), read against Article 15(1) of the Constitution, must be construed to mean that only ratified treaties take precedence over laws of the Russian Federation. This would mean that treaties not subject to ratification fall outside the scope of Article 15(4) of the 1993 Constitution and Article 5 of the 1995 Federal Law.

[37] The issues are summarized in Butler, *Russian Law* (2d ed., 2003), pgs. 92–93.

[38] B. L. Zimnenko, *International Law and the Russian Legal System*, trans. W. E. Butler (2007), pg. 205.

[39] Trans. in Butler, *Foreign Investment Law in the Commonwealth of Independent States* (2002), pgs. 579–84.

[40] *Бюллетень международных договоров* [Bulletin of International Treaties], no. 6 (2001), pg. 52 [hereinafter *БМД*]. Russia has analogous treaties with China and Vietnam.

[41] *See supra* note 23 and accompanying text.

The present writer has taken the view that limiting the operation of Article 15(4) of the 1993 Constitution and Article 5 of the 1995 Federal Law to international treaties ratified by the Federal Assembly produces a result that is unconstitutional.[42] On this view, the 1993 Russian Constitution means exactly what it says: all international treaties of the Russian Federation. The legislative history of the relevant provisions confirms this position. In both the Constitutional Conference,[43] which drafted the 1993 Constitution, and in working groups that prepared the draft 1995 Federal Law, proposals were made to insert the requirements of ratification with respect to this supremacy clause, and both times the proposals were rejected.[44]

This view has been questioned by many Russian jurists.[45] Narrower constructions have been posited, although none accepts the literal meaning of the relevant provisions. One such approach notes that two variations may arise with respect to a treaty establishing rules other than those contained in a federal law. The first arises when a treaty introduces significant changes in legislation by adding to or replacing norms or by laying down different general rules. In the second situation, the treaty establishes other rules only for a specific situation, without affecting the operation of rules of a normative-legal act as a whole, for example by creating an exception from the general legislative norm for a particular case: "In the first instance one speaks of the priority of the rule of a treaty over a rule of law. In the second, about the priority of the application of a rule of a treaty in specific conditions."[46] Understanding these two variations, it is argued, helps to understand why the term *ratification* was excluded from Article 15(4) of the 1993 Russian Constitution and from Article 5 of the 1995 Federal Law. Refusing to apply a treaty concluded without ratification would prejudice

[42] See Butler, The Law of Treaties, *supra* note 4, pg. 41.

[43] For the verbatim transcripts of the Constitutional Conference, see *Конституционное совещание. Стенограммы. Материалы. Документы* [Constitutional Assembly. Verbatim Transcripts. Materials. Documents. 29 April–10 November 1993] (1995–1996, 21 vols.).

[44] See I. I. Lukashuk, in V. M. Zhuikov (ed.), *Международные нормы о правах человека и применение их судами Российской Федерации. Практическое пособие* [International Norms on Human Rights and the Application Thereof by Courts of the Russian Federation. Practical Manual] (1996), pg. 10.

[45] Especially by Russian public lawyers. See, e.g., S. Polenina, who criticized the 1993 Russian Constitution for failing to include the adjective *ratification* in Article 15(4) and urged that the provision be interpreted as though the word had been included. See S. Polenina, in L. A. Morozova, ≪Российская правовая система и международное право: современные проблемы взаимодействия≫ [Russian Legal System and International Law: Contemporary Problems of Interaction], *Государство и право*, no. 2 (1996), pg. 5.

[46] Lukashuk, *supra* note 35, pg. 10.

the authority of the state, which bears state responsibility for the obligations assumed under intergovernmental and interdepartmental treaties, and would severely limit the role of both of the last categories of treaties in the regulation of international relations.

Nonetheless, there is great reluctance to extend this point to intergovernmental and interdepartmental treaties. Both the decrees of the Supreme Court, as noted previously, took the view that interdepartmental treaties enjoy priority only with respect to acts of the respective ministry, state committee, or other department.[47] Another Russian jurist has argued that, first, "only the Russian Federation has been endowed with the legal personality to conclude international treaties; second, an international treaty of the Russian Federation must acquire the form and status of a federal law. Therefore, neither intergovernmental treaties nor treaties of an interdepartmental character fall under the definition... of an international treaty of the Russian Federation."[48]

One reason for the considerable doctrinal disquiet with the proposition that all treaties of the Russian Federation fall under Article 15(4) of the 1993 Constitution originates in Russian concepts of the hierarchy of normative legal acts. Interstate ratified treaties can be reasonably accommodated within the hierarchy because such treaties presumably (1) are consistent with the 1993 Constitution and (2) consent to their being binding on Russia takes the form of a federal law on ratification. Notwithstanding the supremacy formulation of Article 15(4), it is the existence of the federal ratification law that satisfies Russian public lawyers. The absence of such a law with respect to intergovernmental and interdepartmental treaties disturbs, in their view, the hierarchy of sources of Russian law.[49] Their apprehension is that a Russian ministry, for example, may by means of concluding an agreement with the ministry of a foreign state introduce a rule that is not

[47] Also see Lukashuk and Naumov, who observed: "Other treaties also enter the legal system of the country, but only at their own level. Treaties confirmed by the Government have priority with respect to governmental and other inferior acts. Agreements of an interdepartmental character do not fall within the operation of Article 15 of the Constitution at all and enjoy priority only with respect to acts which the department has concluded." *See* I. I. Lukashuk and A. V. Naumov, *Международное уголовное право. Учебник* [International Criminal Law. Textbook] (1999), pgs. 21–22.

[48] V. M. Volozhenkina, *Нормы международного права в российском уголовном процессе* [Norms of International Law in Russian Criminal Procedure] (2001), pg. 78. Volzhenkina goes on to suggest that Article 5 of the 1995 Federal Law, insofar as it does include intergovernmental and interdepartmental treaties within the category of international treaties of the Russian Federation, is unconstitutional.

[49] For details, *see* V. A. Tolstikh, *Иерархия российского и международного права* [Hierarchy of Russian and International Law] (2001).

consistent with a federal law and under the supremacy of treaties doctrine effectively legislate by treaty, whereas the normative-legal enactments of the ministry could not change a federal law and if inconsistent therewith would be invalid. On this view, the ministry could make an end run around federal laws by means of a treaty.

Chernichenko explained the issue as follows:

> automatic incorporation of the provisions contained therein into the internal law of a State (and, consequently, the incorporation of the provisions contained therein into the internal law of a State) is the shortest path to the maximum synchronization of international and municipal-law creation. It should extend to all treaties, taking into account the level of the treaties: treaties of the highest level as a result of incorporation should have the status of laws; those to be concluded by the Government and not subject to incorporation – the status of acts of the Government; and interdepartmental treaties – the status of acts adopted by departments.[50]

The reason for this approach, says Chernichenko, is to determine the priority of incorporated treaties, depending on their level, vis-à-vis municipal acts of the respective level.[51]

The answer to this apprehension lies in the 1995 Federal Law and the internal procedures for reviews and approvals that must precede the conclusion of any international treaty of an intergovernmental or interdepartmental character. If those procedures are properly complied with, there should be no instances of an international treaty at any level being inconsistent with a federal law in an improper manner. Nonetheless, it has been noticed that "the notion has begun to form in doctrine, correct in our view, that a ratified international agreement is a normative act possessing in the municipal sphere legal force equal to the force of that act by which it was ratified."[52]

There is no language in either the 1993 Russian Constitution or the 1995 Federal Law to sustain this view. Moreover, there is disagreement in Russian doctrinal writings as to what should be understood by "laws" in this connection. While nearly all accept that laws at a minimum means federal

[50] *See* S. V. Chernichenko, *Теория международного права: старые и новые теоретические проблемы* [Theory of International Law: Old and New Theoretical Problems] (1999), vol. 2, pgs. 350–51, 357.

[51] *Id.*

[52] See M. A. Pshenichnov, ≪Юридико-технические средства обеспечения соответствия российского законодательства международному праву≫ [Juridical-Technical Means of Ensuring the Conformity of Russian Legislation to International Law], in V. M. Baranov (ed.), *Проблемы юридической техники: сборник статей* [Problems of Legal Technique: Collection of Articles] (2000), pg. 189.

laws, some would extend the word to encompass federal constitutional laws and the 1993 Russian Constitution itself, together with laws adopted by subjects of the Russian Federation and all other normative-legal acts. On this view, treaty norms "affect all laws irrespective of the time of their adoption: before or after the conclusion of the treaty."[53] Others contend that "in recognizing the priority of international law over municipal legislation [this] does not extend . . . to the Basic Law of the country"[54] or to federal constitutional laws.[55]

Russian doctrine and judicial practice recognize that a treaty must have entered into force in order to operate within the spheres of interstate relations and municipal relations. Talalaev observed, "[I]t is essential to distinguish the entry into force of an international treaty, when a treaty begins to operate as a source of international law, that is, create rights and duties for the participants thereof, and entry into force of a treaty for a specific State."[56] The entry into force of an international treaty means, Talalaev observed elsewhere, "that the provisions of the treaty have become binding on its participants and that a violation thereof, the failure to fulfill the treaty, will entail certain international-legal consequences, including responsibility of the offending State."[57] It follows that an international treaty may be a source of international law but not binding on an individual party because that party has not yet expressed its ultimate consent to the treaty, or such consent has been expressed but the sufficient minimum of other states necessary for the treaty to enter into force has not been achieved.

In Russian judicial practice, the position has arisen as follows. In March 1997 the Russian Federation signed a treaty with certain other CIS member countries. Under Article 3 of the treaty, the parties agreed to provide housing for designated individuals who had been discharged from military

[53] V. I. Andrianov, in Iu. V. Kudriavtsev (ed.), *Комментарий к Конституции Российской Федерации* [Commentary on the Constitution of the Russian Federation] (1996), pgs. 80–81.

[54] V. A. Kartashkin, *Права человека в международном и внутригосударственном праве* [Human Rights in International and Municipal Law] (1995), pg. 17.

[55] Lukashuk, *Конституция государств и международное право* [The Constitution of States and International Law] (1998), pg. 69.

[56] A. N. Talalaev, ≪Соотношение международного и внутригосударственного права и Конституции Российской Федерации≫ [Correlation of International and Municipal Law and the Constitution of the Russian Federation], *Московский журнал международного права* [Moscow Journal of International Law], no. 4 (1994), pg. 9.

[57] Talalaev, ≪Два вопроса международного права в связи с Конституцией Российской Федерации≫ [Two Questions of International Law in Connection with the Constitution of the Russian Federation], *Государство и право* [State and Law], no. 3 (1998), pgs. 67–68.

service and their family members. In September 1998 the Russian Government confirmed rules regulating the allocation of housing to individuals discharged from military service. Suit was brought in the Russian courts by an individual who claimed that the rules confirmed in September 1998 were not consistent with the treaty of 1997. The Supreme Court denied satisfaction of the suit on the grounds that the Russian Federation had not at the time ratified the 1997 treaty, and therefore there was no requirement that the 1998 rules necessarily comply with the treaty obligations.[58]

Being a party to the 1969 Vienna Convention, Russia accepts the provisions of Article 25 concerning the provisional entry into force of a treaty if the treaty itself so provides or if the negotiating states have otherwise agreed. Such arrangements are known to Russian state practice; for example, the Agreement between the Russian Federation and the Republic of Kazakhstan on Cooperation and Interaction in Ensuring the Security of the "Baikonur" Complex of Military Formations of the Russian Federation Temporarily on the Territory of the Republic of Kazakhstan and Their Staff.[59] Under Article 15 of this agreement, the treaty applies provisionally from the moment of signature but is subject to ratification. The question nonetheless remains whether under the 1995 Russian Federal Law the Russian-Kazakh agreement is in force within the municipal legal system of the Russian Federation. Talalaev vigorously opposed the proposition that it could be in force. Provisionally applied international treaties, he observed, are not subject to official publication and therefore are not part of the Russian legal system. There may be a good-faith obligation to comply with a treaty provisionally in force, but as a matter of municipal law, the treaty does not exist. If the parties wish to enforce the provisionally agreed treaty at the municipal level, they must arrange for official publication of the document.[60]

Russian courts have been criticized for failing to be rigorous in determining the precise date of entry into force of individual treaties: "One may consider usual the situation when courts of all types do not establish (or in any event do not note in decisions regarding cases) the existence of the legal conditions for the possible application of a specific treaty. One of these is the fact of the recognition of the treaty being binding on the Russian Federation."[61]

[58] Available on Consultant Plus.
[59] Available on Consultant Plus.
[60] Talalaev, *supra* note 56.
[61] S. Iu. Marochkin, ≪К 10-летию Конституции Российской Федерации: проблемы реализации принципа о нормах международного права как составной части правовой системы России≫ [On the Tenth Anniversary of the Constitution of the

This has been emphasized in Russian state practice. The treaties between the Russian Federation and Ukraine on the Russo-Ukrainian Border of January 28, 2003, and on cooperation and use of the Sea of Azov and Kerch Strait of December 24, 2003, were subject to ratification and entered into force from the date of exchange of instruments of ratification. The federal laws on their ratification adopted April 22, 2004, did not provide for their entry into force from the moment of publication. Consequently, they entered into force according to the general rule: on the expiry of ten days after publication. The exchange of instruments of ratification occurred on April 23, 2004, that is, earlier than the completion of the process of ratification. When the treaties were published, the date was indicated of their entry into force – April 23, 2004.[62]

Russia to be sure recognizes the relevance of Article 18 of the 1969 Vienna Convention and the duty of a state that has signed a treaty or exchanged instruments constituting the treaty subject to ratification, acceptance, or approval to refrain from actions that would defeat the object and purpose of the treaty. A celebrated example in Russian state practice is Protocol No. 6 to the 1950 European Convention for the Protection of Human Rights and Fundamental Freedoms, which prohibits the death penalty as a criminal punishment during peacetime. Russia signed the protocol on April 16, 1997, but has not yet ratified it. Application of the death penalty by Russian courts of general jurisdiction has, however, been suspended by reason of signature of the protocol.[63]

Pursuant to the 1995 Federal Law, Decree No. 5 of the Supreme Court, and Decree No. 8 of the Supreme Arbitrazh Court, and Russian doctrinal writings, official publication of an international treaty is regarded as an absolute prerequisite for the realization of the treaty provisions within the sphere of municipal legal relations. Although oral treaties cannot satisfy this

Russian Federation: Problems of Realization of the Principle on Norms of International Law as an Integral Part of the Legal System of Russia], in *Обще-признанные принципы и нормы международного права и международные договоры в практике конституционного правосудия* [Generally Recognized Principles and Norms of International Law and International Treaties in the Practice of Constitutional Justice] (2004), pg. 52.

62 Cited in V. Ia. Suvorova, "Entry of Treaties into Force," *Russian Law: Theory and Practice*, no. 2 (2006), pg. 207.

63 The same appears to be true of the Soviet Union–United States agreement on delimitation of the continental shelf in the Bering Sea, for which formalities have been concluded by the United States but not by the Russian Federation. In the case of the death penalty, there is a presidential edict suspending its application that is binding on Russian courts. If a Russian court assigns the death penalty, it will be commuted to life imprisonment, which happens in practice.

requirement, Russian doctrinal writings cite with approval the state practice of the United States as expressed in the Case Act, which (according to Russian commentators) requires that all oral agreements should be clothed in written form and communicated to the Congress of the United States.[64] As a result, Russian courts would not apply an oral treaty and have insisted that official publication of a treaty be proved in court. Although Russian legislation regulating the publication of federal laws requires that treaties be published in stipulated official gazettes, in practice such publication often has been delayed or simply has not occurred, for reasons unknown. Failure to publish does not appear to relate to questions of secrecy, which is a separate matter. There either has been administrative inertia or priorities have been accorded to other matters.

Ordinarily, a treaty of the Russian Federation is published immediately following entry into force for the Russian Federation. However, the period of time between the entry into force of a treaty and its publication may be as long as several years. The Treaty between the Russian Federation and the Estonian Republic on Legal Assistance and Legal Relations with Regard to Civil, Family, and Criminal Cases entered into force March 20, 1995, but was officially published only in 1998.[65] The Agreement on the Legal Regime of Information Resources of Border Forces of States-Participants of the Commonwealth of Independent States, which entered into force November 25, 1998, was not officially published in the official treaty bulletin until July 2001. The Agreement between the Government of the Russian Federation and the Government of the Kingdom of Spain on Cooperation and Mutual Assistance in Customs Matters of June 14, 2000, entered into force on December 14, 2000. However, it was officially published only in August 2004.

Decree No. 5 of the plenum of the Supreme Court provides:

> Proceeding from the meaning of Article 15(3) and (4) of the Constitution of the Russian Federation and Article 5(3) of the Federal Law "On International Treaties of the Russian Federation," those international treaties which have entered into force and which have been published officially in the Собрание законодательства Российской Федерации [Collection of Legislation of the Russian Federation] or in the Бюллетень международных договоров [Bulletin of International Treaties] in the

[64] *See* Lukashuk, *supra* note 35, vol. 1, pg. 533. Approval notwithstanding, the 1995 Federal Law requires publication only of treaties in written form and makes no provision for oral treaties.

[65] *СЗ РФ* (1998), no. 2, item 229; *БМД*, no. 3 (1998), pgs. 12–32. This example and the two following are drawn from Zimnenko, *supra* note 30, pgs. 225–26.

procedure established by Article 30 of the said Federal Law may be applied by courts directly. International treaties of the Russian Federation of an interdepartmental character shall be published by decision of federal agencies of executive power in the name of which such treaties have been concluded in the official publications of those agencies.

International treaties of the USSR which are binding upon the Russian Federation as the State-continuer of the USSR have been published in official publications of the Supreme Soviet of the USSR and Council of Ministers (or Cabinet of Ministers) of the USSR. The texts of the said treaties also have been published in the collections of international treaties of the USSR, but this publication was not official.

Official communications of the Ministry of Foreign Affairs of the Russian Federation concerning the entry into force of international treaties concluded in the name of the Russian Federation and in the name of the Government of the Russian Federation shall be subject to publication in the same procedure as international treaties (Article 30, Federal Law "On International Treaties of the Russian Federation").[66]

The requirement of official publication is deemed to date from July 15, 1995, the date on which the 1995 Federal Law entered into force, with respect to the sources named in the foregoing quotation. Other official sources for treaties operated from January 1, 1992, to July 15, 1995.

Russian legal doctrine links publication of treaties with the constitutional right of natural and juridical persons to know the law. The 1993 Russian Constitution (Article 15(3)) provides that "any normative legal acts affecting the rights, freedoms, and duties of man and citizen may not be applied if they have not been published officially for general information." An international treaty of the Russian Federation falls into the category of normative legal acts. Lukashuk wrote: "the requirement of publication, promulgation of treaties arises from one of the major principles of law recognized by civilized nations, in accordance with which a person is obliged to comply only with those norms of law which have been published in generally-accessible form. A law does not oblige if not published (*non obligat lex nisi promulgata*)."[67]

[66] Trans. in Butler, *Russian Public Law*, *supra* note 2, pg. 60.

[67] Lukashuk, *Международное право в судах государств* [International Law in the Courts of States] (1993), pg. 133. Zimnenko rightly observes that this does not exhaust the possible applications of an unpublished international treaty. Although an unpublished treaty might not be applied to legal relations involving natural and juridical persons, it might be drawn on when reforming legislation or to assist in interpreting rules of municipal law, among others. *See* Zimnenko, *supra* note 30, pg. 222. In contrast, it would be wrong to treat this as a doctrine intended to impede the domestic judicial enforcement of Russian

Russian courts have been zealous in enforcing the requirement of official publication. In February 2001 a cotton depot filed suit against a customhouse to challenge a demand for the payment of customs charges. The plaintiff contended that it was exempt from customs charges under the terms of the Agreement between the Government of the Russian Federation and the Government of the Kyrgyz Republic on the Principles of Recovery of Indirect Taxes in Mutual Trade, which was concluded on October 10, 2000. The arbitrazh court of first instance ruled in favor of the plaintiff and the customs house appealed. The appellate court found that, even though the treaty had entered into force on January 1, 2001, the treaty remained unpublished in February 2001, when the plaintiff challenged the charges imposed. Since the treaty had not been officially published, the appellate court upheld the position that the agreement was not subject to application.[68]

Moreover, judicial practice demonstrates that the courts are attentive not merely to the fact of official publication but also to the precise date of official publication and its implications for the legal relations of the parties to a case. For example, in one case, the Supreme Arbitrazh Court of the Russian Federation reviewed a decision by the Arbitrazh Court of the Voronezh Region.[69] In that case, the customs collector had imposed an import duty on sugar imported into Russia from Moldova. The importer claimed that the sugar was exempt from customs duties under the Agreement between the Council of Ministers – Government of the Russian Federation and the Government of the Republic of Moldova on Free Trade of February 9, 1993. In contrast, the government contended that the sugar was not exempt from

treaty obligations. Although secret diplomacy and secret treaties as a feature of interstate relations have been criticized for decades in doctrinal writings and lamented, to the extent that international law is brought into municipal legal systems or that individuals or associations thereof are brought under the purview of international law, whether as subjects or otherwise, the relative permissiveness of international law with respect to the registration and publication of treaties can not survive a rule-of-law test insofar as natural and juridical persons are concerned. They must be able to have knowledge of the law, and Russian courts are zealous in enforcing this requirement. One result has been the publication in Russian treaty bulletins and other gazettes of treaties apparently long "forgotten." *See* W. E. Butler, "Foreign Relations Law as State Practice," in W. E. Butler (ed.), *Perestroika and International Law* (Dordrecht: Martinus Nijhoff, 1990), pgs. 109–20.

[68] This decree of the Federal Arbitrazh Court of Volga-Viatka District of August 28, 2001, has not been published. *See* Archive of the Court, Case No. 490/5-K; cited in Zimnenko, *supra* note 30, pgs. 222–23.

[69] *Вестник ВАС РФ* [Herald of the Supreme Arbitrazh Court of the Russian Federation], no. 5 (2005), pgs. 28–34.

customs duties because Russia and Moldova had signed a protocol in May 2001 that modified the 1993 agreement.

The Supreme Arbitrazh Court observed that in accordance with Article 1(1) of the Agreement on Free Trade of February 9, 1993, the contracting parties do not apply customs duties, taxes, and charges on the export and/or import of goods emanating from the customs territory of one of the contracting parties and intended for the customs territory of another contracting party. Exceptions from the trade regime are formalized by bilateral documents that are considered an integral part of this agreement. Later, on May 29, 2001, the protocol was signed on making changes in and additions to the said agreement, in which it was provided that the parties shall inform one another about the introduction of exceptions from the regime of free trade in goods specified in Annexes 1 and 2 (this list included white sugar) not less than two months before their introduction (Article 1(3), Protocol of May 29, 2001).

The file of the case contained a statement of the Ministry of Economic Development and Trade of Russia of January 17, 2002, which might have been regarded as notification concerning the exceptions from the free-trade regime. However, the file did not contain any evidence showing that the statement of January 17, 2002, was published in a manner that brought to general information the exceptions from the free-trade regime. Moreover, the lower court failed to investigate this question, as it should have done.

The government of the Russian Federation did publish the Protocol of May 29, 2001. However, the Court said, the fact of official publication of the protocol cannot serve as evidence that the Russian party provided notice of the exceptions because the protocol provides only for the possibility of the introduction of exceptions. Therefore, the Supreme Arbitrazh Court rejected the government's argument that the exceptions from the free trade regime took effect from January 29, 2002. The Supreme Arbitrazh Court reversed the decision of the lower court because that court did not investigate whether the Russian Federation had fulfilled its municipal procedures to bring to general information the introduction of exceptions from the free-trade regime in goods with the Republic of Moldova.[70]

The attentiveness of the courts to the technicalities of official publication in the foregoing case worked in favor of the liberalization of trade policies in that exceptions from the free-trade regime and concomitant imposition of customs duties and charges were not properly notified and had not entered

[70] *Вестник ВАС РФ* [Herald of the Supreme Arbitrazh Court of the Russian Federation], no. 5 (2005), pgs. 28–34.

into force at the time imagined by the customs agencies. But from the standpoint of the law of treaties, punctilious compliance with the formalities of publication and notice is being required by the Russian courts requested to enforce treaty provisions.

IV. INTERACTION WITH FOREIGN AND INTERNATIONAL COURTS AND TRIBUNALS

A. *Awards of Russian International Arbitral Tribunals*

On July 7, 1993, the Russian Federation adopted the Law on International Commercial Arbitration, partly to take into account the provisions concerning such arbitration contained in international treaties of the Russian Federation.[71] There are hundreds of arbitration courts established in the Russian Federation. Whether they have jurisdiction over foreign matters or not, insofar as they apply Russian law to cases they also apply relevant international treaties of the Russian Federation. Beyond doubt, however, the most important and influential permanently operating arbitration court is the International Court of Commercial Arbitration, known by its Russian acronym MKAC, and its sister tribunal, the Maritime Arbitration Commission (MAK).

Both MKAC and MAK, unlike most arbitral tribunals around the world, perform a signal service by publishing their awards in summary form with commentary, the names of the parties, and proprietary commercial information being excised or obscured. All treaties cited in the published awards have been indexed in the relevant volumes of arbitral practice. For the years 1996 and 1997, the 1980 UN Convention on Contracts for the International Sale of Goods (CISG) was cited in twenty-nine cases at MKAC; the 1972 Moscow Convention, in six cases; the 1961 European Convention on Foreign Trade Arbitration, in one case; the 1958 New York Convention on the Recognition and Enforcement of Arbitration Awards, in one case; and the 1992 Kiev Agreement on the Procedure for the Settlement of Economic Disputes, in one case.[72] For the years 1999 and 2000, the CISG was the basis of awards rendered in twenty-seven cases and was deemed not applicable in two cases. The 1972 Moscow Convention was cited in two awards; the 1961 European Convention on Foreign Trade Arbitration, in three; and the 1958

[71] Trans. in Butler, *Russian Company and Commercial Law* (2003), pg. 839.

[72] See M. G. Rozenberg (comp.), *Арбитражная практика за 1996–1997 гг.* [Arbitral Practice for 1996–1998] (1998), pgs. 274–76. All treaties cited are available on Consultant Plus.

New York Convention, in one.[73] The same treaties for the years 2001 and 2002 were invoked: the CISG, twenty-six cases; the 1972 Moscow Convention, one case; the 1961 European Convention on Foreign Trade Arbitration, two cases; and the 1958 New York Convention in one case.[74] The figures are consistent and analogous for 2003 to 2006.[75]

In summary, international treaties are accordingly routinely applied, interpreted, and enforced in Russian arbitral practice.

B. *Recognition and Enforcement of Foreign Judicial Decisions*

The legislation of the Russian Federation, just as that of the former Soviet Union, is categorical in requiring the presence of an international treaty in force between the Russian Federation and any foreign state whose judicial decisions are to be considered for recognition and enforcement in the Russian Federation.[76] The same applies to foreign arbitral awards. The Russian Federation, however, is party to the 1958 New York Convention on the Recognition and Enforcement of Arbitral Awards (a multilateral treaty with more than 140 parties), which means that in principle foreign arbitral awards enjoy a greater likelihood of being enforced in Russia simply because few countries outside Central Europe, Mongolia, China, Vietnam, and Cuba have bilateral treaties with Russia regulating the recognition and enforcement of judicial decisions.

[73] *See* M. G. Rozenberg (comp.), *Практика международного коммерческого арбитражного суда при ТПП РФ за 1999–2000 гг.* [Practice of the International Commercial Arbitration Court Attached to the Chamber of Commerce and Industry of the Russian Federation for 1999–2000] (2002), pgs. 328–30.

[74] *See* M. G. Rozenberg (comp.), *Практика международного коммерческого арбитражного суда при ТПП РФ за 2001–2002 гг.* [Practice of the International Commercial Arbitration Court Attached to the Chamber of Commerce and Industry of the Russian Federation for 2001–2002] (2004), pgs. 488–89.

[75] *See* M. G. Rozenberg (comp.), *Практика международного коммерческого арбитражного суда при ТПП РФ за 2003 г.* [Practice of the International Commercial Arbitration Court Attached to the Chamber of Commerce and Industry of the Russian Federation for 2003] (2004); Rozenberg (comp.), *Практика международного коммерческого арбитражного суда при ТПП РФ за 2004 г.* [Practice of the International Commercial Arbitration Court Attached to the Chamber of Commerce and Industry of the Russian Federation for 2004] (2005); Rozenberg (comp.), *Практика международного коммерческого арбитражного суда при ТПП РФ за 2005 г.* [Practice of the International Commercial Arbitration Court Attached to the Chamber of Commerce and Industry of the Russian Federation for 2005] (2006); Rozenberg (comp.), *Практика международного коммерческого арбитражного суда при ТПП РФ за 2006 г.* [Practice of the International Commercial Arbitration Court Attached to the Chamber of Commerce and Industry of the Russian Federation for 2006] (2008).

[76] *See* Butler, *Russian Foreign Relations and Investment Law* (2006), paras. 7.120–7.135.

The requirement of an international treaty as a prerequisite for enforcement of foreign judicial decisions was laid down by the Edict of the Presidium of the Supreme Soviet of the USSR on June 21, 1988. That edict continues to be in force, except insofar as it may be contrary to the Code of Arbitrazh Procedure. The 2002 Code of Arbitrazh Procedure (Article 241) and 2002 Code of Civil Procedure (Article 409) confirm the general rule: decisions of courts of foreign states are recognized and enforced when an international treaty of the Russian Federation so provides. In Russian state practice, such treaties routinely take the form of legal assistance treaties and appear with some frequency in published case reports.

In 2005 the Supreme Court issued a ruling that modified a decision of a regional court to execute the decision of a Kazakhstan court.[77] The Kazakhstan court had issued a decision in favor of a Kazakhstan citizen directing a male Russian citizen to pay child support for his son. When the Russian citizen appealed, the Supreme Court explained its ruling as follows. According to Article 409(1) of the Code of Civil Procedure of the Russian Federation, decisions of foreign courts are recognized and executed in the Russian Federation if this has been provided by an international treaty of the Russian Federation. The Russian Federation and the Republic of Kazakhstan (of which the applicant was a citizen) are parties to the Convention on Legal Assistance and Legal Relations with Regard to Civil, Family, and Criminal Cases of January 22, 1993 (hereinafter, the Convention). Under Articles 53 and 54 of the Convention, a court considering a petition to recognize and authorize the enforcement of a decision must first establish whether the conditions provided for by the Convention have been complied with. If the conditions have been complied with, the court renders a decision to enforce. The grounds for a refusal to recognize and execute decisions of courts of the contracting parties are enumerated in Article 55 of the Convention and Article 412(1) of the Code of Civil Procedure of the Russian Federation.

The Supreme Court believed that, in satisfying the petition concerning the recognition and enforcement of the decision of a foreign court on the territory of the Russian Federation, the regional court lawfully proceeded from the fact that grounds for refusal to enforce the decision of the foreign court were absent. However, the ruling of the court indicates that child support should be recovered commencing from September 23, 2004.

[77] Ruling of Judicial Division for Civil Cases, Supreme Court of the Russian Federation (4th Quarter 2005), No. 82-Г05–11. *Бюллетень Верховного Суда Российской Федерации* [Bulletin of the Supreme Court of the Russian Federation], no. 5 (2006), pg. 11.

It is provided in Article 54(3) of the Convention that the procedure for enforcement is determined under the legislation of the contracting party on whose territory enforcement should be effectuated. Decisions of a foreign court are executed in the Russian Federation in accordance with the federal law of July 21, 1997: On an Execution Proceeding. By virtue of Article 70 of the said federal law, the procedure for the recovery of child support and indebtedness with regard to child support obligations is determined by the Family Code of the Russian Federation. Observing that under Article 113 of the Family Code of the Russian Federation, overdue child support is recovered either on the basis of an agreement to pay child support or on the basis of a writ of execution, provided that the writ is presented within three years, or a notarially certified agreement concerning payment of child support. When determining that child support was to be recovered on the territory of the Russian Federation from September 23, 2004, the Court did not take into account the aforesaid norms of the Convention or the Family Code of the Russian Federation. Therefore, the recovery of child support from September 23, 2004, was deemed by the Judicial Division to be incorrect.

In addition, in the resolutive part of the ruling the Court decreed to recover from the debtor child support in the amount of not less than one nonleviable minimum revenues of a citizen (a monthly minimum established by the state that every employed citizen is entitled to be paid; it is adjusted from time to time for inflation). However, the decision of the Kazakhstan court contained no such requirement. Consequently, the regional court actually changed the decision of the foreign court. The court was not endowed by the Convention or by the Code of Civil Procedure of the Russian Federation with this power with respect to the decision of a foreign court. Therefore, the Judicial Division for Civil Cases of the Supreme Court changed the ruling of the regional court by excluding from the resolutive part the reference to recovering child support commencing from September 23, 2004, in the amount as designated.

C. *Decisions of the European Court of Human Rights*

On March 30, 1998, the Russian Federation adopted the federal law On the Ratification of the Convention for the Protection of Human Rights and Fundamental Freedoms and Protocols Thereto, thereby completing the legislative process for ratification of the European Convention on Human Rights of November 4, 1950 (ECHR), with the changes made by Protocols Nos. 3, 5, and 8 and additions contained in Protocol No. 2 and Protocols thereto Nos. 1, 4, 7, 9, 10, and 11. These treaty documents became binding on the Russian Federation from May 5, 1998, except that Protocol No. 7 entered into force for Russia from August 1, 1998. Compliance with obligations under this treaty is ensured by the European Court of Human Rights (ECtHR), which both applies and interprets the Convention. When rendering a decision or judgment, the ECtHR in virtually every case refers to prior decisions and judgments in substantiation of its position. By the end of 2008, the ECtHR had considered more than one hundred cases with respect to the Russian Federation.

Russian doctrinal views concerning the legal nature of ECtHR legal positions, sometimes characterized as legal precedent, are still in the early stages of discussion. Zimnenko is inclined to regard these as "precedents of interpretation." He observes that "as a result of interpretation by the [ECtHR] of convention provisions legal positions are formed which assist the [ECtHR] thereafter in more effectively and efficiently considering a case." One may assume, he says, "that the legal essence" of the positions developed by the ECtHR should be elicited through Article 31(3) of the 1969 Vienna Convention, pursuant to which, for the purpose of interpretation of a treaty, there shall be taken into account, together with the context, any subsequent practice "in the application of the treaty which establishes the agreement of the parties regarding its interpretation." It follows for him that the legal positions of the ECtHR are a "special form of subsequent practice of the States-parties connected with the application" of the ECHR.[78]

Support for this approach is found in Decree No. 5 of the Supreme Court,[79] which states that "according to Article 31(3)(b) of the Vienna Convention, when interpreting an international treaty, together with the context thereof, there should be taken into account subsequent practice in the application of the treaty which establishes the agreement of the parties relative to its interpretation." The Supreme Court noted that the Russian Federation, as a party to the Convention for the Protection of Human Rights and Fundamental Freedoms, recognizes the jurisdiction of the ECtHR as binding with regard to questions involving the interpretation and application of the ECHR and protocols thereto in the event of a purported violation by the Russian Federation of the provisions of these treaty acts when the purported violation occurred after the entry into force thereof with respect to the Russian Federation (Article 1, Federal Law of 30 March 1998, No. 54-ФЗ, On the Ratification of the Convention for the Protection of Human Rights and

[78] Zimnenko, *supra* note 38, pgs. 259–60.
[79] Trans. in Butler, *Russian Public Law*, *supra* note 2, pg. 62.

Fundamental Freedoms and Protocols Thereto). Therefore, the application by courts of the ECHR must be effectuated by taking into account the practice of the ECtHR in avoidance of any violation of the Convention for the Protection of Human Rights and Fundamental Freedoms.[80]

The question arises whether the last sentence of the preceding paragraph means that all decisions and judgments of the ECtHR are part of the legal system of the Russian Federation or only certain of them.[81] This is a question for the Russian Federation, which, as a sovereign state, determines what are the integral parts of its legal system. Although decisions and judgments of the ECtHR are not an international treaty, the Federal Law of March 30, 1998, effectively incorporated them into the Russian legal system as binding with regard to the interpretation and application of the ECHR. Zimnenko contends that three criteria must be satisfied by a judicial act of the ECtHR to become part of the Russian legal system.

First, the case with regard to which the judicial act is rendered must involve the Russian Federation as a respondent. Second, the judicial act must establish the fact of a violation of the ECHR and/or its protocols by the Russian Federation. Third, a judgment rendered against Russia must have entered into legal force. If these three criteria are met, then as a matter of international law, the Russian Federation is bound under the ECHR to execute the final judgment of the ECtHR. With respect to Russian municipal law, given the provisions of the federal law on ratification of the ECHR the judgment of the ECtHR is binding with respect to the interpretation and application of the ECHR. The judgment of the ECtHR is a legal fact on the basis of which municipal legal relations arise, change, or terminate.[82]

From time to time, Russian judicial practice takes into account legal positions of the ECtHR formulated in cases to which the Russian Federation was not a party. Thus, in a decision of October 17, 2003,[83] the Supreme Court pointed out that Article 1 of Protocol No. 1 to the European Convention for the Protection of Human Rights and Fundamental Freedoms does not require a state to maintain the purchasing power of monetary amounts placed in financial institutions. In support of this legal position, the Court

[80] *Id.*

[81] For the view that all decisions of the ECHR, irrespective of whether it was adopted with reference to Russia, become part of the system of law of the Russian Federation, see K. N. Ratsiborinskaia, ≪Применение международного права Российскими судами≫ [Application of International Law by Russian Courts], *Международное публичное и частное право* [International Public and Private Law], no. 1 (2004), pg. 26.

[82] Zimnenko, *supra* note 38, pgs. 263–64.

[83] *Бюллетень Верховного Суда Российской Федерации* [Bulletin of Supreme Court of Russian Federation], no. 12 (2004), pgs. 13–14.

referred to the judgment of the ECtHR of August 29, 2002, in *Apollonov v. Russian Federation*; the decision of the European Commission of March 6, 1980, in *H. v. Federal Republic of Germany*; the judgment of the ECtHR of September 7, 1999, in *Rudzinska v. Poland*; and the judgment of the ECtHR of July 2, 2002, in *Haiduk v. Ukraine.*[84]

The Supreme Court also has directed courts of ordinary jurisdiction to take into account the legal positions of the ECtHR with respect to Article 10 of the ECHR when deciding defamation cases, "having in view in so doing that the concept of defamation used by the European Court of Human Rights is identical to the concept of dissemination of defamatory information not corresponding to reality," which is contained in Article 152 of the Civil Code of the Russian Federation.[85]

D. *Acts of Interstate International Organizations*

In passing, we touch on decisions of international interstate (sometimes called intergovernmental) organizations and their relationship to the Russian legal system by virtue of Article 15(4) of the 1993 Russian Constitution. Such organizations, in the view of many Russian international lawyers, "have the right when complying with certain conditions to adopt decisions that become a source of international law."[86] The competence of such an organization to adopt binding decisions is invariably set out in the treaty establishing the organization. Distinctions are commonly drawn between decisions of an international organization to make changes in the charter thereof, decisions establishing rules governing the behavior of member states outside the organization (external regulation), and decisions adopting rules to regulate the internal affairs of the organization (internal regulation).

The treaty origin of an international organization, it is suggested, means that the failure of a state to comply with a decision properly adopted by the organization may entail a violation of the constitutive treaty of the organization.[87] Zimnenko concludes, "[I]t seems advisable in this connection to regard decisions of international organizations as an integral part of

[84] *Id.*

[85] *Бюллетень Верховного Суда Российской Федерации* [Bulletin of Supreme Court of Russian Federation], no. 4 (2005), pg. 3. For Article 152 of the Civil Code, *see* Butler, *Civil Code of the Russian Federation* (2003), pgs. 69–70.

[86] Zimnenko, *supra* note 38, pg. 227.

[87] Tikhomirov observed that the acts of an international organization "hardly require ratification in a parliament since the right to adopt acts has been delegated to them in the constitutive treaties." Iu. A. Tikhomirov, «Реализация международно-правовых актов в российской правовой системе» [Realization of International Legal Acts in

the [Russian] legal system for the purpose of the proper realization of those decisions and, in consequence, [to ensure fulfillment of obligations under the] international treaty in execution of which the respective decisions were adopted."[88] The formulation of certain legislative acts of the Russian Federation intended to implement the decisions of international organizations, however, suggests a disinclination on the part of the legislator to encourage state agencies and officials to turn directly to the texts of the said enactments when implementing the decisions at the municipal level. The edict of the president of the Russian Federation, On Measures for the Fulfillment of United Nations Security Council Resolution 1373 of September 28, 2001, gives evidence of this approach.[89]

Even if individual decisions of international organizations are not, as a rule, binding and subject to application by domestic law-enforcement agencies, some may be of special significance (e.g., UN Security Council decisions) and should be applied. Even decisions that are not part of Russian law, it is suggested, might be used when interpreting norms of international law.[90]

It should be said that Russian courts cite the resolutions of the UN General Assembly and other documents of international organizations with remarkable frequency.

V. CONCLUSIONS

The three systems of Russian courts have moved assertively, even aggressively, to give substance to the Russian constitutional provision that treaties (as well as generally recognized principles of international law and customary rules of international law) are an integral part of the Russian legal system. At the same time, the courts of ordinary jurisdiction have reacted with reserve to the possibility that any treaties not subject to ratification may have priority over federal laws (although in this writer's view that is precisely what the 1993 Russian Constitution does provide). The position of the Constitutional Court and the arbitrazh courts on this matter has not yet been fully articulated.

the Russian Legal System], *Журнал российского права* [Journal of Russian Law], no. 3 (1999), pg. 91.

88 Zimnenko, *supra* note 38, pg. 242.

89 Edict of 10 January 2002, *СЗ РФ* (2002), no. 2, item 137.

90 Lukashuk, ≪Российская правовая система и международное право: современные проблемы взаимодействия≫ [Russian Legal System and International Law: Contemporary Problems of Interaction], *Государство и право* [State and Law], no. 3 (1996), pg. 25.

Official publication of a treaty in Russia is a sine qua non of treaty enforcement in judicial practice. Russian courts are proceeding from the principle that knowledge of the law is fundamental to a democratic society and to a rule-of-law state (not a position fully developed in the international legal system as yet). So far as the courts are concerned, a treaty not officially published does not exist. The intention is plainly to encourage the disclosure and publication of treaties in a country where historically the state has preferred to keep the texts of normative legal acts[91] and treaties confidential or restricted.

The Russian legal system is not particularly receptive for a variety of reasons to concepts of implied rights or implied duties. In contrast, the existence of Article 15(4) of the Russian Constitution eliminates the need for such concepts, and in doing so makes the Russian Federation a jurisdiction in which the international obligation of states to provide domestic judicial remedies for individuals who have been harmed by a violation of their treaty-based rights is undertaken at a more advanced level than in most countries of the world.

Some questions that arise in the context of the law of treaties in other countries are not particularly pertinent in the Russian context. It is exceptionally uncommon for the executive branch in Russia to express a preferred treaty interpretation in a manner that would affect treaty enforcement; indeed, the term *executive branch* is not a term of Russian constitutional law. It would be difficult to distinguish between the government and the presidency for these purposes, although the Russian distinction is vital to their understanding of state structure and checks and balances. Even if either the president or the government had a preferred interpretation of a treaty provision, the codes of procedure in Russia contain no special provision by which it might be presented to a Russian court.

Whether Russian courts consult foreign judicial decisions with respect to treaty interpretation is unknown (other than the ECtHR, whose decisions are regarded by most Russian jurists as part of the Russian legal system). If Russian courts did consider other foreign judicial decisions, it would not be part of the style of judicial decision drafting to so indicate.

Russian courts are not empowered to apply presumptions with respect to the creation of treaty rights for natural persons, nor are there doctrines or judicial practice in favor of broader protection for private rights.

No distinction is drawn with respect to treaty rights as to whether the matter is civil or criminal. The Russian legal system does not have injunctive

[91] *See* W. E. Butler, "Unpublished Normative Acts in Post-Soviet Legal Space," *Journal of Comparative Law*, vol. 3 (2008).

relief in its Anglo-American understanding, and nothing turns on what remedies may be sought from the Russian court. And while the Russian Federation is a form of federated state, nothing turns on the level of courts within the federation with respect to the law of treaties. Where a treaty is relevant, all Russian courts are expected to apply it.

It is appropriate to close with a case in which two individual Russian citizens successfully sued the government of the Russian Federation for seeking to evade environmental requirements in order to implement a treaty obligation.[92] T and M applied to the Supreme Court to challenge the validity of Regulation No. 1483-p on the grounds that the government had failed to comply with federal environmental legislation. In satisfying this demand, the Supreme Court referred to Article 48 of the federal law On the Protection of the Environment, Article 11 of the federal law On Ecological Expert Examination, and Article 4 of the federal law On Making Additions to Article 50 of the Law of the RSFSR On the Protection of the Natural Environment. On the basis of these enactments, the Supreme Court concluded that the importation into the Russian Federation from a foreign state of irradiated fuel clusters from nuclear reactors in order to process them was authorized only if the state-ecological-expert examination had been carried out. The government failed to submit evidence to the court that such had been done. Accordingly, the Supreme Court ordered the government to delay import of the spent fuel from Hungary, notwithstanding the treaty obligation to import and process the fuel, until after the requisite environmental assessment had been completed.

Here, because the treaties were intergovernmental (and therefore not ratified) and because a federal law imposed the requirement of an obligatory state ecological examination, the Supreme Court gave preference to the federal law over the treaty. In doing so, it followed the principle laid down in Decree No. 5, a principle that the present writer has argued is not consistent with the wording of the Constitution. But under either approach, private rights, perhaps here pursued in the public interest, are amply defended in the treaty context.

[92] *Бюллетень Верховного Суда Российской Федерации* [Bulletin of the Supreme Court of the Russian Federation], no. 1 (2003), pgs. 13–14.

11

South Africa

John Dugard

Honorary Professor of Law, Centre for Human Rights, University of Pretoria; Professor Emeritus, University of Leiden

I. INTRODUCTION

Any study of the role of domestic courts in the enforcement of treaties in a particular state is built on the assumption that the state in question is an active member of the international community, with courts aware of the state's international treaty obligations. Such an assumption is certainly true of present-day South Africa, but it was not always so. From 1948 to 1994, while the country pursued the policy of apartheid, South Africa was an isolated pariah state with few treaties and courts largely unconcerned about the country's international obligations. Although South Africa was a party to the Charter of the United Nations – which was not incorporated into domestic law – it refused to become a party to many multilateral treaties, particularly in the fields of African organization, human rights, and humanitarian law. Bilateral treaties were entered into, but even here difficulties were encountered. For instance, most states outside of southern Africa declined to enter into extradition agreements with South Africa or terminated existing agreements. Both the all-white executive and all-white legislature were positively hostile to the international community as it sought to persuade, and later compel, South Africa to abandon apartheid. The courts were likewise unsympathetic to arguments premised on customary international law or treaty obligations.[1] For instance, the South African Appellate Division refused to be guided by the human rights clauses in the UN Charter in its interpretation of the reasonableness of racial discrimination.[2] While courts were prepared to be guided by International Labour Organization (ILO)

[1] J. Dugard, The South African Judiciary and International Law in the Apartheid Era, 14 *S. Afr. J. Hum. Rts.* 110 (1998).
[2] S. v. Adams; S. v. Werner 1981 (1) SALR 187 (A).

standards[3] and the UN Standard Minimum Rules for the Treatment of Prisoners,[4] they refused,[5] except in one case,[6] to be guided by the International Bill of Rights in the interpretation of the law.

The situation has changed dramatically since 1994. South Africa is today an active member of the international community and is a party to many multilateral and bilateral treaties. The South African Constitution of 1996, an instrument that seeks to remedy the defects of its apartheid predecessors, is positively international law friendly. Moreover, courts nurtured on apartheid legislation and hostility to international law have transformed into courts that apply international norms with regularity and enthusiasm. It is this new South Africa that came into being in 1994 that forms the subject of the present chapter.

II. MONISM AND DUALISM

South Africa is a common law country. Its common law is not Anglo-American common law, however, but Roman Dutch law.[7] Roman-Dutch law is the legal system that applied in Holland during the seventeenth and eighteenth centuries, comprising a blend of medieval Dutch law and the Roman law of Justinian, as received in Holland. Roman Dutch law was transported to the Cape when the Dutch settled there in 1652. Inevitably, the principles of Roman Dutch law have been strongly influenced by English law, following the British occupation of South Africa in the early nineteenth century.

The monist-dualist debate postdates the classical period of Roman Dutch scholarship, led by jurists such as Grotius and Van Bynkershoek. It is clear, however, that Roman Dutch law leaned heavily in favor of monism as jurists failed to draw any distinction between international law and municipal law.[8]

Before 1994, following the British occupation of South Africa in 1795,[9] South Africa's constitutional system was modeled on that of Britain.

[3] D.J.G. Woolfrey, The Application of International Labour Norms to South African Law, 12 *SAYIL* 135 (1986–87).

[4] S. v. Staggie 1990 (1) South Africa Criminal Law Reports 669.

[5] S. v. Rudman 1989 (3) SALR 368 (E) at 376 A–B; S. v. Rudman 1992 (1) SALR 343 (A).

[6] In S. v. Khanyile, 1988 (3) SALR 795 (N) at 801 A-D, Justice Didcott sought to fashion a right-to-counsel rule for the indigent accused by relying on the importance attached to this right in the International Covenant on Civil and Political Rights – to which at that time South Africa was not a party.

[7] *See* H.R. Hahlo and E. Kahn, *The South African Legal System and Its Background* (1968), particularly at 329–31.

[8] J. Dugard, *International Law: A South African Perspective* 48–50 (3d ed. 2005).

[9] From 1803 to 1806 the Cape was briefly returned to the Netherlands, under the Batavian Republic.

During this period, South African courts turned to English law, rather than Roman Dutch law, for guidance on questions of public law, including public international law. Thus, courts accepted the English common law position that customary law forms part of municipal law[10] but that treaties required legislative transformation. The latter rule was clearly spelled out by Chief Justice Steyn in *Pan American World Airways Inc. v. SA Fire and Accident Insurance Co.*,[11] when he stated that it was

> trite law . . . that in this country the conclusion of a treaty, convention or agreement by the South African government with any other government is an executive and not legislative act. As a general rule, the provisions of an international instrument so concluded, are not embodied in our law except by legislative process. . . . In the absence of any enactment giving [its] relevant provisions the force of law, [it] cannot affect the rights of the subject.

III. THE NEW LEGAL ORDER

In 1993, twenty-six political groups assembled at Kempton Park to draft a constitution to bring an end to the apartheid legal order. As these groups were in most instances unelected, and simply reflected the political realities of the time, it was considered inappropriate to confer on them the power to draft a final constitution. Instead, the constitution they fashioned was to serve as an interim constitution, pending the drafting of a constitution by a democratically elected constitutional assembly. This interim constitution became the Constitution of the Republic of South Africa Act 200 of 1993.

On April 27, 1994, the Interim Constitution came into effect to govern South Africa's first democratic elections. The Parliament thus elected served the dual role of legislature and constitutional assembly. From January 1995 to May 1996, the constitutional assembly met regularly to draft the final constitution. The new Constitution – the Constitution of the Republic of South Africa, Act 108 of 1996 – was signed into law by President Mandela on December 10, 1996.

Previous South African constitutions made no mention of the place of international law in the South African legal order. Both the 1994 and the 1996

[10] South Atlantic Islands Development Corporation v. Buchan 1971 (1) SA 234 (C) at 238 B–F. In Nduli v. Minister of Justice, 1978 (1) SA 893 (A), the Appellate Division held that this rule of incorporation of customary international law had its origin in Roman Dutch law (906B).

[11] 1965 (3) SALR 150 (A) at 161 C–D. This dictum was confirmed in S. v. Tuhadeleni, 1969 (1) SALR 153 (A) at 173–75.

constitutions remedy this omission. However, while both expressly affirm that customary international law is part of the law of South Africa,[12] the two constitutions differ in their approach to the relationship between treaties and municipal law. While the 1994 constitution failed to adopt a fully dualist approach, the 1996 constitution, in requiring the incorporation of most treaties into domestic law, is avowedly dualist in nature.

Before 1994, South Africa followed the dualist approach to the incorporation of treaties. Treaties were negotiated, signed, ratified, and acceded to by the executive. Only those treaties incorporated by Act of Parliament became part of South African law. Thus, treaty making fell exclusively within the competence of the executive.

The 1993 Kempton Park negotiators were strongly motivated by considerations of transparency and accountability – which had played little role in the apartheid state. Thus, influenced by the Namibian Constitution,[13] they departed radically from the pre-1993 position in respect of the treaty-making power and the incorporation of treaties. While the executive retained its power to negotiate and sign treaties under the Interim Constitution, the National Assembly and Senate were required to agree to the ratification of and accession to treaties.[14] Treaties ratified by resolutions of the two houses of Parliament became part of municipal law, "provided Parliament expressly so provides."[15] The clear purpose of the Interim Constitution was to facilitate the incorporation of treaties into municipal law. The drafters of the Interim Constitution, however, failed to take into account the bureaucratic mind. Government departments, required to scrutinize treaties before they were submitted to Parliament, refused to present treaties to Parliament for ratification until they were completely satisfied that there would be no conflict between the provisions of the treaty and domestic law. The result was that few treaties were presented to Parliament expeditiously. Consequently, few treaties were ratified by Parliament and incorporated into municipal law.[16] In these circumstances, the drafters of the 1996 Constitution elected to return to the pre-1994 position relating to the incorporation of treaties, without abandoning the need for parliamentary ratification of treaties. Section 231 provides:

[12] Sec. 232 of the 1996 Constitution provides that "[c]ustomary international law is law in the Republic unless it is inconsistent with the Constitution or an Act of Parliament."
[13] *See* arts. 32(3)(e), 63(2)(e), and 144. *See also* 15 *SAYIL* 301 (1989–90).
[14] Sec. 231 (2) of Act 200 of 1993.
[15] Sec. 231 (3) of Act 200 of 1993.
[16] N. Botha, Incorporation of Treaties under the Interim Constitution: A Pattern Emerges, 20 *SAYIL* 196 (1995).

(1) The negotiating and signing of all international agreements is the responsibility of the national executive.
(2) An international agreement binds the Republic only after it has been approved by resolution in both the National Assembly and the National Council of Provinces, unless it is an agreement referred to in subsection (3).
(3) An international agreement of a technical, administrative or executive nature, or an agreement which does not require either ratification or accession, entered into by the national executive, binds the Republic without approval by the National Assembly and the National Council of Provinces, but must be tabled in the Assembly and the Council within reasonable time.
(4) Any international agreement becomes law in the Republic when it is enacted into law by national legislation; but a self-executing provision of an agreement that has been approved by Parliament is law in the Republic unless it is inconsistent with the Constitution or an Act of Parliament.
(5) The Republic is bound by international agreements which were binding on the Republic when this Constitution took effect.

Although this provision ensures that Parliament will continue to play an active role in treaty making, it requires an Act of Parliament or other form of national legislation, in addition to the resolution of ratification, for the incorporation of treaties into municipal law. It represents an abandonment of the idealism of 1993 that sought "to bring international law and domestic law in harmony with each other."[17]

The Interim Constitution suggested that all treaties signed by the executive were to be approved by Parliament.[18] This took no account of the fact that many treaties are intended to come into operation immediately at the international level and that slow parliamentary ratification would undermine the value of such treaties. Consequently, government departments ignored the letter of the Interim Constitution and distinguished between formal treaties that required parliamentary approval and less formal treaties that did not. The 1996 Constitution recognizes this distinction.

[17] R. Keightley, Public International Law and the Final Constitution, 12 *S. Afr. J. Hum. Rts.* 405, at 408 (1996).
[18] Sec. 231(2) of the Interim Constitution provided that "Parliament shall . . . be competent to agree to the ratification of or accession to an international agreement negotiated and signed" by the executive.

While treaties that expressly or by necessary implication require international ratification have to be approved by Parliament after signature, technical, administrative, and executive agreements, and agreements that do not require international ratification or accession, enter into force internationally on signature. In practice, this may give rise to disputes about the precise meaning of the phrase "technical, administrative, or executive" in the context of treaty law.[19] Ultimately, however, it is a question of intention.[20] Where parties intend that an agreement is to enter into force internationally immediately on signature, without ratification at the international level, the South African Parliament will not insist on parliamentary approval.

Section 231(4) represents a return to the pre-1994 position expounded by the Appellate Division in *Pan American World Airways*.[21] An international agreement or treaty does not become part of domestic law until it is enacted into law by national legislation. An Act of Parliament is national legislation but the term also includes subordinate legislation.[22]

Three principal methods are employed by the legislature to transform treaties into municipal law. First, the provisions of a treaty may be embodied in the text of an Act of Parliament; second, the treaty may be included as a schedule to a statute; and third, an enabling Act of Parliament may give the executive the power to bring a treaty into effect in municipal law by means of proclamation or notice in the *Government Gazette*.

A. *Self-Executing Treaties*

The proviso to Section 231(4) introduces the concept of self-executing treaties into South African law. The provisions of a treaty approved by Parliament but not incorporated into municipal law by Act of Parliament, that are self-executing become part of municipal law unless inconsistent with the Constitution or an Act of Parliament.

[19] N. Botha, Treaty Making in South Africa: A Reassessment, 25 *SAYIL* 69, at 75–78 (2000); J. Schneeberger, A Labyrinth of Tautology: The Meaning of the Term "International Agreement" and Its Significance for South African Law and Treaty-Making Practice, 26 *SAYIL* 1, at 5–7 (2001); W. Scholtz, A Few Thoughts on s 231 of the South African Constitution, 26 *SAYIL* 202 (2004).

[20] See art 14 of the Vienna Convention on the Law of Treaties, which emphasizes the intention of parties in deciding whether a treaty requires ratification. This principle was endorsed by the South African Appellate Division in S. v. Eliaso 1967 (4) SALR 583 (A).

[21] 1965 (3) SALR 150 (A). This principle was reaffirmed by the Constitutional Court in Azapo v. President of the Republic of South Africa 1996 (4) SALR (CC), at 688, para. 26.

[22] Sec. 239 of Act 108 of 1996.

Whether the provisions of a treaty are self-executing has troubled the courts of the United States for many years.[23] In 1951, Professor Myres McDougal declared in respect of the position in the United States: "this word self-executing is essentially meaningless, and . . . the quicker we drop it from our vocabulary the better for clarity and understanding."[24] American law therefore offers no panacea for the problems that are likely to confront South African courts in the interpretation of Section 231(4).

South African courts have yet to pronounce on the concept of self-executing treaties, but scholars have expressed divergent views on the subject. Botha states that Section 231(4) was taken over "unwisely" from U.S. jurisprudence "with no regard to its suitability to the South African context."[25] In a similar vein, the present writer has warned that Section 231(4) is "bound to create problems" and that, while American law may offer some guidance, South Africa's different constitutional rules preclude a wholesale adoption of American jurisprudence.[26] No general guideline can be given on this matter. Each case in which it is claimed that a treaty is self-executing will have to be decided on its own merits by the courts with due regard to the nature of the treaty, the precision of its language and the existing South African law (both common law and statute) on that subject.[27]

Ngolele[28] and Olivier[29] adopt a different position, in favor of the concept of self-executing treaties, and suggest that human rights treaties, such as the International Covenant on Civil and Political Rights (ICCPR), may be directly applied by South African courts as self-executing treaties. Ngolele rejects the view advanced by the present writer that the adequacy of existing South African law is a condition precedent for self-execution of a treaty.[30] However, in acknowledging that self-execution has limited effect in South Africa, because treaties will be self-executing only if consistent

[23] *See, e.g.*, Foster v. Neilson, 27 U.S. (2 Pet.) 253 (1829); Sei Fujii v. California, 242 P.2d 617 (1952); 19 ILR 312. *See also* Restatement (Third) of The Foreign Relations Law of the United States § 111 (1987).

[24] 45 *Proceedings of the American Society of International Law* 102 (1951).

[25] N. Botha, Treaty Making in South Africa: A Reassessment, 25 *SAYIL* 69, at 91 (2000). *See also* J. D. van der Vyver, Universal Jurisdiction in International Criminal Law, 24 *SAYIL* 107, at 130 (1999) (describing sec. 231 (4) as "nonsensical").

[26] Dugard, *supra* note 8, at 62.

[27] *Id.*

[28] E. Ngolele, The Content of the Doctrine of Self-Execution and Its Limited Effect in South African Law, 31 *SAYIL* 153 (2006).

[29] M. Olivier, Exploring the Doctrine of Self-Execution as Enforcement Mechanism of International Obligations, 27 *SAYIL* 99 (2002).

[30] Ngolele, *supra* note 28, at 161, 164.

with the Constitution and Acts of Parliament, he comes close to the present writer's position that municipal law must be adequate for a treaty to be self-executing, in the sense that it must not obstruct the application of such a treaty. Olivier adopts a more radical position. She argues that in terms of Section 231(2) a treaty approved by Parliament has direct application in South African law without the need for incorporation – that is, is self executing – provided that it is not inconsistent with the Constitution or an Act of Parliament. This, she further argues, has special importance for human rights treaties, a fact that has "been unappreciated by South African commentators."[31] Olivier's thesis is based on a false assumption – namely that Section 231(2) is designed to give domestic effect to treaties approved by Parliament.[32] In the present writer's opinion, Section 231(2) is intended to establish that an international agreement binds South Africa on the international level only after it has been approved by both houses of Parliament. To apply domestically, a treaty must still be "enacted into law by national legislation," as specified in Section 231(4), unless it is self-executing. And it will be self-executing only if the language of the treaty so indicates and existing municipal law, either common law or statute, is adequate in the sense that it fails to place any obstacle in the way of treaty application.

As to the direct application of human rights conventions: the South African Bill of Rights (discussed subsequently) recognizes most of the rights contained in the ICCPR, with the result that courts apply the Bill of Rights itself, with due regard to the language of the ICCPR and its interpretation by the Human Rights Committee. South Africa is a party to the ICCPR, which has been approved by both houses of Parliament pursuant to Section 231(2). Even so, there are no litigated cases in which parties have argued that the ICCPR is directly applicable, despite the fact that it has not been incorporated into domestic law pursuant to Section 231(4). As South Africa has yet to ratify the International Covenant on Economic, Social, and Cultural Rights, because it has not been approved by Parliament pursuant to Section 231(2), the question of self-execution does not arise in respect of this treaty.

The divergent positions adopted by scholars on self-executing treaties confirm the view of the present writer that this concept will create problems for South African courts when called on to decide the matter.

[31] Olivier, *supra* note 29, at 119.
[32] *Id.*, at 116.

B. *International Agreements or Treaties*

The 1996 Constitution, like the Interim Constitution, uses the term *international agreement* instead of the more commonly used term *treaty*. This creates uncertainty over the meaning of Section 231, as there is strong support for the view that the term *international agreement* is broad enough to include both legally binding agreements (treaties) and nonbinding, informal agreements.[33] This uncertainty surfaced in the *Harksen* case,[34] in which it was argued that Section 3(2) of the Extradition Act,[35] authorizing the president to consent to the extradition of a person to a state with which South Africa has no extradition agreement, gives rise to an international agreement if not a treaty. Consequently, the applicant argued, the procedure for the adoption of international agreements contained in Section 231(2) should be followed in respect of such an undertaking by the president. While the Cape Provincial Division was prepared to contemplate the existence of unenforceable, informal arrangements falling within the scope of an "international agreement,"[36] the Constitutional Court rejected the argument that a presidential undertaking under Section 3(2) of the Extradition Act could be categorized as either an "international agreement" or an "informal agreement."[37] Unfortunately, the Constitutional Court failed to throw light on the meaning to be given to the term *international agreement*.

The prevailing view, however, is that the term *international agreement* in Section 231 is synonymous with *treaty* and refers to legally binding, enforceable agreements as defined in Article 2 of the Vienna Convention on the Law of Treaties of 1969.[38] According to this provision, a treaty is "an *international agreement* concluded between states in written form and governed by international law, whether embodied in a single instrument or in two or

[33] R. R. Baxter, International Law in Her "Infinite Variety," 29 *ICLQ* 549 (1980); A. Aust, The Theory and Practice of Informal International Instruments, 35 *ICLQ* 787 (1986); M. Olivier, Informal International Agreements under the 1996 Constitution, 22 *SAYIL* 63 (1997). *But see* J. Klabbers, *The Concept of Treaty in International Law* 63–64, 122–35, 216–17, 243–50 (1996). For an overview of the literature, *see* J. Schneeberger, A Labyrinth of Tautology: The South African Treaty Law and Treaty-Making Practice, 26 *SAYIL* 1 (2001).

[34] S. v. Harksen; Harksen v. President of the Republic of South Africa; Harksen v. Wagner NO 2000 (1) SA 1185 (C); Harksen v. President of the Republic of South Africa 2000 (2) SA 825 (CC).

[35] Act 67 of 1962.

[36] Harksen v. Wagner NO 2001 (1) SALR 1185 (C), at 1201–1202 (paras. 52–54), at 1204 (para. 59).

[37] Harksen v. Wagner NO, 2000 (2) SALR 825 (CC), at 834, para. 21.

[38] Olivier, *supra* note 33, at 74; Botha, *supra* note 19, at 71; Schneeberger, *supra* note 19, at 32–40.

more related instruments and *whatever its particular designation.*"[39] What is important is that the agreement be between states, in writing, and that the state parties intend it to be governed by international law.[40] Once these requirements are met, an international agreement exists between the state parties, and it matters not whether it is called an international agreement or a treaty.

C. *Statutory Interpretation with Special Reference to Human Rights*

The 1996 Constitution reveals a clear determination to ensure that the Constitution and South African law are interpreted to comply with international law, particularly in the field of human rights. First, the common law presumption requiring a court to interpret legislation in compliance with international law[41] is given form in Section 233, which provides: "When interpreting any legislation, every court must prefer any reasonable interpretation of the legislation that is consistent with international law over any alternative interpretation that is inconsistent with international law." Second, the Bill of Rights, which is modeled on international human rights conventions and occasionally refers directly to international law,[42] is subjected to a special interpretative regime that pays particular attention to international law. Section 39 (Section 35 of the Interim Constitution[43]) declares:

> (1) When interpreting the Bill of Rights, a court, tribunal or forum –
> (a) must promote the values that underlie an open and democratic society based on human dignity, equality and freedom;

[39] Vienna Convention on the Law of Treaties, 1155 U.N.T.S. 331, art. 2 (1969) (emphasis added).

[40] *See* S. v. Harksen, 2000 (1) SA 1185 (C), at 1201, para. 52, in which Justice Van Zyl stated: "It is this very intention and consent that distinguishes treaties from informal or *ad hoc* agreements or arrangements." The Cape Provincial Division held that an arrangement to extradite a person under sec. 3(2) of the Extradition Act 67 of 1962 did not qualify as an international agreement because of the absence of an intent to create reciprocal rights and duties. *Id.* at 1204, para. 59. See also the judgment of the Constitutional Court in Harksen, 2000 (2) SA 825 (CC), at 834, para 21.

[41] S. v. Basson 2005 (1) SALR 171 (CC), at 207, para. 100.

[42] Sec. 37(4) provides that any legislation enacted in consequence of a declaration of a state of emergency may derogate from the Bill of Rights only to the extent that, inter alia, the legislation "is consistent with the Republic's obligations under international law applicable to states of emergency." Sec. 35(3)(1) recognizes the right "not to be convicted of an act or omission that was not an offence under either national or international law at the time when it was committed or omitted."

[43] Sec. 35(1) of the Interim Constitution required "a court of law" to "have regard to public international law."

(b) must consider international law; and
(c) may consider foreign law.

(2) When interpreting any legislation, and when developing the common law or customary law, every court, tribunal or forum must promote the spirit, purport and objects of the Bill of Rights.

(3) The Bill of Rights does not deny the existence of any other rights or freedoms that are recognized or conferred by common law, customary law or legislation, to the extent that they are consistent with the Bill.

Fears that international human rights law might be narrowly construed to cover only clear rules of customary law and those human rights conventions to which South Africa is a party have been dispelled.[44] In one of its earlier decisions, in a case involving the constitutionality of the death penalty, the president of the Constitutional Court ruled:

> In the context of sec. 35(1), public international law would include non-binding as well as binding law. They may both be used under the section as tools of interpretation. International agreements and customary international law accordingly provide a framework within which (the Bill of Rights) can be evaluated and understood, and for that purpose, decisions of tribunals dealing with comparable instruments, such as the United Nations Committee on Human Rights, the Inter-American Commission on Human Rights, the Inter-American Court of Human Rights, the European Commission on Human Rights, and the European Court of Human Rights and, in appropriate cases, reports of specialized agencies such as the International Labour Organization, may provide guidance as to the correct interpretation of particular provisions of (the Bill of Rights).[45]

Since the establishment of the new constitutional order in 1994, both the Constitutional Court and ordinary courts have shown a great willingness to be guided by international human rights law. Decisions of the European Commission and Court of Human Rights interpreting the European Convention on Human Rights have provided the greatest assistance, but courts have occasionally also considered the views of the UN Human Rights Committee on the ICCPR, and UN reports on human rights matters. Section 39(1)(b) is not limited to human rights conventions, as is shown by *Prince v. President, Cape Law Society*.[46] In that case, the Constitutional Court

[44] J. Dugard, The Role of International Law in Interpreting the Bill of Rights, 10 *S. Afr. J. Hum. Rts.* 208 (1994).

[45] S. v. Makwanyane 1995 (3) SA 391 (CC) at 413–14.

[46] 2002(2) SALR 794 (CC) at 824 A–E, 837 E–F, 851 B–C, 858–9; Prince v. President of the Law Society, Cape of Good Hope 1998 (8) Butterworths Constitutional Law Reports 976 (C) at

considered the Convention against Illicit Traffic in Narcotic Drugs and Psychotropic Substances of 1988, a treaty to which South Africa is a party, to help evaluate a claim that a Rastafarian was entitled to possess and use cannabis in the exercise of his freedom of religion.

While a court must consider treaties to which South Africa is not a party in interpreting the Bill of Rights, no such rule exists in respect of treaties to which South Africa is not a party where the Bill of Rights is not an issue. A treaty to which South Africa is not a party is res inter alios acta and may not be considered qua treaty, although it may be considered evidence of a customary rule.[47]

Different considerations apply with respect to a treaty to which South Africa is a party but that has not been incorporated into municipal law. In the first instance, a municipal court may have recourse to an unincorporated treaty in order to interpret an ambiguous statute.[48] Second, an unincorporated treaty may be taken into account in a challenge to the validity of delegated legislation on the grounds of unreasonableness.[49] Although there is no clear judicial support for this proposition, the question has twice been raised and left open by the South African Appellate Division in cases in which it was argued that proclamations issued by the South African government for the mandated territory of South-West Africa (now Namibia) might be tested against the terms of the Mandate for South-West Africa, which

985 C–D. *See also* Director of Public Prosecutions: Cape of Good Hope v. Bathgate 2000 (2) SALR 535 (C) at 543, 546.

[47] This is borne out by the judgment in S. v. Petane 1988 (3) SALR 51 (C), in which Justice Conradie considered the question of whether the principal provisions of a treaty to which South Africa was not a party – Additional Protocol I of 1977 – had been translated into customary law by usage.

[48] Maluke v. Minister of Internal Affairs 1981 (1) SALR 707 (B) at 713; Mabuda v. Minister of Cooperation and Development 1984 (2) SALR 49 (Ck) at 54–5 (discussed in 1984 *Annual Survey of South African Law*, at 82–83). For a discussion of this principle, *see* J. Dugard, International Human Rights Norms in Domestic Courts: Can South Africa Learn from Britain and the United States? *in* Ellison Kahn (ed.), *Fiat Iustitia: Essays in Memory of Oliver Deneys Schreiner* 221, 234–36 (1983). *Cf.* Binga v. Cabinet for South West Africa 1988 (3) SALR 155 (A) at 185F, in which JA Van Heerden restricted the scope of this argument in an obiter dictum in which he found that the presumption in favor of compliance with an international treaty obligation applies only where the statute seeks to give effect to the treaty in question. In limiting this presumption, JA Van Heerden preferred the more restrictive approach of LJ Diplock in Salomon v. Commissioner of Customs and Excise (1966) 3 All ER 871 (CA) at 875–76, to that of Lord Denning MR in R v. Secretary of State for Home Affairs, *Ex parte* Bhajan Singh (1975) 2 All ER 1083 (CA). In support of Lord Denning's position, *see* P. J. Duffy, English Law and the European Court of Human Rights, 29 *ICLQ* 585, 589 (1980).

[49] Molvan v. Attorney-General for Palestine (1948) AC 351 (PC) at 365.

was not incorporated into municipal law.[50] Logically, this would seem to be a sound proposition, since the concept of reasonableness is inextricably linked with presumptions of legislative intent, and there is a presumption that the legislature, in enacting a law, did not intend to violate South Africa's international obligations.

As South African courts are given the power of judicial review of legislation under the 1996 Constitution,[51] it is inevitable that international law will be invoked not only as a guide to statutory interpretation but also to support a challenge to the validity of legislation. This may take the form of a direct challenge, where, for example, it is argued that the procedures for ratification and incorporation of a treaty under Section 231 have not been followed. Or it may assume the form of an indirect challenge, where international law is invoked to support a constitutional interpretation that results in the unconstitutionality of a statute.

Azapo v. President of the Republic of South Africa[52] concerned the latter type of challenge. Here the applicants sought to set aside Section 20(7) of the Promotion of National Unity and Reconciliation Act,[53] which provided for amnesty from criminal and civil proceedings for members of the apartheid regime. Applicants argued that amnesty was inconsistent with Section 22 of the Interim Constitution, which provides that every person shall have the right to have justiciable disputes settled by a court of law or, where appropriate, another independent or impartial forum. In support of this challenge, the applicants argued that the state was obliged by international law, particularly the Geneva Conventions of 1949, to prosecute those responsible for gross human rights violations and that the provisions of Section 20(7), which authorized amnesty for such offences, constituted a breach of international law.[54] In a judgment written by Deputy President Mahomed, the Constitutional Court held that the epilogue to the Interim Constitution, which specifically provided for amnesty, trumped Section 22 of the Interim

[50] Winter v. Minister of Defence 1940 AD 194 at 198 and S. v. Tuhadeleni 1969 (1) SALR 153 (A) at 176–77. In Binga v. Administrator-General, SWA 1984 (3) SALR 949 (SWA), especially at 973 D–G, the court wrongly assumed that Tuhadeleni's case held that delegated legislation might not be tested against the Mandate. (*See* J. Dugard, The Revocation of the Mandate for South West Africa Revisited, 1 *S. Afr. J. Hum. Rts.* 154, 159 (1985)).

[51] Sec. 172 of Act 108 of 1996.

[52] 1996 (4) SA 671 (CC). For criticisms of this decision, see the comments by J. Dugard, C. Braude, D. Spitz and D. Moellendorf in 13 *S. Afr. J. Hum. Rts.* 258–91 (1997); and Z. Motala, The Constitutional Court's Approach to International Law and Its Method of Interpretation in the "Amnesty Decision": Intellectual Honesty or Political Expediency? 21 *SAYIL* 29 (1996).

[53] Act 34 of 1995.

[54] Azapo, *supra* note 52, at 687, para. 25.

Constitution, and that Section 20(7) of the Promotion of National Unity and Reconciliation Act was therefore constitutional. From the perspective of international law, the judgment is disappointing because it fails to address adequately the question whether conventional and customary international law oblige a successor regime to punish the officials and agents of the prior regime for international crimes. From the perspective of the place of international law in the new constitutional order, the judgment is disconcerting because of a dictum that may be construed as a minimization of the role of international law in a constitutional challenge.

In the course of his judgment, Deputy President Mahomed states:

> The issue which falls to be determined in this Court is whether sec. 20(7) of the Act is inconsistent with the Constitution. If it is, the enquiry as to whether or not international law prescribes a different duty is irrelevant to that determination. International law and the contents of international treaties to which South Africa might or might not be party at any particular time are, in my view, relevant only to the interpretation of the Constitution itself, on the grounds that the lawmakers of the Constitution should not lightly be presumed to authorize any law which might constitute a breach of the obligations of the state in terms of international law.[55]

Does this mean that, in a challenge to the constitutionality of a statute involving a rule of international law, it is the duty of the court to ascertain the content of the rule and seek to give an interpretation to the Constitution that accords with this rule, and that the Constitution prevails only if there is a clear inconsistency between the rule of international law and the Constitution? Or does it mean that the court should examine whether the statute in question is compatible with the Constitution, without reference to the rule of international law, and then consider only as an afterthought whether international law supports or is in conflict with such an interpretation? Clearly, Deputy President Mahomed's dictum must support the former meaning, despite the fact that the sequence of his reasoning in *Azapo* might give support to the latter interpretation – as does the following dictum:

> The exact terms of the relevant rules of public international law contained in the Geneva Conventions relied upon on behalf of the applicants would therefore be irrelevant if, on a proper interpretation of the Constitution, sec. 20(7) of the Act is indeed authorized by the Constitution, but the content of these Conventions in any event does not assist the case of the applicant.[56]

[55] *Id.*, at 688, para. 26.
[56] *Id.*, at 689, para. 28.

The former meaning is most likely: first, because it accords more fully with the intention of the framers of the Interim Constitution, as reflected in its international law provisions, to promote harmony between international law and municipal law; and second, because there can be no proper interpretation of the Constitution without a consideration of international law.

The *Azapo* decision was given under the Interim Constitution, which contained no provision equivalent to Section 233 of the 1996 Constitution (although such a presumption applied under common law). Section 233 places the correctness of the interpretation of Deputy President Mahomed's dictum in *Azapo* beyond doubt.[57]

Section 39(2) of the Constitution requires a court, when it develops the common law or customary law, to "promote the spirit, purport and objects of the Bill of Rights." In *Carmichele v. Minister of Safety and Security (Centre for Applied Legal Studies Intervening)*,[58] the Constitutional Court invoked the Convention on the Elimination of All Forms of Discrimination against Women to develop a new rule of common law that the state "has a duty under international law to prohibit all gender-based discrimination that has the effect or purpose of impairing the enjoyment of women of fundamental rights and freedoms and to take reasonable and appropriate measures to prevent the violation of those rights."[59] Commenting on this decision, Neville Botha writes that the Constitutional Court has "shown clearly that the spirit, purport and objects of the bill of rights – which reflects the underlying precepts of the Constitution and the fabric of South African society – are inextricably linked to international law and the values and approaches of the international community and international role-players."[60] The Supreme Court of Appeal later followed the approach of the Constitutional Court.[61]

An increasing number of statutes refer expressly to international law, and some make it clear that the statute is to be interpreted to accord with international law. For instance, the Promotion of Equality and Prevention of Unfair Discrimination Act[62] provides that any person interpreting the act

[57] N. Botha, Treaties after the 1996 Constitution: More Questions Than Answers, 22 *SAYIL* 95, 102 (1997).

[58] 2001 (4) SALR 938 (CC).

[59] *Id.*, at 1016–17, para. 62.

[60] N. Botha, The Role of International Law in the Development of South African Common Law, *SAYIL* 253, 259 (2001).

[61] Minister of Safety and Security v. Carmichele 2004 (3) SALR 296 (SCA) 305, at 319–20.

[62] Act 4 of 2000.

may be "mindful" of international law;[63] the Implementation of the Rome Statute of the International Criminal Court[64] provides that a court applying the act must consider both conventional and customary international law;[65] the Labour Relations Act of 1995[66] proclaims as one of the primary objects of the act "to give effect to the obligations incurred by the Republic as a member state of the International Labour Organization" and requires the act to be interpreted in compliance with the public international law obligations of the republic;[67] the Refugees Act[68] provides that the act "must be interpreted and applied with due regard" to the principal refugee conventions, other relevant conventions, and the Universal Declaration of Human Rights.[69] Such statutes confirm the principle expounded in Section 233 of the Constitution that legislation is to be interpreted in accordance with international law.

D. *Hierarchy: Some Concluding Remarks*

The Constitution is the supreme law of South Africa. A treaty enacted into law by national legislation in accordance with Section 231(4) of the Constitution will enjoy the status accorded to it by the act of incorporation: a treaty enacted into law by act of Parliament will be treated as an act of Parliament, whereas a treaty enacted into law by subordinate legislation will be treated as subordinate legislation. A non-self-executing treaty binding on South Africa internationally but not incorporated into municipal law will have no direct force of law but may be used to interpret an ambiguous statute or to challenge subordinate, delegated legislation. A self-executing treaty will obviously, in terms of Section 231(4), give way to both the Constitution and an Act of Parliament. Probably such a self-executing treaty will take priority over delegated legislation, in the event of a conflict. Whereas apartheid South Africa accepted, and indeed approved, a contradiction between international law and domestic law, the new South African legal order seeks to

[63] Sec. 3(2)(a).
[64] Act 27 of 2002.
[65] Sec. 2.
[66] Act 66 of 1995.
[67] Secs. 1 and 3. *See also* N. Rubin, International Labour Law and the Law of the New South Africa, 115 *SALJ* 685 (1998).
[68] Act 130 of 1998. For an example of judicial examination of the Convention Relating to the Status of Refugees of 1951 in the interpretation of the Refugees Act, see Union of Refugee Women v. Director: The Private Security Industry Regulatory Authority, 2007(4) SALR 395 (CC), paras. 62–67.
[69] Sec. 6.

ensure that there will be no conflict between the two. Sections 233 and 39 of the Constitution and several statutes are designed to achieve such harmony.

IV. METHODS OF INTERPRETATION

A. *The Vienna Convention*

As shown earlier, South African courts are directed to have recourse to international law in their interpretation of South African common law and statute. There is, however, no law directing courts to apply the international law rules of treaty interpretation contained in Articles 31 and 32 of the Vienna Convention on the Law of Treaties when they interpret treaties that form part of South African law.

South Africa is not party to the Vienna Convention on the Law of Treaties. At the international level, it seems that South Africa accepts the substance of the Convention as customary international law and is guided by its provisions in international practice. It is uncertain, though, whether South African courts accept the Vienna Convention as customary law for the purpose of applying it as part of South African law pursuant to Section 232 of the Constitution, which provides that "customary international law is law in the Republic unless it is inconsistent with the Constitution or an Act of Parliament." In *Harksen v. President of the Republic of South Africa*,[70] Justice Goldstone, on behalf of the Constitutional Court, stated that he was prepared to "assume in favour of the appellant" that Article 46(1) of the Vienna Convention, providing that a state may not invoke its internal law to overrule its consent to be bound by a treaty, reflected customary international law, but at the same time, he warned that "the extent to which the Vienna Convention reflects customary international law is by no means settled."[71]

The probable reason for the failure of South African courts to pronounce on the applicability of Articles 31 and 32 of the Vienna Convention to the interpretation of statutes incorporating treaties into domestic law is that South Africa's own rules of statutory interpretation broadly follow the rules contained in the Vienna Convention. Inasmuch as South African law, like most common law systems, recognizes the textual (ordinary meaning), intention, and purposive (teleological) approaches to statutory interpretation, South African courts may comply with the most basic rules of the

[70] 2002 (2) SA 825 (CC).
[71] *Id.*, at 835–36, para. 26.

Vienna Convention by applying their own rules. During the apartheid era, there was open hostility to the use of teleological methods of interpretation on the international plane, as a result of the manner in which the International Court of Justice had recourse to teleological reasoning in all but one (the notorious 1966 decision in the *South West Africa Case Second Phase*[72]) of its opinions and decisions on the subject of South-West Africa (Namibia).[73] This hostility to teleological methods was mirrored in the decisions of South Africa's courts at that time.[74] Today the situation is very different: courts do not hesitate to employ purposive interpretation in constitutional and international matters. In *Abel v. Minister of Justice*,[75] *Luxavia (Pty) Ltd. v. Gray Security Services (Pty) Ltd.*,[76] and *Potgieter v. British Airways PLC*,[77] courts expressly approved a purposive interpretation with respect to extradition and aviation treaties incorporated into municipal law.

Courts have invoked the preparatory works (*travaux préparatoires*) of incorporated treaties in their process of interpretation, as permitted by Article 32 of the Vienna Convention on the Law of Treaties. In *Portion 20 of Plot 15 Athol (Pty) Ltd. v. Rodrigues*,[78] Justice Hussain considered the preparatory work of the International Law Commission in his interpretation of the Vienna Convention on Diplomatic Relations of 1961, which is incorporated into South African law. In *MV Mbashi Transnet Ltd. v. MV Mbashi*,[79] the court held that it might have regard to the *travaux préparatoires* of the International Convention on Salvage of 1989. However, in this case, the court simply gave effect to a provision in the incorporating statute that provided that in interpreting the convention a court may "consider the preparatory works to the convention."[80]

B. *International and Foreign Decisions as a Guide to Interpretation*

South African law is an unusual common law system. Being a blend of Roman, Dutch, and English law, the South African common law has relied on the decisions of foreign courts, comprising both common law and civil law jurisdictions (but particularly common law), for its development since

[72] 1966 ICJ Reports 6, at 48.
[73] *See* Dugard, *supra* note 8, at 418–20.
[74] *See* Dugard, *Human Rights and the South African Legal Order* (1978) (parts 4 and 5).
[75] 2001 (1) SALR 1230 (C) at 1236, para. 22.
[76] 2001 (4) SALR 211 (W) at 222–23, paras. 26–28.
[77] 2005 (1) SALR 133 (C) at 140 I–J.
[78] 2001 (1) SALR 1285 (W) at 1293.
[79] 2002 (3) SALR 217 (D) at 222–23.
[80] Wreck and Salvage Act 94 of 1996, sec. 2(5).

its very inception. Before 1994, this development was confined largely to private law and commercial law. No reference was made to the decisions of international monitoring bodies in the human rights field because South Africa was not party to any human rights conventions. Since the end of apartheid, however, the situation has changed dramatically. Foreign judicial decisions are invoked in all fields. In addition, courts now make frequent reference to the decisions of international tribunals, particularly international human rights monitoring bodies, and foreign courts in the field of human rights. This practice has its origin in one of the earliest decisions of the Constitutional Court, *S. v. Makwanyane*.[81] In that case, the court ruled that in interpreting Section 35 of the Interim Constitution (Section 39 of the 1996 Constitution), which directs courts to consider both international and foreign law in their interpretation of the Bill of Rights, courts should have regard to international agreements providing a framework within which the Bill of Rights can be evaluated. Furthermore, courts should consider "decisions of tribunals dealing with comparable instruments, such as the United Nations Committee on Human Rights, the Inter-American Commission on Human Rights, the Inter-American Court of Human Rights, and the European Court of Human Rights" to provide guidance on the interpretation of the Bill of Rights. South African courts have regard to such decisions in order to interpret their own Bill of Rights but, as the Bill of Rights is modeled on instruments such as the ICCPR, to which South Africa is a party, courts are in effect invoking interpretations placed on the ICCPR, and related instruments, such as the European and American conventions on human rights, in order to ensure that South Africa complies with its international obligations under the ICCPR.

As a result of the new Constitution, it has now become common place for the Constitutional Court and other courts to invoke human rights norms and decisions by international tribunals and human rights supervisory bodies to interpret the Bill of Rights and to set aside laws and administrative practices that violate human rights. It is impossible to examine all the judicial decisions that have invoked international human rights law. Academic writings, however, give some indication of the extent of this judicial practice.[82]

[81] 1995 (3) SALR 319 (CC), at 413–14. *See supra* note 45 and accompanying text (discussing *Makwanyane*).

[82] J. Dugard, The Influence of International Human Rights Law on the South African Constitution, *Current Legal Probs.* 305 (1996); J. Dugard, International Law and the South African Constitution, 8 *EJIL* 77 (1997); J. Dugard, The Role of Human Rights Standards in Domestic Law: The Southern African Experience, in *The Future of UN Human Rights Treaty Monitoring* 269 (P. Alston & J. Crawford eds., 2000); T. Maluwa, International Human

The following cases provide a glimpse of this new feature of South African law.

Before 1994, it was unheard of for a South African court to cite decisions of the International Court of Justice. Though such citations are today rare, they do occur, particularly in cases involving customary international law.[83] In *S. v. Basson*,[84] the Constitutional Court cited *Nicaragua v. United States*,[85] the *Legality of the Threat or Use of Nuclear Weapons*,[86] and *Prosecutor v. Tadić*[87] in the course of examining South Africa's obligations under the 1949 Geneva Conventions, which South Africa ratified in 1952 but has yet to incorporate into domestic law. Decisions of the European Court of Human Rights and the European Commission of Human Rights are undoubtedly the main sources to which South African courts turn for the interpretation of the Bill of Rights. In *S. v. Makwanyane*,[88] in which the Constitutional Court held the death penalty to be unconstitutional, the court invoked *Soering v. United Kingdom*,[89] in which the European Court of Human Rights found the death-row phenomenon to constitute inhuman and degrading treatment. This was followed by *S. v. Williams*,[90] in which the court found that

Rights Norms and the South African Interim Constitution 1993, 19 *SAYIL* 14 (1993/94); N. Botha, International Law in the Constitutional Court, 20 *SAYIL* 222 (1995); N. Botha, Riding the Tide: South Africa's "Regular" Courts and the Application of International Law, 21 *SAYIL* 174 (1996); E. de Wet, The Place of Public International Law in the New South African Constitutional Order: With Special Reference to International Human Rights and Humanitarian Law, 1 *Recht in Afrika* (published by African Law Association) 207 (1998); R.C. Blake, The World's Law in One Country: The South African Constitutional Court's Use of Public International Law, 115 *SALJ* 668 (1998); D. Prévost, South Africa as an Illustration of the Development in International Human Rights Law, 24 *SAYIL* 211 (1999); J. Ford, International and Comparative Influence on the Rights Jurisprudence of South Africa's Constitutional Court, in *Constitutional Democracy in South Africa 1994–2004* (M. du Plessis & S. Pete, eds.) 33 (2004); H. Strydom, South Africa and International Law – From Confrontation to Co-operation, 47 *F.R.G. Y.B. Int'l L.* 160, 193 (2004); D. Brand and C. Heyns (eds.), *Socio-Economic Rights in South Africa* (2005); N. Botha and M. Olivier, Ten Years of International Law in the South African Courts: Reviewing the Past and Assessing the Future, 29 *SAYIL* 42 (2004).

[83] The *Barcelona Traction* case 1970 ICJ Reports 44, paras. 78–79, was cited for the proposition that diplomatic protection is a discretionary right on the part of States in Kuanda v. President of the Republic of South Africa 2005 (4) SALR 235 (CC) at 248–49 para. 23; Van Zyl v. Government of the RSA 2005 (11) Butterworths Constitutional Law Reports 1106 (T) at 1121, para. 31.

[84] 2005 (12) Butterworth Constitutional Law Reports 1192 (CC) at 1241–42, paras. 174–78.

[85] 1986 ICJ Reports 14.

[86] 1996 ICJ Reports 226.

[87] ICTY 1995, case no IT-94-1-AR 72.

[88] 1995 (3) SALR 319 (CC).

[89] ECHR, ser. A, vol. 161, 1989.

[90] 1995 (3) SALR 632 (CC).

Economic, Social, and Cultural Rights. The jurisprudence of the European Court of Justice has also been considered.[116]

South African courts have no hesitation to invoke the judgments of foreign courts in the context of decisions on the country's treaty obligations. Judgments of courts in the United Kingdom, the United States, Canada, Germany, France, Australia, New Zealand, Zimbabwe, Namibia, and India feature prominently in South African jurisprudence. For example, in *Potgieter v. British Airways*,[117] Justice Davis of the Cape Provincial Division invoked decisions of the English House of Lords; the U.S. Supreme Court; the French Court of Cassation; and decisions by courts in Montreal, Ontario, and British Colombia to assist him in interpreting the Convention for the Unification of Certain Rules relating to International Carriage by Air (Warsaw Convention), incorporated into South African law by the Carriage by Air Act.[118] Another recent example is *A. M. Moolla Group Ltd. v. The Gap Inc.*,[119] in which the Paris Convention for the Protection of Industrial Property of 1883, which has been incorporated into South African law, was interpreted in the context of decisions from the United States, England, Australia, Canada, and India. The debate in the United States about the role of international and foreign jurisprudence in constitutional interpretation[120] finds no place in South Africa. Discarding the country's isolationist past, judges and lawyers interpret and develop South African law in accordance with the country's international obligations with the fervor of recent converts.

Although South African courts rely heavily on international and foreign jurisprudence, such decisions are not binding but of persuasive value only. This was made clear by President Chaskalson in *S. v. Makwanyane*,[121] where he stated:

> In dealing with comparative law, we must bear in mind that we are required to construe the South African Constitution, and not an international instrument or the constitution of some foreign country, and that this has to be done with due regard to our legal system, our history and circumstances, and the structure and language of our Constitution. We can derive assistance from public international law and foreign case law, but we are in no way bound to follow it.

[116] A. M. Moolla Group Ltd. v. The Gap Inc. 2005 (2) SALR 412 (SCA), at 418, para. 9; *id.* at 2005 (6) SALR 568 (SCA) at 582 (para. 26), 588 (para. 42).

[117] 2005 (3) SALR 133 (C).

[118] Act 17 of 1946.

[119] 2005 (6) SA 568 (SCA).

[120] *See* Agora: The United States Constitution and International Law 98 *AJIL* 42 (2004).

[121] 1995 (3) SALR 391 (CC) at para. 39.

However, as the Constitutional Court itself declared shortly after *Makwanyane*, "the lawmakers of the Constitution should not lightly be presumed to authorize any law which might constitute a breach of the obligations of the state in terms of international law."[122]

C. *Deference to the Executive*

Before 1994, the application of international law in South Africa was subject to constitutional rules and prerogative powers derived from English law. The position has changed dramatically. South Africa is now a constitutional democracy in which the principles of executive accountability and transparency feature prominently, and courts are given wide powers to review administrative action and legislation. Although the executive retains its nonstatutory powers enabling it to conduct foreign relations, these powers are no longer beyond the reach of judicial review.[123]

In *Kolbatschenko v. King NO*,[124] the Cape Provincial Division stated that it is only in highly exceptional cases that a court will adopt a hands-off approach to reviewing executive action in the conduct of foreign relations, where a discretion has been exercised or an executive or administrative decision made that directly affects the rights and interests of an individual applicant.[125] The court recognized that such exceptional cases included the recognition of foreign states or governments, "the making, or the determination of the existence, of treaties between South Africa and foreign states, the declaration of war[,] and the making of peace" because "such decisions usually involve the relationship between the South African state and the foreign state concerned, directly affecting the interests of such states as states, and are often of so political a nature that the courts have "no judicial or manageable standards" by which to judge them."[126] A more restrictive view was expressed by Justice Patel in *Van Zyl v. Government of the Republic of South Africa*:[127] "The conduct of foreign relations may be one of the rare instances where the Constitution and Bill of Rights provide no ground for effective review. This will be the case where the decision does not limit any

[122] Azanian Peoples Organization (AZAPO) v. President of the Republic of South Africa 1996 (4) SA 671 (CC), paras. 26–28 (per Mahomed DP).

[123] Dugard, *supra* note 8, at 73. *See also* Kaunda v. President of the Republic of South Africa 2005 (4) SA 893 (CC), para. 144(6).

[124] 2001 (4) SALR 336 (C).

[125] *Id.*, at 355 C–D.

[126] *Id.*, at 356–57.

[127] 2005 (11) Butterworths Constitutional Law Reports 1106 (T).

fundamental rights and is concerned primarily with the conduct of foreign relations."[128]

To date, South African courts have not been required to consider the question of whether the executive is to be given a free hand in the interpretation of a treaty binding on South Africa. If the treaty has not been incorporated into domestic law and is binding only on the international plane (except in the limited case of self-executing treaties), it is unlikely that a court would review the executive interpretation of such a treaty, since the treaty would not be part of South African law. Different considerations apply in the case of an incorporated treaty (or a self-executing treaty), particularly one affecting the fundamental rights of the individual. Since such a treaty would be part of South African law, a court would in all probability insist that the question of interpretation fell within its exclusive domain. By definition, such an incorporated treaty would involve not only the relationship between the South African state and a foreign state; it would also affect relations between the state and individuals or between individuals inter se. In this author's view, this would be a matter solely within the competence of the judicial power and beyond the discretionary reach of the executive.

D. *Rights for Private Parties Arising out of Treaties*

A treaty does not create rights or duties for the individual unless incorporated into municipal law in accordance with Section 231(4) of the 1996 Constitution. Once incorporated, the treaty creates rights and duties for the individual in the same way that an ordinary statute creates rights and duties. If not incorporated, the treaty may be taken into account only as an interpretative guide to legislation.[129] A self-executing treaty falls into a different category. In terms of Section 231(4) of the Constitution, it becomes law without the need for any act of incorporation. As pointed out earlier,[130] however, uncertainty prevails over when a treaty will be held to be self-executing. Arguments that unincorporated human rights treaties are self-executing,[131] and therefore create rights and duties for the individual without the need for statutory incorporation, remain untested. No attempt has been made to persuade a court that the ICCPR, which has been ratified but not incorporated into domestic law, creates rights for the individual. The explanation for this lies in the fact that most of the rights contained in

[128] *Id.*, at 1131, para. 54.
[129] *See supra* notes 48–49 and accompanying text.
[130] *See supra* notes 23–32 and accompanying text.
[131] *See supra* notes 28–29 and accompanying text.

the Covenant are guaranteed in the Bill of Rights. Nevertheless, this does show that the argument that unincorporated human rights treaties create rights for individuals remains unproven.

E. *Treaties and the Interpretation of Statutes*

As shown previously,[132] both South African common law[133] and the Constitution[134] require courts to interpret legislation in accordance with international law. Moreover, Section 39 of the Constitution provides that a court "must consider international law" when interpreting the Bill of Rights, and a number of statutes expressly direct courts to have regard to international law when interpreting the statute.[135] Courts have responded positively to these constitutional and legislative directions and, since 1994, have endeavored to ensure that there is consistency between legislation and South Africa's treaty obligations.

V. TREATIES AND JUDICIAL REMEDIES

Many treaties confer rights and duties on natural and legal persons. Human rights treaties confer rights on the individual. Refugee conventions provide rights to persons unable to return to their national state for fear of persecution. Diplomatic and consular conventions accord the privilege of immunity to such officials. Antiterrorism conventions and the Statute of the International Criminal Court make certain acts committed by the individual punishable. Extradition agreements provide for the transfer of suspected criminals to other states but at the same time confer due process rights on the suspect. There are many other examples. Treaties of this kind that have been incorporated into South African law under Section 231(4) of the Constitution not only confer rights but also provide for remedies. For instance, the 1951 Convention Relating to the Status of Refugees is incorporated into South African law by the Refugees Act.[136] Under this act, a person defined as a refugee under the 1951 Convention, who may not therefore be returned to his or her state of origin, is entitled to refugee status in South Africa. Failure of the authorities to grant refugee status is subject to judicial review. Thus, there is a remedy under South African law for a right conferred by

[132] *See supra* notes 41–69 and accompanying text.
[133] *See supra* note 41 and accompanying text.
[134] Sec. 233.
[135] *See supra* notes 62–69 and accompanying text.
[136] Act 130 of 1998.

treaty, but only because the treaty has been incorporated into domestic law. So, too, extradition agreements provide for the extradition of suspected criminals but also confer rights on the suspect to resist extradition – if, for instance, the law of the requesting state applies the death penalty or if the offense is one of a political character. If an extradition agreement is not incorporated into domestic law, no extradition will be allowed. And, if it is incorporated, the suspect may seek to resist extradition on the ground that the offense is one of a political character. Both the procedure for extradition and the legal grounds for resisting extradition, however, have their source in the Extradition Act,[137] and not in the bilateral or multilateral extradition treaty.

Section 231(4) of the Constitution contemplates the application of self-executing treaties in South African law without the need for any legislative incorporation. Presumably, a treaty found to be self-executing that confers rights will be enforceable in the same way as an incorporated treaty. Thus, a remedy will follow from a right. However, as has been shown here,[138] there is still uncertainty as to which treaties qualify as self-executing. At present, no treaty has been found by a court to be self-executing.

The foregoing discussion has dealt principally with remedies for the enforcement of treaty rights. The same principle applies to obligations or punishments. No person may be extradited pursuant to an unincorporated extradition agreement. Similarly, no person may be prosecuted domestically for an international crime in the absence of enabling legislation. Thus, legislation has been enacted to allow the prosecution of hijackers;[139] terrorists;[140] and those who have committed war crimes, crimes against humanity, and genocide.[141] In 1999, there was a failed attempt to prosecute the former dictator of Ethiopia, Mengistu Haile Mariam, for the crime of torture while he was on a visit to South Africa. The attempt failed, although South Africa had ratified the Torture Convention in 1998, because South Africa had not incorporated the convention into domestic law.[142]

[137] Act 67 of 1962.

[138] *See supra* notes 23–32 and accompanying text.

[139] Civil Aviation Offences Act 10 of 1972, incorporating the Hague Convention for the Suppression of Unlawful Seizure of Aircraft of 1970 and the Montreal Convention for the Suppression of Unlawful Acts against the Safety of Civil Aviation of 1971.

[140] The Protection of Constitutional Democracy against Terrorist and Related Activities Act 33 of 2004, incorporating the International Convention for the Suppression of Terrorist Bombing of 1997 and similar conventions.

[141] The Implementation of the Rome Statute of the International Criminal Court Act 27 of 2002, which criminalizes the core crimes contained in the Rome Statute of 1998.

[142] See 1999 *Annual Survey of South African Law* 100.

VI. CONCLUSION

South Africa presents an example of a legal system determined to ensure consistency between international law and municipal law. The 1996 South African Constitution, probably one of the most international-law-friendly constitutions in the world, directs courts to interpret municipal law in a manner that reflects consistency with international law. Under the Constitution, courts must consider international law in their application of the Bill of Rights. Moreover, many statutes direct courts to interpret laws incorporating treaties in full or in part in accordance with international law. Courts apply these prescriptions with enthusiasm. Since 1994, courts have consistently interpreted legislation to accord with international law, in stark contrast with their attitude during the apartheid era. Consistency with international treaty law is achieved by means of dualism. Only those treaties incorporated into South African law confer rights and duties, provide remedies, or permit prosecution of international crimes. Unincorporated treaties, with the exception of as-yet-untested self-executing treaties, may be considered in the interpretation of statutes and possibly as a standard for the review of administrative action, but they confer no rights or duties, provide no remedies, and do not permit the prosecution of international crimes.

It is widely believed that the monist approach to treaty incorporation achieves greater compliance with international law and ensures more effective enforcement of treaties in municipal law. This is, however, questionable. Monism per se does not guarantee compliance with international law or the effective enforcement of treaties. A monist state may fail to become a party to many treaties; its constitution may not expressly direct compliance with international law; its courts may fail to achieve consistency with international law because of hostility to international law or ignorance of international law and international judicial decisions; lawyers may refuse to research international law adequately and to present international law arguments before courts; and its law schools may fail to educate lawyers about international law. A dualist state, such as South Africa, committed to ensuring compliance with international law in its Constitution, statutes, courts, legal profession, and law schools, is more likely to achieve consistency between international treaty law and municipal law than a monist state that lacks the will and historical determination to promote international law. The South African experience therefore contradicts accepted wisdom that monism most effectively promotes consistency between international treaty law and domestic law.

12

United Kingdom

Anthony Aust

Former Deputy Legal Adviser, Foreign and Commonwealth Office

I. INTRODUCTION

When it comes to treaties, the United Kingdom is very much a dualist state.[1] A proper understanding of how treaties are (or are not) implemented and enforced in the English legal system requires a reasonably detailed description of this form of dualism. It is also important because most of the other fifty-two Commonwealth States[2] are former British overseas territories that inherited the same, or very similar, constitutional principles about the place of treaties in domestic law.[3] This will be followed by a description of how the English courts approach the matter of interpretation of treaties, which is central to an understanding of how private rights can (or cannot) be enforced. (We are not concerned with so-called collective rights, such as those set out in the International Covenant on Economic, Social and Cultural Rights 1966.)[4] Then, the question of the extent to which English courts recognize and enforce rights conferred on private parties under treaties will be discussed. Finally, there will be a concise description of the remedies that may be available for the enforcement of private rights.

[1] In contrast, customary international law (CIL) is regarded as part of English law and, unlike foreign law (the law of other states), does not have to be proved in evidence but is a matter for legal argument: for a concise account of CIL, *see* A. Aust, *Handbook of International Law*, Cambridge, 2005, pgs. 6–8.

[2] Currently, Fiji is suspended from the Councils of the Commonwealth following a military coup, and Nauru is a Special Member. Zimbabwe has left the Commonwealth, though it is hoped that it will one day return.

[3] *See also* the chapters in this book on Australia, Canada and India; and the entries for Canada and India *in* D. B. Hollis, M. R. Blakeslee, and L. Ederington (eds.), *National Treaty Law and Practice*, Leiden (2005).

[4] International Covenant on Economic, Social and Cultural Rights 1966, 993 UNTS 3 (No. 14531); UKTS (1977) 6.

Only the position in English law is dealt with here. The legal system in Scotland – and, to some extent, in Northern Ireland – is slightly different (it is a foolhardy Englishman who ventures onto Scottish or Irish turf), though the constitutional place of treaties is the same throughout the United Kingdom and its remaining overseas territories.[5]

II. THE STATUS OF TREATIES IN THE ENGLISH LEGAL SYSTEM

Under its dualist approach, the British constitution (mainly, but not entirely, unwritten)[6] gives no special status to treaties: the rights and obligations they create have no automatic effect in domestic law. This reflects, on the one hand, the constitutional power of the Crown (in effect, the Government) generally to bind the United Kingdom to a treaty without the prior consent of Parliament and, on the other hand, the supreme power of Parliament to make law. This division of powers was a product of the seventeenth-century constitutional struggle between the King of England and Parliament. It resulted in the power to legislate being almost completely vested in Parliament, although the Crown retained in common law certain "royal prerogatives" (the right to act without the consent of Parliament), including the making of treaties.[7]

This means that, with a few minor exceptions, Parliament has no control over the Government when it comes to the making of treaties, apart from the Ponsonby Rule (discussed herein), and certain special cases when legislation is needed before the Government can give consent to be bound by a treaty. I know of no case where the courts have even been asked to rule on whether a treaty has been properly concluded by the Government. In any case, this is likely to arise only in those exceptional cases where the Government has a statutory duty to seek the approval of Parliament before the Government ratifies.[8] But this could change. There have been attempts in the House of Lords (usually by the human rights lawyer Lord Lester) to give Parliament

[5] The *United Kingdom* means the metropolitan territory of England (which includes Wales), Scotland and Northern Ireland. It therefore does not include the Crown Dependences (Channel Islands and the Isle of Man) or the several overseas territories: *see* A. Aust, *Modern Treaty Law and Practice*, 2d ed., Cambridge, 2007, pgs. 206–08.

[6] Of former British overseas territories, probably only New Zealand does not have a written constitution in the normal sense.

[7] *See* D. O'Connell, *International Law*, 2d ed., London, 1970, pgs. 216–17; E. Wade and K. Ewing, *Constitutional and Administrative Law*, 13th ed., Harlow, England, 2003, pg. 309 et seq.

[8] *See, e.g.*, s. 12 of the European Parliamentary Elections Act 2002.

greater power in this area, but they have not found support.[9] In practice, the Ponsonby Rule is effective in giving Parliament advance notice of important treaties, and if a treaty needs legislation before the Government can ratify it, Parliament has to enact that legislation (discussed subsequently).

Under the British Constitution, the provisions of a treaty that are made part of (incorporated into)[10] domestic law have the status only of domestic law,[11] and can be amended or repealed by later legislation. If that were to result in breach of the treaty, there would be no remedy in domestic law since there would have been no violation of that law.[12] This legal position is central to any discussion of how treaties can be enforced in domestic law. Only in certain limited circumstances will the courts have regard to unincorporated treaties.[13]

The various methods by which treaties are incorporated may be better understood by a short explanation of the constitutional practice of the United Kingdom.[14] The treaty-making power of the Crown is exercised by the Secretary of State for Foreign and Commonwealth Affairs (foreign minister). There is generally no constitutional requirement for Parliament to consent before the Crown enters into a treaty. But, under a constitutional convention (known as the Ponsonby Rule), a treaty that is subject to ratification or analogous procedure[15] is "laid before" (notified to) Parliament, with a short explanatory memorandum, for twenty-one days while Parliament is sitting. The Rule is adhered to in all cases to which it applies. But the purpose of the Rule is merely to ensure that Parliament is informed of the treaty; it does not make the treaty part of domestic law.[16] Similarly, although a treaty that has entered into force for the United Kingdom is

[9] However, in April 2009 the British Government tabled a Bill to make the Ponsonby Rule a part of the law. It is likely to be enacted.

[10] Another term sometimes used is *transformation*: see I. Brownlie, *Principles of Public International Law*, 6th ed., Oxford, 2003, pgs. 41–45. But, since *incorporation* is sometimes used to describe the monist approach to treaties – that they become part of (are incorporated into) domestic law automatically (*see* Hollis, *supra* note 3, pg. 40) – this may only confuse an already complex subject.

[11] For example, *see* Lord Hoffmann in *Lyons* ([2002] UKHL 44; [2003] 1 AC 976); [2002] 3 WLR 1562), paras. 27 and 40.

[12] *See* Lord Bingham in *Lyons*, *supra* note 11, para. 14.

[13] *See infra* text at notes 71–85.

[14] *See* the detailed account of U.K. treaty law and practice in Hollis, *supra* note 3, pgs. 727–64; R. Jennings and A. Watts (eds.), *Oppenheim's International Law*, 9th ed., 1992, London, Vol. 1, pgs. 56–63; J. Harrington, "Scrutiny and Approval: The Role of Westminster-Style Parliaments in Treaty-Making" (2006) ICLQ 120, 126–31.

[15] Such as formal notification by one or more of the contracting states that all constitutional procedures have been completed.

[16] For further details, *see* Aust, *supra* note 5, pgs. 189–94.

binding on it in international law, the treaty itself is not part of domestic law, even if some of its provisions may have been made part of that law.

Thus, treaties are not in any way supreme law under the British Constitution; they are not superior, or even equal, to domestic law and can be overridden by it, though this is rare.[17] In short, treaties fall into the domain of public international law; legislation that incorporates the provisions of a treaty remains domestic law.

Incorporation into domestic law can take three main forms:

(1) *An Act of Parliament for the purpose of incorporating the treaty into the law of the United Kingdom.* The text of the whole (or part)[18] of the treaty may be scheduled to the Act (primary legislation), which will provide that the provisions of the treaty set out in the schedule "have the force of law in the United Kingdom." Scheduling the text of the treaty enables those provisions to be seen in their proper context, and so is an aid to interpretation. When there is no authentic English text of a treaty, the practice is to attach the original foreign-language text with an English translation.[19] Sometimes none of the treaty is scheduled. Instead, the Act makes such changes to domestic law as are necessary to give effect to the treaty.[20] The Act may, for example, simply authorize expenditure required by the treaty. In such cases, it may or may not declare that its purpose is to give some effect to the treaty. This can have implications for the interpretation of the legislation. Alternatively, an Act may require that rules made under it conform to a treaty.[21]

[17] *See infra* pgs. 487–88 about the special circumstances of the ECHR and the Human Rights Act 1988.

[18] Both the Diplomatic Privileges Act 1964 and the Consular Relations Act 1968 do not schedule all the (substantive) provisions of the Vienna Conventions of 1961 and 1963 (*see infra* pgs. 489–90). See also s. 50 of, and Schedule 8 to, the International Criminal Court Act 2001, which sets out the definitions of the offences in the ICC Statute.

[19] *See* s. 1 Carriage by Air Act 1961 and s. 1 Carriage by Air (Supplementary Provisions) Act 1962. Both implement treaties modifying the Warsaw Convention 1929, which has French as the prevailing language text.

[20] *See* the State Immunity Act 1978, although its main purpose was to enable the United Kingdom to ratify the CoE State Immunity Convention 1972 (1495 UNTS 182 (No. 25699); ILM (1972) 470; UKTS (1979) 74).

[21] *See* s. 2 of the Asylum and Immigration Appeals Act 1993, which requires that the immigration rules be consistent with the Refugee Convention 1951, as amended by the 1967 Protocol (189 UNTS 137 (No. 2545); UKTS (1954) 39, and 606 UNTS 267 (No. 8791); UKTS (1969) 15).

But, one must be careful not to assume that just because treaty provisions are scheduled to an Act they thereby become part of domestic law. The Geneva Conventions Act 1957 (as amended by the Geneva Conventions (Amendment) Act 1995) has annexed to it the (complete) text of the four Geneva Conventions 1949, and the two Additional Protocols 1977. Those treaties set out in great detail some of the most important rules on the law of armed conflict (sometimes today misleadingly called international humanitarian law), including how prisoners of war and civilians are to be treated. But the Act does not provide that their provisions shall have the force of law in the United Kingdom.[22] The main purpose is to enable "grave breaches" of the Conventions to be prosecuted and to protect the Red Cross emblem. It thus creates only certain criminal offences. Enforcement of the rest of the treaties is left largely to military law and military tribunals.[23]

(2) *An Act of Parliament conferring all the powers necessary to carry out obligations under existing or future treaties.* For example, bilateral air services agreements can be concluded without the need each time for fresh legislation, since existing legislation, both primary and subsidiary, is sufficient to implement the agreements. Under section 60 of the Civil Aviation Act of 1982, an Order in Council (i.e., subsidiary legislation) can be (and has been) made to give effect in domestic law to the umbrella treaty, the Chicago Convention on International Civil Aviation 1944.[24] But it may not always be obvious that this is the reason for an Act or part of it.[25]

(3) *An Act of Parliament that provides a framework within which subsidiary legislation can be made to give effect to a certain category of treaty, often bilateral.* The Act can either:

(a) *authorize the Crown to make subsidiary legislation*[26] *making the text of the treaty part of domestic law.* This is usually done by

[22] *See* Cheng v. Conn, Inspector of Taxes [1968] 1 All ER 779; and P. Rowe and M. Meyer, "The Geneva Conventions (Amendment) Act 1995: A Generally Minimalist Approach" (1996) ICLQ 476–84.

[23] The Geneva Conventions are part of U.K. military law, which is part of the law of England. However, military law applies primarily to members of the armed services, not to the general population.

[24] 15 UNTS 295 (No. 102); UKTS (1953) 8. See the Air Navigation Order 1995 (No. 1038).

[25] *See* Solomon v. Commissioner of Customs and Excise [1967] 2 QB 116, at 127(C).

[26] Subsidiary legislation (also known as subordinate legislation) is legislation made by the Government under a Statute which confers such power. The Statute may either give Parliament the power to negate subordinate legislation that has already been made by the Government (negative procedure) or, though this is less often the case, require that

an Order made by the Queen in Council (Order in Council) to which the text of the treaty is attached and that is subject to a fairly brief Parliamentary procedure. Such legislation is frequently made for bilateral double-taxation conventions,[27] extradition treaties,[28] and social security conventions[29]

(b) *authorize the Crown to make subsidiary legislation to implement obligations imposed by certain categories of treaty.* The treaty is not attached to the subsidiary legislation. Instead, its provisions are converted (sometimes with difficulty) into the language of the Act, and, if necessary, elaborated. Typical of this method is the International Organisations Act 1968, under which Orders in Council are made to give effect to treaties conferring privileges and immunities on international organisations and tribunals, and persons connected with them.[30]

(c) *authorize the making of an Order that is not subject to any form of parliamentary approval or procedure, though Parliament is notified when it has been made.* This is an exceptional measure and an Act will only make provision for such Orders to be made when provision has to be made in domestic law for which there can be no question of approval or rejection of the Order by Parliament. For example, the United Nations Act 1946 has only one (short) substantive section, which empowers the Crown to make such Orders when it is necessary or expedient to enable measures adopted by the UN Security Council to be applied effectively. The power is used extensively to implement measures (e.g., economic and other sanctions, the establishment of international criminal tribunals), adopted by the Security Council under Chapter VII of the UN Charter 1945, since every Member of the United Nations is obliged by the Charter to enforce such measures. (Only another Order or Act of Parliament can revoke the Orders.) But the Act does not make the Charter part of domestic law.

the proposed subordinate legislation be first approved by Parliament in draft before it can be made by the Government (affirmative procedure).

[27] Income and Corporation Taxes Act 1988, s. 788(10); SI 2002 No. 3138 (South Africa).

[28] *See* Extradition Act 1989, s. 4, and SI 1990 No. 1507, which gives effect to the CoE Extradition Convention 1957, including reservations and declarations made by the parties.

[29] *See* the Social Security Act 1975, s. 143, and SI 1991 No. 767 (Norway).

[30] *See, e.g.,* Tribunal for the Law of the Sea (Immunities and Privileges) Order 1996 (SI 1996 No. 272).

III. INTERPRETATION OF TREATIES BY THE ENGLISH COURTS

In practice, most treaties are interpreted by national, not international, courts.[31] At least in the past, English judges have not been at their happiest when confronted by a treaty. Admittedly, they were not helped by the strict separation of treaties from domestic law inherent in the dualist approach. The courts have, however, developed certain principles that alleviate some of the strictness of that approach.[32] In summary:

(1) If the language of legislation implementing a treaty is unambiguous, the courts will not look behind the legislation at the treaty.[33] If the text of the statute is narrower than that of the treaty to which it purports to give effect, the court must follow the statute.[34] This is dualism at its strictest.
(2) If the language of the legislation is unclear, the court will look at the treaty that the legislation was enacted to implement, and if necessary, at all of the treaty. It will do this even if the legislation does not mention the treaty.[35] This is simply common sense.
(3) Unclear legislation will be interpreted in a way that is consistent with any applicable international obligations of the United Kingdom, including customary international law and unincorporated treaties. The U.K. courts applied this principle to the European Convention on Human Rights 1950 (ECHR)[36] even before it was incorporated.[37]

[31] *See* the numerous decisions on international law by national courts recorded in the cumulative indexes to the some 130 (and counting) volumes of *International Law Reports*, published regularly by Cambridge University Press.

[32] *See* R. Higgins on U.K. practice in F. Jacobs and S. Roberts (eds.), *The Effect of Treaties in Domestic* Law, London, 1987, pgs. 123–39; *Oppenheim*, pgs. 60–63; I. Sinclair, "The Principles of Treaty Interpretation and Their Application by the English Courts" (1963) ICLQ 508–51; C. Warbrick, "International Law in English Courts – Recent Cases" (2003) ICLQ 815–24.

[33] The Custom and Excise Act 1952 was in part enacted to enable the United Kingdom to ratify the Valuation of Goods for Customs Purposes Convention 1950 (171 UNTS 305; UKTS (1954) 49), but it did not attach any part of the text of (or even mention) the Convention: see *Solomon, supra* note 25.

[34] *Pepushi* [2004] EWHC (Admin) 798, paras. 18–41. *See also* McKerr [2004] 1 WLR 807 (HL), Lord Steyn at paras. 50–52.

[35] *See* The Jade, The Esherscheim [1976] 1 AER 920.

[36] 213 UNTS 221 (No. 2889); UKTS (1953) 71; ETS 5.

[37] *See* Garland v. British Rail Engineering [1983] 2 AC 751, 771. In 1995, in *Teoh* (183 CLR 273; 104 ILR 466), the High Court of Australia went further and held that ratification of a treaty could create a legitimate expectation as to how public authorities would act: *see* M. Shaw, *International Law*, 6th ed., Cambridge, 2008, pg. 166 et seq, esp. fn. 209. The Australian doctrine of legitimate expectations has not been followed by the English courts. *See also* the views of the European Court of Justice in Marleasing SA (Case 106/89 [1990] ECR 4135;

(4) When a treaty has been incorporated by attaching all or part of it to legislation,[38] since the treaty is a creation of international law the English courts will interpret it according to the rules of international law,[39] in particular Articles 31–33 of the Vienna Convention on the Law of Treaties 1969. This is true even though the Convention itself has not been incorporated into English law. In recent years, British judges have become much better at this.[40] When a treaty has not been incorporated, if the court agrees to consider it, it would also interpret it according to the Vienna Convention. (On unincorporated treaties, see section IV.D below.)

(5) When the interpretation of a treaty is in issue, counsel will inevitably refer the court to other treaties and to decisions of courts of other states or of international courts and tribunals. The court may refer to such material in its judgment, though usually only if it finds it helpful. *Al-Skeine*[41] was a claim brought under the Human Rights Act 1998 (which had incorporated the ECHR into English law). In considering the position under the ECHR, in 2005 the Court of Appeal considered various other treaties, such as the Hague Regulations 1907, the Geneva Conventions 1949 and the Torture Convention 1985. But, since such treaties were not part of the legislation they were construing, they were only persuasive, even if, in practice, they can be decisive. Although the UN Charter has not been incorporated into English law, in 2006 the Court of Appeal in *Al-Jedda*[42] decided that any relevant rights that the defendant had under the ECHR were, because of Article 103 of the UN Charter,[43] subject to the United Kingdom's obligations under

[1992] CMLR 305); and the criticism of it in D. Wyatt and A. Dashwood's *European Union Law*, London, 2000, pgs. 93–94 and 101.

[38] For example, Schedules 1 and 2 to the Child Abduction Act 1985 contain most of the articles of the Hague Convention on the Civil Aspects of International Child Abduction 1980 (1343 UNTS 98 (No. 22514); UKTS (1986) 66), and of the European Convention on the Recognition and Enforcement of Decisions Concerning Custody of Children 1980 (1496 UNTS 38 (No. 25701); ETS 105; UKTS (1987) 35).

[39] *See* R. v. Lambeth Justices *ex parte* Yusufu [1985] Times Law Reports 114; Sidhu v. British Airways [1997] 1 AER 193, at 201–12.

[40] *See* R. Gardiner, "Treaty Interpretation in the English Courts since *Fothergill v. Monarch Airlines*" (1995) ICLQ 620; *Oppenheim, supra* note 14, vol. 2, pg. 1269, n. 2 (significantly, perhaps the longest footnote in that noteworthy work); s. 3(1) of the European Communities Act 1972; and C. Kuner, "The Interpretation of Multilingual Treaties" (1991) ICLQ 953, 960–61.

[41] [2005] EWCA Civ 1609. The House of Lords upheld the judgment (*see* [2007] UKHL 26).

[42] [2006] EWCA Civ 327, paras. 55–87.

[43] Art. 103 provides: "In the event of any conflict between the obligations of the Members of the United Nations under the present Charter and their obligations under any other

the relevant Chapter VII resolution of the UN Security Council, 1546 (2004). Because all the parties to the ECHR are also members of the United Nations, they are necessarily bound by such resolutions, and so if there is any conflict between them and their ECHR obligations, their Charter obligations will prevail.[44]

(6) The English courts do not defer to the British Government's favored interpretation of a treaty; though they will accept a certificate given on behalf of the Government that is about facts within the particular knowledge of the Government.[45] If the Government is represented before the court (and this is unlikely to be so unless the Government is in some way affected or the case raises a matter of general public interest), its counsel has no higher standing than counsel of any other party. This is so even when the Government is represented by the Attorney-General himself. The same goes for the Government's legal arguments. They are not dispositive; whether the court is persuaded by them depends entirely on their merits.

(7) There is no presumption that a treaty does not create a right for a private party, but nor should it be assumed that every treaty which places a duty on government or a public official thereby also creates a private right. Unless a private right is clearly included in implementing legislation, the party asserting such a right has the burden of proving that the treaty creates it and that it is enforceable by the courts.

IV. DOMESTIC LEGAL PRINCIPLES GOVERNING PRIVATE RIGHTS UNDER TREATIES

We are here concerned only with the breach of a private right accorded to a person by a treaty. By "private right" is meant a right conferred on a natural (an individual) or legal person (e.g., a corporate body), as

international agreement, their obligations under the present Charter shall prevail." The reference to "obligations" includes obligations put on Members by Chapter VII resolutions of the Security Council, e.g., about imposing sanctions. These are binding on the British courts by virtue of the Orders in Council (subordinate legislation) made to implement them (see *supra* pg. 481, para. 3(c)).

[44] If the European Court of Human Rights holds that it is bound by a Chapter VII resolution of the UN Security Council, that judgment binds the United Kingdom under international law. Now that we have, by the Human Rights Act 1998, in effect made the ECHR and judgments of its Court part of U.K. law, the British Government and courts are bound by such judgments. *See also* the judgments of the EC Court of First Instance in *Kadi* (T. 315/01) and *Aden* (T. 306/01). But on September 3, 2008, the ECJ reversed the judgment in *Kadi*: see C-402/05P and C-415/05P.

[45] *See Oppenheim, supra* note 14, vol. 2, pgs. 1046–52, esp. pg. 1051.

opposed to the States or international organizations that are parties to the treaty. Whether a remedy is available (and meaningful) in English law for infringement of a private right accorded by treaty depends, first, on whether the treaty itself confers such a right. A private right is not generally conferred as such by treaty, whether bilateral or multilateral, most being more concerned with inter-State relations. Whether a treaty does create a private right will, in practice, be relevant only if there is doubt whether the domestic law implementing the treaty accords such a right in domestic law.

In the bilateral field, one body of treaty law that is important for daily life is the international law governing civil aviation, in which private rights are likely to be accorded to legal persons such as airlines. Because an airline needs prior permission to land or take on board passengers in another State, there has developed an extensive network of bilateral treaties known as air services agreements (ASAs). A typical ASA provides for airlines of each party to operate services on routes between the two States; designation of the airlines to operate the agreed services; fair and equal opportunity for the designated airlines to compete; the capacity (i.e., the size of aircraft) they can operate; a mechanism for approval of tariffs (fares); exemption from customs and other duties and taxes on fuel; freedom to convert and remit each airline's net earnings to its home state;[46] and the right to bring in airline staff and establish sales offices. However, those rights are conferred by the foreign State, not the State of the airline. Disputes about, say, the right of the airline to fly into the other State are matters that the airline's State has to take up with the foreign State under the ASA. If necessary, the matter may have to go to international arbitration.[47]

Thus, the designation of an airline to fly between the two States is done by the State of the airline (not by the foreign State). Although a disgruntled airline may be able to challenge such a designation in court, this should not be seen as a proceeding to enforce a private right under the ASA. Rather, it would be an action to challenge the State's exercise of discretion given to it under the ASA.

The enforcement of private rights conferred by treaties is more likely to arise in the case of multilateral treaties, in particular those concerned with human rights (including refugees) and the law of armed conflict.

[46] Reciprocal exemption from direct taxes is usually provided either in a double taxation convention (*see infra* text at note 96), or in a specific exchange of notes.

[47] *See* United States v. France 1963, 38 ILR 182; United States v. France 1978, 54 ILR 303; United States v. Italy 1965, 45 ILR 393; United States v. United Kingdom 1993, 102 ILR 215.

Given the United Kingdom's dualist approach to treaties, the unwavering practice of the Government is to take each treaty that has been adopted[48] to see whether the United Kingdom should become a party to it. There will be an examination of the treaty in detail. Part of this will be to see whether there will be any need for new legislation to enable a provision to be enforceable in domestic law. It is invariable British practice never to ratify a treaty until any such legislation has first been made, since finding parliamentary time for what may be regarded by other Cabinet ministers as nonessential legislation is never easy, especially when you are in a hurry.[49] In considering these matters, no provision will be made in the legislation for remedies for the breach of private rights unless it is clear from the treaty that domestic law must provide for them. The ECHR was ratified by the United Kingdom as early as 1951 without any domestic provision for the enforcement of the private rights created by it, even though Article 13 expressly provides that there shall be "an effective remedy before a national authority" for any violation of the ECHR. The then British Government considered that all the rights were already well protected by existing common law and legislation, and if compensation was justified, this could always be given ex gratia. The loss by the United Kingdom of many cases before the Strasbourg Court eventually led in 1998 to the incorporation of the ECHR into domestic law, including the provisions in section 8 for courts to give remedies (including, where appropriate, compensation) for breaches of the ECHR.

Whether it takes the monist or dualist approach to treaties, it is the national court that will have to decide whether the treaty does accord a private right. That depends on how the treaty is interpreted by the court. Even in a dualist state like the United Kingdom, a right under the treaty is a right in international law. So to be effective the right needs to be one recognized also as a right in domestic law. This is important given the strictness of the dualist approach. The English courts are not hidebound by Latin tags, such as *ubi jus, ibi remedium* (where there is a right, there is a remedy), though if a court does find that the implementing legislation (not the treaty itself) does confer a private right, it would be rare indeed if it did not also find some sort of remedy. Though, as we shall see, this will not necessarily be an award of compensation (damages). These principles apply equally to both civil and criminal cases.

[48] If it would enter into force on signature, the process would have to be done before signature. Fortunately, most treaties that enter into force on signature are bilateral and either do not need implementing legislation or can be implemented on the basis of preexisting legislation.

[49] *See* Hollis, *supra* note 3, pgs. 733–40.

A private right may be established in various ways:

(a) An express provision in the domestic legislation (which can be primary or subsidiary) by which the treaty was incorporated.
(b) By deduction from the text of the treaty that is attached to domestic legislation or referred to in the legislation.
(c) When the domestic legislation does not even refer to the treaty, by deduction from the terms of the legislation.
(d) When asserting a right under common law, a court might possibly consider the terms of an unincorporated treaty or an MOU[50] to see whether there was an intention to create a private right.

As should be clear from the foregoing, the crucial issue is whether the legislation (or possibly the common law) recognizes a private right. This is very characteristic of the dualist approach to treaties. If the legislation (including any treaty text that is part of the legislation or referred to in it) does not clearly recognize a private right, it will be difficult for the court to infer one.

We will now examine these four possibilities in detail.

A. *Express Provision in the Domestic Legislation by Which the Treaty Was Incorporated*

The legislation may be primary or subsidiary. Some legislation will provide expressly not only that it creates private rights but also that a remedy exists for breach of them. The best example is the Human Rights Act 1998,[51] which effectively incorporated the ECHR into English law. The Act does not formally make the ECHR part of domestic law but requires courts and public bodies to apply existing and future legislation "so as far as possible" in a way "which is compatible with" rights under the ECHR (referred to from now on as a Convention right).[52] Under section 4, if a court determines that a provision is incompatible with a Convention right, it may make a "declaration of incompatibility."[53] Under section 10, subsidiary legislation may then be made[54] (although there is no legal obligation on Parliament,

[50] For a short explanation of this term, *see infra* text at notes 73–75.
[51] Also to be found in ILM (1999) 464. The Act applies also to Scotland and Northern Ireland.
[52] To do this, they also have to "take into account any judgment, decision, declaration or advisory opinion of the European Court of Human Rights": s. 2(1)(a).
[53] *See* Bellinger v. Bellinger [2003] UKHL 21, Lord Nicholls, paras. 50–55; [2003] AC 467.
[54] S. 10 enables the Minister or The Queen in Council to make an order amending either primary or subsidiary legislation that is incompatible with the Human Rights Act. The

because under the British Constitution it remains sovereign) to remove the incompatibility, including an incompatibility determined by the European Court of Human Rights (Strasbourg Court). Section 19 requires a Bill for all Acts of Parliament to be accompanied by a statement regarding compatibility with rights under the ECHR. Since the Human Rights Act commenced in full in 2000, it has been pleaded in many cases that an act of a public authority, or legislation, is not compatible with a Convention right, and in several cases, the plea has been successful.[55]

For present purposes, the real importance of the Act is that section 7 provides a new remedy to a person who claims that a public authority has acted (or proposes to act) in a way that is incompatible with a Convention right. If a person considers that he or she is (or would be) a victim (for the purposes of Article 34 of the ECHR) of such unlawful act, that person can bring proceedings against the authority in an appropriate English court or tribunal and rely on a Convention right in any legal proceeding. The remedy sought may include damages. Section 8 provides that, before damages can be awarded, the court or tribunal must be satisfied that such an award is necessary to afford just satisfaction to the person. This is the test applied by the Strasbourg Court under Article 41 of the ECHR, and the domestic court or tribunal must take into account the principles applied by the Strasbourg Court in awarding compensation (which generally tends to be modest).[56] So far as possible, a victim should thereby be put into the same position as if the breach had not occurred. Sometimes an English court will therefore not consider that a finding of a breach of the Human Rights Act justifies an award of damages. The typical case would be when the breach was purely procedural and, following the jurisprudence of the Strasbourg Court, the court considers that a declaration of breach provides just satisfaction to the claimant.[57] In most areas, the approach of the Strasbourg Court is not significantly different from the rules applied by English courts to the award of damages, but there are some points on which the practice of the

order can be annulled by Parliament after it has been made by the Minister or The Queen in Council. In certain special cases, the Act requires that a draft of the proposed order must first be approved by both Houses of Parliament before the final order can be made. *See* ss. 10 and 20 of the Act.

[55] *See, e.g.*, A(FC) and others v. Secretary of State, UKHL (2004) 56.

[56] *See, e.g.*, R (D) v. Secretary of State [2006] EWHC (Admin) 980, esp. paras. 127–28. In *Anufrijeva* ([2003] EWCA 1406, LCJ paras. 56–78) and *Greenfield* ([2005] UKHL 14, L. Bingham, paras. 17–19), the Court of Appeal and the House of Lords, respectively, decided that the quantum of damages for a breach of the HRA should follow more closely that awarded by the Strasbourg Court.

[57] *See* P. v. South Gloucestershire Council [1 Feb. 2007] CA.

Strasbourg Court differs from that of English courts. For example, it does not award punitive damages, but, in contrast, it does award compensation for some non-pecuniary or intangible losses that have not yet been recognized by English courts. It is expected that no major changes to the English law on damages will be needed, yet English courts are likely to follow the practice of the Strasbourg Court in awarding damages for intangible loss.[58]

The importance of the compensation provisions of the Human Rights Act goes further than might at first be thought, as some of the grave breaches of the Geneva Conventions will have been committed when the persons harmed were subject to the jurisdiction of the United Kingdom (provided they were under the effective control of members of the British armed forces, such as in a military prison abroad),[59] and so would also amount to violations of a Convention right. Compensation may therefore be obtainable under Section 8 of the Human Rights Act.

The United Kingdom is a party to the International Covenant on Civil and Political Rights of 1966,[60] but it did not legislate to incorporate its provisions into domestic law. Because the Covenant is very similar to the ECHR, which at the time was not felt to need incorporation, there appeared to be no need to incorporate any provisions of the Covenant. But, if today there should be a breach by the United Kingdom of the Covenant, since it would probably also amount to a breach of the ECHR, the remedies under the Human Rights Act should be adequate.

In *LaGrand* and *Avena*,[61] the International Court of Justice decided that failure by the United States to inform foreign nationals of their right to communicate with their consular officers was a breach of Article 36 of the Vienna Convention on Consular Relations 1963 and therefore of their individual rights. Thus, Article 36 clearly gives not only (public) rights to a consular officer of a sending State, but also private rights to a national of the sending State who is detained by the receiving State. Yet, although the Consular Relations Act 1968 gives many articles of the Convention the force of law in the United Kingdom, it does not do so for Article 36. Given this (clearly deliberate) exclusion, it is difficult to see how a foreign national detained by the U.K. police, immigration, or other public authorities would

[58] *See generally* 2000 Report of the English Law Commission on Damages under the Human Rights Act 1998 (No. 266), *available at* http:// www.lawcom.gov.uk.

[59] *See* R. (Al-Skeine) v. S of S [2007] UKHL 26.

[60] 999 UNTS 171 (No. 14668); ILM (1967) 368; UKTS (1977) 6.

[61] *ICJ Reports* (2001), pg. 9; ILM (2001) 1069; 118 ILR 37, and *ICJ Reports* (2004); ILM (2004) 581.

have any remedy under the 1968 Act for a breach of Article 36. Instead, any claim may have to be based on some other breach of a Convention right committed while he or she was detained. There may be a right to compensation under the Human Rights Act for breach of Article 5 of the ECHR (right to liberty and security). Alternatively, the right to communicate may well now be regarded as a right in customary international law and, if so, should be recognized and enforced by the English courts.[62]

The U.K. approach in the Consular Relations Act 1968 seems to support the view that a right accorded to a person by a treaty does not necessarily have to be enshrined in domestic law. There are various alternative ways in which certain individual rights can be enforced. Administrative instructions to police and prison officers, whether or not issued pursuant to legislation, can be enforced in the English courts by proceedings for judicial review. It is now firmly established that even the exercise by the Government of prerogative powers (e.g., the issue of passports) is subject to judicial review.[63]

In contrast, the provisions in both the Vienna Conventions on Diplomatic Relations 1961 and on Consular Relations 1963 according immunity to diplomats and consuls have been made part of domestic law. The essence of immunity is that domestic courts cannot enforce a private right unless the immunity is waived. Thus, the basic issue of whether immunity is applicable in the particular circumstances is one that inevitably can also affect private rights. In the United Kingdom, the Government leaves it to the courts to determine on the law and on the facts whether a person is entitled to immunity in a particular case. The most the Government will do is give a certificate of facts that are within its particular knowledge, such as that X has been formally notified to the Government of the State of Y as one of its diplomatic agents. Although the certificate is conclusive as to the facts in it, the court is not bound to conclude that Mr X therefore has immunity in the particular case. For example, it may be satisfied on other evidence before it that X is permanently resident in the United Kingdom and therefore entitled to only limited immunity.[64] In this way, the private rights of a plaintiff may be protected, albeit somewhat indirectly.

Section 2 of the Asylum and Immigration Appeals Act 1993 provides that nothing in the Immigration Rules shall lay down any practice that would be contrary to the Refugees Convention 1951.[65] This is clear recognition

[62] *See supra* note 1.

[63] *See* R. v. S. of S., *ex parte* Everett [1989] 1 QB 811; *see generally* H. Woolf, J. Jowell, and A. Le Sueur, *De Smith's Judicial Review*, London, 2006.

[64] *See generally* E. Denza, *Diplomatic Law*, 3d ed., 2007, Oxford, on art. 31.

[65] 189 UNTS 137 (No. 2545); UKTS (1954) 39.

that private rights could be infringed. Over many years, there have been numerous successful challenges by way of judicial review to decisions on claims to refugee status. Accordingly, the doctrine of legitimate expectation has been held to prohibit prosecution of a refugee applicant for carrying false documentation, because Article 31(1) of that Convention does not permit penalties for arrival without proper authorization, even though that provision may not have been expressly incorporated into U.K. law.[66]

B. *By Deduction from the Text of the Treaty That Is Attached to Domestic Legislation or Referred to in the Legislation*

So, it should not be thought that most treaties, whether bilateral or multilateral, necessarily show an intention to impose a duty on their parties to create private rights in their domestic law. Judicial review proceedings in *Quark* before the English High Court, and later the Court of Appeal,[67] concerned the powers under local legislation of the Director of Fisheries of South Georgia and the South Sandwich Islands (a British overseas territory) to issue fishing licences. Quark was a company that had, in previous fishing seasons, been granted licenses to fish in the waters of the territory. In granting them, the local legislation required the Director to have regard to the Convention for the Conservation of Antarctic Marine Living Resources 1980 (CCAMLR),[68] which applied, inter alia, to fishing in such waters. (The matter came to the English courts because the British Foreign Secretary had instructed the Director as to what he should do, in particular to restrict the number of licenses awarded to Quark.) Whether the Director (as so instructed) had properly carried out his statutory duties depended very much on the provisions of CCAMLR and how the director had applied it in the past. This required a detailed investigation into technical facts. Quark was successful in that the court found that the Director had not properly carried out his statutory powers and, thus, quashed his decision. However, because in English law it is not at all easy to get damages for breach of a public law right, a claim for damages was mounted under the Human Rights Act. The House of Lords eventually rejected it because the application of the ECHR to the United Kingdom had (unlike most other U.K. overseas territories) not been extended to South Georgia and the South Sandwich

[66] Adimi et al. [2001] QB 667, paras. 56–57.
[67] [2002] EWCA Civ 1409; [2002] AER (D) 450.
[68] 402 UNTS 71 (No. 22301); ILM (1980) 837; UKTS (1982) 48; TIAS 10240.

Islands.[69] So, the plaintiff had a somewhat pyrrhic victory. If it had been otherwise, damages would almost certainly have been awarded.

Staying in the same part of the world, the purpose of the Antarctic Act 1994 is, in particular, to implement the 1991 Protocol on Environmental Protection of Antarctica.[70] For this, the Act requires a permit from the Secretary of State to conduct various activities in Antarctica, such as mounting a British expedition; establishing a research station; operating a British-registered ship or aircraft; killing, injuring, capturing, and so on flora or fauna; introducing nonnative animals or plants; or entering protected sites. Although there are criminal penalties for doing those things without a permit, section 15 requires the Secretary of State to have regard to the Protocol when considering a permit application. So, as in the case of CCAMLR, a decision to refuse a permit could be challenged by way of judicial review. Such a review would have to consider the terms of the Protocol and how it had been interpreted and applied, both by the United Kingdom and other parties to it, to decide whether the refusal was reasonable. Today a court might even agree to consider an objection by an environmental group to the grant of a permit. The next two options are much more problematic.

C. *When the Domestic Legislation Does Not Even Refer to the Treaty, by Deduction from the Terms of the Legislation*

The situation here involves interpreting the domestic legislation in light of the terms of the treaty that it is designed to implement, even though it has not been incorporated. This is more likely to occur in a judicial review of action (or inaction) by a public body. But, if the legislation is clear, it is unlikely that the court will look behind it at any treaty it may be designed to implement.

D. *When Asserting a Right under Common Law, or Even under Legislation, a Court Might Possibly Consider the Terms of an Unincorporated Treaty or an MOU*

On the final appeal in *Venables*,[71] one judge in the House of Lords was prepared to consider the legality of the exercise of a statutory power in

[69] [2005] UKHL 57. An Application to the Strasbourg Court was dismissed on Sept. 19, 2006 (Dec. No. 15305/06), also for lack of jurisdiction.

[70] ILM (1991) 1460; UKTS (1996) 6; 1998 ATS 6; *available at* http://www.ats.org.ar.

[71] R. v. Secretary of State for the Home Department, *ex parte* Venables ([1997] UKHL 25; [1998] AC 407; [1997] 3 AER 97), *see* Lord Browne-Wilkinson in the passage on the 1991 Act.

the light of an unincorporated treaty, the Rights of the Child Convention 1989.[72]

This is more likely when the court is deciding whether the conduct alleged to have caused harm to the plaintiff amounted to, say, negligence. This may, at least at the moment, be more problematic, as it raises a thorny issue: whether an English court would examine any material that is neither legislation nor a treaty.[73] International lawyers will think immediately of that strange, widespread, but little appreciated creature, the memorandum of understanding (MOU). An MOU is a bilateral or multilateral instrument made by States and/or international organizations that may, at first sight look like a treaty, but it is not one because the participants do not intend it to be legally binding in any law, whether international or domestic. MOUs range from important political statements, like the Helsinki Final Act 1975,[74] to numerous mundane and technical bilateral instruments. One might also include resolutions of meetings of states parties to treaties; resolutions of the UN General Assembly on matters of international law; and, possibly, reports of treaty-monitoring bodies. No doubt one could add others.[75]

Any English judge would be right to be suspicious at first of anything that is neither a treaty nor domestic or foreign law. Yet the English courts are now more open to arguments that draw on less traditional sources, and English judges will try to look at them, provided always that it may be helpful to them in carrying out their onerous judicial task. One would expect them to ask themselves the following questions:

- Might the instrument be relevant to an issue in this case?
- Does it come from an authoritative source?
- Might it help to do justice in this case?
- Is there a legal hook on which I can hang it?

If an English judge were referred to an international instrument (say, an unincorporated treaty, or even an MOU concluded by the United Kingdom) that might be relevant to an issue before him or her, he would usually agree to look at it and hear argument about its relevance.[76] Whether the judge

[72] 1577 UNTS 3 (No. 27531); ILM (1989) 1448; UKTS (1992) 44.

[73] This passage is based on the author's paper in R. Wolfrum and V. Röben (eds.), *Developments of* [*sic*] *International Law in Treaty Making*, 2005, Berlin, pgs. 487–96. *See also* Gardiner, *supra* note 40.

[74] ILM (1975) 1293.

[75] On MOUs generally, *see* Aust, *supra* note 5, pgs. 20–21, and chap. 3.

[76] *See Solomon*, *supra* note 25.

will cite the instrument in the judgment will depend on how relevant it is and whether the judge can find a legal hook on which to hang it. In 2002, in the celebrated case of *Kuwait Airways v. Iraqi Airways (No. 2)*,[77] the House of Lords (sitting as the highest court of appeal) decided that in English law it would be contrary to public policy to recognize the legal effectiveness of foreign legislation that was in breach of the UN Charter.[78] The legislation in question was an Iraqi decree that purported to transfer to Iraqi Airways legal title to aircraft of Kuwaiti Airways that had been seized by Iraqi forces during the invasion. The judges ignored the fact that the UN Charter had not been incorporated[79] and found that the invasion was contrary to the prohibition in customary international law on the use of force, as reflected in the UN Charter and in various resolutions of the Security Council on Iraq, such as Resolutions 660, 662, and 674, which had not been incorporated either. This is the continuation of a judicial trend apparent since at least *Brind* in 1991.[80] Since then, English judges seem to have been increasingly willing to consider unincorporated treaties (e.g., the Rights of the Child Convention 1989)[81] if they enable them better to do their job, such as deciding whether the exercise of a statutory discretion was reasonable, such as under the Children's Act 1989.

So, although unincorporated treaties usually have difficulty being recognized by the English courts,[82] this does not mean that they will always ignore them. If the terms of an unincorporated treaty are relevant, they may well be considered. This will be so if an unincorporated treaty may be relevant to the factual background, as was done in the celebrated International Tin Council litigation.[83] Furthermore, if one can establish that the rules in an unincorporated treaty have come to be accepted as customary international law, then the English courts will apply them, albeit as customary international law.[84] This is the case with the Vienna Convention on the Law of Treaties 1969, to which the United Kingdom is a party. Unlike other

[77] [2002] UKHL 19.

[78] Public policy is a common law principle developed through case law. It concerns legal acts that are seen by the courts as injurious to the public good, which can change over time. It is not the policy of the British Government. *See Halsbury's Laws of England*, 4th ed. (reissue), vol. 9(1), paras. 841–42.

[79] The United Nations Act 1946 merely authorizes the making of Orders in Council to implement Chapter VII resolutions of the UN Security Council.

[80] [1991] UKHL 4; [1991] AC 696; [1991] 1 AER 720.

[81] 1577 UNTS 3 (No. 27531); ILM (1989) 1448; UKTS (1992) 44.

[82] *See* R (for the Campaign for Nuclear Disarmament) v. Prime Minister of the United Kingdom [2002] EWHC 2777 (Admin).

[83] Maclaine Watson v. Department of Trade [1989] 3 AER 523, 544–45; 81 ILR, 701–02.

[84] *See supra* note 1.

States, the United Kingdom has enacted no legislation to implement that Convention or otherwise to regulate treaty making.[85] There is only internal guidance for government departments.

The fact that an instrument, such as an MOU, was never intended to be a treaty means that an English court will treat it as having a status similar to a treaty to which the United Kingdom is not bound – even lower than an unincorporated treaty. But if, for example, the case concerns legislation conferring discretionary powers on the Government or other public bodies, the court may consider the lawfulness of the exercise of that discretion in the light of an MOU. So, if a court is considering whether a port authority has lawfully detained a foreign vessel, it might well examine MOUs, such as the Paris Memorandum of Understanding on Port State Control 1982,[86] and equivalent ones for the Caribbean (1996)[87] and other parts of the world, because, though they are not treaties but MOUs, they are now considered as reflecting customary international law.[88] But in so doing, the court would be applying customary law, not the MOUs as such.

An MOU like the Helsinki Final Act stands alone. But many less important MOUs are subsidiary to treaties. Even in these deregulated days, there are still thousands of bilateral air-services agreements, and most are accompanied by MOUs. They set out details of what has been agreed on about the actual routes that can be operated and the number of flights, size of aircraft, and seat prices. The MOU form is used so that these (commercially confidential) details can be kept from competitor airlines. Not being a treaty, there is no obligation to publish and register an MOU. Also, very detailed, technical content may need to be changed frequently, and an MOU is much easier and quicker to amend than a treaty.

Such subsidiary MOUs should be seen in light of Article 31 of the Vienna Convention. That favorite article of the International Court of Justice not only helps in the interpretation of treaties but also is a most useful tool for making and using treaties, paragraphs 2(a) and 3(a) in particular. They provide that when interpreting a treaty, in addition to the text, including the preamble and annexes, the context also comprises "'any agreement relating to the treaty that was made between all the parties in connexion with the conclusion of the treaty' or 'any subsequent agreement between the parties regarding the interpretation of the treaty or the application of its

[85] By contrast, *see* the Russian Federal Law on International Treaties, ILM (1995) 1370–1392.

[86] ILM (1982), pg. 1. It has since been amended several times.

[87] ILM (1997), pg. 237.

[88] R. Churchill and V. Lowe, *The Law of the Sea*, 3d ed., Manchester University Press, 1999, pgs. 274–76. On customary international law, *see supra* note 1.

also found in British legislation on extradition, international organizations and double taxation.[96]

Customary international law being part of the common law,[97] the English courts will on occasion examine resolutions of the UN General Assembly. And, if the General Assembly eventually adopts final resolutions bringing to the attention of the Members draft articles on state responsibility or reservations to treaties, they may well be influential in argument before the English courts as to what the international law is on these important subjects.

Last, one should briefly mention authoritative guides to the interpretation of treaties. These would certainly be taken notice of by the English courts. The explanatory reports approved by the government experts involved in drafting conventions of the Council of Europe, and adopted at the same time as the conventions and published with them, provide an invaluable guide to their interpretation and are considered part of the context in which the conventions were concluded.[98] As such, they must be distinguished from official commentaries that are later produced and, depending on the circumstances, may come to be regarded as authoritative. The Handbook on Procedures and Criteria for Determining Refugee Status, published by the UN High Commissioner for Refugees (UNHCR), is generally regarded as an authoritative commentary on the Refugees Convention and is frequently referred to by British courts and tribunals.[99] The detailed commentary on the Geneva Conventions 1949 edited by Pictet for the International Committee of the Red Cross is also highly persuasive.[100]

Although one would like to be able to say that reports of treaty-monitoring bodies would also be highly regarded by the English courts, that may not be so. Much may depend on the treaty, the composition of the monitoring body and, above all, the degree to which it has power to make binding decisions. But the difficulty with such bodies is that, although their members are often very eminent jurists, the bodies are not courts. Their general pronouncements on international law therefore have to be made without the benefit of full legal argument from the parties

[96] Extradition Act 1989, s. 4; International Organisations Act 1968, s. 11(3); Income and Corporation Taxes Act 1968, s. 788(10).

[97] See *supra* note 1.

[98] I. Sinclair, *The Vienna Convention on the Law of Treaties*, 2d ed., 1984, Manchester, pgs. 129–30. For an example, see ILM (1994), pg. 943.

[99] *See* D. Jackson, *Immigration: Law and Practice*, London, 1996, ss. 10–12.

[100] J. Pictet (ed.), *The Geneva Conventions 1949, Commentary*, 4 vols., 1952–1960. *But see* S. Rosenne, *Practice and Methods of International Law* (1984), pgs. 50–51.

to particular cases, and therefore reflect more the personal views of the members.[101]

V. REMEDIES

Here we are here in serious danger of getting into the morass that is the English law of tort and, in particular, the law applicable to public authorities. The law, such as it is, is a product both of common law and legislation as interpreted and applied by the courts. Any comprehensive account of such law is therefore impossible in the space available.[102] Only some suggestions as to the possibilities will be attempted.

An initial point that needs stressing is that it is relatively rare for a treaty to provide expressly that a party must provide for compensation to persons. States often view the problem of treaty implementation and enforcement as one for action by governments by the imposition of criminal or other public measures, not as a matter for civil proceedings by private persons even if they might be affected. This is particularly so for developing states. The Protocol to Prevent, Suppress, and Punish Trafficking in Persons of 2000[103] requires the parties to make acts contrary to the Protocol criminal offences only. In contrast, Article 35 of the UN Corruption Convention 2003[104] goes rather further in providing that "[e]ach Party shall take such measures, in accordance with principles of its domestic law, to ensure that entities and persons who have suffered damage as a result of an act of corruption have the right to initiate legal proceedings against those responsible for that damage in order to obtain compensation." In any case, the means by which a party implements an obligation to provide for compensation is left to each party. This may well be wise given the varying approaches to compensation in different legal systems. In Article 5 of the International Convention for the Suppression of the Financing of Terrorism 1999,[105] each party is given discretion as to the measures it takes against legal entities (e.g., banks) that are liable for an offence under that Convention. Because the liability of corporate bodies is dealt with differently even in the States of Western Europe, the provision requires that liability be criminal, civil, or administrative, and that, on conviction of a legal entity, the sanctions imposed on it can include monetary penalties, but these can

[101] *See* the discussion in the 1997 Report of the ILC (A/52/10, paras. 133–56).
[102] *But see generally* W. Rogers, *Winfield and Jolowicz on Tort*, 17th ed., London, 2006.
[103] UNTS (No. 39574).
[104] UNTS (No. 42146); A/RES/58/422; ILM (2004) 37; UKTS (2006) 14.
[105] 2178 UNTS 229 (No. 38349); ILM (2000) 268; UKTS (2002) 28; 2002 ATS 23.

be criminal, civil, or administrative "in accordance with its domestic legal principles."

In implementing the UN Corruption Convention 2003, the United Kingdom seems to have relied on a person who has suffered loss as a result of corruption to take action at common law for compensation (damages) against a person who caused or was an accessory to the corruption. Although such a claim would have more chance of success if the defendant had been convicted of corruption,[106] civil proceedings may still be possible, albeit expensive. If a serious crime against the person (i.e., bodily injury) has been committed, even if nobody has been convicted of the crime, the injured person can apply for compensation to the Criminal Injuries Compensation Authority, which administers a Scheme.[107] Since 1964, the Authority and its predecessor have paid out more than £3 billion.

In contrast to French law, in English law there is no general right to an award of damages for breach of a public right that causes loss or damage to a private person. Instead, the remedy is more likely to be an application by an affected person for judicial review[108] of the action (or inaction) of a public body. Today, such an application is more easily accepted by a pressure group (e.g., an NGO), provided that it can show that it does have a sufficient interest in the matter. As we have seen in *Quark*,[109] it is not always easy to recover damages, even if a court has held that action by a public official was unlawful. If, however, a public official is convicted of a criminal offence, a person harmed by the offence might be able to receive damages by a separate civil claim.

There has been a need to incorporate in domestic law certain procedural provisions of multilateral treaties that provide for quasi-universal jurisdiction – that is, that place on each party the duty to extradite a person alleged to have committed an offence defined in the treaty or, if it does not do so, a duty to submit the case to its competent authorities for the purpose of prosecution. For example, the Torture Convention 1984[110] requires each party to provide for such quasi-universal jurisdiction. But although domestic law adequately covered the offence of torture committed in England,

[106] The only crimes related to corruption would seem to be under the Public Bodies Corrupt Practices Act 1889, the Prevention of Corruption Act 1906, and the common law offence of bribery.

[107] *See* http://www.cica.gov.uk. *See* the Criminal Injuries Compensation Act 1995.

[108] The remedy is discretionary, and the court must first be asked to grant leave to apply.

[109] *See supra* text at notes 67–69.

[110] 465 UNTS 85 (No. 24841); ILM (1984) 1027; UKTS (1991) 107. *See also* R. v. Bow St. Magistrates Court, *ex parte* Pinochet (No. 3) [2000] 1 AC 147; [1999] 2 AER 97; [1999] 2 WLR 827; ILM (1999) 581; 119 ILR 135.

there was no provision for the prosecution in England of torture committed abroad. So Section 134 of the Criminal Justice Act of 1988 provides that domestic courts have jurisdiction to try a person alleged to have committed torture either in the United Kingdom or abroad, so enabling the United Kingdom to ratify the Convention. Similar provisions were made in U.K. law for the same "extradite or prosecute" provisions of several other counterterrorism conventions[111] and the Vienna Drugs Convention 1988.[112] Although none of this domestic legislation provides for damages to be paid to those harmed by such offences, a criminal conviction in England for such an offence[113] should be sufficient grounds for a successful separate claim of damages against the criminal, assuming of course that he or she has any recoverable assets. In some cases, a payment by the Criminal Injuries Compensation Authority,[114] or merely a conviction, may be enough.

European Community law[115] sometimes provides for the enforcement of private rights. But more often it accords private rights against either the member states or other persons, yet without prescribing how they are to be enforced. Nevertheless, the consistent case law of the European Court of Justice (ECJ)[116] is that, when Community law does not prescribe procedural or remedial rules, two principles apply. First, equivalence: the Member State's procedural rules on enforcement of a Community right must be not less favorable than those that apply to similar domestic actions. Second, effectiveness: a national court must not substitute its own judgment for that of a national authority that is entrusted with application of the Community law and called on to exercise complex assessments, and thus has a wide discretion. In such a case, judicial review is restricted to verifying that the national authority has not committed manifest error or misused its powers

[111] *See* A. Aust, *Handbook of International Law*, 2005, Cambridge, pgs. 284–91.

[112] 1582 UNTS 165 (No. 27627); LM (1989) 293; UKTS (1992) 26.

[113] Apparently, the only known example of the actual use of the "extradite or prosecute" provision was the conviction in England in 2005 of an Afghan national, Faryadi Zardad, for torture and hostage taking committed in Afghanistan between 1992 and 1996, for which he was sentenced to 20 years in prison.

[114] *See* supra n. 107 and accompanying text.

[115] Although there may be a tendency to refer instead to the European Union, strictly speaking the European Union deals only with what are known as second- and third-pillar matters (Common Foreign and Security Policy and Police and Judicial Cooperation in Criminal Matters). *See* Aust, *supra* note 5, pgs. 414–16.

[116] The ECJ is the judicial organ of the European Community and must not be confused with the Strasbourg Court. The ECJ is in Luxembourg.

or discretion.[117] But, the ECJ has also held that, in certain circumstances, the national court may award damages for harm caused by a breach of Community law.[118]

And then, there may be remedies at common law.[119] A right of action for breach of a statutory duty is possible if the court finds that the legislation was intended to create such a right. Because such liability is strict, there is no need to prove malice or negligence. The court may infer such a right of action from the legislation, provided that the statutory duty is similar to other such duties where a private right of action has been accepted. But the court is unlikely to do so when the legislation provides that a particular public body is responsible for enforcing the duty or when the legislation primarily creates criminal offences. Also, a private right will be inferred only if the legislation is intended to protect a particular class of persons rather than the public at large.

But the main ground for seeking damages is under the doctrine of negligence as developed by the courts. This has the disadvantage that the plaintiff has to prove both that the defendant had a duty of care toward the claimant and that the defendant's negligence caused harm to the plaintiff. But the defendant can be a public official, and in deciding whether there was negligence, the courts may consider the terms of a relevant treaty, including an unincorporated treaty. Treaties on environmental protection (whether or not incorporated) may be relevant because their provisions on protection against environmental damage may be relevant to any issue as to whether the defendant was negligent. A court may also take into account MOUs containing certain concepts, such as the precautionary principal as enunciated in the principles of the Rio Declaration on Environment and Development 1992.[120]

There is an interesting link between the ECHR and common law negligence. The Strasbourg Court has imposed affirmative duties on states, for example, to protect those known to be at risk of criminal violence (*Osman*)[121] and children at risk of abuse (*Z v. United Kingdom*).[122] The English common law might otherwise confer immunity on the public authority, but under Strasbourg jurisprudence, the authority will be held to have a duty of care. However, there are limits. In the latest case of

[117] *See* Peterbroeck (Case C-312/93; [1995] ECR I-4599, para. 12; [1996] 1 CMLR 793; [1996] AER (EC) 242); and *Wyatt and Dashwood's European Union* [*sic*] *Law*, 4th ed., London, 2000, pgs. 110–24.

[118] *See further* D. *Wyatt and A. Dashwood, supra* note 117, pgs. 124–30.

[119] *See generally* Winfield, *supra* note 102.

[120] ILM (1992) 876. *See also supra* notes 88 and 95.

[121] Rep. 1998-VIII, fasc. 95 (28 10 98).

[122] Case 29392; ECHR 2001.V (10. 05. 2001).

Lawrence,[123] the Court of Appeal held that the immunity at common law was not affected by Article 8 of the ECHR. Under that article, the question is whether the authority took a proportionate decision to place a child in care; at common law the question is whether the authority should pay damages if it turns out that its decision was careless.

On judicial review of the lawfulness of the act (or omission) of a public official, the English courts have shown a marked reluctance to pronounce by way of an advisory declaration on the international legality of action (actual or proposed) by the Government, when the act (or omission) allegedly violates an unincorporated treaty.[124] The reason goes to the fundamental constitutional principle that the English courts will not enforce obligations on the United Kingdom, unless they have been made part of domestic law.

VI. CONCLUSION

Because of the nature of the dualist approach to treaties in the English legal system, in the absence of legislation to implement a specific treaty (of which there are many examples) and that accords private rights, inevitably there is not that much scope for an English court to find that there is such a right and that the court can accord a remedy for its breach. Although I have ventured to suggest some (hopefully constructive) ways around the problem when there is no such legislation, it should not be assumed that they would necessarily work in any particular case. In contrast, the monist approach to treaties is not necessarily superior. Under it, it may also not be clear whether a private right can be enforced by a domestic court.

[123] [2007] EWCA Civ 446.

[124] *See, e.g.*, Brown LJ in the *CND* [2002] EWHC 2759 QB, paras. 23, 31, and 36; Abassi [2002] EWCA Civ. 1598.

13

United States

David Sloss

Professor of Law and Director, Center for Global Law and Policy
Santa Clara University School of Law

I. INTRODUCTION

This chapter analyzes the practice of U.S. courts in "treaty cases." The term "treaty cases" includes cases where a court engaged in substantive analysis of a treaty provision, as well as other cases where a party involved in litigation invoked a treaty in support of a claim or defense.

Analysis of judicial decision making in treaty cases is problematic because U.S. courts apply two mutually inconsistent models, which the author has labeled the "nationalist" and "transnationalist" models.[1] The two models provide very different answers to three questions: (1) Which treaties have the force of law in the domestic legal system? (2) How should courts interpret treaties? and (3) Under what circumstances are individuals entitled to judicial remedies for treaty violations? In brief, transnationalists hold that treaties generally have the force of law in the United States, that courts should interpret a treaty in accordance with the internationally agreed understanding of its terms, and that individuals are ordinarily entitled to judicial remedies for violations of their treaty-based individual rights. In contrast, nationalists hold that only self-executing treaties have the force of law, that courts should interpret treaties in accordance with the shared understanding of the U.S. political branches, and that there is a background presumption that treaties do not create judicially enforceable individual rights.

An analysis of judicial doctrine related to treaties, without more, would present an incomplete picture of judicial practice because current

[1] *See* David Sloss, *Schizophrenic Treaty Law*, 43 TEX. INT'L L.J. 15 (2007) (discussing application of the nationalist and transnationalist models in cases involving the Geneva Conventions); David Sloss, *When Do Treaties Create Individually Enforceable Rights? The Supreme Court Ducks the Issue in* Hamdan *and* Sanchez-Llamas, 45 COLUM. J. TRANS'L L. 20, 29–37 (2006) (explaining the conflict between the two models).

doctrine provides support for both the nationalist and the transnationalist approaches. Accordingly, this chapter combines doctrinal and empirical analysis in an effort to explain when courts are most likely to adopt a nationalist approach and when they are most likely to adopt a transnationalist approach. The empirical analysis is based on a database of U.S. treaty cases that the author created for the purpose of this project.[2] The analysis demonstrates that, in litigation between private parties, courts are more likely to apply a transnationalist approach than a nationalist approach. However, in cases where private parties are adverse to government actors, courts are more likely to apply a nationalist approach than a transnationalist approach (see Table 2). These conclusions are valid at a 95 percent confidence level.

These conclusions make sense in light of the normative assumptions underlying the two models. For transnationalists, U.S. compliance with its treaty obligations is a paramount objective and the judiciary has an important role to play in promoting that objective. Nationalists do not dispute the importance of treaty compliance, but they place greater weight on the goal of avoiding friction between the judicial and executive branches in implementing U.S. treaty obligations. In litigation between private parties, there is little risk of creating friction between the judicial and executive branches: hence, the transnationalist goal of promoting treaty compliance often guides judicial decision making. However, in cases where private parties are adverse to government actors, the private parties are generally invoking a treaty as a constraint on executive action. In these circumstances, courts might create friction with the executive branch if they zealously pursued the goal of treaty compliance. Hence, courts tend to apply nationalist strategies, such as deferring to the executive's interpretation of a treaty or declining to rule on the merits of treaty-based claims.

The empirical analysis also demonstrates that there is a statistically significant correlation between case outcomes and a court's discretionary decision to adopt a nationalist or transnationalist approach. The party invoking a treaty wins more than 50 percent of the cases in which courts apply a transnationalist approach. In contrast, the party invoking a treaty wins fewer than 20 percent of the cases in which courts apply a nationalist approach (see Table 3). These estimates are valid at a 95 percent confidence level. The fact that the party invoking a treaty has a higher winning percentage when courts

[2]The database includes all thirty-eight U.S. Supreme Court decisions from 1970 to 2006 in which the Court engaged in substantive analysis of a treaty. It also includes 216 other treaty cases decided by U.S. courts during this period. The process for selecting cases for inclusion in the database is described more fully in Section III.

adopt a transnationalist approach, as opposed to a nationalist approach, holds true for both private-party litigation and for cases where private parties are adverse to government actors (see Tables 4A and 4B).

However, if one divides the governmental litigation cases into civil and criminal cases, the observed pattern does not apply to criminal cases. The government wins approximately 98 percent of the criminal cases in which one party invokes a treaty in support of a claim or defense (see Table 5.B). In this category of cases, there is no significant correlation between case outcomes and a court's discretionary choice to apply nationalist or transnationalist tools.

The remainder of this chapter is divided into five sections. Section II provides a doctrinal overview of the status of treaties in the U.S. legal system, emphasizing the tension between the nationalist and transnationalist approaches. The analysis in Section II is purely doctrinal, not empirical. Section III provides an overview of the cases in the database and describes the methodology utilized to create the database. The next two sections present the heart of the analysis. Section IV documents the fact that courts tend to be more transnationalist in private litigation and more nationalist in governmental litigation. Section V analyzes the correlation between case outcomes and judicial decisions to apply nationalist versus transnationalist approaches. The final section of the chapter presents some concluding observations.

II. THE STATUS OF TREATIES IN THE U.S. LEGAL SYSTEM

In the U.S. constitutional system, there are three distinct mechanisms for concluding international agreements. First, international agreements concluded by the president without authorization from Congress are called sole executive agreements.[3] Second, international agreements approved by a majority vote in both houses of Congress – either in advance, before the agreement is concluded internationally, or by enacting legislation after the international agreement has already been negotiated – are called congressional-executive agreements.[4] Third, international agreements approved by a two-thirds majority vote in the Senate pursuant to Article II of the Constitution are called treaties.[5] Under international law, any legally binding agreement between two or more nations is a *treaty*. In U.S. constitutional parlance, though, the term *treaty* refers only to international

[3] *See* Louis Henkin, *Foreign Affairs and the U.S. Constitution* 219–24 (2d ed. 1996).
[4] *See id.*, at 215–18.
[5] *See* U.S. Const. art. II, § 2, cl. 2.

agreements that are approved by the Senate pursuant to Article II of the Constitution.

In the first 150 years of U.S. constitutional history, from 1789 to 1939, the United States entered into 799 treaties and 1,182 nontreaty international agreements (executive agreements).[6] Since that time, though, the use of executive agreements has far outpaced the use of treaties. In the fifty years from 1939 to 1989, the United States entered into 702 treaties and 11,698 executive agreements.[7] In the ten years from 1990 to 1999 the United States concluded another 2,857 executive agreements.[8]

Unless otherwise noted, this chapter uses the term *treaty* to refer only to international agreements approved by the Senate under Article II. The analysis focuses on Article II treaties for two reasons. First, it is not possible in a work of this scope to cover everything, so it was necessary to adopt some criteria for inclusion and exclusion. Second, treaties are the subject of litigation much more frequently than executive agreements. As discussed in Section III, the database includes all Supreme Court decisions in treaty cases from 1970 to 2006, including Supreme Court cases addressing executive agreements. Only three of the thirty-eight Supreme Court decisions in the database involve executive agreements; the other thirty-five cases involve treaties. This twelve-to-one ratio provides a rough approximation of how frequently treaties become the subject of litigation, as compared to executive agreements.

This section is divided into two parts. The first part presents a brief overview of the domestic constitutional framework governing treaties in the U.S. legal system. The second part discusses the doctrine of self-executing and non-self-executing treaties.

A. *The Constitutional Framework*

The Constitution authorizes the president to make treaties "by and with the Advice and Consent of the Senate."[9] The Constitution also stipulates that "all Treaties made, or which shall be made, under the Authority of the United States, shall be the supreme Law of the Land."[10] The Treaty Clause and the Supremacy Clause, taken together, empower the president

[6] Congressional Research Service, Treaties and Other International Agreements: The Role of the United States Senate, S. Prt. 106–71 (2001), at 39.
[7] *Id.*
[8] *Id.*
[9] U.S. Const. art. II, § 2, cl. 2.
[10] U.S. Const. art. VI, cl. 2.

and Senate to create supreme federal law without the participation of the House of Representatives. Federal courts are empowered to adjudicate cases "arising under" treaties.[11] In addition, state courts have a duty to enforce treaties, "any Thing in the Constitution or Laws of any State to the Contrary notwithstanding."[12]

Broadly speaking, there are two types of constitutional limits on the Treaty Power. First, the federal government may not utilize the Treaty Power to create domestic law that infringes on constitutionally protected individual rights.[13] Thus, for example, a treaty provision obligating the United States to restrict constitutionally protected freedom of speech would be unconstitutional.[14] Second, inasmuch as the House of Representatives does not participate in the Article II treaty process, the treaty makers may not utilize that process to create federal law in areas where the Constitution requires legislation approved by both houses of Congress. Thus, for example, when the United States ratifies a treaty that requires expenditure of money, the Constitution requires bicameral legislation appropriating funds in order for the United States to implement its treaty obligation.[15]

Some commentators maintain that the Constitution should also be construed to impose federalism limits on the Treaty Power.[16] In the leading Supreme Court decision on this issue, the Court held that constitutional limits on the scope of Congress's powers under Article I of the Constitution do not apply to the Treaty Power.[17] This does not mean that there are no federalism limits on the Treaty Power.[18] However, it does mean that the president and the Senate, acting together under Article II, have the power to create domestic law beyond the scope of Congress's Article I legislative powers.

[11] U.S. CONST. art. III, § 2, cl. 1.
[12] U.S. CONST. art. VI, cl. 2.
[13] Reid v. Covert, 354 U.S. 1, 16–17 (1957).
[14] The United States is a party to the International Covenant on Civil and Political Rights (ICCPR), Dec. 19, 1966, 999 U.N.T.S. 171. Article 20 of the ICCPR obligates the United States to restrict constitutionally protected speech. The United States adopted a reservation when it ratified the treaty to avoid a conflict between the Constitution and U.S. treaty obligations. Absent the reservation, "the Constitution still would prevail as the law of the United States... but we would be in default as far as our international obligations are concerned." *International Human Rights Treaties: Hearings Before the Comm. On Foreign Relations, U.S. Senate*, 96th Cong. 35 (1979) (statement of Jack Goldklang).
[15] *See* Henkin, *supra* note 3, at 204.
[16] *See, e.g.*, Curtis A. Bradley, *The Treaty Power and American Federalism*, 97 MICH. L. REV. 390 (1998).
[17] Missouri v. Holland, 252 U.S. 416 (1920).
[18] For a concise analysis of other possible federalism limits on the Treaty Power, *see* David Sloss, *International Agreements and the Political Safeguards of Federalism*, 55 STAN. L. REV. 1963, 1975–78 (2003).

In the U.S. constitutional system, there is an established hierarchy among different types of law. Because the U.S. Constitution ranks higher than treaties, any conflict between the Constitution and a treaty is resolved in favor of the Constitution.[19] Treaties rank higher than state laws; therefore, any conflict between a treaty and a state law is resolved in favor of the treaty.[20] Treaties and federal statutes have equal rank. Accordingly, if a treaty and a statute address the same subject matter, courts attempt to interpret both instruments to avoid a direct conflict.[21] If the conflict is unavoidable, though, the so-called later-in-time rule holds that a later-in-time treaty trumps a prior inconsistent statute, and a later-in-time statute trumps a prior inconsistent treaty.[22]

Nationalists would revise the preceding paragraph by adding the word *self-executing* before the word *treaty* in appropriate places. From a nationalist standpoint, a non-self-executing treaty lacks the force of law in the U.S. legal system.[23] Therefore, a non-self-executing treaty does not preempt inconsistent state law, and it does not supersede a prior conflicting statute. Transnationalists agree that some non-self-executing treaties lack the force of law in the U.S. legal system and that a treaty that lacks the force of law does not preempt state law or supersede prior conflicting statutes. However, from a transnationalist perspective, some non-self-executing treaties do have the force of law, and therefore do trump prior inconsistent statutes and preempt conflicting state law. To elucidate this point further, it is necessary to discuss the doctrine of non-self-executing treaties.

B. *The Doctrine of Non-Self-Executing Treaties*

The distinction between self-executing and non-self-executing treaties has been characterized as "the 'most confounding' in the United States law of treaties."[24] The problem stems, in part, from the fact that the doctrine of self-execution has been employed to address two discrete sets of issues without clearly distinguishing between them. The first set of issues involves

[19] *See* Restatement (Third) of Foreign Relations Law § 115(3) (1987).

[20] *See, e.g.*, Ware v. Hylton 3 U.S. (3 Dall.) 199 (1796).

[21] *See, e.g.*, Trans World Airlines, Inc. v. Franklin Mint Corp., 466 U.S. 243, 252 (1984) ("A treaty will not be deemed to have been abrogated or modified by a later statute unless such purpose on the part of Congress has been clearly expressed.") (quoting Cook v. United States, 288 U.S. 102, 120 (1933)).

[22] *See* Chae Chan Ping v. United States, 130 U.S. 581, 602 (1889); Whitney v. Robertson, 124 U.S. 190, 194 (1888); Edye v. Robertson, 112 U.S. 580, 597–98 (1884).

[23] *See* Medellin v. Texas, 128 S.Ct. 1346, 1356–57 (2008).

[24] Carlos M. Vazquez, *The Four Doctrines of Self-Executing Treaties*, 89 Am. J. Int'l L. 695, 695 (1995) (quoting United States v. Postal, 589 F.2d 862, 876 (5th Cir. 1979)).

whether, and in what circumstances, treaties have the force of law within the domestic legal system. The second set of issues involves whether, and in what circumstances, the judiciary is the appropriate branch of government to apply particular treaty provisions.

The two sets of issues are clearly related. If a treaty lacks the force of law within the domestic legal system, then the judiciary will have little or no role in applying that treaty because the judiciary's function is to apply law, not to apply nonlaw. Conversely, if a treaty does have the force of law within the domestic legal system, the judiciary may play a greater role in applying that treaty, although the nature and scope of the judicial role will depend on a variety of other factors, some of which are sometimes analyzed under the rubric of self-execution. This portion of the chapter will address the question whether, and in what circumstances, treaties have domestic legal force. Questions related to the judicial role in treaty application will be addressed in sections IV and V.

An analysis of the domestic legal force of treaties in the U.S. legal system must begin with the text of the Constitution, which states that "all Treaties made... under the Authority of the United States, shall be the supreme Law of the Land."[25] The Supremacy Clause, on its face, seems to say that all treaties ratified by the United States have the force of law in the U.S. legal system. Nevertheless, it is well settled that some treaties ratified by the United States lack domestic legal force. For example, a treaty provision that conflicts with the Constitution or that has been superseded by a later-in-time statute does not have the force of law in the United States. Nationalists and transnationalists agree on this point.

Nationalists and transnationalists also agree that a constitutionally non-self-executing treaty that has not been implemented by legislation lacks domestic legal force. A treaty is "constitutionally non-self-executing" if it obligates the United States to accomplish a goal that, under the U.S. constitutional system, requires bicameral legislation approved by both houses of Congress.[26] The Supremacy Clause specifies that treaties made "under the authority of the United States" are "the supreme Law of the Land."[27] A constitutionally non-self-executing treaty that has not been implemented by legislation is arguably not made "under the Authority of the United States," at least not for purposes of domestic law, because Article II of the Constitution does not grant the president and Senate authority to create

[25] U.S. Const. art. VI, cl. 2.

[26] *See, e.g.*, Restatement (Third), *supra* note 19, § 111(4)(c) (stating that a treaty is not self-executing "if implementing legislation is constitutionally required").

[27] U.S. Const. art. VI, cl. 2.

domestic law in areas where the participation of the House of Representatives is constitutionally required.[28] Thus, in terms of the constitutional text, it is plausible to maintain that constitutionally non-self-executing treaties are not the "supreme Law of the Land."

The Supreme Court has occasionally suggested that a precatory treaty provision (i.e., a treaty provision that does not impose binding obligations on the United States as a matter of international law) is also non-self-executing.[29] If a treaty does not impose binding obligations on the United States as a matter of international law, and the treaty has not been implemented by domestic legislation, then that treaty cannot impose binding obligations on actors within the domestic legal system. Although the Supremacy Clause says that treaties are the "Law of the Land," the Supremacy Clause cannot create binding domestic legal obligations on the basis of a treaty that does not create binding international legal obligations. Reasonable people might disagree about whether a precatory treaty provision is the "Law of the Land." Regardless, a precatory treaty provision does not impose binding obligations on actors within the domestic legal system.

In light of the preceding discussion, the fundamental disagreement between nationalists and transnationalists, with respect to the domestic legal force of treaties, can be summarized as follows. Assume that the United States has ratified a treaty that creates binding international legal obligations, the treaty has not been superseded by a later-in-time statute, it does not conflict with any constitutional provision, and implementing legislation is not constitutionally required. The question arises as to whether such a treaty has the force of law within the domestic legal system (i.e., whether it creates obligations that bind domestic legal actors as a matter of domestic law). Transnationalists maintain that the answer is an unqualified yes, because the Supremacy Clause says so.[30] Nationalists maintain that such a treaty has domestic legal force only if the authors of the treaty intended it to be self-executing.[31]

[28] The author has developed this argument in greater detail elsewhere. *See* David Sloss, *Non-Self-Executing Treaties: Exposing a Constitutional Fallacy*, 36 U.C. DAVIS L. REV. 1, 46–55 (2002).

[29] *See* INS v. Stevic, 467 U.S. 407, 428 n.22 (1984) (stating the "the language of article 34 [of the Protocol on the Status of Refugees] was precatory and not self-executing").

[30] *See* Sloss, *Non-Self-Executing Treaties*, *supra* note 28, at 46–55.

[31] Within the nationalist camp, there is some disagreement about whether the relevant intent is the shared intent of the states that drafted and negotiated the treaty, or the unilateral intent of the United States, as reflected in the shared understanding of the Senate and president at the time of ratification. The term *authors* is deliberately ambiguous on this point.

The Supreme Court's recent decision in *Medellin v. Texas*[32] provides some support for the nationalist position on this point, although that decision is subject to differing interpretations. In *Medellin*, the Court held that Article 94 of the UN Charter is not self-executing.[33] Some commentators maintain that the Court's decision in *Medellin* is best construed to address the judicial role in applying Article 94, not the domestic legal force of Article 94.[34] If one adopts this interpretation, the Court's decision in *Medellin* has no bearing on the conflict between the nationalist and transnationalist positions on the domestic legal force of treaties. Although there are some passages in *Medellin* that support this interpretation, the present author believes that the Court's holding is best interpreted to mean that Article 94 of the UN Charter lacks domestic legal force (i.e., it does not impose binding legal obligations on actors within the U.S. legal system as a matter of domestic law).[35]

Assuming that this is the correct interpretation of what the Court actually held, there is a further ambiguity concerning the rationale supporting that holding. One possible interpretation is that the Court believed that Article 94 is precatory as a matter of international law. There is at least one passage in the Court's opinion supporting this view.[36] As noted previously, a treaty provision that is precatory does not create binding domestic legal obligations because it does not create binding international legal obligations. In this author's view, the claim that Article 94 is precatory is incorrect as a matter of international law.[37] Regardless, if that is the correct interpretation of the

[32] Medellin, 128 S.Ct. 1346 (2008).

[33] Medellin, 128 S.Ct. at 1358–61. *See also* U.N. Charter, art. 94(1) ("Each Member of the United Nations undertakes to comply with the decision of the International Court of Justice in any case to which it is a party.").

[34] *See, e.g.*, Curtis A. Bradley, *Intent, Presumptions and Non-Self-Executing Treaties*, 102 AM. J. INT'L L. 540 (2008).

[35] Space does not permit a detailed defense of this proposition. However, it bears emphasis that the Court held in the second half of its opinion in *Medellin* that the president lacked the authority to order compliance with the subject decision by the International Court of Justice. In this context, the Court said that "[t]he responsibility for transforming an international obligation arising from a non-self-executing treaty into domestic law falls to Congress," not the President. *Medellin*, 128 S.Ct. at 1368. This statement strongly implies that the Court believed that U.S. ratification of the UN Charter, by itself, did not create any legal obligations that were binding on domestic actors as a matter of domestic law.

[36] *See* Medellin, 128 S.Ct. at 1358 (noting that art. 94 of the U.N. Charter uses the phrase "undertakes to comply," and that the text "does not provide that the United States 'shall' or 'must' comply with an ICJ decision").

[37] To the best of this author's knowledge, the U.S. executive branch has never disputed the proposition that the United States has a binding legal obligation, as a matter of international law, to comply with ICJ decisions in cases where the United States is a party.

Court's decision, then *Medellin* provides little support for the nationalist position concerning the domestic legal force of treaties because nationalists and transnationalists agree that precatory treaty provisions do not create binding domestic legal obligations.

However, there is another possible interpretation of *Medellin* that does support the nationalist position. According to this interpretation, the Court held that Article 94 is non-self-executing, not because it is precatory, but because the treaty makers decided, at the time of ratification, that Article 94 would not have domestic legal force in the absence of implementing legislation. There are several passages in *Medellin* that support this interpretation.[38] It is important to clarify precisely what this interpretation signifies. Article 94 of the UN Charter is a treaty provision that presumably does not conflict with the Constitution,[39] has not been superseded by a later-in-time statute, and for which implementing legislation is not constitutionally required. Assuming that Article 94 is not precatory as a matter of international law, and assuming that the Court in *Medellin* understood the term *non-self-executing* to mean that a treaty lacks domestic legal force, the Court's holding that Article 94 is non-self-executing means that Article 94 does not create any obligation that is binding on domestic actors under domestic law, even though it does create obligations that are binding on the United States as a matter of international law.

This position is difficult to reconcile with the text of the Supremacy Clause. The text specifies that "all Treaties . . . [are] the supreme Law of the Land." On its face, the text seems to say that treaty provisions that impose binding obligations on the United States as a matter of international law also impose binding obligations on domestic legal actors as a matter of domestic law, unless the treaty provision at issue conflicts with the Constitution, or has been superseded by a later statute, or implementing legislation is

[38] *See generally* Medellin, 128 S.Ct. at 1356–61.

[39] Scholars have advanced two distinct arguments suggesting that art. 94 may conflict with the Constitution. First, some scholars have suggested that art. 94's delegation of judicial authority to the ICJ, as applied in particular cases, may conflict with constitutional non-delegation principles. *See, e.g.*, Julian G. Ku, *International Delegations and the New World Court Order*, 81 Wash. L. Rev. 1 (2006). Second, some scholars maintain that the specific ICJ decision at issue in *Medellin* conflicts with federalism principles inasmuch as the ICJ ordered the United States to provide judicial review of state criminal convictions that were deemed "final" under applicable state law. *See, e.g.*, Medellin v. Texas, Amicus Curiae Brief of Constitutional and International Law Scholars in Support of Respondent State of Texas, pgs. 18–26, *available at* http://www.cjlf.org/briefs/MedellinIII.htm. The Supreme Court did not explicitly address either of these issues in *Medellin*. Nevertheless, concerns about federalism and international delegations may have influenced the Court's decision that art. 94 was not self-executing.

constitutionally required.[40] Yet the Court in *Medellin* made no effort to reconcile its holding with the text of the Supremacy Clause. Indeed, the Court's opinion tacitly assumes that the clause has no relevance to the question of whether Article 94 has domestic legal force.

This tacit assumption is entirely consistent with the nationalist position. Nationalists maintain that the treaty drafters and/or ratifiers determine the domestic legal force of a treaty at the time of ratification. If the drafters and/or ratifiers decide that a treaty will have domestic legal force, then it does. If they decide that a treaty will not have domestic legal force, then it does not. From a nationalist perspective, the text of the Supremacy Clause is simply irrelevant. In contrast, from a transnationalist perspective, the Supremacy Clause is dispositive. The clause means that treaty provisions that impose binding obligations on the United States as a matter of international law also impose binding obligations on domestic legal actors as a matter of domestic law, unless the treaty provision at issue conflicts with the Constitution, or has been superseded by a later statute, or implementing legislation is constitutionally required.

Not surprisingly, nationalists and transnationalists also disagree about the extent to which judicial precedent before *Medellin* supports their respective positions. Nationalists contend that prior cases related to self-execution support their position.[41] Transnationalists maintain that, before *Medellin*, the Supreme Court had never endorsed the nationalist view.[42] Although *Medellin* seems to provide significant ammunition for the nationalist model, the debate is likely to continue.

III. SELECTION OF CASES FOR REVIEW

For the purpose of this project, the author created a database of U.S. treaty cases. Creation of the database proceeded in three steps. In the first step, the author identified all the U.S. Supreme Court decisions from 1970 to 2006 in which the Court engaged in substantive analysis of a treaty. In the next step,

[40] The qualifiers after the word *unless* generally follow from the textual provision specifying that a treaty is not "the supreme Law of the Land" unless it is made "under the Authority of the United States." *See* Sloss, *Non-Self-Executing Treaties, supra* note 28, at 46–55 (providing a detailed textual analysis of the Supremacy Clause).

[41] *See, e.g., Medellin*, 128 S.Ct. at 1356–57 (providing a summary of self-execution doctrine from a nationalist perspective).

[42] *See, e.g.*, Sloss, *Non-Self-Executing Treaties, supra* note 28 (using the phrase "Restatement doctrine" to refer to the nationalist position, and showing that, as of 2002, the Restatement doctrine had some support among scholars and lower courts but had never been endorsed by the Supreme Court).

the goal was to identify as many cases as possible decided between 1970 and 2006 in which state courts and lower federal courts referenced treaties. In this step, the author identified a total of 3,238 cases decided between 1970 and 2006 in which a U.S. court made reference to a treaty. Then, in the third step, the author utilized a random selection process to select a subset of those 3,238 cases for more detailed review. Section III explains these three steps.

A. *Identifying Supreme Court Cases*

In the first step, the author identified all the U.S. Supreme Court decisions from 1970 to 2006 in which the Court engaged in substantive analysis of a treaty.[43] The year 1970 was the second year that Warren Burger was Chief Justice of the Supreme Court. The year 2006 was the first year that John Roberts was Chief Justice. Thus, the database includes virtually all significant treaty decisions by the Burger and Rehnquist courts,[44] plus cases from the first term of the Roberts Court. Altogether, there were thirty-eight Supreme Court treaty cases during this thirty-seven-year period.[45] Those thirty-eight cases include thirty cases involving multilateral treaties, five cases involving bilateral treaties, and three cases involving bilateral executive agreements (see Table 1).

[43] The criteria for inclusion or exclusion are as follows. The database includes Supreme Court decisions if (1) one or more parties invoked a treaty in support of a claim or defense or (2) the Court engaged in a treaty interpretation analysis. Such cases are included even if the court applied a statutory or constitutional provision as the rule of decision, and merely consulted the treaty for guidance about how best to interpret that statutory or constitutional provision. However, cases were excluded if a judicial opinion contains no explicit reference to a treaty, even if the case references a statute that implements a treaty. Moreover, cases were excluded if the Court merely referenced a treaty in passing but no party relied on the treaty as the basis of a claim or defense, and the Court did not attempt to interpret the treaty. Finally, cases involving treaties with Indian tribes are also excluded.

The following examples of cases excluded from the database illustrate the application of these criteria: Cortez Byrd Chips, Inc. v. Bill Harbert Const. Co., 529 U.S. 193 (2000) (in a statutory interpretation case involving the Federal Arbitration Act, the Court briefly referenced the Convention on the Recognition and Enforcement of Foreign Arbitral Awards); Goldwater v. Carter, 444 U.S. 996 (1979) (in a case where members of Congress challenged the president's constitutional authority to terminate a bilateral treaty with Taiwan, the Court refused to decide the constitutional issue presented).

[44] During Chief Justice Burger's first term as Chief Justice, the Court decided *U.S. v. Louisiana*, 394 U.S. 11 (1969), a case involving application of the Convention on the Territorial Sea and Contiguous Zone. That case is excluded because it was decided before 1970. Otherwise, every significant treaty decision from the Burger and Rehnquist courts is included in the database.

[45] *Medellin v. Texas*, 128 S. Ct. 1346 (2008), is not included in the database because the Court decided *Medellin* after the database was created.

TABLE 1. *Supreme court treaty cases, 1970–2006*

Case	Year	Type	Treaty
Texas v. Louisiana	1973	Bilateral	Land treaties with France, Spain and Mexico
Scherk v. Alberto-Culver Co.	1974	Multilateral	New York Convention
Vella v. Ford Motor Co.	1975	Multilateral	Shipowners Liability Convention
U.S. v. Alaska	1975	Multilateral	Conv. on Terr. Sea & Contig. Zone
Texas v. Louisiana	1976	Multilateral	Conv. on Terr. Sea & Contig. Zone
Dames & Moore v. Regan	1981	Bilateral	Exec. Agmt. w/Iran
Weinberger v. Rossi	1982	Bilateral	Exec. Agmt. w/Philippines
Sumitomo Shoji v. Avagliano	1982	Bilateral	FCN Treaty with Japan
TWA v. Franklin Mint Corp.	1984	Multilateral	Warsaw Convention
INS v. Stevic	1984	Multilateral	Protocol on Status of Refugees
Air France v. Saks	1985	Multilateral	Warsaw Convention
Mitsubishi Motors v. Soler Chrysler-Plymouth	1985	Multilateral	New York Convention
United States v. Maine	1986	Multilateral	Conv. on Terr. Sea & Contig. Zone
Japan Whaling Assoc. v. Am. Cetacean Soc'y	1986	Multilateral	Int'l Conv. for Regulation of Whaling
O'Connor v. United States	1986	Bilateral	Panama Canal Treaty
Soc. Nationale v. U.S. Dist. Ct.	1987	Multilateral	Hague Evidence Convention
INS v. Cardozo-Fonseca	1987	Multilateral	Protocol on Status of Refugees
Volkswagenwerk v. Schlunk	1988	Multilateral	Hague Service Convention
Chan v. Korean Airlines	1989	Multilateral	Warsaw Convention
United States v. Stuart	1989	Bilateral	Tax Treaty w/Canada
Eastern Airlines v. Floyd	1991	Multilateral	Warsaw Convention
United States v. Alvarez-Machain	1992	Bilateral	Extradition Treaty w/Mexico

Itel Containers v. Huddleston	1993	Multilateral	Container Conventions
Sale v. Haitian Ctrs. Council	1993	Multilateral	Protocol on Status of Refugees
Vimar Seguros v. M/V Sky Reefer	1995	Multilateral	Brussels Convention
Zicherman v. Korean Air Lines	1996	Multilateral	Warsaw Convention
Breard v. Greene	1998	Multilateral	Vienna Conv. on Consular Relations
Federal Republic of Germany v. United States	1999	Multilateral	Vienna Conv. on Consular Relations
INS v. Aguirre-Aguirre	1999	Multilateral	Protocol on Status of Refugees
El Al Airlines v. Tsui Yuan Tseng	1999	Multilateral	Warsaw Convention
Amer. Ins. Assoc. v. Garamendi	2003	Bilateral	Exec. Agmts. w/Germany, Austria, and France
Olympic Airways v. Husain	2004	Multilateral	Warsaw Convention
Roper v. Simmons	2005	Multilateral	ICCPR
Spector v. Norwegian Cruise Line	2005	Multilateral	Conv. for Safety of Life at Sea
Alaska v. United States	2005	Multilateral	Conv. on Terr. Sea & Contig. Zone
Medellin v. Dretke	2005	Multilateral	Vienna Conv. on Consular Relations
Sanchez-Llamas v. Oregon	2006	Multilateral	Vienna Conv. on Consular Relations
Hamdan v. Rumsfeld	2006	Multilateral	Geneva Conventions

B. *Identifying Other Treaty Cases*

In the second step, the goal was to identify as many cases as possible decided between 1970 and 2006 in which state courts and lower federal courts made reference to a treaty. For these purposes, the author drew a distinction among executive agreements, bilateral treaties, and multilateral treaties. Since this study focuses on treaties, not executive agreements,[46] the author made no attempt to identify cases decided by state and lower federal courts involving executive agreements. The search for cases involving bilateral and multilateral treaties proceeded along two parallel tracks.

Table 1 includes five Supreme Court decisions involving bilateral treaties: one case involving land boundary and land acquisition treaties,[47] one involving the Panama Canal Treaty,[48] one involving an extradition treaty,[49] one involving a tax treaty,[50] and one case involving a friendship, commerce, and navigation (FCN) treaty.[51] Although cases involving land boundary and land acquisition treaties were a staple of federal court litigation in the nineteenth century,[52] there are very few such cases litigated today. Therefore, the author did not search for cases involving land treaties. In recent years, U.S. courts have adjudicated a substantial number of cases involving extradition treaties, tax treaties, and FCN treaties. Therefore, the author conducted electronic searches in an effort to identify all or most of the judicial decisions between 1970 and 2006 involving extradition treaties, tax treaties, and FCN treaties.[53] These searches yielded a total of 1,433 judicial decisions. The author believes that most of the cases decided between 1970 and 2006 in which state courts and lower federal courts engaged in substantive analysis of a bilateral treaty are included within this set of 1,433 judicial decisions.

Table 1 includes thirty Supreme Court cases involving a total of fourteen multilateral treaties.[54] The author assigned a law student to conduct

[46] *See supra* notes 6–8 and accompanying text.

[47] Texas v. Louisiana, 410 U.S. 702 (1973) (applying 1803 treaty whereby the United States purchased Louisiana from France, 1819 treaty whereby the United States purchased Florida from Spain, and 1828 treaty establishing boundary with Mexico).

[48] O'Connor v. United States, 479 U.S. 27 (1986).

[49] United States v. Alvarez-Machain, 504 U.S. 655 (1992).

[50] United States v. Stuart, 489 U.S. 353 (1989).

[51] Sumitomo Shoji America, Inc. v. Avagliano, 457 U.S. 176 (1982).

[52] *See* Sloss, *Individually Enforceable Rights*, *supra* note 1, at 51–91.

[53] The author conducted three different searches on Westlaw, using the "allcases" database: (treaty /s "double taxation"); (treaty /s extradition); and (treaty /s friendship). For each search, the author set a date limit after 1969 and before 2007.

[54] The figure of fourteen multilateral treaties counts the two container conventions at issue in *Itel Containers v. Huddleston*, 507 U.S. 60 (1993), as a single treaty. It also counts the four Geneva Conventions at issue in *Hamdan v. Rumsfeld*, 548 U.S. 557 (2006), as a single treaty.

electronic searches to identify published judicial decisions[55] in which a court referenced the Panama Canal Treaty[56] or one of those fourteen multilateral treaties.[57] After identifying all of the published decisions by state courts and lower federal courts referencing those treaties, the student searched for other cases involving specific, named multilateral treaties to which the United States is a party.[58] Altogether, the student identified 1,805 published judicial decisions (other than Supreme Court decisions) in which courts referenced more than thirty-five treaties to which the United States is a party. There is one substantial group of cases involving a multilateral treaty that is excluded from this set of 1,805 cases. U.S. courts decided more than 6,600 cases involving the Convention against Torture (CAT)[59] between 1984 and 2006.[60] The author chose to exclude CAT cases because inclusion of

[55] The phrase "published judicial decisions" includes decisions published in an official reporter. It does not include cases that are published only on Lexis and/or Westlaw.

[56] The Panama Canal Treaty was included in this set of electronic searches because cases involving the Panama Canal Treaty can be identified by searching for the named treaty. In this respect, the Panama Canal Treaty is similar to the multilateral treaties covered in the electronic searches described in notes 57–58, and different from the bilateral treaties covered by the searches described in note 53.

[57] The student conducted multiple searches on Westlaw, using the "allcases" database. For each search, the student entered the name of a particular treaty as the search term and set a date limit after 1969 and before 2007. The specific treaties included in these searches are the multilateral treaties listed in Table 1, as well as the Panama Canal Treaty.

[58] The student conducted multiple searches on Westlaw, using the "allcases" database. For each search, the student entered the name of a particular treaty as the search term and set a date limit after 1969 and before 2007. The specific treaties included in these searches are the Berne Convention for the Protection of Literary and Artistic Works, the Convention on Combating Bribery of Foreign Public Officials in International Business Transactions, the Convention against Illegal Traffic in Narcotic Drugs and Psychotropic Substances, the International Convention against the Taking of Hostages, the Convention on the Prohibition of the Development, Production, Stockpiling, and Use of Chemical Weapons and on Their Destruction, the Hague Convention on Civil Aspects of International Child Abduction, the Convention on the International Sale of Goods, the Convention on International Trade in Endangered Species of Wild Fauna and Flora, the Convention Relating to the Carriage of Passengers and Their Luggage by Sea, the Inter-American Convention on Letters Rogatory, the Convention on International Civil Aviation, the Convention on the Settlement of Investment Disputes between States and Nationals of Other States, the Convention for the Suppression of Unlawful Acts against Maritime Navigation, the Convention on the High Seas, the Convention on the Continental Shelf, the Convention on the Prevention and Punishment of the Crime of Genocide, the Convention for the Prevention of Pollution from Ships, the Montreal Convention, the Paris Convention, the Convention on the Elimination of All Forms of Racial Discrimination, the Single Convention on Narcotics, the UN Convention on the Law of the Sea, and the Vienna Convention on Diplomatic Relations.

[59] Convention against Torture and Other Cruel, Inhuman, or Degrading Treatment or Punishment, 23 I.L.M. 1027 (1984), modified, 24 I.L.M. 535 (1985).

[60] A Westlaw search in the "allcases" database with a date limit before 2007, using search terms (torture /3 convention) yields 6,655 documents. This figure includes both published

those cases would overwhelm the other cases in the database. Leaving aside CAT cases, though, the author is confident that the set of 1,805 cases includes the vast majority of published judicial opinions between 1970 and 2006 in which a U.S. court engaged in substantive analysis of a multilateral treaty.

In summary, the electronic searches described above identified 1,805 published judicial decisions referencing specific, named treaties and 1,433 cases referencing extradition, tax, and FCN treaties. Other than CAT cases, the vast majority of published decisions between 1970 and 2006 in which state courts and lower federal courts engaged in substantive analysis of a treaty are included within this set of 3,238 judicial decisions.

C. *Creating the Final Database*

It was neither feasible nor necessary to conduct a detailed review of all 3,238 cases discussed in part B. Therefore, in the third step, the author utilized a random selection process to select a subset of cases for more detailed review. Specifically, I selected 200 of the 1,805 cases involving specific named treaties[61] and 75 of the 1,433 cases involving extradition, tax, and FCN treaties.[62] The reason for conducting a bifurcated search is as follows. Almost 80 percent of the Supreme Court cases listed in Table 1 involve multilateral treaties. In contrast, only about 55 percent of the 3,238 cases noted in part B involve multilateral treaties.[63] The goal was to generate a final database in which the percentage of cases involving multilateral treaties was roughly the same as the 80 percent figure reflected in the Supreme Court cases. Therefore, in selecting a random sample, I selected about 11 percent of the 1,805 cases involving named treaties and about 5 percent of the cases involving tax, extradition, and FCN treaties.

In the process of reviewing the 275 randomly selected cases, I eliminated 59 cases because the courts in those cases did not engage in substantive analysis of any treaty-related issue.[64] Thus, the final database includes 216

and unpublished decisions. *Tel-Oren v. Libyan Arab Republic*, 726 F.2d 774 (D.C. Cir. 1984), was the first judicial decision referencing the Convention against Torture.

[61] I assigned a number between 1 and 1,805 to each of the cases and used the integer generator at http://www.random.org to generate a random set of 200 integers between 1 and 1,805.

[62] I assigned a number between 1 and 1,433 to each of the cases and used the integer generator at http://www.random.org to generate a random set of 75 integers between 1 and 1,433.

[63] This assumes that almost all the 1,805 cases referencing named treaties involve multilateral treaties, and almost all the 1,433 cases referencing extradition, tax, and FCN treaties involve bilateral treaties.

[64] The criteria for determining whether a court engaged in substantive analysis of a treaty-related issue are the criteria identified in note 43, *supra*.

judicial opinions published by state courts and lower federal courts, plus 38 judicial opinions published by the U.S. Supreme Court, for a total of 254 cases.[65] These 254 cases include 204 cases involving multilateral treaties, 47 cases involving bilateral treaties, and 3 cases involving both types of treaties. The discussion that follows in the remainder of this chapter is based primarily on a detailed analysis of the 254 cases in that database.

Two observations about the database merit brief comment. First, there is a distinct upward trend in the number of treaty cases over time. The database includes thirty-one cases from the 1970s, sixty-one cases from the 1980s, eighty-two cases from the 1990s, and eighty cases decided during the period from 2000 through 2006. This upward trend may be partially explained by an upward trend in the overall number of published decisions by U.S. courts during this period. However, it is likely that the trend also reflects an increase in the percentage of cases involving treaties.

Second, there are a relatively small number of treaties that account for a significant percentage of the cases in the database. Specifically, the database includes forty-nine cases involving the Warsaw Convention,[66] thirty-three cases involving the New York Convention,[67] thirty-two cases involving the Vienna Convention on Consular Relations,[68] and twenty-four cases involving bilateral extradition treaties. Thus, cases involving extradition treaties and these three multilateral treaties account for about 54 percent of the cases in the database. This is broadly representative of the pattern of judicial decision-making in U.S. courts: there are a fairly small number of treaties (and types of treaties) that account for the majority of treaty cases decided by U.S. courts over the past few decades.

IV. TREATY APPLICATION

U.S. courts apply a wide variety of "tools" in treaty cases. The term *tools* refers broadly to canons of treaty interpretation and other doctrines of treaty

[65] These 254 cases include 38 U.S. Supreme Court decisions, 78 decisions by federal appellate courts, 93 decisions by federal district courts, 37 decisions by state courts, and 8 decisions by specialized federal courts (including five from the U.S. Tax Court, two from federal bankruptcy courts and one from the U.S. Customs Court).

[66] Convention for the Unification of Certain Rules Relating to International Carriage by Air, opened for signature Oct. 12, 1929, 49 Stat. 3000, T.S. 876, *reprinted at* 49 U.S.C. § 40105 (2000) [hereinafter Warsaw Convention].

[67] Convention on the Recognition and Enforcement of Foreign Arbitral Awards, June 10, 1958, 21 U.S.T. 2517, 330 U.N.T.S. 38 [hereinafter, New York Convention].

[68] Vienna Convention on Consular Relations, Apr. 24, 1963, 596 U.N.T.S. 261 [hereinafter VCCR].

law. This section describes the main tools of U.S. treaty law and analyzes their application by U.S. courts.

Tools are classified as either nationalist or transnationalist. Whereas transnationalists view domestic courts as agents of both the domestic legal system and the international legal system, nationalists view domestic courts exclusively (or primarily) as agents of the domestic legal system. At least two consequences flow from these contrasting perspectives. First, transnationalists believe that courts should adopt an interpretive approach that promotes the common interests of all treaty parties,[69] whereas nationalists believe that courts should adopt an interpretive approach that gives greater weight to the unilateral interests of the United States.[70] Second, transnationalists believe that domestic courts should adopt an interpretive approach that favors the use of international treaties to protect the rights of private parties.[71] In contrast, nationalists believe that courts should be hesitant to apply treaties for the benefit of private parties.[72]

Sections IV and V present an empirical analysis of the application of treaties by U.S. courts, based on the database described in Section III. Courts have broad discretion in choosing whether to apply nationalist tools, transnationalist tools, both, or neither. When courts utilize those tools, though, interesting patterns emerge. In litigation between and among private parties, courts apply transnationalist tools more frequently than they apply nationalist tools. In contrast, in cases where private parties are adverse to state or federal government actors, courts apply nationalist tools more frequently than they apply transnationalist tools. Section IV documents the use of nationalist and transnationalist tools in different types of cases. Section V considers whether, and to what extent, a court's decision to utilize nationalist (or transnationalist) tools correlates with case outcomes in different types of cases.

A. *The Tools of U.S. Treaty Law*

The most frequently cited principle of treaty interpretation is the idea that courts should interpret treaties in accordance with the goals or objectives

[69] This idea has traditionally been expressed in the canon that treaties should be interpreted in good faith. *See infra* notes 73–77 and accompanying text.

[70] This idea is manifested in the canon that courts engaged in treaty interpretation should defer to the views of the executive branch. *See infra* notes 78–81 and accompanying text.

[71] This idea is embodied in the traditional canon of liberal interpretation. *See infra* notes 82–86 and accompanying text.

[72] This idea is expressed in the presumption that treaties do not create individually enforceable rights. *See infra* notes 87–89 and accompanying text.

of the treaty makers. In about 30 percent of the cases in the database, courts justified their decisions by invoking the purpose of the treaty makers to support their interpretation of a contested treaty provision. However, this figure obscures a disagreement about whether courts should focus on the intent of the international treaty drafters (a transnationalist approach) or the intent of the domestic treaty ratifiers (a nationalist approach). Since this teleological approach could be either nationalist or transnationalist, depending how it is applied, the fact that a court employed purposive analysis in a particular case, without more, does not support classification of that case as either nationalist or transnationalist. In contrast, the other primary tools of treaty application tend to divide along nationalist and transnationalist lines.

1. Deference and Good Faith. The canon of good faith expresses one of the core principles of the transnationalist model. In its traditional form, the canon holds that treaties should be interpreted in a manner that "makes for the common benefit of the contracting parties and tends to put them on a footing of equality."[73] In short, treaties should be construed in a manner that promotes the common interests of all parties, not just the unilateral interests of one party. From the late eighteenth century until the early twentieth century, the principle of good faith was the dominant canon of U.S. treaty jurisprudence.[74] Nowadays, courts rarely cite the canon of good faith explicitly.[75] However, U.S. courts sometimes apply the main idea without using the phrase "good faith." For example, in five cases decided since 1970, the Supreme Court has endorsed the principle that courts should construe treaties "in a manner consistent with the shared expectations of the contracting parties."[76] The author coded cases in the database as "good faith" if a court invoked the principle that treaties should be interpreted in accordance with the shared expectations of the parties.

[73] 2 Vattel, The Law of Nations or the Principles of Natural Law, chap. 17, para. 301 (Charles G. Fenwick, trans., Hein 1995) (1883).

[74] *See generally* Michael P. Van Alstine, *The Death of Good Faith in Treaty Jurisprudence and a Call for Resurrection*, 93 Geo. L.J. 1885 (2005).

[75] Courts cited the canon explicitly in only 1 of 254 cases in the database. *See* Sanchez-Llamas v. Oregon, 548 U.S. 331 (2006).

[76] *See* Olympic Airways v. Husain, 540 U.S. 644, 650 (2004); El Al Airlines v. Tsui Yuan Tseng, 525 U.S. 155, 167 (1999); Zicherman v. Korean Air Lines, 516 U.S. 217, 223 (1996); Eastern Airlines v. Floyd, 499 U.S. 530, 540 (1991); Air France v. Saks, 470 U.S. 392, 399 (1985). In one other case, the dissent endorsed this principle. *See* United States v. Alvarez-Machain, 504 U.S. 655, 673 (1992) (Stevens, J., dissenting).

Cases are also coded as "good faith" if a court referred explicitly to Article 31 of the Vienna Convention on the Law of Treaties. Article 31 codifies the primary international rules of treaty interpretation. It states: "A treaty shall be interpreted in good faith in accordance with the ordinary meaning to be given to the terms of the treaty and in the light of its object and purpose."[77] Thus, by citing Article 31, a court is implicitly, if not explicitly, endorsing the canon of good faith. Altogether, courts endorsed the principle of good faith in 19 out of 254 cases in the database.

The canon of deference to the executive branch is the nationalist counterpoint to the transnationalist canon of good faith. The canon states that "the meaning attributed to treaty provisions by the Government agencies charged with their negotiation and enforcement is entitled to great weight."[78] Whereas the canon of good faith has historical roots that pre-date the U.S. Constitution, the canon of deference to the executive branch is a relative newcomer. In the early days of U.S. constitutional history, the courts did not defer to the executive branch on matters of treaty interpretation.[79] The canon of judicial deference to the executive emerged in the first half of the twentieth century[80] as part of a broader historical trend in which foreign affairs power became concentrated in the executive branch.[81]

Nowadays, the deference canon is one of the most frequently cited principles of treaty interpretation: courts cited the canon in 28 out of 254 cases in the database. Whereas the canon of good faith focuses on the shared understanding of all the parties, the canon of deference to the executive focuses on the unilateral understanding of one party. Of course, deference to the executive is not always unilateralist. If the executive branch's interpretation of a treaty is based upon a good faith effort to ascertain the mutual expectations of the parties, then deference to the executive is entirely consistent with the principle of good faith. On the other hand, insofar as executive

[77] Vienna Convention on the Law of Treaties, 1155 U.N.T.S. 331, art. 31 (1969) [hereinafter VCLT].

[78] El Al Israel Airlines, Ltd. v. Tsui Yuan Tseng, 525 U.S. 155, 168 (1999) (quoting Sumitomo Shoji Am., Inc. v. Avagliano, 457 U.S. 176, 184–85 (1982)).

[79] *See* David Sloss, *Judicial Deference to Executive Branch Treaty Interpretations: A Historical Perspective*, 62 N.Y.U. Ann. Surv. Am. L. 497 (2007) (analyzing Supreme Court treaty interpretation cases from 1789 to 1838 and showing that the Court applied a zero-deference approach).

[80] *See* Robert Chesney, *Disaggregating Deference: The Judicial Power and Executive Treaty Interpretations*, 92 Iowa L. Rev. 1723, 1741–49 (2007) (tracing the rise of the deference doctrine in the early twentieth century).

[81] *See* G. Edward White, *The Transformation of the Constitutional Regime of Foreign Relations*, 85 Va. L. Rev. 1 (1999) (documenting the shift of foreign affairs power from Congress to the executive branch between World War I and World War II).

treaty interpretation is influenced by a desire to promote national policy interests, judicial deference to executive treaty interpretations tends to yield a different interpretation than a disinterested good faith analysis.

2. Rights of Private Parties. Writing in 1809, Chief Justice Marshall stated: "Each treaty stipulates something respecting the citizens of the two nations, and gives them rights. Whenever a right grows out of, or is protected by, a treaty, it is sanctioned against all the laws and judicial decisions of the states; and whoever may have this right, it is to be protected."[82] The idea that treaties are crafted to protect the rights of individuals was traditionally expressed in the canon of liberal interpretation. That canon states: "If the treaty admits of two interpretations, and one is limited, and the other liberal; one which will further, and the other exclude private rights; why should not the most liberal exposition be adopted?"[83] The canon of liberal interpretation expresses another core feature of the transnationalist position: that treaties should be interpreted in a way that promotes broader protection for the rights of private parties. Before World War II, U.S. courts routinely relied on the canon of liberal interpretation as a central principle of U.S. treaty law.[84] Recently, though, the canon has fallen into desuetude. Courts cited the canon in only four out of 254 cases in the database.[85]

In cases involving extradition treaties, courts have begun to cite the canon of liberal interpretation to support a presumption in favor of the state's power to extradite.[86] When the canon is applied in this fashion, it has precisely the opposite effect of the traditional canon because it tends to narrow the scope of protection for private rights. Hence, cases that apply the canon in this manner are not coded as "liberal interpretation" cases.

The nationalist counterpoint to the transnationalist canon of liberal interpretation is the presumption that treaties do not create individually

[82] Owings v. Norwood's Lessee, 9 U.S. (5 Cranch) 344, 348 (1809).

[83] Shanks v. Dupont, 28 U.S. (3 Pet.) 242, 249 (1830).

[84] *See* Van Alstine, *supra* note 74, at 1911–14.

[85] United States v. Stuart, 489 U.S. 353, 368 (1989); I.N.S. v. Cardozo-Fonseca, 480 U.S. 421, 449 (1987) (applying a statutory analogue to the canon of liberal interpretation); Royal Ins. Co. v. Emery Air Freight, 834 F. Supp. 633 (S.D.N.Y. 1993); Estate of Burghardt v. Comm'r of Internal Revenue, 80 T.C. 705 (U.S. Tax Ct. 1983). In one other case, a dissenting opinion invoked the canon of liberal interpretation. Itel Containers v. Huddleston, 507 U.S. 60 (1993) (Blackmun, J., dissenting).

[86] *See, e.g.*, United States v. Lehder-Rivas, 955 F.2d 1510, 1520 (11th Cir. 1992); Elcock v. United States, 80 F. Supp. 2d 70, 79 (E.D.N.Y. 2000) (citing canon in support of the proposition that extradition treaties "should be liberally construed to effect their purpose, namely, the surrender of fugitives"); Extradition of Powell, 4 F. Supp. 2d 945, 959 (S.D. Cal 1998) (citing canon and stating that "the Court applies the interpretation that favors extradition").

enforceable rights. As expressed recently by one federal court, this doctrine holds: "Even though treaties may accord enforceable individual rights, most courts accept a 'presumption' against inferring such rights from international treaties."[87] The database of 254 cases includes 11 cases where a court endorsed the presumption that treaties do not create individually enforceable private rights. In litigation before the Supreme Court, the executive branch has claimed that this is a "long-established presumption."[88] In fact, though, the "long-established" rule is the canon of liberal interpretation, which favors treaty interpretations that promote broader protection for individual rights. In contrast, the presumption against individually enforceable rights did not emerge as a feature of U.S. treaty jurisprudence until the late twentieth century.[89]

It is evident that the canon of liberal interpretation and the presumption against individually enforceable rights drive case outcomes in different directions. A court applying the canon of liberal interpretation is more likely to rule in favor of an individual claiming rights under a treaty. A court applying the presumption against private enforcement of treaties is less likely to do so.

3. The Charming Betsy Canon. In the United States, it is a well-established principle of statutory construction that federal statutes should be construed in conformity with the United States' international legal obligations. This canon of statutory interpretation is known as the "Charming Betsy" canon. The name derives from a Supreme Court decision in 1804, where Chief Justice Marshall stated: "An act of Congress ought never to be construed to violate the law of nations if any other possible construction remains."[90] Although the canon as originally formulated referred to the "law of nations," rather than treaties, U.S. courts have routinely invoked the canon to interpret federal statutes in accordance with U.S. treaty obligations. Courts applied the Charming Betsy canon in 18 out of 254 treaty cases in the database. The canon is clearly transnationalist because it encourages courts to exercise their judicial power to harmonize domestic law with the nation's international legal obligations.

[87] Gandara v. Bennett, 528 F.3d 823, 828 (11th Cir. 2008).
[88] Sanchez-Llamas v. Oregon, 548 U.S. 331, 376 (Breyer, J., dissenting) (quoting amicus brief submitted by U.S. government, which asserted "that there is a long-established presumption that treaties and other international agreements do not create judicially enforceable individual rights").
[89] *See* Sloss, *Individually Enforceable Rights*, *supra* note 1, at 106–10 (documenting the origins of the presumption against individual rights in the 1970s and 1980s).
[90] Murray v. Schooner Charming Betsy, 6 U.S. (2 Cranch) 64, 118 (1804).

In contrast to the other transnationalist tools discussed above, there is no nationalist counterpoint to the Charming Betsy canon. Even so, it bears emphasis that U.S. courts have broad discretion to choose when to invoke the canon and when to ignore it. Indeed, there are numerous cases in the database where a court could have invoked the Charming Betsy canon but did not reference the canon explicitly.[91] In theory, one could classify cases where a court invoked the canon as "transnationalist," and classify cases as "nationalist" where a court could have invoked the canon but elected not to do so. However, the author chose not to apply a nationalist label to cases where courts *could have* applied the Charming Betsy canon because the question whether a court *could have* done so is difficult to answer in a consistent, neutral fashion.

4. The Doctrine of Self-Execution. When a domestic court holds that a particular treaty provision is self-executing, the court acts as an agent of the international legal order by applying that treaty provision as a rule of law within the domestic legal system. Hence, cases in which courts stated expressly that a particular treaty or treaty provision was self-executing are coded as "transnationalist." Conversely, when a court holds that a particular treaty provision is not self-executing, the court refuses to apply that provision as a rule of law within the domestic legal order, thereby shielding the domestic legal system from the influence of international law. Hence, cases in which courts stated expressly that a particular treaty provision was non-self-executing are coded as "nationalist."[92]

Some may object to this classification scheme on the grounds that self-execution doctrine differs from the other treaty doctrines discussed above. In particular, the conclusion that a treaty is self-executing or non-self-executing is the result of an analytical process in which a court examines specific treaty text. In contrast, the decision, for example, whether to invoke the canon of good faith is not the result of any analytical process – rather, it is

[91] *See, e.g.*, I.N.S. v. Aguirre-Aguirre, 526 U.S. 415 (1999) (where foreign national sought to avoid deportation by invoking art. 33 of the Refugee Protocol and the UN High Commissioner's interpretation of that article, the Court relied on a domestic statute as the controlling rule and deferred to a federal agency's interpretation of the statute without mentioning the *Charming Betsy* canon); In re Automotive Refinishing Paint Antitrust Lit., 358 F.3d 288 (3rd Cir. 2004) (where defendant invoked the Hague Evidence Convention in support of a motion for a protective order, the court denied the motion and applied federal rules governing discovery in civil suits without mentioning the *Charming Betsy* canon).

[92] Cases where a court applied both nationalist and transnationalist tools are coded as "both." The database includes one case coded as "both" where a court stated expressly that a treaty was self-executing, and two cases coded as "both" where a court stated expressly that a treaty was non-self-executing.

an *a priori* decision that (at least potentially) influences a court's application of a treaty.

This objection misses its mark. Like the decision whether to invoke the canon of good faith, the decision whether to invoke the doctrine of self-execution is also an *a priori* decision that (at least potentially) influences a court's application of a treaty. In fact, courts decided almost 90% of the cases in the database (227 out of 254 cases) without even mentioning the doctrine of self-execution. Courts referenced the doctrine in only 27 cases, and in six of those cases the court did not decide whether the treaty at issue was self-executing.[93] Altogether, a court reached a specific conclusion that a particular treaty was or was not self-executing in only 8 percent of the cases in the database (21 out of 254 cases).[94]

The decision to classify a case as "nationalist" if a court said that a treaty was non-self-executing should not be construed to imply that transnationalists reject the non-self-execution doctrine. Transnationalists acknowledge that some treaty provisions are so vague or ambiguous that there is no rule of law for a court to apply.[95] Similarly, if a treaty merely regulates horizontal relationships between nations, and not vertical relationships between states and private parties, ordinary limitations on standing generally preclude a court from applying that treaty at the behest of a private litigant.[96] The doctrine of non-self-execution is entirely consistent with transnationalist principles insofar as it is invoked to restrain judicial application of treaties in these types of cases.[97]

However, courts frequently justify the conclusion that a treaty is not self-executing by claiming that the treaty drafters intended the treaty to

[93] *See* Sanchez-Llamas v. Oregon, 548 U.S. 331, 346 (2006) (referring briefly to the doctrine of self-execution); Sale v. Haitian Centers Council, Inc., 509 U.S. 155, 167 (1993) (noting that district court said that art. 33 of the Refugee Protocol is not self-executing); United States v. Alvarez-Machain, 504 U.S. 655, 667 (1992) (noting that respondent asserted that extradition treaty with Mexico was self-executing); Avero Belgium Ins. v. American Airlines, 423 F.3d 73, 77–78 (2d Cir. 2005) (discussing the distinction between self-executing and non-self-executing treaties); Holmes v. Laird, 459 F.2d 1211, 1222 (D.C. Cir. 1972) (referencing the doctrine of self-executing treaties); Micronescu v. Costner, 345 F. Supp. 2d 538, 546 (M.D.N.C. 2004) (stating that "both parties have expended significant energy addressing the issue of whether or not the Torture Convention is self-executing" but not deciding the issue).

[94] *See infra* Table 2B and accompanying text.

[95] *See, e.g.*, Vazquez, *supra* note 24, at 713–15 (1995).

[96] *See, e.g.*, Sloss, *Non-Self-Executing Treaties*, *supra* note 28, at 27–29.

[97] This is not an exhaustive list of legitimate reasons for concluding that a treaty is not self-executing. For more detailed analysis, *see id.*, at 19–44.

be implemented by legislation rather than judicial action.[98] This ostensible rationale manifests the court's confusion about the relationship between domestic and international law. Typically, an international treaty obligates a state to accomplish some result; the choice of means for accomplishing that result – legislative versus executive versus judicial means – is left entirely to the discretion of the signatory nations.[99] Thus, when a court says that the treaty language demonstrates that the drafters intended the treaty to be implemented by legislative action, not judicial action, the court is almost always misinterpreting the relevant treaty provision.[100] Moreover, this all-too-common misinterpretation typically promotes a nationalist objective by shielding government action from judicial review on the basis of norms incorporated in treaties.[101] Hence, this consistent pattern of treaty misinterpretation in the service of nationalist objectives supports the decision to classify cases as "nationalist" when courts say that a treaty is not self-executing.

B. *Selective Application of Treaty Tools by U.S. Courts*

For the reasons explained in part A, the canon of deference to the executive branch and the presumption that treaties do not create individually enforceable rights are classified as nationalist tools. The canon of good faith, the canon of liberal interpretation and the Charming Betsy canon are classified as transnationalist tools. The doctrine of self-execution is classified as a nationalist tool if a court stated that a treaty was not self-executing, and as a transnationalist tool if a court stated that a treaty was self-executing.

Table 2 summarizes the application of nationalist and transnationalist tools by U.S. courts. A case is classified as "nationalist" if a court applied one

[98] *See, e.g.*, Int'l Café, S.A.L. v. Hard Rock Café Int'l (U.S.A.), Inc., 252 F.3d 1274, 1277 n.5 (11th Cir. 2001).

[99] *See* 1 Sir Robert Jennings & Sir Arthur Watts, Oppenheim's International Law § 21 (9th ed. 1992). *See also* Sean D. Murphy, Chapter 2 in this volume.

[100] For example, in *Int'l Café*, 252 F.3d 1274, the Eleventh Circuit addressed the Paris Convention for the Protection of Intellectual Property, July 14, 1967, 53 Stat. 1780, 24 U.S.T. 2140. The Eleventh Circuit said: "The Paris Convention is not self-executing because, on its face, the Convention provides that it will become effective only through domestic legislation." 252 F.3d 1274, 1277 n.5. The Court cited art. 17 of the Paris Convention in support of this claim. Art. 17 states: "It is understood that at the time an instrument of ratification or accession is deposited on behalf of a country, such country will be in a position under its domestic law to give effect to the provisions of the Convention." Contrary to the Eleventh Circuit's mistaken interpretation, art. 17 does not obligate states to enact domestic legislation to implement the treaty. Rather, art. 17 obligates states to "give effect" to the Convention through whatever mechanisms are appropriate under their respective domestic legal systems.

[101] *See infra*, pgs. 538–39.

or more nationalist tools in that case but did not apply any transnationalist tools. A case is classified as "transnationalist" if a court applied one or more transnationalist tools, but did not apply any nationalist tools. A case is classified as "both" if a court applied both nationalist and transnationalist tools in the same case, and as "neither" if a court chose not to apply any nationalist or transnationalist tools. In the aggregate, about 67 percent of the cases in the database are included in the "neither" category. The preponderance of cases in which courts did not apply any nationalist or transnationalist tools suggests that U.S. courts have broad discretion in choosing when and whether to apply such tools.

The rows in Table 2 classify cases according to the identity of the parties and the type of case. The first row indicates that the database includes 105 cases that were wholly private (i.e., no government agency or officer was either a party or an amicus in the case). The second row shows that 114 cases count as "government party." In all but one of the government-party cases,

TABLE 2. *Use of nationalist and transnationalist tools*

	Nationalist	Transnationalist	Neither/Both
Private Parties (105 cases)	2.9% [0, 6.1] (3)	18.1% [10.7, 25.5] (19)	79.0% (83)
Gov't Party (114 cases)	27.2% [19.0, 35.4] (31)	8.8% [3.6, 14.0] (10)	64.0% (73)
Gov't Civil (65 cases)	24.6% [14.0, 35.2] (16)	10.8% [3.2, 18.4] (7)	64.6% (42)
Gov't Criminal (49 cases)	30.6% [17.6, 43.6] (15)	6.1% [0, 12.9] (3)	63.3% (31)
USG Amicus (21 cases)	19.0% [1.8, 36.2] (4)	19.0% [1.8, 36.2] (4)	61.9% (13)
Other (14 cases)	0	7.1% [0, 21.1] (1)	92.9% (13)
Total (254 cases)	15.0% [10.6, 19.4] (38)	13.4% [9.2, 17.6] (34)	71.6% (182)

the government actor was adverse to a private party.[102] The government-party cases include sixty-five civil cases and forty-nine criminal cases;[103] these cases are analyzed separately in rows 3 and 4. Row 5 shows that the database includes twenty-one cases in which the U.S. government appeared as an amicus.[104] The fourteen cases categorized as "other" include nine cases where private parties were adverse to foreign states[105] and five cases that involved suits between domestic governmental entities.[106]

The cells in Table 2 present estimates of the rate at which courts apply nationalist and transnationalist tools in different types of cases. For example, the upper left cell provides an estimate that courts adopted a nationalist approach in 2.9 percent of the private-party cases (3 out of 105 cases in the database).[107] The figures in brackets provide a 95 percent confidence interval for that estimate.[108] The figures in brackets in the upper-left cell indicate that, for the broader universe of cases from which the sample was selected, one can say with 95 percent confidence that courts applied a nationalist approach in fewer than 6.1 percent of the private-party cases.

Compare the first row in the left-hand column to the second row in the left-hand column. The best estimate is that courts apply nationalist tools in about 27.2 percent of government-party cases compared to only 2.9 percent

[102] The one exception is Federal Republic of Germany v. United States, 526 U.S. 111 (1999), where a foreign government sued the United States.

[103] Cases in which individuals file suit against government officers seeking postconviction relief after having been convicted of a criminal offense count as criminal cases.

[104] This figure includes three state criminal cases, two civil cases involving state government officers, one case in which a foreign state was a party, one case in which the United Nations was a party, and fourteen cases involving conflicts between private litigants.

[105] The total of nine foreign-state cases excludes one case involving a foreign state that is included in the "USG amicus" category and one case involving a foreign state that is included in the "government party" category. The nine cases in this category are all cases where the foreign state was adverse to a private party.

[106] These five cases include three cases where the federal government was adverse to a state government and two cases between state governments. All five cases involve disputes over title to land beneath oceans, bays, or rivers. Four of the cases involve the application of the Convention on the Territorial Sea and Contiguous Zone.

[107] The three private party cases in the database that are classified as nationalist are: Int'l Café v. Hard Rock Café, 252 F.3d 1274, 1277 (11th Cir. 2001) (in trademark dispute between private parties, court concluded that the Paris Convention is not self-executing); Denlinger v. Chinadotcom Corp., 110 Cal.App.4th 1396, 1403 (Cal. App. 2003) (in suit by U.S. citizen against foreign corporation, court deferred to executive's interpretation of Hague Service Convention in ruling on a motion to quash service); Cocron v. Cocron, 375 N.Y.S.2d 797 (1975) (in divorce action involving Austrian consul, court deferred to executive's interpretation of bilateral FCN treaty and rejected husband's immunity claim).

[108] The presentation of data regarding confidence intervals follows recommended guidelines in Lee Epstein, Andrew D. Martin & Matthew M. Schneider, *On the Effective Communication of the Results of Empirical Studies, Part I*, 59 Vand. L. Rev. 1811, 1827–38 (2006).

of private-party cases. That is about a nine-to-one ratio. One can say with high confidence that the actual ratio in the broader universe of cases is at least three-to-one because the high end of the private-party confidence interval is 6.1 percent and the low end of the government-party confidence interval is 19.0 percent.

The difference between two groups of cases in the same column is statistically significant if the confidence intervals do not overlap. Note that there is no statistically significant difference between the government civil cases and the government criminal cases (because the confidence intervals do overlap). However, still focusing on the left-hand column, courts apply nationalist tools in both criminal and civil cases more frequently than they do in private party cases, and this difference is statistically significant for both criminal and civil cases. In other words, the fact that courts apply nationalist tools more frequently in government litigation than in private litigation holds true for both civil and criminal cases.

It is also instructive to compare the first column to the second column in Table 2. Courts adopted a transnationalist approach in 18.1 percent of the private-party cases in the database (19 of 105) and they applied a nationalist approach in 2.9 percent of those cases (3 of 105). These figures suggest that, in private-party litigation, courts are about six times more likely to apply a transnationalist approach. If one compares the high end of the nationalist confidence interval (6.1) to the low end of the transnationalist confidence interval (10.7), one can say with high confidence that, in the broader universe of private party cases, courts apply a transnationalist approach at least 1.8 times as often as they apply a nationalist approach. A similar analysis indicates that, in the broader universe of government-party cases, courts apply a nationalist approach at least 1.4 times more often than they apply a transnationalist approach.

In summary, the data show that, in cases where private parties are adverse to each other, U.S. courts are more likely to apply transnationalist tools than nationalist tools. However, in cases where government actors are adverse to private parties, courts are more likely to apply nationalist tools than transnationalist tools. These findings are statistically significant at a 95 percent confidence level.[109]

[109] One might wonder how certain heavily litigated treaties influence the overall numbers. The 105 private party cases include 40 Warsaw Convention cases and 27 New York Convention cases. Those sixty-seven cases include eleven that are classified as transnationalist and zero that are classified as nationalist. Comparing these figures to the numbers in Table 2, it seems that cases involving these two treaties may push the private party category further in the transnationalist direction.

TABLE 2A. *Deference and good faith*

	Court applied Deference canon	**Court applied** Good-faith canon
Private Parties (105 cases)	2.9% [0, 6.1] (3)	10.5% [4.6, 16.4] (11)
Gov't Party (114 cases)	14.0% [7.6, 20.4] (16)	1.8% [0, 4.2] (2)
USG Amicus (21 cases)	42.9% [21.2, 64.6] (9)	28.6% [8.8, 48.4] (6)
Other (14 cases)	0	0
Total (254 cases)	11.0% [7.1, 14.9] (28)	7.5% [4.3, 10.7] (19)

Tables 2A–2C present a different perspective on the same data, focusing on the usage of particular tools in specific categories of cases. Table 2A compares the usage of the canons of good faith and deference in different types of cases. Note that courts invoked both canons fairly frequently in cases where the United States appeared as an amicus. This data can be explained, at least in part, by the fact that most of the USG amicus cases are Supreme Court cases,[110] and the Supreme Court applies the canons of good faith and deference with greater frequency than the lower courts.[111]

Leaving aside the USG amicus cases, there are three points worth noting in Table 2A. First, courts apply the deference canon more frequently in governmental litigation than they do in private litigation. Second,

Twenty-three of the forty-nine criminal cases involve the VCCR. The twenty-three VCCR cases include five nationalist cases and two transnationalist cases. Comparing these figures to the numbers in Table 2, it seems that VCCR cases may push the criminal category further in the transnationalist direction.

[110] Fifteen of twenty-one cases in the "USG amicus" category are Supreme Court cases. The database includes 38 Supreme Court cases and 216 other cases. The U.S. government appeared as an amicus in 15 of 38 Supreme Court cases (39 percent) but only 6 of 216 other cases (3 percent).

[111] The Supreme Court applied either the canon of good faith, or the canon of deference, or both, in about 34 percent of the Supreme Court cases in the database (13/38). In contrast, the other courts applied one or both canons in only 12.5 percent of the other cases in the database (27/216).

courts apply the good-faith canon more frequently in private litigation than they do in governmental litigation. Third, in government-party cases (where private parties are adverse to government actors), courts are much more likely to apply the deference canon than the good-faith canon. All three of these comparisons are statistically significant.[112] Thus, the data in Table 2A reinforce the point that courts are more likely to apply nationalist tools in government litigation than in private litigation. Conversely, courts are more likely to apply transnationalist tools in private litigation than in government litigation.

The fact that courts rarely cite the canon of deference in litigation between private parties is understandable. If the government does not appear in a case as either a party or an amicus, the court is unlikely to be aware of the government's views unless one of the parties presents those views to the court. Clearly, a court cannot defer to the executive's interpretation if it does not know the executive's interpretation.

The fact that courts rarely cite the canon of good faith in governmental litigation is potentially more problematic. In cases where the United States and other parties agree on the correct interpretation of a treaty, a court's failure to invoke the canon of good faith is inconsequential. But in cases where the U.S. executive branch has adopted a treaty interpretation that differs from the views of other parties, the lack of any reference to good faith may indicate a judicial tendency to favor the U.S. interpretation. Nationalists argue that such a preference for the U.S. interpretation is necessary to ensure that the United States "speaks with one voice" on matters involving foreign affairs.[113] However, from a transnationalist perspective, the paucity of references to the canon of good faith in treaty cases where government actors are adverse to private parties raises the disturbing prospect that courts may not be acting as neutral arbiters in such cases.

Table 2B presents data about judicial application of the doctrine of self-execution. The most revealing data point in Table 2B is the fact that courts held treaties to be non-self-executing in 11.4 percent of the government-party cases in the database. For the broader universe of cases, one can say with 95 percent confidence that the true figure is at least 5.5 percent. This

[112] In contrast, if one compares the two cells in the first row, the difference between application of the good-faith and deference canons in private party cases is not statistically significant at the 95 percent confidence level.

[113] *See, e.g.*, John Yoo, The Powers of War and Peace: The Constitution and Foreign Affairs after 9/11, at 191 (2005) ("Functionally, interpreting American treaty obligations is such a critical part of setting and implementing day-to-day foreign policy that it is difficult to imagine how it could be separated from the president's responsibility to represent the nation in foreign affairs.")

TABLE 2B. *Doctrine of self-execution*

	Court mentioned Self-execution doctrine	**Court said** Treaty was not self-executing	**Court said** Treaty was self-executing
Private Parties (105 cases)	6.7% [1.9, 11.5] (7)	1.0% [0, 2.9] (1)	4.8% [0.7, 8.9] (5)
Gov't Party (114 cases)	15.8% [9.1, 22.5] (18)	11.4% [5.5, 17.3] (13)	0.9% [0, 2.6] (1)
USG Amicus (21 cases)	9.5% [0, 22.4] (2)	0	4.8% [0, 14.1] (1)
Other (14 cases)	0	0	0
Total (254 cases)	10.6% [6.8, 14.4] (27)	5.5% [2.7, 8.3] (14)	2.8% [0.8, 4.8] (7)

is significantly higher than the rate at which courts held treaties to be non-self-executing in private-party litigation. It is also significantly higher than the rate at which courts held treaties to be self-executing in governmental litigation.

The database includes fourteen cases where a court said that a treaty was not self-executing. In twelve of those fourteen cases, an individual invoked the treaty as a constraint on the exercise of governmental powers.[114] The

[114] I.N.S. v. Stevic, 467 U.S. 407, 428 n.22 (1984) (where alien petitioner invoked art. 34 of the Refugee Convention in support of argument to avoid deportation, Court said art. 34 is not self-executing); In re Rath, 402 F.3d 1207, 1210 (Fed. Cir. 2005) (where German citizen invoked Paris Convention in support of appeal from administrative decision of the Trademark Trial and Appeal Board, court said Convention is not self-executing); Al Odah v. United States, 321 F.3d 1134, 1147 (D.C. Cir. 2003) (Randolph, J., concurring) (where aliens detained at Guantánamo Bay invoked Geneva Convention in support of habeas corpus petition, judge said Convention is not self-executing); United States v. Duarte-Acero, 208 F.3d 1282, 1284 n.8 (11th Cir. 2000) (where defendant in federal criminal trial invoked International Covenant on Civil and Political Rights (ICCPR) as a defense to criminal prosecution, court said that ICCPR is not self-executing); Bertrand v. Sava, 684 F.2d 204, 218–19 (2d Cir. 1982) (where Haitian nationals detained in immigration detention facility invoked Refugee Protocol in support of habeas corpus petition, court said Refugee Protocol is not self-executing); United States v. Williams, 617 F.2d 1063, 1089–90 (5th Cir. 1980) (where defendant in federal criminal trial invoked Convention on the High Seas in support of defense to criminal prosecution, court said Convention is not self-executing);

database includes seven cases where a court said that a treaty was self-executing.[115] In only one of those seven cases did an individual invoke the treaty as a constraint on the exercise of governmental powers.[116] The pattern is clear: courts are more likely to say that a treaty is non-self-executing in situations where an individual invokes a treaty as a constraint on the exercise of executive power.[117] Since the conclusion that a treaty is non-self-executing means that a court will not apply the treaty as a rule of decision, the data suggest that U.S. courts may be hesitant to utilize their judicial power to enforce treaty-based constraints on the conduct of executive officers. In contrast, they appear to be more willing to utilize their judicial power to enforce treaty-based constraints on the conduct of private parties.

Table 2C compares judicial application of the canon of liberal interpretation and the presumption against individually enforceable rights. Note that

Jocham v. Tuscola County, 239 F. Supp.2d 714, 730 (E.D. Mich. 2003) (where plaintiff invoked ICCPR in support of civil rights claim against county government, court said ICCPR is not self-executing); United States v. Bridgewater, 175 F. Supp. 2d 141, 147 (D.P.R. 2001) (where defendant in federal criminal invoked ICCPR in support of defense to criminal prosecution, court said ICCPR is not self-executing); Maria v. McElroy, 68 F. Supp. 2d 206, 231 (E.D.N.Y. 1999) (where alien petitioner invoked ICCPR in support of argument to avoid deportation, court said ICCPR is not self-executing); Extradition of Sandhu, 886 F. Supp. 318, 323 (S.D.N.Y. 1993) (where foreign national invoked Refugee Protocol in support of argument to avoid extradition, court said Refugee Protocol is not self-executing); United States v. Noriega, 746 F. Supp. 1506, 1532–34 (S.D. Fla. 1990) (where defendant in federal criminal trial invoked various treaties in support of defense to criminal prosecution, court held that relevant provisions of the UN Charter, OAS Charter and Hague Conventions were not self-executing); *Ex parte* Pressley, 770 So.2d 143, 148 (Ala. 2000) (where death row prisoner invoked ICCPR in support of challenge to capital sentence, court said ICCPR is not self-executing).

The two exceptions are Int'l Café v. Hard Rock Café Int'l, 252 F.3d 1274, 1277 n.5 (11th Cir. 2001) (in trademark dispute between private parties, court said Paris Convention for the Protection of Industrial Property is not self-executing); and United States v. Feld, 514 F. Supp. 283, 288 (E.D.N.Y. 1981) (where government invoked Single Convention on Narcotic Drugs (SCN) in support of federal criminal prosecution, court said treaty was not self-executing).

[115] Trans World Airlines v. Franklin Mint Corp., 466 U.S. 243 (1984); Vagenas v. Cont'l Gin Co., 988 F.2d 104 (11th Cir. 1993); United States v. Torres Del Muro, 58 F. Supp. 2d 931 (C.D. Ill. 1999); Filanto v. Chilewich Int'l Corp., 789 F. Supp. 1229 (S.D.N.Y. 1992); Pochop v. Toyota Motor Co., 111 F.R.D. 464 (S.D. Miss. 1986); Davidoff Extension v. Davidoff Int'l, 612 F. Supp. 4 (S.D. Fla. 1984); Mizugami v. Sharin West Overseas, 583 N.Y.S.2d 577 (NYAD 1992).

[116] United States v. Torres Del Muro, 58 F. Supp. 2d 931 (C.D. Ill. 1999) (where defendant in federal criminal trial invoked art. 36 of VCCR in support of pretrial motion to suppress self-incriminating statements, court said VCCR is self-executing but suppression is not an appropriate remedy for an art. 36 violation).

[117] The data in Table 2B support this claim. Compare the figures in the first two rows of the middle column.

TABLE 2C. *Rights of private parties*

	Court applied Canon of liberal interpretation	**Court applied** Presumption against individual rights
Private Parties (105 cases)	1.0% [0, 2.9] (1)	0
Gov't Party (114 cases)	2.6% [0, 5.6] (3)	9.6% [4.2, 15.0] (11)
USG Amicus (21 cases)	0	0
Other (14 cases)	0	0
Total (254 cases)	1.6% [0.1, 3.1] (4)	4.3% [1.8, 6.8] (11)

courts applied the canon of liberal interpretation most frequently in cases where the U.S. government was a party. This fact is somewhat anomalous: since liberal interpretation is a transnationalist canon, one might expect courts to apply it less frequently in cases where the U.S. government is a party. The anomaly can be explained, in part, by the fact that the canon has morphed from a rule designed to protect the rights of private parties to a rule that promotes more liberal use of extratextual sources.[118] In any

[118] *See* Van Alstine, *supra* note 74, at 1916–19. In one of the liberal interpretation cases in the database, a court invoked the canon to justify reliance on international negotiating history, although that history supported an interpretation of art. 29 of the Warsaw Convention that effectively restricted the rights of a litigant raising a third-party claim under the Convention. *See* Royal Ins. Co. v. Emery Air Freight, 834 F. Supp. 633, 636 (SDNY 1993). In another case, the Supreme Court invoked the canon of liberal interpretation to support its conclusion that a bilateral tax treaty with Canada granted Canadian authorities expansive "rights" to demand bank records from a U.S. bank, over the objection of Canadian citizens who did not want the records released. U.S. v. Stuart, 489 U.S. 353, 368 (1989). The database contains only two cases where a court invoked the liberal interpretation canon to support broader rights for a private litigant, and in one of those cases the Court really relied on a "statutory cousin" of the liberal interpretation canon. *See* I.N.S. v. Cardozo-Fonseca, 480 U.S. 421, 449 (1987) (referring to the "longstanding principle of construing any lingering ambiguities in deportation statutes in favor of the alien"); Estate of Burghardt v. Comm'r of Internal Revenue, 80 T.C. 705 (U.S. Tax Ct. 1983) (applying the liberal interpretation canon in favor of a nonresident alien who claimed entitlement to a tax credit under a bilateral tax treaty with Italy).

case, the canon is utilized so infrequently that data about its relative use in different types of cases is not statistically significant.

In contrast, the data in Table 2C tell an interesting story about judicial application of the presumption against individually enforceable rights. When courts apply this presumption, they typically use language suggesting that the presumption operates as a limitation on the power of individuals to invoke treaties in judicial proceedings. Interestingly, though, the database does not contain a single case in which a court applied this presumption to limit private enforcement of a treaty against other private parties.[119] Rather, courts apply this presumption almost exclusively in situations where an individual invokes a treaty as a constraint on the exercise of governmental powers.[120] Thus, in practice, courts utilize this presumption to limit

[119] The author conducted an electronic search in an effort to identify cases where courts have applied the presumption in the context of litigation between private parties. Although courts have applied the presumption in dozens of cases, the author found only one case where a court applied the presumption to limit private enforcement of a treaty against private parties. *See* Gross v. The German Foundation Industrial Initiative, 499 F. Supp. 2d 606, 659 (D.N.J. 2007) (invoking presumption in support of decision to dismiss claims against German companies that allegedly supported slave labor during World War II).

[120] *See* United States v. Diaz, 179 Fed. Appx. 938, 943 (6th Cir. 2006) (where defendant invoked VCCR in appeal from federal criminal conviction, court applied presumption and affirmed conviction); Cardenas v. Dretke, 405 F.3d 244, 252–54 (5th Cir. 2005) (where Mexican national on death row in Texas invoked VCCR in support of federal habeas petition, court applied presumption and denied petition); United States v. Williams, 617 F.2d 1063, 1089–90 (5th Cir. 1980) (where defendant in federal criminal case invoked Convention on the High Seas in support of appeal from criminal conviction, court applied presumption and affirmed conviction); Bell v. True, 413 F. Supp. 2d 657, 729–32 (W.D. Va. 2006) (where Jamaican national on death row in Virginia invoked VCCR in support of federal habeas petition, court applied presumption and denied petition); Diaz v. Van Norman, 351 F. Supp. 2d 679, 680–82 (E.D. Mich. 2005) (where Mexican national invoked VCCR in support of civil rights claim against state and federal officers, court applied presumption and dismissed claim); United States v. Rashed, 83 F. Supp. 2d 96, 104–05 (D.D.C. 1999) (where criminal defendant raised a treaty-based defense under the Convention on Suppression of Unlawful Acts against the Safety of Civil Aviation, court held that the treaty did "not extend any benefit or protection to defendant"); Extradition of Sandhu, 886 F. Supp. 318, 324–25 (S.D.N.Y. 1993) (where Indian nationals invoked extradition treaty in support of defense to extradition, court applied presumption and ruled in favor of India); United States v. Noriega, 746 F. Supp. 1506, 1533 (S.D. Fla. 1990) (where individual invoked various treaties in support of defense to criminal prosecution, court said "individuals lack standing to assert violations of international treaties in the absence of a protest from the offended government"); Matta-Ballesteros *ex rel.* Stolar v. Henman, 697 F. Supp. 1040, 1043 (S.D. Ill. 1988) (where Honduran national sought habeas relief on grounds that U.S. agents violated extradition treaty, court said "only sovereign nations have the authority to complain about violations of extradition treaties"); Gomez v. Commonwealth, 152 S.W.3d 238, 242 (Ky. 2004) (where defendant in state criminal trial invoked VCCR in support of motion to exclude evidence, court applied presumption and affirmed trial court's decision to deny motion); Kasi v. Commonwealth, 508 S.E.2d 57, 63–64 (Va. 1998) (where Pakistani national

the judicial application of treaty-based norms as a standard for judicial review of governmental conduct. In this respect, judicial application of the presumption against individually enforceable rights appears to serve a function similar to non-self-execution doctrine.

In summary, a straightforward doctrinal analysis would suggest that the nationalist doctrine of non-self-execution and the presumption against individually enforceable rights are generally applicable doctrines of treaty law that apply, in principle, in every case where a private litigant invokes a treaty before a domestic court. In practice, though, these doctrines are almost never utilized in litigation between private parties. Rather, courts apply these doctrines almost exclusively in cases where an individual invokes a treaty as a constraint on the exercise of governmental powers. When a court applies one or both of these doctrines in such a case, the court is effectively telling the individual: "We will not utilize our power of judicial review to evaluate your claim that the government's action is inconsistent with U.S. treaty obligations." Thus, in practice, the doctrine of non-self-execution and the presumption against individually enforceable rights function as abstention doctrines that shield government actors from judicial review of government compliance with treaty-based norms. From a nationalist perspective, this application of the doctrines is justified because it helps ensure that the government "speaks with one voice" on matters affecting foreign relations. From a transnationalist perspective, though, these doctrines are problematic because the courts are abdicating their constitutional responsibility to ensure that government actors comply with the law of the land.

V. TREATY TOOLS AND CASE OUTCOMES

Section IV examined the application of nationalist and transnationalist tools by U.S. courts in different types of cases. Overall, the analysis showed that, in litigation between private parties, U.S. courts are more likely to apply transnationalist tools than nationalist tools. However, in cases where government actors are parties, courts are more likely to apply nationalist tools than transnationalist tools. Section V analyzes the correlation between case outcomes and the application of nationalist versus transnationalist tools. Throughout Section V, a key measure of case outcomes is the percentage of cases in which the party invoking a treaty won the case. The analysis is divided into three parts: (1) overall assessment, (2) a comparison of private

on death row in Virginia invoked VCCR on appeal to Virginia Supreme Court, court applied presumption and affirmed capital conviction).

litigation with governmental litigation, and (3) a comparison of criminal versus civil cases.

A. *Overall Assessment*

The key question to be answered is this: in what percentage of cases did the party invoking a treaty win the case? To obtain an accurate measurement, it is necessary first to eliminate three types of cases. First, there are fifty-seven cases in the database where both parties invoked a treaty in support of their respective positions. Second, there are two cases where a nonparty invoked a treaty.[121] Third, the database includes twelve other cases that were effectively mixed outcomes, where neither party won or lost.[122] In these three types of cases, it is not possible to conclude that the party invoking a treaty won or

[121] Republic of Philippines v. Marcos, 665 F. Supp. 793 (N.D. Cal. 1987) (where Central Bank of Philippines sued former President Marcos, and Marcos sought discovery from the solicitor general, a nonparty, the solicitor general claimed diplomatic immunity on the basis of the Vienna Convention on Diplomatic Relations); Orlich v. Helms Bros., Inc., 560 N.Y.S.2d 10 (NY 1990) (in a product liability suit, where plaintiff sought discovery from a nonparty, the nonparty invoked the Hague Evidence Convention in support of its motion for a protective order).

[122] It is difficult to specify precise criteria for determining what counts as a win or a loss. The following cases, all of which are included in the database, exemplify the types of cases that do not count either as a win or a loss: Medellin v. Dretke, 544 U.S. 660 (2005) (writ dismissed as improvidently granted); Spector v. Norwegian Cruise Line, Ltd., 545 U.S. 119 (2005) (remanding case for further consideration by lower court); Mozes v. Mozes, 239 F.3d 1067 (9th Cir. 2001) (where father invoked Hague Convention on International Child Abduction in support of petition for return of children to Israel, Ninth Circuit remanded case for further consideration by district court); U.S. v. Chanthadara, 230 F.3d 1237 (10th Cir. 2000) (where Laotian national invoked VCCR in support of appeal from death sentence, court rejected treaty argument but reversed death sentence on other grounds); Forman v. Korean Air Lines, 84 F.3d 446 (D.C. Cir. 1996) (in Warsaw Convention case where district court awarded various categories of damages, appellate court affirmed some damage awards and reversed others); Coriolan v. I.N.S., 559 F.2d 993 (5th Cir. 1977) (where Haitian nationals invoked Refugee Protocol and sought relief from deportation, court remanded for immigration judge to reconsider in light of changed political conditions in Haiti); NORML v. Drug Enforcement Agency, 559 F.2d 735 (D.C. Cir. 1977) (where nonprofit group sought "rescheduling" of marijuana, and government invoked the Single Convention on Narcotic Drugs in support of its position, the court ruled in favor of government on some issues and against government on other issues); *In re* Greater Ministries Int'l., 282 B.R. 496 (Bkptcy Ct. M.D. Fla. 2002) (in a bankruptcy proceeding where the trustee attempted to serve two Canadian defendants, and both invoked the Hague Service Convention in support of motions to quash, the court granted one motion and denied the other); Streeter v. Bruderhof Cmtys., 852 A.2d 889 (Conn. 2003) (where plaintiff filed state law claims in state court, and defendant argued that Warsaw Convention preempted state law claims, court ruled that Convention preempted some claims, but not others); Servin v. State, 32 P.3d 1277 (Nev. 2001) (where individual who was sentenced to death invoked International Covenant on Civil and Political Rights in support of argument to vacate death sentence, court rejected treaty argument but ruled in favor of individual on other grounds).

TABLE 3. *Treaty tools and case outcomes: overall assessment*

	Party invoking treaty Won	**Party invoking treaty** Lost
Court Applied Only Transnationalist Tools (23 cases)	69.6% [50.4, 88.8] (16)	30.4% [11.2, 49.6] (7)
Court Applied Only Nationalist Tools (34 cases)	8.8% [0, 18.5] (3)	91.2% [81.5, 100] (31)
Court Applied Neither or Both (126 cases)	42.1% [33.4, 50.8] (53)	57.9% [49.2, 66.6] (73)
Total (183 cases)	39.3% [32.2, 46.4] (72)	60.7% [53.6, 67.8] (111)

lost. If one subtracts these 71 cases from the total of 254 cases in the database, that leaves 183 cases where one can reasonably conclude either that the party invoking a treaty won or that the party invoking a treaty lost.

Table 3 presents data on these 183 cases. The data show that the party invoking a treaty won 69.6 percent of the cases in which a court applied a transnationalist approach but only 8.8 percent of the cases in which a court applied a nationalist approach. Thus, for the limited sample of cases in the database, the party invoking a treaty was almost eight times more likely to win when a court adopted a transnationalist approach versus a nationalist approach. In the larger universe of cases, one can say with 95 percent confidence that the party invoking a treaty is at least 2.7 times more likely to win when a court applies a transnationalist approach versus a nationalist approach. (This figure is derived by comparing the lower bound of the confidence interval for transnationalist cases with the upper bound for nationalist cases.)

It is instructive to compare the nationalist row in Table 3 to the baseline case where courts elected to apply neither nationalist nor transnationalist tools (or applied both types of tools).[123] There is a stark difference between the baseline cases, where the party invoking a treaty won 42.1 percent of the cases, and the nationalist cases, where the party invoking a treaty won only 8.8 percent. For the limited sample of cases in the database, the party

[123] The 126 cases in the "neither/both" category in Table 3 include 117 cases where courts applied neither type of tool and 9 cases where they applied both types.

invoking a treaty was about 4.8 times more likely to win in the baseline cases compared to the nationalist cases. In the larger universe of cases, one can say with 95 percent confidence that the party invoking a treaty is at least 1.8 times more likely to win if a court applies neither nationalist nor transnationalist tools, rather than adopting a nationalist approach. In contrast, the difference between the transnationalist cases and the baseline cases is not statistically significant, as evidenced by the overlap between the 95 percent confidence intervals for these two sets of cases.

The available data do not support any inference about causality. It may (or may not) be true that a court's decision to apply nationalist tools is a causal factor contributing to the result that the party invoking the treaty loses. It may (or may not) be true that courts first decide who should win the case, and then choose to apply nationalist or transnationalist tools, as appropriate, to support conclusions that they reached for other reasons. Regardless, as discussed in Section IV above, U.S. courts have virtually unlimited discretion to decide whether to apply nationalist tools, transnationalist tools, both, or neither. Moreover, the data in Table 3 show clearly that the party invoking a treaty rarely wins a case in which the court chooses to adopt a nationalist approach.[124]

B. *Private Party Litigation versus Governmental Litigation*

Recall that Table 2 divided cases into four groups: "private party," "government party," "USG amicus," and "other."[125] If one divides the 183 cases included in Table 3 into the same four categories, and eliminates the "USG amicus" and "other" cases, one is left with a total of 162 cases, including 68 "private party" cases and 94 "government party" cases. Tables 4A and 4B compare the outcomes in these two sets of cases.

The 68 cases included in Table 4A are all cases where private parties were adverse to each other. All but one of the 94 cases included in Table 4B are

[124] The party invoking a treaty won only 3 of 34 cases in Table 3 where a court employed a nationalist approach. Interestingly, the federal government was effectively the winner in all three cases. *See* Am. Ins. Assoc. v. Garamendi, 539 U.S. 396 (2003) (court deferred to views of U.S. government, appearing as an amicus in the case, and U.S. government views supported the plaintiffs' claims against a California state official); *In re* Extradition of Tuttle, 966 F.2d 1316 (9th Cir. 1992) (court deferred to views of U.S. government where government invoked extradition treaty as a basis for its power to extradite fugitive); Matter of Extradition of Hamilton-Byrne, 831 F. Supp. 287 (S.D.N.Y. 1993) (court deferred to views of U.S. government and upheld government's power to effectuate provisional arrest of prisoners on the basis of an extradition treaty).

[125] *See supra* notes 102–06 and accompanying text (explaining these categories).

TABLE 4A. *Treaty tools and case outcomes: private party litigation*

	Party invoking treaty Won	Party invoking treaty Lost
Court Applied Only Transnationalist Tools (13 cases)	69.2% [43.1, 95.3] (9)	30.8% [4.7, 56.9] (4)
Court Applied Only Nationalist Tools (3 cases)	0	100% (3)
Court Applied Neither or Both (52 cases)	57.7% [44.1, 71.3] (30)	42.3% [28.7, 55.9] (22)
Total (68 cases)	57.4% [45.6, 69.2] (39)	42.6% [30.8, 54.4] (29)

cases where private parties were adverse to government actors.[126] Both tables exclude cases in which the United States appeared as an amicus, the adverse parties both relied on a treaty to support their litigating position,[127] or there was no clear winner because the case yielded a mixed outcome.[128]

If one compares the third row of Table 4A with the third row of Table 4B, there is a significant difference between the private party cases and the government party cases. In baseline cases (where courts adopt an approach that is neither nationalist nor transnationalist), the party invoking a treaty has a much better winning percentage in private party cases than in governmental litigation: 57.7 percent versus 24.1 percent. This difference is statistically significant. This means that party structure has some independent explanatory power in explaining case outcomes, even in cases that are neither nationalist nor transnationalist.

It is also instructive to compare categories within tables, rather than across tables. Table 4A shows that, in private-party litigation, the party invoking a treaty has a greater chance of winning if the court applies a transnationalist approach rather than a nationalist approach. Similarly, Table 4B shows that, in governmental litigation, the party invoking a treaty has a greater chance of winning if the court applies a transnationalist approach

[126] The one exception is Federal Republic of Germany v. United States, 526 U.S. 111 (1999), where a foreign government sued the United States.

[127] The database includes fifty-seven cases where adverse parties both invoked a treaty to support their respective positions.

[128] *See supra* note 122.

TABLE 4B. *Treaty tools and case outcomes: government party litigation*

	Party invoking treaty Won	**Party invoking treaty** Lost
Court Applied Only Transnationalist Tools (8 cases)	62.5% [26.6, 98.4] (5)	37.5% [1.6, 73.4] (3)
Court Applied Only Nationalist Tools (28 cases)	7.1% [0, 16.8] (2)	92.9% [83.2, 100] (26)
Court Applied Neither/Both (58 cases)	24.1% [13.0, 35.2] (14)	75.9% [64.8, 87.0] (44)
Total (94 cases)	22.3% [13.8, 30.8] (21)	77.7% [69.2, 86.2] (73)

rather than a nationalist approach. The difference between the nationalist and transnationalist rows in Table 4B is statistically significant.[129] Thus, after controlling for party structure, it remains true that there is a statistically significant correlation between case outcomes and a court's discretionary decision whether to adopt a nationalist or transnationalist approach.[130]

Recall that the ninety-four government-party cases in Table 4B do not include cases in which both parties invoked a treaty. Table 4C includes the ninety-four cases from Table 4B, plus fifteen other government-party cases where both parties invoked a treaty. Table 4C displays the government's winning percentage in those 109 cases.[131] (In contrast, the previous tables

[129] In Table 4B, the difference between the nationalist and transnationalist categories is statistically significant because the confidence intervals do not overlap. In Table 4A, it is not possible to calculate a confidence interval for the estimated winning percentage in nationalist cases because the estimate is zero.

[130] By applying more sophisticated statistical tools, one could develop a more analytically rigorous approach for comparing the explanatory power of party structure as an independent variable versus the explanatory power of the nationalist/transnationalist dichotomy as an independent variable. That type of statistical approach is beyond the scope of this chapter.

[131] The perceptive reader will note that Table 2 showed 114 government party cases, whereas Table 4C shows only 109 such cases. The difference between 114 and 109 is attributable to 5 cases that were effectively mixed outcomes, which are excluded from Table 4C. *See* United States v. Chanthadara, 230 F.3d 1237 (10th Cir. 2000); NORML v. Drug Enforcement Agency, 559 F.2d 735 (D.C. Cir. 1977); Coriolan v. I.N.S., 559 F.2d 993 (5th Cir. 1977); *In re* Kasper-Ansermet, 132 F.R.D. 622 (D.N.J. 1990); and Servin v. State, 32 P.3d 1277 (Nev. 2001).

TABLE 4C. *Treaty tools and case outcomes: governmental litigation*

	Government won	Government lost
Court Applied Only Transnationalist Tools (9 cases)	44.4% [10.0, 78.8] (4)	55.6% [21.2, 90.0] (5)
Court Applied Only Nationalist Tools (31 cases)	100% (31)	0
Court Applied Neither/Both (69 cases)	87.0% [79.0, 95.0] (60)	13.0% [5.0, 21.0] (9)
Total (109 cases)	87.2% [80.9, 93.5] (95)	12.8% [605, 19.1] (14)

measured the winning percentage for the party invoking the treaty, not the winning percentage for the government).

Remarkably, the government won all thirty-one cases in which a private party was adverse to a government actor, one or both parties invoked a treaty, and the court applied a nationalist approach. Technically, it is not possible to calculate a confidence interval if the sample yields an estimate of 100 percent. Therefore, one cannot say that there is a statistically significant difference between the 100 percent estimate for nationalist cases in Table 4C and the 87 percent estimate for the baseline cases (where courts adopt an approach that is neither nationalist nor transnationalist). Even so, the data show clearly that the government occasionally loses cases in which courts choose not to apply nationalist or transnationalist tools. However, in cases where a government actor is adverse to a private party and the court applies a nationalist approach, the government (almost) always wins.

Table 4C also shows that there is a statistically significant difference between the government party cases where courts applied transnationalist tools and the baseline cases where courts applied neither or both types of tools. One can say with high confidence that the government wins at least 79 percent of the baseline cases where courts adopt an approach that is neither nationalist nor transnationalist. In contrast, the government's winning percentage is lower in transnationalist cases, although the estimate for how much lower is quite uncertain because the sample size is very small.

TABLE 4D. *Treaty tools and case outcomes: private party invokes treaty against government*

	Party invoking treaty Won	**Party invoking treaty** Lost
Court Applied Only Transnationalist Tools (7 cases)	57.1% [17.5 , 96.7] (4)	42.9% [3.3, 82.5] (3)
Court Applied Only Nationalist Tools (26 cases)	0	100% (26)
Court Applied Neither/Both (50 cases)	14.0% [4.3, 23.7] (7)	86.0% [76.3, 95.7] (43)
Total (83 cases)	13.3% [6.0, 20.6] (11)	86.7% [79.4, 94.0] (72)

The ninety-four cases summarized in Table 4B include eighty-three cases where a private party invoked a treaty in support of its claim or defense against a government actor and eleven cases where a government actor invoked a treaty in support of its claim or defense against a private party. Table 4D presents data about the eighty-three cases where a private party invoked a treaty against the government. It shows that private parties who invoked treaties against the government had a 13.3 percent success rate. In contrast, the government won 90.9 percent of the cases in which a government actor invoked a treaty in support of its claim or defense against a private party (ten of eleven cases).[132] Typically, when the government invokes a treaty in support of its litigating position, the government argues that the treaty expands or enhances governmental power. In contrast, when a private party invokes a treaty in litigation against a government actor, the private party argues that the treaty should be applied as a constraint on the exercise of government power. Thus, the government's 91 percent success

[132] The 95 percent confidence interval for this estimate is [73.1, 100]. The ten cases that the government won are Weinberger v. Rossi, 456 U.S. 25 (1982); Dames & Moore v. Regan, 453 U.S. 654 (1981); Martin v. Warden, 993 F.2d 824 (11th Cir. 1993); Matter of Extradition of McMullen, 989 F.2d 603 (2nd Cir. 1993) (en banc); In re Extradition of Tuttle, 966 F.2d 1316 (9th Cir. 1992); Antunes v. Vance, 640 F.2d 3 (4th Cir. 1981); Matter of Extradition of Powell, 4 F. Supp. 2d 945 (S.D. Cal. 1998); Matter of Extradition of Hamilton-Byrne, 831 F. Supp. 287 (S.D.N.Y. 1993); United States v. Feld, 514 F. Supp. 283 (E.D.N.Y. 1981); United States v. One 43-Foot Sailing Vessel, 405 F. Supp. 879 (S.D. Fla. 1975). The one case the government lost was Bell v. Office of Personnel Management, 169 F.3d 1383 (Fed. Cir. 1999).

rate suggests that courts have no objection to applying treaties that augment government powers. However, the 13 percent success rate for private litigants suggests that U.S. courts may be hesitant to apply treaties to constrain the exercise of government power.

Row 3 of Table 4D shows that the party invoking a treaty won 14 percent of the cases where the court's approach was neither nationalist nor transnationalist. If one compares this figure to the comparable figure in row 3 of Table 4A, it is clear that, for the cases in the sample, a private party who invoked a treaty against another private party was four times more likely to win than a private party who invoked a treaty against a government actor (57.7 percent versus 14.0 percent).[133] For the universe of cases as a whole, if one compares the 44.1 percent lower bound of the confidence interval in Table 4A with the 23.7 percent upper bound of the confidence interval in Table 4D, one can say with 95 percent confidence that a private party who invokes a treaty against another private party is at least 1.8 times more likely to win than a private party who invokes a treaty against a government actor. In sum, a private party who invokes a treaty in litigation has a much better chance of winning if he or she is adverse to another private party rather than to a government actor.

There are several possible explanations for the fact the government has a higher winning percentage than private parties. First, the government probably has more expertise than private litigants with respect to treaties. Second, the government is more of a repeat player than most private parties, so the government has more opportunities to learn from its litigation mistakes. Third, the government has substantially more resources than most private parties, so the government can afford to hire better litigators and pay for a more intensive litigation effort than can most private parties. Whereas these explanations are entirely plausible, there is a less benign explanation that is also plausible: it may be true that the courts' tendency to adopt a nationalist approach in cases where government actors are parties tilts the playing field in favor of the government. Further study is needed to test this proposition.

C. *Civil versus Criminal Cases*

Table 4C above presented data about the government's win-loss rate in 109 cases where government actors were adverse to private parties. Those cases can be divided into two groups: forty-seven criminal cases and sixty-two

[133] This calculation controls for the effects of the nationalist-transnationalist dichotomy by excluding cases in which the court adopted either a nationalist or transnationalist approach.

TABLE 5A. *Treaty tools and case outcomes: government litigation, civil cases*

	Government won	Government lost
Court Applied Only Transnationalist Tools (6 cases)	16.7% [0, 49.3] (1)	83.3% [50.7, 100] (5)
Court Applied Only Nationalist Tools (16 cases)	100% (16)	0
Court Applied Neither/Both (40 cases)	80.0% [67.4, 92.6] (32)	20.0% [7.4, 32.6] (8)
Total (62 cases)	79.0% [68.8, 89.2] (49)	21.0% [10.8, 31.2] (13)

civil cases.[134] Tables 5A and 5B show that there are significant differences between these two groups of cases. First, comparing the bottom rows in the two tables, the government won 97.9 percent of the criminal cases versus 79.0 percent of the civil cases. This difference is statistically significant at the 95 percent confidence level. However, if one compares the third row in Tables 5A and 5B (where courts applied neither or both types of tools), the difference between civil and criminal cases is not statistically significant. The most striking difference between the civil and criminal cases involves the small number of cases where courts applied transnationalist tools. In the criminal category, the government won all three cases where courts applied transnationalist tools.[135] In the civil category, though, the government won

[134] Cases in which individuals file suit against government officers seeking post-conviction relief after having been convicted of a criminal offense count as criminal cases. The sixty-two civil cases include fifty-eight cases involving federal government actors and four cases involving state government actors. The forty-seven criminal cases include thirty cases involving federal government actors and seventeen cases involving state government actors. There do not appear to be significant differences between the state and federal cases, but the small number of cases involving state government actors makes it difficult to draw firm conclusions in this regard.

[135] United States v. Marino-Garcia, 679 F.2d 1373 (11th Cir. 1982) (applying *Charming Betsy* canon to construe statute in accordance with international law); United States v. Torres-Del Muro, 58 F. Supp. 2d 931 (C.D. Ill. 1999) (stating that VCCR is self-executing); Silva v. Superior Court, 52 Cal.App.3d 269 (1975) (applying *Charming Betsy* canon and construing federal statute to conform to treaties).

TABLE 5B. *Treaty tools and case outcomes: government litigation, criminal cases*

	Government won	Government lost
Court Applied Only Transnationalist Tools (3 cases)	100% (3)	0
Court Applied Only Nationalist Tools (15 cases)	100% (15)	0
Court Applied Neither/Both (29 cases)	96.6% [89.8, 100] (28)	3.4% [0, 10.2] (1)
Total (47 cases)	97.9% [93.7, 100] (46)	2.1% [0, 6.3] (1)

only one out of six transnationalist cases.[136] This difference between the transnationalist civil cases and the transnationalist criminal cases helps explain why there is a statistically significant difference between civil and criminal cases in the bottom row of the two tables, even though the difference in the third row is not statistically significant.

Table 5B shows that the government won forty-six out of forty-seven criminal cases in the database.[137] Within the class of criminal cases, a court's

[136] The one case the government won was Weinberger v. Rossi, 456 U.S. 25 (applying *Charming Betsy* canon and construing the word *treaty* in a federal statute to include executive agreements). The cases the government lost are: Hamdan v. Rumsfeld, 548 U.S. 557 (2006) (construing federal statute in accordance with Geneva Conventions); I.N.S. v. Cardozo-Fonseca, 480 U.S. 421 (1987) (construing federal immigration statute to conform to Refugee Protocol); Mojica v. Reno, 970 F. Supp. 130 (E.D.N.Y. 1997) (applying *Charming Betsy* canon and construing federal immigration statute to conform to U.S. obligations under ICCPR); SDI Netherlands v. Comm'r of Internal Revenue, 107 T.C. 161 (U.S. Tax Ct. 1996) (construing statute to conform to tax treaty); Estate of Burghardt v. Comm'r of Internal Revenue, 80 T.C. 705 (U.S. Tax Ct. 1983) (applying canons of good faith and liberal interpretation to construe a tax treaty).

[137] The one criminal case where a private party prevailed was Roper v. Simmons, 543 U.S. 551 (2005). In *Simmons*, the Supreme Court cited the Convention on the Rights of the Child, the International Covenant on Civil and Political Rights and the American Convention on Human Rights in support of its holding that the Eighth Amendment prohibits capital punishment for individuals who were younger than eighteen years old when they committed crimes. *Simmons* is classified as "neither nationalist nor transnationalist" because the Court did not apply any of the nationalist or transnationalist tools discussed in Part III.A *supra*. One could argue that *Simmons* is properly classified as transnationalist because the Court utilized international law as a tool of constitutional interpretation. However, the

discretionary choice to apply nationalist tools, transnationalist tools, both, or neither does not correlate with case outcomes. In criminal cases where one or both parties invoke a treaty in support of a claim or defense, the government wins virtually every case, regardless of whether courts adopt a nationalist or transnationalist approach.[138]

There are several possible explanations for the government's remarkably high winning percentage in criminal cases. The government's success may be partially attributable to a tough-on-crime attitude that is prevalent among U.S. judges, and that has nothing to do with judicial attitudes about international law. It may be true, though, that the data manifest a view shared by some judges that it is inappropriate for U.S. courts to rely on international law as a source of rights for criminal defendants because the Constitution provides all the rights to which those defendants are legitimately entitled. Finally, it may also be true that criminal defense attorneys tend to raise treaty-based defenses disproportionately in cases where defendants have a very weak case. Further study is warranted to help explain why criminal defendants consistently lose when they raise treaty-based defenses.[139]

In contrast to criminal cases, the civil cases in Table 5A do manifest a statistically significant correlation between case outcomes and a court's discretionary choice to apply nationalist or transnationalist tools. Comparing the "transnationalist" row in Table 5A to the "neither/both" row, it is clear that the government is less likely to win cases in which courts adopt a transnationalist approach; this difference is statistically significant. Table 5A does not show a 95 percent confidence interval for the nationalist cases because the government won 100 percent of those cases in the database. However, one can say with 95 percent confidence that the government wins at least 87.8 percent of the government civil cases in the larger universe

database utilized for this project did not track the use of international law in constitutional interpretation.

[138] Twenty-two of the forty-seven cases summarized in Table 5B are cases where criminal defendants raised a defense based on the VCCR. The defendants lost all twenty-two cases. In this respect, the VCCR cases do not appear to be significantly different from the other cases in which criminal defendants raised treaty-based defenses. The database includes cases where criminal defendants raised defenses based, inter alia, on the ICCPR, the Geneva Conventions, the Convention on the High Seas, bilateral extradition treaties, and bilateral FCN treaties. Criminal defendants lose consistently when they raise treaty-based defenses, regardless of which treaty is involved.

[139] Forty-six of the forty-seven criminal cases summarized in Table 5B are cases where criminal defendants raised treaty-based defenses. The one exception is United States v. Feld, 514 F. Supp. 283 (E.D.N.Y. 1981), where the government invoked the Single Convention on Narcotic Drugs to support its preferred interpretation of a federal criminal statute.

TABLE 5C. *Treaty tools and case outcomes: governmental litigation, civil cases*

	Party invoking treaty Won	**Party invoking treaty** Lost
Court Applied Only Transnationalist Tools (5 cases)	100% (5)	0
Court Applied Only Nationalist Tools (13 cases)	15.4% [0, 35.8] (2)	84.6% [64.2, 100] (11)
Court Applied Neither/Both (29 cases)	41.4% [23.2 59.6] (12)	58.6% [40.4, 76.8] (17)
Total (47 cases)	40.4% [26.2, 54.6] (19)	59.6% [45.4, 73.8] (28)

of cases.[140] This is significantly higher than the government's winning percentage in civil cases where courts apply transnationalist tools. Thus, in civil cases where government actors are parties, there is a statistically significant correlation between case outcomes and a court's discretionary choice to apply nationalist or transnationalist tools.

Table 5C presents a different perspective on the civil cases summarized in Table 5A. Table 5C measures the win-loss record for the party invoking a treaty instead of measuring the government's win-loss record. To make this calculation, it is necessary to eliminate fifteen cases where both parties invoked a treaty. Thus, Table 5C presents data on forty-seven (vice sixty-two) civil cases in which government actors were adverse to private parties.

It is instructive to compare the data in Table 5C to the corresponding data for private party litigation in Table 4A above. Overall, the party invoking a treaty won 57.4 percent of the private party cases in Table 4A, compared to 40.4 percent of the government civil cases in Table 5C. Focusing solely on the cases in the "neither/both" row, the party invoking a treaty won 57.7 percent of the private-party cases, compared to 41.4 percent of the government civil

[140] If the government won only 15 of 16 of the nationalist cases in Table 5A, that would yield a point estimate of 93.7 percent, with a 95 percent confidence interval of plus or minus 12.2. The 12.2 figure provides an overestimate of the 95 percent confidence interval for the actual sample (where the government won 16 of 16). 100 – 12.2 = 87.8. Therefore, one can say with 95 percent confidence that the government wins at least 87.8 percent of the cases in this category in the broader universe.

TABLE 5D. *Treaty tools and case outcomes: governmental litigation, criminal cases*

	Party invoking treaty Won	**Party invoking treaty** Lost
Court Applied Only Transnationalist Tools (3 cases)	0	100% (3)
Court Applied Only Nationalist Tools (15 cases)	0	100% (15)
Court Applied Neither/Both (29 cases)	6.9% [0, 16.3] (2)	93.1% [83.7, 100] (27)
Total (47 cases)	4.3% [0, 10.1] (2)	95.7% [89.9, 100] (45)

cases. Neither of these differences is statistically significant at the 95 percent confidence level.

In contrast, there are substantial differences between the criminal cases summarized in Table 5D and the private-party cases summarized in Table 4A. In total, the party invoking a treaty won 57.4 percent of the private party cases in Table 4A, compared to 4.3 percent of the criminal cases in Table 5D. This difference is statistically significant.[141] There is also a statistically significant difference between the winning percentages for the "neither/both" category in Tables 4A and 5D: 57.7 percent versus 6.9 percent. Thus, the contrast between governmental litigation and private-party litigation that was summarized in Tables 4A and 4B is attributable primarily to criminal cases rather than government civil cases.

VI. CONCLUSION

Domestic litigation involving treaties frequently implicates a complex set of interrelated issues involving U.S. compliance with international norms,

[141] As shown in Table 5D, the party invoking a treaty won only two of the criminal cases in the database. Those two cases are Roper v. Simmons, 543 U.S. 551 (2005) (defendant invoked treaty and won case); United States v. Feld, 514 F. Supp. 283 (E.D.N.Y. 1981) (government invoked treaty and won case).

domestic separation-of-powers concerns, and the rights of private parties. In cases where state or local government actors are parties, federalism issues may also be implicated. In practice, U.S. courts have manifested a schizophrenic attitude toward treaty cases. In some cases, courts adopt a nationalist approach that preserves executive control over foreign affairs and (sometimes) promotes federalism values. Transnationalists criticize this approach on the grounds that it gives insufficient weight to the value of treaty compliance and inadequate protection for private rights. In other cases, courts adopt a transnationalist approach that promotes treaty compliance and protects the rights of private parties. Nationalists criticize this approach on the grounds that it encourages judicial interference with the executive's conduct of foreign affairs and (sometimes) leads to excessive judicial intervention in matters committed to state or local regulation.

Although the split between nationalist and transnationalist camps may initially appear random or inexplicable, the preceding analysis suggests that the party structure in a given case provides at least a partial explanation for the courts' tendency to oscillate between nationalist and transnationalist poles. The data show clearly that U.S. courts are more likely to adopt a nationalist approach when they decide cases in which private parties are adverse to government actors. Conversely, they are more likely to adopt a transnationalist approach when they decide cases involving litigation between private parties (see Table 2).

The empirical analysis also demonstrates that there is a statistically significant correlation between case outcomes and a court's discretionary decision to adopt a nationalist or transnationalist approach. The party invoking a treaty has a fairly good success rate when courts apply a transnationalist approach and a very poor success rate when courts apply a nationalist approach (see Table 3). The fact that the party invoking a treaty has a higher winning percentage when courts adopt a transnationalist approach, as opposed to a nationalist approach, holds true for both private party litigation and for cases where private parties are adverse to government actors (see Tables 4A and 4B). However, if one divides the governmental litigation cases into civil and criminal cases, the observed pattern does not apply to criminal cases. In criminal cases, there is no significant correlation between case outcomes and a court's discretionary choice to apply nationalist or transnationalist tools (see Table 5B).

Finally, it bears emphasis that there is a discrepancy between the application of certain nationalist tools and the rhetoric describing those tools. In particular, courts and commentators describe the doctrine of non-self-execution and the presumption against individually enforceable rights as generally applicable doctrines of U.S. treaty law. In practice, though, these are not generally applicable doctrines: courts apply these nationalist doctrines almost exclusively in the context of litigation that pits private parties against government actors (see Tables 2B and 2C). Moreover, courts utilize these nationalist doctrines to rationalize decisions to refrain from addressing the merits of allegations that federal, state or local government officers are violating or have violated treaty-based norms. Thus, in practice, the doctrine of non-self-execution and the presumption against individually enforceable rights function as abstention doctrines that shield government actors from judicial review of compliance with treaty-based norms.

14

The Role of Domestic Courts in Treaty Enforcement

Summary and Conclusions

Michael P. Van Alstine

Professor of Law and Associate Dean for Faculty Development
University of Maryland School of Law

I. INTRODUCTION

The legal world at the dawn of the twenty-first century finds itself in a period of profound, and for some, unsettling, transition. It is of course a truism that one of the most enduring features of the law – as a system designed to regulate constantly inventive and adaptive human systems – is change. But certain transformations are of a more seismic nature. As international law continues to expand in both depth and breadth, the consequent friction over its penetration into domestic law portends one such fundamental shift in the modern legal world. Perhaps no better fact highlights the significance of this tension than the existence of more than fifty-five thousand formal treaties worldwide (and nearly triple that number of derivative acts of international law significance).

The foundation (or significant expansion) of any autonomous system of laws inevitably creates tension with the legal orders that abut or precede it. In this sense, the increasing friction between international and municipal law is not a novel phenomenon. For example, as new nation-states coalesced in nineteenth-century Europe and South America, of necessity the drafters of the new civil codes had to address the continued vitality of the preexisting statutory and customary norms. The issue was perhaps even more immediate for twentieth-century legal architects in newly reconstituted, yet broadly multicultural states such as Russia and China. But similar challenges in resolving the friction between new and old arose as well for the numerous postcolonial legal orders founded throughout the twentieth century.

The modern phenomenon of a rapidly expanding international legal system nonetheless diverges from these antecedents in certain fundamental respects. Except for extreme monists, international law does not claim a sovereignty that entirely displaces the legal autonomy of its constituent states. Framed another way, the international legal system does not purport to arrogate to itself, as a foundational principle, an autonomous power to subsume the municipal legal systems without regard to their consent.

Moreover, modern international law remains under the influence of the principles from which it emerged. In the traditional view, the constituent states of the international system were its subjects in the sense that only states had the power to conclude treaties under international law.[1] States likewise traditionally sought vindication of their international law rights vis-à-vis other states at an international level (whether in international tribunals or through interstate negotiation and settlement). As a result, as Professor Murphy explains in this work, even under modern views, international law generally does not compel a state either to submit to suit in the domestic courts of another[2] or to permit suit against itself in its own.[3]

Nonetheless, through a process that began more than two centuries ago but found broad traction in the past fifty years, it is now well established that international treaties may also create rights and obligations for private individuals and entities (i.e., that individuals may be the objects of treaties).[4] In other words, although by definition treaties come into being through the consent of states,[5] international law now clearly recognizes that individuals may be third-party beneficiaries of that consent.[6] Moreover, individuals now may be the beneficiaries of international law rights and obligations in their own right, without the traditional necessity of state intercession, or in international law terms, of states "espousing" individual claims on their behalf.[7]

The problem arises with the proper forum for the vindication of individual treaty rights. International tribunals of their nature lack a direct legal connection to a sovereign entity with the powers of an executive department. As a result, these tribunals cannot bring about immediately enforceable results on their own.

The most prominent alternative, of course, would be the judicial and administrative enforcement mechanisms of state law. At the international law level, it is now well established that states may bind themselves to

[1] *Cf.* Vienna Convention on Treaties (hereinafter, VCLT), art. 4.

[2] *See* Chapter 2, pgs. 71–85 and in particular 72–74 (citing the ancient maxim *par in parem non habet jurisdictionem*).

[3] *See id.*

[4] *See id.*, at 85–87.

[5] *See* VCLT, arts. 11–17. As the VCLT reflects, this principle has relaxed in recent years to embrace treaties concluded by international organizations. *See* VCLT, art. 5.

[6] *See* Chapter 2, pgs. 69–71.

[7] *See id.*, at 73.

provide this vehicle for treaty enforcement. As Professor Murphy explains, it has been an accepted principle of international law since at least a 1928 advisory opinion of the Permanent Court of International Justice that a treaty may express state consent to opening its own domestic courts for the vindication of individual treaty rights.[8] And a number of extant treaties expressly do just that.[9]

Moreover, an obligation of domestic treaty enforcement may arise by implication from the object and purpose of a treaty. The Vienna Convention on the Law of Treaties (VCLT) expressly permits such an inquiry.[10] There is perhaps no better illustration of this point than the recent decisions of the International Court of Justice (ICJ) on the interpretation of the Vienna Convention on Consular Relations (VCCR). In its well-known *LaGrand*[11] and *Avena*[12] decisions, the ICJ concluded that the VCCR created individual rights that the treaty parties were bound to protect in domestic law. Moreover, because it found a violation of those rights by the United States in the specific circumstances at issue, the Court ordered the United States to provide an individual remedy through appropriate domestic judicial proceedings.[13] Unfortunately, the Supreme Court of the United States subsequently refused to recognize a domestic law right to enforce these very decisions of the ICJ.[14]

The tension between international law right and domestic law enforcement demonstrates the importance of this book project. Until fully effective mechanisms develop on the international level, the enforcement of treaties

[8] *See id.*, at 85–87.

[9] *See id.*, at 87–96 (canvassing the numerous treaties that address the rights of individuals to assert rights in domestic courts). Perhaps the clearest example of this phenomenon, as Professor Murphy notes, are treaties of friendship, commerce, and navigation (so-called FCN treaties), which commonly contain provisions that ensure access to host-country courts for nationals of the treaty partners. *See id.*, at 88–89.

[10] *See* VCLT art. 31(1)("A treaty shall be interpreted in good faith in accordance with the ordinary meaning to be given to the terms of the treaty in their context and in the light of its object and purpose.").

[11] LaGrand Case (Ger. v. U.S.), 2001 I.C.J. 466, para. 77 (June 27), *reprinted in* 40 I.L.M. 1069 (2001) (concluding that the relevant provision of the VCCR "creates individual rights").

[12] Avena and Other Mexican Nationals (Mex. v. U.S.), 2004 I.C.J. 12, para. 139 (Mar. 31), *reprinted in* 43 I.L.M. 581 (2004) ("The rights guaranteed under the Vienna Convention are treaty rights which the United States has undertaken to comply with in relation to the individual concerned").

[13] *See* Avena, paras. 138–44. For a more detailed review of the ICJ's analysis in the LaGrand and Avena cases, *see* Chapter 2, pgs. 97–105; Chapter 1, pgs. 52–56.

[14] *See* Medellín v. Texas, 128 S.Ct. 1346 (2008).

will remain a matter of great significance for domestic law. As the differences between Professor Sloss's introduction and Professor Murphy's international law chapter reveal, however, a substantial amount of controversy remains about the precise modalities of the state obligation to enforce in domestic law the rights and obligations founded in international treaties.

The international legal system nonetheless is in transition. As Professor Murphy notes in his concluding remarks, subtle movements are afoot that may suggest a greater penetration of international law in the future.[15] Scholars have pushed hardest in this regard in the field of fundamental human rights, where notions such as *jus cogens* have their most potent appeal.[16] As with predictions in general, however, the future of these incipient trends remains uncertain.[17]

In the meantime, and likely for the intermediate future, scholars and practitioners of international treaty law will be required to develop ever more nuanced understandings of the domestic legal systems on which they focus. It is for this reason that the present work is so significant and timely.

The states studied in the individual country chapters (eleven in all) represent a broad cross-section of legal systems, cultures, and traditions. They have emerged under the influence of the common law tradition (e.g., the United Kingdom, Canada, the United States), the civil law tradition (e.g., Germany, the Netherlands, Poland), as well as a mixture of both (e.g., India, Israel, South Africa). Viewed in another way, even a sample from the states studied (compare India, Poland, the United States, Russia, and Australia) reveals a broad variety of politico-economic backgrounds. The states are widely dispersed from a geographic angle as well (consider Canada, South Africa, Australia, Germany, and Israel).

This diversity provides a broad perspective on the role of domestic courts in the interpretation and application of international treaties throughout the world. But it also highlights the fact that a full understanding of international treaty law requires a deep and thorough appreciation of the diverse constitutional, cultural, and legal approaches to domestic recognition and enforcement. That is precisely the purpose of the individual country chapters that make up this work. The goal of this chapter is to offer a summary of those chapters – to highlight commonalities and mark out differences. For

[15] *See* Chapter 2, at 109–15.

[16] Principal among these trends may be the 2006 Basic Principles and Guidelines on the Right to a Remedy and Reparation for Victims of Gross Violations of International Human Rights Law and Serious Violations of International Humanitarian Law, which were adopted by consensus by the U.N. General Assembly. *See* Chapter 2, at 112–13.

[17] *See id.*, at 115–18.

by reflecting on the convergences and divergences, we may better understand how international treaty rights and obligations may best be phrased and framed to ensure enforcement in actual practice.

To be sure, such generalizations of their nature carry a risk of overlooking nuance. But a careful review of the country reports reveals significant commonalities and differences, and ultimately provides insights into how domestic courts confront the challenge of applying treaty law in the disparate traditions, cultures, and legal orders that comprise the international law system.

II. CONSTITUTIONAL FRAMEWORK AND INTERNATIONAL LAW

A. *Constitutional Systems and Treaties in General*

A full appreciation of the role of domestic courts in applying treaties first requires a basic understanding of the constitutional systems in which they operate. It should hardly come as a surprise that substantial diversity exists among the states studied herein, even with respect to the very foundations of their constitutional systems. The diversity ranges from the largely unwritten British constitution distilled from ancient traditions to long-standing framework constitutions substantially amplified by judicial interpretation (the United States, Australia) and to very modern written constitutions of considerable detail (Poland, South Africa, Russia).

The age of a state's constitutional system in large measure also seems to align with the depth in which it addresses the domestic law effects of international law. In the unwritten British constitution of considerable vintage, the subject falls entirely within the traditional allocation of institutional authority, and in particular the principle of parliamentary sovereignty.[18] The constitutions from the beginning or middle of the past century are a mixed bag. Some – most commonly those of the former British Empire (e.g., Australia,[19] Canada[20]) – contain only general references to allocation of authority over external affairs. Others (e.g., Israel[21]) do not address the domestic force of international law at all. But still others from this period

[18] *See* Chapter 12, pg. 477 (observing that the British constitution "gives no special status to treaties" and that the domestic law effect of treaties falls within "the supreme power of Parliament to make law").

[19] *See* Chapter 3, pgs. 123–28.

[20] *See* Chapter 4, pgs. 169–72.

[21] *See* Chapter 7, pg. 276 ("Neither the Basic Laws nor ordinary statutes of the *Knesset* contain provisions relating to the status of international law in the domestic legal system.").

have more detailed provisions on the subject (e.g., Germany,[22] India,[23] and the Netherlands[24]).

In contrast, but perhaps not surprisingly, the modern constitutions of the past decade and a half are exemplars of textual transparency on the integration of international treaties into domestic law. Poland's Constitution of 1997, South Africa's Constitution of 1996, and the Russian Federation's Constitution of 1993 all contain detailed provisions.[25] In the case of the Russian Constitution, this fact takes the form of a broad statement on the force of international law: It declares as a fundamental proposition that "[g]enerally recognized principles and norms of international law and international treaties of the Russian Federation shall be an integral part of its legal system."[26]

The possible anomaly on this chronological alignment is the U.S. Constitution of 1789. That early written constitution expressly addresses the force of international treaties in a variety of places.[27] But the generality of its provisions has fomented interpretive controversies that have raged to this day over the force of treaties and the proper role of courts in their application in the domestic legal system.[28]

B. *The Power to Negotiate Treaties*

Substantial uniformity exists among the states studied regarding which domestic institution has authority over treaty negotiation and the drafting and conclusion of a treaty's text. All of the state chapters report that these matters are within the control of the national executive. It is worth noting in this regard that this allocation of authority obtains whether a

[22] *See* Chapter 5, pgs. 214–17.
[23] *See* Chapter 6, pgs. 243–44.
[24] *See* Chapter 8, pgs. 326–35.
[25] *See* Chapter 9, pgs. 375–78; Chapter 10, pgs. 410–12 (citing art. 15(4) of the Constitution but also noting that derivative legislation has defined detailed rules on the conclusion and force of treaties and on the obligation of domestic courts to apply treaties); Chapter 11, pgs. 450–52, 456–58.
[26] *See* Chapter 10, pgs. 410–11 (citing art. 15(4) of the 1993 Constitution). The Polish Constitution of 1997 states a similar fundamental principle: "The Republic of Poland shall respect international law binding on it." *See* Chapter 9, pg. 376 (citing art. 9 of the Constitution).
[27] *See* Chapter 13, pgs. 506–08 (citing arts. II, § 1, II, § 2, III, § 1, and VI, § 1 of the Constitution). *See also* U.S. Const. art. I, § 10.
[28] *See* Chapter 13, pgs. 509–14 and passim. *See also infra* notes 305–09, 315–18, 331–36 and accompanying text.

state follows a parliamentary system[29] or has a formally separate executive branch.[30]

The means by which this constitutional arrangement came into being differ greatly, however. For some states (especially those that emerged from the British tradition), executive control over negotiation came about by constitutional tradition;[31] for others (e.g., Poland), it arose by virtue of a special statute governing treaty law and practice;[32] and for still others (especially the states with recently reformed constitutions), the matter is resolved by express constitutional provision.[33]

The executive authority over the negotiation of treaties is, however, quite a distinct matter from the power to express final, binding consent to treaty obligations on behalf of the state.[34] As we shall see in detail in Sections III.B and C., some states permit the national executive to express that consent without any involvement of the legislature.[35] Others, by contrast, require advance legislative approval for at least some treaties before the executive may formally bind the state to international treaty obligations.[36] And this issue, in turn, is itself distinct from whether, and if so how, even an accepted international law treaty may have relevance as a matter of internal, domestic law.[37] We will turn to these latter issues in Section III.

C. *Treaties and the Allocation of Authority in Federal States*

The internal allocation of lawmaking authority in federated states raises special constitutional issues for the domestic application of treaty law. Some of the states studied (Australia, Canada, Germany, India, Russia, the

[29] *See, e.g.*, Chapter 4, pgs. 167–69; Chapter 8, pgs. 326–27; Chapter 12, pgs. 477–79; Chapter 6, pg. 243.

[30] *See, e.g.*, Chapter 13, pg. 507 (noting that art. II., § 2, of the Constitution empowers the President "to make treaties"); Russian Constitution of 1993, art. 86.

[31] *See, e.g.*, Chapter 3, pg. 120; Chapter 4, pg. 167; Chapter 7, pgs. 280–81.

[32] *See* Chapter 9, pgs. 376–78 (citing the International Treaties Act of April 14, 2000).

[33] *See* Russian Constitution of 1993, art. 86; South African Constitution of 1996, art. 231(1).

[34] Executive control over negotiation may include a power to adopt and authenticate the text of a negotiated treaty. *See* VCLT, arts. 9–10. But the signing of a treaty may also alone constitute consent to be bound to the treaty obligations. *See id.*, art. 11 ("The consent of a State to be bound by a treaty may be expressed by signature"); *id.*, art 12 (describing the circumstances in which signature may constitute consent).

[35] *See infra* Section III.B.1.

[36] *See infra* Section III.C.1.

[37] *See infra* Sections III.B.2., III.C.1.

United States) are fundamentally founded on a federal system in which domestic lawmaking competence is distributed between the national government, on the one hand, and municipal subunits (provinces, states, *Länder*) on the other. Nonetheless, in all of these states, the authority over the expression of consent to international treaties is delegated to the national government,[38] subject to constitutional procedures and requirements for treaty making in general (about which more in Section III).[39] Indeed, the U.S. Constitution expressly forbids its individual states from concluding international treaties.[40]

The same is true, with the noteworthy exception of Canada,[41] regarding the force of treaties in municipal law. We will have much more to say below about the various approaches to the domestic law effect of treaties in general.[42] What is important for immediate purposes is that the chapters for the federalist states – again, with the exception of Canada – report that their internal allocations of power do not impose any special limitations on the effect or implementation of treaties by the national government.

The point seems clearest in the constitutions of Russia and India. Treaties in the Russian Federation have the direct force of domestic law by express constitutional provision.[43] The Indian Constitution of 1949 likewise delegates to the national Parliament exclusive power "to make any law for the whole of any part of the territory of India for implementing any treaty, agreement or convention with any other country or countries."[44]

Ambiguous language in the German Basic Law (*Grundgesetz*) makes the matter a bit more complicated in light of express grants of lawmaking competences to the *Länder*.[45] Nonetheless, the Germany report concludes

[38] *See* Chapter 3, pgs. 121–26 (observing that section 51(xxix) of the Constitution delegates the foreign affairs power to the national government); Chapter 4, pgs. 166–67 (stating that the national executive has the power to conclude treaties under international law); Chapter 5, pgs. 216–17 (citing art. 32 of the *Grundgesetz*); Chapter 6, pg. 243; Chapter 10, pgs. 411–12 and Russian Constitution of 1993, art. 71); Chapter 13, pgs. 507–08.

[39] *See infra* Section III.A., B.

[40] *See* U.S. Const., art. I, § 10.

[41] *See infra* notes 52–54 and accompanying text.

[42] *See infra* Section III.

[43] *See* Chapter 10, pgs. 410–11 (citing art. 15(4) of the Russian Constitution of 1993). *See also* Federal Law of the Russian Federation on International Treaties of the Russian Federation, art. 3(1). For more on this point, see *infra* notes 116–122 and accompanying text.

[44] Chapter 6, pgs. 243–44 (quoting art. 253 of the Indian Constitution of 1949). Indeed, this power to implement treaties even extends to decisions "made at any international conference, association or other body." *Id.*

[45] *See infra* notes 111–113 and accompanying text.

that the dominant view among courts and commentators is that "the federal legislature is empowered to regulate matters that would domestically be regulated exclusively by *Länder* legislatures."[46]

The chapters for Australia and the United States report more nuanced approaches. Nonetheless, both conclude that their respective constitutional systems ultimately do not impose any generalized federalism constraint on the conclusion and implementation of treaties. The Australian written constitution of 1900 delegates the external-affairs power to the Commonwealth as a whole.[47] The Australia chapter reports that the High Court of Australia has interpreted this delegation as empowering the Commonwealth to implement international treaty obligations in domestic law, provided the implementing legislation is "appropriate and adapted" to the terms of the treaty.[48]

The U.S. Constitution of 1789 likewise grants to the national government the exclusive power to conclude treaties.[49] But it also expressly accords treaties the force of supreme federal law that preempts the law of the individual states.[50] Its chapter thus concludes that, though some controversy remains among scholars, the otherwise-applicable substantive limits on national lawmaking apply neither to the direct effect of treaties nor to the power of the national government otherwise to implement international treaty obligations.[51]

Federalism plays a more significant role in Canada. That chapter reports that, under the prevailing interpretation of Sections 91 and 92 of the Constitution Act of 1867, the same division of domestic legislative competence for standard domestic legislation applies for the implementation of treaty obligations.[52] As a result, "if the subject matter of a treaty falls within federal

[46] *See* Chapter 5, pg. 217. With regard to those international agreements that the national executive may conclude without advance legislative approval (see *infra* Section III.C.2), the implementation authority follows the otherwise-applicable allocation of competences between the national government and the *Länder*. *See id.*, at 217–19.

[47] *See* Chapter 3, pgs. 121–26 (citing sec. 51(xxix) of the Constitution).

[48] *See id.*, at 123–24.

[49] *See* Chapter 13, pgs. 507–08.

[50] *Id.* (noting that treaties under art. VI, cl. 2, of the U.S. Constitution, treaties concluded under the authority of the national government "shall be the supreme Law of the Land"). *See also id.* (also observing that the same provision expressly requires state courts to enforce treaties, "any Thing in the Constitution or Laws of any State to the Contrary notwithstanding").

[51] *See id.*, at 508 (citing Missouri v. Holland, 252 U.S. 416 (1920)). As the U.S. Chapter notes, some federalism limits founded in specific constitutional provisions (e.g., those relating to the sovereignty of the individual states) nonetheless remain. *See id.*

[52] *See* Chapter 4, pgs. 171–72.

legislative jurisdiction, [the national] Parliament may implement it alone. If, however, the treaty falls partly or entirely within provincial legislative jurisdiction, it must be implemented by each provincial legislature."[53] In some cases, the Canada chapter observes, this has limited Canada's ability to participate in treaty projects.[54]

III. THE STATUS OF TREATIES IN DOMESTIC LAW

A. *Introduction*

Section II examined the basic constitutional arrangements concerning treaties and their negotiation at an international level. Although important in its own sphere, the primary value of this exercise for present purposes is to set the context for the more challenging, and practically significant, issue of the status and force of international treaties in or as domestic law.

An analysis of these issues will benefit from a reminder of the subject of this book project. Recall that our task here is to analyze the role of domestic courts in treaty enforcement. Stated differently, the question is when and under what circumstances courts may recognize treaty-based law as within their authority, in the famous 1803 words of Chief Justice Marshall of the Supreme Court of the United States, "to say what the law is."[55]

It is traditional at this point to draw a sharp distinction between the so-called monist and dualist understandings of the interaction between international and municipal law. In crude terms, the monist view holds that international and domestic law are part of a single system, with the result that municipal institutions may apply binding norms of international law (including treaties) just like any other form of domestic law. A pure dualist approach, in contrast, views international and domestic law as separate systems. The consequence is that treaties do not operate of themselves in domestic law; rather, municipal lawmaking bodies must first adapt or adopt domestic law (subject as well to requirements and procedures prescribed by domestic law) to conform to the international treaty obligations.

Unfortunately, blunt generalizations over monism and dualism carry a risk of oversimplification, not least because the terms can mean different

[53] *Id.*

[54] *See id.*, at 204 (observing that if the subject of a treaty "falls within provincial jurisdiction, the federal government will normally hold off on ratifying or acceding to the treaty until it has persuaded all the provinces to ensure implementation of the right in their jurisdictions").

[55] Marbury v. Madison, 5 U.S. (1 Cranch) 137, 177-78 (1803)("It is emphatically the province and duty of the judicial department to say what the law is.").

things to different observers.[56] This is particularly true on the issue – which is foundational for the subject of this work – of the role of domestic lawmaking institutions in the approval of international treaties. Viewed from one perspective, all of the states studied in this work share the premise that the advance or subsequent approval of the legislature is required, in at least some cases, as a condition to the enforcement of international treaty obligations in or as domestic law. The chapters for Australia,[57] Canada,[58] Germany,[59] India,[60] Israel,[61] the Netherlands,[62] Poland,[63] Russia,[64] South Africa,[65] United Kingdom,[66] and the United States[67] all report that legislative involvement in some form is necessary for either the direct application or, as the case may be, the domestic implementation of some or all international treaties. This applies either for all treaties that touch on domestic law or those that otherwise address certain significant subject matters.

To view the states only from this angle, however, both overdraws the similarities among them and understates the potential influence of treaties in actual practice. To focus on the force of treaties in domestic law, for example, courts in all of the states studied, as we shall see in much more detail,[68] have recognized a range of domestic law effects even for treaties that lack the required formal legislative approval. Included among these are interpretive presumptions for domestic law to favor treaty obligations; the power of executives to enforce at least some treaties without legislative sanction; the *quasi-incorporation* or implied incorporation of treaties; limits on the

[56] At a more theoretical – though related – level, the monism versus dualism debate revolves around the question of whether international and domestic law comprise a single, unified legal order. For an introduction to the classical debates on this score, *see* J.G. Starke, *Monism and Dualism in the Theory of International Law*, 17 Brit. Y.B. Int'l L. 66 (1936) (reviewing the debate); Hans Kelsen, The Pure Theory of Law 328–47 (Max Knight trans., 1967)(advocating for a monist approach).

[57] *See* Chapter 3, pgs. 121–23.

[58] *See* Chapter 4, pgs. 169–72.

[59] *See* Chapter 5, pgs. 214–16.

[60] *See* Chapter 6, pgs. 244–45.

[61] *See* Chapter 7, pgs. 276–80.

[62] *See* Chapter 8, pgs. 326–27.

[63] *See* Chapter 9, pgs. 376–78.

[64] *See* Federal Law of the Russian Federation on International Treaties of the Russian Federation, art. 15. As noted subsequently, the author of the Russia Chapter expresses a contrary view on the requirement of legislative approval for treaties. *See infra* notes 121–122 and accompanying text.

[65] *See* Chapter 11, pgs. 451–53.

[66] *See* Chapter 12, pgs. 477–79.

[67] *See* Chapter 13, pgs. 506–09.

[68] *See infra*, especially Sections IV.A and IV.C.2.

discretion of administrative bodies derived from treaties; and even a recognition of individual treaty rights not otherwise established in domestic law.

Moreover, a generalization about the required role of domestic legislatures in approving treaties overlooks important differences of substance and procedure. Indeed, a more nuanced analysis reveals that the states studied in this work in fact tend to distill into two broad groups with reference to the substance of the dualism-monism dichotomy. The states in one group, following the British tradition, retain a clearer dualist separation between international and domestic law (see Section III.B). The states in another group, though they follow disparate and hybrid procedures, share the basic theme that international treaties may take direct effect in domestic law, most commonly on advance legislative approval (see Section III.C).

Although we may profitably draw a formal distinction between the two groups of states, our analysis will benefit from pulling apart two separate issues that they both address. First, we will see that they differ on the requirements and procedures for expressing consent to treaties under international law in the first instance. Second, they also diverge in noteworthy ways on the means by which international treaties (or the substance of treaty obligations) become cognizable in or as domestic law.

A final word of caution is nonetheless in order before we proceed. Although there is a value in recognizing a formal distinction between what are referred to here as traditional dualist and hybrid monist states, we will see in Section IV that substantial functional similarities exist in how their respective courts interpret and apply treaty-based law. These similarities are equally valuable in appreciating the role of domestic courts in treaty enforcement.

B. *Traditional Dualist States*

1. The Respective Roles of the Executive and the Legislature. A fundamental principle that defines a dualist system is a clear separation of international treaty making from domestic treaty implementation. Five of the states studied in this work (Australia, Canada, India, Israel, and the United Kingdom) emerged from a British constitutional tradition that most clearly conforms to this separation.[69] For ease of description, we may thus properly refer to these countries as following a "traditional dualist" approach to treaties.

[69] *See* Chapter 3, pg. 128 (observing that constitutional tradition "has seen Australia adopt essentially a dualist approach toward international law"); Chapter 4, pg. 168 (confirming with regard to treaties "Canada's so-called dualist approach to international law"); Chapter 6, pg. 244 (stating that the basic view on treaties in India "is based on the dualist theory");

Under this system, treaty making – the power to express binding consent to treaty obligations under international law – falls exclusively within the so-called royal prerogative. The Canada chapter concisely captures this principle:

> In British constitutional tradition, certain functions are recognized as belonging entirely to the Crown, i.e., the executive branch of government. Such royal prerogatives may be exercised without the need for parliamentary approval or even parliamentary involvement. Among these prerogatives is the conduct of foreign affairs, including the negotiation and conclusion of treaties.[70]

The chapters for each of the other four fundamentally dualist states contain similar declarations.[71] In these states, in other words, the executive has the constitutional power to bind the state to treaty commitments under international law without the advance (or even subsequent) consent of the legislature.

The lawmaking power of the legislature, on the other hand, is equally clear. The "supreme power of Parliament to make law,"[72] as the U.K. chapter observes, carries with it the corollary, as declared by the Canada chapter, that "domestic laws cannot be made by executive action alone."[73]

This principle applies as well to treaties. Even if the executive binds the state to treaty obligations under international law, those obligations are not cognizable in the domestic legal system unless the legislature implements them through formal lawmaking procedures. It is thus entirely possible for a treaty to bind a traditional dualist state under international law through the action of the executive but have no formal effect in domestic law without the action of the legislature.[74]

The Supreme Court of Israel has provided among the clearest descriptions of this approach for treaties (i.e., conventional international law) in its so-called *VAT* opinion:

Chapter 7, pgs. 276–80 (confirming that Israel follows the British tradition, which separates executive treaty making from legislative treaty implementation); Chapter 12, pg. 476 (observing that "[w]hen it comes to treaties, the United Kingdom is very much a dualist state").

[70] Chapter 4, pg. 167.

[71] *See* Chapter 3, pgs. 120–21; Chapter 6, pg. 243; Chapter 7, pgs. 276–80; Chapter 12, pgs. 477–79.

[72] Chapter 12, pg. 477.

[73] Chapter 4, pg. 167.

[74] As the Israel Chapter thus observes, "[m]any treaties that have been ratified by the government and are consequently binding on Israel in international law have not been incorporated by domestic legislation." Chapter 7, pg. 283.

> [T]he rules of conventional international law are not automatically incorporated, and they do not become part of the law that applies in Israel until they have been adopted or incorporated by the process of legislation, and thereby become part of the law which applies in Israel on the strength of the provisions of statutes or subsidiary legislation that derives its validity from the enabling legislation *praeter legem.*[75]

This dualist separation of international treaty making from domestic treaty implementation has important implications for the function and powers of domestic courts. However implemented (see Section III.A.2), in a strict sense it is the legislation, not the treaty itself, that becomes domestic law. The U.K. chapter states this point quite starkly: "[A]lthough a treaty that has entered into force for the United Kingdom is binding on it in international law, *the treaty itself* is not part of domestic law, even if some of its provisions have been made part of that law."[76]

As we shall see, this approach has had derivative effects on the treaty jurisprudence of the courts. Most prominently, the courts in these states have not engaged in noteworthy discussions over whether the particular terms of a treaty – as opposed to the implementing legislation – are of a nature that would permit direct enforcement in domestic law.[77]

Nonetheless, we must be careful not to exalt form too greatly over function. Left alone, the statement that only the implementing legislation, not the treaty, becomes domestic law in the traditional dualist states paints a quite misleading picture of the potential influence of treaties in actual practice. After disclaiming direct effect without legislation, for example, the Canada chapter emphasizes that "treaties do influence Canadian law indirectly, even in cases where they are not implemented."[78] Indeed, we shall see that some courts in this tradition have readily looked to the international law genesis of treaty implementation statutes.[79] Moreover, they have recognized a whole variety of effects even for treaties that have not been implemented in domestic law in a formal sense.[80]

2. The Means of Implementing Treaty Obligations in Domestic Law. Because treaties fall within the standard allocation of lawmaking authority

[75] *See* Chapter 7, pg. 282 (quoting Abu Ita v. IDF Commander, 37 PD (2) 197). *See also id.* pgs. 281–82 (examining this decision in greater detail); Chapter 6, pg. 244 ("[I]f a treaty covers new ground or is inconsistent with existing law, new legislation is necessary to give effect to the terms of the treaty.").

[76] Chapter 12, pgs. 478–79 (emphasis in original).

[77] *See infra* Section IV.C.1.

[78] *See* Chapter 4, pgs. 172–74.

[79] *See infra* Section IV.A.1.

[80] *See infra* Section IV.C.3.

to the legislature, the adoption of domestic law to conform to treaty obligations most commonly is accomplished through standard legislation by both houses of the parliament (or legislature or Knesset).[81] The chapters for the traditional dualist states speak in this sense of the "implementation,"[82] or more commonly "incorporation,"[83] of treaties by subsequent legislative action. Nonetheless, some of the country reports for the traditional, dualist states also describe a high state of refinement in the forms of parliamentary implementation. The most straightforward means is through appending the entire treaty text to a legislative act (so-called scheduling).[84] Alternatively, the legislature may craft a more detailed statute to amend existing legislation or create a new statute to conform to the substance of the treaty obligations.[85]

Finally, a legislative act may delegate power to the executive to implement – via secondary legislation or administrative regulations – either a specific treaty or a whole category of treaties in domestic law.[86] But again, the prohibition on executive lawmaking means that any delegated power to implement treaty obligations exists only within the confines of the legislative approval. As the Canada chapter observes with specific reference to treaty implementation, "[d]elegated legislative power is created by statute and is invalid if it exceeds its authority."[87]

C. *Hybrid Monist States*

1. The Role of the Legislature: International and Domestic Law. A second group of states studied in this work differ markedly among themselves on the domestic law procedures for and status of international treaties. They

[81] *See, e.g.*, Chapter 3, pg. 138; Chapter 12, pgs. 479–81. *Cf.* Chapter 4, pgs. 169–72 (noting that the Constitution sets forth no special procedure for parliamentary approval of treaties); Chapter 6, pgs. 244–45 (merely noting that parliament must implement treaties in domestic law); Chapter 7, pgs. 283–85 (same).

[82] *See* Chapter 4, pgs. 169–71.

[83] *See* Chapter 3, pg. 123 (but also elsewhere using the term "implementation"); Chapter 6, pgs. 244–45; Chapter 7, pgs. 283–85; Chapter 12, pg. 479.

[84] *See, e.g.*, Chapter 3, pg. 138 (referring to "full implementation"); Chapter 4, pg. 169; Chapter 7, pgs. 283–84; Chapter 12, pg. 479. One of the hybrid states analyzed here, South Africa, shares many of the attributes of the dualist tradition and in fact reports a similar practice. *See* Chapter 11, pg. 455 (describing a similar procedure for the implementation of some treaties).

[85] *See, e.g.*, Chapter 3, pg. 138; Chapter 4, pgs. 169–70; Chapter 7, pg. 238; Chapter 12, pgs. 479–80.

[86] *See, e.g.*, Chapter 4, pgs. 169–170; Chapter 7, pgs. 284–85; Chapter 12, pgs. 480–81. Some hybrid monist states report the same practice. *See* Chapter 8, pgs. 336–37; Chapter 11, pg. 455.

[87] *See* Chapter 4, pg. 167. note 6.

nonetheless share an attribute that distinguishes them, as a group, from the traditional dualist states: each requires advance legislative approval for some or all treaties as a condition to ratification or accession under international law; in return, each permits treaties approved in that way to function as directly applicable domestic law.[88] In this sense, therefore, these states share the monist perspective that treaties may simultaneously function as law in both the international and the domestic legal systems (or, more theoretically, in a unified international legal system). The requirements for achieving this end diverge significantly, however, and not all treaties may be enforceable in domestic law in any event. Because of the shared principle, but different procedures for consent to and implementation of treaties, we shall refer to this group here as *hybrid monist* (or simply hybrid) states.

A. GERMANY, THE NETHERLANDS, POLAND, AND THE UNITED STATES. As one might expect from the preceding summary, valid generalizations among the hybrid monist states are difficult. Nonetheless, the basic principles of law are clearest in four states in this group (Germany, the Netherlands, Poland, and the United States). Each of these states follows the general approach that the national executive has authority over the negotiation of treaties.[89] But what is also common among the first four hybrid monist states is a standard procedure for advance legislative approval of some or all treaties as a condition to ratification or accession under international law in the first instance.[90] In return, this advance endorsement also permits international treaties to function, in the monist fashion, as directly applicable domestic law without further legislative action.[91]

The U.S. Constitution of 1789, for example, provides for a special procedure for advance legislative consent to treaties. Under this procedure, treaties first made by the president require the approval of one house of the legislature (the Senate), a body structured to protect the interests of the individual states in its federal system.[92] But the required threshold is

[88] Often, formal publication is also required. *See, e.g.*, Chapter 8, pg. 340 (observing that the Constitution "contains a requirement of publication of treaties as a precondition for direct application"); Chapter 10, pgs. 433–37.

[89] *See supra* Section II.B.

[90] *See* Chapter 5, pgs. 214–15; Chapter 8, pgs. 330–31; Chapter 9, pgs. 377–80; Chapter 13, pgs. 506–08.

[91] As we shall see here, the legal systems in Russia and South Africa also permit advance legislative approval for some treaties. *See infra* Section III.C.1(b). The particularities for this option in these states nonetheless defy easy generalization and thus warrant separate treatment.

[92] The U.S. Supreme Court has separately recognized that the president can conclude certain international agreements without following the Senate consent procedure in art. II of the Constitution. For more on this, *see infra* notes 141–142 and accompanying text.

two-thirds of that body as a condition to subsequent ratification by the president under international law.[93] The consequence is that treaties obtain the force of "supreme Law of the Land"[94] and thus may become immediately enforceable in domestic law in accordance with their nature and substance (about which much more in Section III.B.2[95]). It is nonetheless appropriate to describe the United States approach as hybrid, for it is not uncommon for Congress also to adopt subsequent implementing legislation when a treaty by its substance does not become immediately enforceable domestic law. It also seems reasonably clear that advance approval of treaty ratification could come through standard legislation by both houses of Congress (so-called congressional-executive agreements), although the Supreme Court as yet has not formally sanctioned the practice.[96]

The Netherlands chapter likewise reports that advance legislative approval is required before treaties may bind the state under international law.[97] In general, the voting threshold for such approval is the same as for statutes – a simple majority of both houses of the legislature.[98] With such approval, as the Netherlands chapter explains, treaties may take direct effect in domestic law: "All treaties that are binding on the Netherlands as a matter of international law are automatically incorporated and thus have the force of law in the domestic legal order."[99] As a demonstration of its general receptivity to international law, Dutch law also provides for a special voting procedure and threshold for treaties that conflict or may conflict with the Constitution itself.[100] As we shall see in more detail here, a treaty approved through this procedure may even prevail over the Constitution.[101]

Special care is required in the description of the system followed by Poland. The Polish Constitution of 1997 states as a fundamental principle that treaties are "part of the domestic legal order and shall be applied directly, unless [their] application depends on the enactment of a statute."[102] But

[93] *See* U.S. Const. art. II. § 2. *Cf.* Chapter 13, pg. 507 (noting that treaties made by the President require the "Advice and Consent of the Senate").

[94] *See id.*, at 507–08 (citing art. VI, cl. 2, of the U.S. Constitution).

[95] *See infra* Section IV.B.2.

[96] *See* Chapter 13, pgs. 506–07.

[97] *See* Chapter 8, pg. 328 (citing art. 91 of the Constitution to the effect that "[t]he Kingdom shall not be bound by treaties . . . without the prior approval of the Parliament").

[98] *See id.*, at 328 ("Treaties are approved by a simple majority vote in both Chambers of Parliament.")

[99] *See* Chapter 8, pg. 331.

[100] *See id.*, at 329.

[101] *See id.* (citing art. 91(3) of the Constitution). *See also infra* notes 156–157 and accompanying text.

[102] *See* Chapter 9, pg. 378 (citing article 91(1) of the Constitution).

as the Poland chapter explains, the Constitution also draws a distinction between treaties that require advance legislative approval before a treaty may bind the state under international law (i.e., full ratification) and those that do not (i.e., small ratification).[103] Full ratification, through standard legislative procedures,[104] is required for certain expressly identified categories of important treaties, including those that involve military alliances, constitutionally protected individual rights, significant financial obligations for the state, or "matters regulated by statute or those in respect of which the Constitution requires the form of statute."[105] Treaties not in these described groups, in contrast, may be ratified merely through the cooperation of the premier and the popularly elected president (subject to the informal oversight of the legislature).[106] As a result, legislative approval is not required for these small ratification treaties to bind the state under international law.

With advance legislative approval, treaties may operate as directly applicable domestic law.[107] As the Poland chapter explains, the Constitution "clearly establishes the principle of direct applicability of all ratified treaties."[108] In contrast, treaties subject only to small ratification have only limited force in domestic law. As the Poland chapter concludes, the breadth of the full ratification list – including the reference to those subjects that would otherwise require "the form of a statute" – means that, as a practical matter, legislative approval is required for all treaties "that are meant to be directly applicable in domestic courts."[109]

German law draws a similar distinction. As its chapter describes in detail, Article 59(2) of the *Grundgesetz* requires advance legislative approval, according to standard procedures,[110] for those treaties "that regulate the political relations of the Federation or relate to subjects of federal legislation."[111] The former category addresses those treaties that "directly affect the existence of the state, its territorial integrity, its independence and its position or prominent weight within the community of states."[112] But the

[103] *See id.*, at 376–78.
[104] *See id.*, at 376.
[105] *See id.*, at 376–77 (citing art. 89(1) of the Constitution).
[106] *See id.*, at 379–80.
[107] *Id.*
[108] *Id.*, at 378 (referring to art. 91, sec. 1 of the Constitution).
[109] *Id.*, at 377.
[110] *See* Chapter 5, pg. 216 (referring to the approval of the legislature "in the form of a federal law").
[111] *See id.*, pgs. 216–17.
[112] *See id.*, pg. 217 (citing, *inter alia*, BVerfGE 1, 372 at 382; 90, 286 at 359).

latter category – those that "relate to subjects of federal legislation" – also captures all other treaties that are designed to function as domestic law. As the Germany chapter thus observes, "Whenever a single provision of a treaty touches upon a matter that would require legislation when regulated domestically, the treaty itself is subject to legislative consent prior to ratification" by the national executive under international law.[113] In accordance with the monist premise, treaties so approved in advance in turn operate as directly applicable domestic law (although the precise descriptive model remains subject to some debate).[114]

B. RUSSIA AND SOUTH AFRICA. The approaches of Russia and South Africa defy easy categorization, and it is for that reason only that they are grouped together here. What they have in common is only that both permit treaties to function in some sense as directly applicable domestic law. Although they share some attributes that parallel the other hybrid monist states analyzed here, each follows a distinctive set of rules and procedures for the adoption and implementation of treaties. To facilitate description, we will discuss them according to the ease by which a treaty may function as directly applicable domestic law.

The law of the Russian Federation would appear to embrace the direct effect of all treaties. In conformance with the common practice among all states studied here, the president of the Russian Federation has authority over the negotiation and signature of international treaties.[115] Article 15(4) of the Russian Constitution of 1993 then provides that all "international treaties of the Russian Federation shall be an integral part of its legal system."[116] A special law likewise directs all courts of the Russian Federation to give effect to "international treaties of the Russian Federation."[117]

As the Russia chapter explains, however, the actual force of Article 15(4) of the Constitution requires more careful analysis. First, for purposes of international law, the special Federal Law of the Russian Federation on International Treaties of the Russian Federation expressly requires the advance approval of the national assembly for the ratification of certain categories

[113] *Id.* at 217. The Germany chapter also notes that this advance approval creates a "self-binding" by the legislature to enact any required implementing legislation. *See id.*, at 218.

[114] *See* Chapter 5, pgs. 215–16.

[115] *See* Federal Law of the Russian Federation on International Treaties of the Russian Federation, art. 12(1).

[116] *See* Chapter 10, pgs. 410–11.

[117] *See id.*, at 412 (citing the Federal Constitutional Law on the Judicial System of the Russian Federation (1996)).

of important interstate treaties, including those that would require new domestic legislation.[118]

For purposes of domestic law, treaties with such advance legislative approval then enjoy the force prescribed by Article 15(4) of the Constitution and prevail over otherwise-applicable statutory law.[119] In contrast, the Supreme Court of Russia has held that so-called intergovernmental and interdepartmental treaties not approved by the legislature do not have this preemptive force in domestic law.[120] Notwithstanding the weight of authority on this point,[121] the author of the Russia chapter in this work takes the view that all treaties accepted by Russia under international law, including those lacking advance legislative consent, operate as directly applicable and preemptive domestic law (provided that they are properly published in the official gazette).[122]

The "hybrid" label is particularly apt for South Africa. Its Constitution of 1996 generally[123] requires – like the hybrid states analyzed in the immediately preceding section – the advance approval of both houses of Parliament before the national executive is able to bind the state to international treaty obligations in the first place.[124] With this advance approval, some treaty provisions may function directly as domestic law in a monist fashion. In specific, Article 231(4) of the Constitution declares that "a self-executing provision . . . is law in the Republic."[125] Generally, however, the South Africa chapter explains that – in conformity with the dualist tradition – "[a]n international agreement or treaty does not become part of domestic law until it is enacted into law by national legislation."[126] Also in parallel with the traditional dualist states, this legislative act of implementation may take the form of simply appending the treaty to a statute (i.e., scheduling), a more carefully structured statute, or a delegation of implementing authority to the national executive.[127]

[118] *See* Federal Law of the Russian Federation on International Treaties of the Russian Federation, art. 15.
[119] *See* Chapter 10, pgs. 420–21.
[120] For more on this point, *see infra* notes 176–78 and accompanying text.
[121] *See* Chapter 10, pgs. 428–31.
[122] *See id.*, at 428.
[123] With regard to treaties of a "technical, administrative or executive nature," *see infra* Section III.C.2.
[124] *See* Chapter 11, pgs. 450–51.
[125] *Id.*, at 452 (citing art. 231(4) of the Constitution). For more on the "self-execution" debate, *see infra* Section IV.B.2.
[126] *Id.*, at 455 (citing art. 231(4) of the Constitution).
[127] *Id.*

2. The Independent Authority of Executives to Conclude Some International Agreements: International and Domestic Law. Although the hybrid states generally require some form of legislative approval for treaties, their chapters also commonly report a category of exceptions in which the executive may act alone. As we turn to these exceptions, however, we must carefully keep in mind the distinction between international law consent and domestic law effect.

Let us turn first to the authority of executives to bind the state under international law. By way of background, recall that in the traditional dualist states examined in Section III.B, the basic allocation of authority permits the executive to bind the state to all treaties under international law.[128] Although the structure of authority is different, the chapters for the hybrid states likewise report that their executives (or executive departments) have an independent power to express binding consent under international law for at least some categories of treaties. We see this most clearly with Germany, Poland, and South Africa. The constitutions of all three expressly identify the categories of treaties that require advance legislative approval.[129] By negative inference in both Poland[130] and Germany,[131] the executive can – with the formal cooperation of the head of state or other constitutional institution – conclude treaties that are binding under international law[132] on other subjects without prior legislative consent.

The Constitution of South Africa expressly provides that the executive may conclude "international agreement[s] of a technical, administrative or executive nature" without advance legislative approval.[133] A similar result obtains in the Netherlands by special statute;[134] in the United States by constitutional tradition (so-called sole executive agreements);[135] and in the Russian Federation both by special statute and general approach.[136]

[128] *See supra* Section III.B.1.

[129] *See supra* notes 102–113 and accompanying text.

[130] *See* Chapter 9, pgs. 376–78. *See also id.*, at 376 (noting that "[n]o ratification is required for agreements of a purely administrative nature" but stating that such agreements do not function directly as domestic law).

[131] *See* Chapter 5, pgs. 216–17.

[132] The term *treaty* here, as contemplated by the Vienna Convention on the Law of Treaties, embraces all "international agreement[s] concluded between States in written form and governed by international law." *See* VCLT, art. 2(1)(a).

[133] *See* Chapter 11, pgs. 452–53 (citing sec. 231(3) of the 1996 Constitution).

[134] *See* Chapter 8, pgs. 328–29.

[135] *See* Chapter 13, pgs. 506–07.

[136] *See supra* notes 116–22 and accompanying text.

The extent to which such executive agreements may apply as law in the domestic legal system, in contrast, is substantially less clear. The South African Constitution prescribes that only those international agreements approved by the legislature may have direct domestic law effect.[137] The Poland chapter likewise reports that as a practical matter the full ratification procedure (i.e., with legislative approval) is required for all treaties "meant to be directly applicable in domestic courts."[138]

The remaining hybrid monist states leave only limited room for the direct effect of treaties not approved by the legislature. German law generally permits executive agreements for purposes of international law; but its chapter reports that, without legislative approval, the German *Grundgesetz* "narrowly circumscribes the competences of the executive branch" regarding enforcement in domestic law.[139] The law of the Netherlands, while it generally gives effect to all binding treaties, similarly limits the executive authority to conclude treaties without legislative approval to a narrow subset of issues.[140]

The legal situation in the United States and Russia for purposes of domestic law effect is less clear. The Supreme Court of the United States has long held that sole executive agreements – those international agreements that lack the express approval of Congress – may take effect directly as domestic law and in such a case will displace the subnational law of the individual states.[141] In a recent case, however, it has emphasized that this domestic force of sole executive agreements depends significantly on the extent of past acquiescence by Congress.[142]

In Russia, it seems clear that intergovernmental and interdepartmental treaties may likewise function as domestic law.[143] As we will explain in more detail in the following Section, however, these executive treaties have a rank of priority in the domestic law hierarchy that is significantly below those treaties expressly approved by the national legislature.[144]

[137] *See* Chapter 11, pgs. 455–56 (citing sec. 231(4) of the 1996 Constitution).
[138] *See* Chapter 9, pg. 377.
[139] *See* Chapter 5, pgs. 216–17.
[140] *See* Chapter 8, pg. 328 (observing that legislative approval is required except "for treaties that execute treaties approved earlier; for short-term treaties; for secret treaties; or for changes to execution annexes that are an integral part of a treaty").
[141] *See* United States v. Belmont, 301 U.S. 324 (1937); United States v. Pink, 315 U.S. 203 (1942); Dames & Moore v. Regan, 453 U.S. 654 (1981); Garamendi v. American Ins. Ass'n 539 U.S. 396 (2003). In contrast, a sole executive agreement should not be able to displace statutory law adopted by Congress.
[142] *See* Medellín v. Texas, 128 S.Ct. 1346, 1371–72 (2008).
[143] *See* Chapter 10, pgs. 428–29.
[144] *See infra* notes 173–179 and accompanying text.

D. *The Hierarchy among the Constitution, Statutes, and Treaties*

The general rule among the states studied is that the law derived from international treaties – whether by direct force or through subsequent implementing legislation – is of a legal nature that is equivalent to domestic statutory law. The legal structures by which this general principle obtains, however, differ significantly among the traditional dualist states and what I have referred to here as the hybrid monist states.[145] Moreover, as the following Section explains, the general rule of equivalence is subject to important exceptions in some states.

1. The Traditional Dualist States. As noted in Section III.B., in the traditional dualist states the implementation of treaties in domestic law most commonly is accomplished through standard legislation adopted by both houses of the legislature.[146] Because of this requirement of legislative implementation, a treaty, in a strict sense, has no formal rank in the normative hierarchy of such states, for it is only the implementing legislation that functions as domestic law. The creation of domestic law on the foundation of international treaty obligations thus occurs in the same way and to the same extent as standard domestic legislation. Legislation implementing treaty obligations, in other words, has the same status in law as any other standard statute.

As a consequence, treaty implementation legislation generally supersedes any prior inconsistent legislation. But the reverse is true as well.[147] That is, like any other statute, the law adopted to implement a treaty is itself subject to revision or repeal simply by subsequent parliamentary action. The approach of the United Kingdom is illustrative of this general later-in-time rule in the traditional dualist states. As its chapter reports, "the provisions of a treaty that are made part of (incorporated into) domestic law have the status only of domestic law, and can be amended or repealed by later legislation."[148]

[145] In federal states, treaties properly implemented by the national government clearly will prevail over all provincial legislation, whether prior or subsequent. *See* Chapter 3, pgs. 130–35; Chapter 6, pg. 243; Chapter 13, pgs. 507–08. As noted earlier, a different rule obtains in Canada, where the standard division of legislative competence between the federation and the provinces limits the power of the national government to implement some treaties. *See supra* notes 52–54 and accompanying text.

[146] *See supra* Section III.B.2.

[147] *See* Chapter 4, pgs. 169–70, 190–92; Chapter 6, pgs. 244–45; Chapter 7, pgs. 276–77; Chapter 12, pg. 480. *Cf.* Chapter 3, pg. 138 (observing that treaties are implemented via parliamentary legislation).

[148] Chapter 12, pg. 478.

2. The Hybrid Monist States. The common theme among the hybrid states studied in this work is that each permits at least some treaties to function directly as domestic law.[149] The procedure for the required legislative approval of treaties nonetheless differs markedly among these states, as we have seen.[150] Some provide for special and distinctive procedures.[151] In the majority of these states, in contrast, the legislature expresses its consent to treaty ratification – with the result that the treaty may itself function as domestic law – through a legislative procedure that is roughly equivalent to that for standard statutes.[152]

The basic concept that treaty law is of a legal nature equivalent to domestic statutory law generally obtains in the hybrid states as well. A clear consequence of this is that treaties – even those the legislature has expressly approved in advance of ratification – may not contravene the Constitution.[153] This rule is accomplished in some states (e.g., Poland) by express constitutional provision[154] and in others (e.g., the United States) by constitutional interpretation.[155]

The prominent exception to this rule is the Netherlands. As its chapter explains, Article 91(3) of the Dutch Constitution provides for a special parliamentary procedure by which a properly ratified treaty may supersede the Constitution itself.[156] This procedure – which is somewhat less demanding than for a formal amendment to the Constitution – requires a two-thirds vote in both chambers of Parliament.[157]

The principle of equivalence likewise means that treaties approved by the legislature generally have a legal status that is of equal dignity with

[149] For elaboration on this point, *see infra* Section IV.B.1 (referring to the reception of treaties in domestic law).

[150] *See supra* Section III.C.1.

[151] *See* Chapter 13, pgs. 506–08; Chapter 11, pgs. 453–54 (providing for a special advance legislative approval procedure).

[152] *See* Chapter 8, pgs. 328–29 (for treaties approved by standard legislation); Chapter 5, pg. 217.

[153] *See, e.g.*, Chapter 8, pgs. 328–30 (for treaties approved by standard legislation); Chapter 5, pgs. 218–19; Chapter 9, pgs. 381–82 (but also noting that the Constitution permits the court to leave even an unconstitutional law in effect for twelve months to permit legislative correction); Chapter 11, pgs. 452–54; Chapter 13, pg. 508.

[154] *See* Chapter 9, pg. 381 (observing that the clear implication of arts. 91 and 188 of the Constitution is "that international treaties (whatever the procedure for their ratification) do not have precedence over the Constitution").

[155] *See* Chapter 13, pg. 508 (citing Reid v. Covert, 354 U.S. 1, 16–17 (1957)).

[156] *See* Chapter 8, pg. 329.

[157] *See id.*

standard domestic legislation.[158] As a result, in most of the hybrid states, the later-in-time rule will give precedence to later-approved treaties, and vice versa, although an interpretive presumption (about which more in Section IV.A.3.) that statutory law conforms with international obligations may create obstacles for any conclusion that a statute actually conflicts with an earlier treaty.[159]

Some of the country reports nonetheless describe noteworthy exceptions to this principle of equivalence. Once again, the most prominent in this regard is the Netherlands. As its report explains, Article 94 of the Dutch Constitution provides that "[s]tatutory regulations in force within the Kingdom shall not be applicable if such application is in conflict with provisions of treaties that are binding on all persons."[160] This latter clause, as will be examined in Section IV.B.2.,[161] is significant for the question of whether a treaty, although it generally functions as domestic law, may be immediately enforceable in domestic courts. Nonetheless, the supremacy of treaties in the Dutch legal system means that properly accepted treaties – even those not approved by the special super-majority vote of the legislature[162] – will prevail not only over prior statutes but also over subsequent legislation adopted by Parliament.[163]

Poland follows a similar approach. As described previously, for certain categories of important treaties the Polish Constitution of 1997 requires the advance approval of the legislature (so-called full ratification).[164] By express constitutional provisions, treaties approved in this fashion take precedence over statutory law.[165] Indeed, such treaties "enjoy a suprastatutory rank."[166] The Poland chapter thus declares that "the courts are not

[158] *See* Chapter 5, pg. 217 ("The domestic rank of treaties concluded with legislative consent is equal to that of domestic legislation."); Chapter 11, pgs. 452–54; Chapter 13, pg. 509 (citing, *inter alia*, Whitney v. Robertson, 124 U.S. 190, 194 (1888), for the well-established later-in-time rule in the United States).

[159] *See infra* Section IV.A.3. The Germany Chapter, for example, thus observes that in the case of a later-in-time statute, "it cannot be assumed that the legislature, insofar as it has not clearly declared otherwise, wishes to deviate from the Federal Republic of Germany's international treaty commitments or to facilitate violation of such commitments." Chapter 5, pg. 229 (quoting the decision of the Federal Constitutional Court reported at BVerfGE 92, 91 *et. seq.*).

[160] *See* Chapter 8, pgs. 335–36.

[161] *See infra* notes 301–04 and accompanying text.

[162] *See supra* notes 156–57 and accompanying text.

[163] *See* Chapter 8, pgs. 335–36.

[164] *See supra* notes 103–05 and accompanying text.

[165] *See* Chapter 9, pgs. 379–81 (citing art. 91(2) of the Constitution).

[166] *Id.*, at 379.

only invited to apply directly the provisions of such treaties, but also are obliged to grant them priority over a conflicting statutory norm, whether prior or subsequent to the treaty."[167] In contrast, the Constitution leaves some doubt about the effect of those treaties approved with only the cooperation of the president and the prime minister (i.e., small ratification). The Poland chapter notes that, although "it is obvious . . . that such treaties cannot take precedence over statutes," scholars are divided on whether small ratification treaties are equal or subordinate to ordinary statutes.[168]

South Africa, in contrast, takes a more limited view regarding a conflict between directly enforceable treaty provisions and standard legislation. As we have seen,[169] Section 231(4) of its 1996 Constitution provides that a "self-executing provision" of a treaty ratified with the advance consent of Parliament may take effect directly as domestic law.[170] As a matter of hierarchy, however, the same section of the Constitution declares that such a treaty provision is not effective in domestic law if it is "inconsistent with the Constitution or an Act of Parliament."[171]

Finally, the hierarchy of treaties in Russia requires careful analysis.[172] We have noted that Article 15(4) of its 1993 Constitution provides that all "international treaties of the Russian Federation shall be an integral part of its legal system."[173] Indeed, in case of conflict, the same provision states that treaties take precedence over domestic law.[174] In accordance with the decisions of the Supreme Court of the Russian Federation and the weight of authority among commentators, however, only those treaties ratified with the advance approval of the legislature – or otherwise implemented by legislation – may "take precedence over laws of the Russian Federation."[175]

In contrast, intergovernmental and interdepartmental treaties – those concluded by the national executive or executive branch agencies without express legislative approval – do not have this preemptive effect over otherwise applicable national law.[176] According to the weight of authority, such

[167] *Id.*
[168] *Id.*, at 380–81.
[169] *See supra* note 125 and accompanying text.
[170] *See* Chapter 11, pgs. 453–54.
[171] *See id.* (citing section 231(4) of the Constitution).
[172] *See supra* notes 118–122 and accompanying text.
[173] *See* Chapter 10, pgs. 410–11.
[174] *Id.*
[175] *See id.*, at 421, 428–31.
[176] *See id.*

treaties do not prevail over inconsistent statutory law unless confirmed by subsequent legislation.[177] Instead, they have priority only over the "subordinate normative-legal acts issued by the agency of state power" that concluded the treaty at issue.[178] Some commentators, including the author of the Russia chapter in this work, however, argue that even intergovernmental and interdepartmental treaties enjoy the preemptive force described in Article 15(4) of the Russian Constitution.[179]

E. *Excursus: The Direct Effect of Customary International Law*

One of the interesting results from the chapters in this work is the contrast between the force of international treaties – which are subject to individualized consent – and the treatment of customary international law. Almost irrespective of the general approach to the domestic law effect of treaties – whether traditional dualist or hybrid monist – a number of the country chapters report that domestic courts afford some form of direct effect for the rules of customary international law without any required sanction by domestic lawmaking institutions.[180]

This result is expressly prescribed by the constitutions of some states (e.g., South Africa,[181] Germany,[182] and Russia[183]). The German *Grundgesetz* is illustrative. Its Article 25 explicitly provides that the general rules of international law are incorporated into federal law and may create directly enforceable rights and obligations for individuals.[184] By special provision, the *Grundgesetz* also leaves all decisions about the domestic effect of nonconventional international law solely to the Federal Constitutional Court.[185]

[177] *See id.*, at 429.
[178] *See id.*, at 421, 429.
[179] *See id.*, at 428–31.
[180] *See* Chapter 3, pg. 129; Chapter 4, pg. 168; Chapter 6, pgs. 244–45; Chapter 7, pgs. 278–79; Chapter 8, pgs. 332–33; Chapter 9, pgs. 376–77; Chapter 10, pgs. 410–11; Chapter 11, pg. 452; Chapter 12, pg. 498.
[181] *See* Chapter 11, pg. 464 (noting that sec. 232 of the 1996 Constitution provides that "[c]ustomary international law is law in the republic unless it is inconsistent with the Constitution or an act of Parliament").
[182] *See* Chapter 5, pgs. 218–19.
[183] *See* Chapter 10, pgs. 410–11 (quoting art. 15(4) of the 1993 Constitution, which provides that "[g]enerally-recognized principles and norms of international law . . . shall be an integral part" of the Russian legal system).
[184] *See* Chapter 5, pg. 221.
[185] *See id.*

In states that follow the common law tradition (e.g., Australia, Canada, India, the United Kingdom, the United States), the direct effect of customary international law has come about through the role of the courts in developing the common law. Interestingly, this is true even in the particularly purist states of the dualist tradition such as Australia[186] and the United Kingdom.[187]

The Supreme Court of India has a particularly well-developed jurisprudence on this score. The India chapter reports that, under the Court's doctrine of incorporation, the customary rules of international law automatically apply in domestic courts, provided that they do not conflict with express statutory provisions: "The comity of nations," the Indian Supreme Court has explained, "requires that rules of international law may be accommodated in the municipal law even without express legislative sanction, provided they do not run into conflict with Acts of Parliament."[188]

As the latter clause of this quotation reflects, however, a common approach among the states studied in this work is that the rules of customary international law must yield to domestic law norms generated through legislative sanction.[189] The same approach obtains even in international-law-friendly the Netherlands. The Supreme Court there has concluded based on the drafting history of the Constitution that the preeminence of treaties over domestic law does not extend to "the enforcement of unwritten international law if that clash[es] with national statutes."[190]

F. *Constitutionalism and Delegations to International Institutions by Treaty*

Some of the states studied report special constitutional arrangements for treaties that delegate domestic lawmaking or interpretive authority to international institutions. Not surprisingly, the member states of the European Union provide the most prominent examples. In each of the four member

[186] *See* Chapter 3, pg. 129 (quoting Brennan, J., in Mabo v. Queensland [No. 2], (1992) 175 C.L.R. 1 at 42, to the effect that "international law is a legitimate and important influence on the development of the common law").

[187] *See* Chapter 12, pg. 498 (stating that "[c]ustomary international law [is] part of the common law"); Chapter 4, pg. 168 (observing that dualism "does not extend to rules of customary international law").

[188] *See* Chapter 6, pg. 245 (quoting Gramophone Company of India Ltd. v. Birendra Bahadur Pandey and Others, 21 February 1984, AIR 1984 SC 667, (1984) 2 SCC 534, [1984] 2 SCR 664).

[189] *See, e.g.*, Chapter 3, pg. 129; Chapter 6, pgs. 244–45; Chapter 8, pgs. 333–35, 349; Chapter 11, pg. 452.

[190] *See* Chapter 8, pg. 358 (quoting HR 18 September 2001, NJ 2002, 599, para. 4.6).

states studied (Germany, the Netherlands, Poland, and the United Kingdom), decisions of EU institutions created on the foundation of treaties may have an effect in some form without subsequent formal ratification by domestic lawmaking institutions.

Perhaps the most explicit and expansive approach to this power of treaties is Germany. As its country chapter explains, the *Grundgesetz* expressly permits Germany to transfer domestic lawmaking authority to international institutions by treaty confirmed in law: "The Federation may by a law transfer sovereign powers to international organizations."[191] Although founded on less elaborate constitutional arrangements, the law of the Netherlands likewise permits the direct application of law created by EU institutions (narrowly, European Community Law) within their areas of competence.[192]

The Polish Constitution of 1997 has similar special provisions. Its chapter explains that Article 90 of the Constitution requires a two-thirds vote of both houses of Parliament (or a referendum if the parliament so decrees) for delegations of lawmaking competence to international organizations.[193] As a result, because Poland properly ratified the EU Accession Treaty through this enhanced procedure, the subsidiary norms of EU institutions "shall be applied directly and have precedence in the event of a conflict with statutes."[194]

The application of European law nonetheless remains subject to the individual constitutions of the member states (with the exception of the Netherlands[195]).[196] Of special note is the approach of Germany. As its chapter explains, the German legislature amended the *Grundgesetz* in the early 1990s to provide explicitly that transfers of legislative competence to European Union institutions must "guarantee[] a level of protection of basic rights essentially comparable to that afforded by this *Grundgesetz*."[197] As a result, as the German chapter explains, "[i]n cases where European organs act beyond the scope of their legitimate authority, the Federal Constitutional Court maintains that it may decide that such an act does not have effect on

[191] *See* Chapter 5, pgs. 218–19 (observing that "there is no doubt that treaties . . . may provide for the direct intervention of international organizations in domestic affairs without implementing legislation").
[192] *See* Chapter 8, pgs. 367–71. *See also* Chapter 12, pgs. 501–02.
[193] *See* Chapter 9, pg. 377.
[194] *See* Chapter 9, pgs. 385–87 (citing art. 91(3) of the Constitution).
[195] *See supra* notes 156–57 and accompanying text.
[196] *See* Chapter 5, pgs. 219–22; Chapter 9, pg. 384; Chapter 12, pg. 479 (observing that "treaties are not in any way supreme law under the British Constitution").
[197] *See* Chapter 5, pgs. 236–38 (quoting art. 23 of the *Grundgesetz*).

German territory."[198] The Constitutional Court also has retained for itself – at least rhetorically – the final authority over the conformity of decisions of the European Court of Justice (ECJ) with the German Constitution. It thus has declared that the decisions of the ECJ must adhere to a "minimum standard" of the human rights and dignity protected by the *Grundgesetz.*[199]

On the role of courts in treaty enforcement, the close integration of the members of the European Union has led to a specialized jurisprudence that is not easily generalized beyond the scope of community law. Nonetheless, because of its special relevance for the broader analysis in Section IV, the approval and implementation of the European Convention on Human Rights (ECHR) is worthy of special emphasis here. On the foundation of legislative approval of the ECHR, domestic courts have directly enforced the individuals rights protected there on a great number of occasions, including with reference to decisions of the European Court of Human Rights.[200]

Perhaps not surprisingly, a bit more nuanced analysis is necessary for the United Kingdom on this point. With its strict dualist requirement of parliamentary implementation of treaties in general, we must look to the implementing statute for guidance on the role of the ECHR in domestic law. But on this score, the Human Rights Act of 1998 is remarkably accommodating. Its Article 8 creates a private right of action, including a right to damages, for governmental violations of rights secured by the ECHR (which in substance also folds in numerous other international human rights norms).[201] Where statutory law conflicts with the ECHR, the Human Rights Act permits a court only to issue a "declaration of incompatibility." But such a declaration in turn empowers the executive to remove the incompatibility by adopting subsidiary legislation without further action by the Parliament.[202]

[198] *Id.*, at 227. As the Germany Chapter notes, however, this possibility thus far has remained of theoretical interest only, for the Federal Constitutional Court has never declared a European legal act inapplicable in the German legal order because an institution has exceeded its delegated authority. *See id.*

[199] *See id.*, at 227–28.

[200] *See* Chapter 5, pgs. 228–33 (referring to the "special role of the Convention in the German legal order"); Chapter 8, pg. 347 (noting that Dutch courts now apply the ECHR on "an almost daily basis"); Chapter 9, pgs. 389–91. *See also* Chapter 10, pgs. 441–44 (noting that Russia is a party to the ECHR and that, although some uncertainly remains, it appears that decisions of the ECHR in cases to which Russia is a party may have some direct force in the domestic legal system of Russia).

[201] *See* Chapter 12, pgs. 489–91.

[202] *Id.*, at 487–89.

IV. THE ROLE OF DOMESTIC COURTS IN THE INTERPRETATION, APPLICATION, AND ENFORCEMENT OF TREATIES

A. *The Commonalities Among States*

1. Judicial Recognition of the International Law Foundations of Treaty Law. The basic structure of the foregoing analysis has focused on the distinction between traditional dualist states and what I have referred to as hybrid monist states. The fundamental dividing point between the two groups is whether treaties may operate directly – that is, of their own status and force – in domestic law. We have seen that, although procedures differ, the hybrid states generally permit this result; in the traditional dualist states, in contrast, even when treaties concluded by the executive are implemented by legislative action, it is the implementing legislation, not the treaty, that functions as domestic law.

Given this formal divergence, among the most striking conclusions from a review of the chapters in this work is the extent of the functional similarities in the actual interpretation of treaty-based law by domestic courts. These begin in the basic recognition of the international law foundations of treaties or, as the case may be, the statutes that implement them. That this should be true in the hybrid states – which permit direct application of at least some treaties in any event – is not surprising. Thus, for example, the Germany report declares that the "straightforward" task of domestic courts "is to allow Germany to fulfill its international obligations by faithfully interpreting German law in accordance with Germany's international obligations, in particular treaty obligations."[203]

The one note of exception on the hybrid monist states is the United States. As the U.S. chapter relates, domestic courts have applied a variety of nationalist tools – non-self-execution doctrine, deference to executive treaty interpretations, and a presumption against individually enforceable rights – to "shield government actors from judicial review of government compliance with treaty-based norms."[204] Notwithstanding a general interpretive presumption in favor of treaty obligations,[205] the effect of this practice is to undermine in a troubling way the influence of the international law foundations on the application of treaty obligations in domestic law.

[203] Chapter 5, pgs. 209–10.
[204] *See* Chapter 13, pgs. 538–39. For more on this point, *see infra* notes 305–309 and 331–336 and accompanying text.
[205] *See* Chapter 13, pgs. 526–27 (citing the "Charming Betsy Canon").

In contrast, what is significant from a review of the country reports is that the courts in traditional dualist states also have recognized the international law foundations of treaties. The Canada chapter provides a good example. Although it observes that treaties do not function as domestic law on their own, the chapter quotes at length the leading decision of the Canadian Supreme Court that recognizes the international law foundations of a treaty implementation statute:

> Since the purpose of the [provision of the domestic statute] is to implement the underlying Convention, the Court must adopt an interpretation consistent with Canada's obligations under the Convention. The wording of the Convention and the rules of treaty interpretation will therefore be applied to determine the meaning of [the statutory provision] in domestic law[.][206]

The chapters for the other traditional dualist states studied in this work make similar observations. The domestic courts even in these states have recognized the propriety of having recourse to the international law foundations of the underlying treaty for interpretive guidance (unless the implementing statute unambiguously conflicts).[207] This is particularly true where implementation occurs through the scheduling of the entire treaty to the legislative act.[208] In such a case, as the U.K. chapter explains, "since the treaty is a creation of international law the English courts will interpret it according to the rules of international law."[209] The Supreme Court of Israel has made a like pronouncement,[210] although the Israel chapter offers

[206] *See* Chapter 4, pg. 177 (*quoting* Pushpanathan v. Canada (Minister of Citizenship and Immigration), [1998] 1 SCR 982). *See also id.*, at 176–77 (quoting a lower court in the same case to the effect that "[i]t is also accepted that in interpreting a treaty-implementing statute one may have regard to the treaty and the means for its interpretation even if the implementing statute is not on its face ambiguous").

[207] *See* Chapter 3, pgs. 139–40 (quoting the Australia High Court to the effect that Australian courts "will endeavour to adopt a construction" of an implementing statute, "if that construction is available," that "conforms to" the underlying treaty); Chapter 6, pg. 264 (reporting recent jurisprudence in which "the Supreme Court had recourse to the original treaty in order to satisfy itself that the treaty provisions had been faithfully transformed into municipal law"); Chapter 12, pg. 482 (describing a variety of similar principles to the effect that if the implementing statute is ambiguous, domestic courts "will look at the treaty that the legislation was enacted to implement").

[208] *See supra* note 84 and accompanying text.

[209] *See* Chapter 12, pg. 483.

[210] *See* Chapter 7, pgs. 291–92 (observing that "[w]hichever incorporation technique is employed, the courts will try to interpret the legislation according to the terms of the [underlying] convention").

noteworthy words of caution concerning application in cases involving the Occupied Territories.[211]

Domestic courts from both traditions have extended this shared recognition of the international law foundations of treaty-based law into a variety of more specific interpretive principles. Included among these are resort to the rules of the VCLT (see Section IV.A.2(a)); a common – though uneven – willingness to look to other treaty member-state courts for interpretive guidance (see IV.A.2(b)); and a widespread, though not universal, refusal to defer to executive interpretive views (see IV.A.2(c)). More broadly, domestic courts have sought to interpret all domestic law – including in some cases constitutional law – to advance conformity with international treaty obligations (see Sections IV.A.3 and IV.A.4). On each of these points, substantial functional similarity exists among the states studied in this work, almost without regard to whether they follow the traditional dualist or hybrid monist traditions on the domestic force of treaties.

2. Treaty Interpretation by Domestic Courts

A THE ROLE OF THE VIENNA CONVENTION ON THE LAW OF TREATIES. The VCLT reflects the principal effort to define the international law governing treaties. Its rules on the interpretation of treaties in Articles 31 through 33 of necessity are of significance in a work such as this. To summarize briefly, Article 31(1) provides that "a treaty shall be interpreted in good faith in accordance with the ordinary meaning to be given to the terms of the treaty in their context and in the light of its object and purpose." The remainder of this article elaborates on this "general rule of interpretation" by requiring consideration of related agreements between the parties,[212] their subsequent practices and agreements as well as general rules of international law,[213] and any special interpretations intended by them.[214] Article 32 authorizes interpreters to have recourse to "supplementary means of interpretation," including the preparatory work of the treaty (the *travaux*

[211] *See id.*, at 292–94 (noting that "in cases relating to the [Occupied Territories], for a long time the Supreme Court in fact adopted the interpretation of the [the Fourth Geneva Convention] favored by the authorities, even when this meant changing the theory of interpretation from case to case."); *id.*, at 314–25 (examining the role of international law in cases involving the Occupied Territories, but cautioning in conclusion that "[i]t should not be thought that the Court has always been receptive to arguments based on international law, nor has the manner in which it has interpreted this law always been compatible with accepted modes of interpretation. Far from it.").

[212] *See* VCLT, art. 31(2).

[213] *See id.*, art. 31(3).

[214] *See id.*, art. 31(4).

préparatoires). Finally, Article 33 provides for equal treatment of languages where a treaty is concluded in more than one language.

On the surface, it would appear from the country chapters that little conformity exists on the role of these interpretive rules in the application of treaty-based law by domestic courts. One might expect, moreover, that the formal distinction between the dualist and monist approaches to the domestic force of treaties would divide the states on the role of the VCLT. Finally, while most of the states studied have formally ratified or acceded to the VCLT,[215] four have not (two, interestingly, from each tradition).[216]

Closer examination reveals, however, that substantial similarities exist on the influence of the VCLT almost irrespective of tradition and member-state status. To start with the clearest example, it should not surprise that courts from hybrid monist states that also have ratified the VCLT have directly applied its interpretive rules in Articles 31–33 on that basis.[217] Thus, for example, a 2003 decree of the plenum of the Supreme Court of Russia expressly instructs domestic courts to apply the interpretive principles of the VCLT.[218]

Some member-state courts from the dualist tradition likewise have directly applied the VCLT.[219] Interestingly, as the approach of the United Kingdom illustrates, this is true even if the VCLT itself has not been implemented through domestic legislation. The U.K. chapter reports that, if Parliament has implemented a treaty by appending the text to the legislation (i.e., scheduling), English courts "will interpret it according to the rules of international law, in particular Articles 31–33 of the Vienna Convention on the Law of Treaties . . . even though the Convention itself has not been incorporated into English law."[220]

But the courts of some non–member states, ironically, also have directly applied VCLT Articles 31–33. They have done so through a recognition of the VCLT, at least in this respect, as customary international law.[221] (As we have

[215] Australia, Canada, Germany, the Netherlands, Poland, Russia, and the United Kingdom have all ratified or acceded to the VCLT. *See* Status, Vienna Convention on the Law of Treaties, U.N. Treaty Collection, *available at* http://untreaty.un.org/ilc/texts/getter.asp.

[216] India, Israel, South Africa, and the United States are not member states to the VCLT. *See id.*

[217] *See* Chapter 5, pg. 222, n. 64; Chapter 8, pgs. 361–62; Chapter 10, pg. 418.

[218] *See* Chapter 10, pg. 418 (referring to Decree No. 5 of the plenum of the Supreme Court of October 10, 2003).

[219] *See* Chapter 3, pgs. 151–52; Chapter 4, pgs. 175–82; Chapter 12, pg. 483.

[220] *See id.*

[221] *See* Chapter 7, pgs. 297–88 (but also noting that the instances in which Israeli courts have expressly referred to the interpretive rules of the VCLT are "few and far between"); Chapter 11, pg. 464 (observing that "[a]t the international level, it seems that South Africa accepts

seen, the courts in the states studied commonly apply accepted principles of customary international law.[222])

To be sure, some chapters, even for some VCLT member states, report that domestic courts generally have not applied the interpretive rules in the VCLT by express reference.[223] Nonetheless, these chapters also have observed that their courts commonly apply the substance of VCLT Articles 31–33 because this substance largely corresponds to domestic interpretive norms in any event.[224]

In short, therefore, one can safely generalize that – whether by express reference or by accepted practice – domestic courts in the states studied in this work have interpreted the law derived (directly or indirectly) from treaties in a manner largely consistent with the principles reflected in the VCLT.[225] That is, in conformance with the basic principle in Article 31(1), courts have approached treaty interpretation beginning with an examination of the text[226] but informed by the objects and purposes of the treaty. The High Court of Australia aptly summarized this fundamental approach to treaty interpretation (especially regarding multilateral treaties) in one case as follows:

> The effect of Art 31 is that, although primacy must be given to the written text of [a treaty], the context, objects and purpose of the treaty must also be considered. The need to give the text primacy in interpretation results from the tendency of multilateral treaties to be the product of compromises by the parties to such treaties.[227]

the substance of the Convention as customary international law" but noting that whether its courts actually apply the treaty "is uncertain").

222 *See supra* Section III.F.

223 *See* Chapter 9, pgs. 388–89; Chapter 11, pgs. 464–66.

224 *See* Chapter 9, pgs. 388–89; Chapter 11, pgs. 464–66 (proffering that the likely reason its courts have not expressly referred to VCLT arts. 31 and 32 is that the domestic principles of statutory interpretation "broadly follow" the substance of those rules). *See also* Chapter 4, pgs. 183–84 (observing that Canadian courts follow the VCLT but that domestic interpretive techniques are similar in any event).

225 The country chapters report only rare express citations to the force of the principle of good faith in interpretation. *See, e.g.*, Chapter 9, pgs. 400–01 (referring to the influence of the principle of good-faith interpretation in Polish courts); Chapter 13, pg. 523 (observing that "U.S. courts sometimes apply the main idea [of VCLT art. 31] without using the phrase 'good faith'").

226 *See, e.g.*, Chapter 3, pgs. 151–52; Chapter 4, pgs. 179–80. *See also* Chapter 9, pgs. 387–88 (observing that although Polish courts have not directly cited VCLT art. 31, "in practice they first try to give the ordinary meaning to the terms of the treaty when interpreting it"). The U.S. Supreme Court emphasized the significance of text in the interpretation of treaties in a recent opinion. *See* Medellín v. Texas, 128 S.Ct. 1346, 1357–60 (2008).

227 *See* Chapter 3, pgs. 151–52 (citing Morrison v. Peacock, [2002] HCA 44 at [16]).

As this quotation makes clear, "the context, objects and purpose" of the treaty also play a significant interpretive role.[228] Canada may be cited as an exemplar in this regard. Its chapter reports that the courts of Canada frequently resort to the VCLT "to interpret Canadian treaty obligations," including for statutes that implement international treaties in the fields of taxation, extradition, human rights, and investment.[229] In particular, Canadian courts have made active use of the object and purposes of treaties in domestic practice. Although it also has noted the importance of text, the Canadian Supreme Court has even observed that the "starting point of the interpretive exercise" for a disputed article in an international treaty is "to define the purpose of the Convention as a whole and, second, the purpose and place of [the article] within that scheme."[230]

Some domestic courts also have affirmed that treaties are to be construed in a more liberal manner than standard domestic legislation and with more flexible interpretive norms.[231] This results from both the teleological (or purposive) approach noted previously and the separate direction in VCLT Article 32 that treaty interpreters may refer to "supplementary means of interpretation."[232] Included here in particular is an endorsement of reliance on the drafting records and other preparatory work in interpreting treaties (the so-called *travaux préparatoires*).[233] This more liberal resort to drafting records has found approval even in the United States, where there is a continuing controversy over the propriety of judicial reference to legislative history for statutes.[234]

[228] *See* Chapter 3, pgs. 151–52; Chapter 7, pgs. 290–91; Chapter 9, pgs. 388–89; Chapter 11, pgs. 465–66; Chapter 13, pgs. 522–23 (observing that "[t]he most frequently cited principle of treaty interpretation is the idea that courts should interpret treaties in accordance with the goals or objectives of the treaty makers").

[229] *See* Chapter 4, pgs. 181–82.

[230] *See id.* at 178 (quoting [1998] 1 SCR 982 (Pushpanathan), at para. 56).

[231] *See* Chapter 3, pgs. 151–52; Chapter 4, pgs. 179–80; Chapter 9, pg. 400 (observing that on the principle of good-faith interpretation, Polish courts apply a "presumption in favor of broader protection for private rights" under a treaty). *See also* Chapter 13, pg. 525 (citing the "canon of liberal interpretation," but noting that "[r]ecently, . . . the canon has fallen into desuetude").

[232] *See* Chapter 3, pgs. 151–52; Chapter 4, pg. 174.

[233] *See, e.g.*, Chapter 4, pgs. 177–80, 181–82 (observing that "[i]n particular, the practice of resorting to *travaux préparatoires* is accepted" in interpreting treaties). *See also* Chapter 11, pgs. 465–66.

[234] *See, e.g.*, El Al Israel Airlines v. Tseng, 525 U.S. 155, 167 (1999) ("Because a treaty ratified by the United States is not only the law of this land . . . but also an agreement among sovereign powers, we have traditionally considered as aids to its interpretation the negotiating and drafting history[.]") (quoting Zicherman v. Korean Airlines, 516 U.S. 217, 226 (1996)). *See also* Chapter 13, pg. 537 (observing that the traditional canon of liberal interpretation of treaties "has morphed from a rule designed to protect the rights of private parties to a rule that promotes more liberal use of extra-textual sources").

Finally, some states have a special judicial practice of providing advance guidance on treaty interpretation. The chapter for Russia, for example, describes a procedure by which the Russian Supreme Court may issue general or specific directives to lower courts on the interpretation of treaties.[235] The broadest in this regard may be the 2003 Decree No. 5 by the plenum of the Supreme Court of Russia "[o]n the Application by Courts of General Jurisdiction of Generally-Recognized Principles and Norms of International Law and International Treaties of the Russian Federation."[236]

B REFERENCE TO THE DECISIONS OF OTHER COURTS. A second more specific interpretive norm commonly reported by the individual country chapters is reference to relevant opinions of other national and international courts. This includes in particular interpretive decisions by the courts of other treaty member states.[237] The frequency of citation and the persuasive force of such decisions, however, have been uneven.[238]

Interestingly, even the chapters for some traditional dualist states report this practice. As we shall examine in more detail, the interpretive exercise in these states commonly begins with the implementation statute itself.[239] Nonetheless, the chapters for Australia, Canada, Israel, and the United Kingdom note that their courts, although to different degrees, have referred to decisions of courts from other treaty member states.[240] The Israel chapter, for example, reports that, "[i]n interpreting a convention that has been incorporated into Israeli law, the courts refer extensively to decisions of courts in other jurisdictions relating to the convention."[241]

Reference to decisions of international tribunals is also a commonly cited practice.[242] Once again, however, the frequency and effect of this

[235] *See* Chapter 10, pgs. 415–21.

[236] *See id.*

[237] *See* Chapter 3, pgs. 151–52; Chapter 4, pgs. 185–86; Chapter 7, pgs. 291–92; Chapter 9, pg. 398; Chapter 12, pgs. 483–84 (observing that courts may refer to decisions of other member state courts in their judgements).

[238] *See, e.g.*, Chapter 4, pgs. 185–86 (observing that "Canadian precedent for having regard to foreign interpretations of the state's treaty obligations is scarce"); Chapter 9, pg. 398 (stating that Polish courts "only occasionally" refer to such other court decisions as persuasive evidence); Chapter 12, pgs. 483–84 (observing that courts refer to decisions of other member state courts "only if it finds [them] helpful").

[239] *See infra* Section IV.C.1.

[240] *See* Chapter 3, pgs. 151–52; Chapter 4, pgs. 185–86; Chapter 7, pgs. 292–93; Chapter 12, pgs. 483–84.

[241] Chapter 7, pgs. 291–92.

[242] *See, e.g.*, Chapter 4, pgs. 183–86; Chapter 5, pgs. 235–36; Chapter 7, pgs. 298–301; Chapter 8, pgs. 346–47; Chapter 9, pgs. 386–88.

practice are irregular. In some states, decisions of international tribunals within their jurisdiction are accorded considerable force.[243] A quite positive example is that provided by the Constitutional Court of Germany. As the Germany chapter develops in considerable detail, the Federal Constitutional Court has declared that, in light of the German Basic Law's "friendliness" toward international law, German courts are required "to 'take into account' decisions of the International Court of Justice when binding on Germany" pursuant to a relevant treaty.[244] Even when a decision of an international tribunal is not technically binding, it nonetheless functions as a "normative guideline" for German courts in interpreting the treaty.[245]

In other states, in contrast, the practice of citing international tribunals is only occasional or quite circumscribed in the degree of its deference.[246] The most prominent – if unfavorable – recent example in this regard comes from the Supreme Court of the United States. As noted earlier, in 2003 the ICJ rendered a binding decision under international law on the interpretation of the VCCR.[247] The Supreme Court nonetheless refused to follow the ICJ's decision and instead applied its own interpretation that gave precedence to certain principles of domestic law.[248]

C. DEFERENCE TO THE EXECUTIVE. We noted early in this summary chapter that there is effective uniformity among the states studied on the principle that the executive (or government) controls the negotiation of treaties.[249] Nonetheless, most of the country chapters report that domestic courts do not broadly defer to executive views on issues of interpretation.[250] Indeed, the Poland chapter observes that complete deference to the executive on treaty interpretation "would be incompatible with the principle of independence of the judicial branch" set forth in the Polish Constitution.[251]

[243] *See, e.g.*, Chapter 5, pgs. 235–36; Chapter 9, pgs. 385–86.
[244] *See* Chapter 5, pgs. 235–36.
[245] *See id.*
[246] *See* Chapter 4, pgs. 183–84 (observing that "Canadian courts have, on occasion, considered the state's treaty obligations in light of pronouncements by international and/or foreign judicial or quasi-judicial bodies").
[247] *See also supra* notes 11–14 and accompanying text.
[248] *See* Sanchez-Llamas v. Oregon, 126 S. Ct. 2669, 2685 (2006); Medellín v. Texas, 128 S.Ct. 1346 (2008).
[249] *See supra* Section II.B.
[250] *See* Chapter 4, pgs. 186–88; Chapter 8, pgs. 363–64; Chapter 9, pgs. 399–400; Chapter 11, pgs. 472–74; Chapter 12, pg. 484.
[251] *See* Chapter 9, pgs. 399–400.

A small number of the states studied, however, follow a contrary path. Perhaps the most prominent example of this is the United States, where it is not at all uncommon for the Supreme Court to cite a principle of deference to the executive branch in treaty interpretation cases.[252] As the U.S. chapter reports, the effect of this principle can vary greatly depending on the involvement of the U.S. government and the subject matter – civil versus criminal – of the dispute.[253] But in cases involving claims against government officers, the chapter relates a clear practice of deferring to the interpretive views of the executive branch.[254] Similarly, the report for Israel observes that, although its Supreme Court generally views interpretation as solely a judicial task, in practice it has deferred to the executive on significant matters related to the Occupied Territories.[255]

3. Interpretation to Promote Conformity with International Law. The country chapters in this work also report functional similarity on the broader and more fundamental principle that courts should interpret domestic law to advance conformity with their state's treaty obligations under international law. Although the precise extent and formulation vary, this common feature among the states studied also bridges the formal dualist-monist dichotomy. The chapters for the traditional dualist states (Australia, Canada, India, Israel, and the United Kingdom[256]) as well as the hybrid monist states (Germany, the Netherlands, Poland, Russia, South Africa, and the United States[257]) all confirm that, at a minimum, national

[252] *See* Chapter 13, pg. 524 (quoting the Supreme Court in El Al Israel Airlines, Ltd. v. Tsui Yuan Tseng, 525 U.S. 155, 168 (1999), to the effect that "the meaning attributed to treaty provisions by the Government agencies charged with their negotiation and enforcement is entitled to great weight"). *See also id.* at 524 (observing that "[n]owadays, the deference canon is one of the most frequently cited principles of treaty interpretation").

[253] *See id.*, at 533 (concluding that "courts apply the deference canon more frequently in governmental litigation than they do in private litigation"); 539–52 (providing and analyzing empirical data on how courts employ nationalist tools in cases involving the government and in civil vs. criminal cases).

[254] *See id.*, at 533–34.

[255] *See* Chapter 7, pgs. 292–95.

[256] *See* Chapter 3, pgs. 152–56 (but noting some disagreement among the justices of the High Court of Australia on this score); Chapter 4, pgs. 188–89; Chapter 6, pgs. 247–55; Chapter 7, pgs. 287–90 (reporting a "presumption of compatibility" with international law); Chapter 12, pg. 282 (observing that "[u]nclear legislation will be interpreted in the way that is most consistent with the international obligations of the United Kingdom, including... unincorporated treaties"). *See also id.*, at 487–89 (observing that in particular the Human Rights Act instructs courts to apply a presumption of conformity with the underlying ECHR).

[257] *See* Chapter 5, pg. 209 ("German courts are also bound to interpret domestic law, as far as possible, in a way that avoids the breach of international legal obligations"); Chapter 8,

courts will prefer an interpretation of domestic law that will avoid conflict or, more broadly, promote consistency with international law in general and treaties in specific.

For the hybrid states – which generally require advance legislative approval for binding treaties – this interpretive principle has its most immediate effect in avoiding conflicts between a treaty and a later-enacted statute.[258] But what is striking is that courts in traditional dualist states have applied the conformity norm even to treaties that the legislature has not yet implemented in domestic law.[259] To be sure, such treaties must yield to clear and unambiguous domestic legislation; but the country chapters report that domestic courts will, wherever possible, seek to avoid such conflicts in a way to favor conformity with international law obligations, including those in unimplemented treaties. The reasoning of the Supreme Court of India provides a good example:

> International treaties have influenced the interpretation of Indian law in several ways. This court has relied upon them for statutory interpretation where the terms of any legislation are not clear or are reasonably capable of more than one meaning. In such cases, the courts have relied upon the meaning which is in consonance with the treaties, for there is a prima facie presumption that Parliament did not intend to act in breach of international law, including State treaty obligations.[260]

As this quote makes clear, domestic courts commonly have founded this approach on a presumed intent of the legislature.[261] But some courts have gone further, most notably the Supreme Court of Canada. As the Canada chapter explains, "the presumption is described as a rule of judicial policy – as opposed to an interpretive rule founded in the actual or presumed intent

pgs. 335–36 (noting that properly accepted treaties even trump later legislation); Chapter 9, pg. 404 (noting a similar "co-application" doctrine); Chapter 11, pgs. 457–58 (quoting sec. 233 of the Constitution to the effect that "[w]hen interpreting any legislation, every court must prefer any reasonable interpretation of the legislation that is consistent with international law over any alternative interpretation that is inconsistent with international law"); Chapter 13, pg. 526 (observing that "[i]n the United States, it is a well-established principle of statutory construction that federal statutes should be construed in conformity with the United States' international legal obligations" and referring to this principle as the "Charming Betsy canon").

[258] *See supra* note 159 and accompanying text.

[259] *See, e.g.*, Chapter 4, pgs. 175–76; Chapter 6, pgs. 247–55; Chapter 7, pgs. 287–90; Chapter 12, pgs. 483–84. *Cf.* Chapter 3, pgs. 152–56 (observing some controversy in the High Court of Australia on this principle).

[260] *See* Chapter 6, pgs. 250–51 (quoting the 2005 opinion of the Supreme Court of India in People's Union for Civil Liberties v. Union of India).

[261] *See* Chapter 3, pgs. 152–53.

of the lawmaker whose law is in question."[262] As a result, the presumption applies even to a statute that predates the treaty obligations in question.[263] Although exceptional, the Canadian Supreme Court has even been open to revising its established case law in light of new, though unimplemented, international treaty obligations.[264] The German Constitutional Court has been an exemplar in this regard as well.[265]

The jurisprudence of the Supreme Court of Canada on "implied incorporation" on the foundation of this robust presumption of conformity is also worthy of special note here. As its country chapter describes in detail, the Supreme Court of Canada has held that even a formally unimplemented treaty may obtain domestic law effect if Parliament leaves in place preexisting legislation that covers the same subject matter and that is not directly inconsistent with the later treaty.[266] The judicially applied presumption of conformity thus may operate to effect an implied implementation of the treaty through the nonobjection of parliament.[267]

4. **Treaties and Constitutional Interpretation.** Some domestic courts have been willing to look to international treaties even in the interpretation of domestic constitutions. The practice is by no means universal (only slightly more than half of the state chapters report some form of it);[268] but it is interesting to note that it has found a footing in the jurisprudence of courts from both the dualist and monist traditions. Perhaps the best example from the hybrid monist approach is the South African Constitution of 1996. Section 39(1) of that Constitution expressly provides that in interpreting the Bill of Rights, a court or other tribunal "must consider international

[262] *See* Chapter 4, pgs. 189–90.

[263] *Id.*

[264] *See* Chapter 4, pg. 205 (citing Health Services and Support – Facilities Subsector Bargaining Ass'n v. British Columbia, 2007 SCC 27).

[265] *See* Chapter 5, pgs. 228–31 (noting that the presumption of conformity applies both to legislation adopted before and after a relevant treaty); *id.*, at 229 (observing that on at least one occasion the Constitutional Court has revised its own case law based on a subsequent treaty).

[266] *See* Chapter 4, pgs. 203–04.

[267] *See id.* For more detail on the force of the general presumption of conformity, *see infra* Section III.C.1.

[268] Significant discussion and noteworthy controversy exist on this score in both Australia and the United States. For Australia, see Chapter 3, pgs. 156–58; for the United States, see Roper v. Simmons, 543 U.S. 551, 575–78 (2005) (a case in which a majority of the U.S. Supreme Court extensively referred to foreign and international law in the interpretation of the U.S. Constitution); *but see* Roper v. Simmons, 543 U.S. at 604–05, 622–28 (in which four of nine justices expressly disagreed with such a practice).

law." On this basis, the South Africa chapter reports that "both the Constitutional Court and ordinary courts have shown a great willingness to be guided by international human rights law" in interpreting the constitution itself.[269] This willingness of domestic courts to look to international law includes both treaties that are formally binding on South Africa and those that are not.[270] Germany and Poland report analogous interpretive approaches by their highest constitutional courts.[271]

A similar result is achieved in dualist India through an innovative interpretive mechanism set forth in its Constitution of 1949. The India chapter explains that Part IV of the Constitution sets forth certain "Directive Principles of State Policy."[272] Although not formally enforceable by domestic courts, these principles nonetheless are deemed "fundamental in the governance of the country" and state organs are enjoined "to apply these principles in making laws."[273] Included among these is a mandate that the state "endeavor to . . . foster respect for international law and treaty obligations in the dealings of organised peoples with one another."[274]

The Supreme Court of India has read this directive principle as a command to interpret not only domestic law generally, but also the fundamental rights protected by the Constitution, under the influence of the obligations of the state under international law. Through this vehicle, even unimplemented treaties have come to play a significant role in the interpretation of the Indian Constitution.[275] Thus, the Court has recognized that, although formally binding only under international law, such treaties may serve as an interpretive supplement to the fundamental rights established in the Constitution: "It is now an accepted rule of judicial construction that regard must be had to international Conventions and norms for construing domestic law when there is no inconsistency between them and there is a void in the domestic law."[276]

Another express provision in the Indian Constitution also has contributed to a broad influence of unimplemented treaties in the interpretation of

[269] *See* Chapter 11, pgs. 458–60.

[270] *See id.*, at 458–59 (citing the landmark decision of the Constitutional Court in S v. Makwanyane 1995(3) SA 391 (CC) at 413–14).

[271] *See* Chapter 9, pgs. 401–02; Chapter 5, pgs. 229–30. *See also id.*, at 235 ("German courts tend to interpret constitutional provisions in harmony with treaties and international court decisions, rather than risking a conflict.").

[272] *See* Chapter 6, pgs. 245–246.

[273] Indian Constitution of 1949, art. 37 (quoted in Chapter 6, pgs. 245–46).

[274] *Id.*, art. 51(c) (quoted in Chapter 6, pg. 246).

[275] *See* Chapter 6, pgs. 244–46.

[276] *Id.*, at 257–58 (quoting Visaka v. State of Rajasthan, 13 August 1997 [1997] 3 LRC 361).

fundamental constitutional rights. Article 32 expressly empowers the Court to issue directions, orders, and writs to ensure relief in matters pending before it. As the India chapter explains, the Court has seized on this mandate to issue a variety of broad decrees to protect fundamental rights in the voids left by parliamentary inaction.[277] On the same basis, it has greatly relaxed procedural requirements to permit public interest litigation initiated by the most informal means.[278] And as we have seen previously, the Court has approved the use of even unimplemented treaties to inform the content of the fundamental rights at the foundation of these innovative exercises of judicial power.

Other dualist tradition states have adopted a similar approach without express constitutional sanction. The Israel chapter thus relates that its courts often look to ratified though unimplemented treaties for guidance in developing the "material common law constitution" regarding gaps in the Basic Laws of the country.[279] The reports for Canada and Australia describe similar, though perhaps less well-grounded, practices.[280]

B. *The Hybrid Monist States: Treaty Enforcement and the Judicial Role*

1. Monism and the "Reception" of Treaties in Domestic Law. Section IV.A reviewed the substantial functional similarities that exist among the states studied in this work on certain general issues of treaty interpretation. In broad measure, these similarities flow from a recognition by domestic courts from both traditions – traditional dualist and hybrid monist alike – that the interpretive context for treaties or, as the case may be, treaty implementation statutes, is to be found in their international law origins. Nonetheless, the ability of treaties in the hybrid monist states to penetrate directly into domestic law marks a significant difference of principle with the traditional dualist states. This difference creates a variety of special challenges for the domestic courts in the enforcement of treaties in hybrid monist states.

Before we proceed, the analysis of these challenges will benefit from a careful review of the foundational principle of treaty enforcement in the hybrid monist states (see Section III.C). The common principle among all of these states is that at least some treaties approved by the legislature may

[277] *See* Chapter 6, pgs. 266–70.
[278] *Id.*, at 270–72.
[279] *See* Chapter 7, pgs. 300–01. *See also id.* at 298 ("In interpreting Basic Laws . . . the courts regularly refer to conventions that have not been incorporated in domestic law.")
[280] *See* Chapter 4, pgs. 197–201 (although noting some debate on this issue); Chapter 3, pgs. 156–58.

themselves have the force of law in the domestic legal system. Unfortunately, commentators and courts have employed a variety of different, and sometimes overlapping and even contradictory, terms to describe this threshold question.[281] Distilled to its essence, however, one may best conceive of this primary legal effect of treaties in the hybrid monist states – or any other similar monist state for that matter – as the "reception" of treaties in domestic law. With this term, we focus the analysis on the elemental point that the constitutional structure in these states recognizes properly approved treaties in themselves as law in the domestic legal system.

We have seen this most clearly in Germany, the Netherlands, Poland, Russia, and the United States, each of which prescribes such a reception by express constitutional provision.[282] As an illustration, there is value in repeating here the observation in the Netherlands chapter that "[a]ll treaties that are binding on the Netherlands as a matter of international law are automatically incorporated and thus have the force of law in the domestic legal order."[283]

The reception of treaties into the law of South Africa requires a bit more elaboration. Recall that under a specific provision in the South African Constitution "a self-executing treaty provision is law in the Republic."[284] When carefully considered, this provision both embraces the principle of reception and establishes a requirement for a more detailed substantive analysis of the provisions of each specific treaty (about which more follows[285]).

As an abstract matter, some uncertainty remains over the precise descriptive model for the principle of reception. The Germany chapter, for example, relates a continuing academic dispute over whether the legislative approval "transforms" a treaty into domestic law or "executes" it as international law in the domestic realm.[286] Although the practical consequences of the distinction may not be large,[287] the German Constitutional Court has wavered

[281] The most prominent among these are self-execution, direct effect, and validity. *See also, e.g.*, Chapter 8, pgs. 331–33 (using the term *validity* in this sense); Chapter 9, pg. 381 (referring to the direct applicability of treaties); Chapter 13, pgs. 509–14, 527–29 (describing the confusion over the meaning of *self-execution*). *But see* Chapter 5, pg. 222 (employing the term *self-execution* to describe "whether [a treaty] creates directly enforceable rights and obligations for individuals").

[282] *See supra* Section III.C.1(a) and notes 115–17 and accompanying text (for Russia).

[283] *See* Chapter 8, pg. 331.

[284] *See* Chapter 11, pg. 454 (citing art. 231(4) of the Constitution).

[285] *See infra* Section IV.B.2.

[286] *See* Chapter 5, pgs. 217–18.

[287] *Cf.* Chapter 5, pg. 222 (observing that "[t]ensions between the transformation theory and the execution theory are largely irrelevant to the concrete analysis of the impact of international treaties on domestic affairs").

on the theoretical dispute.[288] In any event, it seems reasonably clear that the domestic courts in all of the hybrid monist states have reserved to themselves a final, independent role in the interpretation and application of treaties in domestic law – although the degree of deference accorded international institutions within their assigned jurisdiction has varied.[289] The one exception in this regard is the special case of the interpretive authority of the ECJ within its delegated competence under the treaties that make up the European Union.[290]

Although significant, the principle of reception in the hybrid monist states results in only the elemental proposition that treaties penetrate into domestic law of their own force. It does not mean that domestic courts necessarily are the sole or immediate enforcement agencies for all treaties, any more than for other forms of domestic law. Consider as a parallel illustration a standard domestic statute that delegates rule-making discretion to an administrative agency. The statute undoubtedly has the force of law. Nonetheless, it may not be susceptible – as determined, of course, by applicable rules of interpretation – to immediate or direct enforcement by domestic courts. The same is true of a treaty that has the basic force of law in the domestic legal system through the principle of reception.

The reception of treaties, in other words, reflects only a necessary, but not in all cases a sufficient, condition for their application by domestic courts. The more challenging practical issue, as we shall see, is whether specific treaties, from their design, substance, and nature, are appropriate for direct enforcement in domestic law by domestic courts.

2. Special Issues for Judicial Enforcement of Treaties: Understanding the Debates over Direct Effect and Self-Execution. The special challenges that face domestic courts in the enforcement of treaties in the hybrid monist states arise principally from the distinctive processes for legislative approval. Recall that the law in these states permits or requires the legislature to grant advance, wholesale approval for the ratification of at least some treaties.[291] But in these states, as well, the negotiation of treaties is within the control of the executive.[292] Moreover, the negotiation and drafting process

[288] *See id.*, at 217–18.
[289] *See supra* notes 242–48 and accompanying text (describing in particular the recent example of the ICJ's interpretation of the Vienna Convention on Consular Relations).
[290] For more on this point, *see supra* Section III.F.
[291] *See supra* Section III.C.1.
[292] *See supra* Section II.B.

for treaties – most important, the need for consensus driven by the inability of a majority to impose its will on a minority – can be strikingly different from that for standard domestic legislation.[293] And at the end of the drafting process, domestic legislatures effectively have no ability to amend a treaty's agreed text and only limited room for reservations.[294]

The principle of the reception of treaties in the hybrid monist states nonetheless means that treaties penetrate with the force of law with only the wholesale approval of the legislature. The challenge for domestic courts charged with enforcement is only compounded by the fact that treaties of their nature represent state obligations under international law, with the result that a misfire in interpretation may compromise a state's foreign relations. Without the familiar foundation of standard domestic lawmaking processes, in other words, the distinctive origins of treaties require that courts in hybrid monist states confront the special interpretive issue of whether particular treaties – or particular treaty provisions – are of a nature to permit direct enforcement without further legislative implementation (as in traditional dualist states[295]).

It should not surprise, therefore, that an almost parallel debate exists on this score in the hybrid monist states studied in this work. Unfortunately, the precise idiom and structure of the debate differ, and this tends toward confusion. Most commonly, one finds the term *self-execution* to describe treaties that are enforceable directly by domestic courts,[296] but this term has variously been employed also to cover the principle of reception (see Section IV.B.1), the issue of judicial enforceability (which we address here), and the more focused question of individual treaty rights (see Section IV.B.3). An alternative term, *direct effect* can suffer from a similar ambiguity.[297]

To focus our analysis here, the essential question at this point is whether a treaty provision of itself is directly enforceable by domestic courts (or other institutions) to resolve specific legal disputes over which they otherwise have jurisdiction. What is remarkable is that the chapters for effectively all of the hybrid monist states studied in this work report a basic distinction between

[293] *See generally* Michael Pg. Van Alstine, *The Death of Good Faith in Treaty Jurisprudence and a Call for Resurrection*, 93 GEO. L.J. 1885, 1923–25 (2005).

[294] *See* VCLT, arts. 19–23.

[295] *See infra* Section IV.C.1.

[296] *See, e.g.*, Chapter 5, pgs. 222–24; Chapter 9, pgs. 401–09; Chapter 11, pgs. 455–57; Chapter 13, pgs. 527–29 (with reference to the opposite proposition of a "non-self-executing" treaty).

[297] *Compare* Chapter 8, pgs. 341–46 (referring to "direct effect") with Chapter 10, pgs. 416–17 (referring to "direct operation").

treaties of this nature and those that are not directly enforceable.[298] The difficulty, of course, is to articulate a precise legal standard to guide the analysis of this distinction.

Stated in broad terms, the common focus in the direct enforceability (or self-execution or direct effect) of a treaty provision is whether, as the Netherlands chapter states, it is "clear enough to serve as objective law."[299] The chapter for Poland further refines the point by focusing on whether a provision is "complete":

> The court must examine whether the treaty provision has been drafted in a "complete manner," i.e., in a manner allowing its use as an exclusive legal basis for resolving an individual case or controversy. In other words, the legal norm can be drawn from the text of the treaty and it is not necessary to enact domestic legislation to implement or concretize the treaty provisions.[300]

The chapter for the Netherlands reports a particularly well-developed jurisprudence on whether a treaty is directly enforceable by domestic courts (which it refers to as direct effect).[301] The Dutch constitution generally gives domestic effect to all treaties, but only to the extent that they are "binding on all persons by virtue of their contents."[302] On this basis, courts and scholars have identified two factors to assess the direct effect of treaty provisions: (1) the intent of the parties to the treaty and, perhaps more important, (2) whether the treaty provision at issue "is sufficiently clear from its content that it can serve as 'objective law'" without formal legislative implementation.[303] The Netherlands chapter even concludes that this "doctrine of direct effect . . . often has a significant limiting effect on the application of treaties by the courts and the executive."[304]

In the United States, the debate over what have come to be known as self-executing treaties has existed in some form since the early 1800s. As noted previously, the Constitution of 1789 expressly describes "all Treaties" as "the

[298] *See* Chapter 5, pgs. 222–24; Chapter 8, pgs. 341–46 (referring to the direct effect of treaties); Chapter 9, pgs. 401–06 (analyzing the self-execution of treaties); Chapter 10, pgs. 416–17 (referring to the issue of "[w]hether a treaty is of direct operation or not"); Chapter 11, pgs. 455–57 (referring to self-execution); Chapter 13, pgs. 527–29 (same).

[299] *See* Chapter 8, pg. 342.

[300] *See* Chapter 9, pg. 401.

[301] *See* Chapter 8, pgs. 341–46.

[302] *Id.*, at 332 (citing art. 93).

[303] *See id.*, at 332–33, 341.

[304] *Id.*, at 369.

supreme Law of the Land."[305] The courts of the United States have nonetheless recognized, as the U.S. chapter extensively describes, a doctrine of non-self-executing treaties.[306] The Supreme Court has itself recently restated the distinction between a treaty that "operates of itself without the aid of any legislative provision" and one that does not.[307] Unfortunately, the precise standard for distinguishing between the two categories remains the subject of confusion.[308] In any event, the U.S. chapter relates (with empirical support) that domestic courts have employed a "non-self-execution doctrine" as a "nationalist tool" where they have prevented the direct enforcement of treaties in domestic law and a self-execution doctrine where they have come to a contrary conclusion.[309]

The South African Constitution likewise permits the direct enforcement of those treaty provisions that are self-executing.[310] Unfortunately, as that chapter notes, "South African courts have yet to pronounce on the concept."[311] The chapters on Poland (as noted) and Germany also describe a parallel debate over self-execution as developed by judicial interpretation of more general constitutional norms.[312] Even in Russia,[313] the courts have concluded that not all treaty provisions may be directly enforced in domestic courts. That chapter reports that "[w]hether a treaty is of direct operation . . . can be determined, inter alia, by whether there are indications in the treaty text that the treaty obliges state parties to make changes in their domestic legislation."[314]

[305] *See supra* note 94 and accompanying text. *See also* U.S. Const. art. VI, § 2.

[306] *See* Chapter 13, pgs. 509–14.

[307] *See* Medellín v. Texas, 128 S.Ct. 1346, 1356 (2008). *See also* Chapter 13, pgs. 512–14 (analyzing the case in detail).

[308] *See* Chapter 13, pgs. 509–14, 527–29.

[309] *See id.*, at 527–29 and 534–36 (analyzing in specific Table 2B.). For an analysis of the same doctrines with specific reference to individual treaty rights, *see infra* notes 331–36 and accompanying text.

[310] *See* Chapter 11, pgs. 455–56 (citing sec. 231(4)).

[311] *Id.* at 456. *See also id.*, at 456–57 (describing scholarly debates on the subject).

[312] *See*, Chapter 5, pgs. 222–24 (noting a similar issue in domestic courts over whether a treaty provision is self-executing); Chapter 9, pgs. 402–05 (observing that judicial enforcement even of a provision in a treaty approved by the legislature is subject to "[t]he substantive condition" that "requires that completeness of the treaty provision that enables its operation without any additional implementation") (citing a decision of the Supreme Court of November 21, 2003).

[313] Recall that the Constitution of the Russian Federation provides that "international treaties of the Russian Federation shall be an integral part of its legal system." *See supra* notes 116–22 and accompanying text.

[314] *See* Chapter 10, pg. 416 (citing Decree No. 5 of the plenum of the Supreme Court of October 10, 2003, on the application of treaties by domestic courts).

Nonetheless, it would be error to emphasize the abstract debate over direct effect or self-execution without tempering the analysis with the actual practice of courts. In many cases, domestic courts enforce treaty rights (and obligations) without any serious question about their effect as domestic law. In contrast, domestic courts have considerable tools at their disposal to avoid recognizing and applying treaty law in actual practice. The chapter for the United States demonstrates this point with an extensive empirical analysis. It describes how courts have used the "transnationalist tools" of good-faith interpretation,[315] a presumption in favor of interpreting domestic statutory law to conform to international legal obligations, and the doctrine of self-execution to vindicate treaty-based rights and duties.[316] In contrast, domestic courts commonly have employed the "nationalist tools" of deference to the executive (as we have seen in Section IV.A.2(c)), a presumption against individual treaty rights, and the doctrine of non-self-execution where they have refused to enforce treaty-based law.[317] In actual practice, in short, the evidence summarized by the U.S. chapter demonstrates a noteworthy correlation in case outcomes between, on the one hand, judicial reliance on transnationalist tools and a successful invocation of treaty rights and, on the other hand, judicial reliance on nationalist tools and a rejection of treaty-based legal claims.[318]

3. Judicial Enforcement of Individual Treaty Rights. Among the most significant goals of this work is to examine the role of domestic courts in the enforcement of treaties by individuals. Even ancient legal societies recognized the maxim *ubi jus, ibi remedium* (where there is a right, there is a remedy).[319] As noted at the beginning of this summary chapter, it is now well established that international treaties may create rights for private

[315] *See* Chapter 13, pgs. 533–34 and Table 2A. The U.S. Chapter includes under this concept the cases in which courts have referred to the "shared expectations of the parties." *See id.*, at 523. *See also id.*, at 529–32 and Table 2 (summarizing the data on the use of the nationalist and transnationalist tools).

[316] *See id.*, at 522–29; *id.* at 534–36 and Table 2B.

[317] *See id.*, at 536–39 and Table 2C. (comparing cases that have invoked the nationalist tool of presumption against individual rights with the transnationalist tool of liberal interpretation).

[318] *See* Chapter 13, pgs. 539–52 (summarizing the data on the use of the nationalist and transnationalist tools on case outcomes). *See also id.*, at 505 (concluding that the empirical analysis "demonstrates that there is a statistically significant correlation between case outcomes and a court's discretionary decision to adopt a nationalist or transnationalist approach").

[319] *See* Chapter 2, pgs. 83–85 (noting the maxim in Roman law).

individuals and entities.[320] But as Professor Murphy's chapter on international law notes, this does not mean that a person with a treaty-protected right necessarily is entitled to vindicate that right in any particular forum.[321] This fact brings to practical significance the question of whether, and if so under what circumstances, domestic law will recognize that an individual may vindicate treaty rights through a direct action in domestic courts.

In large measure, the rights of individuals derived from treaties may be subsumed within the structure of the analysis of direct enforceability examined in Section IV.B.2.[322] Indeed, the Poland chapter observes that its courts have shown "a considerable readiness" to enforce treaties directly and that "[t]his trend is particularly visible in regard to treaties establishing rights of individual persons."[323] The Russia chapter similarly offers the straightforward observation that "[i]ndividuals and juridical persons may invoke treaty rights directly in Russian courts" and that in fact "[j]udges are encouraged as part of their training to draw on international legal acts when appropriate" even if private litigants do not raise the issue.[324]

When carefully considered, however, whether an individual may invoke a treaty obligation in domestic courts is a conceptually distinct question from the more general notion of direct enforceability. (A treaty may, for example, create directly enforceable rights or powers in favor of governments. Mutual Legal Assistance Treaties (MLATs) are a good example.)[325] Moreover, even the Netherlands chapter observes that the invocation of treaty obligations by individuals faces "a major hurdle because it is still widely (but perhaps mistakenly) assumed that the provisions of most treaties are primarily concerned with the legal relations between nation states."[326]

The Netherlands again has a quite well-developed jurisprudence on invocation of treaty rights by individuals.[327] That chapter describes an analysis of this issue that parallels direct enforceability but is more focused. "Above

[320] *See supra* notes 4–6 and accompanying text.

[321] *See* Chapter 2, pgs. 83–85.

[322] As the Netherlands Chapter thus observes, "In many cases" the questions of direct effect and of invocation by individuals "will coincide since, if a private party raises a matter of international law, a court will have to decide both whether that party is entitled to do so and whether the provision lends itself to a judicial ruling." *See* Chapter 8, pg. 346.

[323] *See* Chapter 9, pg. 400.

[324] *See* Chapter 10, pg. 410.

[325] *See, e.g.*, http://travel.state.gov/law/info/judicial/judicial_690.html (listing the numerous such treaties ratified by the United States).

[326] *See* Chapter 8, pg. 345.

[327] *See id.*, at 347–51.

all," the chapter notes, courts will examine – as a matter of treaty interpretation – whether the parties to the treaty "intended to grant rights to individuals."[328] If that intent is not clear from the treaty and its negotiating history, then the courts "will analyze the nature and content of the treaty to ascertain whether its provisions are designed to protect the interests of individuals."[329] And in actual practice, the Netherlands chapter observes that its courts "have identified a large number" of such treaties that create rights that individuals may invoke directly in domestic courts.[330]

The U.S. chapter, in contrast, reports a troubling trend in domestic courts against the invocation of treaty rights by individuals, at least in cases adverse to the interests of the government. Its chapter describes how domestic courts increasingly have applied certain nationalist doctrines to prevent the full enforcement of individual treaty rights. The principal such nationalist strategy is a presumption recently recognized by some lower courts that "treaties do not create judicially enforceable private rights" in the absence of express language to the contrary.[331] The precise origin of this jurisprudence is not at all clear; but the Supreme Court of the United States itself recently referred to this supposed presumption (although without express endorsement).[332]

This presumption has also operated in tandem with the broader doctrine of non-self-execution, noted previously,[333] to avoid recognizing individual treaty rights. As the U.S. chapter demonstrates through a broad empirical study of treaty cases, this practice is most pronounced in cases adverse to the interests of the government.[334] The chapter thus observes that the twin nationalist doctrines of non-self-execution and presumption against individual treaty rights "are almost never utilized in litigation between private parties" but instead apply "almost exclusively in cases where an individual invokes a treaty as a constraint on the exercise of governmental powers."[335] Overall, the U.S. chapter concludes that the two doctrines "function

[328] *Id.*, at 347.
[329] *Id.*, at 347–48.
[330] *Id.*
[331] *See* Chapter 13, pgs. 536–39 and Table 2C (comparing cases that have invoked the nationalist tool of presumption against individual rights with the transnationalist tool of liberal interpretation). *See also id.*, at 525–26 (describing this nationalist tool as one by which domestic courts are viewed as agents of the domestic legal system in interpreting and applying treaties).
[332] *See* Medellín v. Texas, 128 S.Ct. 1346, 1357 n.3 (2008).
[333] *See supra* notes 306–09 and accompanying text.
[334] *See* Chapter 13, pgs. 542–47.
[335] *Id.*, at 539.

as abstention doctrines that shield government actors from judicial review of government compliance with treaty-based norms."[336]

C. *The Traditional Dualist States: Treaty Implementation and the Judicial Role*

1. Special Issues from the Judicial Application of Treaty Implementation Statutes. We have noted that the animating principle of the traditional dualist states studied in this work is a clear separation between international treaty making by the executive and domestic treaty implementation by the legislature.[337] Even when the legislature implements a treaty, therefore, in a strict sense it is the legislation, not the treaty itself, that functions as domestic law. As the U.K. chapter explains, although in this tradition a treaty may be binding under international law, "*the treaty itself* is not part of domestic law, even if some of its provisions may have been made part of that law."[338]

This formal separation of international from domestic law has important implications for the work of domestic courts in relation to treaties. In particular, the chapter reports for the traditional dualist states contain no serious discussion of the direct enforceability (or direct effect or self-execution) of treaties – that is, whether the design, nature, or substance of particular treaty provisions permit direct enforcement by domestic courts. One need not speculate too greatly about the reason for this absence. In the typical case of a specifically designed implementation statute (as opposed to wholesale adoption), the substance of the treaty is filtered through standard legislative processes. In consequence, the legislature has an opportunity to craft the implementation statute to accommodate the special legal concepts, terminology, and structures of the domestic system.

The Australia chapter helpfully explains this point in this way: "The more common situation . . . is where a statute seeks to give partial effect to a treaty provision such that the treaty has been 'adapted and adopted' for the purposes of Australian law. In these instances, the treaty right may have been modified to reflect Australian circumstances, or a distinctive statutory scheme may have been developed around it."[339]

With this familiar legal foundation, the courts in such cases look primarily to the implementing legislation, and not to the treaty, to determine

[336] *Id.*
[337] *See supra* Section III.B.1.
[338] *See* Chapter 12, pgs. 478–79 (emphasis in original).
[339] *See* Chapter 3, pg. 138.

rights and remedies.[340] In fulfilling this interpretive task, they may (as we have seen[341]) seek guidance in the international law background of the underlying treaty, especially where the legislation is unclear.[342] But where the implementing legislation is unambiguous (whether in a positive or a negative sense), the interpretive enterprise in the traditional dualist states in large measure is at an end.[343]

The recognition of individual rights derived from a treaty likewise follows standard interpretive rules for legislation. Without legislative implementation, the basic principle is that individuals may not vindicate their treaty rights founded in international law directly in domestic courts.[344] As the U.K. chapter thus explains, "to be effective, [a treaty] right needs to be one recognized also as a right in domestic law. This is important given the strictness of the dualist approach."[345] The Canada chapter similarly declares that "[w]here a treaty right is not, for whatever reason, implemented in Canadian law, the orthodox rule is that judicial remedies will not be available."[346] This does not mean that the domestic legislation must expressly endorse individual rights founded in treaties; for, as some chapters observe, such individual rights may arise by deduction from legislation even when it does not expressly refer to the treaty.[347]

[340] *See, e.g.*, Chapter 4, pgs. 203–04; Chapter 12, pg. 482 ("If the language of legislation implementing a treaty is *un*ambiguous, the courts will not look behind the legislation at the treaty. ... This is dualism at its most strict"); *id.*, pg. 487 (extending the same observation to private rights of action).

[341] *See supra* Section IV.A.1.

[342] *See* Chapter 3, pgs. 151–52 (observing that where a legislative act is ambiguous, a special interpretive statute expressly authorizes a court to refer to "any treaty or other international agreement that is referred to in the act"); Chapter 4, pgs. 202–04; Chapter 7, pgs. 290–91; Chapter 12, pgs. 487, 492. *See also id.*, at 487 (referring to the possibility of a treaty-based remedy arising "by deduction from the terms of ... legislation" that does not even refer to the treaty).

[343] *See* Chapter 4, pg. 202 ("Where the treaty right upon which a claimant seeks to rely is implemented in Canadian law, there may be no need to refer to the international aspect of the right at all."); Chapter 7, pgs. 289–91; Chapter 12, pgs. 482, 487.

[344] *See, e.g.*, Chapter 4, pg. 204; Chapter 7, pg. 280 (citing the "undisputed principle that domestic courts in Israel may not enforce treaties that bind the state in international law unless the provisions of such treaties have been incorporated by parliamentary legislation"); Chapter 12, pgs. 486–87 (concluding that "to be effective [a treaty] right needs to be one recognised also as a right in domestic law"). *See also* Chapter 3, pg. 136 (observing that in absence of an implementing statute, "an applicant will have a much diminished chance of success in securing [a] treaty-based remedy").

[345] Chapter 12, pgs. 486–87.

[346] Chapter 4, pg. 204.

[347] *See, e.g.*, Chapter 12, pg. 487 (referring to this process of deduction); Chapter 3, pgs. 151–52 (referring to judicial enforcement where legislation makes only a partial or indirect reference to a treaty).

The one area in which the traditional dualist approach nonetheless begins to overlap with the direct enforceability debate in hybrid monist states is through the practice of scheduling. This involves the legislature simply appending the entire text of a treaty to a legislative act (or otherwise simply declaring that the treaty itself has the force of law).[348] In other words, this practice reflects a subsequent wholesale endorsement of a ratified treaty that parallels the advance wholesale endorsement common in the hybrid monist states.

Perhaps not surprisingly, therefore, we find a discussion in some of the traditional dualist states as well of whether a scheduled treaty itself is designed to create rights directly in favor of individuals. We have already noted that in the case of scheduling, domestic courts have been especially inclined to look to the underlying treaty for interpretive guidance.[349] But as reflected in the U.K. chapter, courts from traditional dualist states also have recognized the possibility that a formal individual right may arise "by deduction from the text of a treaty which is attached to domestic legislation or referred to in the legislation."[350] And one may presume that the standards for such a deduction directly from a treaty would parallel those applied by courts in the hybrid monist states to determine whether a treaty creates individual rights.

2. The Surprising Influence of Unimplemented Treaties. Given the fundamental importance of legislative implementation for the traditional dualist states, among the most remarkable conclusions from the country reports is that domestic courts have accorded broad influence even to treaties that have not been so implemented in domestic law. We have already seen one such meta-rule of interpretation above. As Section IV.A.3 explained, a broad presumption applies in traditional dualist states as well that courts should interpret domestic law wherever possible to advance conformity with their state's treaty obligations under international law. This presumption also applies to treaties that, although ratified by the executive, have not been implemented in domestic law by the legislature.[351] In other words, even formally unimplemented treaties may have a significant influence in domestic law. Indeed, in Canada even legislative inaction may

[348] *See supra* note 84 and accompanying text. *See also* Chapter 3, pg. 138; Chapter 4, pgs. 169–70; Chapter 7, pgs. 276–77; Chapter 12, pg. 487.

[349] *See supra* notes 208–09 and accompanying text.

[350] *See* Chapter 12, pg. 487. *See also* Chapter 3, pg. 138 (referring to the full implementation of treaties as domestic law).

[351] *See supra* Section IV.A.3.

result in the implementation of a treaty through the doctrine of implied incorporation.[352]

But as we shall see here, the effect of unimplemented treaties may extend beyond the basic interpretive presumption of conformity with international law. Courts in traditional dualist states also have relied on such treaties to limit the discretion of administrative bodies and even to recognize individual rights not otherwise established in domestic law. Curiously, the discussion of these issues has not been as robust in hybrid monist states.

A. QUASI-INCORPORATION, IMPLIED INCORPORATION, AND CONSTRAINTS ON ADMINISTRATIVE DISCRETION. Among the more interesting results from the chapter reports is that some courts in traditional dualist states have afforded influence to unimplemented treaties (as well as customary international law[353]) in a variety of functionally significant ways beyond the interpretive principles and presumptions previously described in Section IV.A. Prominent among these is a recognition that unimplemented treaties may function to limit the discretion delegated by the legislature to executive or administrative agencies. The chapters for Australia,[354] India,[355] and the United Kingdom[356] each report some form of this proposition. The Israel chapter also notes a continuing debate on the subject.[357] (Interestingly, the chapter for hybrid-monist South Africa describes a similar principle with reference to otherwise-unenforceable treaties that the legislature has not implemented in a dualist fashion.)[358]

The most notable example of this is the *Teoh* doctrine in Australia.[359] As that chapter relates, the High Court of Australia found in a case of the same name that, even in absence of a direct or even indirect reference in formal legislation, a ratified treaty may operate to limit the discretion of administrative agencies:

> [R]atification by Australia of an international convention is not to be dismissed as a merely platitudinous or ineffectual act, particularly when the instrument evidences internationally accepted standards to be applied by courts and administrative authorities in dealing with basic human rights

[352] *See supra* notes 266–67 and accompanying text.
[353] *See supra* Section III.C.
[354] *See* Chapter 3, pgs. 145–51, 158–64.
[355] *See* Chapter 6, pgs. 251–55; Chapter 4, pgs. 193–97.
[356] *See* Chapter 12, pgs. 495–96.
[357] *See* Chapter 7, pgs. 277, 298–301.
[358] *See* Chapter 11, pg. 459 (observing that an unimplemented treaty "may be taken into account in a challenge to the validity of delegated legislation on the grounds of unreasonableness").
[359] *See* Chapter 3, pgs. 138–39, 145–51.

> affecting the family and children. Rather, ratification of a convention . . . is an adequate foundation for a legitimate expectation, absent statutory or executive indications to the contrary, that administrative decision makers will act in conformity with the Convention[.][360]

The Australia chapter observes, however, that subsequent decisions of the High Court have left some doubt about the continuing force of this "legitimate expectations" doctrine.[361] Similarly, the Canada chapter states that this principle has not (yet) received a warm reception by the courts there.[362]

The Australia chapter also reports on a doctrine of "quasi-incorporation" of international treaty obligations.[363] This actually involves three distinct, yet related mechanisms by which legislation indirectly or informally empowers courts to measure rights or obligations against international treaties otherwise not formally incorporated into domestic law. The first is where domestic statutes are "based, either substantially or partly, on international instruments and are clearly designed to give effect to international obligations." The second is where "government departments and administrative decision makers are given directions to take into account the provisions of" international treaties. Finally, legislation may "indicate[] that it is to operate subject to international obligations under international law."[364] The Australia chapter concludes that this practice of "quasi-incorporation" (or "partial incorporation") will have a significant, although in some respects uncertain, impact on the power of the judiciary to enforce international treaties in the country.[365]

Interestingly, the notion of "quasi-incorporation" parallels developments in other traditional dualist states examined above. Prominent among these is the jurisprudence of the Supreme Court of Canada on "implied incorporation," by which a formally unincorporated treaty may obtain domestic law effect through parliamentary inaction on related legislation.[366] In the same vein is the possibility recognized by the United Kingdom report that implied treaty rights may arise by interpretive deduction even where legislation does not expressly refer to the treaty.[367]

360 Minister of State for Immigration and Ethnic Affairs v. Teoh (1995) 128 ALR 353 (per Mason, CJ, and Brennan, J) (quoted in Chapter 3, pg. 148).

361 *See* Chapter 3, pgs. 148–51.

362 *See* Chapter 4, pgs. 193–97.

363 *See* Chapter 3, pgs. 158–64.

364 *See id.*, at 158–61.

365 *See id.*, at 161–64.

366 *See supra* notes 266–67 and accompanying text.

367 *See* Chapter 12, pg. 492.

B. THE INFLUENCE OF UNIMPLEMENTED TREATIES FOR NEW COMMON LAW RIGHTS. Domestic courts in traditional dualist states also have recognized an indirect influence of unimplemented treaties with respect to the rights and remedies of individuals. Interestingly, but not surprisingly, the five states in this group emerged not only from the British constitutional tradition but also from its common law tradition. This judge-made common law has presented a vehicle for domestic courts to recognize individual rights or remedies even for treaties that have not yet been implemented in domestic law by the legislature.

To be sure, the level of enthusiasm for this use of the common law differs. The Israel chapter, for example, broadly states that "in discussing principles of Israel's common law, the courts regularly refer to conventions that have not been incorporated in domestic law."[368] The Supreme Court of India likewise declared in a maritime case that, because certain relevant treaties "embody principles of law recognized by the generality of maritime States," they "can therefore be regarded as part of our common law."[369] Significantly, the Court endorsed this principle even though India had not formally implemented the treaties at issue.[370] The chapter for Australia also suggests that its courts "have become more open" to use of unimplemented treaties in this way.[371]

The U.K. chapter, in contrast, reports a more tepid judicial reaction, observing only that a domestic court "might possibly consider" an unimplemented treaty in recognizing common law rights.[372] The courts of Canada likewise have not yet expressly embraced the proposition,[373] but the Canada chapter elsewhere notes in broader fashion that the particularly powerful

[368] *See* Chapter 7, pgs. 298–301.

[369] *See* Chapter 6, pgs. 255–56 (quoting M.V. Elizabeth v. Harwan Investment and Trading Pvt.).

[370] *See* Chapter 6, pgs. 255–56 (examining the principle that "an international convention may play a part in the development by the courts of the common law").

[371] *See* Chapter 3, pgs. 136–37 (observing that although unimplemented treaties generally may not found domestic rights, "one clear trend is that the courts have become more open to hearing matters based on the existence not only of a treaty right recognized under Australian law, but also of a right that exists entirely under international law by way of a treaty to which Australia is a party").

[372] *See* Chapter 12, pg. 487, (explaining that "[w]hen asserting a right under common law ... a court might *possibly* consider the terms of an <u>un</u>incorporated treaty or [a memorandum of understanding] to see whether there was an intention to create a private right"); *id.*, at 492–99 (examining the point in more detail). *But see id.* at 478 ("Only in certain limited circumstances will the courts have regard to unincorporated treaties.").

[373] *See* Chapter 4, pgs. 191–92 (noting that Canadian courts have not yet formally extended the fundamental presumption of conformity with international treaties to the common law).

presumption of conformity there has "further erod[ed] support for the proposition that treaties always require legislative implementation before taking effect in domestic law."[374]

V. CONCLUSION

One might be tempted to conclude from the individual chapters in this work that the differences among the states studied preclude any reliable generalizations about the role of domestic courts in enforcing international treaty law. To be sure, the eleven states diverge, often in substantial ways, over constitutional framework, methods of approval and implementation, and judicial tradition on the domestic law effect of treaties.

In no way is this clearer than in the difference between the traditional dualist and hybrid monist approaches to the penetration of international treaties in domestic law. In the traditional dualist states, the separation of international treaty making from domestic treaty implementation has led domestic courts to focus primarily on the treaty implementation statutes, not the treaties themselves. In the hybrid monist states, in contrast, the basic reception of treaties directly into domestic law has generated distinctive debates over whether particular treaties or treaty provisions are of a design, substance, or nature to permit direct enforceability by domestic courts without further legislative endorsement.

Nonetheless, we have seen in this work that the formal difference between the traditional dualist and hybrid monist approaches can obscure significant functional similarities in the actual practice of domestic courts. At a fundamental level, courts even in traditional dualist states have readily turned to the international law foundations of treaties in the interpretation of implementation statutes. Moreover, almost irrespective of the fundamental approach, domestic courts have applied basic principles of interpretation that largely conform to the norms in the VCLT. Finally, the country chapters in this work report a broadly accepted principle that courts should interpret domestic law to advance conformity with their state's treaty obligations under international law. This applies, interestingly, even in traditional dualist states and even for treaties not formally implemented by the legislature.

This does not mean that domestic courts, even in hybrid monist states, always have been enthusiastic about applying the law derived from treaties in actual disputes, much less to recognize and enforce individual rights on that basis. Indeed, as the Netherlands chapter observes, "The attitude

[374] *See id.*, at 188–89.

of courts themselves may be as important as the formal features of the constitutional system."[375] Stated differently, as is clear from the evidence on the actual practice of courts described in the U.S. chapter, there is a discrepancy between the rhetoric that accompanies seemingly neutral principles on the analysis of treaty-based claims and the judicial application of those principles in actual practice.[376]

But what is said often serves as a forerunner for what is done. And the country chapters in this work reveal that much, in fact, has been done toward enforcing the international law obligations derived from treaties either in or as domestic law. Through ever more detailed constitutional provisions, a heightened awareness of the issue among treaty drafters, and greater judicial familiarity with the subject, domestic courts have developed an increasingly sophisticated jurisprudence on the interpretation and application of treaty-based law. To be sure, the progress has been and continues to be uneven. Indeed, recent trends in judicial practice in some traditionally international law friendly states (e.g., the United States) and transitional challenges in some rapidly reconstituting states (e.g., Russia) are sources of serious, continuing concern. But on the foundation of enhanced democratic legitimation and more transparent judicial practice, the chapters in this work strongly indicate that domestic courts will play an ever more significant role in recognizing and enforcing rights, powers, and obligations that trace their origins to international treaties.

[375] Chapter 8, pg. 369.
[376] Chapter 13, pgs. 553–54.

Index